TO THE NORTH POLE

Peary

Arctic Circle

HUDSON STRAIT

Henry Hudson

JAMES BAY

JAMESTOWN

ATLANTIC

Columbus

Cook

James

Captain

Lindbergh

Magellan

BAHAMAS

CAPE BOJADOR

BATHURST

NATAL

Vasco da Gama

Pizarro   Orellana

Lange

Darwin

LA PLATA RIVER

SIERRA DEL FUEGO

Shackleton   SOUTH GEORGIA

ELEPHANT ISLAND

OCEAN

Whymper
(MATTERHORN)
VENICE

Cousteau

Herodotus

Marco Polo

Hedin

Harrer
LHASA
Herzog
ANNAPURNA

Marco

CALICUT

Polo

Du Chaillu

Speke
UGANDA
Tippu
Tib ZANZIBAR
Livingstone

MADAGASCAR

Cook

INDIAN

OCEAN

THE
GREAT
EXPLORERS

THE
GREAT
EXPLORERS

by Helen Wright
and
Samuel Rapport

HARPER & BROTHERS, PUBLISHERS
NEW YORK

Contents

vi   Contents

Introduction

The story of exploration is crowded with happenings as dramatic as any in human history. Inevitably the discoverers of new lands have come into conflict with savage and unrelenting nature and even more savage human enemies. Death by starvation and thirst, by disease and cold have been commonplace. Cannibalism and massacre have been by no means rare. And perhaps most dramatic of all, mutiny and treacherous murder have been eventualities which all the great commanders have had constantly to guard against. Everyone has read about the murmurs against Columbus by his men. Compared with the problems of such leaders as Magellan and Hudson, they sink into triviality.

Yet out of this welter of bloodshed and melodrama, there arises a narrative which is majestic in tone and inspiring in accomplishment. The great explorers have, in the very nature of things, been heroic adventurers whom we cannot fail to admire for their determination and courage. By our own standards many of them, particularly the Portuguese and Spanish conquerors, have been bloody and sadistic killers. By the standards of their own day, they are to be judged on a different level. The conquistadors were driven by a desire for gold and often wiped out entire tribes to get it. But they were also inspired by the sincere need to bring lost souls to salvation and to increase the power and glory of their own nations—motives which even in our own day are considered admirable.

It must be acknowledged nevertheless that the prime historical motive for exploration has been the desire for gain. Dominating the Mediterranean, the Venetians controlled the enormously profitable commerce with the Orient. A sea route to the Indies would open such commerce to Spain and Portugal and England, and this basic need lay at the bottom of the relentless search which resulted in the mapping of the great waters of the earth. The conquistadors, as we have said, desired gold. The whalers and sealers who penetrated Arctic and Antarctic waters went in search of skins and blubber. The mountain men who explored the American West were trapping for pelts. And the modern geologists and prospectors who explore both the surface of the earth and underneath it, hope to find oil or gold or uranium.

Yet other finer impulses have played their part. Of these one of the most admirable has been the search for pure knowledge, the desire to know which is the foundation of scientific research. Of this company were men like Darwin and Humboldt and Wallace. So, too, was Henry the Navigator, from whose imagination, as we shall see, stemmed the exploits of the greatest of the explorers—Columbus, Da Gama and Magellan. David Livingstone, who did more to illuminate the map of Africa than any other man, began his travels as a missionary but later became consumed with a thirst to travel to places which no other civilized human had seen. Even Henry Morton Stanley, whose search for Livingstone began as a pure journalistic stunt, became imbued with this desire to know. And William Dampier, a bloodthirsty pirate, was a careful observer of the plants and animals of the strange tropic lands he explored.

Often allied with scientific curiosity has been a sheer love of danger and desire for fame. The British pioneers in Arabia, the polar explorers like Amundsen and Stefansson and Shackleton, the mountain climbers like Mallory and Tenzing and Herzog, the divers like Beebe and Cousteau, the fliers like Lindbergh, have all felt such impulses. They are basic in human character.

We have mentioned religion as a prime cause of exploration. Hundreds of Catholic priests suffered hardships and even martyrdom to carry the word of God to parts of China, Japan, the Indies and Tibet at a time when these lands were hardly more than legends and fantasies to Western Europe. Protestant missionaries to darkest Africa and the islands of the Pacific have often been equally fearless and well meaning, although as recent literature has told us, the results of their ministrations to the heathen have not always been happy. One of the purest examples of selfless religious zeal is Saint Isaac Jogues, whose tragic story appears in the pages that follow. And there is another aspect of religion which must be taken into account—the desire for freedom of worship and conscience that motivated the Pilgrims and the Puritans and helped to open up the New World.

It is manifestly impossible in one volume to tell all the great adventures in exploration. We have therefore attempted to select those highlights which dramatize the story and show its progress from the days of Herodotus to modern times. These highlights illuminate the spirit of discovery and communicate its excitement better than a mere chronicle of events. In some cases, the discoverers tell their own stories. In others, the best accounts by historians and biographers have been chosen. In all cases, the interest of the material rather than the amount of information has been a prime consideration in making a choice.* The running commentary which precedes each selection is intended to bind them them into a connected whole.

A word is necessary about the point of view of the authors, which with hardly an exception is that of Western civilization. In earlier centuries the Arabs and the Chinese traveled great distances in Africa and Asia. The Polynesians sailed far over the vast Pacific, and the Eskimos of today traverse the North on their fabulous hunting expeditions. But the main stream of history has up to now been dominated by the white Caucasian peoples of Europe. These peoples have also been the most articulate, and have recorded their explorations in a way which others could understand and follow. And thus the story of exploration as it is here presented is that of such Europeans as the Spanish and the Portuguese, the Norse and the British—and more recently the Americans.

* The editors have also edited the original texts, often of considerable length, in such wise as to permit their inclusion in this volume.

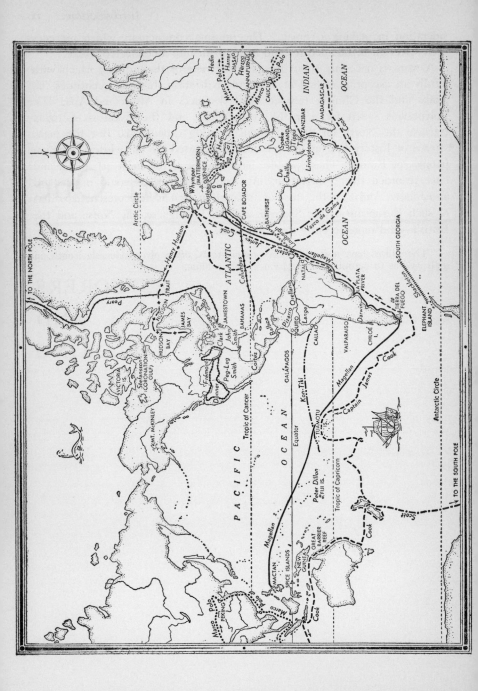

Part One

EXPLORERS
AND
EXPLORING

THE
SPIRIT OF ADVENTURE

by Theodore Roosevelt

George Leigh-Mallory is reported to have said, when asked why he climbed mountains, that he did so because the mountains were there. Despite its apparent profundity, the statement says very little, either about the adventurer—and for this word we can substitute explorer—or about his motivations. What actually is he like? Why does he do what he does? There have been many attempts to answer these questions and this section opens with one of the most graphic, by a former President of the United States.

THE man should have youth and strength who seeks adventure in the wide, waste spaces of the earth, in the marshes, and among the vast mountain masses, in the northern forests, amid the steaming jungles of the tropics, or on the deserts of sand or of snow. He must long greatly for the lonely winds that blow across the wilderness, and for sunrise and sunset over the rim of the empty world. His heart must thrill for the saddle and not for the hearthstone. He must be helmsman and chief, the cragsman, the rifleman, the boat steerer. He must be the wielder of ax and of paddle, the rider of fiery horses, the master of the craft that leaps through white water. His eye must be true and quick, his hand steady and strong. His heart must never fail nor his head grow bewildered, whether he face brute and human foes, or the frowning strength of hostile nature, or the awful fear that grips those who are lost in trackless lands. Wearing toil and hardship shall be his; thirst and famine he shall face, and burning fever. Death shall come to greet him with poison fang or poison arrow, in shape of charging beast or of scaly things that lurk in lake and river; it shall lie in wait for him among untrodden forests, in the swirl of wild waters, and in the blast of snow blizzard or thunder-shattered hurricane.

Not many men with wisdom make such a life their permanent and serious occupation. Those whose tasks lie along other lines can lead it for but a few years. For them it must normally come in the hardy vigor of their youth, before the beat of the blood has grown sluggish in their veins.

Nevertheless, older men also can find joy in such a life, although in their case it must be led only on the outskirts of adventure, and although the part they play therein must be that of the onlooker rather than that of the doer. The feats of prowess are for others. It is for other men to face the peril of unknown lands, to master unbroken horses, and to hold their own among their fellows with bodies of supple strength. But much, very much, remains for the man who has "warmed both hands before the fire of life," and who, although he loves the great cities, loves even more the fenceless grassland and the forest-clad hills.

The grandest scenery of the world is his to look at if he chooses; and he can witness the strange ways of tribes who have survived into an alien age from an immemorial past, tribes whose priests dance in honor of the serpent and worship the spirits of the wolf and the bear. Far and wide, all the continents are open to him as they never were to any of his forefathers; the Nile and the Paraguay are easy of access, and the borderland between savagery and civilization; and the veil of the past has been lifted so that he can dimly see how, in time immeasurably remote, his ancestors—no less remote—led furtive lives among uncouth and terrible beasts, whose kind has perished utterly from the face of the earth. He will take books with him as he journeys; for the keenest enjoyment of the wilderness is reserved for him who enjoys also the garnered wisdom of the present and the past. He will take pleasure in the companionship of the men in the open; in South America, the daring and reckless horsemen who guard the herds of the grazing country, and the dark-skinned paddlers who guide their clumsy dugouts down the dangerous equatorial rivers; the white and red and half-breed hunters of the Rockies, and of the Canadian woodland; and in Africa the faithful black gunbearers who have stood steadily at his elbow when the lion came on with coughing grunts, or when the huge mass of the charging elephant burst asunder the vine-tangled branches.

The beauty and charm of the wilderness are his for the asking, for the edges of the wilderness lie close beside the beaten roads of present travel. He can see the red splendor of desert sunsets, and the unearthly glory of the afterglow on the battlements of desolate mountains. In sapphire gulfs of ocean he can visit islets, above which the wings of myriads of sea fowl make a kind of shifting cuneiform script in the air. He can ride along the brink of the stupendous cliff-walled canyon, where eagles soar below him, and cougars make their lairs on the ledges and harry the big-horned sheep. He can journey through the northern forests, the home of the giant moose, the forests of fragrant and murmuring life in summer, the iron-bound and melancholy forests of winter.

The joy of living is his who has the heart to demand it.

HOW I BECAME AN EXPLORER

by Roald Amundsen

We go from the general to the particular, from discussion of explorers as a class to portraits of three men which, each in its individual way, illuminate some special aspect of the explorer's personality or way of life. The young man is rare who does not dream of visiting unknown, distant places. Usually the pressures of existence or the first taste of adversity result in a permanent cure. Not so in the case of the explorer with an authentic flair. Young Amundsen, for example, nearly lost his life in his first attempt. He found only stimulation in the adventure and went on to a career of polar exploration which culminated in his discovery of the South Pole. His story, exciting in itself, illuminates the explorer's compulsion to follow his hard and hazardous way of life.

HOW did I happen to become an explorer? It did not just happen, for my career has been a steady progress toward a definite goal since I was fifteen years of age. Whatever I have accomplished in exploration has been the result of lifelong planning, painstaking preparation, and the hardest kind of conscientious work.

I was born a few miles south of Oslo in Norway, and when I was three months of age my parents removed to the capital, where I was reared and educated. I passed without incident through the usual educational routine of Norway, which is divided into a primary school for the ages of six to nine, a "gymnasium" for the ages of nine to fifteen, and college from the age of fifteen to eighteen. My father died when I was fourteen, and my older brothers went out into the world to care for themselves. I was thus left at home alone with my mother, by whom I was directed toward a course to prepare me to practice medicine. This ambition, however—which originated with her and for which I never shared her enthusiasm—was never to be realized. When I was fifteen years old, the works of Sir John Franklin, the great British explorer, fell into my hands. I read them with a fervid fascination which has shaped the whole course of my life. Of all the brave Britishers who for four hundred years had given freely of their treasure, courage, and enterprise to dauntless but unsuccessful attempts to negotiate the Northwest Passage, none was braver than Sir John Franklin.[1] His description of the return from one of his expeditions thrilled me as nothing I had ever read before. He told how for three weeks he and his little band had battled with the ice and storms, with no food to eat except a few bones found at a deserted Indian camp, and how before they finally returned to the outpost of civilization they were reduced to eating their own boot leather to keep themselves alive.

Strangely enough the thing in Sir John's narrative that appealed to me most strongly was the sufferings he and his men endured. A strange ambition burned within me to endure those same sufferings. Perhaps the idealism of youth, which often takes a turn toward martyrdom, found its crusade in me in the form of Arctic exploration. I, too, would suffer in a cause—not in the blazing desert on the way to Jerusalem, but in the frozen North on the way to new knowledge in the unpierced unknown.

In any event, Sir John's descriptions decided me upon my career. Secretly —because I would never have dared to mention the idea to my mother, who I knew would be unsympathetic—I irretrievably decided to be an Arctic explorer.

More than that, I began at once to fit myself for this career. In Norway, in those days, there were no organized athletic sports as there are now everywhere. The only sports at all were football and skiing. Although I did not like football, I went in for it as part of the task of training my body to endure hardship. But to skiing I took with perfect naturalness and intense

[1] Sir John Franklin, who in 1845 sailed in search of the Northwest Passage and who ultimately perished in the Arctic.—Eds.

enthusiasm. At every opportunity of freedom from school, from November to April, I went out in the open, exploring the hills and mountains which rise in every direction around Oslo, increasing my skill in traversing ice and snow and hardening my muscles for the coming great adventure.

In those days, houses were kept tightly closed in winter, so I was regarded as an innovator and something of a freak because I insisted on sleeping with my bedroom windows wide open, even in the bitterest weather. My mother anxiously expostulated with me about this practice. To her I explained that I liked fresh air, but of course it was really a part of my conscientious hardening process.

At eighteen I graduated from the college, and, in pursuance of my mother's ambition for me, entered the university, taking up the medical course. Like all fond mothers, mine believed that I was a paragon of industry, but the truth is that I was a worse than indifferent student. Her death two years later, in my twenty-first year, saved her from the sad discovery which she otherwise would have made, that my own ambitions lay in another direction and that I had made but poor progress in realizing hers. With enormous relief, I soon left the university, to throw myself wholeheartedly into the dream of my life.

Before I could realize it, however, I had to discharge the duty of all young men in Norway, of performing my tour of military service. Military service in Norway occupies only a few weeks of the year, so I had plenty of time to carry on my own course of special training for my future career of explorer. One incident of this training very nearly wrote "finis" to my life, and involved dangers and hardships fully as severe as any I was destined ever to encounter in the polar regions.

This adventure happened in my twenty-second year. It was in an effort to achieve a sort of Arctic passage not many miles from Oslo itself. To the west of the capital there rises a line of steep mountainsides surmounted by a plateau of about six-thousand-feet elevation. This plateau extends westward nearly to the coast of Norway, in the neighborhood of Bergen, and is marked on that side by an even more abrupt descent—so difficult, in fact, that only two safe trails down its side exist. In summer the plateau was frequented only by Lapp herdsmen pasturing their nomadic herds of reindeer. No farmers lived there, so the only building of any sort in many miles was a hut erected by these herdsmen for shelter from cold rainstorms in the fall of the year. In the winter, the Lapps descended to the valleys, and the plateau was deserted. There was no record of any person having ever crossed the plateau in winter, from the mountain farm called Mogen on the east to the farm called Garen on the west coast. I determined to make this crossing.

Choosing a single companion, I proposed that we make the venture together. He agreed, and we left Oslo during the Christmas holidays. We made our way rapidly over the snow on our skis to the little farm called Mogen. Here we stopped at the last farmhouse that we expected to see on the whole trip. It was a tiny affair of only one room in which were crowded an old man and his wife and their two married sons—six people in all. They were, of course, of the simplest peasant type. There were no tourists in those days in any season of the year, so that our descent upon them would have been a surprise at any time. Coming as we did in the dead of winter, they were doubly astonished. We had no difficulty in persuading them to allow us to stay overnight with them. They were hospitable folk and made room for us on the floor near the fireplace, where we rolled ourselves up in our reindeer sleeping bags and slept very comfortably.

On the morrow, however, it was snowing, and this storm turned out to be a regular blizzard. It lasted for eight days, and we spent the whole of this time in the farmhouse.

Of course, our hosts were curious to know what errand could have brought us to their remote home. When we told them our plan to ascend to the plateau and cross it to the coast, they were first incredulous and then greatly alarmed for our safety. All three of the men were familiar with the plateau and joined in earnestly warning us not to attempt to cross it in winter. It had never been done, and they were sure it could not be done. Nevertheless, we were determined to push on and attempt it, so on the ninth day they accompanied us to the foot of the plateau at the head of their valley and showed us the best way to ascend. They bade us good-by sadly, and we understood that they feared they would never see us again.

Of course, we were lighthearted about the enterprise. To us it seemed simple enough. The plateau was only about seventy-two miles wide, and with our skill on skis and any decent luck with the weather, we counted at most on two days to make the crossing. Our equipment for the venture was based upon this theory, and accordingly was of the sketchiest character. Besides our skis and ski sticks, we each had a reindeer sleeping bag that we carried on our backs. We took no tent. Each of us had a small bag containing our provisions and a small alcohol lamp. This bag was rolled inside the sleeping bag. Our provisions consisted of a few crackers, some bars of chocolate, and a little butter—at the best scant rations for perhaps eight days. We had a pocket compass and a map of the region printed on paper.

We had no difficulty in ascending to the plateau. It was not a perfectly level plain that we found, but, for the practical purpose of travel, it might as well have been, for it offered no distinguishing landmarks to guide our course. There was nothing to be seen but an endless succession of small and indistinct hills.

We set our course by the compass. Our destination for our first day's travel was the herder's hut which was about in the middle of the plateau. At that time of the year in Norway, the daylight is little better than twilight, but with our compass we had no difficulty in getting along, and early in the evening we found the hut.

Our elation at this discovery was rather short-lived, for we found that the door and window of the hut had been nailed up and the top of the chimney covered over with heavy boards. We were pretty well tired with our day's exertions, the wind had started to blow again, and the thermometer was about ten degrees Fahrenheit below zero. With these handicaps, it was the hardest kind of work to get into the hut and later to clamber onto the roof and clear the top of the chimney so that we could start a fire. Both of us got our fingers badly frostbitten, and my companion, for some weeks after, was in grave danger of losing one of his.

We had the good fortune to find firewood stacked up in the hut. It took us some time, however, to make it of any use to us—if you have ever tried to build an open fire under a cold chimney with the thermometer below zero, you will understand the difficulty we had in getting a draft going. The cold air settles down on your fire like a blanket, and you have to get a pretty brisk blaze going before the heat displaces the column of cold air in the flue. Meanwhile, of course, in our efforts to do this, we had filled the little hut with smoke that got into our eyes and throats and caused us much discomfort.

We felt pretty good after we had the fire blazing and had eaten a supper. At length, we rolled up in our sleeping bags in the bunks on the opposite wall and slept very comfortably.

In the morning, we found that our troubles had only begun. The wind of the night before was still blowing, and it was now snowing heavily. The storm was so severe that it would obviously be folly to venture out in it. We therefore settled down to sit the storm out before the fireplace. Further exploration of the hut revealed another bit of good luck—it disclosed a small sack of rye flour that had been left behind by some herdsman. As we now realized that our own provisions must be husbanded, we made a thin porridge of this flour, which we cooked in an iron kettle over the open fire.

We spent two days in the hut, and the only food we took in that time was this weak porridge. At best, it was not very nourishing, and neither was it palatable.

On the third day, the storm had somewhat abated, and we decided to resume our march westward toward Garen. We now had to set our course very carefully, as there were only two places on the west coast at which a descent from the plateau was at all possible, and as these places were several miles apart, we had now definitely to choose one of them and reject the other. Having made this choice we set forward.

We had not gone far before it started snowing again and the weather grew milder. We had frequently to consult the map to take our bearings, and the wet snow falling on the flimsy paper soon reduced it to pulp. After that, we had to proceed as best we could by the compass alone.

Night overtook us before we reached the edge of the plateau and, of course, there was nothing to do but to camp where it found us, out in the open. That night nearly finished us. When we had unrolled our sleeping bags, we took out our provision bags and laid them at our feet. Alongside them we set up our ski sticks as markers to indicate in the morning where the bags were if the overnight snow should cover them. We spent the night in extreme discomfort. The soft snow had melted on our clothing and had saturated it with moisture. When we got into our sleeping bags, the heat of our bodies turned enough of this moisture into steam so that it permeated the inside of the sleeping bags as well. It was a wretched experience. Worse yet, it turned cold again in the night. I woke up in the darkness feeling half frozen, and was so uncomfortable that I could not go back to sleep. It finally occurred to me that, if I got up and drank some of the alcohol out of the lamp in my provision bag, it would restore my circulation. I climbed out of the sleeping bag and felt around in the dark until I got hold of my ski stick, and then I clawed about for my provision bag. To my astonishment and chagrin, it was not to be found. When morning broke, we both resumed the search and could find neither of the bags. To this day I have not been able to make a reasonable conjecture that would explain what became of them. There was, however, no doubt of the fact—they were gone.

Our plight now was worse than uncomfortable, it was extremely dangerous. Unless we could speedily reach shelter and food, we should certainly freeze to death. With this alarming situation confronting us, we headed west again in hopes of reaching the edge of the plateau before night fell.

Luck was still against us. It soon began to snow so heavily that we could not see our way more than a few feet ahead. We decided now that the only thing to do was to turn around and try to make our way east across the plateau to our starting point. We made a few miles on this new course when night again overtook us.

Again the night was wet. We were drenched, and our bags were still heavy with moisture. Snow was still falling. When night came on, we had reached a small peak that thrust up out of the plateau. We sought out its lee side, figuring that we might be reasonably comfortable if we could keep out of the wind. We found that it did make a good deal of difference. I decided to improve even on that. I dug into the snow and made myself a small cave not much larger than my body, and into the cave I climbed head first and pulled my bag in after me. I soon congratulated myself on this idea, for I escaped altogether the gusts of wind outside.

In the night, the weather turned cold suddenly. The wet snow had settled down on me in my cave and over its entrance at my feet. When the temperature dropped, it froze. In the middle of the night I woke up. I was lying on my back with my right wrist across my eyes and the palm of my hand up—as one often sleeps to keep the morning light out of his eyes. My muscles felt cramped and I made the instinctive move to change my position. I could not move an inch. I was practically frozen inside a solid block of ice! I struggled desperately to free myself, but without the slightest effect. I shouted to my companion. Of course he could not hear.

I was now stricken with horror. In my panic, I naturally thought he likewise had been frozen in the wet snow that had fallen in the night and that he was in a like predicament with me. Unless a thaw immediately set in, we should both soon freeze to death in our ghastly coffins of ice.

My shouts quickly died away, as I found it impossible to breathe deeply. I realized that I must keep quiet or I would suffocate. I do not know whether it was the heaviness of the little air I had to breathe, or what was the reason, but I soon dropped off into either sleep or unconsciousness. When I came to I could hear faint sounds. My companion, after all, had not been imprisoned. Probably the only reason he had not emulated my example and built himself a cave the night before was that he was too tired, and from exhaustion too indifferent, to go to the trouble. In any event, his failure to do so saved both our lives. When he awakened and looked about, he found himself alone in an ocean of snow. He called to me, and I did not answer. Then he began a frantic search for some trace that would show him where I had gone. There was only one, and providentially his eye fell upon it—a few hairs of the reindeer skin of my sleeping bag were visible in the snow. At once he began digging with his hands and ski stick to extricate me from my prison. It took him three hours to dig me out.

Both of us were now getting pretty weak. It was still night when he got me out, but we were too much upset to think of trying to rest further. Though it was still dark, the sky was clear and we were able to set a course and travel by the stars. We had been going two hours, with my companion in the lead, when suddenly he disappeared as if the earth had swallowed him up. Instinctively, I realized that he had gone over a precipice, and, instinctively, I acted instantly to save myself. I threw myself flat on the ground. A moment later, I heard his voice calling up, "Don't move. I have dropped over a precipice." He had indeed fallen about thirty feet. Fortunately, he had landed on his back, so that the sleeping bag which he carried as a pack on his shoulders had broken the force of the fall and he did not suffer more than a severe shaking up. Naturally, we did not attempt to go farther until daylight. Then we plowed ahead on our seemingly hopeless travels.

We had now been four days without food of any sort, and the two days before that our diet of weak rye porridge had not been much better, so far as sustenance was concerned. We were getting nearly exhausted. The only thing that had saved us from collapse was our ability to get drinking water. On the plateau were numerous little lakes connected by small streams, and at these streams we had been able to keep our stomachs filled with water, and this saved us from the extreme effects of starvation.

At nightfall we came upon a little shanty filled with hay. There were ski tracks around the shanty. This discovery renewed our courage and proved that we were certainly back near civilization. It gave us hope, that, if we could keep ourselves going, on the morrow we might find food and shelter. The hay offered us a luxurious bed, and we spent the night burrowed into the heart of it.

The next morning I turned out to explore our surroundings. My companion was now so exhausted and dispirited that he seemed unequal to the effort and I left him in the haymow while I followed the ski tracks. After an hour's trudging, I saw a man in the distance. I surmised correctly that he was a peasant farmer making the morning rounds of the snares he had set for ptarmigan. I called loudly to him. He gave a startled look and, to my dismay, proceeded to run as fast as he could away from me. These lonely peasants are a superstitious folk. While they are courageous enough in the presence of real danger, they suffer many terrors of their own creation.

Doubtless his first impression of me was of a ghostly apparition haunting the uninhabited plateau.

I called again and threw my whole soul into the cry. My tone must have conveyed my desperation, for the man stopped running and, after some hesitation, came back to meet me. I explained our plight and asked him where we were. I had a little difficulty in understanding his explanation, and even when I did, could hardly believe my senses, for it showed that we were now not more than an hour's travel from the farmhouse above Mogen from which, eight days before, we had started on our misadventure.

Heartened by this information, I hurried back for my companion. The news put fresh vigor in him, too, and soon, with no great trouble, we made our way down the little valley to the familiar farmhouse. We knocked at the door, were invited to enter, and went in. I was puzzled at our reception —until later I saw myself in the mirror. In the single room of the farmhouse the women were busy at their spinning and the men at wood-carving. They looked up hospitably, but merely greeted us with a brief "How do you do," in an entirely impersonal and inquiring manner. It was soon apparent that they did not recognize us. Little wonder, as I later realized, for our scraggly beards had grown, our eyes were gaunt and hollow, our cheeks were sunken, and the ruddy glow of color had changed to a ghastly greenish yellow. We were a truly awful spectacle. Our hosts at first would not believe us when we explained that we were the two young fellows who had left them eight days earlier. They could see no resemblance to their former guests in the gaunt specters before them. At length we convinced them, and they showed us every kindness. We spent a couple of days with them, eating and sleeping until our strength returned, and then, with many expressions of gratitude, we took our leave of them and made our way safe into Oslo.

The sequel of the story I did not myself learn until a year later, when I discovered it was known that the farmer who owned Garen, on the westerly edge of the plateau at the head of the trail we had intended to descend, had come out of his house one morning and found ski tracks within a few yards of his doorway coming from the east and not from the west. He could not credit his eyes, because he knew no one had ever come that way in the winter, nor did he believe it was possible. Those tracks could have been none other than ours, for the date also matched.

Think of it! We had been unknowingly within a hundred yards of our destination and had turned back to recross the plateau after being within ten minutes' walk of a safe haven on its western edge!

As I said when I started to describe this adventure, it involved as many hardships and dangers as anything I later encountered in my polar expeditions. It was a part of my preliminary training for my polar career. The training proved severer than the experience for which it was a preparation, and it well-nigh ended the career before it began.

ADVENTURER
EXTRAORDINARY—
SIR FRANCIS DRAKE

by A. L. Rowse

If ever an adventurer typified the spirit which Theodore Roosevelt describes in the first selection, it was Sir Francis Drake, darling of Elizabethan England and special favorite of its red-haired Queen. Drake singed the beard of King Philip of Spain and in so doing helped change the course of history. When his time was on him, he rose to put on his armor so that he might die like a soldier. Drake was of that company which included Grenville, Hawkins and Frobisher. He ranged farther, indeed around the world, than any of the others. About him there was an élan, a spirit "palpably heroic" and romantic, that clings to his name even at the present day.

ON HIS third voyage [to the West Indies] Hawkins[1] had ten ships, big and small, including two ships of the Queen's, the *Jesus* and the *Minion*. He made a successful trading voyage, the colonists again being only too glad to trade with him by connivance, against the commands of their remote master. Hawkins was ready to return, when gales sprang up and the leaky hulk of the *Jesus* nearly foundered. She was in urgent need of repair, if she was ever to get home, and the only harbor was the port of Mexico, San Juan de Ulloa. While the English were in harbor, the new

From *The Expansion of Elizabethan England* by A. L. Rowse. Reprinted by permission of Macmillan & Co., Ltd. and St. Martin's Press Inc.
[1] Sir John Hawkins.—Eds.

Viceroy arrived with a large fleet. Hawkins, with his superior gun-power, could have kept him out. But that would have been an open declaration of war, and Hawkins was the Queen's representative. With misgivings in his heart, he made way and made room. Don Martín Enríquez gave his written word that all should be well—and then seized the opportunity, with overwhelming manpower, to board the English ships. It was an act of simple and black treachery which was never forgotten or forgiven by any of the Elizabethan seamen—though it was in keeping with much else that the Spaniards did in this high noonday of their power, like Menéndez's promise to the French garrison in Florida and, then, slaughtering them.

The immediate consequences for the English were terrible. The *Jesus*, the occasion of the disaster, was left there disabled. Such of her crew as survived the sudden onslaught leaped into the *Minion*, which got away—with two hundred men on board and hardly any victuals or water. The little *Judith*, whose captain was the young Drake, "forsook us in our great misery." (Drake was one to look out for himself; but, indeed, what could he have done?) It was the end of the Anglo-Spanish friendship that had endured since the early days of Henry VII. Henceforth, Spain had a vigorous and clever and tenacious enemy to deal with.

For the next eight years the West Indies were kept in a ferment of reprisals and irregular warfare by the privateers: the English had penetrated into the Caribbean, "and in one capacity or another they have been there ever since." The key figure in this phase is the young Drake. With his early career we enter the realm of the romantic—it is like *Treasure Island* translated back into history—as, with his later, we enter the region of the palpably heroic. Those characteristics in Drake's unique career were of the essence of the age—as we can see from the way it took Drake to its heart and made of him the most famous Englishman of his day. Along with many other incidents and gestures of the time, flashes of Drake's personality, images of him at revealing moments, have become part of the myth of the English people. Drake was one of those rare persons in history who had a magic about him: he possessed an aura, along with a charmed life. There is no doubt about it: Spaniards bore witness to the quality in their most dangerous enemy, no less than the English. The simple inhabitants of the coasts he visited thought of him as something more than human, a demon; instructed Spaniards could not withhold their admiration from the combination of fighting courage with humanity, of a natural force —like a thunderbolt coming out of the blue—with debonair good manners that charmed all those he captured. Lope de Vega, who devoted a whole epic to recounting his misdeeds, could not forbear a tribute to the man. And Juan de Castellanos, who witnessed the havoc Drake made in the Indies in 1585, wrote a narrative poem that bears witness to the nobility that was in the subject of the poem.

The English have so many moments of him imprinted on their mind: of the early August Sunday in 1573, about sermon time, when the news ran over the town at Plymouth that the Captain was back from Nombre de Dios, and all the congregation poured out of St. Andrew's, their minds were so surpassed "with desire and delight to see him that very few or none remained with the preacher." Or perhaps it is at Nombre de Dios itself, outside the King's treasurehouse, and Drake telling his men that he had brought them to the mouth of the treasurehouse of all the world; or climbing that tree from which he first saw the Pacific and praying, if God would give him life and leave, that he might sail an English ship once upon those waters; or listening in the silent night for the sound of mulebells outside Venta de las Cruces; or, at the end, taking a gold quoit out of his doublet, "Thank God, our voyage is made." Or we think of him on the voyage round the world, discovering that there was sea to the south of the American Continent, going out to the uttermost point of land, flinging himself on the ground and reaching out over as far as he could go; or preaching his sermon to the quarreling ship's company, "I must have the gentleman to haul and draw with the mariner, and the mariner with the gentleman." Or hovering in the haze behind St. Nicholas's Island—that is now called after his name—on his return, with his first question, "Is the Queen alive or dead?"; and the scene on board the *Golden Hind* with the Queen threatening to cut off his head and handing the sword to the French ambassador to knight him—by way of inculpating France a little. Or we think of the sad last voyage, ending where he had begun in those familiar, colored, hurricane-visited seas and, checkmated and dying, rising out of delirium to put on his armor and "meet death like a soldier." His body was committed to the sea there, but his spirit can never be far away from Plymouth Hoe. Or we may think of him in the end as the first governor in Newfoundland, when a boy at home in Devon, remembered seeing him

As he was walking up Totnes' long street:
He asked me whose I was? I answered him.
He asked me if his good friend were within?
A fair red orange in his hand he had;
He gave it me, whereof I was right glad,
Takes and kissed me, and prays God bless my boy.

We recall that he had no children of his own.

His children were his exploits. They were the fruit of careful planning and preparation. The Hawkins brothers sent Drake out in the winter of 1570-71 as a first step toward recouping their losses: he despoiled Venta de las Cruces. Later in 1571, in the twenty-five ton *Swan*, he made a rapid reconnaissance voyage on which he burnt a ship in Cartagena and brought the owner back to Plymouth for ransom. Next year, 1572-73, with the *Swan* and the *Pasco* of seventy tons, he carried out the campaign he planned, for which he had gathered information and made his preparations. It involved more than campaigning: it necessitated first-class seamanship: "the crews of those days included carpenters, smiths and sail-makers, who could do wonders of shipbuilding on desolate beaches, all with the tools and materials they carried with them." They took back some forty thousand pounds in treasure.

Meanwhile, at home, schemes for long-range discovery and overseas settlement were beginning to take shape. By far the most important was Grenville's carefully planned, and very nearly made ready, project for such a voyage into the Pacific, the first of its kind. The two problems of the Pacific that exercised the keenest minds at the time were that of the existence of *Terra Australis*, a great continent in the Southern Hemisphere to balance the land mass of Europe and Asia in the Northern; and that of the whereabouts of a supposed Strait of Anian leading from the Pacific end to the North-West Passage into the Atlantic. The main object of the voyage was to discover this continent, open up trade with it and plant settlements there

In 1574 circumstances were not propitious for such a challenge to the Spanish Empire, and the Queen refused to grant Grenville a licence. Three years later they had changed: she was willing to grant to the upstart young captain what she had refused to an aristocratic Grenville. According to Drake, she had said, "Drake! So it is that I would gladly be revenged on the King of Spain for divers injuries that I have received." To the Spanish ambassador she said, "The gentleman careth not if I disavow him." In fact, "the business was as fully a state undertaking, although capable of disguise, as Hawkins's West Indian expeditions had been."

It was only this fact and the authority it gave him that enabled Drake to surmount the critical difficulties of venture "which becomes ever more astonishing as we learn more about it." The strain of the voyage was tremendous, and not merely physical. There was the latent opposition of Doughty,[2]

---

[2] Later in the voyage, Drake beheaded him for treachery.—Eds.

coming gradually into the open and issuing in disloyalty and disaffection that might well have wrecked the voyage, as similar divisions wrecked so many others. The objectives had been kept absolutely secret: when they were revealed at the Equator, those who objected to the course (they had been told they were going to Alexandria) provided a party in support of Doughty —mainly the landsmen on board against the seamen, who were with Drake. None of them had crossed the Equator before, and nerves were on edge in the equatorial calms in which they made no progress; the baffling winds and calms off the coast of Brazil the men put down to Doughty's conjuring; the furious storms they met with once they were through the Strait and in the belt of Brave West Winds threatened to drive them back onto the coast or into the Strait again for shelter—from which Winter in the *Elizabeth* could not emerge, though he tried again and again. Drake in the *Golden Hind* had had his usual luck and made the exceedingly dangerous navigation of the passage in sixteen days—the shortest record of the century. (Magellan had taken thirty-seven days, Cavendish and Richard Hawkins were to take forty-nine and forty-six: they were repeatedly blown back at the exit by the head wind from the west.)

Once through into the Pacific—"as a pelican alone in the wilderness—" Drake made a lunge westward to find the coast of *Terra Australis,* but the winds were dead against. It was then, too, that he discovered that there was a sea passage around the southernmost tip of the American Continent; but he made nothing of it: perhaps because he did not want the Spaniards to get hold of his discovery. Off Panama, his voyage was "made" by the capture of the richly laden treasure ship the *Cacafuego*: "we found in her great riches, as jewels and precious stones, thirteen chests full of reals of plate, four score pound weight of gold, and six and twenty ton of silver." Drake's young cousin, John—they were often painting together in Drake's cabin—was the first to catch sight of her from the top and so to earn Drake's gold chain. This lad was wrecked on the Plate coast a few years later; made prisoner by the Inquisition, he was reconciled to the Church, married safely in the country and lived the rest of his life there—so Drake blood is there still.

We can now see the famous voyage from the Spanish side, from the subsequent evidence of the prisoners whom Drake invariably released, after little acts of courtesy and kindness that conquered their hearts. They all spoke well of the English corsair who apologized as he took a cross of emerald from one or some porcelain and silks from another—but we must not call him a "corsair," for that made him angry: he insisted to all and sundry that he was the Queen's officer holding her commission. And he told his captives exactly how he viewed things and what was the ground of dispute: if the King would not permit trade in the Atlantic, then he would suffer depredations in both oceans; he himself intended to go on until he recovered the two millions his cousin had lost at San Juan de Ulloa. He meant to plant settlements. Don Francisco de Zarate was sailing along in the moonlight just before dawn, off Acapulco, when he found the *Golden Hind* beside him. There was no resistance and, when Don Francisco was brought on board, Drake was walking up and down on deck. "He received me with a show of kindness and took me to his cabin, where he bade me be seated and said, 'I am a friend of those who tell me the truth, but with those who do not I get out of humor.'" Drake asked if there were any gold or silver, or anything belonging to Don Martín Enríquez, on board. On being told that there was not, he said, "Well, it would give me greater joy to come across him than all the gold and silver in the Indies. You would see how the words of gentlemen should be kept." At dinner, "he ordered me to sit next to him and began giving me food from his own plate, telling me not to grieve, that my life and property were safe. I kissed his hands for this. . . . Of that which belonged to me he took but little. Indeed he was quite courteous about it. Certain trifles of mine having taken his fancy, he had them brought to his ship and gave me, in exchange for them, a falchion [a broadsword] and a small brazier of silver, and I can assure your Excellency that he lost nothing by the bargain. On his return to his vessel he asked me to pardon him for taking the trifles, but that they were for his wife."

To each of the Spanish sailors and of the poor among the passengers Drake gave a handful of reals—which we may contrast with the Spanish treatment of the French in Florida, or the English at Lima. Zarate gives us the most intimate view into the *Golden Hind* that we have: Drake's men were under strict discipline—the clue to his success where so many others broke down; "when our ship was sacked, no man dared take anything without his orders: he shows them great favor, but punishes the least fault. . . . Each one takes particular pains to keep his arquebus clean. He also carries painters who paint for him pictures of the coast in exact colors. He carries trained carpenters and artisans, so as to be able to careen the ship at any time. . . . He is served on silver dishes with gold borders and gilded garlands, in which are his arms. He carries all possible dainties and perfumed waters: he said that many of these had been given him by the Queen. He dines and sups to the music of viols." There was always music

and musicians on board these ships—singing and dancing were a chief solace
of the sailors: on Cavendish's voyage round the world "they played and
danced all the forenoon among the Negroes" on shore (who can think of
sailors dancing without a leap of the heart?). After Drake's death there
was taken from his ship "a chest of instruments of music . . . lute, oboes,
sackbuts, cornets and orpharions, bandora and suchlike." But that was
happily twenty years on. When Don Francisco managed to ascertain
"whether the General was well liked, all said that they adored him."

And so on up the Pacific coast beyond California into higher latitudes—
to the coast of present-day British Columbia—until the weather grew rough
and cold: possibly Drake was looking for the Strait of Anian through which
to come direct home. Turning back again, he found a good anchorage near
modern San Francisco where to give the ship a refit before crossing the
Pacific. Here the white men were worshiped as gods by the local Indians—
embarrassing for a rather devout Protestant like Drake, who took Foxe's
Book of Martyrs with him (as other ships did), and pointed out victims
of the Inquisition to insufficiently inquisitive Spaniards. At this spot Drake
raised a monument with an inscription proclaiming California one of the
Queen's dominions under the name of New Albion. Thence he made a
prosperous passage across the Pacific to the Moluccas, crossed the Indian
Ocean and so back to Plymouth Sound.

The voyage had reverberating effects in every direction. It was a sudden
and brilliant demonstration that a new power had arrived on the oceans.
Drake was not only the first Englishman to sail the Pacific, but the first
to cross the Indian Ocean—familiar to the Portuguese since Vasco da Gama.
That showed how backward the English had been—and also with what a
sudden swoop they were now catching up: for Drake had accomplished in
one voyage what Dias, da Gama and Magellan had done separately over
years. It enormously raised the prestige of England in Europe and the
confidence of England in herself, on the threshold of the eighties that
were to see the country not afraid to come to grips with the world empire
. . . Spain.

THE
OLD FRONTIERSMAN—
GEORGE ROGERS CLARK

by Walter Havighurst

Often, though not always, it is the fate of the explorer to see the world catch up with him. Perhaps, like many an American frontiersman, he has been driven on his journeys by a need for space, for room to move around. Perhaps, like Daniel Boone when elbow room was lacking, he moves along to places where fences do not exist. More likely, he resigns himself to the inevitability of change.

George Rogers Clark is a name synonymous with the settlement of the Ohio, adventure in the Kentucky wilderness, conquest of the frontier lands of Illinois and the winning of the West for a new nation. At the end, the famous old General built himself a house by the river and watched the endless stream of settlers, traders, soldiers and bad men go by, where once there had been endless forests inhabited only by Indians and wild beasts.

IN ALL his roving life George Rogers Clark had owned just one home of his own; it was a lean-to hut, dim as a cave, where Fish Creek flowed into the great Ohio. He won territory that gave homes to multitudes of Americans, but for thirty years he had no place of his own. At last, in the autumn of his life, he built a small log house on the north side of the Falls of the Ohio. So he became a citizen of the Northwest Territory which he had won for his country.

There he went to live in 1803 with three faithful Negro servants, Kitt, Cupid, and Venus. The house stood on a wooded hill above the river; it looked down at the thickets of Corn Island where once he had readied his little army for the great campaign. Inside the door was a littered living room, in bachelor disorder, strewn with books, maps, surveying records, drawings of forts and Indian mounds, crumbs of tobacco, old pencil stubs, and wooden shavings. Before a blackened fireplace a bearskin rug lay on the rough floor. There, or on the small square porch outside, rocking slowly in a creaking chair, the old warrior sat with his memories. Back in the kitchen Venus sang as she poured corn meal into a baking tin, and from the garden came the clink of a hoe where Kitt was hilling up the bean vines. But the sound that never ceased was the roar of the rapids, and the old man heard it night and day. It was an ancient sound; it filled the valley before the first white hunters found the Indian trails, before the first French explorers journeyed down the Ohio, before the Indians hollowed their first log canoes, before the ancient mounds were heaped above the ancient dead. It was an unchanging sound, but it came to the old general with many voices. Sometimes it rose loud and high like a storm wind in a forest, sometimes it was a far-off thunder, sometimes a throbbing of many Indian drums.

On fine days the old soldier walked down to the river, through thickets of dogwood, wild plum, and willow, with his rifle cradled in his arm. His hands were still steady and his eyes were true; he brought back a brace of ducks for Venus to brown in the kitchen oven. After supper he sat in his worn chair watching the sunset over the far dark line of forest and the blue dusk veiling the hurrying water. Two miles away, at the head of the islands, Louisville lay like stars on the dark riverbank.

In the bright light of October, 1803, a white pirogue, built that summer at Pittsburgh, waited under the hill while two young travelers sat on the porch with the old commander. Their eyes kept lifting to the West, and the West was all they talked of—Meriwether Lewis, looking more youthful than his twenty-six years, erect, fair-haired, with gentle mouth and serious deep-set eyes, awkward in his movements but with strength and chivalry in his face; and tall, lean, red-haired William Clark, rugged and resourceful, generous and hearty, his gray eyes lighted with distance and excitement. Between them sat George Rogers Clark. No one knew more than the old general of the land and lore of the Old Northwest, but these two captains were talking about strange far rivers—the Platte, the Snake, the Yellowstone, the Columbia. Now they were bound for St. Louis where they would recruit their men and gather stores and equipment for the epic journey. Ahead of them lay distance and danger, hardship and hunger, promise and discovery. They gripped the old man's hand and strode down the steep riverbank. Their pirogue swept into the current—the same current that had carried a fleet of barges on the way to capture Kaskaskia twenty-five years before. On the little porch the chair creaked slowly and the old man's eyes looked westward.

Three years and one month later, on a chill day in November, 1806, a boat pulled up the strong current and made fast to Clark's landing. Up the hill strode two men, lean, brown, hardened, with a new fortitude in their faces. They found the old man on his porch, wrapped in a faded blue coat, and they gripped his gnarled hand. Captains Lewis and Clark had come back from their discovery. They had seen fierce Sioux warriors in deerskin leggings fringed with scalp locks of their enemies, herds of antelope skimming like swallows across the prairie, dark masses of buffalo making the earth rumble as they ran. In the desolate Dakota winter they had stared at sundogs on the skyline and three pale rings encircling the ice-white moon. After hundreds of miles of gaunt and lonely plains, they saw the Shining Mountains like a drift of clouds across the Western sky. They had followed huge game tracks and faced grizzly bears that rose up eight feet tall, waving great hairy paws like a boxer. At night they had heard a quaver of wolves in the buttes and at dawn the roar of mating buffalo like a thunder in the valley. They had stared silent at the flow of the Columbia in its solemn gorge and at the Pacific crashing on the rocks of Oregon. . . . Now all these pictures were in the strewn room where an old man listened, his hooded eyes staring at the fire. He had crossed one wilderness; his tall young brother had completed the journey that led from Virginia to the Western Sea.

In those years a man sitting above the Ohio could watch the march of America. This was the only great river that flowed west (except the far-off, fabulous Columbia) and so it was a highway like no other. Young George Rogers Clark had seen it lonely and vast, rolling in grandeur past his Fish Creek camp. Now old George Rogers Clark saw it laden with the life of a new nation. It carried rafts and keelboats, pirogues and barges, arks and broadhorns, "Kentucky boats" bound only for the Falls and "New Orleans boats" bound all the way to the Gulf of Mexico. It brought soldiers and settlers, pirates and preachers, artisans and aristocrats. At Pittsburgh an endless throng waited for passage west, and mountains of trade goods grew on the landings. Flour, salt, iron, cider, whisky, barrel staves, pottery, bricks, wheels, door and window frames, all moved down the Ohio; molasses, sugar, coffee, lead, and hides made the slower journey against the river current.

Floating gristmills called at the river towns. Floating tinsmiths mended pots and kettles on the landings. A floating blacksmith shop traveled up and down the river, its anvil clanging like a pilot's bell. Sawmills and furniture shops plied the Ohio, spilling a stream of yellow sawdust on the current. Store boats clanged bells at the landings, and women trooped down to buy salt, soap, mustard, muslin. The first newspaper in the West was printed on a flatboat, the first library was a barge lined with bookshelves, the first theaters were flatboats with the audience seated on the sloping river bank.

Coming round a bend, the flatboatmen blew a long wooden horn; its soft sad notes carried for miles over the water. The crews sang a flatboat song:

> Hi-o
> Away we go,
> Floating down the river
> On the O-hi-o.

And the crews of the faster keelboats mocked the plodding flatboatmen:

> Hard upon the beech oar!
> She moves too slow!
> All the way to Shawneetown,
> A long time ago.

Then the keelboatmen were humbled by the steamboat. In fine October weather in 1811 down the Ohio came a wonderful craft, 138 feet long, 26 feet wide, painted blue as the Kentucky sky, with two tall chimneys towering upward. Just seventy hours out of Pittsburgh, it reached Louisville on a moonlit night, its paddles churning, its ranked windows all agleam, the pent-up steam seething from its boilers. At Louisville it waited for high water; after a heavy autumn rain it ran the rapids and steamed on toward the Mississippi.

So the first steamboat, the *New Orleans*, in command of its builder and captain, Nicholas J. Roosevelt, passed the house above the river in November, 1811. That was a strange, historic month—the month when William Henry Harrison fought the Indians at Tippecanoe in the Wabash bottoms; when the earth of Kentucky trembled with "the great shake" and the Mississippi, throwing up huge jets of reddish mud, changed its ancient course; when a fiery comet passed through the northern sky.

Many times George Rogers Clark had traveled the empty Ohio, but now the river was never empty. Each year the tide increased, people from

Virginia and Pennsylvania, from New York and New England, from England, Scotland, Ireland, and Wales, from France and Germany. The Northwest had been won from the British, but now the London newspapers advertised great tracts of land in Kentucky, in Ohio, in the Western territories. Already Kentucky had been established as a state. The old trails had become broad turnpikes with stage lines rattling from town to town. The old fort stations had grown into graceful elm-shadowed villages with the stockades sinking to ruin and only the old men remembering the quaver of war cries in the "year of the bloody sevens." The forest that Clark had surveyed in 1773 was now the capital city of Frankfort. At the site of the Zane cabins on Wheeling Creek, where Clark had beached his canoe and surveyed wild country, there was a clamor of horns, bells, and teamsters' cries. In place of the council ring at Chillicothe was a busy Ohio town; the battlefield at Piqua was owned by land speculators. Vincennes was the territorial capital of the Northwest, and Kaskaskia was soon to be the capital of the new state of Illinois.

So many changes—so quickly the wilderness became a tamed and settled land. An old man could remember when the Great Forest covered it like a rug, threaded by Indian trails and trampled at the licks by the big game animals. Now towns grew up where the hunting trails had crossed; the stagecoach passed morning and afternoon. Roadside markers directed a traveler on his way; "To Lexington," "To Frankfort," "To Louisville" replaced the old savage signs and blazes, the rude drawings of deer, bear, and buffalo, of sun and moon.

"Clark's Land" was the name given the 149,000 acres granted to his troops. But it was *all* Clark's land, and it was Jefferson's land, also. Thomas Jefferson had never seen the vast slow rivers of the West or the green avenues of its forest paths, but in his mind's eye he could see its farms, villages, and towns, and he had pushed the land acts through Congress. Now land offices were spaced from Pittsburgh to the Mississippi; the whole country was open to settlement and purchase at two dollars an acre. When Henry Clay, Kentucky's eloquent young statesman, journeyed home from Washington, he stepped out of the stagecoach, bent over in the road, and put his ear to the ground.

"What are you listening for, Mr. Clay?" the driver asked.

"I am listening," said Henry Clay, "to the tread of unnumbered thousands of feet that will come this way westward."

From his porch above the river the man who had won the Northwest watched the future claim it. Sometimes an old soldier came to see him, on land business in Clark's Grant or just to think about old times—lean times, hard times, but the best times—when they were young in a wild, disputed country that demanded all their strength and hardihood. They filled their pipes and slowly emptied their glasses, and for a little while the old flames flickered in Clark's hooded eyes. Occasionally a moody chief sat with him, smoking in Indian silence, staring across the river to the busy streets of Louisville where people had forgotten the fear of scalping knives. They were two primitives, left over from another time.

One visitor brought another kind of memory. Once in a while young John James Audubon came in from the woods or the river. A man of many wanderings, he was not yet twenty-five when he sat with the brooding general above the river. Tall and slender, with a swinging stride that could carry him through miles of swamp and bottom timber, he had dreamy gray eyes and fair hair falling to his shoulders. He was a courteous man in a drawing room and a tireless man on the trail. In him burned a passion for the wilderness, even then disappearing, and so he had a bond with the old woodsman. He knew the wilds as well as any scout, though he had never lifted a rifle in warfare. For twenty years he was to live on the frontier, seeking birds and passionately painting them in a huge folio that he would at last take to England for publication.

To Louisville young Audubon had come with his soft-voiced wife Lucy; they lived in the Indian Queen Tavern, and Audubon worked in a frontier store. But his mind was not on the lanterns and axes, the gingham and muslin, the spools of thread and the packets of needles on the rough shelves; his thoughts were of egrets and herons wading the Ohio shallows, of vireos, linnets, and warblers in the canebrakes. Some days he failed to appear at the store. He was off with a rifle in the river bottoms to add a new hawk or a new heron to his collection. After a long day in the woods he might come to Clark's door, tired, wet, and hungry, and ready for a sundown glass of spirits while his jacket steamed by the fire. He would tell about a new species of kingfisher, and while he talked, he would take a pencil from the littered table and begin to draw; with swift sure strokes the bird took form on the back of a land plot in Clark's Grant. Or he would tell of a hunt he had made with a party of Shawnee and explain how he had learned to make the call of the wild turkey through a piece of hollow bone. He had quick eyes, quick slender hands, and he talked with hurrying words in English strongly accented with French. An ardent and companionable youth, he some way warmed the mind of the old warrior until he talked with his own urgency about the wilderness of forty years before, the game at the licks and the fowl in the marshes. All his life Clark had been a naturalist. He had observed carefully and he remembered well. Now he needed only to close his eyes to see the wild glades of the Kanawha, the great trees and the tiny sedges, the wary wild tracks beside a shadowed stream. He could draw a quick map for young Audubon showing all the bends of the Licking or the Wabash, marking the ancient mounds beside the rivers. The young man and the old one had much to talk about as dusk gathered beyond the window.

They did not discuss the growth of Louisville, the new line of keelboats bringing flour and pork to the landings, or the barrel-stave shops springing up in Indiana towns. They talked about the back country, the still wild regions, the sites of Indian villages, and the mysterious burial mounds. Some travelers had speculated that the great mounds were not built by Indians but rather by the legendary Welsh prince Madoc in his legendary search for Utopia, or by De Soto and his Spanish expeditions. Clark had written his own rebuttal to that fantasy. He had seen many hundreds of mounds, from the Monongahela to the Mississippi, and now he shook his rumpled head as he said to Audubon, "Madoc and De Soto must have had a busy time if they built all the mounds I can remember."

So the young man with a bird skin in his pocket ready for mounting with wire and clay, and the old man with memory in his eyes talked over their food and drink. Audubon had never stalked an Indian or fought his way out of ambush, but a visit from him was as good as talk with an old comrade.

By 1810 the old comrades were few and widely scattered. The loud-voiced men who thronged Louisville's landing, the heavy-jowled men who sat in the Indian Queen talking about the Embargo Act and the rising price of Illinois acres were a different race from those who had traveled the trails with all their possessions in a game sack. The lean men, the silent men who left no sign—where were they now?

For Daniel Boone, Kentucky had become a land too tame. After the wars he raised a crop or two on his farm at Marble Creek, but his heart was not in that. He had claims to 100,000 rich Kentucky acres, all of it tangled in legal complications. Smarter men, with pre-emption papers and deeds of entry, took possession. The lithe old hunter made no great complaint; perhaps his heart was not in that either. He was lined and gray, but he had not lost his hunger for new country. In 1780 he left Kentucky to find "elbow room" beyond the Mississippi; he followed the bear and the buffalo to the

West. While George Rogers Clark sat on his porch above the river, Daniel Boone was hunting in the Ozark Mountains and learning the language of the Osage tribes. He had made the first trace over Cumberland Gap, marking the way with white slashes on dark forest trees, but Kentucky had no need of him now.

Tall Chief Tobacco's Son, the "Grand Door of the Wabash," had died many years before. He kept the treaty he had made with Clark, and he remembered the "Big Knives'" friendship. A year after the victory at Vincennes he died in his ancestral Wabash Valley, where morning mists rise from the meadows and sycamores lean above the water. He asked to be buried among the Americans at Vincennes.

Simon Kenton, the fair-haired giant with a gentle smile, had become a scarred and dented man. Already he was a legend in the Ohio settlements. *Eight times*, they said, *he was forced to run the gantlet, three times tied to a stake, once left for dead after an ax had felled him.* But he was still treading the trails, trading knives, traps, and blankets for the Indians' peltry, ginseng, and cranberries, going on long hunts with the Wyandots, losing land in lawsuits that he could not fathom. Finally he was sentenced to debtor's prison but the sheriff reported that "he refused to be arrested," and so he kept his freedom. He knew all the Ohio country, the long lake road through the forest of the Seneca and past the rivers where the fishing camps were pitched in spring, the dark woods of White Woman Creek and the deep gorges of the Cuyahoga, the wild green ridges of the Olentangy and the dark wastes of the Black Swamp. When war came again in 1812, he was fifty-eight years old and limping on a broken leg. But he rode off to a new campaign, joining the American troops moving on Detroit (Clark's dream fulfilled at last, by other men). In enemy country across the Detroit River he took a day off to visit an old friend and an old enemy: he found Simon Girty old, abject, and brooding in a little farm on the Canadian shore.

Simon Girty, terror of the border, had become before his death a dark legend. The white man who had led howling Indians against the settlements lived a long life and died in bed. Once he had been a scout with Clark and Kenton, strong on the trail, wise and crafty in the woods; now he was twisted with rheumatism and smoldering with memories. His hair was white as ashes, the skin lay wrinkled on his bull-like neck, his eyes were darkening to blindness. Girty the renegade was dying like Clark the conqueror—old, obscure, helpless, brooding, in a house above a river. Sometimes a moody Indian stopped to visit him, but there was no more strategy to plan against the white militia, no traps to spring on defenseless settlements. The "Big Wind," General Wayne, had been dead for twenty years. Chief Blue Jacket was buried beside the Auglaize River in Ohio. Old Tarhe the Crane was in his grave beside the Sandusky, and Little Turtle lay under the grass of Kekionggay near Fort Wayne, in the new state of Indiana. In February, 1818, while swirling snow hid the river outside his door, Simon Girty died. They had to hack the ground with pickaxes to dig his grave.

The lean men—comrades and enemies—it was like a roll of drums to call their names. Sitting in his gray room, with the fire sinking and snow outside his window, Clark could even remember the drummer boy trudging on in cold and misery, stubbornly pounding his wet drum as the men floundered toward Vincennes. Now the roar of the winter river came to him vaguely, like a muffled beat of drums.

On such a day he slumped suddenly in his chair, his big head nodding and his right leg jerking out. When he woke he was numb, as though half his body had gone to sleep. He tried to move his arm, his hand, his knee, his foot. He was paralyzed.

His people in Louisville begged him to leave the lonely house, but Clark was an independent man. He stayed there, like a bear in his cave. But one cold day, hobbling across the room to mend the fire, he fell. Kitt and Venus found him, his leg badly burned by the embers on the hearth. When an infection grew, the doctors said his leg must go.

George Rogers Clark had seen men maimed, scalped, mangled. Now he stared stonily as the surgeon made ready. There was no anesthetic to draw a curtain on pain, but he asked for a fifer and drummer. While the surgeon worked, they marched round and round the house; Clark lay staring at the hewn rafters, the fingers of his live hand keeping time to the music. A hundred times he had marched past the border of exhaustion; he had endured hunger, cold, and pain. Now he lay stolid as an Indian while his leg was cut away. . . .

His life was darkening. Another stroke of paralysis left him voiceless. He was an old man, maimed, mute, helpless, but he could not die. Always he had been too strong to surrender. So he hung on, year after year, his mind growing dim, his eyes staring out of memory and silence.

Only the lasting memories could be left him then. The criticism must have faded, the bitterness must have gone. The busy towns, the commerce-laden roads and rivers, the grasping men in land offices and courthouse halls—these could be forgotten. The deep memories remained: a smoke-blue ridge of mountains darkening against the sunset, a grassy road dipping past Fort Necessity and leading to the Forks of the Ohio, the silent burial mounds in forest shadows, the sharp spiced smell of the woods at daybreak, the murmur of creek water under the willows, the faint print of a moccasin on a sandy shore, the creak of saddle leather, boots steaming and stiffening by the fire, the quaver of turkey cries around a besieged station, an enemy flag on a blockhouse and men creeping up with rifles ready, a chief blowing smoke to the four winds, a bare room in a stockade with a map of disputed country on the wall. These were more lasting than humiliation—but even these faded before the end.

He could not live easily and he could not die easily. But at last the stubborn heart faltered. He died on February 13, 1818, and was buried two days later in the private cemetery at Locust Grove. Guns were fired over his grave, but the sound was softened by a falling snow. Snow was falling in the little burial plot, covering the mound of frozen earth, whitening the thorny branches of the locust trees. It was falling in the streets of Louisville and where the river made its everlasting crying on the rocks. It was falling on the house above the river, on the little porch where an old man had sat in his rocking chair, and falling on the gray prairies of Illinois and in the Wabash bottoms. It whitened the streets of Kaskaskia and the churchyard at Vincennes. It was falling on the camps of the Indians and the old burial mounds beside the Mississippi. It fell silently on the flag-draped coffin that was lowered into Kentucky earth at Locust Grove.

In that same month, while the same snow was falling, Simon Girty died in his farmhouse beside the Detroit River. In that year, 1818, a woman named Nancy Hanks Lincoln died at Pigeon Creek, Indiana, and eight-year-old Abe Lincoln whittled pegs for her coffin. In that year Illinois became a state, and at St. Marys, Ohio, a treaty was signed by Wyandot, Shawnee, and Ottawa chiefs, defining their last reservations in the Ohio country. In that year crews of Irish workmen began digging the Erie Canal, the first Great Lakes steamship, *Walk-in-the-Water*, voyaged between Buffalo, Cleveland, and Detroit, and the National Road was opened to traffic over the mountains to Wheeling on the Ohio, where George Rogers Clark had once built a lean-to cabin on the empty shore.

MAPS

by Lloyd A. Brown

What are the tools of the explorer? There is the basic equipment—food, clothing, shelter, medicines—which he needs in order to survive. There are the guns and trinkets and knowledge of primitive human nature which protect him from or endear him to the natives of the territories he invades. There are the compasses which tell him the direction in which he is going and compasses, possibly an original invention of the Chinese, were used by Western navigators as early as the twelfth century. There are the maps which show him where he is and where his objective lies.

To make accurate maps, accurate determinations of latitude and longitude are necessary. The history of map making is therefore a history also of the improvement of instruments for making these determinations. To find his latitude the navigator must have an instrument that can be pointed at the heavenly bodies to measure their altitude above the horizon, for as the latitude changes, so obviously does the angle of altitude. At first this was done with the astrolabe, a circle marked with a scale in degrees and a diametrical pointer in the center that could be moved and set on sun or star. The quadrant, similar to the astrolabe, was a quarter of the complete circle. On land these instruments had fair accuracy. At sea, on a tossing ship, it was a different story. In the seventeenth century the great English navigator, John Davis, combined the principle of the quadrant with that of the cross-staff, an instrument for measuring angles between heavenly bodies which had first been described by the Persian Avicenna in the eleventh century. This "Davis quadrant" was widely used on English ships. The greatest advance, however, came with the development by Thomas Godfrey in America and John Hadley in England of the "reflecting quadrant" in which mirrors were used to determine the angle between light rays coming from the heavenly bodies and the horizon. Out of this more accurate instrument grew the highly precise modern mirror sextant.

The determination of longitude proved to be even more difficult than that of latitude. At first the only means of finding this distance east or west of the prime meridian was based on methods that depended on the moon. The results were unreliable. Soon, therefore, navigators began to wonder if they could not take Greenwich time with them. If they could compare the time of astronomical events such as the rising of the sun in their own positions with the known time of their happenings in Greenwich, the difference in time would be a measure of the longitude. At first they tried to keep track of time with hourglasses. This meant that the sailor on watch must remember to turn the glass at the exact moment when the sand ran out (usually every half-hour). Sometimes he would forget, or, eager to finish his watch, would turn the glass before the time was up. Finally, in 1732, a young cabinetmaker turned watchmaker arrived in London. His name was John Harrison and he decided to try to win the huge sum of twenty thousand pounds which had been offered by the British government to anyone who could solve the difficult problem of longitude. Up to that time no clock had been devised that could keep accurate time on a moving ship as it sailed through all sorts of climates and weathers. Harrison, however, designed a small pendulum clock with two pendulums. It was tried out on several voyages; it kept good time in calm and storm, in the tropics and in regions of intense cold. The enigma was solved but John Harrison was not given the prize. The influential Astronomer Royal, Nevil Maskelyne, was still devoted to the old lunar methods and refused to award it. Harrison, disappointed but undaunted, continued to design more and better chronometers, as his clocks were called, and finally when he was eighty-three, he received the great prize. Strangely, many seamen as stubborn as Maskelyne were loath to adopt Harrison's new instrument and continued to sail by the old inaccurate methods for years. When finally they surrendered and carried chronometers as well as sextants, they could sail almost anywhere over the world's oceans.

Supplemented by modern radio and electronic devices these instruments are still in use today. Without them, cartographers would be unable to achieve any high degree of accuracy in their craft. Such accuracy is important in many ways, for maps are the tools not only of the explorer, but also of the warrior, the trader and the scientist. Lloyd Brown, who is an expert on the history and the use of maps for many purposes, tells some curious facts about them in the article which follows.

WHEN hostilities began in Europe in 1939, every map collection of any consequence in the United States and abroad was quickly dusted off, and even some of the smaller, little-known collections in private hands were ferreted out. It was discovered that the world had been mapped, to be sure, but how? Obsolete maps and charts of remote, forgotten islands, lagoons, plateaus and jungle trails suddenly became prized possessions, guarded with unremitting vigilance. The world had been mapped, yes. Nevertheless, there was something radically wrong. The old familiar paths were there (though the scale was often too small to have any great military value), but the theater of war did not always follow the old familiar pattern, and it shortly developed that the world, all of it, had not been mapped after all. History tells us why.

The recent world war brought about this new interest in world cartography because, regardless of our political views regarding isolationism, the vast, unfamiliar world with which we have lately had to deal has relentlessly closed in around us. Our interest in it is no longer the casual interest of neutral observers; it is the interest of persons who have come to realize that the map of the world is our map and that it is time to learn a little more about it.

Maps, charts and globes are expendable; and there is an abundance of evidence to prove that countless numbers of them were destroyed through sheer carelessness and indifference. But there are other reasons why original map sources are scarce, and why there are wide gaps in the chronological sequence of map development.

Ancient maps were designed primarily for travelers, soldiers and mariners. Traveling in ancient times was a hazardous business. Conveyances were crude when available and the condition of the roads, up to the development of civil engineering in Rome, negated the small comfort to be had from a crude wagon or iron-shod chariot. Highwaymen were as common as hostels were rare; consequently many "traveler's pictures," road maps and itineraries rotted by the wayside with their owners' bodies. Fire, flood and shipwreck accounted for many more.

The very material used in the making of maps, charts and globes contributed to their destruction. No medium or material has yet been discovered which can be used for map making and nothing else. For example, both Charles the Great (Charlemagne), Roman Emperor and King of the Franks, and King Roger of Sicily, ordered maps made on solid silver plates. Servants and conquering soldiers might not be interested in such productions from the standpoint of geography, but solid silver—! Copper and brass were just as tempting. The brass globes of Archimedes and others made in his day were natural bait for a thief looking for bright metal. Or, as one writer has suggested, a hollow metal globe, cut in two, would make two fine camp kettles for an invading army. Lead could be made into bullets;

parchment and vellum would make good cartridges, also a strong spine for a bookbinding. If a map were old and obsolete and parchment was scarce, the old ink and rubrication could be scraped off and the skin used over again. This practice, accounting for the loss of many codices as well as valuable maps and charts, at one time became so pernicious because of the scarcity of writing material that in 691 A.D. a synodical decree was handed down forbidding the mutilation or destruction of any of the Scriptures or writings of the Church Fathers by such means.

A part of the map known as the Peutinger Table, a rare example of Roman cartography, was found in use as a flyleaf of a book in the city library of Treves, generally considered the oldest German city. Another rare fragment of a Roman map of Spain, cut in stone, was found built into the wall of the Abbey of Saint John, near Dijon in France. Stones bearing inscriptions make just as good building material as those without scratches on them. A fishmonger near the British Museum once discovered that parchment or limp vellum, though defaced by ancient ink and paint, was better than oiled paper for wrapping fish. Before the authorities caught up with him, numerous rare manuscripts had found their way into London kitchens, and from thence to the trash bin.

Large maps have always been inconvenient to store flat and open, so they were often folded, many of them into books. This practice accounted for the loss of many important cartographic documents. Continued folding and unfolding produced wear and tear, and if a map were stout enough to withstand this sort of treatment, a guillotine wielded by a careless or indifferent bookbinder often completed the dissection if not the total destruction of the document.

At the beginning of the Christian era, and for the next twelve hundred years or so, only the brave and the pagan indulged in geographic speculation. It was impious if not downright sinful to probe the mysteries of the universe, and the explanations set forth by the Church in regard to the heavens and the earth, as well as the maps produced under the supervision of the clergy, were sufficiently vague and awe-inspiring to satisfy all but the most skeptical observers of natural phenomena. So while both ecclesiastical and pagan manuscripts were collected openly, maps were made furtively, studied secretly, and in many cases destroyed promptly.

Heretics and barbarians, meaning whoever happened to be the enemy at the time, were not the only ones to destroy maps. It seems to be an assumption of long standing that the latest map is the best one, regardless of the area involved or the compiler; but this is frequently not so. An original map may be the product of a careful survey while a later, more resplendent *copy* may be a hasty, inaccurate job produced to sell in quantity at a large profit. Unfortunately the out-of-date map is usually discarded or destroyed when a new one comes along, even though military campaigns have been won with the aid of "obsolete," long-forgotten maps and charts, a statement which holds good as of this date.

With the exception of commercial publications designed to entertain as well as edify, maps and charts have always been surrounded by an aura of mystery and secrecy which has had much to do with their destruction, and retarded at the same time the dissemination of geographic knowledge. They were dangerous things to have around. The earliest extant records show that the informative nature of a map has always been fully appreciated. If your neighbor coveted your ox or your ass, your hidden granary or your secret supply of salt, your treasure chest or your harem, it was not sensible to leave a papyrus roll lying around showing the exact location of your possessions. Let the thief "case" the place himself before raiding it. Thus, there are no examples extant of the cadastral surveys made by the "geometers" of early Egypt. Chances are they were destroyed by members of the families who ordered the surveys made.

Since the beginning of time, maps have been associated with military intelligence as well as local adventure and intrigue. Because they were potential sources of information to the enemy, maps of an empire or even a city were closely guarded. The location of roads and navigable streams by which an army might threaten the security of a city, the location of military objectives such as arsenals, barracks, water mains, dockyards and public buildings, was not information to be divulged any more than necessary to a hostile world. For this reason the Roman Emperor Augustus, who ordered the compilation of a detailed survey of his empire, had all maps and related data locked up in the innermost vaults of the palace, and allowed only partial copies to be distributed, and then only on the advice of his imperial councilors, to generals going off to the wars or to the schools of the provinces for educational purposes. Domitian is said to have punished severely one of his councilors for indiscreetly divulging information contained on such maps, and later history tells of many persons who suffered death for similar treasonable offenses. The situation today remains essentially unchanged. The legends concerning the secrecy attached to navigational charts and ships' logbooks which stud the maritime history of every nation are timeless. In emergencies, all such confidential and informative documents take precedence over cargo, the ship itself and the safety of the crew.

One story tells of a loyal Carthaginian sea captain whose ship was pursued and intercepted by a Roman squadron. Rather than let his log and charts, keys to the secret of a lucrative Carthaginian trade, fall into Roman hands, he ran his ship on the rocks and drowned his crew. When he finally reached home he was given a hero's welcome. This is by no means an isolated example.

The old Spanish custom of weighting charts, not to mention log and code books, with lead so that they could be quickly jettisoned is still as popular as it is effective should the enemy try to board. This sort of practice, combined with the general reluctance of statesmen and sovereigns to duplicate and distribute important maps and charts, has contributed to their scarcity and has left the historian to guess what maps were made and what was on them. Often it is necessary to accept second- or third-hand evidence that a map was actually made; its contents must therefore be conjectural or hearsay.

From the beginning of Spanish exploration of the New World, in fact from the first voyage of Columbus, all maps and charts of the New World were deposited for safekeeping in the archives of Seville, and only a limited number of copies were made for the use of the most trustworthy Spanish sea captains. None of the original maps or charts made by the great explorers was allowed to be engraved and printed, so that today, for one reason or another, the primary documents relating to Columbus, Cortés, Magellan and countless others, are lost, probably forever. What maps and charts we do have of the great maritime explorations and discoveries have been compiled from miscellaneous notes and drawings that escaped the vigilance of the Spaniards and Portuguese.

Representatives of foreign powers were not the only offenders when it came to the illegal appropriation of maps and charts that were not meant for public distribution, for a chart showing a new trade route or the details of a newly discovered harbor was always a negotiable document. The "Casa de la Contratación de las Indias" was a noble attempt on the part of its founders, in the reign of Ferdinand of Spain, to pool all information relating to the seven seas, so that the best maps and charts would be available to the Spanish mariners responsible for the establishment of new sea routes to the New World and the Orient. But human frailty often prevailed and money talked. Information was withheld from the pool and sold on the side; Portuguese gold assayed as heavily as Spanish.

Whole editions of books and maps were brought up and destroyed by the Spanish authorities because they told too much or pictured the wrong things, and there was always a prison cell or a little machine waiting for the author and publisher of confidential maps and charts. In the sixteenth century genuine Spanish charts of any part of the Americas were real maritime prizes, rated as highly by the French and English as the gold bullion which might be in the ships' strong rooms. One such priceless haul was made by the English adventurer and freebooter Woodes Rogers. While cruising in behalf of some merchants of Bristol along the coast of Peru and Chile he captured some charts which were so "hot" that they were immediately engraved in London and published by John Senex. Other nations, especially those that made any pretense of carrying on a maritime trade, have been guilty at one time or another of this same thirst for knowledge, and piracy is the term which most adequately describes the technique employed in acquiring it.

The history of science as a whole is the record of a select group of men and women who have dared to be wrong, and no group of scientists has been more severely criticized for its errors than cartographers, the men who have mapped the world. Hundreds of weighty tomes have been written to prove how very wrong were such men as Ptolemy, Delisle and Mitchell. For every page of text, for every map and chart compiled by the pioneers in cartography, a thousand pages of adverse criticism have been written about them by men who were themselves incapable of being wrong because they would never think of exposing themselves to criticism, let alone failure. Yes, the early cartographers, without exception, were wrong, gloriously wrong in the same way Columbus was wrong when he thought he had made a landfall on the coast of Asia; the way Harrison was wrong when he built his first timekeeper; the way Edison was wrong when he used a bamboo filament in his incandescent lamp instead of tungsten. The remarkable achievements of early scientists, not to mention their personalities, have become lost in a maze of critical commentaries and ponderous verbiage. And yet the men who mapped the world were colorful figures from all walks of life. Some were astute and learned scientists: astronomers, mathematicians, physicists and naturalists, men of high ideals and ability. Others were military men, local burghers, river pilots, religious zealots, merchant seamen and resourceful rascals. For the most part they led interesting and exciting lives; some were starkly tragic. A few perpetrated swindles, falsifying data and withholding information at the cost of lives, fortunes and even empires. Some suffered ostracism for their radical views regarding the universe, others died in their defense.

The world has been mapped, after a fashion, and this story tells how the job was done, stressing methods and apparatus rather than the end product, the hundreds of thousands of maps and charts produced, representing centuries of trial and error. Each early map and chart is a story in itself, often incorporating a little folklore and philosophy, some art both good and bad, and a smattering of scientific fact. Most of them contain enough errors to delight the critical scholar; consequently a great many individual maps have been written up in minute detail, adding valuable fragments to the picture as a whole. But how was the framework built? How did "they," meaning the early map makers, do such accurate work centuries before they were supposed to have the necessary knowledge and equipment?

The mapping of the world, with every coastal outline, every river, lake and mountain, town and city in its proper place with regard to distance and direction, depends upon a simple geometric proposition, namely, that the intersection of two lines is a point. In other words, to "locate" a spot on the earth, to "fix" it cartographically, it is only necessary to know two things: its latitude and longitude, two lines which intersect at the desired spot, and lo and behold, it is done. But right here simplicity breaks down and complications begin to set in.

There is only one way to compile an accurate map of the earth and parts thereof, and that is to go into the field and survey it; likewise, there is only one way to establish a series of base lines of reference from which such surveys can be made, and that is to send out expeditions to the far corners of the earth equipped with astronomical apparatus and surveying instruments. This represents a tremendous undertaking requiring time, centuries of it, and money. It also requires an incentive. The nations that have been most interested in the establishment of colonies and a world trade have contributed more than others to the establishment of a science of cartography; those nations which have resisted exploitation and the intrusion of outsiders, regardless of their mission, have hindered the cause. The net result today is a map of the world which is spotty, both literally and figuratively. Much remains to be done. Writing in 1932, Kenneth Mason, an English geographer, said, "I have hinted that the world is discovered, but I doubt whether a hundredth part of the land surface of the globe is surveyed in sufficient detail for modern requirements. If the pioneer's day is nearly over, the specialist-explorer's dawn is only breaking."

SURVIVAL ON
LAND AND SEA

Prepared for the United States Navy

A small booklet entitled Survival on Land and Sea has been responsible for the saving of thousands of lives of men who have been cast away on hostile shores or in the jungles and forests of enemy lands. The booklet was prepared for the United States Navy by the Ethnogeographic Board and the Staff of the Smithsonian Institution, with contributions by the Bureau of Aeronautics and Bureau of Medicine and Surgery, United States Navy. It is primarily a weapon of warfare. But the conditions it describes have been faced by numberless explorers past and present. The methods of survival it suggests may prove useful to future explorers. For that reason, the selection from it which follows has a proper place in this book.

Introduction

THOUSANDS of men whose ships have been sunk or whose planes have come down in uncivilized areas of the world have made their way back to friendly territory.

The greatest obstacle that will confront you in the wilderness or at sea is fear of the unknown. As you meet and solve each problem you will find that it was not half so bad as you thought it was going to be and that after all you are doing pretty well. Just remember that many men, and women too, have already undergone such experiences and have come through. What they did, you too can do.

First stop and think things over. Size up the situation and plan your course of action. If you are adrift at sea you cannot hurry and there should be the emergency kit and set of instructions in the boat or raft to help you. On land, however, there will be the temptation to rush off immediately in some direction, any direction, and attempt everything at once, thus using up valuable energy and adding to your own confusion. If you are cast ashore on a beach—actually the best place to be—the problem, perhaps, will not seem so pressing as when you are lost in the interior, especially if it is bush or jungle country where it is difficult to see very far. On the other hand, if you are stranded on the desert, the fact that you can see so far and so little may make you want to start out at once in an effort to cover as much ground as possible in a short time. Regardless of the nature of the location in which you find yourself, take time to consider your plight and the best ways to go about improving it.

"Men Against the Sea"

The most important factor in survival at sea is being prepared when the order to abandon ship comes, or if all communications have been broken down, when your judgment tells you you must leave. To be prepared, first, *always* have a sheath knife on a lanyard in your belt, a police whistle around your neck, and a light pair of leather gloves in your hip pocket. Second, have a small knapsack or kit bag, with shoulder straps, prepared so that you can take it to your battle station. This should contain a filled canteen, a flashlight with a transparent rubber sheath tied over it (you can buy such a rubber sheath in a drug store in the States), a blanket, sweater, shirt, and socks (the latter also in a waterproof wrapper), first-aid packet, and dark glasses.

In abandoning ship wait until the ship comes to a stop; try to get away in a lifeboat, and jump only when it is impossible to go down a hose, line, cargo net, or ladder. Remember to put on your gloves and go down hand-over-hand. Don't slide and burn your hands! You'll need them later. If it is necessary to jump get rid of your helmet, fold your arms tight across your life jacket, and, selecting a clear area below, jump with legs extended and feet together.

If you have a cork life jacket, throw it over first and jump after it. Don't wear it when you jump or it may knock you out. If you have a pneumatic rubber jacket and are a good swimmer, jump in before you inflate it and swim as far away from the ship as seems safe before you do. If you are wearing a kapok life jacket, be sure the lower drawstring is drawn tight and tied securely before you jump.

Swim or paddle slowly toward a lifeboat, raft, or any floating object that will support you.

Half the battle is won when you get safely aboard your rescue craft, whether it be a raft or lifeboat. Despite lurid newspaper accounts of exceptional cases, actual statistics show that of boats adrift for more than twenty-four hours nearly half have reached safety within five days. It is the exception for any lifeboat not to be picked up within three weeks. If you have foresight, knowledge, and initiative your chances are excellent. From now on, the way you act will affect not only your own physical comfort and chances of survival but those of your companions as well.

Do not exhaust yourself by getting excited. Do not sing or shout for it uses up strength and valuable moisture. If a mass of men are around a raft, hang on but don't try to climb on it. Help get the wounded on. No matter how close-packed or uncomfortable you may be, do your best to be cheerful and, if you can't, be quiet. Make the best of it, for your survival depends on everyone carrying out routine cheerfully and promptly. It is highly important that everyone aboard a boat or raft should be allocated some job, however small. Only the badly wounded or very exhausted should be excused. Watches should be set on a definite routine.

As soon as possible, if you are in a raft or boat, squeeze out all your wet clothing but do not take off all your clothes unless the weather is warm and dry, and the wind moderate. Undress and dry your clothes layer by layer. Pay special attention to your feet. If you have on boots and socks remove and dry them. If possible, put on dry socks. Carrying a pair of dry socks in waterproof wrappings while at sea would here yield big dividends. Your feet should be kept dry and covered if possible. If your rescue craft is wet, keep your shoes on, but if you notice your feet swelling remove your shoes.

To protect yourself against cold winds, rain, spray, or, in the tropics, the sun, put up canvas or other screens, or rig up an awning with whatever is available. Do not take off too many clothes. They protect you against sunburn, which may occur even in cloudy weather. The experiences of men who have lived for weeks on rafts, to be rescued eventually, indicates that, for the tropics, systematically building up a resistance to sunshine in advance of any emergency will lessen the hardships of exposure.

Drinkable water will be your most essential need. Try to estimate how long you may be adrift and ration your water accordingly. A man needs about a pint a day to keep fit, but he can survive on two to eight ounces. A man in good health can live from eight to twelve days without water. Water will go farther if you hold it in your mouth a long time—rinse, gargle, and swallow. If you have no water, do not eat, since digestion uses up body moisture.

In the Arctic and Antarctic, pools of water from ice melted in the sun and ice on floes over a year old are drinkable if not made brackish by salt water spray. Your water ration should be based on careful estimates of your chances of being picked up and the probability of catching rain water.

Do not drink sea water. It will increase your thirst and make you violently sick.

Food is not so important as water. A man with water can survive several weeks without food. However, the more food you have, the better are your chances. A strict watch should be kept over food and water at all times. A trustworthy man should be delegated to take charge of the preservation and rationing of food and water.

If fish can be caught they will provide you with both food and water. The flesh of fish caught in the open sea is good to eat, cooked or raw. It is healthy and nourishing. Many tribes and some nations commonly eat fish raw and like it.

If and when you have caught more fish than you can eat, chew out the juice from the flesh. To do this, put a piece of fish in your mouth. Chew it small. Suck out the juice and swallow it, and then spit out the pulp that is left. Keep it up as long as you are thirsty and have fish.

In case you find that your lifeboat or raft does not have a fishing kit or if by chance you lose it through accident, you probably will be able to fashion equipment that will be serviceable out of materials that you have at hand. Have everyone empty his pockets and contribute whatever he may have in the way of stickpins, safety pins, campaign bars, collar and other insignia to a pool where it may be inspected for useful articles.

Take a square of canvas and cut carefully with a sharp knife along the weave of the fabric so that strands about a yard long can be drawn. When eight or ten have been obtained, fasten them at one end or have someone hold them. Then, taking an equal number of strands in each hand, grasp them between the thumb and forefinger of each hand and roll or twist each strand clockwise, at the same time passing those held in the right hand counterclockwise around those held in the left. It is important that each strand be twisted tightly and the two wound firmly together, so that the completed line will not unravel. This will form a small line with a breaking point well over one hundred pounds. Unraveled rope or the ravelings from a trouser leg may be used if you have no canvas.

Very efficient fishhooks can be made from wood, preferably hardwood. First shape the shaft and cut a notch near the end in which to seat the point. Shape the point and sharpen it so that the hardest part of the grain will form the extreme tip as well as the barb. Seat the point in the notch on the shaft. This section should form an angle of about thirty degrees with the long axis of the shaft and should be firmly lashed in position, using single strands from the canvas, to prevent slipping. A good point also can be made by using a nail from the rubber heel of your shoe. Excellent hooks may be fashioned from pins of all kinds. A safety pin may be used, or a bobby pin may be hammered to a flat point and cut diagonally using a knife blade as a cold chisel, and then shaped into a hook. A pin from a campaign bar, marksman bar, collar insignia, or other military insignia may be used.

Lures are often more successful than live bait and should be tried frequently. If game fish are in the neighborhood they will take lures without hesitation. Lures can be made from clothing or such trinkets as are at hand.

All birds are good to eat. There are numerous cases of men in lifeboats and on rafts catching birds, so if any come near make every effort to catch them. Some kinds can be caught on a baited hook and line. Their blood is both nourishing and thirst quenching. The intestines make good bait, and bird skins and feathers may be used for improvised hats or garments. Turtles are also good to eat and their blood is suitable for drinking.

Navigation in a rubber life raft is of necessity most elementary. As a survival factor its role is generally a minor one. Fine distinctions as to courses, bearings, speeds, etc., have little value due to the extremely limited maneuverability of a raft. However, a general knowledge as to one's approximate whereabouts is surely a matter of interest in any case and under certain circumstances can be of tremendous importance to survivors.

Prior to abandoning surface ships, a slip giving course and distance to the nearest land is supplied to each boat officer. In case of a plane crash or forced landing, occupants of each raft (if there is more than one) should be given the same information—if only in approximate terms. This is the responsibility of the navigator, first or second pilot, or of whoever may have the information.

For the greatest part, the movement of a raft will be governed by prevailing winds and currents. These, of course, cannot be altered by survivors. However, they sometimes can be intelligently utilized if the survivor knows the direction he desires to go.

Wind and current do not necessarily move in the same direction in a given area. One may be favorable, the other unfavorable.

The lower the raft rides in the water and the lower its occupants remain, the greater will be the effect of current. This effect can be increased by the use of a sea anchor or drag if the current is setting toward land or toward an area in which your patrols are operating.

On the other hand, if the wind should be favorable, the raft should be lightened as much as practical. Survivors should sit erect to offer wind resistance. Any sort of makeshift sail would be of help.

Landfall and Island Survival

In looking for land remember that cumulus clouds in an otherwise clear sky are likely to have been formed over land. Since they may have drifted from their original position steer to the windward rather than to the leeward of them. "Lagoon Glare," a greenish tint in the sky caused by the reflection of sunlight from coral reefs, may often be seen from a long distance. It is often more easily noted by looking slightly to one side of the point rather than directly at it. Driftwood and floating plants are a good indication of land. Coral reefs often cause difficulty in landing and should be approached cautiously. The surf is not so great if you make your landing on the lee side of an island. Breaks in the reef are indicated by calm gaps in the long line of breakers. If the pass is deep the color will be clear blue. If shallow it will be uniformly or blotchy brown. For navigation in shoal coral waters it is always desirable to have the sun anywhere except dead ahead. The ideal condition is to have the sun over one's shoulder or even directly overhead.

Men adrift, especially in northern latitudes, sometimes imagine they can see things which are not there, such as smoke, sails, ships, or land. This is a form of mirage, the same phenomenon that occurs in the desert, and if you experience it, it does not mean that you are out of your mind or even light-headed.

If you land on an island which is not in enemy territory and has natives on it, the worst of your troubles are over; they know what to do and will help you.

Footgear is important here, for cuts made by live coral are always painful and slow to heal. Your main needs will again be water, food, and shelter.

On most islands in the tropics some protection from the sun is necessary to prevent sunstroke and severe sunburn. Should you lack normal clothing or equipment there are several expedients which will minimize these dangers. Keep out of the sun as much as possible during the middle of the day. If green leaves are available tie them on to protect your head from the sun. Coconut oil smeared over exposed portions of the body also helps.

Many islands in the Pacific have a good water supply, others do not. In this regard it is interesting to note that many native peoples live permanently on islands that lack streams, springs, wells, or even coconuts. They get their water in a number of ways. In some cases there are holes and hollows in the rocks that collect rain water; always look for these. Shallow pits or holes are also dug to catch rain or the seepage of water after rains, or water is obtained by digging holes along the shore at low tide. If you are forced to dig such a well, in the absence of better tools a large shell lashed to a stick makes a serviceable implement. *Do not* go deeper than the first water found. Fresh water, being lighter than sea water, has a tendency to remain on the surface of salty water and that seeping through the sand may be a bit fresher than the sea water.

A *little* salt is good for you in the tropics where excessive perspiration robs the body of natural salts, but remember that *too much salt is bad.* Very limited quantities of the brackish water should be taken the first day or sickness will result. This is equally true of any other water drunk after a long period of thirst. Sip it up slowly or you will throw it up.

Upon atolls or coral islands which do not have enough rainfall to support trees, you will find a weed known as pigweed, or purslane. To alleviate thirst, chew the fleshy, reddish-green leaves and stems. The weed stands eight inches high and covers the ground in patches. No other atoll plant is like it.

On islands covered with jungle there are often air plants in the trees. The bases of the leaves of these air plants hold water for a long time. It is necessary to strain out bugs, wrigglers or an occasional frog but the water is good. The tips of the aerial roots of the pandanus tree may also be chewed for their moisture content. On islands where cactus grows, moisture may be obtained from the pulp of that plant.

Where there are coconuts your problem is much simpler. That the coconut is a valuable source of food and drink is well known. It also provides coconut oil, strong fibers which can be used in an emergency to manufacture cordage, and fronds or leaves for sandals, baskets, and building shelters.

The coconut grows in clusters on a tall palm. The first problem in the use of the coconut is to get it down from the tree. You may find yourself badly in need of a coconut for food or drink, but unable to climb the tree. Some coconut palms are very difficult to climb unless you have had considerable practice, but there is a simple device known as "the climbing bandage." It consists of a belt or rope which is a little larger around than the circumference of the tree.

If you have a belt or rope or even a piece of cloth put it around the trunk of the palm tying it so as to leave enough room for your feet, and step on it with both feet. The loop will catch on the other side of the trunk and will support your weight. Reach up with your arms and grasp the trunk with both hands. Pull yourself up, doubling your knees and sliding the "bandage" up to a higher position with your feet. Straighten up, resting your weight on the "bandage" to get a new position. By repeating this process you can climb to any height. You will note that this permits free use of your hands when you reach the top, so that you can pick the nuts. Let them drop. They won't be hurt, but don't lie under a coconut tree or they may hurt you!

If a tree can be felled (not a recommended procedure, obviously, where trees are sparse), a large amount of edible celery-like material known as the heart of the coconut, or "cabbage," may be obtained from the center of the trunk at its juncture with the sprouting leaves.

Anyone stranded on a beach or shore should have little difficulty in maintaining himself for an indefinite period on shellfish or mollusks. These are an abundant source of food much appreciated by all native peoples. All you need to do is work along the beach when the tide is out and gather a supply. There will be no difficulty in finding mollusks by turning over blocks of coral rock or picking them up in exposed situations. If you do not see anything but empty shells walk slowly along the beach and watch for bubbles in the sand—like those seen in the bottom of springs. When you see them dig down and you will find your mollusks. Shellfish can be eaten raw, as we eat oysters, and the juice coming from clams is not only nutritious but serves to quench thirst as well. The shells can be crushed with a rock or a piece of wood and the animal be extracted. Shellfish can be cooked by covering them with sand or earth and building a fire over the pile. When this is done they steam in their own juices. They can also be cooked by being dropped in a container of boiling water. Sections of bamboo can serve this purpose. Cut a section from a large bamboo stem, preserving one of the joints to form the bottom. The green shell is so durable that water can be boiled in it before the bamboo burns. If the container is held over the fire on a slant rather than straight up and down, the water heats faster.

Crabs and lobsters can most easily be caught at night, as that is the time when they generally move about. They may be stunned with a stick or stone, caught in the hands, or trapped. They often can be taken on a line baited with dead fish or spoiled meat. Tie the bait on just above a sinker of some kind and pull in from time to time, not too hard or the crab will let go, to see if you have caught one.

As far as is known all crabs and lobsters, whether marine, fresh-water, or land forms, are fit for human consumption provided they are fresh. Salt water forms can be eaten raw with little likelihood of bad effects, but *all land crabs*, particularly in Asia and the closely adjacent islands, *should be thoroughly cooked*, since they are infected with lung parasites that are often fatal to human beings if the animals are eaten raw. The best way to cook crabs and lobsters is to drop them alive into boiling water and keep them boiling for twenty minutes to half an hour. Thus there is no danger of decay before cooking and they become sterilized at the same time.

Still another source of sea food is *sea urchins* or *sea eggs*. Sea urchins are found on all tropical reefs and along all rocky shores and form an important source of food in many regions, especially in southern Europe, the West Indies, southern South America, parts of the Indo-Pacific region, and the Aleutian Islands. They are globular in shape, usually somewhat flattened, from two to six inches in diameter and are covered with spines. The edible portion consists of the masses of eggs within their bodies. These eggs usually form five finger-like, more or less yellow colored processes on top of the body inside the shell. They may be eaten either raw or boiled.

Fish are one of the most abundant types of food available on the reefs, in the lagoons, and in the sea. At night some species of fish come close inshore and swim along the surface. By remaining still, a person can hit them with sticks or spear them with a sharpened pole as they surface.

The outer margins of reefs usually contain channels, while on the surfaces of reefs are pools among the rocks and coral blocks. Fish frequently swim into these places at high tide, leaving as the water recedes. It is possible to trap them at such times by blocking the opening with rocks, sticks, or leaves from palm trees. Stones also may be built into low walls extending out into the water and forming an angle with the shore. Fish can be driven into this neck or narrow channel and into a pool at its inner end, and there be confined in the manner mentioned above.

When more fish are caught than are required to satisfy immediate needs, it is possible to preserve them for a time by cutting the flesh into small thin strips, washing with clean water, then hanging in the wind and sunlight to dry.

Never eat a fish that has slimy gills, sunken eyes, flabby flesh or skin, or an unpleasant odor. If, upon pressing the thumb against the fish it remains deeply dented, the fish probably is stale. Do not use it. Good flesh should be firm and not slimy.

Most fish are edible, palatable, and wholesome. However, there are a few with flesh that is *definitely poisonous* and it is important that everyone recognize these.

All of the important fish with poisonous flesh belong to one large group, the Plectognathi, of which there are many kinds in the tropics. *All these fish lack ordinary scales* such as occur on bass, grouper, and sea trout. Instead, these poisonous fish are covered with bristles or spiny scales, strong sharp thorns, or spines, or are encased in a bony boxlike covering. Some of them have naked skin, that is, no spines or scales. Never eat a fish that blows itself up like a balloon.

Certain other fish should be avoided for a different reason. They have sharp spines on their heads and in their fins. These spines may cause a burning or stinging, even an agonizing pain, that is out of all proportion to the apparent severity of the wound. This is the result of venom that is injected when the spines penetrate the flesh. The venom varies greatly in quantity and in power. In the most venomous varieties it is as deadly as that of the most dangerous snakes.

Natives

If you are in a region inhabited by native peoples make every effort to get in touch with them and ask them for help. You run little danger if you approach them in a friendly manner. Never show fear, or threaten, or flourish a gun. As a rule it is fear on the part of natives that makes them attack strangers and if you do nothing to cause concern you will be perfectly safe. Go up to them as you would to individuals of your own race and color, smile, offer a cigarette if you have one, and make your wants known. You may need to use signs to show them what you want—food, water, or directions —but natives are accustomed to such procedure, as they often communicate in that fashion themselves and will understand. The important thing is to treat them with dignity. Most of them have a strong sense of self-respect and do not regard themselves as "natives" or primitive. They will appreciate being treated as human beings just like yourself, neither as inferiors nor as superiors.

Should the natives be inclined to be shy or unapproachable do not rush matters by going right up to them. Stop where you are. Sit down and light up a smoke. If you know any tricks with string, take out a piece and proceed to do things with it. Most natives have and are fond of an elaborate variety of string figures, such as the familiar cat's cradle, which they make for their own amusement and on some occasions for ceremonial purposes. They also are very curious and in a short time some of them may not be able to hold back any longer and will come to see what you are doing. When they do, hand them the string and they will probably show you a few tricks. If you don't have string take out some trinket and show interest in it. They will want to see, too. Once the ice is broken, you can go ahead and ask for what you need. This method of approach has been used many times in many parts of the world by those going to study native peoples and rarely has it failed to produce the desired results.

Most native houses are small and crowded and more often than not are infested with fleas, lice, bedbugs, and other disease-carrying creatures. It is strongly advised that you do not stay in them unless compelled by extreme circumstances. If it is apparent that you are to be there for some time they can and probably will be willing to build you a shelter in short order. Of course, one should never enter a native house without being invited. They don't like to have strangers come barging into their homes any more than you would. *Without making it seem that you are doing so*, it is advisable to avoid as much as possible all physical contacts with the natives. They often suffer from serious skin diseases, syphilis, tuberculosis, and other communicable ailments. If it can be done without giving offense, one should prepare his own food and drink in such surroundings.

Should it be necessary for you to remain with a native group for any length of time you must be very observant and learn from experience what you can and cannot do. Respect their customs and manners. They have an entirely different form of etiquette from ours, but one that they believe in as strongly as we do in ours. In general you will find that the less civilized the natives are, the stronger the local taboos or restraints will be and the more you will be expected to conform to them. Respect for personal property, as well as for privacy, is very important. Never pick fruits, kill pigs, or take other food without first ascertaining their ownership, gaining permission and paying for them. Remember that in isolated regions money has little value; paper money is actually worthless and coins only are a medium of exchange insofar as they have trinket or jewelry value. Oftentimes matches, cigarettes, empty containers, or other odds and ends that you may have in your pockets are worth more to the native than any form of money. An exception, of course, would be a group that is living close to the outposts of civilization and white man's stores. Under such conditions money may be the preferred medium of exchange, but unless it is, don't try to force it on them. Be sure, however, that you make some form of payment. Also, if you make a promise of any kind, keep it literally. You can't pull a fast one on a native and get away with it.

One thing above all to bear in mind is to *leave the native women alone*. More white men have been killed by natives for trying to make some dusky dame than for any other reason. Even if the circumstances are favorable, which they may be under certain conditions with a father, brother, or husband offering a woman to you, it is better to skip the opportunity, as a case of venereal disease usually can be expected as a follow-up, this being one of the "benefits" of civilization bestowed by the white man wherever he has gone. If you must play with fire regardless of all considerations, do your dickering with the men and pay them first. Native women are often considered as chattels and do not have free say in such matters. Permission in such cases must come from some male relative as well as the woman herself. Also remember that among native peoples there is frequently little secrecy about such affairs. They usually become a matter of common village gossip.

When staying with natives there are certain things you can do that will help you to become accepted as a member of the group more quickly than if you hold aloof. Entertain them with match tricks, games, feats of skill, dances and songs. Unless you are unusually strong and proficient along that line, don't try to impress them with plain bull strength, as the natives probably are better equipped than you are in that respect and might show you a thing or two. They like to entertain too, so be a good audience and let them perform for you and be duly appreciative of their efforts. Show admiration for products of native handicraft, but don't be too profuse in your praise or they may feel they should give the object to you. Most "primitive" peoples are rather fond of playing practical jokes and probably will do so at your expense. If you find yourself the victim of some native form of "hot-foot," join them in their laughter; don't lose your temper and show anger even though they have hurt you. Another thing that is of great help in winning favor is to learn as many words of the native language as you can pick up. They will take delight in teaching you if you show a willingness and desire to learn. *Whatever you do, leave a good impression* because other white men may come along later and need help. If you have abused your privileges or taken advantage of the people those who follow will suffer for it.

Should you be stationed where you have time ashore and there are natives, make friends with some of them and have them show you the many useful tricks they know—how they fish, how they make snares and traps to catch birds and small animals, what plants are good for food, and how they cook their various dishes. This not only will help you pass the time, but it may give you a fund of knowledge that will some day save you.

Tropical Forests

Most of us think of the "jungle" in terms of a Tarzan movie. The word originally meant a "tract of uncultivated land," but now it is used more specifically to mean a dense tropical thicket of bamboos and palms as in India, of brush and vines as in Australia, of gigantic tangled grasses as in Africa, or to indicate a parklike woodland of tropical trees, a forest choked with undergrowth, or a tangled and impenetrable swamp.

Remember that the tropical forest is just another woods on a grand scale and that the man who learns how to use it has more chance of survival in it, over a long period of time, than he probably would have in the forest areas of our own country. *If it seems to have more alarming noises than you have ever heard before don't get excited.* Most of them are caused by frogs, monkeys, and insects, and other small creatures that exist there in greater numbers than you will ever find in the more northern countries. Even though the movies have taught you that life in the jungle is just one narrow escape after another from leopards, tigers, elephants, and other unpleasant creatures, you probably won't see any of them at all because many places don't have them, and where they are present they make every effort to avoid contact with man. The most you can expect to see in the way of animals will be birds, squirrels, hares, monkeys, and other small forms that are active during the day. None of them is dangerous, if left alone.

Water will not prove to be so much of a problem in most tropical forests as on small atolls and desert islands. In areas of heavy rainfall the earth is so soaked with moisture that a small hole dug in any low spot will yield water. Then there are streams, ponds, springs, and places where water collects from rain and seepage. The main problem is one of purity and *no surface water should be drunk without being boiled or chemically treated.* In higher portions of the mountains on large islands and the mainland the water from swiftly flowing streams and springs may be used without treatment if absolutely necessary, but even then you will be taking a chance.

As in our own country, following a stream down is certain eventually to lead you to human settlements, and the larger the stream the sooner they will be reached. Streams also lead to the coast and that is where you want to go, arriving as soon as possible. If you are in the mountains, it is probably better to follow the ridges as the stream beds are often precipitous.

If you follow a stream you will not only be provided with water, but with such edible creatures as crabs, shrimps, mollusks, and fish. If it is a large stream build a raft and float it down. Use soft woods, the lighter the better, for the raft. Lash the pieces together with vines or fibrous strips of bark. Sections of bamboo, because of their hollow air-filled segments, make the best rafts if that type of growth is available.

Always remember to take your time. You will make better headway if you do. If you come to a bog or swamp, *go around it*; don't try to fight your way through; you might get caught hip deep in muck. If a tree has fallen across a trail, travel around it, not through its branches. If you come to a fork, take the path that seems to have had the most travel. Never follow one that is closed by a string, rope, grass mat, or some other obvious barrier. It may lead to the scene of native religious rites that are forbidden to strangers, or you may fall into a pit or other dangerous trap set for large game.

In the open sun, even on a cloudy day, wear something on your head. If you have lost your hat or helmet a layer of green leaves under a knotted handkerchief or piece of cloth will give you protection. Do not expose yourself to sunburn as it may seriously incapacitate you. During the hottest hours of the day it is well to follow the example of the natives and rest quietly under a tree. Remember the old song "Mad dogs and Englishmen go out in the midday sun." Your camp should be on rising ground, well back from the stream and away from swamps and bogs, where mosquitoes and sand flies and gnats will be less numerous. Should there be any breeze stirring put your camp where you will get full benefit from it.

A crude lean-to or A-type shelter with a frame of sticks or bamboo with large leaves of leafy branches for walls and a roof will give protection from the cold dew of the tropics and also from prowling animals. Where there is any form of construction the latter will suspect a trap and keep away.

A fire is advisable and should be built in front of the open side of your shelter. Starting a fire may be a problem; it will prove doubly so if you have no matches, and to avoid such a contingency you should *always keep some matches about your person in a waterproof container*. It is even better if the heads have been dipped in paraffin.

When you don't have matches or a lighter there are a number of ways of starting fires. Natives as a rule are quite adept in the matter, but the average white man needs considerable practice and it may take you a long time to master the art. If you persist, however, you probably will succeed. Making fire by friction is not easy. Perhaps the method most likely to be productive, certainly the most efficient of the friction methods, is that of the fire thong. Its use has been widespread throughout southeastern Asia, the East Indies, and West Africa, and at one time it was employed in northern Europe. All that is needed in the way of equipment is a strip of dry rattan, preferably about one-quarter inch in diameter and about two feet long, and a dry stick about three-fourths inch in diameter and long enough so that it can be held on a rock or another piece of wood with the foot, one end being off the ground. The latter end should be split, the split being held open by a piece of twig or a pebble, and a good sized pinch of tinder wedged snugly, but not too tightly into the open part of the split. The rattan is then held firmly, one end in each hand, and is looped under the split so that the contact will be directly beneath and with the tinder. The rattan is then drawn rapidly back and forth with as much pressure as can be applied, the stick being held firmly in place with the foot. Within a few seconds the tinder should start to smoke. When it is smoking well, withdraw it and blow on it until a red coal appears and finally a flame. Beforehand gather shavings, bits of bark, and small twigs that can be added until a blaze sufficient to start larger pieces of wood has been developed.

Much easier, of course, is a burning glass if you have one and are where you can get enough sun to use it. In the absence of a regular glass, which is an excellent thing to carry in your pocket, a suitable substitute can be made if two of the members of the party have watches with crystals of approximately the same size. Take the two crystals, place them back to back and fill the space between with water. This will focus the sun to a point sharp enough to start a blaze.

The creatures that are most dangerous to man are small and inconspicuous for the most part and belong to the insect world. Mosquitoes generally are the most prevalent kind of noxious insect and in many cases are the carriers of yellow fever and malaria. You don't have to worry about yellow fever, as you have been inoculated against it, but there is no such protection against malaria. Hence you should guard against mosquito bites as much as possible. Since mosquitoes fly only in the evening and at night, the best way to escape infection is to get under a net as soon as possible after sunset. This, of course, is not always possible, particularly if you have lost part of your equipment and have no nets. Under such conditions one should cover all exposed parts of the body as far as possible and build a smudge of heavy smoke to help drive off the mosquitoes.

There are various kinds of scorpions and centipedes and they are common in most tropical countries. Their sting is painful but rarely is there any serious consequence if the bite does not become infected. Spider bites may cause local pain and swelling, yet they rarely have serious results.

The thought of snakes usually is uppermost in the minds of most people at the mention of the word "jungle." There is no need to be unduly concerned about them, however, as you may go for months without seeing a snake even in areas where they may be abundant. If you do see one it will probably be a fleeting glimpse as the snake will be making every effort to get away from you and disappear in the vegetation. Your chances of being bitten by one are about on a par with those of being struck by lightning. That does not mean that you should be careless of the possibility of snake bites, but ordinary precautions against them are sufficient. Just be particularly watchful when clearing ground for a camp site, trail, or the like, and when roaming in the bush gathering firewood. Many snakes are non-venomous, but the safest plan is to leave them all alone. If you should happen to be bitten don't worry over what kind of a snake it was but go ahead and treat the bite as though it were from a venomous variety.

There are three steps that should be taken. (1) Immediately apply a tourniquet above the wound, that is, between the bite and the heart. Release the pressure for five or ten seconds out of every ten or fifteen minutes so as not to stop circulation completely. (2) Make four or five parallel incisions, each about two inches long, as close to the snake bite wound as possible, and extending through the skin and fat and into the muscle. These cuts should be made with a razor, a razor blade or sharp knife, and should run lengthwise rather than across the limb. If the incisions are boldly made, bleeding and seepage of serum will be free and much of the venom will thus be eliminated. *Do not place permanganate crystals in the wound.* (3) Keep quiet; take hot fluids such as tea and coffee if available. *Do not take alcohol or morphine.* Have your comrades get you to a doctor as quickly as possible.

In some areas there are crocodiles in the streams. They can be avoided by not going into the water, or, when it is necessary to cross larger rivers, by doing so on improvised rafts. Authentic cases of crocodiles attacking human beings are practically impossible to find, so you don't need to worry over that.

Some of the South American streams have fish called caribe, palometa, or piranha that will attack men or animals entering the water and inflict dangerous wounds. They are infuriated by blood or sores but often do not attack persons without these conditions. They, too, can be avoided by staying out of streams where natives say they occur and by crossing on rafts.

Food in the Tropics

The matter of food is one that will be extremely important. If, as previously suggested, you have made contact with the natives you will have little to worry about. However, it may be some time before you come to a settlement or meet up with any of the local inhabitants, and in that case you may be forced to make out the best that you can. It may not be pleasant to contemplate, but in an emergency you will find that many unconventional creatures are edible and are, as a matter of fact, eaten by the people of the country. Among them are lizards and snakes. The meat from the hind quarters and tail of the lizard is the best. It is somewhat dry and stringy but is very much like the white meat from chicken. No lizard is poisonous, except the North American Gila monster and the beaded lizard of Mexico, although the larger ones have good biting teeth and a person should take care not to be bitten by them. All snakes are edible, but they are not found so frequently as might be expected. They also taste much like the white meat of chicken, although the flesh may be a bit stringy and slightly salty flavored. In using snakes be sure that the head is cut off immediately. It is dangerous to hold some species by the back of the head as they have the ability to throw their jaws out of joint and reach around to the hand. With both snakes and lizards, you skin, remove the viscera, and cook like any other meat.

All birds are edible, but some are not desirable. Carrion-eating birds, such as vultures should be used only in cases of last resort. They are in no way harmful, yet their usual source of food is such that it imparts an unpleasant taste to the flesh. Some birds, particularly parrots and hawks, are likely to be tough, but they can be stewed and used for soup. All birds' eggs are good for food, although some may be more palatable than others. If you want to be certain of fresh eggs remove all but one from the nest and take the fresh ones as they are laid. Along the shores and particularly on the smaller islands where birds lay their eggs in great numbers a section of previously laid eggs can be cleared, the area marked, and those left there subsequently gathered and used.

Animal life differs in its distribution. In some areas there is considerable variety and individuals are fairly numerous. Other places have only a few forms and not many of each. Too much reliance should not be placed on animals as a source of food because they are difficult to find and probably will be hard to kill with the equipment at hand. If you have a rifle or a revolver you may be able to shoot enough to keep going, but often it may not be desirable to use firearms. Most of the smaller animals can be killed with clubs, may be trapped by making noose snares, constructing deadfalls of logs, or by digging pits and covering them with light branches, twigs, and leaves. Natives generally thrust sharpened split-bamboo or other sticks in the bottom of such pits to impale the animals when they fall into the hole. Such pits, of course, are placed in game trails. All animals are good to eat; the flavor of some may not be all that you would desire but they are edible. Monkeys are good if you can shoot or catch them.

Should you be fortunate enough to get a sizable animal and have more meat than you can use at one time, the extra may be preserved for future use by drying. One method of making this jerked meat is to cut the flesh into long, thin strips not more than an inch in width and a half an inch in thickness. Soak these strips in brine, if salt is available to make it, an hour or two. String the strips of salt-soaked meat on the limb from a small tree and hang over a smoking fire until thoroughly dry. Where sea water or salt is not available the meat can be dried by exposure to the sun.

There are other living things that also may be used as food. The white grubs of the palm weevils and other wood-infesting beetles are highly prized by many native people. Their larvae, often as big as your thumb, are found in rotting wood and around freshly cut places on palm trees. Split and broiled over the coals of a fire, they are quite palatable and have a flavor somewhat like that of oysters. Natives rarely bother to cook them, preferring to pop them into their mouths as they find them.

Plants are one of the main sources of food in the tropics. The natives eat many wild and cultivated plants that are unknown to white men not familiar with the different areas where they grow. It is not possible to name and describe all of the forms suitable for emergency or general use but a few of the more common and obvious ones, those readily identified, are discussed in the following pages. One rule that can be relied upon is that *whatever the monkeys eat is safe for human beings.* Monkeys are not present everywhere, although they do occur in many of the places where you may go. Birds are more widely distributed but they are not a safe guide as they will occasionally feed on things harmful to man.

Food plants are more abundant in some localities than others and your chances of finding them vary according to the nature of the place where you are forced to look for them. Seashores, abandoned clearings, margins of streams, and swamps are more likely places than deep tropical jungles or mountaintops. The best places to find food plants, of course, are those where men are or have been growing them. In cultivated regions you can depend upon the natives for food, if you have made the proper contacts in the manner already described in the discussion of natives. Where there are no natives you will have to fall back on your own resourcefulness.

In many cases the need for emergency food plants may arise along a seashore. As a general rule such places are better supplied in that respect than other locations. This is in part because of the fact that in less civilized regions the people tend to live near the sea and as a consequence there are numerous cultivated plants, although they actually may not longer be cared for, as well as various wild forms. Many of the sandy, tropical shores have plants which are found all over the world. Coconuts characteristically line many tropical coasts. Other kinds of palms are also a valuable source of food. The tender growing tips, usually found at the tops of the stems in the bases of the leaves, may be cut out and eaten.

Far more dangerous than any of the poisonous tropical plants are those which—although in themselves perfectly harmless—carry the germs of disease. In all inhabited areas in the tropics the danger of contracting disease through the eating of contaminated food is ever present. Germs are left on fruits and vegetables when they are handled. Vegetables frequently are contaminated by the earth in which they are grown because in many countries the fields and garden plots are fertilized with human dung which, of course, carries the germs of the ailments from which the natives suffer and provides a ready source of reinfection. Fruits and vegetables should be eaten raw *only when they are peeled or the outer surface is cut off with a knife by the person eating them.* Even then care must be taken not to reinfect the freshly exposed portions. Vegetables and plants found in abandoned clearings may be contaminated from the soil. Even though appearances suggest that the place has not been occupied for some time, you should be on your guard and prepare your food as carefully as though people were actually living there. Thorough cooking kills all disease germs; hence to be safe you should cook all vegetables. This is good protection against dysentery, cholera, and diarrhea. If flies are present the food should be protected from them, as they can reinfect it after it is cooked.

The Arctic

There are no large sections of the American Arctic in which Eskimos, Indians, or white men have not lived. These people have not been stranded or forced there, but have lived there by choice, and usually without hardship. Though you need not be an expert woodsman or know all the tricks an Eskimo knows, some knowledge of how others have lived in these regions will be of great assistance to you in an emergency.

There are three principal requirements for survival in the Arctic: (1) knowledge of the country, (2) suitable clothing and equipment, (3) calm judgment and knowledge of what to do.

When stranded in unfamiliar territory, whether forced down in a plane or shipwrecked, your first thought will be for the care and comfort of any who may be injured. You should next consider what action on your part will lead to rescue in the shortest time. If you have been forced down from an airplane in the interior, stay by the plane unless you have definite knowledge of the location of a camp or settlement and know that you can reach it in a short time. If you start off at random you will be in much greater danger than if you stay where you are. Searching planes will not be able to see you and almost certainly you will become hopelessly lost. On the other hand, the grounded plane will be easily visible from the air and if you establish a camp near by and build a fire as a signal, your chances of rescue are good. If there is not too much wind, the smoke from a good fire will be visible for ten miles or more. As an additional means of attracting the attention of planes, spruce branches should be arranged on the snow to form letters a hundred feet across or more. Fire your signal pistol only when planes are heard approaching.

In the north, native villages and camps as well as white settlements are generally found along the coasts. Therefore, if you are stranded on a beach your chances of rescue are good. However, if there are rivers that cannot be crossed or if for any other reason it is not practicable to set out on foot along the coast, the best procedure will be to select a suitable camping place, build a smudge fire and await rescue. Wood for the fire—driftwood or growing timber—will almost certainly be available, and the chances are that food also can be obtained with little difficulty.

For winter travel back from the coast, snowshoes of some sort are usually essential. These can be improvised after a fashion from flat airplane or boat parts. The natives, in a pinch, use flat spruce boughs lashed onto their feet. Stick to the ridges or streams where the wind-blown snow is thin, wherever possible. In the spring and fall the snow may be soft in the daytime but form a crust at night which will permit easier travel.

Several packages of matches in waterproof containers, a lighter, and candles are among the most necessary items of your equipment; some should be carried in your pockets and some in the emergency kit. It is much better to take this simple precaution than to be forced later to the difficult and uncertain expedient of making fire by primitive methods. This warning is particularly applicable to those who may be lost in the Arctic where snow in winter and rain and mist in summer may make it difficult to obtain suitable dry materials for producing fire.

Outside the forested areas the best fuel is driftwood. This is usually abundant on northern beaches, though it is scarce in some localities in the central Canadian Arctic and in the western Aleutians. It may also be found, though in smaller quantities, along lake shores and rivers in the interior, even in the so-called Barren Grounds. If driftwood is not to be had, dwarf or ground willow will provide an acceptable substitute.

If matches or a lighter are not available, fire can be made by the strike-a-light method with flint and steel. Better than flint is iron pyrites, known as "fool's gold," a yellowish mineral found in lumps along Arctic stream beds. A piece of pyrites and steel or flint, or two pieces of pyrites, when struck together will give a good shower of sparks; this method of fire making is employed by most of the interior Eskimos and northern Indians. The flint or steel should be struck against the pyrites, not violently but with a sharp scraping motion. For making fire in this way a soft, dry, powdery tinder must be used. In an emergency cloth can be unraveled and shredded. Very dry dead grass, cedar or birch bark, or moss may be used, but it must be finely shredded or pulverized.

If stranded in deep snow without equipment, a trench can be dug to a depth of several feet and the floor packed down by stamping until it is solid. The top of the trench can then be covered with a parachute or whatever may be available. Such a shelter breaks the wind for its occupants. Northern Indians when unable to get back to their camp or village often burrow a sleeping hole into the side of a snow bank. A breathing hole should be left open and one should be on the watch and ready to move if deep drifts form. The Indians also make a snow house by piling up a heap of snow about the size of a small haystack, patting down the surface with their snowshoes. After standing for about thirty minutes, in very cold weather, the outer surface freezes into a thin crust which makes a good roof when the pile of snow is hollowed out. To do this they tunnel into one side of the heap, one man passing the snow out to the others, until only a shell some six or so inches thick is left. The snow floor is packed and, when possible covered with spruce boughs. It is important to have an air hole at the top and at least a small crack where the door is covered by a block of snow, ice, or other object. Otherwise those inside might suffocate. Such a shelter, if properly made, will hold several people comfortably. The Eskimos make a more elaborate snow-block house, but this calls for considerable skill and the method of construction should be learned from the natives themselves.

If a tent or other closed shelter is used, it must be carefully ventilated. A fire of any kind burning in a closed and poorly ventilated space may produce carbon monoxide, a deadly poisonous gas.

For cooking, the fire should not be too large. If possible it should be built between two logs or stones on which the cooking utensils may rest. Another method is to suspend the pot over the fire from a pole, the lower end of which is stuck into the ground.

Boiling is the simplest and most practical method of cooking. Long boiling is not necessary. If meat is cut into small pieces and put in cold water it will be cooked sufficiently by the time the water has boiled a couple of minutes. Drink the water in which the meat is cooked.

Drinking water is not a fundamental problem in the North. In summer water can be obtained from streams, lakes, or ponds. On the tundra pond water may have the color of tea because of stain from grass roots and other plants, but it is good to drink.

In winter, snow and ice are melted for drinking. Whenever possible avoid eating snow or ice directly for it lowers body temperature and cuts down endurance.

On the sea you can obtain good drinking water from old sea ice. Young sea ice is salty, like the water from which it was formed, but after a year it loses its salt and becomes fresh. Old sea ice can be distinguished by its smooth rounded corners and bluish color.

Living off the country is not difficult in the North if one has or can make the necessary weapons or other means for killing or capturing land animals and fish. In the summer, shellfish can be collected along the shore. Fish are abundant in fresh water lakes, streams, and in the sea. Caribou and other land mammals may be found, and millions of ducks, geese and smaller birds come to breed on the tundra or the sea cliffs. Since the sea freezes over in the winter and most of the birds go south, food resources then are more limited, and specialized hunting techniques are necessary.

Edible shellfish are relatively abundant on the Arctic and Bering Sea coasts of America, but are scarce in the Arctic regions of Europe and Asia. In regions where there is great variation in water level between high and low tides, shellfish can usually be obtained easily at low water, either by digging them with a stick on the tide flats or by collecting them from exposed pools and off-shore reefs. On open sandy beaches with a low tide range, shellfish are often cast up by storm waves. Before eating them, however, make sure they are not spoiled. Generally speaking, the bivalves, such as clams and mussels, are more palatable than those with spiral shells, like snails, though all are edible.

The eggs of the spiny sea urchins are excellent food. In early days enormous quantities were consumed by the natives of the Aleutian Islands and South Alaska. Sea urchins are easily collected among the rocks and in the tide pools at low water. The bright yellow eggs or roe are obtained by breaking the shell between two stones. One adult may contain as much as a tablespoonful of eggs.

Salmon, cod, sculpin, trout, whitefish, herring, flounder, and other salt-water fish are abundant in the Arctic and along nothern Atlantic and Pacific shores. Some of these can be caught by surf casting from the beach with a long hand line. In spring and summer salmon enter many of the northern streams to spawn—often in such numbers that they can be speared from the bank. An improvised gig or spear—a long pole with two or three sharp wooden barbs lashed to the end—can be used effectively in shallow water.

Small trout, grayling, and other fresh water fish will take any kind of bait —worm, bug or piece of meat—and can be caught with the simplest of makeshift tackle, such as a bent pin or a small sharp wooden hook attached to a thread or raveling.

The simplest form of hook, one used by primitive peoples in many parts of the world, is the gorge. This is a straight sliver of wood or bone sharpened at both ends and with the line attached at the middle. It is entirely covered with bait and is swallowed lengthwise by the fish. A pull on the line then turns it crosswise in the gullet.

In winter fish can be caught at open leads or through holes cut in the ice. The hook should be barbless so that the fish can flop off as soon as it is hauled out, for in cold weather it is difficult to remove a barbed hook with bare fingers.

The caribou is the best all-round food animal on land in the American Arctic. Some caribou move south to forested country in the fall, but many remain on the northern islands and Barren Grounds throughout the winter. Approach them carefully, taking advantage of any cover, and try to get within two hundred yards before firing. Be certain that you are downwind from them so that they cannot get your scent.

Wolves, foxes, snowshoe rabbits, lemmings, weasels, and field mice remain the year round and may be shot or trapped for food. Ground squirrels are found in summer but hibernate in winter. Musk-ox provide excellent food but are now found in only a few remote localities in the Far North.

Polar bears live on the ice floes and feed on seals. They can be shot without much trouble but it takes a bullet in the heart or brain to kill them. *Polar bear liver is poisonous and should not be eaten.*

Seals are hard to approach but every effort should be made to get them for they provide the best meat. In spring seals come up to bask on the ice beside their breathing holes. They sleep restlessly, raising their heads about every thirty seconds to look around for their enemy, the polar bear. In approaching the seal, the Eskimo hunter crawls forward cautiously while the seal is sleeping, being careful to keep downwind of it. When the seal moves the hunter stops and imitates its movements, lying flat on the ice, raising his head up and down and wriggling his body slightly. In order to look as much like a seal as possible the hunter approaches the seal sideways instead of head on and keeps his arms close to his body. Since the seal is lying on smooth ice and usually at an incline near the edge of the breathing hole, it must be killed instantly by a shot through the brain, for with the least movement of its body it will slide into the water. Therefore, it should be shot through the head at close range, twenty-five to fifty yards, so that the hunter can dash up and seize it before it reaches the water and sinks.

The Deserts

Deserts are usually large, barren, dry, hot in the daytime, cool at night, and relatively free from dangerous large animals. Being too large to walk out of easily, deserts force you to plan carefully and to conserve your strength and supplies to the utmost. Being barren, deserts cannot be expected to supply you with vegetable food; you cannot count on any growing thing to eat. Being dry, deserts deplete rather than replenish your precious water supply. Being hot in the daytime, and cooler at night, deserts force you to *lie quietly during the sunlight hours* and to *travel at night*. Being fairly free of large dangerous animals, deserts relieve you of the necessity of carrying heavy weapons, which would otherwise add to your load. Be sure to keep light arms in case you are lucky enough to find birds or other small game.

The two most important things to remember are:

1. Save your water supply. Do not swallow large mouthfuls but merely moisten your lips and throat with a small sip now and then.

2. Conserve your strength by staying quietly under cover during the heat of mid-day. Walk during the early evening, night, and early morning, when it is more comfortable and when you can avoid the risk of sunstroke or heat prostration and get along on less water.

If you have more equipment than you can carry, sacrifice anything but water. The amount of water you carry is the amount of insurance you have against desert disaster. Use what water you have for drinking. You can wash when you are safe again. Of course, if you have any wounds, scratches or sores you must keep them clean even at the expense of your precious drinking supply. If you have any salt tablets with you, take them from time to time, the interval depending on how many tablets you have and how far from help you estimate you may be. They will help combat fatigue and heatstroke, and also enable you to get along on less water. Do not smoke. Smoking increases thirst. Carrying a smooth pebble in the mouth will reduce thirst by stimulating the flow of saliva.

There are several aids to finding water that may be present in some desert areas. If there are any dried-up stream beds, which look like long, fairly narrow and rather shallow ditches, choose the lowest place in the bottom of the ditch and dig. If there is any water within a few feet of the surface you will soon feel that the sand is lightly damp. If you find this to be so, dig further and you may find water. The same is true for dried-up lake beds. These are usually pond-shaped fairly level areas, called "pans" in some deserts, around the edges of which are slightly raised ridges. Again find the lowest spot and dig. Remember that water runs downhill and that it seeks the lowest place it can reach either on or under the surface.

Plants are good indicators of water. As a rule the denser the growth of such desert grasses as salt grass and reedlike grasses, the closer to the surface the water probably is. In those deserts of the Western United States where the desert palm is found, its presence is a sure indicator of water, usually not more than a foot or two away from its base.

Do not drink all your water when you see a lake or stream. Wait until you get to it. It may be a mirage and leave you in a far worse plight than before.

If you come to a water hole or small oasis you can replenish your supplies of water and food. Boil all the water before using it or storing it in your canteens for the next trek. Cook any food you may get from natives at an oasis. Do not trust ready-cooked food or raw fruits and vegetables.

Go over what food you have and decide on a daily ration. Eat as little as possible. The more you eat the more water you will want, and the sooner you will be out of both food and water. The heat of the desert will tend to reduce your appetite. Food spoils rapidly when once it is opened, so make your meals of one can or package at a time.

If the wind causes a dust storm, cover your nose and mouth with any cloth you may have to act as a filter for the air you inhale. Keep your back to the wind; it helps protect your eyes and your breathing.

Be sure to keep your head and body covered from the sun during the day. The nights are apt to be cool and you should have warm enough clothing. Remember this if you have to decide how much of your clothing you can afford to discard to lighten your load. In the daytime always wear a woolen cloth around your abdomen to prevent chills, especially when it is very hot and there is a rapid evaporation of perspiration. Chilling of the abdomen may bring on diarrhea and other complaints.

Wear clothing as loose as possible. Any flapping as you move helps create a little breeze which aids in evaporation of your perspiration. This, in turn, helps maintain your normal body temperature, and helps to keep you from overheating.

If you think you may be found where you are, stay there. Otherwise travel at night and do not try for too great speed. Remember the marathon runner. He conserves his strength for distance and does not try to sprint. In the daytime rest quietly, covered from the sun by shade, if any, or by a make-shift blanket. If you have a compass, trust it rather than yourself. If you do not have one, never forget the importance of keeping on a straight path. When resting, always sit facing the direction you want to go. When lying down have your head in that direction, so that you won't forget which way you were going. Or arrange a stick or a line of pebbles as a pointer.

If you have matches and any burnable material, make a bright fire as a signal at night, or a smoky smudge as a signal in the daytime. If you have gasoline, you can scratch large letters in the sand, fill these trenchlike lines with gasoline and ignite when planes pass overhead.

Part Two

THEY
SAILED
THE
SEVEN
SEAS

THE GREEKS
AND THE VIKINGS

by Jeannette Mirsky

In that great saga of exploration the Odyssey, Homer portrayed in Ulysses a man typical of his breed in every age and clime. Always Ulysses insists that he is anxious to return to home and family. Always he searches for new adventures and strange new lands. While the actual account is no doubt mythical, much of it is based on actual fact. Here is the world of the Mediterranean as it was known or imagined by the ancient Greeks. And the voyages of Ulysses are the prototypes of many that were to follow, in which the Phoenicians and the Minoans, the Egyptians and the Carthaginians traveled from Africa to Asia Minor.

To these voyagers, the world beyond their inland sea was utterly unknown, a region populated with unimaginable dangers. It remained for Pytheas, an early genius of exploration, to be the first to venture beyond the protective Mediterranean shore into the world of the northern mists. Jeannette Mirsky tells his story and those of other early explorers in "The Greeks and the Vikings." It is difficult for moderns to comprehend what daring such voyages required, in days when the earth was supposed to be the center of a circular disc suspended in the heavens, with a vast ocean flowing about it and darkness surrounding all.

Pytheas was the forerunner of others who summoned the courage to venture outside. Gradually some knowledge of the coast of France and the regions around the British Isles was gained. Caesar's Gallic conquests and his trips to the island of tin helped to popularize this knowledge. But the darkness of ignorance still covered the great waters of the Western Ocean. Then around 1000 A.D., the Vikings, exhibiting a bravery unique among ancient peoples, sailed vast distances to discover the islands which lay to the west. Perhaps they reached the Continent of North America itself, that land of grapes which they named Winland. The tales of their feats were preserved from generation to generation in the great Norse sagas which have come down to us. Drawing on these sagas, and on recent excavations which have uncovered their ships, Jeannette Mirsky tells us something about them and what their voyages were like.

THE stage is set, the curtain rises, in ancient Greece. The first precise information about the Britons, the most northerly people known to antiquity, and the earliest tidings of the Arctic regions were brought to the warm civilization of the Mediterranean by one Pytheas, who was born in the Greek colony at Massilia that is now known as Marseilles.

He was a great navigator and an able astronomer but, above all else, a remarkable observer. His writings, unfortunately, have mostly disappeared; they have come down to us only as fragments "on the stream of time, as chance wreckage, partly distorted and perverted by hostile forces." From them three impressive facts emerge: Pytheas introduced the method for determining geographical location exactly by astronomical measurement; he noted the relation between the moon and the tides; and he was chosen head of an elaborately equipped expedition sent out to find the remote sources of tin and amber. The imagination and energy of those Greek merchants of Massilia who organized the quest were stirred by a desire to know from what lands came the strange and valuable products that were finding their way to the southern market.

At a time when Aristotle was meeting his classes under the ilex trees and Alexander the Great was marching toward India, Pytheas, "one of the most intrepid explorers the world has seen," set sail to the North. Between the Pillars of Hercules he went, out into the unknown.

Sailing northward he passed Cape Finisterre, the extreme point that Himilco the Carthaginian had probably reached a century before, and this course brought him to the island of the Britons. He stayed a long while in this land he had discovered. Making extensive trips into the interior, he noted that only on the hills could people escape the forests and swamps that filled the valleys, that they raised wheat and corn and barley and made a "wine" from fermented grain, that they had domestic animals, that they had tools and weapons of iron and adorned their wooden chariots with bronze and gold. He visited the tin mines. Coasting farther north, he saw how agriculture diminished and finally disappeared. He skirted the coast of Scotland and passed the last straggling skerry of the Orkneys. Still he sailed on, eager to verify the information he had received of the land that lay beyond all these—Thule, where night did not exist during the summer, where the winter never knew of daylight. But a barrier stopped further progress. It is impossible to say whether Thule was one of the Shetlands and this obstruction a thick fog that seemed "neither earth, air, nor sky, but a compound of all three"; or whether it was Iceland and this barricade sludge ice "which can neither be traversed on foot nor by boat." Pytheas was absent almost six years from his home by the blue Rhone. When he died, his work died with him. Rome knew him only as a ridiculous liar. His detractors had their way and made of his capable and intrepid work a nonsensical hash that persisted as long as men "chewed the cud of knowledge that had been collected in antiquity." It is only in the light of our present-day knowledge that Pytheas emerges as a great man wearing the sober habit of courage and truth.

When Rome was smashed, the geographical researches of the Greeks disappeared for almost a thousand years. The concept of the earth as a globe and all the precious lines of exploration that had been traced across its surface were gone. The world was as clean as a schoolroom blackboard in the morning. Then little by little quaint new starts were made. Naïve early maps show Europe and Northern Africa as a little island of the known surrounded by monsters and devils and anchored in unnavigable oceans. Fables and myths were put forward in the garb of fact, while facts could be felt under heavy draperies of imaginative presentation.

Twelve hundred years after Pytheas crossed the threshold of the Arctic, Ottar, a Viking nobleman, first rounded the black table mountain that marks the North Cape and sailed around the Kola Peninsula into the White Sea. He tells of the tribes he met with and their mode of life. So straightforward is the narrative, so clear and precise, that it is possible to trace his exact course.

The Vikings! the Norsemen! a tribe of stalwart men and women to whom conquest was an integral part of living. From the time—two centuries before Christ—when they appeared on the Scandinavian peninsula, subjugated the native Finns, and learned to love that northern arm of Europe as home, on till their ships had mastered the open seas and carried them to Russia, France, England, and Italy, there to rule, their story is consistently one of splendor and wild freedom.

Faced with the difficulty of communicating with the settlements that dotted the winding fiords by overland route, the Vikings were forced to build ships, to perfect them, that they might be safe in northern seas. And the pattern they evolved, the rigging and sails, is still so excellent as to be used today, eleven hundred years later. They were the first of whom there is any record who left the comparative security of coastwise sailing for the danger and peril of venturing across wide waters out of sight of land. Out into the huge, empty, unknown ocean they went in boats seventy-eight feet long, sixteen feet wide, and only four feet deep. They had no compass, nor any instrument with which to take their position. They had to depend upon their own guesswork, had to reckon by the sun, the moon, the stars, the winds. Yet in those open, square-sailed boats they ranged from Novaya Zemlya and Spitsbergen to Greenland and Newfoundland. The outspread limits of their courageous seafaring—their discoveries, their pioneering, and their colonizations—are immortalized in the stirring cadences of the Icelandic sagas. In skill and daring and achievements the Vikings were five hundred years ahead of the rest of Europe.

The legends tell us that a little after the middle of the ninth century a man set out from Norway to the northwest in search of new lands. Lacking a compass, he took three consecrated ravens. When he had sailed a while, he let loose the first raven. Without hesitation it flew back to shore, and from this the man knew that he had not gone far enough. He sailed on and then let loose the second raven. It circled over the ship as though undecided whether to go back or forward to the nearest land and then flew home. This told the man that he must have gone about halfway. On he sailed and then gave the third its liberty. The raven flew straight forward. Following in its direction the man made the new land in triumph. His name was Rabna Floki, or Floki of the Ravens. He had come to Iceland.

But the real colonists did not follow immediately. It was during the long reign (860-930) of Harold Haarfager (Fairhair) who, completing a task which his father, Halfdan the Black, had begun, "murdered, burnt, and otherwise exterminated all his brother kings who at that time grew as thick as blackberries in Norway, first consolidated their dominions into one realm . . . and then proceeded to invade the udal rights of the landholders." Rather than submit to this invasion of their liberty, some of the more powerful nobles preferred to look for a new home and, trusting to the vague, whispered report of land to the northwest, forsook the dear hills of their native land and set out across the icy seas. It was by men "with possessions to be taxed, and a spirit too haughty to endure taxation" that Iceland was settled. They sent word to those chafing at home that cattle could live the year round in the new land and that its encircling waters abounded with fish. The flow of newcomers increased. They were men who had tasted the refinements of life, who were conversant with the pleasures of learning. Their isolation safeguarded their culture from being swamped by the bloody convulsions that in ensuing centuries swept over a distracted Europe. "They were the first of any European nation to create for themselves a native literature. . . . Almost all the ancient Scandinavian manuscripts are in Icelandic. Thanks to these indefatigable and delightful chroniclers, two of man's most impressive deeds have been preserved for us: the colonization of Greenland in the tenth century and the discovery of America at the start of the eleventh.

The Saga of Ara Frode (1067-1148) says: "The land which is called Greenland was discovered and settled from Iceland. Eric the Red was the name of the man from Breidafjord, who sailed thither from thence and there took land at the place which is since called Eiriksfjord. He gave the land a name and called it Greenland, and said that having a good name would entice men to go thither."

From the tales, Erik the Red emerges from a mere name to the full stature of a man. Besides being as fierce and lawless as any of the warlike and hard Vikings, he had all the necessary requirements of the true explorer, the born leader. In addition he had all the shrewdness of a successful realtor. His was a stormy life. Born in Norway about 950, he was twenty when he and his father were forced to flee for having committed murder. They went to Iceland, where his father died. Here Erik hoped to settle, for he married, cleared land, and knew some peaceful years. But then he quarreled and killed, lay low for a time, and then quarreled and killed again. Erik was declared an outlaw. Where should he go? He could not return to Norway, he could not stay in Iceland. His escape, his one path of hope, lay to the west; always to the west, where new lands beckoned, lay hope. He was thirty-three when, with his family and retainers, he set out.

This first voyage of Erik the Red is outstanding in the history of Arctic expeditions. With a masterly hand he loaded his scanty equipment and provisions into the open Viking ships and set out for an unknown land almost within the Arctic Circle, beyond the ice. There he lived for three years and found time for reconnoitering the new country. He coasted along the southwestern shore from the "outermost belt of the skerries to the head of the long fiords." He noted that the shores of the fiords in the summertime bore a rich vegetation, that there were groves of dwarf willows and birch trees and bushes thick with berries, that there was pasturage for cattle and sheep. It looked very good to him. He decided that it was a land worthy of colonists. He gave it an alluring name, hoping thus to induce men to leave an Iceland for a Greenland. He returned to Iceland under the protection of a strong friend and succeeded in finding families to emigrate. In 985 the path that his few ships had taken was retraced. Now there were many ships, filled with brave, eager people, laden with horses, cattle, goats, sheep, and with the most precious of their household goods. In Greenland Erik the Red was a great leader, the chief of a new free state. They called that southwestern stretch East Bygd.

Years passed, the settlement grew larger, more people came. It throve with the miraculous speed of a healthy infant. Erik the Red's son grew to manhood. He was a match for his father in fearlessness, in skill, but above all he was lucky. Leif Eriksson is the man who brought Christianity to Greenland. They called him Leif the Lucky when he found more good land to the west.

His trip to Wineland the Good—identified as the eastern coast of Newfoundland—is debatable ground. It is a matter that has claimed the attention and research of able and learned scholars—some saying he made it, others of the opinion that he could have but did not. It is safer to steer a middle course and say that, because of his birth, his daring, and his association with the introduction of the White Christ to Greenland, Leif became the outstanding figure, the hero on whom the saga writers could fasten the mighty epic of that voyage of discovery. "Leif Eriksson becomes the personification of the first ocean voyager in history, who deliberately and with a settled plan steered straight across the Atlantic, without seeking to avail himself of harbors on the way. . . . It must be remembered that the compass was unknown and that all ships of that time were without fixed decks. This was an exploit equal to the greatest in history; it is the beginning of ocean voyages. . . ."

By 1055 the Greenland colony of East Bygd had spread beyond its northern limit, Frederikshaab, into new settlements—West Bygd. Together they were large and important enough to support their own bishop and a flock of new priests. At their height there were two hundred and eighty homesteads containing about two thousand persons, boasting seventeen churches. The life of these colonists, while not luxurious, was not precarious. They had stables filled with horses, cattle, sheep, and goats, and big barns filled with hay. They fished, caught seals, walrus, and whales. They could pay for necessaries and luxuries imported from Europe. They even explored along the coast toward the north.

The eleventh, the twelfth, the thirteenth centuries saw the colonies flourish and prosper; and then quickly, mortally, they declined, so rapidly that by 1400 the colonies of Greenland, with their bishops and priests, the many people who composed the one hundred and ninety townships, the fine churches and spreading homesteads, were completely gone, like rain in deep snow. Gone suddenly like a note cut short. Gone the very memory of their existence. And the sagas that sing of them came to be regarded not so much as history, but as the recitals of happy dreams of a Never-Never Land, pleasant, pious lies. No one knows what calamity befell, whether they died in the Black Plague of 1349, whether the ice overwhelmed them, or whether they were killed by armies of Eskimo. No one shall ever know, so mysteriously, so utterly, did they perish. By the close of the fourteenth century the Scandinavian maritime supremacy had been completely superseded by the Hanseatic League. Less and less did the Norsemen's ships rove the northern seas. Soon it was as if the very knowledge of Greenland had disappeared. The well-known routes were deserted and lost, and those northern lands and seas that had been familiar were again desolate. Once more the "perilous edges of the world [were] invested with strangeness, and mystery, and romance."

'The standing-stone on the mound bears no mark,
and Saga has forgotten what she knew.'

THE LAND
OF PRESTER JOHN

by Elaine Sanceau

Myths have played an important part in the history of exploration. One such legendary tale, described by Elaine Sanceau in the selection which follows, is that of Prester John, the fabulous monarch whose realm was supposed to lie somewhere in the East. He was, it was thought, the only Christian ruler in that heathen section of the world. Surrounded by satellite emperors, he sat on a throne of rubies, pearls and emeralds. His story helped

Reprinted from *The Land of Prester John* by Elaine Sanceau, by permission of Alfred A. Knopf, Inc. and Hutchinson & Company. Copyright 1944 by Elaine Sanceau.

inspire Henry, son of King John, to become the father of Portuguese exploration. Very early in his career, Henry decided that the way to exploration and conquest was by sea. He studied all the lore of navigation then available. He sent voyage after voyage to find a sea road to the Spice Islands of the East and to the land of Prester John. As a result he earned the famous title of "Henry the Navigator," though he himself never embarked on the voyages he planned. From his school of navigation at Sagres came theories which were to inspire explorers for generations to come. The expeditions which these explorers undertook resulted in a new knowledge of the known world and a new science of geography emerging out of medieval darkness. The tiny country of Portugal, largely as a result of his pioneering, was to become with Spain the foremost seafaring nation of the world, the center of a vast empire whose influence was felt in the most distant parts of the earth.

The voyages of those three greatest of explorers—Columbus, Vasco da Gama and Magellan—which are the subjects of selections which follow, all had their inceptions in the imagination of Prince Henry. At his birth, the map of the known world consisted of little beyond Europe, the vaguely understood routes through Asia reported by Herodotus and Marco Polo, the northern reaches of Thule and the northern coasts of Africa. These three great disciples of Henry, with others less important, created a new world and dispelled forever the darkness of the Ptolemaic world which had preceded them.

A WORLD of phantoms floated around medieval Christendom. Europe saw itself as a small oasis—a spot of light where true religion reigned and life was normal, while mystery and magic veiled everything beyond.

To the west surged the ocean which no man had crossed, impassable and enigmatic as infinity; to the east and south all trailed away into the outer dark. The earth went on, men knew, but none could say just how. It was a wonderful and wicked world that lay beyond the Christians' ken—a world of paynims and of infidels, of sorcery and enchantment. Strange stories filtered through from time to time like echoes from another planet; strange apparitions now and then broke forth, as when a man of unknown race from the world's end was seen on the confines of Christendom, or else sometimes a Christian, greatly daring, would himself disappear into the shades. At other times, more terrible than all, was heard the gallop of horses bearing wild yellow warriors across the eastern steppe, and Europe trembled lest she might be swamped by those demoniac hordes let loose from some region of nameless horror.

The Crusades served to lift a corner of the veil. The crusaders, touching the fringe of the unknown, heard and saw many things. Thus Europe was made aware of Far Cathay and the Great Khan, the Old Man of the Mountain and his Assassins, and so it was that from the dim light of far away there rose and grew the tale of Prester John.

Nobody was sure exactly where might be the realm of Prester John, sole Christian ruler in a heathen continent, but no one doubted his existence. There was no king on earth like Prester John. His robes were washed in fire and woven by the salamander. He lived in an enchanted palace in the mountains, and in front of it a magic mirror stood where he could see his vast dominions at a glance. Seven kings waited constantly on Prester John, as well as sixty dukes, three hundred and sixty counts, and knights and noblemen beyond compute. Thirty archbishops sat at his right hand, and twenty bishops on his left. A king and abbot was his cook, a king bishop his butler, an archimandrite his master of horse, an archbishop his pantler. Surrounded by menials of such exalted rank, how could he also style himself a king? Besides, this mighty potentate was perfect, therefore humble. So he was known as Presbyter or Prester John.

Such was the mirage that shone before the eyes of the twelfth century. Its colors faded as the years passed by, but still the myth endured. As a night wanderer follows a will-o'-the-wisp, medieval imagination pursued Prester John, whose kingdom in like manner moved from end to end of Asia. Sometimes it was alleged to lie beyond the Persian mountains, sometimes in India, and sometimes on the far-off Mongolian steppes near China.

By the fourteenth century it had traveled west. The fact had dawned on Europe that a Christian kingdom existed in Africa. Abyssinian pilgrims sometimes visited the Holy Land, but nobody was certain where they come from. Inaccessible mountains, it was rumored, locked their kingdom round. What could it be if not the land of Prester John? Prester John of the Indies they called him still, the vague geography of the time confusing India with East Africa.

The realm of Prester John had ceased to be a synonym for fairyland, but it remained alluringly remote. This outpost of the faith, lost and cut off, was almost as appealing to imagination. When medieval dreams gave way to the pursuit of facts, then men set out to seek for the reality.

It was a prince of Portugal who led the way. Henry the Navigator stood between two worlds—the dying Middle Ages and the dawning Renaissance. The mysticism of the one and the insatiable curiosity of the other were the driving forces which controlled his life. He was a crusader and a man of science rolled into one.

Dom Henrique was born in 1394—the end of an age—to a nation on the threshold of new destinies. He was third son of the King João I, that valiant bastard who had upheld the independence of the realm against the armies of Castile and so won for himself his father's crown.

The Infante Dom Henrique inherited the martial instincts of his father, and the earnest devotion of his mother, Philippa of Lancaster. There was intellectual ancestry on either side; Dom Henrique and his brothers developed a thirst for knowledge at an early age, and from childhood they read and collected books. . . .

All knights and gentlemen had to be soldiers, but Henrique's generation had inherited a tradition of fighting for the right. Their fathers' swords had won their country's freedom; the sons who grew up in a land at peace aspired to win their maiden spurs in the defense of a good cause.

For men of the Iberian Peninsula, a good cause was never far to seek. Their kingdoms were the buffer states of Christendom against the Moslem hordes outside the pale. Close to their gates still raged a holy war, which had known intervals of truce, but never peace, during six hundred years. It is true that the Moor had been pushed out of Portugal, but across the narrow straits, beyond the sea, his palmy cities flourished almost within Christian sight. When Dom Henrique and his brothers wished to win their knightly spurs, it seemed to them that a high and holy enterprise would be the conquest of Ceuta.

Queen Philippa backed up her sons' suggestions to their father. "Since God in His mercy has been pleased to give them strength of mind and body," said she, "I would not for the world that they should fail to execute works such as these, however difficult!"

So it was that, carrying with them a dying mother's blessing, Dom Henrique and his brothers sailed across the straits and were knighted by their father in the conquered Moorish town.

That hour fixed a nation's destiny. A young man with an inquiring mind had his first taste of Africa, and found that he was gazing at a mystery.

Ceuta was the fairest town along the Moorish coast. It overflowed with lovely things from far away. It was rich with pearls from the Persian Gulf, with rubies from Ceylon, perfumes of Syria, and silks of Egypt. Within the flat-roofed houses faced with colored tiles were carpets from the Persian looms and embroideries from India. Behind the houses there were mosaic courts, scented with orange trees and musical with fountains; behind the town were fields of sugar cane, orchards, and trailing vines; behind the orchards were the hills, and then behind those—what?

Ceuta, divided from the Christian world by a few leagues of sea, was the last link of a long chain that began in the totally unknown. And this chain could be followed back, Henrique knew, to Satan's seat—those lands where Islam reigned unchallenged and supreme. How far into this mysterious land did the accursed Crescent hold its sway? Had Africa an end, or did it run from pole to pole? Where beyond those hills of darkness lay the realm of Prester John, that isolated champion of the faith who would surely welcome help against the common foe? If Prester John could but join forces with the Christians of the West, could they not then destroy Islam? And the land of Prester John was on the way to India, that fabled treasurehouse of spice and gold. Had not St. Thomas found his way to India and planted there a Christian church?

Dom Henrique went home with his mind full of questions. How to reach Prester John and get in touch with that mysterious India that Alexander's armies had seen long ago? The land routes of the Orient were closed to Europe. Everywhere the Crescent barred the way, and so to reach the Christians of the East, Dom Henrique chose the path of the Dark Ocean.

That was a fearsome undertaking. "No man sailing south of Cape Bojador returns alive!" declared medieval wisdom. A region of nameless horror stretched beyond. The Middle Ages formulated theories and left the matter there, but the Renaissance was seized with the desire to prove. Intellectually, Dom Henrique was of the Renaissance though he lived and died a generation earlier. When he began to wonder, then he must find out.

He gave his life up to this end. He established his abode in the far south of Portugal, on the Cape of Sagres, the last point of Europe. There, "where two seas, the Mediterranean and the Great Ocean, fight together," he set himself to solve the riddle of the universe and so "attain the purpose that he had in mind, to discover from the western side the navigation to Oriental India."

Pleasure, political power, even family ties meant nothing to the recluse of Sagres, and all the revenues of the Order of Christ, of which he was Grand Master, were devoted to his quest. Upon his wind-swept rock the Infante gathered about him a unique court: mathematicians, astronomers, cartographers, makers of instruments of precision, builders of ships, collected there from far and wide, each contributing his own particle of skill or wisdom to the task. With the men of theory came the men of action—all the seamen, pilots and adventurous young *fidalgos* of Portugal, as well as foreign wanderers out to see the world and seek their fortune. And mingling with the sages and the sailors of the West were more exotic types. The Infante by his largesse lured into his orbit pilgrims from the Levant who came to visit Occidental shrines—Syrians and Copts and other dwellers on the confines of Christendom who carried with them echoes of the world beyond. From such he gathered news about the Arab trade with the Far East, and how their treasure-laden *djelbas* sailed up to Suez bringing the spices of India to Alexandria and Cairo. But the strangest tales were brought by captives such as the Moor Adahu, who told of inland seas far in the heart of Africa, of how salt caravans crossed the Sahara into the Sudan, and how hundreds of camels laden with gold went down to the Red Sea from Timbuktu.

Thus surrounded by *"men of diverse nationalities,"* the Infante Dom Henrique spent his days and nights co-ordinating all his clues, meditating upon travelers' reports, poring over old maps, compiling others, wrestling with mathematics, studying the stars, and from all this deducing a new science—how men might find their path on trackless seas. And continually he sent forth ships—each year more ships—with orders to sail farther and farther south until they found the end of Africa.

They sailed cautiously at first—for might not any kind of monster haunt the South Atlantic?—and then with reckless ease, for after all no bogy put in an appearance, and though they sailed into the tropics, the ocean never boiled as those supposed to know affirmed it would. They even found out with a shock that Ptolemy—that oracle of all learned mediaevals—"the illustrious Ptolemy, who wrote so well of many things," says one of Dom Henrique's men, "was quite mistaken here!" Ptolemy had declared the tropics to be "uninhabited because of the great heat, and we found quite the contrary!" Such was the crumbling up of perconceived ideas. Even the demon Cape Bojador turned out to be an overrated terror. It is true that a ship could not sail home against the current that ran down the coast, but the answer was to lose all sight of land and sweep a circle out to sea.

The Dark Ocean soon ceased to frighten Henrique's navigators. They engulfed themselves far from all continents and found the lovely islands lost in the Atlantic. They defied one by one the capes of Africa—Bojador, Branco, Palmas, and beyond. They saw the desert shores give way to tropic green, they saw all Arab traces fade away and Berber types succeeded by the genuine Negro—yet the intriguing coast ran on and on, apparently forever.

Dom Henrique never showed signs of discouragement. He colonized Madeira and the Azores; he built fortresses and trading factories on the coast of Africa, and sent his caravels far out to sea toward the unknown west. Whether they reached the Antilles forty years in advance of Columbus, or Brazil fifty years before Cabral, is a question that historians are debating still. It is certain that the Infante sought to penetrate the undiscovered world in all directions, but he never lost sight of the East and Prester John.

Exactly how much he did upon the eastern side is wrapped in even deeper mystery than the Atlantic explorations that he organized. His messengers must have succeeded in some penetration overland. We can speculate as freely as we choose about all this. It is a puzzle with too many pieces missing to be reconstructed otherwise than by imagination.

When Dom Henrique died, in 1460, the problems that he had set himself were still mostly unsolved. The land of Prester John had hardly ceased to be a legend. The dream of a sea route to India was not substantiated yet. But in his lifetime Dom Henrique had changed the world. His hand had swept away forever the phantoms with which men's imagination peopled the Atlantic. A nation had lost all terror of the ocean. And the nation that the Infante had trained in seamanship was young and strong—a people yet unspoiled by luxury, who had lived by agriculture and the sword. Their fathers had bequeathed to them a great fighting tradition. Few in number, they were used to overcoming fearful odds. Sons of the vanquishers of both Moors and Castilians, they felt themselves to be invincible. As for the perils of the deep, a sea voyage was no longer a haphazard adventure, but a problem to be worked out by the rules of an exact science. Portugal thus faced the unknown world and feared it not at all.

The great quest was carried on. Afonso V, the African, engrossed though he was in the conquest of Morocco, did not forget it altogether; and his son, the future Dom João II, on attaining manhood, brought to bear upon the problem all the vigor of his restless intellect. "He was determined," we are told, "to pursue the discovery of the Guinea coast that his predecessors had begun, for by that coast it seemed to him that he would find the land of Prester John of which he heard reports, and by that way he might reach India."

So the little ships continued seeking new horizons. In 1471 Alvaro Esteves had crossed the Equator. In 1484, a stone pillar was erected near the Congo River by Diogo Cão. Finally, in 1486, Bartholomeu Dias struck boldly out to sea and sailed far south of the discovered world. For thirteen days his fifty-ton caravels ran blindly before wild winds and raging seas, and the long-sought cape was turned at last, unknowingly amid the shrieking storm. "Cape of Tempests," the sailors called it when they saw the giant upon their homeward way. "Call it rather Cape of Good Hope!" said Dias, with visions of the golden East before his eyes, and so the name remained. But they had gleaned no news of Prester John upon those savage shores.

CHRISTOPHER COLUMBUS, MARINER

by Samuel Eliot Morison

A child's first introduction to the history of exploration is often the information that Columbus discovered America. Yet, as Samuel Eliot Morison, the authority on maritime history explains, this idea requires qualification if by America we mean the continental mass itself. On his first voyage, Columbus landed on the Bahamas, then Cuba and Haiti, and concluded that he had reached an Asian port. He did not know of the existence of either North or South America.

Long before Columbus sailed, as we have seen, the Vikings may have reached the coast of North America. Now in the fifteenth century, while Columbus sailed toward the south in the hope of reaching the Indies, John Cabot, an Italian turned Englishman, aimed for the same goal by sailing north. We must credit Cabot with the "discovery" of the North American Continent— he reached Newfoundland—unless we accept the story of the Vikings or of an expedition sent out by Henry the Navigator which may have touched the coast.

Columbus was never to understand the real meaning of his discovery. On a later voyage he concluded that the land he found was only "nineteen days' sail from the Ganges." Why then has Sir Percy Sykes, the explorer, called his discovery "the greatest event in the history of exploration"? Professor Morison, in his graphic account of the first voyage, gives us some of the reasons. He shows us also Columbus the man, proud and sensitive, son of a weaver who became one of the master mariners of all time.

CHRISTOPHER COLUMBUS, discoverer of the New World, was first and foremost a sailor. Born and reared in Genoa, one of the oldest European seafaring communities, as a youth he made several voyages in the Mediterranean, where the greatest mariners of antiquity were bred. At the age of twenty-four, by a lucky chance he was thrown into Lisbon, center of European oceanic enterprise; and there, while employed partly in making charts and partly on long voyages under the Portuguese flag, he conceived the great enterprise that few but a sailor would have planned, and none but a sailor could have executed. That enterprise was simply to reach "The Indies"—Eastern Asia—by sailing west. It took him about ten years to obtain support for this idea, and he never did execute it, because a vast continent stood in the way. America was discovered by Columbus purely by accident and was named for a man who had nothing to do with it; we now honor Columbus for doing something that he never intended to do, and never knew that he had done. Yet we are right in so honoring him, because no other sailor had the persistence, the knowledge and the sheer guts to sail thousands of miles into the unknown ocean until he found land.

This was the most spectacular and most far-reaching geographical discovery in recorded human history. Moreover, apart from the magnitude of his achievement, Columbus was a highly interesting character. Born at the crossroads between the Middle Ages and the Renaissance, he showed the qualities of both eras. He had the firm religious faith, the a priori reasoning and the close communion with the Unseen typical of the early Christian centuries. Yet he also had the scientific curiosity, the zest for life, the feeling for beauty and the striving for novelty that we associate with the advancement of learning. And he was one of the greatest seamen of all time.

The little we know about the Discoverer's childhood and early youth can be quickly told. He had very little formal schooling, spoke the Genoese dialect, which was almost unintelligible to other Italians, and never learned to read and write until he went to Portugal. As everyone who described him in later life said that he had a long face, an aquiline nose, ruddy complexion and red hair, we can picture him as a little, freckle-faced redhead with blue eyes. One imagines that he was a dreamy little boy and very religious for one of his age, and he must have disliked working in his father's loom shed, as he took every opportunity to go to sea.

In later life Columbus said that he first went to sea in 1461 when he was ten years old. Probably his seafaring at that age did not amount to much; maybe his father let him sail with a neighbor to Portofino to load dried fish, or even over to Corsica, which would have seemed like a foreign voyage to a little boy. What sailor can forget his first cruise? Every incident, every turn of wind, every vessel or person you meet stays in your memory for years. What pride and joy to be given the tiller while the skipper goes below and the mate snoozes on the sunny side of the deck! What a thrill to sight five mountains above the horizon, to watch them rise, spread out and merge into one as you approach! Then, to go ashore, to swap your jackknife for a curiosity, to see the island gradually sink below the horizon on the homeward passage, and to swagger ashore feeling you are a real old salt! Such things a sailor never forgets.

In May, 1476, in his twenty-fifth year, came the adventure that changed the course of Christopher's life. Genoa organized an armed convoy to carry a valuable cargo to Northern Europe, and in this convoy Christopher sailed as seaman in a Flemish vessel named *Bechalla*. On August 13, when it had passed the Strait of Gibraltar and was off the southern coast of Portugal, the fleet was attacked by a French task force. The battle raged all day, and by nightfall three Genoese ships and four of the enemy's had gone down. *Bechalla* was one of the casualties. Christopher, though wounded, managed to grasp a floating sweep and, by alternately kicking it ahead and resting on it, reached the shore six miles distant. The people of Lagos, near which he landed, treated him kindly, and on learning that his younger brother Bartholomew was living at Lisbon, sent him thither as soon as he could travel.

That was one of the best things that could have happened to Christopher Columbus.

Portugal was then the liveliest and most progressive country in Europe, and Lisbon the center for exploration and discovery. Almost half a century earlier the Infante Dom Henrique, the Portuguese prince whom we call Henry the Navigator, had set up a combined hydrographic and marine intelligence office at Cape St. Vincent, which attracted ambitious seamen from all over the Mediterranean. He subsidized voyages out into the Atlantic and down along the west coast of Africa. His captains discovered the seven islands of the Azores, one-third of the way to America; the Portuguese colonized not only the Azores but the Madeira group which had been discovered earlier, and the Cape Verde Islands off Africa.

Lisbon, moreover, was a learned city where it was easy for a newcomer like Columbus to learn Latin and modern languages and to acquire books that increased his knowledge of the world. Bartholomew, who had already joined the Genoese community there, was employed in one of the chart-making establishments, where he got a job for Christopher, and before long the Columbus brothers had a thriving chart business of their own. That put them in close touch with master mariners and the like, for all charts at that time were based on information and rough sketches that seamen brought home. The two brothers would manage to be on hand whenever a ship returned from Africa or the Western Islands to invite the master or pilot to dine or drink with them, and would extract from him all the data they could for correcting their charts of known countries or extending those of the African coast. It may well be that in one of these conferences a grizzled captain, looking at a chart of the known world, remarked. "I'm sick of sailing along the fever-stricken Guinea coast, chaffering with local chiefs for a cargo of blackamoors; why can't we sail due west beyond the Azores, till we hit the Golden East, and make a real killing? . . ."

We do not know how Columbus came by the idea of sailing west to reach the East, but once he had it, that was the truth for him; he was the sort of man in whom action is the complement of a dream. Like the pioneers of aviation, he was considered a little touched in the head: one who would fly in the face of God. And the worst of it was that he had to persuade stupid people in high places that his Enterprise of the Indies, as he called it, was plausible, because he wanted money, men and equipment to carry it out. More maritime experience than that of foremost hand and apprentice chartmaker was needed before he could hope to convince anyone. And that he obtained, under the Portuguese flag.

Christopher Columbus, now aged thirty-one or -two, had "arrived," according to the standards of his day. He was a master mariner in the Portuguese merchant service, then the finest and most far-ranging merchant marine in the world. He had sailed from above the Arctic Circle to the Equator, and from the eastern Aegean to the outer Azores. He had learned all of practical navigation that could be acquired by entering ships "through the hawse hole" and working up to the captain's cabin. He could make charts and figure latitude from the North Star. Besides, he was an avid reader of books on geography and cosmography. He was connected by marriage to two important families of Portugal. He had business connections with a leading merchant-banker house of Genoa. Columbus had only to continue in this career, persevere in the African trade with its many opportunities to make something on the side, and retire after a few years, a rich man. Or the King might give him one of the royal caravels to explore the African coast, as Diego Cão was doing in 1482-83; and Cão, for discovering a new farthest south on the African coast, was knighted and ennobled in 1484.

But Christopher had other ideas and a vaster ambition. His mind was seething with the notion of sailing west to the Orient, acquiring wealth beyond the dreams of avarice, and glory exceeding that of any earlier mariner. . . .

In 1484 he made his first effort to interest a prince—John II, King of Portugal, a nephew of Henry the Navigator who was intensely interested in new discoveries. According to the contemporary Portuguese historians and chroniclers, the Columbian project was exactly the same then as later—to reach Japan by sailing west and to discover other islands en route. "The King," says one of the historians, "as he observed this *Christovão Colom* to be a big talker and boastful . . . and full of fancy and imagination with his Isle *Cypango* . . . gave him small credit." Nevertheless, the King committed the project to a junta consisting of a prominent churchman and two Jewish physicians of reputed skill in celestial navigation. They turned it down, flat. Their reasons for so doing are not recorded, but we may assume that they had a more accurate idea of the distance to be covered than did Columbus.

In 1485, the same year that the Portuguese committee turned him down, his wife Dona Felipa died at Lisbon. That broke his strongest tie with Portugal. Nobody there would stake him if the King would not, so Columbus decided to try his luck in Spain. He knew no one there except a sister of his late wife who was married to a Spaniard in Huelva, so to that part of Spain, the County of Niebla adjoining Portugal, Columbus took ship with his five-year-old son Diego.

It must have been with sinking heart that Columbus entered the Rio Saltés and sighted the sleepy little ports of Huelva and Palos, a sad contrast to bright, bustling Lisbon. As his ship rounded into the Rio Tinto, he observed on a bluff the buildings of the Franciscan friary of La Rábida. That suggested a solution to his problem of what to do with Diego, as the Franciscans were known to take "boarders." So, after landing at Palos, he walked with his little son four miles to the friary, knocked at the gate and asked the porter for a drink of water and some bread for the boy. Fortunately, Antonio de Marchena, a highly intelligent Franciscan who had studied astronomy, came to the gate and got into conversation with Columbus. He invited both father and son to stay, accepted Diego as a pupil and introduced Columbus to the Count of Medina Celi, a grandee of Spain and also an important shipowner of Cadiz.

Medina Celi, of whom Columbus asked "three or four well-equipped caravels, and no more," had almost decided to underwrite the enterprise when it occurred to him to ask permission of the Queen. He did so, and

Isabella refused, believing that so important an enterprise as that of Columbus should be conducted by the crown. But this transfer from Count to Queen postponed Columbus's voyage some six years.

On May Day 1486, almost a year from the time he had first set foot in Spain, Columbus was received by the Queen in the Alcazar that still stands at Cordova. Isabella the Catholic was one of the ablest European sovereigns in an age of strong kings. She had an intuitive faculty for choosing the right man for a job, and for doing the right thing at the right time. She was very close to Columbus's age and similar to him in temperament, and in coloring—blue eyes and auburn hair. Her marriage with Ferdinand of Aragon had united all "the Spains," excepting Portugal, to which she was allied, and the remnant of the Moorish Caliphate of Cordova, which she had resolved to conquer. Some spark of understanding evidently passed between Christopher and Isabella at their first meeting, and although she turned down his enterprise more than once, he found that he could count on her in the end. On this occasion she appointed a special commission under Hernando de Talavera, her confessor, to examine the Great Project and recommend whether she should accept or reject it, or allow Medina Celi to back it.

Then began a period of almost six years, the most unhappy in Columbus's entire life. He had to sustain a continual battle against prejudice, contumely and sheer indifference. A proud, sensitive man who *knew* that his project was feasible and that it would open new pathways to maritime achievement and opportunity, he had to endure clownish witticisms and crackpot jests by ignorant courtiers, to be treated worse than a beggar, and at times actually to suffer want. Worst of all, perhaps, he learned by experience the meaning of the phrase *"cosas de España,"* the irritating procrastination of Spaniards, who never seemed to be able to make up their minds, to carry out a plain order, or to make a firm decision without fees or favors. In later years he often alluded bitterly to these experiences and tactlessly contrasted the enormous wealth and power he had conferred on Spain with his pitiable and protracted efforts to obtain a fair hearing.

At about Christmas time 1491, Columbus again appeared at court, which was then being held in the fortified camp of Santa Fe during the siege of Granada. A new commission was appointed, and the Royal Council reviewed their findings. The exact details are not known, but it seems probable that the commission, reading the Queen's mind, recommended that Columbus be allowed to try this project, and that the Council rejected it because of the price he asked. For this extraordinary man, despite poverty, delays and discouragement, had actually raised his demands. In 1485 he had been willing to sail west for Medina Celi on an expense-account basis, without any particular honors or emoluments. Now he demanded not only ennoblement and the title of admiral, but also that he be made governor and viceroy of any new lands he might discover, that both titles be hereditary in his family, and that he and his heirs be given a ten per cent cut on the trade. He had suffered so many outrages and insults during his long residence in Spain that—by San Fernando!—he would not glorify Spain for nothing. If the sovereigns would grant him, contingent on his success, such rank, titles and property that he and his issue could hold up their heads with Spanish grandees, well and good; but no more bargaining. Take it, Your Majesties, or leave it.

Leave it they did, in January, 1492, immediately after the fall of Granada. Ferdinand and Isabella told him this at an audience that the King, at least, intended to be final. Columbus saddled his mule, packed the saddlebags with his charts and other exhibits, and started for Seville with his faithful friend Juan Pérez, intending to take ship for France and join Bartholomew in a fresh appeal to Charles VIII.

Just as, in Oriental bargaining, a storekeeper will often run after a departing customer to accept his last offer, so it happened here. Luis de Santangel, keeper of King Ferdinand's privy purse, called on the Queen the very day that Columbus left Santa Fe and urged her to meet Columbus's terms. The expedition, he pointed out, would not cost as much as a week's entertainment of a fellow sovereign, and he would undertake to raise the money himself. As for the honors and emoluments, Columbus asked only for a promise of them in the event of his success, and if he did succeed, they would be a small price to pay for the discovery of new islands and a western route to the Indies. Isabella, who had probably felt that way all along, jumped at this, her really last chance. She even proposed to pledge her crown jewels for the expenses, but Santangel said that would not be necessary. And she sent a messenger who overtook Columbus at a village four miles from Santa Fe, and brought him back. . . .

Although it was now settled in principle, the success of the Enterprise depended on an infinite number of practical details. First, it was decided to fit out the fleet and recruit the men at Palos, the little port in the Niebla where Columbus had first set foot in Spain, and for several reasons. Columbus had made friends there of the Pinzón family, leading shipowners and master mariners; both ships and sailors were available. And Palos had committed some municipal misdemeanor for which the Queen conveniently fined her two well-equipped caravels. Columbus made a public appearance in the Church of St. George, Palos, on May 23, 1492, with his friend Fray Juan Pérez, while a notary read the royal order that "within ten days" the two caravels were to be provided and crews recruited, with four months' advance pay.

Ten days, of course, was preposterous, and it actually took about three months for Columbus to get to sea. He had been promised three caravels, not two, but it so happened that a ship from Galicia, owned and captained by Juan de la Cosa, was then in port, and Columbus chartered her as his flagship.

Santa María, as this ship was called, is the most famous of Columbus's ships. She left her bones on a reef off Hispaniola, and no picture or model of her has survived, but several conjectural models have been made and two full-size "replicas" have been constructed in Spain. The original *Santa María* was probably of about one hundred tons' burthen, which meant that her cargo capacity was one hundred "tuns" or double hogsheads of wine.

A Spanish ship in those days had an official name, usually that of a saint, and a nickname which the sailors used; *Santa María* was *La Gallega*, "The Galician." One of the two caravels provided by the town of Palos was named *Santa Clara*, but she is universally known by her nickname *Niña*, so given because she belonged to the Niño family of Palos. *Niña* was Columbus's favorite.

Pinta, also a locally built caravel, was probably a little larger than *Niña*, and square-rigged from the first. Her real name we do not know; *Pinta* probably was derived from a former owner named Pinto. She was a smart sailor; the New World was first sighted from her deck and she was first home to Spain.

Almost all the enlisted men—stewards, boatswains, calkers, able seamen and "gromets," or ship's boys—were from the Niebla or near-by towns of Andalusia like Seville, Cordova and Jerez de la Frontera. Each seaman received about the equivalent of $7 in gold per month, the petty officers twice that and the boys about $4.60. The only foreigners, besides Columbus, were another Genoese, one Portuguese and a Venetian. The story that Columbus had an Englishman and an Irishman on board is a myth, but there is some foundation for the tradition that the crews included jailbirds. Three lads who had been given life imprisonment for helping a condemned murderer to break jail were set free in order to ship with Columbus; they turned out to be trustworthy men and went with the Admiral on later voyages, as did a large number of the others. On the whole, the crews of these ships were good, capable fellows from the neighborhood, with members of three leading families in key positions. Encouraged by an ancient pilot who was sure he had just missed the Indies on a Portuguese voyage westward forty years earlier, these men and boys overcame the natural conservatism of a mariner in the hope of glory, gold and adventure. Those who survived won plenty of the first two, and all shared in one of the greatest adventures of history—Columbus's First Voyage.

By the second day of August, 1492, everything at last was ready. That night every man and boy of the fleet confessed his sins, received absolution and made his communion at the church of Palos, which by happy coincidence was dedicated to Saint George, patron saint of Genoa. Columbus went on board his flagship in the small hours of Friday the third and gave the signal to get under way. Before the sun rose, all three vessels had anchors aweigh, and with sails hanging limp from their yards were floating down the Rio Tinto on the morning ebb, using their long sweeps to maintain steerageway. As they swung into the Saltés and passed La Rábida close aboard, they could hear the friars chanting the ancient hymn "*Iam lucis orto sidere*" with its haunting refrain "*Et nunc et in perpetuum,*" which we render "Evermore and evermore."

This fleet of good hope, whose achievements would radically alter world history, sailed parallel to another fleet of misery and woe. On the very same tide there dropped down the Saltés the last vessel carrying the Jews whom Ferdinand and Isabella had expelled from Spain. August 2 was their deadline; any who remained thereafter were to be executed unless they embraced Christianity. Thousands of pitiful refugees, carrying what few household goods they could stow in the crowded ships, were bound for the more tolerant lands of Islam, or for the only Christian country, the Netherlands, which would receive them. Columbus in all his writings dropped no word of pity for the fate of this persecuted race, and even expressed the wish to exclude them from the lands he discovered. But if there had been a new prophet among the Spanish Jews, he might have pointed out the Columbian fleet to his wretched compatriots on that August morning and said, "Behold the ships that in due time will carry the children of Israel to the ends of the earth."

Columbus's plan for the voyage was simple, and its simplicity insured his success. Not for him the boisterous head winds, the monstrous seas and the dark, unbridled waters of the North Atlantic, which had already baffled so many Portuguese. He would run south before the prevailing northerlies to the Canary Islands, and there make, as it were, a right-angle turn; for he had observed on his African voyages that the winter winds in the latitude of the Canaries blew from the east, and that the ocean around them, more often than not, was calm as a millpond.

On September 2 all three ships were anchored off San Sebastián, the port of that island. Columbus then met for the first time Doña Beatriz de Bobadilla, widow of the former captain of the island. Beatriz was a beautiful lady still under thirty, and Columbus is said to have fallen in love with her; but if that is true, he did not love her warmly enough to tarry to the next full moon. Additional ship's stores were quickly hoisted on board and struck below, and on September 6, 1492, the fleet weighed anchor for the last time in the Old World. They had still another island to pass, the lofty Ferro or Hierro. Owing to calms and variables Ferro and the twelve-thousand-foot peak of Tenerife were in sight until the ninth, but by nightfall that day, every trace of land had sunk below the eastern horizon, and the three vessels were alone on an uncharted ocean. Columbus himself gave out the course: "West; nothing to the north, nothing to the south."

Before going into the details of the voyage, let us see how those vessels were navigated, and how a day was passed at sea. Celestial navigation was then in its infancy, but rough estimates of latitude could be made from the height of the North Star above the horizon and its relation to the two outer stars (the "Guards") of the Little Dipper. A meridian altitude of the sun, applied to available tables of the sun's declination, also gave latitude, by a simple formula. But the instruments of observation—a solid wood or brass quadrant and the seaman's astrolabe—were so crude, and the movement of a ship threw them off to such an extent, that most navigators took their latitude sights ashore. Columbus relied almost completely on "dead reckoning," which means plotting your course and position on a chart from the three elements of direction, time and distance.

The direction he had from one or more compasses which were similar to those used in small craft until recently—a circular card graduated to the thirty-two points (N, N by E, NNE, NE by N, NE, and so on), with a lodestone under the north point, mounted on a pin and enclosed in a binnacle with gimbals so it could swing freely with the motion of the ship. Columbus's standard compass was mounted on the poop deck where the officer of the watch could see it. The helmsman, who steered with a heavy tiller attached directly to the rudder head, was below decks and could see very little. He may have had another compass to steer by, but in the smaller vessels, at least, he was conned by the officer of the deck and kept a steady course by the feel of the helm. On a sailing vessel you can do that; it would be impossible in any power craft.

Time on the vessels of that day was measured by a half-hour glass which hung from a beam so the sand could flow freely from the upper to the lower half. As soon as the sand was all down, a ship's boy turned the glass and the officer of the deck recorded it by making a stroke on a slate. Eight glasses made a watch; the modern ship's bells were originally a means of marking the glasses. This half-hour-glass time could be corrected daily in fair weather by noting the moment when the sun lay due south, which was local noon.

One reason Columbus always wanted two or more vessels was to have someone to rescue survivors in case of sinking. But he made an unusual record for that era by never losing a ship at sea, unless we count the *Santa María*, grounded without loss of life. Comforts and conveniences were almost totally lacking. Cooking was done on deck over a bed of sand in a wooden firebox protected from the wind by a hood. The diet was a monotonous one of salt meat, hardtack and dried peas. For drink they had wine, while it lasted, and water in casks, which often went bad. Only the Captain General and the ships' captains had cabins with bunks; the others slept where they could, in their clothes.

In those days, sailors were the most religious of laymen. On each vessel a boy was charged with singing a ditty at daybreak, which began:

> Blessed be the light of day
> And the Holy Cross, we say;

after which he recited the Lord's Prayer and the Ave Maria, and invoked a blessing on the ship's company. Every half-hour a boy sang out when turning the glass. For instance, at what we would call five bells, he sang:

> Five is past and six floweth,
> More shall flow if God willeth,
> Count and pass make voyage fast.

After sunset, and before the first night watch was set, all hands were called to evening prayers. The service began with the boy whose duty it was to light the binnacle lamp singing:

> God give us a good night and good sailing;
> May our ship make a good passage,
> Sir Captain and Master and good company.

All hands then said the Lord's Prayer, the Creed and the Ave Maria, and concluded by singing the *Salve Regina*. As Columbus himself said, "Seamen sing or say it after their own fashion," bawling it out in several keys at once and murdering the stately Latin words. But was it the less acceptable to the Virgin, under whose protection all sailors felt secure?

Now the boy who turns up the glass for the eighth time sings:

> The watch is called,
> The glass floweth.
> We shall make a good voyage
> If God willeth.

And as the vessels sail westward through the soft tropic night, rolling and pitching, sails bellying and slatting, cordage straining, bows throwing foam, every half-hour is marked by this chantey:

> To our God let's pray
> To give us a good voyage,
> And through the Blessed Mother,
> Our advocate on high,
> Protect us from the waterspout
> And send no tempest nigh.

So much for the sea ritual that went on every day, whatever the weather. Now for the events of the voyage.

On September 9, the day he dropped the last land below the horizon, Columbus decided to keep a true reckoning of his course for his own use and a false one to give out to the people, so that they would not be frightened at sailing so far from land.

During the first ten days (September 9 to 18), the easterly trade wind blew steadily, and the fleet made 1,163 nautical miles westward. This was the honeymoon of the voyage. *"Que era plazer grande el gusto de las mañanas"*—"What a delight was the savor of the mornings!" wrote Columbus in his Journal. That entry speaks to the heart of anyone who has sailed in the trades; it recalls the beauty of the dawn, kindling clouds and sails rose color, the smell of dew drying on a wooden deck, and, something Columbus didn't have, the first cup of coffee.

On September 19, only ten days out from Ferro, the fleet temporarily ran into an area of variable winds and rain. But the seamen who, on the tenth day of the northeast trades, were beginning to wonder whether they could ever beat back home were cheered by the change of wind.

During the next five days only 234 miles were made good. During this spell of moderate weather it was easy to converse from ship to ship and to talk about this or that island, St. Brendan's or Antilia, which they might pick up. In the middle of one of these colloquies, a seaman of *Pinta* gave the "Land Ho!" and everyone thought he saw an island against the setting sun. Columbus fell on his knees to thank God, ordered *"Gloria in excelsis Deo"* to be sung by all hands, and set a course for the island. But at dawn no island was visible; there was none. It was simply a cloud bank above the western horizon resembling land, a common phenomenon at sea. Martin Alonso Pinzón apparently wished to beat about and search for this island, but Columbus refused, because, he said, "his object was to reach the Indies, and if he delayed, it would not have made sense."

The trade wind now returned, but moderately, and during the six days September 26 to October 1, the fleet made only 382 miles. Under these circumstances the people began to mutter and grumble. Three weeks was probably more than they had ever been outside sight of land before. They were all getting on each other's nerves, as happens even nowadays on a long voyage to a known destination. There was nothing for the men to do in the light wind except to follow the ship's routine, and troll for fish. Grievances, real or imaginary, were blown up; cliques were formed; Spain was farther away every minute, and what lay ahead? Probably nothing, except in the eye of that cursed Genoese. Let's make him turn back, or throw him overboard!

On October 7, when there was another false landfall, great flocks of birds passed over the ships, flying west-southwest; this was the autumn migration from eastern North America to the West Indies. Columbus decided that he had better follow the birds rather than his chart, and changed course accordingly that evening. That was "good joss"; it was his shortest course to the nearest land. Now, every night, the men were heartened by seeing against the moon (full on October 5) flocks of birds flying their way. But by the tenth, mutiny flared up again. No land for thirty-one days. Even by the phony reckoning which Columbus gave out they had sailed much farther west than anyone had expected. Enough of this nonsense, sailing west to nowhere; let the Captain General turn back or else—! Columbus, says the record, "cheered them as best he could, holding out good hope of the advantages they might gain; and, he added, it was useless to complain, *since he had come to go to the Indies, and so had to continue until he found them, with Our Lord's help.*"

Signs of land, such as branches of trees with green leaves and flowers, became so frequent that the people were content with their Captain General's decision, and the mutinous mutterings died out in the keen anticipation of making a landfall in the Indies.

As the sun set under a clear horizon October 11, the northeast trade breezed up to gale force, and the three ships tore along at nine knots. But Columbus refused to shorten sail. He signaled everyone to keep a particularly sharp watch, and offered extra rewards for first landfall in addition to the year's pay promised by the sovereigns. That night of destiny was clear and beautiful with a late rising moon, but the sea was the roughest of the entire passage. The men were tense and expectant, the officers testy and anxious, the Captain General serene in the confidence that presently God would reveal to him the promised Indies.

At 10 P.M., an hour before moonrise, Columbus and a seaman, almost simultaneously, thought they saw a light "like a little wax candle rising and falling." Others said they saw it too, but most did not; and after a few minutes it disappeared. Volumes have been written to explain what this light was or might have been. To a seaman it requires no explanation. It was an illusion, created by overtense watchfulness. When uncertain of your exact position, and straining to make a night landfall, you are apt to see imaginary lights and flashes and to hear nonexistent bells and breakers.

On rush the ships, pitching, rolling, throwing spray—white waves at their bows and white wakes reflecting the moon. *Pinta* is perhaps half a mile in the lead, *Santa María* on her port quarter, *Niña* on the other side. Now one, now another forges ahead, but they are all making the greatest speed of which they are capable. With the sixth glass of the night watch, the last sands are running out of an era that began with the dawn of history. A few minutes now and destiny will turn up a glass the flow of whose sands we are still watching. Not since the birth of Christ has there been a night so full of meaning for the human race.

At 2 A.M., October 12, Rodrigo de Triana, lookout on *Pinta*, sees something like a white cliff shining in the moonlight, and sings out, "*Tierra! tierra!*" "Land! land!" Captain Pinzón verifies the landfall, fires a gun as agreed, and shortens sail to allow the flagship to catch up. As *Santa María* approaches, the Captain General shouts across the rushing waters, "Señor Martín Alonso, you *did* find land! Five thousand maravedis for you as a bonus!"

Yes, land it was this time, a little island of the Bahamas group. The fleet was headed for the sand cliffs on its windward side and would have been wrecked had it held course. But these seamen were too expert to allow that to happen. The Captain General ordered sail to be shortened and the fleet to jog off and on until daylight, which was equivalent to a southwesterly drift clear of the island. At dawn they made full sail, passed the southern point of the island and sought an opening on the west coast, through the barrier reef. Before noon they found it, sailed into the shallow bay now called Long or Fernandez, and anchored in the lee of the land, in five fathoms.

Here on a gleaming beach of white coral occurred the famous first landing of Columbus. The Captain General (now by general consent called Admiral) went ashore in the flagship's boat with the royal standard of Castile displayed, the two Captains Pinzón in their boats, flying the banner of the Expedition—the green crowned cross on a white field. "And, all having rendered thanks to Our Lord, kneeling on the ground, embracing it with tears of joy for the immeasurable mercy of having reached it, the Admiral rose and gave this island the name *San Salvador*"—Holy Savior.[1]

VASCO DA GAMA AND THE PORTUGUESE CONQUEST OF THE EAST INDIES

by Henry H. Hart

In approximately 1460, the year that Henry the Navigator died, there was born in Portugal a child who was destined to realize the Prince's lifelong dream. By the time Vasco da Gama reached manhood, only the ignorant believed that the earth was anything but round. The Indies could be reached by sailing west in the path of Columbus, but a voyage in the opposite direction should reach the same destination. First, however, the great land mass to the south had to be circumnavigated, if indeed that could be done. In voyage after voyage the attempt was made. Year after year saw the slow accretion of information about the route, and with the triumphant journey

[1] Although there is still some difference of opinion, the generally accepted identification of Columbus's island is the one formerly called Watlings. It has been officially renamed San Salvador.

past the Cape of Good Hope by Bartholomeu Dias, the way lay clear for a passage to the East.

There are authorities who believe that Dias's voyage was a greater feat of pioneering than that of Da Gama; many feel that the voyages of both were more difficult of accomplishment than those of Columbus. Certainly they took far more time; certainly the problems faced were far more varied. But this was a time of greatness in exploration and all were giants.

Henry H. Hart is an authority on exploration to the East. In his book Sea Road to the Indies, he tells how Da Gama won his way to the Orient, how he found there riches beyond his most optimistic calculations and how in the process he set a pattern of ruthlessness and cruelty which was to persist for centuries and darken the name of Portugal in history.

Da Gama voyaged three times to the East. His experiences were rich in the qualities which make the story of exploration so exciting. One of the most famous episodes deals with his incredibly brutal destruction of an Arab ship and one of the most unusual of these episodes with his attempt to stem the excesses for which he had set a pattern. These are here described.

A S WITH his first expedition, no record is in existence compiled or written by Dom Vasco himself about his second voyage to India. The first landfall of the voyage was the group of the Canary Islands, and thence the course was set southeast. At the end of February the Cape Verde Islands were sighted, and the ships put in at Porto Dala for wood and water.

Continuing the voyage after a short stop at Mozambique, the fleet arrived at the island of Kilwa, at the mouth of the Coavo River. It was a rich city, with fine houses of stone, whose people "all goe naked," or very slightly clad. Gama remembered that the Emir Ibrahim had treated Cabral[1] badly and had refused to accept Christianity on his demand. This natural refusal was taken for impudence and hostility. Gama sent word that he would burn the town to the ground if Ibrahim would not submit to the Portuguese and pay tribute to Manuel. The helpless Emir was forced to submit and swear fealty to the king. As guarantee for the payment of the tribute demanded, one Mohammed Ankoni, citizen of Kilwa (whom the Emir suspected of plotting to usurp his throne), was handed over to Gama. Mohammed knew that the sheik had no intention of paying the tribute from his own treasury and that the Portuguese would kill him, so he paid out the two thousand mitcals demanded and was released forthwith. The Admiral received the money and never inquired who paid it. The important

---

[1] The leader of an expedition which followed Gama's first voyage.—Eds.

thing for him was that he had obtained both the submission of Kilwa's ruler and the coveted tribute.

The ships next arrived at Cannanore; and there Gama awaited the ships from Mecca, "and these are the ships which bring spices to our lands, and we wished to destroy them and thus the King of Portugal would alone have the spices there [in India] brought together."

After some days an Arab ship, the *Meri*, was sighted coming from the west. It was a vessel on its return voyage from Mecca. In addition to a cargo of merchandise it carried 380 passengers, men, women, and children, mostly people returning from a pilgrimage to the holy city to their homes in Calicut. The Portuguese commander gave chase and quickly overhauled the Arab ship, which surrendered without resistance, as it would have been futile against such overwhelming numbers. Gama ordered the cargo to be handed over and all arms surrendered. The Arabs thereat denied possessing anything of value. Thereupon the Admiral had two of them thrown into the sea, whereat the others confessed that they did carry some valuable cargo. The best of this was loaded on the ship of Diogo Fernandes Correa for the King, and the rest was distributed among Gama's crews. The transfer of cargo occupied two days. The Admiral suspected that much was still concealed by the Mohammedans and that perhaps all the weapons had not been handed over. Thereupon, though he had met with no resistance and had pillaged a peaceful ship of a country with which he was not at war, Gama terminated this inexcusable act of piracy with the most dastardly and ferocious act of his whole career. Cold-bloodedly he ordered the passengers to be locked in the hold of the *Meri*, the ship to be set afire, and all on it burned to death. This, says Castanheda, he did in revenge for attacks made by the Moors on Cabral.

The bombardiers to whom the horrible task was assigned set fire to the ship in several places, and the Portuguese vessels drew away far enough to be safe from the flames. The doomed Arabs, hearing and smelling the fire, managed to break out and rushed about the deck with buckets and axes, stamping out the fire which had entered the hull through the shot holes made by the Portuguese. Realizing the horrible fate awaiting them, they prepared to sell their lives dearly with the few weapons which they had managed to conceal. But first they made one more despairing plea for mercy. The women ran to the bulwarks, shrieking, wailing, and holding up their babies in their arms, pointing to them and to the few ornaments on their arms and fingers, lamenting pitifully in their native tongues and trying with wild gesticulations to melt the heart of the cruel unbeliever. It was all of no avail. Gama, who was on Estavão's ship, gave orders to grapple with the Arab craft and to set it afire again. He stood at a window of his cabin, looking stonily out onto the deck of the doomed vessel—a scene out of the Inferno, with black smoke and red and orange flames billowing out from the decks and hold of the *Meri;* the men, singed and fire-blackened, struggling pitifully to beat out the flames; the women and children screaming, running about to escape the flames and the missiles the Portuguese were now showering on them, while above all rose the derisive howls and shouts of the Portuguese pirate crews. In their frenzy the Arabs seized blazing sticks and timbers and flung them onto the decks of the Portuguese vessels, and Gama's men were kept busy extinguishing the flames. Dom Vasco could not be moved from his bloody decision. He brutally gave the order to board the ship and fire it again where the flames had been extinguished. The Portuguese vessels again closed in, the crews leaping from their high bulwarks onto the low-lying deck of the Arab. They met a fierce, insane resistance, the resistance of men fighting for their very lives and for those of their loved ones. The decks were slippery with blood, and again and again they repulsed the waves of Portuguese coming over the side.

Night fell, and the Portuguese ships drew off in fear that they in turn might be boarded or set afire by the despairing Arabs. The latter, exhausted and helpless, clung to the slender hope that wind and current might carry them far enough away during the hours of darkness to make good their escape even though the Portuguese vessels were all about them. Throughout the night the Arabs could be heard praying to Allah and calling upon Mohammed to save them. So the unequal struggle, unbelievable as it appears, continued for four days and four nights, the Portuguese repeatedly setting the ship on fire and the Arabs doggedly stamping out the flames. Though much of the ship was burned and many Arabs had been drowned when they threw themselves from the blazing deck into the sea, Gama's crews were beginning to weary of the fight, for they were losing men, ammunition, and time over a single looted vessel, no longer of any value to them. At this critical moment the Mohammedans were betrayed and destroyed by one of their own people. Lopes tells the tale:

The admiral went to the ship *Leonanda* and discussed the matter with six or seven other leaders of the fleet . . . that they had pursued [the fight] for four days and four nights with none of them being able to grapple with it, and only as they passed by it could they fire on it with bombards, and already our people were resolved not to continue further, when one of the Moors who had leaped into the sea came to tell our captain that if he would spare his life he would swim out and attach a rope to the hinge of the rudder of the ship, so as to set fire to it, and putting this into effect the admiral granted him his life and handed him over to João de Vera. He had with him coins [*xerafims*] of gold, and told of the great wealth which had been on the ship, and which had been thrown into the sea, moreover of the great quantities of provisions which it carried: he told us also that in the casks of honey and of oil they had hidden much gold, silver, and jewels, throwing everything overboard when they saw that we did not intend to spare their lives. And their fury was such that several times, in the midst of the melee we saw men wounded by arrows tear them out and fling them back at us by hand, and continuing to fight as though they felt no pain. And so, after so many struggles the admiral set that ship ablaze with much cruelty and without the least pity, and it burned with every one aboard.

Of all that shipload of helpless humanity, only some twenty boys were spared to be converted to Christianity and become monks at Belém! And none of all this atrocity was done in an outburst of passion, wrath, or revenge, but with cold, calculated, and unfeeling ferocity. It is an ineffaceable stain on the grim character of Dom Vasco da Gama, though the contemporary accounts do not seem to have found his action reprehensible.

After the destruction of the ship from Mecca, Gama sailed for Cannanore, with whose rajah he had sealed a pact of friendship on his first voyage—a man who was overjoyed at finding in the Portuguese an ally against his enemy the Samorin[2] of Calicut. A commercial treaty was discussed, and shortly thereafter the fleet sailed on, anchoring off Calicut on October 30, 1502.

The Samorin was now aroused and frightened, for Gama was before his city with a large fleet; and the ruler at last realized that he had made a fatal error in scorning the admiral on his first voyage and in not preventing the treacherous attack on Cabral's men. He moved with alacrity and sent out officials with offers of friendship. Dom Vasco treated the envoys with contempt, telling them that his king could carve out a ruler equal to the Samorin from the trunk of a palm. He demanded as the price of peace the immediate banishment of every Mohammedan in Calicut. To impress the Samorin that he meant to follow up his ultimatum with action, the Admiral perpetrated another inexcusable and inhuman outrage. On the arrival of the fleet a number of fishermen had put out in their boats to sell their catch to the crews. Gama had thirty-eight of the poor innocent fellows

[2] The sovereign lord.—Eds.

seized. Protesting and struggling, they were dragged on the ship and hanged from the yardarms. At the same time Gama ordered his ships to bombard the city, which possessed but few, if any, cannon with which to reply.

At nightfall Gama ordered the bodies of the hanged men taken down. Their heads, hands, and feet were cut off and heaped up in a boat, and their dismembered bodies were flung overboard to be washed inshore by the tide. A message in Arabic was fastened to the heap of hands, feet, and heads, pointing out that this was but a warning and a forecast of the fate of the city if it resisted. The chronicler Correa adds that the letter suggested that the Samorin make a fine curry of the severed heads and limbs. The boat was then cast off to drift ashore.

The picture of the horrible night that followed is painted in lurid colors by Lopes. The inhabitants of Calicut gathered in crowds along the shore, staring at the ghastly sight; while many waited at the water's edge as the headless and limbless torsos were rolled up on the sand by the incoming tide, trying in the light of smoky torches to recognize their kin by their clothing or otherwise. When any were recognized they were carried off by their relatives, and the monotonous death chants of the Hindus could be heard rising and falling through the night.

On the following day the bombardment of the city was renewed, and a heavily laden ship which had been seized at the shoreline the day before was looted and then burned.

After committing this further act of piracy, Gama sailed off with his fleet to Cochin to load spices, leaving six ships and a caravel, under the command of Vicente Sodré, before Calicut to cut off any entry there by ships. Dom Vasco arrived at Cochin on November 7 and began loading his vessels with spices and other goods while he entered into a trade agreement and an exchange of gifts with the Rajah of Cochin.

Meanwhile, the Rajah of Cannanore sent a messenger with the information that he, too, had enough cargo to fill several of the Portuguese ships, and Gama dispatched two ships to take on the merchandise.

On January 3 a Brahmin and his son, together with two distinguished citizens of Calicut, arrived in Cochin, bringing letters from the Samorin, who had tried in vain to attack and break Sodré's blockade, asking that the admiral return to Calicut to sign a treaty of peace and commerce. Gama departed in the *Flor de la Mar*, commanded by his nephew, dispatching a caravel at the same time to his uncle at Cannanore, ordering him to join the *Flor de la Mar* at Calicut. The invitation of the Samorin was a trap set to capture or kill Gama. During the night the latter found his ship surrounded by Arab vessels, and it was with difficulty that he escaped destruction from their fire. Had not Vicente Sodré come swiftly to his rescue with a ship and two caravels, the Portuguese would have fared very badly in the encounter.

Gama immediately took his revenge. He had released the Brahmin, but he strung up the boy and the other two prisoners at his yardarm and sailed up and down several times before the city with his ship's gruesome ornaments swinging in the wind. Then he returned to Cochin and completed the loading of his vessels. As the work was drawing to an end, word was received that the Arabs were gathering a great fleet to attack the Portuguese. Gama immediately summoned all the ships of his armada to Cochin, and on February 10, 1503, sailed away to Calicut again. There, on the twelfth of the month, he engaged the Rajah's fleet in combat. It was evidently not a very serious engagement. After a short encounter the Arab vessels fled, and with the dropping of the wind the heavier Portuguese ships could not pursue.

And now the Admiral deemed that he had finished the task assigned him. The monsoon favorable for the return voyage was at hand, and on February 20 the fleet sailed from Cannanore straight for Mozambique.

Thus ended the second voyage of Dom Vasco da Gama to India. Again he had brought his sovereign added glory and gold. He had signed treaties and added far-off vassals and tributaries to the Portuguese crown, and he had laid the foundations of the conquest and exploitation of the East African coast and the Indian seas for his people. But in so doing he had left behind him a hideous broad trail of fire, blood, and hatred—of the blood of innocents, needlessly shed, and of hatreds that could have been avoided by the exercise of tact, patience, and prudence. He had sown the wind. His successors were to reap the whirlwind, and in a few short generations his countrymen were to be stripped of the most valuable of their conquests and possessions. For himself, Dom Vasco had again given all too much evidence of the steely ruthlessness of his character, of his cold-blooded cruelty indulged in even when needless or futile. One seeks in vain in the record of the second voyage to India to find traits that might redeem him and soften the judgment of history and of ethics on this man who seemed to be, as Garcia da Orta remarked of Magellan, "the devil entered into a Portuguese."

The Portuguese people had an unparalleled opportunity to expand and develop through Gama's discovery of India. Unfortunately, they possessed certain characteristics which, from the first, militated against their success. They seem to have had no fixed ideals, a too easy willingness to compromise with ethical principles, an unbelievably cold-blooded cruelty, combined with a stupidity and ineptitude in dealing with foreign, particularly with native, peoples, together with fanaticism and absolute hatred of peoples not of their faith. These foredoomed their empire in the Indies, in spite of dazzling successes at the outset, to a short life and a speedy decline.

The fleets which the king of Portugal sent out to India between 1500 and 1504 were merchantmen—armed, it is true—for no conquest seemed to be contemplated. All that was desired was the obtaining of monopolistic control of the export trade of India. During the first years of the century an effort was made to establish factories (warehouses and shipping facilities) in the friendly cities of Cochin, Cannanore, and Coalão. The king relied on the friendly rajahs and petty princes to protect the factories and the Portuguese who remained to carry on the trade. The constant quarrels and fighting with the Samorin of Calicut, the most powerful state on the Malabar coast, not only made trade with that port almost impossible, but had a very deleterious effect on the relations between the Europeans and their Indian allies.

After several attacks by the Rajah of Calicut on the Portuguese in Cochin, King Manuel realized that dependence on scattered factories and the looting of native vessels could not continue. If Portugal was to maintain her place in the Indian trade, some sort of a system was necessary to maintain law and order and to assure a steady stream of merchandise flowing into Lisbon. It was decided to create a new office, that of Viceroy of India, the term of the viceroy to be three years. Dom Francesco d'Almeida was chosen. A wise and tried soldier, he sailed from Lisbon in March, 1505, clothed with full power to make treaties, regulate commerce, and, if necessary, to wage war.

Almeida's first act was to build and man a fort at Kilwa, on the East African coast, the second was to loot and destroy several towns near by! On his arrival in India a fort was built at Cannanore, which Gama had visited on his first voyage, and Portuguese were landed to settle in Cochin. Meanwhile, his ships had treated the Mohammedan traders with a high hand, killing and looting indiscriminately.

The Portuguese control of the sea was challenged by the Mameluke Sultan of Egypt, whose fleet, in 1508, attacked a Portuguese squadron and killed Almeida's son. The Viceroy swore vengeance, and, meeting the

Egyptian fleet at Diu, off the west coast of India, soundly defeated it on February 3, 1509, the artillery of the Europeans being far more than a match for the primitive weapons of the Egyptians and their allies from Calicut. Shortly after this victory Almeida's term as viceroy came to an end, and he was succeeded by Affonso d'Albuquerque, though he held his office until 1509.

D'Albuquerque had come out to the Indies in 1507, with orders to subdue the Persian city of Hormuz. Though there was no quarrel between Manuel and the boy king of Hormuz, D'Albuquerque saw no reason not to attack. Three towns were ruthlessly sacked and burned, and the slaughter of the helpless natives was horrible. The prisoners taken were all mutilated, the women having their noses and ears cut off, the men their noses and right hands. All this was done in cold blood, for the Portuguese were the aggressors, and very few of them had been killed. Hormuz surrendered after the Portuguese artillery had attacked the Persian fleet, an annual tribute was exacted, and a fort was built. To terrify the Persians still more completely, D'Albuquerque threatened the emissaries of the king that if he was interfered with he would "build the walls [of his fort] of Mohammedans' bones, nail their ears to the door, and set up his flagstaff on their skulls." Finally the Hormuz expedition failed because of the disloyalty of some of the Portuguese captains and D'Albuquerque sailed for India. After a defeat by the Nairs of Calicut, the Viceroy began to put into execution a plan for the control of the East. We are interested here only in the Indian portion of his policy, which involved the occupation of Goa as a colony and as the center of Portuguese power on the Indian coast.

Goa (from the Hindu *Gomant*, "the district of cowherds") is an old city on the central west coast of India, just north of 15° N. latitude, and was, next to Calicut, the principal seaport on the coast. It is situated on an island formed by tidal creeks. Its soil is fertile and it was easily defended by a fleet. It was a most strategic place in which to found a colony. D'Albuquerque sailed for the city in January, 1510, with a fleet of twenty-three ships. The town, to his surprise, surrendered after one of its small forts was captured, and on March 1 the governor entered the city and took possession of it, with all its warehouses, horses, elephants, and dockyards.

After only two months of peace a Mohammedan force of sixty thousand attacked the forts. When D'Albuquerque saw that he was in danger of being defeated, he retreated from the island, but first ordered a massacre of the inhabitants. He spared a few of the richest men for ransom, "the more beautiful of the women to marry, and some of the children to turn into Christians." He and his men then fought their way to their ships. Fortunately for the Viceroy, fourteen ships arrived from Portugal, and he pressed them into his service. Attacking the city on November 20, D'Albuquerque forced his way in and succeeded in retaking the island. After a solemn religious service of thanksgiving had been held, he issued orders to sack the city and to destroy every Mohammedan man, woman, and child remaining in it. Three hideous days of slaughter, rape, and torture followed. D'Albuquerque sent a dispatch to his sovereign that six thousand men, women, and children had been massacred. In February, 1512, while D'Albuquerque was away at Malacca, Goa was again besieged by the Shah of Bijapur, ruler of Goa, who had been driven out of the city. Caught between the governor's fleet and the fire from the walls, the Mohammedans were driven off. They surrendered nineteen Portuguese deserters. D'Albuquerque promised to spare their lives. He kept his word, but in a letter to his king he wrote, "I gave them their lives . . . but I ordered their noses, ears, right hands, and left thumbs to be cut off, for a warning and in memory of the treason and evil that they did." Half of the poor wretches died under the tortures, and the others dragged out a miserable existence. D'Albuquerque devoted much of his time to putting the administration of the Indian factories in a satisfactory condition. The fear inspired by his cruelty and efficiency was such that even the ruler of Calicut permitted the building of a Portuguese fort in his city.

In 1515, while campaigning in the Persian Gulf, D'Albuquerque received word that his term had expired (he had served as viceroy six years) and that his successor was to be Lopo Soares de Albergaria. A harsh and cruel man, D'Albuquerque nonetheless must be recognized as the real founder of the Portuguese dominion in India. With a small fleet and badly trained and armed men, D'Albuquerque had established and maintained the control of the trade routes of the Indian Ocean. He had founded a colonial empire and had an understanding of the political and economic aspects, problems and duties of government. He was a real leader, and men followed him. His was a brutal, savage, fanatical, and ruthless age, and it did not judge him harshly. All in all, he must be considered one of the greatest among all those Europeans who have ruled in India.

One of D'Albuquerque's colonial schemes for colonizing the Indies should be mentioned here, for it had a devastating effect on later efforts of the Portuguese to hold their dominions. It was the plan to colonize by bringing men to India and having them marry native women. To D'Albuquerque and his fellow countrymen this was nothing abnormal. African slaves had been brought into the country from the time of Prince Henry the Navigator and had been absorbed into the population. The native women in India became nominally Christians but maintained their relations with their people. The Portuguese quickly lost their vigor in the enervating climate. Symptoms of decay set in very early.

Lopo Soares de Albergaria, the successor of D'Albuquerque, was his very opposite, and his weakness, after D'Albuquerque's strength, quickly had its effect on Portuguese relations with their allies and subjects. Where D'Albuquerque would not allow Portuguese to trade, Soares opened the door to every kind of abuse by permitting rascals of all types to prey on legitimate Indian commerce, and even piracy was soon rampant. Soares interfered in the administration at every point; and finally many of D'Albuquerque's finest officers, disgusted with such proceedings as the auctioning off of D'Albuquerque's private property to fill Soares's own treasure chest, left India. After a thoroughly discreditable administration, Lopo Soares departed in 1518, hated and unregretted.

Lopo Soares was succeeded as governor by Diogo Lopes de Sequeira. His term, from 1518 to 1522, was not distinguished by any great events (in India), and he himself extorted wealth on every hand.

The fifth governor of India was Dom Duarte de Menezes, a thoroughgoing rascal, licentious and greedy even for his times. He arrived in India just three months before the death of King Manuel. After carrying on what seems to have been a perpetual war with Hormuz, Menezes turned his attention to Indian affairs.

The Portuguese historians are strangely silent about most of the events of Menezes' governorship. The most famous event seems to have been the "discovery" of the tomb of the Apostle St. Thomas near Madras.

The Portuguese government by this time had finally become aware of the terrible straits into which the Portuguese administration had fallen, and realized that a thorough housecleaning had to be made. It would be almost impossible, were it not for many records of the time, to believe that such deterioration could have set in in two decades. Several narratives have supplied most vivid descriptions. The Portuguese captains would often receive money from the King to buy provisions and would steal half the money, forcing the men to live on half-rations throughout the voyage. One Italian who visited India wrote: "There come from Portugal every year 2,500 or 3,000 men and youths of the lowest class imaginable. Most of them come to a bad end." An old Portuguese soldier describes the horrors of the voyage, often lasting seven months, and how the crews and soldiers, landing half-dead, were received with a salvo of greeting and cries and foul names, not only from the boys and natives, but from the people of their own nation and fatherland. "He who has no money or letter for friend or relatives sleeps under the eaves of the church, or within the boats drawn up on the shore . . . the second and third day are spent pawning or selling their cloak or sword. . . . And they go, four by four or six by six, entering houses, stupefied and starving, so that many . . . die." Incredible stories are told of thefts and false entries by tax collectors and other officers, who would bribe messengers to show them secret dispatches from which they could derive profit, shamelessly pocketing public funds and extorting all they could from the hapless natives. These people lived, as one chronicler has it, "in the luxury of a sultan and the greed of a rag-picker. . . . At the end of the three-years' term of one of the early viceroys [the Count of Vidigueira, grandson of Gama] . . . the ships [taking him back to Portugal] hardly sufficed to take all the baggage and chests of the viceroy and those near him, and were overflowing with precious things and infamy."

The practice of rewarding men like Gama and later officials with grants made for personal commerce, or of money, and so forth, finally made the official positions less public offices than royal liberality, a drain that neither the homeland nor the colonies could long sustain. Almeida, the first viceroy, advised against permitting private trading by officials, but no steps were ever taken to enforce decrees designed to put an end to the abuse. The salaries of officials were small, but in their stead were given captaincies, commands of fortresses, auditorships, rights of trade, and so forth.

The soldiers who were sent to garrison the Indian settlements were in general a poor lot, and their fate in India was a pathetic one. They were recruited from the farms and the slums. They brought nothing with them to India, where they were jeeringly called *descamisados* (literally, "men without shirts"). Many of them became robbers and thieves, for there were in India none of the controls which had kept them in their place in Portugal. With them worked the desperate adventurers and jailbirds who had enlisted in the crews. Cheating, gambling, debauchery were the common pleasures of the Portuguese in the India of King Manuel. One traveler who wrote shortly after this period bitterly remarked that "the prevailing characteristic of the first fifty years [of the Portuguese in the East] was ferocity." Added to all the evils enumerated above was the growth of slavery in the colony. The slaves were bought, sold, and treated like animals. Both men and women were stripped naked on the auction block on the rua Direita, in Goa, to exhibit their good points. In order to prevent trickery, girls offered as virgins were examined by women before they were purchased as concubines by the Portuguese. African women were preferred to Asiatics. Some Portuguese kept as many as five or six of these women. Slaves were brought to Goa from every part of the Indies, as well as from Africa. In addition to the female slaves, Goa swarmed with native women, who consorted with the soldiers, crowding the taverns and cheap lodgings. These women are quaintly described by Garcia da Orta, a famous botanist of the time, who lived many years in India, as "ardent Malabar she-dogs, many pretty, of tropical temperament, perfumed with sandal, aloes, camphor, musk . . . and rose water. They could converse in bad Portuguese, dance, play, and sing with much grace."

One of the great causes of the severity and difficulty of life for the Portuguese in India was the almost complete absence of women from the homeland. Most of the men took native or half-caste women as their wives. These sat around in idleness, waited on by slaves, and having no conception of the real position of a wife.

Added to all of these evils, the Portuguese were an easy prey to tropical diseases. Weakened as they often were by the long voyage, bad food, and outbreaks of scurvy, they fell easy victims to cholera, dysentery, and malaria, as well as to syphilis and other diseases which they had themselves brought to the Indies.

The Portuguese empire in India was, because of all these forces, rapidly becoming decadent, though not even a generation had passed since the opening of the sea route. The colony was in sad straits. The feudal evils of the Portuguese system in Lisbon had found their counterpart in India. No one was concerned with the common weal. From the governor down to the lowest official it was each for himself, and greed and lust ruled instead of moderation and an efficient administration.

What India needed, and needed badly, was a wise governor and an efficient, honest administration, if, indeed, it were not too late. The new king, John III, was certainly not a man of great parts, and made many errors of judgment in government, but the blame for the debacle in India cannot be placed altogether on his shoulders. The enterprises of Manuel had grown too large for a tiny nation like Portugal to carry. The effort was too great; the crash was bound to come. And more profound than all else was the disintegrating effect of India on Portugal. The enterprise was not an ordinary colonization of a virgin land, or one inhabited by an inferior people. India had a civilization as high as that of Portugal of the sixteenth century, but a civilization that was far different. The contact of the two was fatal to the Portuguese efforts. India had a civilization which combined fabulous riches with widespread and abject poverty, the opulence of the few accompanied by the starvation of the many, clamoring for a handful of rice. It was a country of absolute rulers, where a head was lopped off at the nod of a prince. In the picturesque words of a Portuguese narrator: "It was a mixture of perfume and the odor of blood, and of duplicity and cruelty with abject cowardice, all of which accorded with the base passions of the conquerors."

It was to this Portuguese India that Vasco came as viceroy in 1524.

The ships sailed from Lisbon and crossed the Tagus bar on April 9, 1524, Vasco da Gama leading the way on his flagship, the *St. Catherine of Mount Sinai*.

Gama was welcomed with real joy by the better class of both Portuguese and natives, for they felt that his coming would bring a change for the better. He was received under a rich canopy, with festivities and speeches, and was led in a great procession, first to the cathedral and then to the fortress. The council of the city dispatched a letter to King John, announcing the Admiral's arrival and rejoicing that at last an honest and efficient administrator had arrived.

The Viceroy had been granted plenary powers, executive, judicial, and legislative. His reputation had preceded him, and he was much feared and respected. He immediately set about using these powers in an earnest effort to correct the abuses that he found rampant and to restore respect and obedience for the government. One of the first things he discovered was that the King's officers had sold many pieces of artillery to the merchants of the colony. He immediately issued an order commanding the return of all such property within thirty days, under the penalty of losing both property and life. Most of the artillery was quickly returned! In the words of a letter from the Council of Goa to the King, he refused, when "many persons went to him with gifts such as is customary to make to newly arrived governors, to take anything from Christian or Moor, and still less from this city, which we all look upon as strange, as it is the custom for all to be accepted." He found the hospital crowded with men who were using it as a lodging, and drove them out. He forbade the hospital to receive anyone wounded in a brawl, "saying that they brawled on account of women." Crews of ships were to remain aboard while in harbor and receive their rations there.

The next step was to make an example of three women who had shipped in the fleet at Lisbon and who had been locked up ever since they had been turned over to him at Mozambique. He issued an order that the three women be flogged in public, while the government crier proclaimed: "The justice of the King, our Lord, It commands that these women be flogged because they did not fear his justice, coming to India contrary to his prohibition." Upon the announcement of the approaching punishment, people of all classes, "gentlemen," bishops and friars and the Brothers of Mercy, interceded on behalf of the women and offered a large sum of money to buy them off. He even refused, on the day of the carrying out of the sentence, to listen to priests carrying a crucifix from the Franciscan church. The order for flogging was carried out; and though he was adjudged a cruel man, it had a very salutary effect among would-be evildoers.

Just before his death, Gama did his best to mitigate the fate of the three women. He sent each of them 300,000 reis, "which were to be given them with much secrecy, and if they should not choose to accept them, this sum was to be doubled and given to the Santa Casa de Misericórdia. These women, with this money, found good husbands and were married and became honest women." Thus the chronicler Correa.

The Viceroy was already ailing but persisted in his task of reorganizing the government of the Portuguese Indies. After spending some time in restoring law and order in Goa, Gama sailed south to confer with the Portuguese Governor of Cochin. He labored unceasingly and, in spite of the heat and his increasing illness, did not take the customary siesta, but worked through the entire day. . . .

And now the great Viceroy's illness was becoming more severe, being aggravated by the heat, his overwork, and the strain of his struggles with dishonest or inefficient officials. The Viceroy, realizing the gravity of his illness, had himself carried from the fortress of Cochin, where he had been lodging, to the house of Diogo Pereira. There he summoned his secretary and other responsible officials and made the last disposition of official matters, including memoranda for the governor who might succeed him. The official business finished and put aside, "he confessed and partook of the Holy Sacrament, with much perfection as a Catholic Christian." He then summoned his sons and made his testament, and

set his affairs in order, like a good Christian, with all the Sacraments of the Church, and ordered that his bones should be conveyed to the Kingdom [of Portugal], as they were conveyed later. Speaking always with his full understanding, he ended the number of his days when he surrendered up his soul on the eve of Christmas of the holy birth of

Christ, at three o'clock after midnight, on the twenty-fourth day of December of this present year of 1524. God be praised.

Vasco da Gama, unlike Columbus, had forerunners, and because of their labors had a clean-cut problem given to him to solve, a problem based on the voyages of Bartholomeu Dias and his predecessors. Nonetheless, his nautical performance was not inferior to that of Columbus, though Magellan's was greater than that of either. To solve Gama's problem required great seamanship, personal courage and fortitude and a driving personality, one that could face all odds and not recede a foot's breadth.

As a seaman, Gama's greatest claim to fame probably lay in his courage-ous decision to abandon the timid creeping southward along the African coast that had characterized the voyages of his predecessors, and to steer instead boldly west-southwest out into the middle of the unknown Atlantic. His daring lay in his doing this at a period when that portion of the Atlantic had not been explored and when there were great uncertainties of navigation—for there was no means available of accurately ascertaining longitude. Moreover, the charts of the African coast were, when in existence, extremely inaccurate. He sailed thousands of miles out of sight of land, going into regions whose winds and currents were all either unknown or a matter of conjecture. This took him almost within sight of South America, which was later accidentally (?) discovered by Cabral on his Indian voyage.

The route thus followed by Vasco da Gama through trial and error is still the true sailing route from Europe to the Cape of Good Hope, and it was followed as long as sailing ships plowed the South Atlantic. He was three months out of sight of land, and even the unfamiliar stars and con-stellations could not be of the assistance that those visible in the Northern Hemisphere were to Columbus. Considering the type and size of his vessels, the long, alternating spells of storm and calm, and his absolute ignorance of his environment, his choice of route has, in the words of the former Director of Operative Staff of the British Admiralty, "a strong claim to rank as the finest feat of pure navigation ever accomplished."[3]

The casual reader of the story of Vasco da Gama will probably be impressed mostly with the lurid tales of murder and rapine that fill its pages. But that would not alone have secured for him the place he occupies in history. Besides his seamanship he contributed much. His command of men, harsh and unrelenting though it was, accomplished results. He always kept on the course he had laid out for himself, and none of his men dared

[3] Admiral G. A. Ballard.

swerve, "because the captain-major did not choose." With all his cruelty and other faults, he was the embodiment of the conquering spirit of Portugal, the spirit which enabled a tiny nation to make miraculous conquests—and, it must be added, sadly enough, the cruel and fanatic spirit that aroused the hatred of the Westerner in the hearts of the natives of Africa and Asia which has not ceased until this very day.

Gama, like Columbus and Magellan, is one of the heroes of that period which came once in the world's history but which can never be repeated, that era which marked the sudden expansion of the knowledge of the world by the Western nations through daring and unprecedentedly long sea voyages. These discoveries shifted the center of gravity of European civilization from the shores of the Mediterranean, where the great scenes of the ancient and medieval world had been enacted, to the coast of the Atlantic, and the centers of commerce and political activity moved thenceforth westward. One historian has well called this era of exploration "one of the most important and fateful epochs in man's history on earth."[4]

Vasco da Gama was one of the greatest figures of this era. The immediate results of his voyage far exceeded those of Columbus. The latter discovered a land which required many generations for its development and a profitable return. Gama's discovery brought Europe in contact with a rich civilization, and the returns on the investment were speedy and fabulous.

Gama's voyages not only revolutionized the history of Europe, but also ushered in a new era in Asia, and for the first time the sea became important in Indian political history.

We have examined what references his contemporaries and later historians have made to Vasco da Gama. When all his great exploits have been weighed against his defects of character and personal attitudes, Gama appears as one of history's great figures, "fit for all that was intrusted to his conduct as Captain, as Discoverer and as Viceroy." He belongs not only to the history of Portugal, his tiny homeland, and to the history of India, but to world history.

[4] Arthur P. Newton, in *The Great Age of Discovery.*

HOW TO
QUELL A MUTINY—
FERDINAND MAGELLAN

by A. S. Hildebrand

When Vasco da Gama first set out, Ferdinand Magellan was still a page in the court of the Queen of Portugal. His forerunner, the ship chandler *Amerigo Vespucci, whose name was given to the New World, was exploring the coasts of South America, making observations that would change the face of Spanish maps.*

Here, with Arthur S. Hildebrand, we see how Magellan first became imbued with the idea of a trip around the world; how Balboa's first sight of the hitherto unknown great South Sea convinced him of the rightness of his plans; how he faced hardships of storm and mutiny with consummate leadership; how after passing through the straits north of Tierra del Fuego, he sailed into the ocean which Balboa had seen and which Magellan named "Pacific." He himself did not live to circumnavigate the globe. Attacked by savage tribesmen, he died in the Philippines. Other members of the crew sailed his ship home to his adopted country of Spain.

Today, however, Magellan is known with justice as the first circumnavigator. His was the vision, his the courage, his the broad outlook that carried him to the point where he could prove that East and West do meet, and that the world indeed is round. The story of this wonderful voyage with all its hazards, which corrected once and for all Ptolemy's theories about the size of Asia and showed the magnitude of the Pacific, was told first by a member of Magellan's crew, Antonio Pigafetta, a great admirer of his leader, and his "constancy in adverse fortune."

Of Magellan's determination to find the straits at any cost, he writes:

"Had we not discovered that Strait, the Captain General had determined to go as far as 75 toward the Antarctic Pole." After his death on that Pacific island Pigafetta records: "In the midst of the sea he was able to endure hunger better than we. Most versed in nautical charts, he knew better than any other the true art of navigation, of which it is a certain proof that he knew by his genius, and his intrepidity, without anyone having given him the example, how to attempt the circuit of the globe, which he had almost completed."

MAGELLAN had been six years in the East. There had been much of seafaring in his six years. He had made that tremendous voyage around the Cape[1]—something unprecedented in history before his time, utterly beyond the imagination of previous generations. The visits to the coast cities of Africa, the crossing of the Indian Sea, the coasting off Malabar, the hazardous sailing among the Eastern Islands, were things new to him, and amazing. They had given him a feeling of a special bent, as if he were on a road alone.

Magellan had been surprised to find at Malacca so organized and definite an arrangement of life, so old and established a civilization. He had expected it in India; in the Archipelago, the ships were still farther east. And the natives suddenly became startlingly familiar, as if he had seen them before; naked savages in their canoes, bought with a red cap or a ball of thread, childishly pleased with a bit of colored glass or a tinkling bell. They were not the men Columbus had seen—it had not been demonstrated that the world was much too large for that—but they were similar. The ships of Portugal had come so far to the East—farther than any European ships had ever come before—and there they began to find the characteristics which had already been found in the West. So it appeared.

It might not be true. But at any rate the suggestion which it offered was a valid one. The East and the West approached each other—if not closely, then remotely. That the world was round no sensible man any longer doubted, and any sailor knows that a ship will go west as well as east, if there is a hand on her helm. There was no chart anywhere to tell him what lay between the West and the East. Well, if it was sea, a man could sail it. If it was a continent, a man could go around it. He was the man. That decision reflects his genius and his greatness. He had felt the East as a kind of inspiration, and while under that domination, he had seen the thing which his times needed to have done and had selected himself as the man to do it.

[1] On Vasco da Gama's second voyage to India.—Eds.

Magellan set about his project. To get back to the East, by crossing the South Sea—this was what he wanted, and he undertook it in all the lightheartedness of a man with a dominating desire. He studied longitude. Longitude was the essence of his scheme, since all conception of the size of the earth depended upon this measure of it. As to what lay between East and West, over there on the other side of the Moluccas, he could only guess, but his guess would be helped if he could know how much space there was —how much space between the farthest east and the farthest west that men had reached.

Moreover, to demonstrate practicability, it was necessary to have something more than a firm, but unsupported, conviction. Some scholars must be found who were willing to admit the feasibility of the project, and their opinions must be quoted, and defended very ably, if the King's favor was to be gained.

Don Manuel did not seem disposed to grant his favor, however. Magellan's seven years of service in the East and his wounds received in action seemed to count for nothing with the King. He treated him coldly; "he always hated him."

Considering one phase of the matter, it would seem likely that whoever could show King Manuel or any other monarch a new road to the East would be sure of a hearing and adequate support. For the road to the East was the chief concern of every maritime nation in the world; Spain was exploring the Carribbean; England was seeking the Northwest Passage; Portugal had found her road, indeed, but it was a road twelve thousand miles long.

During the progress of these events something had happened in the New World. It was important, indeed, in itself. But to Magellan it was like a roll of thunder. Vasco Núñez de Balboa had crossed the Isthmus of Panama and had seen the ocean that lay on the other side.

It was a sea that lay between East and West.

To go around the world, across the South Sea, to the Spice Islands— this much was his own. As for its public aspect: if Portugal did not care to know of a new route, then Spain could settle the question of longitude, once for all time, and claim the Moluccas, with all new lands east of them. It depended, now, on one last interview with the King.

He asked once more if his *moradia*[2] might be increased. It would not be increased. Might he hope for some command that would give him an opportunity to serve his sovereign? He might not. Was he to understand that his country had no further use for him? That was the fact. Did His

[2] Living allowance.—Eds.

Majesty realize that he was then forced to offer his loyalty to someone who would be disposed to make use of it? He might do as he pleased. The audience was concluded.

Magellan had spent more than five years in perfecting his project, in organizing his first vague ideas into a definite program. Now the plan was ready, and he took action. In 1517, the thirty-seventh year of his age, he renounced his Portuguese citizenship and went to Spain.

In Seville, there was a considerable group of men, from every walk and condition of life, who were bound together by the fact that they had once been Portuguese, and had now come to try for better fortune here in Spain. Of these the most conspicuous was Diego Barbosa, alcaide of the arsenal. His son, Duarte, had voyaged extensively in the far East, and in the previous year he had completed his book of travels.

The three men gained friendship and mutual trust, and out of this there grew a program of action. To go to the King, unknown and unassisted, would be folly; a man would get no farther than some officious chamberlain, and then he would become a pest, like other too-persistent seekers of favors, and would spend his days in pursuit of a cheap and fading hope. There must be found someone whose name would open a door, whose reputation would gain respect, whose recommendation would be predisposed for acceptance. Señor Barbosa suggested Don Sancho Matienzo and Juan de Aranda, chiefs of India House. He knew them, and their support, if they gave it, would lead toward the throne.

Magellan's first step then was to present his plan to India House, the Casa de Contratación. Here was the affair begun. It hardly seemed possible. It had been so very easy and simple; all the difficulties which apprehension had dreaded had been strangely escaped, and the courtesy and confidence of Señor Aranda surely indicated success. The proposals were forwarded to the court. It was perfectly clear to the King that some such enterprise as this was exactly what was needed to further his own interests with the nation. Though King Charles expressed himself with difficulty, his perception was very clear and quick. A *capitulation*[3] was prepared, duly signed, and delivered.

Señor Aranda was sent to Cadiz to purchase ships. He brought back the five vessels which had been authorized by the King's capitulation. Magellan stood on the quay and watched them come up the river, in charge of the

[3] A certificate of approval from the King.—Eds.

pilots from San Lucar, and anchor off the city. These were his ships. They meant more to him than anything else in life. There they were.

He went aboard at once. The largest of the fleet was the *San Antonio*, of one hundred and twenty tons; she would be rather unhandy, and a dull sailer. The *Trinidad*, of one hundred and ten tons, was the most capable vessel of the five; she was sound, and in as good condition as could be expected; she was smart and well found; he chose her at once for his flagship. The fleet would follow her lantern. For two years . . . around the world. . . . Well. The *Concepción* was of ninety tons, the *Victoria* of eighty-five, the *Santiago* of seventy-five. There they were.

The officers were assigned to their several ships. In the *Trinidad* Estaban Gomez was King's Pilot, and Juan de Punzarol Master; in the *San Antonio*, Juan de Cartegena, fleet captain, was Captain and Juan de Elorriga Master; in the *Concepción* Gaspar de Quesada was Captain, and Juan Sebastian el Cano Master; in the *Victoria* Luiz de Mendoza, the Treasurer, was Captain, and Anton Salomon Master; in the *Santiago* Juan Serrano was Captain, and Ballasar Ginoves Master.

These were the men on whom everything depended. There were traitors among them, or among the crew—somewhere. It would come to the surface; it would creep up on him, at some moment when he was not on guard against it. When? Off what coast, or in what lonely roadstead? What would happen before he came again to Seville? Well. See about those extra charts.

On the tenth of August the pilots were summoned, and the ships went down the river to San Lucar.

There was a special Mass at Nossa Señora de Barremeda, and all went to Confession. The Captains swore loyalty. They prayed together, for God's blessing on them, for protection in peril, for steady purpose and courage. *Ora pro nobis.* Amen. The flag, the flag!

On Tuesday, September 20, 1519, they sailed.

From San Lucar the fleet proceeded on a southwest course for the Canaries. Five ships, with a fair wind in pleasant weather, surging over the long rollers . . .

The watches were arranged for sea routine, and signals for communication between the several ships. Each night, just after sunset, when the weather permitted it, the ships were to close within hailing distance of the *Trinidad*, to receive the orders for the night and to salute: *"Dios vos salve, señor Capitan General y maestre, é buena compania."*

On the sixth day out of San Lucar they sighted a patch of thick dark mist on the horizon ahead, and the Peak of Tenerife came looming up out of the sea.

The fleet remained three days at Tenerife, taking in meat and wood and water, and then they went to Punta Rasca, at the southern end of the island, and loaded pitch. All day long the trade wind went shouting across the mountain, bending the trees; the boats came and went between the ships and the shore.

And a caravel, flying the standard of Spain, rounded the point and stood up for the anchorage. The men on the beach straightened their backs; the oarsmen lay on their oars; the captains stood at their rails; word was taken to the Captain General, who came to his quarter-deck and watched. She rounded up and backed her foresail; men were busy in her waist, getting a boat over; the boat left her side and rowed to the *Trinidad*. A messenger from India House. He went into the cabin with the Captain General.

The letter was from Diego Barbosa. "Keep a good watch, since it has come to my knowledge that your captains have told their friends and relations here that if there is any trouble they will kill you . . . your captains have resolved not to obey you, particularly Juan de Cartegena." Magellan gave the messenger a simple acknowledgment: he was grateful for the warning, but he would go on, of course. The boat went back to the waiting caravel and was hoisted aboard; she filled away on the starboard tack and disappeared behind the headland, bound around the island on her way home. Across the intervening space between their two ships Captain Mendoza looked questioningly at Captain Cartegena. The work went on again.

At midnight, on the third of October, the order was given to get under way, and the ships hove their anchors out of Spanish ground and stood away to the southward, following the Captain General's lantern. At dawn the Peak of Tenerife was a patch of thick dark mist on the horizon astern.

All down the Guinea coast they met with rough water and hard head winds and violent squalls. The demonstration concluded with a howling gale. It was impossible to set a rag of sail; the ships went wallowing off before it under bare poles. Each night the *Trinidad's* lantern showed ahead, reeling over the waves, half hidden by flying mist and level rain; each day dawned on a dim wild world of low dark sky and hissing water. It was discouraging work, endless and hopeless; they were swamped in dread and despair. But one black night St. Elmo's fire appeared; pale flames streamed from the mastheads, and a glaring ball of light hung at the flagship's maintop, sputtering, wavering in the wind, lighting the decks and the men's faces, and showing tears in their eyes. The good omen promised that the gale would end. A heavy rain succeeded, killing the wind and flattening out the seas, and the sun shone brightly in the morning.

The trades blew fresh, the water sparkled, the distant mountains in Africa stood up sharp and blue in the clear air. The ships made sail, all together, and the *Trinidad* set the course: south by west. Now this was not the course that had been mentioned and agreed upon, and Captain Cartegena —wanting, perhaps, to see how matters stood—crowded sail on the *San Antonio* and drew up abreast the flagship. He hailed and asked the course. South by west. And then he asked why it had been changed. "Follow the flagship and ask no questions," was the reply. The *San Antonio* dropped back again where she belonged. And when the course was changed again, no questions were asked.

The routine was resumed. But when the *San Antonio* ranged up to salute, it was a quartermaster who hailed. *"Dios vos salve, señor capitan y maestre, é buena compania."* Magellan called Captain Cartegena on deck; he was "Captain General," and not "Captain," and he expected to be properly addressed. "I sent the best man in the ship to salute you," shouted Cartegena, "and another day, if you like, I will salute you through one of the pages." The *San Antonio* dropped back to her place, and for three days thereafter offered no salutes at all.

On a certain day not long following, the flagship hove to and set the signal: all captains report on board. They gathered, accordingly, in the Captain General's cabin; the matter in hand was the trial of a sailor in the *Victoria*—the report of it having been carried to the Captain General by the same process of keeping in touch decreed for the beginning of each first watch of the night—and the investigation of the case being finished, Captain Cartegena spoke again of that change of course. He said that the agreement had been for a southwest course, but the Captain General had altered it, as if he were keeping near Africa for some reason of his own; now, they were standing across the Atlantic on a course that was taking them to the nearest point of South America, which was Portuguese territory. What was the reason for this, and why had not the captains been consulted?

Magellan wanted no words with him. He clutched him by the jacket. "You are my prisoner," he said, and turned him over to Captain Luiz Mendoza for custody. There were the two of them together.

The command of the *San Antonio* was given to Antonio de Coca.

On November 29 they made their landfall in the New World—Cape

St. Augustine, on that outreaching sweep of coast that approaches most closely to Africa.

Magellan issued very particular instructions in respect to the treatment of inhabitants: there must be no fighting, at whatever provocation, in the domain of the King of Portugal. There was no provocation.

On December 13 the fleet entered Santa Lucia Bay at Rio de Janeiro. The people were cannibals, and the custom had come about in a curious way. They did not eat human meat because it was good—which, in fact, it was not—but as a ceremonial revenge against their enemies. Some years before, during a war with another tribe, a young man had been taken prisoner. His mother, in an explosion of wild rage, had caught one of the enemy and bitten him in the shoulder; back in the village he said that she had tried to eat him, and showed his wounds. Since then, both tribes had always eaten prisoners.

In other respects, too, the people were not without interest. Their formal dress was a ridiculous and gaudy tail of parrot feathers, sticking out behind. They pierced their lower lips and wore stone ornaments in them. They lived in long houses, divided for several families by hanging mats of rushes; there was a smoke hole in the roof, but none of the smoke went out; it seemed that they never slept, for the racket and jabber was ceaseless.

The next anchorage was at Río de la Plata. A man appeared on the beach. It seemed incredible—yet it was true that he was almost a giant in size. In the old books there had been travelers' tales of giants in these outlandish parts. Others appeared, both men and women, and stood staring, plainly afraid. The Capain General sent a hundred men ashore, and the giants ran so fast that they could not be overtaken. They were gone. Had they really been giants?

Further down the coast they came upon a group of small islands, literally swarming with enormous geese. To replenish the food supply the ships selected a convenient bay and rounded in and anchored. Some men were sent to the islands, well armed. But there proved to be no need for arms; the geese could be knocked down with a stick. Certainly, they were extraordinary geese; they stood almost as high as a man's waist; they were black, with white markings on their breasts, and their feathers were all of the same sort, both on wings and bodies. They did not fly at all, but they swam wonderfully, diving even more cleverly than ducks, and using their wings as flippers. No one in the fleet had seen penguins before.

By the time the fleet reached forty-nine South the season was well advanced—it was early in March—and the weather was growing steadily worse. There were frequent squalls, with flurries of snow and hail—a merciless, dispiriting process of exhaustion. Each hour brought the limit of endurance—and a worse hour followed.

Then there came a howling gale from the southeast. It blew as no man in that fleet had ever seen it blow before. The seas swept in at thirty miles an hour, boiling white, and each succeeding hill of water caught up the ships and set them nearer shore. To look for shelter would be simple folly. No man, unless he had resolved on death, would run a ship blindly for that yelling beach in the faint hope that some way would open up before her through the banks, or some chance gap in the coast would lead her into the protecting land. They set what sail they dared to risk, came about onto the offshore tack, and went sagging away to sea. They were laying over buried up in foam, jumping like mad things, leaking, groaning with the strain, steering wild. But they got offshore.

St. Elmo's fire appeared again.

When it was over, the fleet reached back in toward the land, with a northerly wind. An opening appeared. There was a bar across it, with a broad bank of sand in the center and an intricate channel with swirls of tidal current on either side. The *Trinidad* yawed in the swift current; the rollers caught her and shot her forward, head down, roaring. Then almost in a single instant she was through. The others fell in line and followed. Behind the point the water gradually shoaled, and the fleet dropped anchor. Port St. Julian, the winter quarters. It was the last day of March, 1520.

The aspect of the shores was desolate, but there was firewood in evidence and a plentiful supply of fish and seafowl. The ration of bread and wine was reduced. Alvora de la Mezquita was appointed to the command of the *San Antonio* to replace Antonio de Coca.

The reduction of rations brought an immediate protest. In the men's view of it, the rations should have been increased, not reduced; they had had all the hard treatment they were disposed to stand, and now that they were in harbor for the winter, were they not to live easy? The captains were of the opinion that the expedition had already failed. Were they all to die in this horrible place?

Magellan replied that they would assuredly die—if not here, then somewhere farther on—or accomplish what they had set out for. There was a strait; the King had ordered him to discover it, and he would discover it. As for food, there was plenty of it in the country; the bread and wine had not failed them, and would not, so long as they adhered to the rations which he had ordered. Had they no faith in the spring? Were they

Castilians? What had become of the valorous spirit of Spain?

Then let them have done with such fainthearted talk, and set about their business. The day following, the first of April, would be Palm Sunday; let all captains, masters, pilots, and officers of the fleet go ashore to celebrate the Mass. Afterward, they would dine with him on board the flagship.

Luiz de Mendoza and Gaspar Quesada did not come to Mass, and the Captain General dined with Alvora de la Mezquita alone. The two men were cousins. They sat in the cabin, with candles on the table before them, and conversed very soberly in Portuguese. The wind moaned in the rigging, the water talked noisily under the bows, the ship swung and surged at her cable. It was black starless midnight when Captain de la Mezquita rowed back to the blur of yellow light that marked the position of his ship.

Early on the morning of April second the Captain General ordered out a boat. They were to go to the *San Antonio* for men and then proceed to shore to look for water. Within five minutes the boat came back.

It had happened.

The boat had rounded up beside the *San Antonio,* and had been told to keep off. But they came with orders from the Captain General. This was not the Captain General's ship; nor the *Concepción,* nor the *Victoria.* "For whom are you?" cried the coxswain. Gasper Quesada appeared on deck. "For the King and for myself," said he.

Magellan did not ask about the *Santiago.* She was commanded by Juan Serrano.

During the night, Gaspar Quesada, Juan de Cartegena, and Juan Sebastian el Cano, with thirty men from the *Concepción,* had gone aboard the *San Antonio.* They entered the Captain's cabin, where Mezquita, just returned from the *Trinidad,* faced them. They had drawn swords in their hands. They had seized the *Concepción* and the *Victoria,* they said, and they demanded his surrender. They had been hazed long enough, under pretext of the King's orders; now they were through. If it kept up, they were all dead men. There was a sound of confused scuffling on deck; the men who would not join were being put in irons. Was it yes, or no?

Just at that instant there appeared in the black doorway behind them Juan de Elorriaga, Master of the *San Antonio.* In all the three ships, this brave Basque was the only man who spoke a word for loyalty and duty. "In the name of God and of the King Don Carlos," he said, "I summon you to go to your ship. This is no time to go through the fleet with armed men. Release our captain."

Quesada whirled on him. "Must our work remain undone because of this madman?" he cried, drawing his dagger. He stabbed Elorriaga and stabbed him thrice again as he fell. Mezquita surrendered.

Quesada remained in charge of the San Antonio; Mendoza had gone to the *Victoria*; Cartegena took the *Concepción*.

That was all. It was bad enough, indeed. It was bad enough that three ships out of the five should have turned against him. The forces were ninety-eight against one hundred and seventy.

In the evening, a message came from the mutineers. They had done this in order that he might no longer ill-treat them. If he would agree to fulfill the King's instructions, they promised obedience. If not—they had three ships.

Magellan replied that he was willing to treat with them; if they would come to the flagship he would hear what they had to say. With this message the boat returned to the *San Antonio*. He watched them climb aboard; they stood consulting for a moment in the nipping wind. Then they dropped into the boat again and came rowing back to the flagship. The light was fading from the sky and from the surrounding shores; the boat crawled like a black bug across a sheet of pallid silver. A bleak and desperate twilight.

The mutineers could not consent to come to the flagship.

He sent for Duarte Barbosa, and . . . a man for dangerous work . . . yes . . . the Master of Arms, Gonzalo Gomez de Espinosa. He wrote out an order to Luiz de Mendoza: report at once on board the flagship for conference. Espinosa was to deliver it; he was to have six men with him, with hidden weapons. They were to keep together while the note was handed over; if Mendoza refused to obey the summons, they were to kill him. At once, before he had time to shout "To arms!" Espinosa understood. Meanwhile, Duarte was to take fifteen men in the *Trinidad's* spare boat and row up under the *Victoria's* stern. If they heard a sound of a fight—a cry, or noise of naked steel—they were to board and take the ship. They were to kill no one, except as might be necessary to defend themselves; they were to trust any man who seemed to warrant it, but they were to remember that it was easy for any mutineer to say that he had appeared to consent to mutiny in order to save his life. Having the ship, they were to shift her berth nearer the harbor mouth, so as to prevent the escape of the *Concepción* and *San Antonio*. They must not fail.

The boats were put over and the men dropped into them; their faces showed for a second in the lantern light, and then they vanished utterly. The whole anchorage was perfectly black. Duarte's men were very quiet, but Espinosa's oars thumped loudly, and grew fainter in the distance. The wind was moaning, and outside—as always, day or night—the surf boomed loudly on the beaches. A hail was heard beside the Victoria and a light showed for a second over the rail.

Aboard the Victoria, in the Captain's cabin, Espinosa delivered the note. The six men stood around him. No one spoke nor moved while Mendoza unfolded the paper. Then he laughed. "Ho!" he said, "I'm not to be caught that way!" Instantly Espinosa stabbed him. He struck at his throat—it was likely that he wore a chain mail under his cloak, and Espinosa was the man to know it.

There was a moment's silence, and then Duarte and his fifteen men came piling in over the rail. An extra ration of wine had been served out to all the Victoria's hands, which did not improve their courage. They surrendered at once, without resistance. It was impossible to tell who had mutinied and who had not, but the men who were found in chains were sure, at any rate, and these were released.

On the morning of April third the Trinidad, the Victoria, and the Santiago lay in a line across the harbor mouth, and the mutineer's ships were like bears at bay. In the night's brief interval the situation had been completely reversed; the balance of power had shifted to the Captain General's side; the rebel ships were trapped; and, now that they knew what they might expect, and saw the chances turned against them, the mutineers' courage changed to despair.

Quesada and Cartegena made the best plan they could. To send men with a message to the Captain General would simply be weakening their forces so much, for the men would be seized. But Alvora de la Mezquita might be sent; he was not to be trusted as a mutineer, no matter what might be the outcome and he was moreover, a kinsmen of the Captain General's. He was under hatches, in chains, knowing nothing of what had happened.

Quesada went down. He was going to release him, he said, and send him to Magellan to ask for terms. Mesquita replied that there would be no terms. This was obviously true, on second thought; the more so since Mezquita gave up his chance of life to say it. Well then, they would go to Spain. They would slip out in the darkness, that night, and Mezquita, stationed up forward for the purpose, would hail the Captain General as they passed, and ask him, once more, as a last chance, to give up the voyage. Mezquita saw that this was folly. Then he saw himself as a witness in a court of piracy, and, at the same instant, saw that Quesada saw it. Then he was left alone again.

That night it came on to blow. The wind was south, along the coast, and directly out of the anchorage. It was a black night, of course—all nights were black in Port St. Julian. It was quite plain that this was the mutineers' chance.

The three ships, like sentries before a prison door, loaded their cannon, got out their grappling irons, and stood under arms. The whole world was a pocket of black. There were no light on the *Concepción* and the *San Antonio*, and it was impossible even to keep fixed in the mind the positions where they lay. There was no sound anywhere except the dreary wind and that eternal roar of surf. Hours passed. They stood there, waiting, unable to see or to hear, forbidden to speak; they reached out their hands from time to time to feel their comrades near them.

Just before midnight a faint sound was heard—a confused clatter and clumping. Then all was still again. Then there came a sudden guarded shout. And all at once the *San Antonio,* invisible, lurching through the dark, dragging her anchor, unable to turn or steer or make sail, drifted stern first into the *Trinidad.* The ships reeled, and every man braced his feet. The gunners fired a broadside. The grappling hooks were thrown across. Torches flared up blindingly. The *Victoria's* men boarded from the other side, and the mutineers surrendered.

The crew of the *Santiago* were sent to take the *Concepción,* and, having done so, mounted guard. Not a man was wounded. Only Juan Rodriguez de Mafra, sitting in chains in the hold of the *San Antonio,* saw a cannon ball come splintering through the side of the ship and go humming across between his legs.

In the morning the body of Luiz de Mendoza was quartered and impaled on stakes on the shore.

The mutineers were tried and sentenced. Gaspar Quesada was beheaded and quartered; his servant, Luiz de Molino, was offered pardon if he would consent to act as executioner, and did so. Juan de Cartegena and Pedro Sanchez de la Reina, a priest, were sentenced to be marooned. They, and more than forty others found guilty, were put in chains until the fleet should leave. The forty were ultimately pardoned, but Cartegena's and la Reina's sentences were carried out.

Then winter began in earnest.

The weather had been the real cause of the mutiny. The wind and the cold and the desperate coast had discouraged them all, except the Captain General himself, and those few who were able to take what came without being crushed by it.

An earnest attempt was made to determine the longitude. It failed of any intelligent result. But it was certain, at least, that Port St. Julian was in Spanish territory. It would be a criminal neglect of opportunity if the land were not explored; no one had been there before, and it was hard to say when anyone would come again; but the land was Spain's, and worth investigating. He determined, therefore, to send an expedition to explore the coast to the south, to examine the country, to avoid subsequent delay of the fleet, and to find—perhaps—the strait.

The *Santiago* was ordered ready for sea. She was a small and handy ship, and drew less water than the others. Serrano, of course, would take her; he knew the ship, to begin with, and there was no one in the entire fleet, save only the Captain General himself, who had had more experience. And this, certainly, would require all the skill and judgment that a man could bring to it.

Toward the end of April, Serrano was ready. When the *Santiago* hove anchor and made sail the entire fleet turned out to watch her go. It was the first separation, and it gave them all a feeling of self-reliance and independence; St. Julian was a headquarters now, and they had a world of their own.

In all this time at Port St. Julian, no one had been seen on shore. There was reason enough, indeed, to consider the country uninhabited. But late in May a man appeared on the beach, dancing. He was a giant, and he danced mightily, stopping now and again to catch up handfuls of sand, which he threw on his head. This might reasonably be assumed a sign of welcome and of submission. The Captain General sent a man ashore alone, with instructions to meet the demonstration in the spirit in which it was intended. The man landed; the giant paused to watch him step out and draw up his boat. Then the two danced together for some time. Then they got into the boat, and the man rowed the giant to the islet where the smithy was.

When the Captain General arrived at the islet the giant was utterly astonished at his appearance, and made it plain by signs that he thought they came from heaven. But the giant's appearance was even more extraordinary. He was huge; the Spaniards came hardly to his waist. His face was painted red, with yellow about the eyes, and there were heart-shaped patches painted on his cheeks. He had a short heavy bow with a gut string, and flint-tipped arrows. He was clothed in skins, very neatly sewn, and he wore enormous fur boots. It was Magellan who gave these people the name of Patagones—"Big-feet." They gave him some food, for which he seemed grateful, and showed him a large steel mirror. He was badly frightened at the sight of his own face, jumped back, and upset four men. The mirror was presented to him, with a comb and some bells, and he was set ashore. He disappeared over the hills toward the west.

Six days later another came. He also danced lustily; his feet sinking in the ground to the ankles at every leap. He seemed to like the Spaniards, and remained for a long time; they baptized him, and gave him the name of Juan, which he learned; he was able also to say "Jesus," "Ave Maria," and "Pater Noster," very clearly and loudly. He was given presents, and disappeared into the west.

Then two men appeared together. They shouted and waved their arms and while the boat was coming for them they sat down on the sand. The boat brought them back to the *Trinidad*. They were very sick-looking men; they were haggard, in tatters, hardly recognizable. They were from the *Santiago*.

Their comrades were safe—that is, they were on shore. Except that one man had lost his life.

They had gone down the coast for about sixty miles, and found it low land, covered with scrubby bushes, and fronted by a shingle beach. Then they had come to a large river, which Captain Serrano had named the Santa Cruz, and there they had entered. The water was salt, and they thought at first that they had found the strait, but when the tide ebbed the water became fresh, and they did not go far inland. They spent a week in catching fish, with which the river was swarming, and then they prepared to return.

They were caught in a heavy onshore gale. Their rudder was broken, and the ship, unable to get about to claw off, drove ashore. She struck broadside on, swung on her heel, and put her bow in the breakers; every wave picked her up and dropped her on the sand; she opened like a basket, and her whole rig went by the board. There was no hope for her, and they climbed out into the head rigging and dropped on the beach. A Negro had been drowned by jumping too soon. They huddled together on the beach, soaked with the spray, deafened by the roar of savage breakers with tumbling rocks in them, choked by flying sand; the scrub behind them shrieked like a million jangled harps. The ship went to pieces before their eyes.

They were thirty-seven men. They caught fish, and managed to keep alive, and when the sea went down they saved what they could from the wreck. They made a raft of planks to cross the river, and for eight days they waited for the stream to grow quiet enough for them to risk the passage. But there were no quiet intervals.

Finally, these two had volunteered to make the attempt to go back to St. Julian for help. They had crossed, cautiously, but paddling hard to fight the vicious current, and looked back only when they had made the shore and tied the raft. Their comrades had been watching them breathlessly; they saw caps waving. Then they had struck north over the tops of the cliffs.

They had been eleven days on the way. They had slept in the scrub, and had found no water fit to drink. Swamps stopped them, and they had been forced to make wide detours inland. They were nearly dead but they had done it.

Magellan called for volunteers, and selected twenty-four men, who took a two months' supply of biscuit, and set out. . . .

The crew of the *Santiago* returned. The rescuing party had found the shipwrecked men intact and safe, though they had suffered greatly from privation and exposure.

Serrano reported. The coast was not so desperate as the first messengers had said, and it would have been perfectly possible to send the fleet to effect the rescue—indeed, this was what Serrano had expected when he sent the men north, and he had been watching the sea for his deliverance, rather than the land. The anchorage was good; if it had not been for his broken rudder he would not have lost his ship. In his opinion, the fleet might profitably proceed to Santa Cruz.

Juan de Cartegena and Pedro de la Reina were given a large supply of bread and wine, and put ashore.

Sails were brought out and bent, and the ships were made ready for sea. It was only a two days' journey that they contemplated—but it was two days of Patagonian winter. The crew of the *Santiago* was distributed among the other ships, and the commands were rearranged: Duarte Barbosa took the *Victoria*, Alvora de la Mezquita the *San Antonio*, and Juan Serrano the *Concepción*. No one knew what was coming; before them was awful weather, a dangerous coast, the reminder of one shipwreck, and uncertainty in every changing hour—but every man in the fleet was glad to escape from the curse of Port St. Julian.

The passage was without incident. It did blow very hard, and the ships very nearly went ashore—it was like falling from a terrifying height, or sinking in quicksand, or expecting uncertain death each second of twelve long hours—but they did not go ashore, and the passage was without incident. On the twenty-sixth the fleet crossed the bar at the mouth of the river and anchored opposite the island behind the second point on the south shore.

The Captain General felt his impatience grow, and with it there grew a realization of the need of haste. He was near the strait—perhaps. But he had done nothing toward finding it. If it was near; if he might, two weeks from that day, or a month from that day, discover it and pass through it and be on his way across the South Sea . . . Was it not folly to wait? Or—for this also was possible—if it was to be months away, and the South Sea should be set back far into the future, on the other side of long hardship and weary struggle . . . Why not begin it now? He could not wait forever. He could not guess what he had to face. It was easiest to go to meet it. It was inaction and uncertainty that were unendurable. Make sail.

On the eighteenth of October the fleet left the Santa Cruz.

It was on Saint Ursula's day, the twenty-first of October, that the cape was sighted, and the Captain General named it the Cape of the Eleven Thousand Virgins. Beyond it was a low sandy point covered with tangled and matted kelp which had been blown out of the water. Beyond the point there was a great indentation in the coast.

They were four miles from the beach, and protected only by the sand banks. The tide rose forty feet, and covered the banks. And during the night it came on to blow.

There could not be a worse position. The Captain General showed four lights: get under way. The ships made sail, hove up, and stood off and on, under easy canvas, in the center of the bay, well clear of the land. To be jammed in on a lee shore, in an encircling bay, with no room to reach out and nowhere to run, is a situation which has its only remedy in a shift of wind. And this was in black night, with the shores invisible.

By noon of the following day it had moderated somewhat. The *San Antonio* and the *Concepción* were sent to leeward to look at the head of the bay. The other two ships hove to and awaited them very impatiently. The sooner the fleet was out of this the better.

The *San Antonio* and the *Concepción* reached over to the north shore of the bay; they were nearly out of sight. The changing light hid them and then revealed them; it was only between two waves, and when they chanced to roll so that the light was reflected from their sails, that they could be seen at all. They were at the very head of the bay. Then their sails showed as square notches cut in the coast behind them; they were coming back.

The Captain General watched them come. There was a point of land under their lee, and they seemed to be trying to keep off it—it was a continuation of the same line of shore where the sand banks were. If there was a shoal under their bows, with the wind they were carrying, they were gone. A current, and their own leeway, was sweeping them down; they drifted with terrible speed and seemed to draw nearer very slowly. A line of white water now lay right across their path. They must do something—soon. Then all at once they swung off, both together. They squared their yards and ran straight for the point. In an instant they were out of sight behind it.

Early in the morning of the second day the wind shifted and blew off-shore. All at once the *San Antonio* and the *Concepción* came flying around the point. They were ten miles away, but coming very fast; they ran out beside the point of shoals and headed straight down the bay. They were carrying every rag of sail they owned: topsails, spritsails, mizzens, bonnets on the courses, crowding along like clouds, stamping over the long swells of the storm, thundering through white water, flying flags and banners from every truck. They were firing bombards. As they got nearer they cheered. The crews lined the rails, yelling like madmen, waving their caps. Serrano stood on his quarter-deck. He ran the *Concepción* down past the flagship's stern; she went plunging by, rolling thunder before her, flinging up her head in streamers of foam, lurching, reeling, wallowing, smoking through it in one tremendous dash, with everything cracking aloft—it was as if she were cheering herself. Mezquita took the *San Antonio* through on the other side and rounded her up, surrounded by a halo of whistling spray, her canvas rumbling like volleying cannon, her banners snapping in the wind. Everyone was cheering. They had found it. It was there. The straight was behind that point of land.

That navigation of the strait was a marvelous achievement. In all the years since 1520, the passage from Cape Virgins to the Pacific entrance, even by smart and able fore-and-afters, has rarely been attempted. And Magellan's ships were square-riggers, and of a type absolutely at its worst under these conditions. Indeed, Magellan Strait is the end of the earth. No portion of the world frequented by man has worse weather; there is no fine season, and winter and summer alike, snow, hail, rain, and wind are absent only for very brief periods; every feature which can add difficulty and danger to navigation is here present in a superlative degree. Bold coasts, of a complexity utterly unknown elsewhere; passages so narrow that a lee shore is never more than five miles away, and is generally much nearer; water so deep that it is impossible to anchor, except too close to the shore for safety; sudden and violent squalls in which no ship is manageable and which no canvas can endure; an atmosphere too thick for visibility; submerged rocks and heavy overfalls and whirlpool currents—and, for these ships, no charts, no courses, no basis of experience; nothing but a blind decision of expediency, made in the last moment before disaster. But Magellan took them through.

On November 28, 1520, the ships cleared Cape Deseado and set a course northwest into the great South Sea.

HOW NOT TO QUELL A MUTINY— THE MAROONING OF HENRY HUDSON

by Llewellyn Powys

Directly to the west of Europe lay the American continents. Directly to the east lay the land mass of Siberia. Only by going far to the south or far to the north and then turning east or west, could the Spice Islands be reached by ship. So reasoned the geographers. We have seen the results of the journeys south in the great accomplishments of Columbus, Da Gama and Magellan. The journeys north were barren, for no feasible route to the Indies existed in that direction. But it was only as the result of numerous expeditions and untold hardship and suffering that this information was gained.

Like the Spanish and Portuguese, John Cabot had dreamed of finding a passage to Cathay. He convinced the merchants of Bristol, then the center of English sea trade, that his plans were sound, and in the spring of 1497 set out. He made a landfall on Cape Breton and like Columbus in that same year, felt sure he had struck the coast of Asia. It was bitterly cold and he therefore decided he had reached a point north of those fabulous regions described by Marco Polo. He headed south, along the coast of Maine, to Cape Cod and perhaps even to the mouth of the Delaware, but of course never reached the wonderful palace of Kublai Khan. He did discover valuable new lands and cod fishing banks, but he felt that his voyage was a failure and therefore others felt so too.

His son Sebastian had sailed with him and later decided to outfit an expedition to find a northeast passage to Cathay. In 1553 he set up his famous list of ordinances to govern the voyage, but wise as they were, they could not save it from disaster. Sir Hugh Willoughby and Richard Chancellor were the leaders. On the Lapland coast Willoughby and his crew were frozen to death. Chancellor sailed on to the White Sea and to that region where he "found no night at all." This, it turned out, was a part of northern Russia, and Chancellor was the first Englishman ever to penetrate that unknown, secret land. He traveled on to Moscow and negotiated a trade monopoly for the Muscovy Company for which Sebastian Cabot was agent. But he did not find the Northeast Passage.

Sebastian Cabot himself sailed not only north but also far to the south. He searched for a passage through Central America. Failing that, he sailed to Brazil and to the mouth of the river which, because of the silver ornaments he found there, he named the Río de la Plata.

The dream persisted. Eighty years after John Cabot, Martin Frobisher again went searching to the northwest. He sailed further than anyone before him and was driven by a storm into a large body of water which seemed to lead westward. It was what is now known as Hudson Strait but Frobisher was forced to turn back and never learned whether he had found the route to Cathay. John Davis, another brilliant navigator, likewise tried and failed.

In *1794*, Willem Barents made an attempt to the east, hoping that he would "saile into the North Seas to discover the kingdoms of Cathaia and China." He reached the coast of Novaya Zemlya and spent the winter there. It was a winter such as no European had ever faced before. "The heroic Barents," writes Sir Percy Sykes, "who died during the homeward voyage, certainly ranks among the great Arctic explorers."

And still the dream persisted. Twelve years later, Henry Hudson made his first northern voyage—an unsuccessful attempt to reach Japan via the North Pole. The selection which follows describes the end of his second voyage north. We see him as he enters Hudson Bay, convinced that he has found the Northwest Passage.

Most of us know Hudson as the commander of the Half Moon, which sailed up the river that bears his name. Few of us know of his other exploits or his personality. He was as different in every way as possible from Magellan. One was a brilliant leader, the other a vacillator. One quelled mutiny with an iron hand. The other first encouraged revolt by his actions, then proved utterly unable to deal with the situation. As we read the tragic story told by Llewellyn Powys, we wonder how he could have contributed as much as he did to the history of exploration.

HERE can be no doubt that Henry Hudson, as he sailed through the narrows between Cape Digges and Cape Wolstenholme, considered that the most difficult part of the voyage was over, and that he had actually discovered the long-desired passage. On his left towered the dizzy ledges of the famous Labrador headland, a headland that terminates in a point two hundred feet high, but is immediately backed by a jagged perpendicular cliff that rises to an elevation of nearly two thousand feet. Before him was no river nor ice-filled sound, but an open sea, wide and full, which must surely lead to where dark-skinned men, who knew nothing of snow and frost, employed themselves in packing their priceless merchandise in boxes of almug wood.

Opposite Cape Wolstenholme, two miles away, rose the vertical cliff of Cape Digges, itself over a thousand feet high; and it was between these two magnificent promontories that the small ship passed, on that day in August when was written the last entry preserved for us in Hudson's journal. For instead of sailing, as he surmised, toward the balm-bearing East, he was, as a matter of fact, being drawn surely and inevitably forward to his own damnation.

Before the prow of the *Discovery* extended a limitless sea "with water like whay." He began sailing southward, "confidently proud that he had won the passage." From Cape Wolstenholme the coast level falls to Cape Dufferin, and then rises again as it approaches Cape Jones, past which Hudson had to steer before entering James Bay. Here he spent several weeks sailing to and fro, but never finding the desired passage. He took in water and ballast, probably at Agoomska Island. The crew began to murmur, reasoning amongst themselves "concerning our coming into the bay and going out."

Such discontent obviously cast reflection upon Hudson's competence as a navigator, and the fact that he *was* uncertain as to what to do next rendered him perhaps more than usually sensitive. On this occasion he spoke out his mind to Juet, accusing him of disloyalty. Juet, perhaps relying upon the dissatisfaction of the sailors, with whom he had spoken, asked to be given an open trial before the whole crew. The trial took place on September tenth. Hudson first examined and heard "with equitie" all that Juet had to say in his own defense, and then listened to the charges brought against him. Bennett Mathues asserted that upon their approaching Iceland, Juet had said to him "that hee supposed that in the action would bee manslaughter, and prove bloodie to some." Others testified that soon after they had left Iceland he had "threatened to turne the head of the ship home from the action." Arnold Lodlo and Philip Staffe swore with their hands on the ship's Bible that Juet persuaded them to keep their swords in their cabins, together with their muskets, saying that the latter would be "charged with shot ere the voyage was over." Finally he was accused of having been at the bottom of the trouble with the men in the strait, when he had derided Hudson's hope of reaching Java by the second day of February.

Such damning evidence of bad faith put Hudson in a strong position. The crew sided with him in thinking "it was fit time to punish and cut off farther occasions of the like mutinie"; and that very afternoon Hudson deposed Juet from his position as mate, and put Robert Bylot into his place at the same rate of wages. Also, Francis Clemens, the boatswain, "who had basely carried himself to our master and to the action," was replaced by William Wilson, while Adrian Motter was made boatswain's mate, and John King and William Wilson, who had both "very well carryed themselves to the furtherence of the businesse," were promised a rise in their pay out of the boatswain's "overplus of wages."

Meanwhile Hudson assured the disgraced men that if they behaved themselves in the future, "he would be a meanes for their good, and that he would forget injuries." It may well be imagined that vague assurances of this kind carried little weight with sailors who had had their wallets tampered with, nothing in the world being more calculated to stir up that stagnant mire of evil blood, present in the hearts of all mortal men, than money, the gain of it, or the loss of it. Robert Juet nursed his hatred like a red-eyed ferret in the hutch of his dark soul, but for the present he was powerless to do evil.

But even when the sensation of this "ship's row" had subsided, the course of the *Discovery* remained as much of a mystery to the crew as ever.

At Michaelmas they were in Hannah Bay, but came out of it almost directly, and stood to the north again, where they met with foul weather, and lay anchored for more than a week. As soon as ever the wind abated, Hudson, impatient of delay, ordered the men to heave up the anchor.

Philip Staffe warned Hudson of the danger of rocks, and sure enough they presently ran on a rift and remained stranded upon it for twelve hours, "but (by the mercy of God) we got off unhurt but not unscarred." We may believe that Hudson's prestige was in no way strengthened by this misadventure. They afterward crossed to the southeast corner of James Bay and dropped anchor in a harbor where stood three hills. This harbor is now called Rupert's Bay. It is in latitude 51° 10', and is sheltered on the north by a granite hill, four hundred feet high, which has since been named Sherrick Mountain.

November first, they hauled their ship aground close in to shore, and by the tenth of the month the *Discovery* was frozen in.

It would be hard to conceive a more desolate landscape than that which now surrounded the marooned company. The ship still contained a good supply of victuals, but not enough to get them through the winter and bring them back again to England. For this latter purpose they already relied upon the number of birds that they had seen nesting on the cliffs at Cape Digges and at Cape Wolstenholme. Hudson began regulating the distribution of the provisions, "for it behoved us to have a care of what we had; for that we were sure of, but what we had not was uncertain": also, to increase the supply of food, he offered rewards for any bird or beast brought back to the ship; at the same time giving instructions that no sailor should go hunting by himself, but always two together, the one carrying a gun, the other a pike. Some time before this, John Williams, the gunner, died. Now, it was the custom amongst sailors, in those days, that if any of their number died on a voyage, his clothes were forthwith sold before the mast to the highest bidder. The unlucky gunner had possessed a mariner's gaberdine of gray homespun; but instead of following the usual practice Hudson promised to sell this garment to Greene, who was without clothes other than the one supplied to him by Master Venson. This arbitrary disposal of the prized clout formed a fruitful subject for discussion amongst the rest of the crew. However, as it was in the province of the captain to arrange as he thought best, the matter rested there.

Hudson now decided to build a house on shore, in spite of the fact that when this very step had been suggested at the end of October, he had refused to consider it. Philip Staffe, realizing the difficulties of putting up even the roughest shelter in the dead of winter, when every plank would freeze to the ground, and the nails, when he held them in his mouth, would take the very skin off his lips, sent back word to the master "that he neither would nor could goe in hand with such worke." When these words of the carpenter were reported to Hudson, he lost his temper and went down to Staffe "and ferreted him out of his cabbin to strike him, calling him by many foule names, and threatning to hang him," thereby once more revealing a fatal weakness in the management of his crew. Men, like animals, respond best to reasoned firmness. A policy of "frightfulness" is dangerous, but nothing is so dangerous as conduct that vacillates between propitiation and a show of false force.

The next day, while still out of favor, Staffe, who was one of the best hunters in the ship, took his fowling piece and went on land. Henry Greene went with him; and this so displeased Hudson, that to punish Greene, he allowed Robert Bylot, who at this time seems to have been in high favor, to have the gunner's gown. It was a method of retaliation unworthy of the great explorer, and one calculated to excite bad feeling. As soon as Greene heard about it, he went to Hudson and challenged his former promise, at which Hudson began railing against his favorite, telling him that he was a rascal whom no one would trust with twenty shillings, and that unless his manners improved he would not receive from him a penny in wages.

It seems that after this, a reconciliation took place between Hudson and Staffe; for the latter went to work and, like the skillful ship's carpenter that he was, soon put together some kind of shelter.

So the dark hours of the winter slowly passed over the heads of the stricken and dejected men. Scurvy, that unrelenting bane of sailors, broke out. The blackened gums of their jawbones rotted round their teeth, and their limbs swelled; and Prickett grew lame and the nails were frozen off the feet of Francis Clemens. And ever about the isolated men was the same dismal landscape, the same dismal and monotonous sea.

As the days drew on toward Christmas, Hudson and his crew came to subsist more and more upon ptarmigans, birds provided by God for these, His chosen people, after the same manner that He had sent down quail to satisfy the hunger of the Children of Israel long ago among the sandhills of Mount Sinai. But no token of divine dispensation was capable of softening the hearts of Juet, Greene, and Wilson, hearts harder than ever was the heart of the obdurate Pharaoh of old. However, as long as Bylot stood by Hudson, all was well. The hour of darkness was nigh, but had not yet struck. In the secret crevices of their minds they fed their black thoughts and watched them grow. . . .

At the first indications of the approach of spring, the willow ptarmigan, "white as milk," became scarce, its place being taken by migratory waterfowl such as the swan, the goose, and the duck, flying toward their incredibly remote breeding haunts far in the North. Already Juet and Greene and Wilson realized that there was danger of starvation; and we may be sure that not one of these three men would be content to die whistling through his fingers. Eat they must, but eat what? The animals were fleet of foot and the brant geese swift of wing.

They wandered into the woods, up over the hills, and down into the valleys, searching like knavish foxes for "all things that had any show of substance in them, how vile soever." They ate moss, "than the which," writes

Prickett, "the powder of a post be much better." They ate frogs, those grotesque bladder-bellied caricatures of humanity.

Then, when the ice was beginning to melt in good earnest, their sense of absolute and unrelieved solitude was suddenly broken by the appearance of a native, "coming to the ship as it were to see and be seen." This unexpected event, in the time of their utmost destitution, filled Hudson with hope. He made a great deal of the savage, and tried to get from the crew certain knives and hatchets for him to carry back as gifts to the place from which he had come. John King and Prickett responded to Hudson's appeal, and the savage went away with a knife, some buttons, and a looking glass, making signs to the effect that after he had slept he would come again.

When he returned, which he did shortly, he came drawing behind him a sled, on which were two deerskins, two beaver skins, and some meat. He was also carrying a script under his arm, from out of which he presently drew the things that Hudson had given him, gravely laying the knife upon the beaver pelts, and the mirror and buttons on the deerskins, as though he did not realize them to be presents, taking them rather to be tokens of future benefits.

This simple honesty, and the fact that he had returned as he had promised, so reassured Hudson, that he now felt himself—his communications with the Indians being assured—in a position to drive a good bargain. He had limed the branch and the bird had come to settle. When, therefore, the Indian offered to barter one of the deerskins for a hatchet, Hudson insisted that the implement was worth both the skins. The native consented to the explorer's exaction at the time, but evidently formed a secret resolution never to come near him again. One authority asserts that he was "badly treated" by Hudson; and although this is improbable, there can be small doubt that he detected in the overbearing attitude of the Englishman that latent avarice presently to have so great an influence on the fortunes of his race.

As the native never returned, Hudson and his men were once more thrown upon their own resources. James Bay was now almost free of ice, and Hudson sent Greene, Wilson, Perse, Thomas, Motter, Mathues, and Lodlo out in the shallop to fish. Here were some brave fishermen to go casting nets in this Sea of Galilee! The first day their draft of fishes numbered five hundred, made up of trout and some other kind "as big as herring." Immediately they assumed that their anxiety on the score of food was at an end. It was said afterward that Hudson, had he shown prudence, would have begun salting down fish for the return voyage. Everyone was profoundly relieved. "They were in some hope to have our wants supplied and our commons mended."

Alack! Their confidence was premature. Try as they might after that day, their efforts were never rewarded with the same plenty.

For little or no reason, save his own ill-humor, Hudson seems at this time to have committed the grave error of deposing Bylot from his position as mate and placing John King, the quartermaster, in his place. We can hardly doubt that in doing this he was playing into the hands of the malcontents. With Bylot disaffected, those in favor of mutiny were in a stronger position than ever. Certain words they uttered as they got the ship ready for leaving its winter haven have been preserved for us, words muttered by ragged sailors holding to the lanyards or standing by the capstan bars. John King was an ignorant man, who could neither read nor write, and yet it was he who was now in Hudson's confidence. With scant provisions on board, they weighed anchor on June 12, the men with many an oath declaring "that the master and his ignorant mate would carry the ship whither the master pleased."

Before sailing Hudson had taken stock of the provisions that were left. He collected what bread remained, and divided it amongst the men with his own hands; and the share of each man came to one pound, "and hee wept when hee gave it unto them." He also sent the boat out once more to see what could be caught in the net; but it came back, after having been gone two days, with only four score small fish, "a poore reliefe for so many hungry bellies."

As soon as they sailed, the demand for food again became pressing; and this time, "to stop a gap," he brought out what cheese remained, and divided it into equal portions, which came to three and a half pounds for seven days. The crew believed that there were more cheeses in the storeroom than had been divided. Hudson apportioned the cheeses all at one time, because he found they were not of one goodness, and in this way he thought to insure to each man an equal share of the good and the bad. The plan did not prove a success, because when the food was once in the men's possession, nothing could restrain some of them from eating up their fortnight's ration in one or two days. Greene, for example, gave his ration to one of his mates, to keep for him, but presently demanded it of him again and devoured it. William Wilson ate the whole of his allowance in a single day, and "laid in bed two or three days for his labour."

The mutual distrust that now pervaded the ship was not improved by the fact that Hudson had in the boat certain favorites, amongst them the young surgeon, whom he used to ask into his cabin, to enjoy, so the hungry men imagined, ampler fare. Indeed, it seems almost certain that Hudson did not act with complete honesty over the distribution of the remaining stores. Afterward, in their evidence, the mutineers affirmed that he had "a scuttle" between his cabin and the hold, through which he could receive separate supplies "to serve his own turn." The matter came to a head through the simplicity of Philip Staffe, who, being approached by Wilson to explain "why the master should so favour to give meate to some of the companie, and not to the rest," answered in justification of Hudson's action that "it was necessary that some of them should be kepte upp." We can guess the effect that those innocent words had upon the consciousness of Wilson. "It was necessary that some should be kepte upp!" So that was the idea, was it! But if some were to be "kepte upp," what was to happen to Robert Juet, Greene, and the rest of them? That was the question that offered itself for consideration in out-of-the-way corners of the deck, in the darkened gangways, and in ill-ventilated bunks.

On Saturday night, June 23, while the *Discovery* was moored in ice, Wilson and Greene entered Prickett's cabin. There, in the confined space of that dim cubicle, with choked water of the great bay murmuring and lapping on the other side of a few inches of sound English oak, was conveyed to the intelligence of the serving man one of the foulest plots that has ever defiled the records of exploration. In hushed voices the conspirators told how they and their associates were determined to put Hudson and the impotent men out of the ship into the shallop, "and let them shift for themselves." The two declared that they had not eaten for three days, and at best there was not left more than a fortnight's victuals for all the company; and as for themselves, "they would go through with it, or dye."

Though Abacuk Prickett was weak in the legs, his mind was as clear as ever. He expressed his astonishment at what had been communicated to him and appealed to the two men, for the sake of their wives and children, "not to commit so foule a thing in the sight of God and man as that would bee." Bachelor Greene, after listening to this pious "chat" for a few minutes, told him to hold his peace; for that "as the master was resolved to overthrow all," he knew it to be a matter of starving or hanging, and of the two he preferred to risk the gallows.

They then imparted to Prickett the comfortable news that it had been decided by the ringleaders that he would be allowed to remain on the ship, at which Prickett began to mutter something about not having come into the ship for the purpose of mutiny. They countered him by saying that if he felt like that about the matter, perhaps it would be best for him after all to try his luck in the shallop. To which the worthy Prickett answered, "The will of God be done." Greene, at that pietistical utterance, lost his temper and flung out of the cabin, swearing that he would cut the throat of any man who double-crossed them. The boatswain remained, telling Prickett "that he intended to goe on with the action whilst it was hot," and explaining that it was too late now to change their plans, seeing that if what they plotted came to Hudson's ears, they themselves might be served with the same mischief they were devising for the others.

In a little while, back came Greene, to inquire whether Prickett had been won over. To whom Wilson answered, "He is in his old song, still patient." Prickett again attempted to reason with them, pleading with them to delay the execution of their plan for three days, for two days, for twelve hours, adding that if they would only wait till the following Monday, he would then join with them in insisting upon having the provisions of the ship equally divided. He told them that he suspected that "it was some worse matter that they had in mind," seeing that they were impatient to carry through their deed at such a time of night. Whereupon Henry Greene, the professed freethinker, to prove that it was not "bloud and revenge hee sought," took up the Bible that Prickett ever kept near his bedside, and swore on his oath that "hee would doe no man harme, and what he did was for the good of the voyage, and for nothing else."

The other mutineers now came in and did likewise, each swearing to keep a promise which itself was nothing but a sanctimonious prevarication. There they stood together, those secretive and bloody-minded mariners, each vying with the other in assurances that there was no evil in the murder they planned. The old man Juet, whose skill and judgment they relied upon for their return voyage, went so far as to assert that he, when he reached England, would justify the deed. John Thomas and Michael Perse took the false oath, and after them Bennett Mathues and Adrian Motter. When these last two appeared, Prickett asked them "if they were well advised what they had taken in hand," and they answered him that they were, "and therefore came to take the oath."

Prickett was now curious to know what other members of the crew would presently appear in his cabin to take his famous oath. But no one else came. The exact words that Prickett had invented for the men to say were: "You shall sweare truth to God, your prince and countrie: you shall doe nothing, but to the glory of God and the good of the action in hand, and harme to no man."

Remembered long afterward, in retrospect those whispering midnight hours, so critical, nay, so fateful, were able to impart even to Prickett's graphic style a new glamour. "It was darke," he writes, "and they in readinesse to put this deed of darknesse in execution. . . . Now every man would go to his rest, but wickednesse sleepeth not."

They at first feared that John King, the new mate, was with Hudson, but were reassured to learn that he was talking with Staffe, who was sleeping "on the poope," and immediately Bylot was sent to meet him, as if by chance, so as to get him if possible into his cabin. Henry Greene, meanwhile, kept company with Hudson, watching over him like a deathhouse jailor, lest he, growing suspicious, should take steps to prevent the villainy they had in hand. Only once did he leave him, and then to bring to the mutineers a piece of bread that the cabin boy had given him. Well can we see him haunting the sleeping man, this dangerous and depraved youth whose black lawless spirit knew naught of pity.

And while the small tunneled ship rocked to and fro at anchor, on the perfect balance of her keel, the whisperers with restless impatience awaited the coming of the dawn, awaited the hour when their vigil would be over, and they would be free to perpetrate their crime without further fear of surprise. The death-watch beetle was silent; no scratch was heard from the tiny feet of the bugs, as, led by an obscure instinct, with the utmost deliberation they moved from one dark beam to another. No sound was made by the deep-swimming fish, as they touched with their blunt noses the slippery keelson far under the ice-bearing water. All was stillness. Treachery and slumber lying together had brought forth silence.

And then, as the first indications of sunrise appeared over Charlton Island and over the cold stretches of water that lay between the ship and the eastern shores of the great bay, there was audible in each wan chamber the cheerful familiar sound of Mathues, the cook, going out, kettle in hand, to fetch water from the butts. This was the signal. John King was beguiled into entering the hold, and the bolt of its door slipped fast upon him. Greene and another went on deck, to divert the attention of Philip Staffe "with a talk"; for although they had no intention of putting him out of the ship, they did not feel at all certain as to how he might act in the face of open rebellion.

Henry Hudson now came out of his cabin. Immediately the sound of a scuffle was heard. John Thomas and the cook had leapt upon him, and before he had time to resist, Wilson, from behind, had pinioned him with a rope. The Portsmouth surgeon, hearing a noise, looked out of his door. He shouted to Hudson, to ask what was happening, and Hudson answered that they had bound him. Immediately the mutineers turned upon Wilson, and inquired of him if he was well; and when he answered that he was well, then they said to him, with the sinister reticence of dangerous men, that "yf he were well he should keepe himself soe." Hudson now asked the men what they intended, and they answered him that he would know "when he was in the shallop."

The moment for swift action had come. The shallop was hauled alongside the ship, and Hudson was put into it, under the care of Bennett Mathues and John Thomas. Many of the men were ignorant as to what had been arranged. Bylot, who kept himself below deck, afterward declared that he was under the impression that they intended to hold Hudson in the shallop only for as long a while as they would take to search the vessel for food.

To the majority it was "utterlye unknowen who should goe or who should tarrye," Greene, Wilson, and Juet acting as "affection or rage did guide them in that furye." Greene, for example, now that Mathues and Thomas were in the shallop, had a mind that they should stay there; and he would have carried this double treachery through, had not Silvanus Bond and Francis Clemens, realizing what he was up to, had them back "with much adoe," and forced Arnold Lodlo and Michael Butt to take their places, men who, only a few moments before, had themselves been railing against Hudson.

"The authors and executors" of the plot now seized upon Wydowse, who had sufficient imagination to envisage what was in store for him, and went to his doom "in the greatest distress," calling out that they could have his keys and share his goods, if only they would allow him to remain on board. He was followed by Adame Moore and Syracke Fanner, mariners too sick to make trouble, and also by John Hudson.

While Greene, with oaths and curses, was superintending matters on deck, Robert Juet had gone down to the hold to bring up John King, but the old man had undertaken more than he could manage, for no sooner had he slipped the bolt back than he was attacked by the former quartermaster, who had his sword with him, and held Juet at bay, and would have killed him had not other mutineers come to his rescue and helped him to get King on deck and out into the shallop.

The shallop had now been manned to the satisfaction of the mutineers. But it was destined to hold yet one other. Philip Staffe, the Ipswich carpenter, who seems at first hardly to have understood, now delivered himself of his simple commentary upon the proceedings that were taking place. This honest man, from the banks of the River Gipping, had not heard the bells of St. Mary-at-Key "knoll to church" for nothing. He knew what was right, and what was wrong—no one better; and he was not a man who could be easily budged from the narrow path. Rough and illiterate as he was, he became gradually aware that his own personal pride was in some way involved by what was happening. It is true that he was at liberty —at liberty, and yet at the same time bound by a stouter and more inextricable sailor's knot than could ever have been contrived by the quick fingers of young Master Greene. To his unsophisticated intelligence there seemed no doubt as to his present duty. Suddenly, deep down in the heart of this rude man, born and bred in Suffolk clay, the celebrated categorical imperative of Immanuel Kant became audible; and he turned upon the mutineers, and in the curious dialect of East Anglia, told them plainly what was in his mind. "As for himselfe, hee said, hee would not stay in the ship unlesse they would force him." Let him have his chest of carpenter's tools and be damned to them, for he chose rather to commit himself to God's mercy and "for the love of the Master go down into the shallop, than with such villaines to accept of likelier hopes." The mutineers could not dissuade him from his purpose, and down he went into the doomed boat, with his chest, his musket, some meal, and an iron pot.

And now, the shallop still being in tow, they stood out of the ice; and when they were nearly out of it, "they cut her head fast from the stern of the ship," and with topsails up, steered away into an open sea, leaving their captain and his son, with seven poor sailors, abandoned and exposed, "without food, drink, fire, clothing, or other necessaries," in the great unexplored bay. There he sat in the tiny boat, dressed "in a motley gown," the possessed sea captain who had sailed to the North, and sailed to the East, and sailed to the West in his endeavor to find a passage through the ice-bound ramparts of the planet itself. There he sat, this dreamer, in his coat of many colors, until to the eyes of the mutineers, who watched the shallop grow smaller and smaller in the wake of their stolen vessel, he became a mote, a speck, a nothing, lost to sight on the unresting waves of the wharfless wilderness that had been by him, so resolutely, so desperately discovered.

Thus Henry Hudson and his companions went to an unknown fate; as no trace of them or their shallop has ever been discovered. The mutineers managed to make their way back to London, where they inflamed the citizenry with the belief that the Northwest Passage, and thus a new route to the untold wealth of the Indies, had been discovered. Partly as a result, although there was an investigation and trial none of the mutineers was ever punished for Hudson's death, and some of them were permitted to embark on other voyages to confirm what was considered to be the original discovery.

CAPTAIN COOK AND THE PINCERS OF THE GREAT BARRIER REEF

by John Gwyther

When John Gwyther, author of the selection which follows, joined the Royal Navy during the Second World War, he eventually reached the Pacific. There he became fascinated by the adventures of Captain Cook and realized how much of our knowledge of the Pacific still depends on Cook's navigational discoveries. When he returned to England, Gwyther studied all available records. As he worked, life aboard ship in the eighteenth century came to life for him, and the result is the account of the voyage of the Endeavour from which the present selection is taken.

It was a century and a half after Drake's famous voyage round the world, that Cook's first expedition began. Its main purpose was to observe the transit of Venus which took place in 1769 and which could be seen from Tahiti; and the crew included a distinguished group of scientists from the Royal Society. When Cook was far out to sea, however, he opened his sealed orders and discovered that after the transit he was to head southward to explore the mysterious "southern Continent" which was supposed to be as large as Europe and Asia combined.

Cook successfully observed the transit and then began an extended trip. He journeyed completely around New Zealand. Then he sailed westward and reaching the eastern coast of Australia, sailed north. It is this portion of his

From *Captain Cook and the South Pacific* by John Gwyther. Reprinted by permission of Houghton Mifflin Company and Hutchinson & Co., Ltd.

expedition which Gwyther describes. Weathering almost certain disaster, Cook reached the Torres Strait. Voyaging through them between New Guinea and Australia, he proved that Torres, who two hundred years before had suggested the possibility of such a passage, was correct. And by his exploration of Australia, he showed its true nature, dispelling the myth of a great Southern Continent.

It is likely that William Janszoon had sailed down a part of the Australian coast before Cook, calling it New Holland. It is known that Abel Tasman discovered New Zealand. Long after in 1699, the buccaneer Dampier revisited these shores on a scientific expedition for the British Admiralty. His account of his voyages was widely read. Europe was fascinated by the picture of an earthly paradise, where life was idyllic and beautiful women could be taken for the asking. Other English voyages, under Wallis and Carteret, were undertaken. The Frenchman Bougainville sailed to Tahiti, which Wallis had discovered the previous year.

Yet it remained for Cook to make the first really scientific survey of this huge area. He charted countless islands as well as the great mass of Australia, which he named New South Wales and claimed in the name of King George. On his second voyage he ventured far to the south and suggested the existence of the Antarctic Continent, of which more will be told in the section on polar exploration. Later, he ventured along the Western North American Continent as far north as Point Barrow and Bering Strait. When he sailed southward for the last time, Cook discovered Hawaii, or the Sandwich Islands as he called them. Here he was killed by a pilfering band of native tribesmen. So died one of the greatest navigators and explorers of his day.

COOK was the first explorer of the eastern coast of Australia, but perhaps if he could have glanced at a chart of the coast and seen the nightmarish dangers that lay ahead, he might have been tempted to turn back. Running parallel to the coast is the formidable Great Barrier Reef, a reef that draws gradually tighter into the coast the farther north it goes, like a deadly pincer, forcing ships nearer to the pitiless rocks of the mainland—a jagged coral wall of destruction, inexorably squeezing in on the little boat. Every mile northward narrowed the strip of water between the reef and the mainland, every day the space in which to maneuver shrank.

Looking north and east, the sea was studded with innumerable tiny islands, each one certain destruction, with the huge Pacific swell crashing

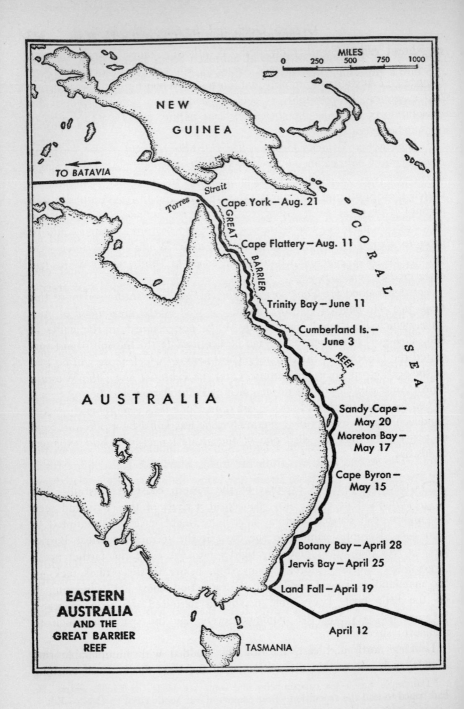

MILES
0   250   500   750   1000

NEW GUINEA

TO BATAVIA

Torres *Strait*

Cape York — Aug. 21

GREAT BARRIER

Cape Flattery — Aug. 11

Trinity Bay — June 11

Cumberland Is. — June 3

CORAL SEA

REEF

AUSTRALIA

Sandy Cape — May 20

Moreton Bay — May 17

Cape Byron — May 15

Botany Bay — April 28

Jervis Bay — April 25

Land Fall — April 19

April 12

TASMANIA

EASTERN AUSTRALIA AND THE GREAT BARRIER REEF

the might of thousands of miles of unbroken ocean against them, spuming up into a glittering, silver spray, coldly beautiful, but as deadly as exploding gunpowder. Yet for every reef that could be seen, there were ten submerged, rising sheer from the ocean bed to within a few feet of the surface.

To navigate in those completely unknown waters called for a constant vigilance on which their lives depended. A boat was always kept ahead, passing back soundings to the Captain, but so irregular were the reports, jumping from twenty fathoms to two, that they never knew from one moment to the next which way they would have to steer.

It was fantastically dangerous, like a man hanging by his hands above a thousand upturned swords, knowing that sooner or later he must drop and certain that unless the million-to-one chance comes off, he could not hope to fall between the points, but must impale himself on them. This was the situation that faced Cook, and to stick to it calmly without once allowing signs of strain or worry to show on his face needed vast reserves of physical and mental toughness few men possess.

Nor had the Captain any idea how many miles of this grueling navigation lay ahead. Tomorrow might see the end of it, or they might still be floundering around in the maze three months hence. He possessed only two scrappy pieces of evidence on the coastline ahead, neither of which could be much relied on. The first was from Quiros, the optimistic, cranky explorer who refused to give his helmsman a course because the Almighty would look after them. He was supposed to have sighted the islands they were now passing, "and which," as Cook cuttingly remarked, "some geographers, for what reason I know not, have thought fit to join to this land." The second hint was from the highly unreliable Dalrymple,[1] for in the secret chart he had given Banks just before they sailed, there was shown a strait between northern Australia and New Guinea.

Whatever Cook's personal feelings about Dalrymple might have been, searching anxiously for a break in the coast to the northwest and a release from the dangers they found themselves in, he must have hoped desperately that his information was correct. Every mile of the shore was hopefully scanned, but there was no "indication of a passage to the North West." Ahead of them as far as the eye could see loomed danger, with a strong possibility of shipwreck and death. Even the iron will of the Captain was appalled at their future prospects and shows itself in his writing.

Hitherto we had safely navigated this dangerous coast where the sea in all parts conceals shoals that suddenly project from the shore, and

[1] Dalrymple was a sea captain who had some knowledge of Pacific waters. He had hoped to lead the expedition whose command was finally given to Cook.—Eds.

rocks that rise abruptly like a pyramid from the bottom, for an extent of two-and-twenty degrees of latitude, more than one thousand, three hundred miles; and therefore hitherto none of the names which distinguish the several parts of the country that we saw, are memorials of distress; but here we became acquainted with misfortune, and we therefore called the point which we had just seen farthest to the northward "Cape Tribulation."

[May-June, 1770]

As the hard glare of sunlight softened into the evening dusk, Cook took his ship farther out to sea, not wishing to attempt the dangers ahead until he had a clear day before him. From six o'clock to nine he gently edged *Endeavour* away from the land, pacing the deck in clear moonlight, with a fine, light breeze blowing from the west that exactly suited his purpose; and with a satisfying regularity, the soundings deepened gradually from fourteen to twenty-one fathoms and remained steady.

At nine o'clock, feeling happier about the situation than he had for some time, the Captain went below to snatch a quick supper, but he had scarcely seated himself before he was summoned frantically on deck again. Within the space of minutes the sea bed had suddenly shoaled from twenty-one fathoms to twelve, ten, and eight, or, when Cook jumped up hastily from his supper, there was a hundred and twenty-six feet of water beneath the ship and by the time he reached the upper deck only forty-eight feet. "I immediately ordered everybody to their station," and all was made ready to turn the ship back into deeper water and drop anchor to stop her, while the ground ahead was investigated by one of the boats. "But meeting at the next cast of the lead with deeper water again, we concluded that we had gone over the tail of the shoals which we had seen at sunset, and that all danger was past." Long before ten o'clock they were back to deep, steady sounding, drawing farther from the land into safer water. "Then gentlemen left the deck in great tranquility, and went to bed!"

But again a few minutes before eleven, the water shallowed from twenty to seventeen fathoms, and within the seconds it took to swing the lead, *Endeavour*, with a shuddering, jarring shock struck the reef, grinding herself to a standstill on the knife-sharp coral.

In a few moments everyone was on deck "with countenances which sufficiently expressed the horrors of our situation." The ship remained immovable, except for the merciless heaving of the swell that beat her against the crags of rock on which she lay. "We had too much reason to conclude that we were upon a rock of coral, which is more fatal than any other, because the points of it are sharp, and every part of the surface so rough, as to grind away whatever is rubbed against it, even with the gentlest motions."

Immediately Cook ordered all the sails to be taken in and the boats hoisted out to examine the depth of water around the ship. They soon found that their position was even worse than they had at first feared, for the vessel had been lifted over a ledge of rock and lay in a hollow basin of coral, the edges of which, in some places, were no more than three feet below the surface. *Endeavour* was well and truly aground, ironically enough in the exact latitude in which Bougainville had approached the coast two years previously.

Every man aboard knew just how perilous was their situation. Scarcely beneath the horrified expressions of their faces lay a mad, murderous panic, for seamen of those days, highly superstitious as they were, obeyed only two laws in the face of imminent shipwreck and death. They refused to learn to swim, because it was only a means of prolonging the agonies of drowning, and they immediately broke into the wine and spirit stores, to get as drunk as possible in the short time left them to live.

But the calm efficiency of the Captain, reflected in his officers, checked their fears and kept the panic under control. With cool steadiness Cook gave his orders, anticipating dangers and keeping a couple of moves ahead, putting into operation the long tried and practical maneuvers carried out under such conditions. The longboat was already out, sounding round the ship to discover where the deepest water lay, and the anchor was carried to that point, then, provided the anchor held, the capstan was turned in the hopes that the ship would wind herself toward the anchor, pulling her off the reef at the same time. But though the men pushed against the stubborn capstan spars till their hearts were fit to burst and the sweat poured off them, they could not budge her. They worked under terrible conditions, with the ship beating so violently against the rocks that they could hardly keep their feet. It seemed impossible that anything made by man could long withstand such a terrible battering; she must break up, and to complete the scene of distress they could see, by the light of the moon, great chunks of the vessel floating away around them; first the protective sheathing boards, specially added before they left England to protect the real ship's bottom, then with a sickening wrench the false keel broke away and drifted off "so that every moment was making way for the sea to rush in which was to swallow us up."

Their only chance was in lightening the ship, but they had missed the best opportunity, for she had struck right at high tide and as stores were thrown overboard the water also shallowed. Indirectly it helped. She settled more firmly on the coral and was not beaten against it with such violence. Their great hope lay in the next high tide, "but it was doubtful whether she could hold together so long, especially as the rock kept grating her bottom under the starboard bow with such force as to be heard in the fore store-room." Cook well knew it was an equal danger his men might break under the mental strain. "This, however, was no time to indulge in conjecture, nor was any effort remitted in despair of success." That strong attitude of determination, coupled with Cook's superb qualities as a leader, inspired his men. The gentlemen, too, acted with typical English phlegm. Green continued to take observation as though nothing had happened. Banks quietly lent a hand wherever necessary, nevertheless admitting that the Captain's firm handling of the situation impressed him more than anything on the voyage, for he speaks of "the cool and steady conduct of the officers, who, during the whole time, never gave an order which did not show them to be perfectly composed and unmoved by the circumstances however dreadful they might appear."

Immediate action was taken in preparation for the next high tide; the pumps were started in the hold, for they were leaking badly and everything that could be spared was jettisoned:

. . . six of our guns, being all we had upon the deck, our iron and stone ballast, casks, hoop staves, oil jars, decayed stores and many other items that lay in the way of heavier materials, were thrown overboard with the utmost expedition, everyone exerting himself with an alacrity almost approaching to cheerfulness, without the least repining or discontent, yet the men were so far impressed with a sense of their situation that not an oath was heard among them.

They labored unceasingly through the night to the accompaniment of the groans of a dying ship. As day broke, they could see land about twenty-five miles away, without any island between them and the shore, precluding the possibility, if *Endeavour* should go to pieces, of scrambling to safety while the boats ferried them to the mainland. With immense relief, however, they realized the wind was gradually dying away and early in the forenoon it was dead calm. If it had blown hard the ship must inevitably have been destroyed.

The next high tide was expected at eleven o'clock and the men waited tensely for the supreme effort they would have to make. Nearly fifty tons of equipment had been thrown overboard, but as the tide started to rise the water began to pour into the ship, for while they had rested securely on the bottom, the leak had not been too bad, but now it rushed in so fast that two pumps, worked incessantly, could scarcely keep pace with it.

Long before it was time, the sailors were waiting by the capstan; no orders were necessary, they longed for the word "go." Then at a signal from the Captain they threw themselves against the spars, pushing till their muscles throbbed, ached, and went numb with the strain and their heads lolled stupidly between their arms. But *Endeavour* still stuck fast, immovable as a mountain—"to our inexpressible surprise and concern, she did not float."

Cook did not allow his men to think about this second failure for an instant, but put them to work immediately, preparing for the next high tide. He now realized himself that the midday flood fell some feet short of the night tide and cheered his men on with the information. They worked on numbly, taking out two more anchors, hoping that by shortening the length of cable between the three anchors and the ship they might draw her off the ledge on which she rested toward deeper water. But they still had hours to wait before the attempt could be made.

By two o'clock in the afternoon, *Endeavour* was heeling giddily over to starboard, swaying drunkenly on the coral rocks. At five in the evening the tide began to rise. At the same time the leak increased so alarmingly that two more pumps were brought into action, but only one would work. Three pumps were kept going, and by a prodigious effort they managed to keep level with the inrushing water. By nine the ship was on an even keel, but the leak was gaining on them. It was only the terrific strength of the Captain's character that kept the men going, for fear gripped icily at their hearts. And that was the real victory: the unshakable respect of the ship's company for Cook was stronger than their combined fears.

But they were all aware of the real danger, for with the leak steadily gaining on them, it was more than likely that if *Endeavour* could be freed she would lose the support of the rocks she lay on and almost certainly sink.

This was a dreadful circumstance, so that we anticipated the floating of the ship not as an earnest of deliverance, but as an event that would probably precipitate our destruction. We well knew that our boats were not capable of carrying us all on shore, and that when the dreadful crisis should arrive, as all command and subordination would be at an end, a contest for preference would probably ensue, that would increase even the horrors of shipwreck, and terminate in the destruction of us all by the hands of each other; yet we knew that if any should be left on board to perish in the waves, they would probably suffer less upon the whole than those who should get on shore, without any lasting or effectual defense against the natives, in a country where even nets and fire-arms would scarcely furnish them with food; and where, if they should find the means of subsistence, they must be condemned to languish out the remainder of life in a desolate wilderness, without the possession, or even hope, of any domestic comfort, and cut off from all commerce with mankind, except the naked savages who prowled the desert, and who perhaps were some of the most rude and uncivilized upon the earth.

In fact, no other ship visited that part of the coast for the rest of the century.

In that dreadful state of suspense they waited for death. The long day dragged by and the crucial moment that was to determine their fate drew near. They could read in each other's faces the horrible fears that were in their own minds.

By about twenty past ten that night, the tide had risen sufficiently to float the ship, and as many hands as could be spared from the pumps were sent to man the capstan and windlasses. They knew that if they failed this time *Endeavour* would certainly not survive another twenty-four hours of cruel battering she had taken. But with the last desperate effort, "she was heaved into deeper water." For a tense, immeasurable moment the level of water in the hold was watched, the seconds that were to decide their fate. Miraculously the leak did not increase; there was still a shred of hope, still life. The men, "having now endured excessive fatigue of body and agitation of mind for more than four-and-twenty hours, and having but little hope of succeeding at last began to flag." None of them could stand the back-breaking toil at the pumps for more than five or six minutes at a time. Then, totally exhausted and quivering with fatigue, their breath coming in harsh, wheezing gasps, they flung themselves on the deck, though a stream of water was running over it from the pumps. A few moments of respite, till their mates threw themselves down and the others jumped to fight the inrushing sea, relieving each other until an accident very nearly tipped the scales from hope to despair.

The planking which lines the inside of a ship's bottom is known as the ceiling and between this and the outside planking there is a space of about eighteen inches. The man who had been taking the depth of water in the hold had done so to the inside planking, but on being relieved the next seaman took the depth to the bottom planking, so that within the space of a few minutes it appeared to the weary men at the pumps that the leak had gained eighteen inches. Exhausted to near breaking point, even the bravest were on the point of giving up the unequal struggle and in a few moments everything would have been in a state of complete confusion. This accident, however dreadful its consequences might have been, was soon righted, and instead of the murderous panic which the Captain knew only too well would be likely to follow, the men were imbued with a sudden joy that acted like a charm, inspiring fresh vigor:

. . . they renewed their efforts with such alacrity and spirit, that before eight o'clock in the morning the leak was so far from having gained upon the pumps, that the pumps had gained upon the leak. Everybody now talked of getting the ship into harbour as a thing not to be doubted.

By eleven o'clock, with a fair breeze from seaward, they got under sail and stood toward the land.

It was, however, quite impossible to sustain very much longer the terrific effort that had been made at the pumps. They had been at it ceaselessly for nearly thirty-six hours and their faces were lined and drawn with fatigue. In this situation one of the midshipmen made a suggestion—quite new to Cook—which eventually saved them. He took a piece of sail and stitched lightly to it handfuls of chopped-up wool and oakum, smearing sheep dung and other filth on it. The sail thus prepared was hauled under the ship's bottom by ropes which kept it extended, and when it came under the leak, the suction which carried in the water sucked in the sail, effectively bunging up the hole. "By the success of this expedient our leak was so reduced, that instead of gaining on three pumps, it was easily kept under with one."

Nor was the mat the midshipman's own idea; he had, in fact, seen it used by the master of a merchantman, who had such faith in it that he sailed his ship right across the Atlantic from Virginia to London, though he could have had the leak properly repaired before leaving Virginia. Such a feat must undeniably have left a strong impression on the midshipman's mind, yet, so strong was the iron curtain around commanding officers of those days, Cook included, that *Endeavour's* leak was perilously near to beating them before the young officer dared to make a suggestion to his Captain.

Like a faithful, old, wounded dog, *Endeavour* started to limp over the painful twenty-five miles between her and the shore. A brave little ship kept afloat by a few square feet of canvas and sheep's dung: humble enough articles to save the southern Pacific from plunging back into its age-old obscurity. A bit of sailcloth preserving for Britain the secrets and ultimate possession of the mighty continent of Australia and the rich lands of New Zealand.

[*June-August, 1770*]

Very gently Cook edged his ship to within two miles of the shore, sending ahead a couple of boats to hunt for a suitable bay, for it was absolutely essential to beach *Endeavour* as soon as possible.

The first bay investigated proved too shallow, but at nine o'clock that night the pinnace returned with the news that they had found an ideal harbor with fresh water and a high enough rise and fall of tide to allow the ship to be put ashore. They weighed anchor at six o'clock the next morning, keeping two boats ahead as an essential precaution, but despite every possible care they only just missed running aground again, skimming over the top of a reef with barely four feet of water between the ship's bottom and the rocks.

They were in a better position than when lying on the rocks, but still in great danger, for the ship was not working well, answering the helm with sluggish indifference. The wind was freshening to gale force and they were entangled among the shoals onto which Cook feared they might be driven before his boats could mark the channel entrance to the bay. To speed up the operation the Captain went personally in the pinnace to buoy the entrance, but by the time he had finished the weather had so far worsened that an attempt to get inside the harbor that night would have been suicidal. There was nothing for it but to anchor and let the gale blow itself out.

Every conceivable precaution was taken for their safety, "for in all the joy of our unexpected deliverance, we had not forgot that at this time there was nothing but a lock of wool between us and destruction."

For two days they lay strung out on the end of their cable, unable to move, silently wondering at the strange freak of the weather that had preserved them while they lay hopelessly floundering twenty-five miles out to sea on the reef. It blew hard before they grounded; it blew hard for the rest of their stay on the coast. "It was calm only when we were upon the rock, except once; and even the gale that afterwards wafted us to the shore, would then certainly have beaten us to pieces."

Cook desperately wanted to get his ship safely into the harbor, for troubles were heaping themselves on him.

The scurvy now began to make its appearance among us, with many formidable symptoms. Our poor Indian Tupia, who had sometimes before complained that his gums were sore and swelled, and who had taken plentifully of our lemon juice by the surgeon's directions, had now livid spots upon his legs, and other indubitable testimonies that the disease had made a rapid progress, notwithstanding all our remedies. . . . Mr. Green, our astronomer, was also declining; and these, among other circumstances, embittered the delay which prevented our going on shore.

On the morning of the seventeenth, though the wind was still blowing hard and only the absolute necessity of getting into the bay prompted Cook, he ventured to weigh anchor and push into the harbor. Twice during the attempt they ran aground, their nerves strained to breaking point. The first time they slid off easily, but the second time stuck fast and only freed themselves by making a raft of some of the masts alongside the ship; this, with a rising tide, saved them, and by evening they were safely moored alongside the steep beach of the little bay. "It is remarkable, that in the whole course of our voyage we had seen no place which, in our present circumstances, could have afforded us the same relief." Small wonder he wrote those words; any safe anchorage was a paradise after the grueling battle they had fought.

When everything possible had been done for the sick members of the crew, Cook turned his attention to the wounds of his ship. The forge was landed, the blacksmith and armorer set to work making nails, bound to be needed in the repair; and to the merry chink of hammer on anvil, the ship's company set to work clearing stores from the forward end, where the leak was, to the beach, and moving some to the stern, so as to rear up the bows of the ship and drop the stern. Thus, bows up, stern down, assuming the position of a motorboat at high speed. At the apex of a high tide, *Endeavour* was pulled onto the steep beach.

As they gazed in numb silence at her injuries they realized, fully now for the first time, how hairbreadth had been their escape, how relentlessly the sharp, jagged coral had sawed into the ship: "there was not a splinter to be seen, but all was smooth as if the whole had been cut away by an instrument." Yet their preservation had finally depended on the most extraordinary, million-to-one chance. Cook, and many others aboard, had fully expected *Endeavour* to go to the bottom once she lost the support of the rocks, and so she would have done had not a piece of coral broken off and remained sticking in the planking as the ship slid off the reef: "one of the holes, which was big enough to have sunk us, if we had had eight pumps instead of four, and been able to keep them incessantly going, was in a great measure plugged up by a fragment of the rock, which, after having made the wound, was left sticking in it."

It was to take them six weeks to restore *Endeavour* to seaworthiness; six weeks during which their main attention was directed to living off the land, for it was essential to preserve the small remaining stock of feeding stuffs. . . .

Inevitably, contact with land animals meant contact with the aborigines, in this part of the coast as in others—timid, furtive creatures, almost animal. Seldom seen, but often sensed and heard, darting swiftly out of sight at the approach of the English. They did manage, however, to extract from the natives a name for the strange, hopping animals. "Kanguroo," Cook called it (an amusing mistake that has endured to the present day). Years later, if only we had been fortunate enough, we should have seen learned naturalists and dignified naval officers in frock coats hopping about the beach of Endeavour River, before an astonished crowd of aborigines. "The word 'kangaroo' was repeatedly used to them last year, accompanied by an imitation of the leap of the animal, which the natives readily understood." But after each splendid series of exhausting hops and the word "kangaroo," the natives sadly shook their heads. "Men-u-ah," they repeated again and again. A fairly accurate translation from Cook's word "kanguroo" is, "I don't know," or, "I don't understand you." Still, it stuck and to this day the animal remains a "kangaroo," an "I-don't-know."

Endeavour's bows were now patched up, but already three unsuccessful attempts had been made to refloat her, each one a maneuver taking days of preparation. With the fourth try they were successful but she had been floating only a few minutes before it was obvious that the awkward position in which she had lain—bows ashore, stern floating—had strained her badly amidships, causing another serious leak and leaving the Captain no option but to go through the tedious operation of laying his ship back on shore.

What was going to happen once, and if, they got to sea? Cook knew their only chance lay in threading a way north through the tangled coral reefs, for the wind blew constantly from the south, and a return home by the route they had come, beating back into the wind, frequently blowing at gale force, for two thousand miles amid the hazards of reef and shoal, was completely, hopelessly impossible. It was north or nothing. But what a terrifying prospect loomed ahead.

Consequently, the Master was sent out day after day in a boat to take soundings and see if he could discover the start of a passage to the northward, getting as far as twenty to twenty-five miles from the ship. On occasions his reports were hopeful, sometimes not, but finally, "the Master returned with the discouraging account that there was no passage for the ship to northward." Cook shrugged his shoulders; it made no difference, that was their only escape route. It would have been just the same to tell a man in a burning room with the door blocked that he must not jump out of the window.

By the beginning of August they were ready for sea, waiting for the weather to moderate and the water across the bar of the harbor to deepen sufficiently to let them out; but they never seemed to come right at the same time, either there was a sufficient depth of water and a howling gale stopped them, or it was the other way round. At last, at five o'clock in the morning of the fourth of August, they passed over the bar and got under sail.

Overhead it was gray and hazy, and a steady monotonous rain fell. The day before the carpenter had examined the pumps and "to our great mortification found them all in a state of decay." No pumps, no protective sheathing, false keel gone, food stocks perilously low, and before them the dreaded teeth of the Great Barrier Reef, a vicious enemy that had already tasted their blood.

[August-Sept., 1770]

"At low-water I went to the mast-head and took a view of the shoals which made a very threatening appearance." Indeed, as far as the eye could see, the ocean was studded with hundreds of islands. On his west side the mainland of Australia; north and south, innumerable reefs; and to the east, the outside edge of the Great Barrier Reef, on which the might of the Pacific hurled itself with a thunderous, exploding surf, bursting skyward in a glittering fan of silver spray.

Their progress was painfully slow, Cook giving his steering direction from the masthead, always with a boat ahead to give forewarning of danger. It was only safe to venture forward when the tide was practically out, exposing the reefs, and frequently, when the tide was right, the wind blew at gale force, making movement impossible; or again, tide and wind were right but visibility too hazy to allow progress. At such times Cook would call from the masthead for some of the officers to come aloft. There they would sit among the mist-drenched sails and sheet vainly straining their eyes for sight of a way out.

After a time they thought they could detect a clear opening before them and hoped they were once more out of danger; "in this hope, however, we soon found ourselves disappointed, and for that reason I called the headland Cape Flattery." They steered along the shore until one o'clock for what they thought was an open channel, when the petty officer at the masthead cried out that he could see land stretching menacingly right across their path, and between the ship and the mainland, another reef.

Whether the obstacle ahead was mainland or islands, Cook was not prepared to turn back without investigating what lay beyond. He anchored for the night and went forward the next day, "in the pinnace, accompanied by Mr. Banks, whose fortitude and curiosity made him a party in every expedition." The Captain did not want the pessimistic chatter of his officers; Joseph Banks was the ideal companion, the sort of sympathetic friend to whom Cook could think aloud and express his doubts, knowing that Banks was not waiting to fan the slightest smolder of indecision, and urge him to turn back, as his officers would. About one o'clock they reached the loftiest of the islands "and immediately ascended the highest hill, with a mixture of hope and fear, proportioned to the importance of our business, and the uncertainty of the event." When they looked round they could see reefs and islands stretching out of sight with the ocean swell breaking in a dreadful surf, "and I conceived hopes of getting without these, as I perceived several breaks or openings in the reef and deep water between."

The Captain returned on board determined to get outside rather than "run the risk of being locked in by the great reef," and to keep pressing northward in the hopes that a few days' sailing might see the end of the reef and a speedier passage to the East Indies, "as we now had but little more than three months provision on board at short allowance."

The next morning Cook placed his ship abreast a gap in the reef while the Master went ahead to make a final check. Through this opening the tide rushed with a smooth, oily speed, narrowing to the characteristic V-shape of fast-flowing water. Either side of this "eye in the needle" rose the sharp teeth of coral. Cook was taking a calculated risk; when the moment came to shoot the gap he would have no control over his ship. He waited quietly, received the Master's "go-ahead" signal, and aimed the bows of *Endeavour* for the middle of the gap. The tide gripped her and she shot through like a cork in a millrace . . . into deep, bottomless water, cradled on a huge swell rolling in from the southeast.

That night Cook stood well out to sea but the next morning came back toward the coast, "in order to get within sight of land, that I might be sure not to overshoot the passage; if passage there was, between this land and New Guinea" (the elusive Torres Strait).

Now they found themselves in worse danger than when they were inside the reef, for the moment the wind dropped and the tide started to flow toward the land, they were carried inexorably toward the reef.

About four o'clock in the morning we plainly heard the roaring of the surf and at break of day saw it foaming to a vast height, at not more than a mile's distance. Our distress now returned upon us with double force; the waves which rolled in upon the reef, carried us towards it very fast; we could reach no ground with an anchor and had not a breath of wind for the sails.

All three boats were out ahead desperately trying to pull *Endeavour* away from the danger, but losing ground rapidly, and at six o'clock that evening they were only a "hundred yards from the rocks upon which the same billow which washed the side of the ship, broke to a tremendous height the very next time it rose; so that between us and destruction there was only a dreary valley, no wider than the base of one wave."

This time it seemed their luck was at an end, there was no escape. But a gentle breeze sprang up, "so light that at any other time we should not have observed it," and gave the men pulling in the boats just that tiny bit of help which enabled them to get clear.

A mile ahead they could see a narrow opening in the reef and all their hopes were centered on getting back inside, but the breeze that had helped them temporarily for ten miles, dropped, and they were rushed back toward the rocks. Again, when they were no more than a stone's throw from destruction, a scarcely perceptible breeze sprang up, and by its help they got *Endeavour* opposite the gap, just as the tide turned. Instead of being swept through, she was hustled two miles out to sea on the current. It gave them a temporary break, a chance to regain their breath, but only until the tide turned. Then they were sucked back toward the rocks; this time a little farther north, but again opposite a gap in the coral. "We struggled hard with the flood, sometimes gaining a little and sometimes losing, but every man still did his duty."

Then carried irresistibly on the powerful current, which but for the opening in the rocks would have smashed them to matchwood on the coral, they were swept back inside the reef with "amazing rapidity, by a torrent that kept us from driving against either side of the channel."

And now, such is the vicissitude of life, we thought ourselves happy in having regained a situation which, but two days before, it was the utmost object of our hope to quit. Rocks and shoals are always dangerous to the mariner, even where their situation has been ascertained; they are more dangerous in seas which have never before been navigated, and in this part of the globe they are more dangerous than in any other: for here there are reefs and coral rocks, rising like a wall almost perpendicular out of the unfathomable deep . . . and here the enormous waves of the vast Southern Ocean meeting with so abrupt a resistance, break with inconceivable violence.

Cook was now certain their only course was northward, inside the reef, for during their brief spell outside another unpleasant fact had been forced on him: "We could not safely put the same confidence in our vessel as before she had struck: for the blows she had received had so widened her leaks, that she admitted no less than nine inches of water an hour." This, without pumps, and "the danger of navigating in unknown parts of the ocean was now greatly increased by our having a crazy ship." Their survival lay in moving forward with even more caution than before.

For nearly three weeks *Endeavour* moved steadily forward, but as the end of her appalling ordeal approached, she did not burst suddenly into the freedom of the Indian Ocean. The coast started to trend westward, the soundings became more regular, until, passing between two points, "we could see no land, so that we conceived hopes of having at last, found a passage into the Indian Sea." Cook landed on one of the numerous islands and, climbing to the highest point, knew that Torres Strait was no myth,

which gave me great satisfaction, not only because the dangers and fatigues of the voyage were drawing to an end, but because it would no longer be in doubt whether Australia and New Guinea were two separate islands.

As I was now about to quit the eastern coast of New Holland, which I had coasted from latitude thirty eight degrees to this place, and which I am confident no European had ever seen before, I once more hoisted the English colours, and though I had already taken possession of several particular parts, now took possession of the whole eastern coast, from latitude thirty eight degrees to this place, latitude ten and a half South, in the right of his Majesty King George the third, by the name of New South Wales, with all the bays, harbours, rivers and islands situated upon it: we then fired three volleys of small arms, which were answered by the same number from the ship. Having performed this ceremony upon the island, we named it Possession Island.

At last, after a year and a week, *Endeavour* was back on the map. She had made a great sweeping arc into the unknown, uncharted ocean of the South Pacific, the last four months of which had strained the nerves, minds, and bodies of them all beyond the prudent limit of human endurance.

But now, released from the horrors of the Great Barrier Reef, they felt free as birds. They could cram on all canvas and sail along the western shore of New Guinea in long, unhindered tacks, making for Batavia.

MASSACRE AT FIJI

by Peter Dillon

On March 10, 1788, the Boussole and the Astrolabe, under the command of the great French navigator, the Comte de la Pérouse, sailed out of Botany Bay after a frightful massacre at Tutuila, in which twelve of his men were killed and many others wounded. They were never heard from again. King Louis XVI sent out a search expedition, but the mystery remained unsolved for years.

La Pérouse had made extensive explorations in the Pacific. From Cape Horn he sailed to Easter Island and Hawaii, then up to Alaska and down the American coast to California. He explored the Philippines, Formosa and Kamchatka before sailing to Samoa where the massacre occurred. After his disappearance an account of his voyages was compiled from reports he had sent back to France, and was published in 1799.

Ten years after the publication of this book, Peter Dillon, "a gigantic, dashing Irishman," sailed out of Ireland to trade in the Pacific and the Orient. On one of these voyages he came across an ancient sword guard which he believed must have belonged to La Pérouse. As a result the East India Company, the most powerful trading company in the world, sent him out in search of further remains. This led to his discovery of the wreckage of the ill-fated ships on the reefs of Vanikoro in the Santa Cruz group.

The "Massacre at Fiji" actually occurred when Dillon was a sandalwood trader in his early days in the Pacific. It is included in his Narrative and Successful Result of a Voyage in the South Seas . . . to Ascertain the Actual Fate of La Pérouse's Expedition.

IN 1812 and 1813 I sailed as an officer in the Calcutta ship *Hunter*, Captain Robson, on a voyage from Bengal to New South Wales, the Beetee Islands (commonly called the Fiji Islands), and Canton. I had before visited these islands in 1809, and remained among them for four months, during which time, being in the habit of associating very much with the natives, I made a considerable progress in learning their language. On joining the *Hunter* I found Captain Robson had been at these islands twice before, and had obtained considerable influence over the natives of a part of the Sandalwood Coast, by joining them in their wars and assisting them to destroy their enemies, who were cut up, baked, and eaten in his presence. The chief with whom he was most intimate was Bonasar, of the town of Vilear and its dependencies in the interior.

On the afternoon of the 19th February, 1813, the ship *Hunter* anchored in Vilear Bay, at a distance of a quarter of a mile from the entrance of a small river that led to the town. The town of Vilear is about a mile, or perhaps one and a half, from the anchorage, situated on the verdant banks of a beautiful stream. The sides of the river are covered with thick forests of mangrove bushes to within a short distance of the town, where the land is somewhat elevated and clear of wood.

Before the anchor was let go, the chief's brother came on board to congratulate the captain on his return; and shortly after, the chief, with several other chiefs and priests, with a lascar or East Indian sailor, who had deserted from the *Hunter* at this place about twenty months before. The chief informed the captain that shortly after his departure for Canton last voyage, the towns which he had conquered on the coast and interior by the captain's assistance revolted, and being joined by the powerful tribes who reside on the banks of a large river, called Nanpacab, they had waged a furious war against him.

The chief then hinted at the impossibility there was of obtaining sandalwood until this powerful alliance was put down by force of musketry, and requested the commander to join him in a new campaign. To this request he did not then accede. The chief urged the danger to which his subjects would be exposed while they were in straggling parties cutting the sandalwood for us, as the enemy would lay wait for them and cut them off when they least expected it. I went on shore with the captain and chief to the town, where we were exceedingly well received, and got presents of a hog, yams, and coconuts. We were visited next day by Terrence Dun and John Riley, British subjects: the former was discharged from the *Hunter* last voyage, and the latter from an American brig at the same time.

They informed me that they had resided during their time on shore at various parts of the islands, and were exceedingly well treated by the inhabitants; but that their countrymen who resided on the neighboring island of Bow had become very troublesome to the islanders. Such was their bad and overbearing conduct that the natives rose on them one day and killed three of them before the King of Bow had time to suppress the wrath of his people, who wished to destroy all the Europeans on the island. Dun was therefore of opinion that the surviving Europeans would be prevented from visiting the ship.

It is here necessary to explain how so many sailors of different countries got on shore to reside at these islands. In 1808 an American brig from the River Plate was lost on one of the islands with forty thousand Spanish dollars on board. The crew were saved in the vessel's boats, and part of them joined an American ship then lying at Myanboor Bay, on the Sandalwood Coast; others escaped to the neighboring island of Bow, with as many of the dollars as they could conveniently carry off. Shortly after the above shipwreck several vessels, English, Indian, American, and New South Wales men, came to the coast for the purpose of procuring sandalwood. The seamen on board these vessels became allured by the report of so many dollars being on shore at the neighboring islands. With a view of enriching themselves, some deserted and others were regularly discharged by their commanders and proceeded to the field of wealth. Some of those men, with the few dollars then procured, bought firearms and gunpowder, with which they rendered important assistance to the king of the neighboring island of Bow, and were on that account thought highly of by the islanders, from among whom they procured wives and lived very comfortably, until their insolence and cruelty induced the natives to destroy a part of them; and it will shortly be seen what a dreadful fate awaited the others in consequence of Captain Robson's proceedings.

From the time of our arrival up to the end of March following, the sandalwood came in but very slowly. The natives in our neighborhood begged several times of the captain to assist them in their wars and promised, as a reward for such service, to load the ship with the desired article in two months after their enemy was conquered. Captain Robson consented; and we accordingly set out for the island of Nanpacab, situated about six miles up the river of the same name, and distant from the ship forty or fifty miles. The armament consisted of three armed boats carrying twenty musketeers, and in one of the boats there was a two-pound cannon mounted. We were accompanied by forty-six large canoes, carrying I suppose near a thousand armed savages, besides three thousand more that marched by land to the scene of action. The weather being wet and stormy, we were obliged to rendezvous at an island near the entrance of the Nanpacab until the morning of the fourth, at which time we entered the river, and were saluted by showers of arrows and stones from slings by the enemy who were standing on its banks.

On getting near the island of Nanpacab we found it fortified. After a few discharges of the two-pounder, the defenders abandoned the fortress and escaped to the mainland, from whence they were soon driven by the fire of the musketry. There were eleven of the Nanpacab people killed on this occasion, whose bodies were placed in the canoes of our party, excepting one, which was immediately despatched in a fast-sailing canoe to Vilear, to be there devoured.

After this short skirmish we proceeded fifteen miles up the river, and destroyed the towns and plantations on its banks. In the evening we returned to a landing place, where the islanders began to cook their yams in a kind of oven which will be hereafter described. The dead bodies were placed on the grass and dissected by one of the priests. The feet were cut off at the ankles, and the legs from the knees; afterward the private parts; then the thighs at the hip joints; the hands at the wrists, the arms at the elbows, the shoulders at the sockets; and lastly, the head and neck were separated from the body. Each of these divisions of the human frame formed one joint, which was carefully tied up in green plantain leaves, and placed in the ovens to be baked with the taro root.

On the morning of the fifth we proceeded along the coast to the eastward, but found the towns, forts, and plantations abandoned. On the night of the eighth we returned to the ship.

Early in May we were joined by our tender, the *Elizabeth* cutter, Mr. Ballard master, which had sailed from Port Jackson before us for the Sandwich Islands, and in a few days after we were visited by the Europeans who resided at Bow. The captain employed them to work in the ship's boats, for which they were to be paid at the rate of four pounds per month, in cutlery, glass beads, ironmongery, etc. at a fixed price, and to return to Bow when the ship was prepared to proceed on her voyage.

May, June, July, and August passed over, and we had only procured one hundred and fifty tons of sandalwood from the islanders, which was not more than one-third of a cargo. They then declared their inability to procure more wood, as the forests were exhausted by the great number of ships which had frequented the coast for some years past.

The chiefs and men of consequence kept away from the ship, being apprehensive they might be detained as hostages until their engagements of loading the vessel were fulfilled. Captain Robson was very much displeased at this trick played on him by a savage and cunning people, and vowed vengeance against his old and faithful allies, whose stomachs he had so often helped to glut with the flesh of their enemies.

Early in September two large canoes from Bow, carrying about two hundred and twenty or two hundred and thirty men, visited the ship for the purpose of taking home the Europeans and their wives that joined us in May. Captain Robson, about that time being sixty miles distant from the ship in the tender, attacked a fleet of Vilear canoes, and took fourteen of them; on which occasion a native of the latter place was shot dead by a small cannon shot. On the ship and cutter rejoining company, the captain proposed to heave the cutter down, to repair some damage she had sustained in her bottom. However, he deemed it prudent, before doing so, to endeavor to possess himself of the remainder of the Vilear canoes, to prevent, as he said, their attacking the people while employed about the cutter, as it would be necessary to haul her on shore at high water.

On the morning of the sixth of September the Europeans belonging to the ship were all armed with muskets, also those Europeans from Bow, and placed under the direction of Mr. Norman, the first officer. We landed at a place called the Black Rock, a little way to the eastward of the river: the two canoes shortly after landed at the same place. We were joined by the Bow chiefs and a hundred of their men. The canoes and boats then put off into deep water, which precaution was used to prevent their getting aground by the tide ebbing.

On landing, the Europeans began to disperse into straggling parties of two, three, and four in a group. I begged of Mr. Norman, our commander, to cause them to keep close together in case of a sudden attack from the islanders; but no attention was paid to my remonstrance. We proceeded by a narrow path over a small level plain without interruption until we arrived at the foot of a hill, which we ascended, and soon gained the level or tableland on its top. There a few natives showed themselves, and by shouts and gestures tried to irritate us.

Mr. Norman turned to the right along a narrow path, which led through a thicket to some native houses: I followed him with seven other Europeans and the two Bow chiefs, with one of their men. Here a few natives tried to dispute our passage: they were fired at, one shot dead, and the others retreated. Mr. Norman then directed the chief's house with some others to be set on fire. The order was immediately complied with, and all were in flames in a few seconds. A few minutes after we heard dreadful yells and shoutings of the savages proceeding from the road by which we had ascended to the tableland. The Bow chiefs understood from the yells that some of their men as well as Europeans were killed by the Vilear people, who lay concealed in ambush until they got us on the tableland, where they attacked our straggling parties, who having discharged their muskets, were killed before they had time to reload. Others, I afterward understood, on seeing themselves nearly surrounded by the savages, threw down their muskets and ran toward the boat: only two of whom escaped. In Mr. Norman's party there were ten musketmen, with the two Bow chiefs and one of their followers. We determined to keep close together and fight our way to the boats.

We immediately got out of the thicket onto the tableland, where there were not more than three of the islanders, who shouted and called out to us that several of our men were killed, as also a number of the Bow men, and that we should immediately share a similar fate. On reaching the brink of the path by which we were to descend to the plain, we found Terrence Dun lying dead with his brains beaten out by a native club, and the whole plain between us and the boats covered with thousands of infuriated savages, all armed. Before descending to the plain, a young man named John Graham separated from us, and ran into a thicket of bushes on the left-hand side of the road, where he was quickly pursued by the three savages above mentioned, who despatched him. This young man was the son of a publican at Port Jackson, and had served his time to the sea; he had joined an American brig about two years before, as interpreter for these islands, and after procuring a cargo for her, was paid off and discharged at his own request. The remainder of us proceeded down the precipice. On getting to the bottom the savages prepared to receive us; they stood in thousands on each side of the path, brandishing their weapons, with their faces and bodies besmeared over with the blood of our slaughtered companions.

At this moment a native who came down the precipice after us threw a lance at Mr. Norman, which entered his back and passed out of his breast: he ran a few yards and fell down apparently dead. I fired at this native and reloaded my musket as soon as possible, when on turning round I found my companions had all run off by different routes. Taking advantage of the absence of the natives, who had all quitted the path and pursued our unfortunate flying men, I dashed along with all the speed that was possible, but had not proceeded more than a few yards when I came on the dead body of William Parker, who was prostrated across the path with his musket by him, which I took up and retreated with.

About this time the natives observed me and gave chase. One of them came up so close to me that I was obliged to throw Parker's musket away, as also a pistol which I had in my belt. In a moment after this I reached the foot of a small steep rock that stood on the plain. Finding it impossible to get to the boat through the crowds of natives that intercepted the pathway, I called out to my companions (some of whom were on my right), "Take the hill! Take the hill!" We then got to the top of it, where I joined the following persons: Charles Savage, Luis a Chinaman, and Martin Bushart, with Thomas Dafny and William Wilson. The three former men resided at Bow, and joined us at this island for the purpose before mentioned; the two latter were seamen belonging to the ship. Mic Macabe, with Joseph Atkinson and the two Bow chiefs, were killed: those men had joined us also here. Dafny fired his musket on the plain and then broke it off at the butt in defending himself. He was wounded in several parts of the body, and he had four arrows stuck in his back: the point of a spear had pierced his shoulder, having entered from behind and came out in the fore part under the collar bone.

It fortunately happened that the rock or hill to which we escaped was so steep that few persons could ascend it at a time; and it was too much elevated for the natives to annoy us much with their spears or slings. They however shot several arrows at us, which were impeded by a strong gale of wind that blew them off their intended course. Our chief officer having fallen, I now, as next in rank, took command of the party, and stationed them in the best way I could to defend our post. I did not allow more than one or two muskets to be fired at a time, and kept the wounded man loading for us. Several of the natives ascended the hill to within a few yards, and were shot by us in self-defense as fast as they approached. After some of them had been killed in this manner the rest kept off. Having but little ammunition left, we were as sparing of it as possible; besides which we did not wish to irritate the natives more than they already were by firing, except when driven to it by necessity. From our elevated situation we had a clear view of the landing place, the boats at anchor waiting our return, the two Bow canoes, and the ship. This we had but little prospect of ever again rejoining, though I had some hopes that Captain Robson would make an effort to rescue us, by arming himself, six Indian soldiers that were on board, two or three Europeans, and the Bow people in the canoes. These hopes soon vanished, when I saw the Bow canoes set sail and steer toward their island without passing alongside the ship.

The plain which surrounded the rock was covered with the armed savages assembled from all parts of the coast, amounting to several thousands, who had been in ambush waiting for us to land. This assemblage now exhibited a scene revolting to human nature. Fires were prepared and ovens heated for the reception of the bodies of our ill-fated companions, who, as well as the Bow chiefs and their slaughtered men, were brought to the fires in the following manner.

Two of the Vilear party placed a stick or limb of a tree onto their shoulders, over which were thrown the bodies of their victims, with their legs hanging downward on one side, and their heads at the other. They were thus carried in triumph to the ovens prepared to receive them. Here they were placed in a sitting posture, while the savages sung and danced with joy over their prizes, and fired several musket balls through each of the corpses, all the muskets of the slain having fallen into their hands. No sooner was this ceremony over than the priests began to cut up and dissect these unfortunate men in our presence. Their flesh was immediately placed in the ovens to be baked and prepared as a repast for the victors, after the manner already described; meanwhile we were closely guarded on all sides but one, which fronted the thick mangrove forest on the banks of the river.

Savage proposed to Martin Bushart to run for that, and endeavor to escape to the water's side and swim for the ship. This I opposed, threatening to shoot the first man dead that left the hill, and my threat for the present had the desired effect.

By this time the fury of the savages was somewhat abated, and they began to listen attentively to our harangues and offers of reconciliation. I reminded them that on the day the fourteen canoes were seized and taken, eight of their men had been made prisoners on board the ship, where they were now confined. One of them was the nambety (or high priest) of Vilear's brother. I represented to the multitude that if we were killed, the eight prisoners would be put to death on board; but that if I with my five companions were not sacrificed, we would cause the eight prisoners to be released immediately. The head priest, who is regarded as a deity by these savages, immediately asked if I was speaking truth, and if his brother and the other seven men were alive? I assured him they were, and that I would send a man on board to the captain to order them to be released, if he would convey the man safe down to the boat from among the multitude. This the priest promised to do immediately.

As Thomas Dafny was wounded and had no arms to defend himself, I prevailed on him to venture down the rock with the priest, and thence to the boat. He was then to inform Captain Robson of our horrid situation, which may be more easily imagined than described. I also directed him to tell the captain that it was my particular request that he should release one-half of the prisoners, and show them a large chest of ironmongery, whales' teeth, etc. which he might promise to deliver to the remaining four prisoners with their liberty, the moment we returned to the ship.

This man proceeded as directed, and I did not lose sight of him from the time he left us until he got on the ship's deck. A cessation of arms took place in the meantime, which might have continued unbroken had it not been for the imprudence of Charles Savage, who put a greater temptation in the way of the natives than they could withstand. During this interval several native chiefs ascended the hill, and came within a few paces of us, with protestations of friendship, and proffered us security if we would go down among them. To these promises I would not accede, nor allow any of my men to do so—till Charles Savage, who had resided on the islands for more than five years, and spoke the native dialect fluently, begged of me to permit him to go down among the natives with the chiefs to whom we were speaking, as he had no doubt their promises would be kept, and that if I allowed him to go he would certainly procure a peace, and enable us all to return safe to the ship.

Overcome by his importunities, I at last gave my consent, but reminded him that I did not wish him to do so, and that he must leave his musket and ammunition with me. This he did, and proceeded about two hundred yards from the foot of the rock to where Bonasar was seated, surrounded by chiefs, who were happy to receive him, their secret determination being to kill and eat him. They conversed with him, however, for some time, and then called out to me in the native dialect, "Come down, Peter, we will not hurt you: you see we do not hurt Charley!"

I replied that I would not go down until the prisoners landed. During this discussion the Chinaman, Luis, stole down the opposite side of the hill unknown to me, with his arms, for the purpose of placing himself under the protection of a chief with whom he was intimately acquainted, and to whom he had rendered important service in former wars. The islanders, finding they could not prevail on me to place myself in their power, set up a screech that rent the air. At that moment Charles Savage was seized by the legs, and held in that state by six men, with his head placed in a well of fresh water until he was suffocated; whilst at the same instant a powerful savage got behind the Chinaman, and with his huge club knocked the upper part of his skull to pieces. These wretched men were scarcely lifeless when they were cut up and put into ovens ready prepared for the purpose.

We, the three defenders of the hill, were then furiously attacked on all sides by the cannibals, whom our muskets however kept in great dread, though the chiefs stimulated their men to ascend and bring us down, promising to confer the greatest honors on the man who should kill me, and frequently inquired of their people if they were afraid of three white men, when they had killed several that day. Thus encouraged, they pressed close on us. Having four muskets between three of us, two always remained loaded: for Wilson being a bad shot, we kept him loading the muskets, while Martin Bushart and I fired them off. Bushart had been a rifleman in his own country and was an excellent marksman. He shot twenty-seven of the cannibals with twenty-eight discharges, only missing once: I also killed and wounded a few of them in self-defense. Finding they could not conquer us without a great sacrifice on their part, they kept off and vowed vengeance.

The human bodies being now prepared, they were withdrawn from the ovens and shared out to the different tribes, who devoured them greedily. They frequently invited me to come down and be killed before it was dark, that they might have no trouble in dissecting and baking me in the night. I was bespoken joint by joint by the different chiefs, who exultingly brandished their weapons in the air, and boasted of the number of white men each had killed that day.

In reply to all this I informed them that if I was killed their countrymen confined on board our vessel would be killed also, but that if I was saved they would be saved. The ruthless savages, "Captain Robson may kill and eat our countrymen if he please; we will kill and eat you. When it is dark you cannot see to shoot at us, and you have no more powder."

Myself and companions, seeing no hope of mercy on earth, turned our eyes toward heaven and implored the Almighty Ruler of all things to have compassion on our wretched souls. We had now not the most distant hope of ever escaping from the savages, and expected to be devoured as our companions were but a few minutes before. The only thing which prevented our surrendering quietly was the dread of being taken alive and put to the torture.

These people sometimes, but not very often, torture their prisoners in the following manner. They skin the soles of the feet and then torment their victims with firebrands, so as to make them jump about in that wretched state. At other times they cut off the prisoner's eyelids and turn his face to the sun, at which he is obliged to look with his bare eyes: this is said to be a dreadful punishment. From the fingers of others they pull off the nails. By all accounts, however, these punishments are very rare, and only inflicted on persons who have given the greatest provocation—such as we had done this day, by shooting so many men in our own defense.

Having no more than sixteen or seventeen cartridges left, we determined, as soon as it was dark, to place the muzzles of our muskets to our hearts with the butts on the ground and discharge them into our breasts, thus to avoid the danger of falling alive into the hands of these cannibal monsters.

At this moment the boat put off from the ship and soon got close to the landing place, where we counted the eight prisoners landing from her. I could not imagine how the captain could have acted in this strange way, as the only hope presented of our lives being spared was by allowing a part of the prisoners to land, who would, of course, intercede with their friends on shore to save us, that we might in return protect their countrymen when we returned to the ship. But this precaution not having been attended to, all hope seemed now fled, and the only means of relief left consisted in the dreadful determination of destroying our own lives in the mode already mentioned.

Shortly after the eight prisoners landed, they were conveyed unarmed up the rock to me, preceded by the priest, who informed me that Captain Robson had released the eight men, and sent a chest of cutlery, ironmongery, etc. on shore for the chiefs, with orders that we were to deliver our muskets to them, and that he would see us safe to the boat. I replied that as long as I lived I would not part with my musket, which was my own property, as I was certain they would slaughter me and my companions, as they had done Charles Savage and Luis.

The priest then turned to Martin Bushart and harangued him on the policy of our complying. At this moment the thought entered my head of making the priest a prisoner, and either to destroy him or regain my liberty. I tied Charles Savage's musket with my neck-handkerchief to the belt of my cartridge box, and presenting my own musket to the priest's head, told him that I would shoot him dead if he attempted to run away, or if any of his countrymen offered to molest me or my companions. I then directed him to proceed before me to the boat, threatening him with instant death in case of noncompliance. The priest proceeded as directed, and as we passed along through the multitude, he exhorted them to sit down, and upon no account to molest Peter or his countrymen, because if they attempted to hurt us he would be shot, and they of course must be aware they would consequently incur the wrath of the gods in the clouds, who would be angry at their disobedience of the divine orders, and cause the sea to rise and swallow up the island with all its inhabitants.

The multitude treated their priest's injunctions with profound respect and sat down on the grass. The nambety (which is the term for priest) proceeded as directed toward the boats, with the muzzles of Martin Bushart's and Wilson's muskets at each of his ears, while the muzzle of mine was placed between his shoulders. Finding that night was approaching, and anxious to prolong life, I had recourse to this dreadful expedient, being aware of the influence and sway which the priests in all barbarous nations have over their votaries.

On getting to the boats, the nambety made a sudden stop. I ordered him to proceed. This he refused doing in the most positive manner, declaring that he would go no further and that I might shoot him if I liked. I threatened to do so, and asked him why he would not go to the water's edge? He replied, "You want to take me on board alive and put me to the torture." There being no time to spare, I told him to stand still, and turned my face to him with my musket presented, threatening to shoot him if he attempted to move until I got into the boat. We then walked backward to the waterside, and up to our breasts in water, where we joined the boat, and had no sooner got into her than the islanders came down and saluted us with a shower of arrows and stones from slings.

Being thus once more out of danger, we returned thanks to Divine Providence for our escape, and proceeded toward the ship, which we reached just as the sun was setting. I expostulated with Captain Robson on his extraordinary conduct in causing so many human beings to be unnecessarily sacrificed. He made use of some absurd apologies, and inquired if we were the only persons who had escaped. I replied, yes; but that if the natives could have made proper use of the muskets which fell into their hands on that occasion, we must all have been killed.

KON-TIKI

by Thor Heyerdahl

Whatever the truth of the theory which Thor Heyerdahl set out to prove in 1947, and there are doubts as to its validity, there can be no doubt whatever that this voyage itself is one of the most thrilling and remarkable in man's long story of battle against the sea. The present selection is taken, not from his book, but from a preliminary account which appeared in Natural History. It is fitting that this section, which begins with a selection dealing in part with the ancient Vikings, should close with an article written by a modern Viking who also was noteworthy for both enterprise and valor.

FOREWORD
By the Editors of *Natural History*

Authorities generally agree that the ancestors of the American Indians came from Asia by way of the Aleutian Islands or Bering Strait. The earliest of these people may have come as much as twenty thousand to forty thousand years ago. But up to fifteen hundred years ago the vast island domain of the Central Pacific known as Polynesia apparently remained uninhabited. There seem to have been two migrations into these islands, one perhaps around A.D. 500 and the other around A.D. 1000.

The question of where these Polynesian people came from has long occupied the attention of anthropologists. Obviously they must have come from either Asia or America. Almost all specialists in this field of science have considered it more likely that they came from Asia.

The present article is written by a man who, after several years of study including approximately a year in Polynesia, a year among the Indians of the Northwest Coast, and many months in South America, became convinced that the Polynesians came from the American side of the Pacific. So firmly did certain cultural similarities lead him to this theory that he resolved to duplicate this long voyage from Peru to Polynesia with the same primitive equipment that the Peruvians are known to have had prior to the first European contacts. The present article is the story of this voyage.

Neither the author nor the editor would have felt it within the scope of this article to present or evaluate the various complex arguments bearing on this migration riddle. The author has assembled his own arguments in a sizeable book, and there they will be judged by scholars on their own merit. Here we have opportunity to see, as if at firsthand, the actual problems that would have been met by a group of prehistoric Peruvians if they embarked or were cast adrift on one of their large rafts. As such, the voyage of Mr. Heyerdahl and his five companions provides new information on one of the significant aspects of this question, and it can be considered one of the most enterprising expeditions of recent years.

USUALLY men who have embarked on an ocean raft in modern times have been shipwrecked sailors whose sole desire was to escape the perils of the open sea and reach the nearest coast. But this was not the case in April of last year, when the tugboat *Guardian Rio* towed a clumsy raft away from the sheltered docks of the Peruvian port of Callao and left it adrift well outside the harbor entrance. The six of us that were left aboard the raft were filled with one single hope—that the wind and current would push our primitive craft far away from the South American mainland and right into the wide-open span of the vast Pacific Ocean.

Our purpose was not to flee the Republic of Peru. Leading officials of many nations had bidden us hearty farewell at the dock as the Peruvian Navy tugged us to our point of departure. Nor did we possess any desire to establish a world record in hazardous ocean drift. Yet the betting went high at the docks when we left.

Some claimed that we would be picked up off the coast in a few days or would never be seen again. The nine logs of porous balsa wood upon which we floated were too fragile and would break asunder in the heavy coastal swells, or they would at least be waterlogged and sink underneath us far short of the halfway mark to Polynesia, whose nearest islands lay some four thousand miles from Peru. With a foot and a half of freeboard at the highest section of the bamboo deck, and with an open bamboo hut with thatched roof as our only shelter, we would be at the constant mercy of the waves and the weather and be lost in the first storm.

Others claimed that ropes were no good in the tropic sun and in the sea water and that the complete absence of nails, pegs, and wire in our raft would allow it to tear to pieces as soon as the constant movements of the logs started to chafe the hemp-rope lashings. And if a balsa-wood raft, against all the warnings of the experts, should prove to be seaworthy, it would still not be navigable with its clumsy, square sail and primitive steering oar. How, then, could we possibly expect to hit one of the tiny, farflung islands? The distance ahead was twice the journey of Columbus and the clumsy raft not even comparable.

All these sinister but well-meant warnings were haunting my mind the first night after the last smoke of the tugboat had dissolved behind the horizon. When I was relieved from watch and tried to sleep, I realized how everything was in motion, not so much the pitching and rolling, as the restlessly undulating movement of the bamboo matting on which we lay on top of the great logs. Each time the stern was lifted by the seas, I saw dancing black hills of water, silhouetted against the stars as they chased along both sides of our raft, with whitecaps hissing at us as they passed. I listened to the squeaking and gnawing of a hundred ropes and the splashing and hammering of water everywhere. At regular intervals heavy seas thundered on board astern, but I noticed with comfort how the water, after whirling up to the waists of the two steersmen, instantly dwindled by falling between the open logs or over the sides of the raft. The seas fell in a pit before they could reach the unprotected bamboo hut lashed on deck a few feet from the stern. Therefore, we struggled to hold the stern to the weather and never let the seas in from the sides.

Gradually I felt happy and proud of our peculiar craft. But I could not quite get away from the complaining music of all the light and heavy ropes as everything aboard moved slowly up and down and even sideways as far as the ropes would permit.

What would the future bring us? How would the raft behave after a week, a month, or perhaps a year at sea?

I was not a sailor, and only one of my companions was experienced in handling an ordinary boat at sea. I had not been able, word by word, to answer the pessimistic warnings of naval authorities and other experts before we put out to sea. I was, nevertheless, firmly convinced that our raft could float across the ocean and bring us safely to some distant Polynesian shore. The secret of my stubborn confidence was that I felt certain that this same ocean route had been covered before by prehistoric men on the very same type of craft.

Already in 1937, after leaving the University of Oslo, I had made a zoological-ethnological survey on the lonely Marquesas Islands in the Southeast Pacific. What I found led me to suspect that an influence from early Central or South America had somehow preceded the present Polynesian culture in this area. It is well known that a number of striking similarities in the culture of South America and Polynesia have been noted. These include two of the important cultivated plants—the sweet potato and the bottle gourd—and many cultural features. The theory has therefore frequently been advanced—and again as frequently rejected—that there must have been a prehistoric contact between these two areas.

There can be no possibility of any land bridge having existed in human times, for a comparative study of the animal life of Polynesia proves its hoary isolation. The island people, when first discovered by Europeans, possessed good seagoing canoes, whereas the natives of Peru had only clumsy balsa rafts for their coastal navigation. Because of this, it has usually been assumed by the few who believe there was a cultural transfer that the South American cultures were influenced by the island people rather than vice versa. This view has never been fully accepted and is even doubted by competent scholars of the present day. It is too obvious that some of the Peruvian constructions, artifacts, and food plants in question date from an earlier period in America than A.D. 500, which is commonly accepted, through comparative genealogy, as the approximate date when the first Polynesians spread into the East Pacific.

Thus I had found myself inescapably drawn toward the alternative theory to explain the striking parallels between Peru and Polynesia—namely, that an offshoot from the amazing cultures of early Peru drifted, intentionally or otherwise, into the Pacific.

I was instantly met by one killing argument: How could the Peruvians have covered the thousands of miles of intermediate ocean when their only means of navigation in prehistoric times was an open balsa raft?

To me, there was only one satisfactory answer, and that was to build such a balsa raft and see if it could survive this journey.

I selected five dependable men who volunteered to join me on the experimental voyage. One of them, Herman Watzinger, was a technical engineer, and he directed the building of the balsa raft, guided by detailed accounts and sketches left in the earliest records after the conquest of Peru. First we had to get into the heart of the Ecuadorian jungle to find present-day balsa trees that would match the dimensions of the prehistoric rafts. We cut down nine giant trees, and floated on them down a jungle river to the Pacific coast. With the blessings of the President of Peru and his Naval Minister, the prehistoric type of craft was built in the main naval harbor of Callao under our own supervision.

The nine balsa logs were lashed together side by side with many separate pieces of hemp rope. The bow of the raft took an organ-pipe design, with the longest log in the middle measuring forty-five feet and projecting beyond the others both in the front and in the stern. In the stern it supported a big chunk of balsa holding tholepins for the steering oar. Of the two-foot cross section of these logs, more than half was submerged in the water, but nine smaller crossbeams of light balsa covered with bamboo lifted the highest portion of the deck (including the floor of the open hut upon which we slept) eighteen inches above the sea. The little plaited bamboo hut with thatched roof; two hardwood masts side by side, with a square sail; five centerboards two feet wide and six feet deep, inserted at irregular intervals between the logs; and a long wooden steering oar astern completed our replica of the colorful prehistoric craft.

We named our raft *Kon-Tiki* in honor of the mythical sun king who the Incas claim built the enormous stone constructions near Lake Titicaca before he was defeated in war by local tribes. After the defeat, according to legend, he fled with his light-colored people down to the coast and then westward into the Pacific Ocean, never again to return to Peru. Throughout the Polynesian islands, Tiki is remembered as the mythical hero who was first in the line of aboriginal chiefs to settle the islands and to claim direct descent from the sun. The Peruvian prefix "Kon" means Sun.

The six of us went aboard on April 28 and were left at the mercy of the elements in the old Inca fishing grounds outside the port of Callao. Our ages ranged from twenty-five to thirty-two. Herman Watzinger, second-in-command, was in charge of testing and hydrographic and meteorologic measurements. Erik Hesselberg, an artist, was responsible for plotting our drift. Our radio operators were Knut Haugland and Torstein Raaby, both famous for their sabotage activities during World War II (instrumental, respectively, in the important sabotage of the German Heavy-Water Plant and the battleship *Tirpitz*). Bengt Danielsson, lonely Swede on our Norwegian expedition, was an ethnologist from the University of Upsala who joined us in South America after an expedition in the jungles of Brazil.

Our voyage would carry us through a vast span of ocean that was very little known, since it was outside all the usual shipping lines. We had therefore been requested to make continuous observations and transfer them via the amateur radio network to the United States Weather Bureau. But unless we should use the radio for calling help, it would not alter the primitive conditions of our experiment in any way.

The first weeks at sea were hard. One man was seasick for several days and confined to the hut; consequently, with the ocean breaking over us, two of us at a time constantly had to battle with the clumsy steering oar, trying to hold our stern against the short, racing seas of the Humboldt Current. We were soon caught by the offshore trade winds and were then only able to sail before the wind. We now realized that we had cut all our bridges and that there was no road back to the coast.

We had been at sea only a couple of days when an airplane flew out to bring us a last farewell. We never saw the plane (our horizons were narrowly fenced in with watery hills on all sides), nor did they see us, but we spoke to them for several hours with our little radio.

After the first weeks we came into calmer seas with long, rolling swells. The great blue ocean was dotted with whitecaps, and trade wind clouds drifted across the blue sky. We had soft days with swimming and rest, and we traveled along in comfort. Our drift turned from northwest to west as we left the green and cold Humboldt Current and entered the blue and increasingly warm South Equatorial Current. We made as much progress as seventy-two miles in one day, with a daily average of forty-two miles for the entire voyage. The surface drift exceeded the current drift and occasionally blew us out of the main sweep of the central current.

We found little wearing on the ropes and learned the reason why. The balsa was too soft to chafe them. In case of friction, a rope would soon work itself into the waterlogged surface of the balsa logs and thus remain protected. It was more discomforting to observe that splinters cut from the surface of the logs had become waterlogged and sank when thrown overboard. It had been common opinion in Peru that the logs would be completely submerged before we sighted the islands.

Archaeologists no longer doubt that the prehistoric Peruvians used sails. Not only are there good historical descriptions of rafts equipped with sails, but centerboards of late pre-European date have been found. Our testings with centerboards clearly proved that they are useless on a raft if it is merely paddled or carried along by the current.

The first real excitement we ran into after entering the South Equatorial Current was the largest monster of the seas—the rare but famous whale shark. Accompanied by a shoal of pilot fish, this giant among all fishes slowly caught up with us from astern, and the water splashed around its enormous, white-speckled back as though on a small reef. The fish bumped into the steering oar and placed its huge, frog-like head, with tiny eyes and a five-foot mouth, right up against the raft. The whale shark has been measured to a length of forty-five feet and undoubtely grows larger. We would never have dared such an estimate, but while the head appeared on one side of the raft, the tail simultaneously appeared on the other.

The whale shark kept us company for several hours, and the excitement on board was great, with everybody prepared with spears, hand harpoons, and motion picture camera. The peaceful visit ended when the excited navigator ran his harpoon with all his strength down between his legs and into the cartilaginous head of the monster. During the terrific commotion the whale shark dived, broke the harpoon, snapped the rope, and disappeared.

Only at one other time were we visited by what we suspected to be whale sharks. It was during a fairly calm night when three immensely large and phosphorescent bodies swam in circles under us. But occasionally we ran into schools of whales. The huge, snorting animals rolled right up beside us without the slightest fear. They could have splintered our raft with a single blow of their mighty tails, but after an exhibition of their swimming ability, they left us behind.

Some six hundred miles southwest of the Galápagos we were twice visited by giant sea turtles. One was under constant attack by a dozen furious dolphins which tried to snap at the turtle's neck and fins. After sighting the raft, the turtle made its way right up to our side but swam away as soon as it saw us. Three of our men, equipped with rope, pursued the turtle in a tiny, inflatable rubber float, but our visitor escaped while the bewildered dolphins concentrated all their attention on the bouncing little float.

Weather permitting, we often got into our rubber float, two or three at a time, and took a "vacation" from our sturdy log raft to study our craft from a distance. We could imagine the sight that early Peruvian seafarers must have had when they sailed their flotillas of rafts side by side along the coast—or into the ocean like Inca Tupac Yupanqui, who according to legend discovered some East Pacific islands before the Spanish Conquest. Particularly at night, we experienced an unforgettable sight. Night-black seas, billowing on all sides, and twinkling stars formed our entire world.

The year 1947—A.D. or B.C.—what did it mean? We were at least alive. Time had little meaning; we were lost in the endless dark. Ahead of us *Kon-Tiki* rose and then sank between the seas. In moonlight there was an unbelievable atmosphere around the raft. The huge, wet logs fringed with seaweed, the square contour of the sail, the bushy jungle hut with a petrol lamp astern looked like something cut from a fairy tale rather than from reality . . . Now and then the raft would disappear entirely behind the black sea; then, with water pouring from the logs, it would rise high to be silhouetted against the stars.

Although we spent 101 days and nights drifting on our raft, we never sighted a ship or any floating debris left by mankind. If a ship had crossed our path during an average day at sea, it would have found us slowly dancing up and down over great rolling swells dotted with minor waves that were stirred up by the trade winds, which constantly blow from the New World into the island domain. A tanned and bearded man, devoid of clothing, would have been sighted at the stern of the raft, either desperately struggling with the ropes of a long steering oar or, if the wind were steady, sitting and dozing in the sun. Bengt would be found on his stomach in the doorway of the hut reading one of his seventy-three sociological books. Herman would be seen busily occupied anywhere, at the top of the mast, underneath the logs, or running around with instruments to measure wind and water. Knut and Torstein were always struggling with the weather-beaten radio sets, repairing damage and sending out reports at night to the amateur stations that could hear our signals. Erik was always mending sail and splicing rope and sketching fishes and bearded men alike. And each noon he grabbed his sextant and gazed at the sun to determine how far we had moved since the day before. As to myself, I was writing logs, collecting plankton for food experimentation, and fishing or filming.

The day started with a glorious sunrise over the sea, the cook being relieved by the last night watchman to collect the flying fish that had flown on board during the night. These were fried on a small primus stove and devoured at the edge of the raft after a quick morning dip in the sea. Extra flying fish were used as bait for the great colorful dolphin fish that followed the raft day in and day out across the ocean. Dolphins that we did not eat were used as bait for the great sharks that calmly swam around us day and night. When the sea was high, we could see them sideways as though through a perpendicular glass wall raised high above the level of the raft. Then the raft tipped up and let the water and the slowly moving sharks pass beneath us. They never seemed treacherous except when we cleaned fish, and they scented blood. Then they would wake up in a fury. Yet we never quite trusted them, and in one day we pulled aboard nine six- to ten-foot sharks just to dispose of their intimate company.

When we slid the sharks up onto our shallow and slippery logs, the remoras, clinging to the sharks' skin by suction, would jump off and attach themselves to the side of the raft; and the pilot fish, having lost their king and master, would find a substitute in *Kon-Tiki*, joining us in nice formation before the bow or between the centerboards. If a big blue shark passed, they would occasionally follow him away, but more than forty of them tailed us right across the ocean until our raft was shattered on the reef.

Although we carried our rations lashed to the logs beneath the bamboo deck, it was still of great importance to me to find out whether primitive man, accustomed to hardship as he was, would have been able to renew his supply of food and water on such a long-lasting drift. The answer was affirmative. After the fourth day at sea, there was not a single day throughout the journey when we were not accompanied by numbers of dolphin fish. They kept to the side of the raft or beneath us and could be fished, speared, or hooked whenever we desired. Edible barnacles and seaweeds grew all over the huge logs and could be picked like garden greens. And they often housed tiny, edible pelagic crabs or very small fishes. A dozen or more flying fish, often accompanied by baby squids, came aboard almost every night, sailing through the air in schools right above the surface if pursued by dolphins or sharks. Twice in mid-ocean on dark nights, a long snakelike fish with huge eyes and carnivorous jaws jumped right into our sleeping bags inside the bamboo hut and caused a great commotion. It was probably the *Gempylus,* which was seen this way by man for the first time, only a couple of skeletons having previously been found on South American shores. Soaked shark meat, delicious bonito, and yellow-fin tuna completed our seafood menu and made it clear enough that early, hardy raftsmen were not menaced by hunger.

We carried two hundred coconuts and samples of the Peruvian sweet potato and gourd, which were important food plants that the aborigines of Peru shared with those of Polynesia. Those not eaten en route were successfully planted upon our arrival on the islands, to prove that they could be carried on a raft without loss of germinating power. These prehistoric food plants could never have drifted across the ocean without the aid and care of human hands, and the aboriginal name for sweet potato was *Kumara*—both in Peru and on the Polynesian islands.

The early raftsmen along the dry South American coast carried their water supply in gourds or pottery containers and in huge canes of bamboo with the joints pierced out. Left in the shade underneath the bamboo deck, where they were constantly washed by the seas, we found that our plain Peruvian spring water was preserved for more than two months before the first samples began to rot. At that time we had already entered a part of the ocean where drizzles were frequent and rains occasional, and we were able to collect sufficient rain water for our daily needs. We consumed a ton of water on the journey, along with more than ample rations, and the buoyancy of the balsa logs would have permitted us to double our water supply in easily stored bamboo canes under the deck. With the warm climate creating a demand for salt, we could mix up to 40 per cent of sea water with our drinking water without evil effects. Like our early predecessors and many sailors shipwrecked during the war, we found several simple methods of abstracting the thirst-quenching juice from raw fish, a supply that never ran short.

In this way, with the days full of testings and practical experiments, we found ourselves carried across the ocean bit by bit. By the forty-fifth day we had drifted from the seventy-eighth meridian to the one hundred-eighth and were exactly halfway to the first islands. During those days we were more than two thousand miles away from the nearest shore in any direction. When the ocean was smoothly rolling, we could leave our raft in the little float and row away into the blue space between eternal sea and sky. As we watched our grotesque craft growing smaller and smaller in the distance, an oppressive sense of loneliness came over us. It was as though we were suspended in space, like disembodied spirits. When we rowed back to our distant raft, we felt a strange feeling of relief and were happy to crawl on board our precious, weather-beaten logs and find shade from the glaring sun inside the bamboo hut. The now familiar scent of bamboo and thatched roof made us feel that we were back in our earthly home again, inside a jungle dwelling that was far away from the limitless sea.

We enjoyed our evening meals as the glorious sun sank into the sea before our bow, while sky and water became a dream of colors. Small, striped pilot fish would rush to the surface to snap at our crumbs, and they were occasionally followed by a lazy shark, like kittens by a bulldog.

As darkness came we would light our petrol lamp, and Erik would fetch his guitar. Then merry song and music from the raft spread with the dim light over the nearest waves of a trackless, endless ocean. We would soon roll up on the bamboo matting inside the hut, leaving the watchman alone with the stars and the steering oar.

We hit two storms when we approached the end of the journey. The first lasted one day and the second five. With sail down and ropes shrieking, *Kon-Tiki* rode the breaking ocean like a duck. A raft in high seas with wet and slippery logs and no railing requires careful stepping. The second storm had just begun when Herman went overboard. When visible again, he was seen struggling behind the stern. He struck for the blade of the steering oar, but a strong wind pushed us ahead, and he missed. We could not turn our raft around to go back a single inch. There was no possibility of even stopping our stubborn craft in its reckless trek to the west. The airy float would blow like a feather ahead of the raft if put to sea in such a wind. We threw out a life belt, once, twice, but it blew right back on board. We became desperate as Herman, our best swimmer, was left farther and farther behind. With a line in one hand Knut leaped into the sea, and slowly the two friends worked their way toward each other. Thirty yards behind the raft they joined hands, and the four of us on board pulled them in.

We had a green parrot as ship's pet. It was a perfect sailor and a joyous companion, until a big sea stole it on the sixtieth day.

At the end of the third month, we were constantly visited by Polynesian frigate birds and boobies in increasing numbers. Then we sighted a rising cumulo-nimbus cloud, revealing the existence of some hidden, sun-baked isle beneath the western horizon. We steered for the cloud as best we could, and as the golden sun rose from the sea on the ninety-third day, the blue haze of land was outlined against a reddish sky. We were passing the tiny atoll of Pukapuka, but wind and current would not permit us to turn around. We had covered four thousand miles of ocean heading west, and yet we could not force ourselves four miles to the east to reach the island. More than ever was this a plain and unmistakable lesson, stressing the fact that in this ocean a drifting craft and a natural migration would inevitably be pushed to the west. And it was with strange feelings that we sat quietly down on our raft and saw the little, solid speck of land—the first and only for twelve weeks—slide away on our port stern. For a moment the wind carried a mild whiff of verdant tropical foliage and smoky native household odors, and we filled our salty lungs before the fata morgana—the mirage of our hopes—sank into the sea.

On the ninety-seventh day another island grew up out of the ocean, straight ahead of us in line with the bow. As we approached, we saw from the top of the mast that a roaring reef was twisted like a submerged snake all around the island, blocking the approach to the palm-clad beaches behind. All day long we struggled in the current alongside the island to keep clear of the boiling reef and yet be close enough to attempt a landfall wherever an opening might be seen.

Late in the afternoon we sighted the first natives on a beach, and we hoisted all our flags in joy. A great commotion was seen on the beach, and shortly after, the first Polynesians in small outrigger canoes slid through a passage in the reef and swarmed aboard the *Kon-Tiki*. A strong wind blew up, and our ocean raft struggled away from land as the sun went down in the sea. There was a desperate fight against the elements, in which we were assisted by all the friendly natives who were able to get out and join us in the open sea. As the dark night engulfed the island and the sea, a great campfire was lit on shore to show us the direction of the entrance through the reef. But the wind increased its grip, and won another battle. When the glare of the great fire dwindled like a spark in the distance and the roar of the reef was no longer heard, our excited native friends jumped into their canoes to return to their homes on Angatau for fear of drifting with some crazy strangers into the open sea. And we drifted farther into the heart of the Tuamotu, or Dangerous Archipelago.

One night an unusual motion of the raft awakened me, and I suspected land ahead. Next morning, our one hundred-first at sea, we were alarmed by the watchman on the top of the mast, who had sighted an enormous reef that spanned the entire horizon ahead of us. It was the treacherous twenty-mile reef of Raroia Atoll. With white spray shooting high into the air, the surf battered the endless reef in fury.

As we rode directly into this boiling inferno, we had three hours to prepare for all eventualities. We lowered the sail and threw out an improvised anchor on a long rope that kept sliding along the bottom. We carried valuable cargo into the hut and lashed it fast in watertight bags. We cut off all ropes holding the centerboards in position and pulled them up to get a shallow draft. With shoes on for the first time in one hundred days, we concentrated on the last order: Hang on—hang onto the raft whatever happens!

The first walls of thundering water broke down upon us from above as soon as our logs ran against the solid coral reef. Tons of crashing water tore up the deck, flattened the hut, broke the hardwood mast like a match, and splintered the steering oar and stern crossbeam, while we were thrown in and dragged out, thrown in and dragged out, by the furious ocean. During these minutes, when we cramped every existing muscle to withhold the deadly grasp of the passing seas, we made up for all the leisure of the average ocean day. I felt the last of my strength giving away when a wave larger than the others lifted *Kon-Tiki* free of the water and tossed us high up on the reef. Other waves pushed us closer to shore, until we could jump off the raft and wade the shallow coral reef to a tiny, uninhabited coconut island. Never did any tiny piece of land embody paradise so perfectly to me as this verdant, palm-clad isle with its white and shiny beach facing a crystal-clear lagoon, calm as green glass.

A week later we were found by natives who had detected from another island six miles across the lagoon the drift wreckage and the light from our campfire. And about the same time *Kon-Tiki* was carried by high seas right across the solid reef and left becalmed inside the lagoon. The nine main logs that had carried us 4,300 miles across the ocean in 101 days were still intact, and after an unforgettable two-week Polynesian welcome party on lonely Raroia, our battered raft was towed to Tahiti by the French Government schooner *Tamara*, which was sent expressly to pick us up.

We shall never forget the welcome on these Polynesian islands.

From Tahiti the *Kon-Tiki* was carried as deck cargo back to the Norwegian Museum of Navigation in Oslo.

Part Three

LAKES
AND
RIVERS,
PLAINS
AND
JUNGLES

HERODOTUS—THE FIRST SIGHT-SEER

by Edith Hamilton

Why do men explore? Sometimes it is out of sheer curiosity, and a desire to see wonders hitherto unknown. It was such an urge that led Herodotus, the "Father of History," to go out to see the world. In the first of the next two selections, Edith Hamilton, authority on the Greek and Roman Way, tells us something of the man; in the second Herodotus himself relates, in an astonishingly modern manner and spirit, his observations of the peoples of the ancient world which led him to divide the lands around the Mediterranean into the continents of Europe, Asia and Africa. Over a century after Herodotus, Alexander the Great crossed the Persian Empire and reached the Punjab in India. He explored the Indus and sailed on the Indian Ocean. Alexander's primary object was conquest; yet his great explorations revolutionized the Greek outlook on the world and led to that new age, foreseen by Herodotus when he saw that the theory of the earth as a flat, circular disc was false, and the limits of the world must extend far beyond the lands then known.

SOCRATES, when the young Theætetus was introduced to him as a lad of brilliant promise, said to him that he felt sure he had thought a great deal. The boy answered, Oh, no—not that, but at least he had wondered a great deal. "Ah, that shows the lover of wisdom," Socrates said, "for wisdom begins in wonder."

There have been few men ever who wondered more than Herodotus did. The word is perpetually on his pen: "A wonder was told me"; "In that land there are ten thousand wonders"; "Wonderful deeds, those"; "It is a thing to be wondered at." In this disposition he was the true child of his age—the great age of Greece.

Herodotus, spiritually an Athenian although a native of Halicarnassus, summed up in himself the vigor of his times. He set out to travel over the earth as far as a man could go. What strength of will and also of body that called for under the traveling conditions of the day, it is impossible for us to realize. The first part of St. Paul's journey to Rome gives a picture of the hazards that had to be faced at sea four hundred years after Herodotus, and a companion picture for the land is Xenophon's description of the endless miles on foot or horseback through the burning wastes of Asia Minor to Babylon. It required a hungering and thirsting for knowledge and all the explorer's zest to send a man on the travels Herodotus undertook; undertook, too, with keen enjoyment. He was the first sight-seer in the world, and there has never been a happier one. If he could see something new, discomforts and difficulties and dangers were nothing to him. He seems never to have noticed them. He never wrote about them. He filled his book with the marvels to rejoice a man's heart—marvels of which the great earth was full. Oh, wonder that there were such goodly creatures in it!

Just how far he traveled is hard to say. What he heard he gives with as great interest as what he saw, and he is so objective, so absorbed in whatever he is describing, he generally leaves himself out. But he certainly went as far east as Persia and as far west as Italy. He knew the coast of the Black Sea and had been in Arabia. In Egypt he went up the Nile to Aswan. It seems probable that he went to Cyrene; his descriptions often read like those of any eyewitness. That is less true of Libya and Sicily, but it is quite possible that he had been in both countries. In fact, his journeys practically reached to the boundaries of the known world, and the information he gathered reached far beyond. He knew a good deal about India. For instance, there were wild trees that bore wool, superior in whiteness and quality to sheep's wool. The Indians made beautiful fine clothing from it. With India his information about the East stopped. He had heard a report of great deserts on the further side, but that was all. Of the West he writes:

I am unable to speak with certainty. I can learn nothing about the islands from which our tin comes, and though I have asked everywhere I have met no one who has seen a sea on the west side of Europe. The truth is no one has discovered if Europe is surrounded by water or not.

I smile at those who with no sure knowledge to guide them describe the ocean flowing around a perfectly circular earth.

This is an example of the way the Greek mind worked. The great river Ocean encircling the earth had been described by Homer, the revered, even sacred, authority, and by Hesiod, second only to Homer, and yet Herodotus with never a qualm at possible impiety permits himself a smile. Everything everywhere in the world of men was of interest to him. He tells us how the homely girls in Illyria get husbands, how the lake dwellers keep their children from falling into the water, what Egyptian mosquito nets are like, that the King of Persia when traveling drinks only boiled water, what the Adrymachidæ do to fleas, how the Arabians cut their hair, that the Danube islanders get drunk on smells, how the Scythians milk their mares, that in Libya the woman with the most lovers is honored, how the streets of Babylon are laid out, that physicians in Egypt specialize in diseases, and so on, and so on. Bits of information that have nothing to do with what he is writing about keep straying in; but he is so intensely interested in them himself, the reader's interest is caught too. Is not that really extraordinary? he says to us—or extremely diverting—or remarkably sensible? And we follow him; we are surprised and diverted and approving. Of course this is only to say that he has the *sine qua non* of a writer— he is never dull; but to avoid dullness in what is often a guidebook is an achievement. Some part of it is due to his perfect, his unsurpassed, ease in writing. He has no mannerisms, not a particle of self-consciousness; he is always simple, direct, and lucid, alway easy to read. His countryman, Dionysius of Halicarnassus, said he was the first to give Greece the idea that an expression in prose could have the worth of a verse of poetry.

He is often accused of being credulous even to the point of silliness. It is said that he accepted with the naïve simplicity of a child everything he was told, no matter how preposterous. There is no truth whatsoever in the charge. Precisely the contrary is true: his turn of mind was skeptical; he was a born investigator. The word "history," which was first used in our sense by him, means "investigation" in Greek. His book begins, "This is an account of the investigations [historia] made by Herodotus of Halicarnassus." He started on them prepared to scrutinize everything he heard. When different and equally probable accounts of an event were given him he wrote them all down and left the final judgment to his reader. "I cannot positively state whether this was done or that," he will say. "For myself," he remarks in a notable passage, "my duty is to report all that is said, but I am not obliged to believe it all—a remark which applies to my whole History."

Even these few quotations show the temper of his mind, his sense of responsibility as a reporter, and his care in weighing evidence. But of course in his day the unknown was so great, what was actually known was so limited, no borderline had yet been drawn between the credible and the incredible. It is often impossible to make out why Herodotus accepts one thing and rejects another purely on the ground of what can and cannot happen. Doves, he says firmly, do not ever speak even though the holy women at Dodona declare that they do, but he does not question the story that a mare gave birth to a rabbit. He is sure that no matter what the Egyptian priests assert, it is not true that the phoenix wraps up the dead body of his parent in a mass of myrrh and carries it from Arabia to the Temple of the Sun in Heliopolis where he buries it. On the other hand it seems to him quite reasonable that there are headless creatures in Libya with eyes in their breasts, and that cats in Egypt have the singular habit of jumping into the fire. He had a standard of what was possible and what was not, but it was so different from ours it escapes us. After all, wherever he went he saw so many strange things, it was easy to believe there were even stranger ones in the vast beyond.

But when he was on ground he knew he was a shrewd judge of the improbable. He writes:

> In the highest tower in Babylon, in the topmost chamber, there is a great couch on which the god himself is reported to sleep. So the priests told me, but I do not believe it.
>
> I cannot say with confidence how the man escaped, for the account given me made me wonder. They say he jumped into the sea and swam eighty stadia under water, never rising to the top. If I may give my own opinion, it is that he got off in a boat.

But he is always mildly tolerant of other people's explanations and never dogmatic about his own. Of the storm that wrecked Xerxes' fleet he writes:

> It lasted three days. At length the Magi charming the wind and sacrificing to the Nereids succeeded in laying the tempest—or perhaps it ceased of itself.

When he was sight-seeing in Thessaly he was told that a famous gorge he visited was caused by Neptune, and he remarks:

> It seemed plain to me that it was the result of an earthquake. Many people think earthquakes are the work of Neptune.

The last part of the History has to do with the Persian Wars. Two-thirds of the book are taken up with Herodotus' journeys and what he learned on them. These earlier chapters have the effect, more and more as one reads on, of a slowly unrolling stage setting. The whole of the known world is presented as the fitting background to the tremendous conflict that is to decide whether freedom or tyranny is the stronger, whether the West is to be enslaved by the East. Darius, the Great King, makes his appearance. He is ruler of most of the world. Myriads of men serve him; his wealth is limitless; his magnificence fabulous; his cruelty fantastic. He is the Orient in person, its barbaric pearl and gold, its helpless millions, its disregard for human life and suffering. Over against him stands Greece, "a rocky land and poor," a speaker in Herodotus tells Darius, where, as Pericles puts it, the people "love beauty with economy"; economy, the very opposite to the lavishness and exaggeration of the grandiose East.

Herodotus describes the amused astonishment of the Persian Army at learning that the prize for an Olympic victory was a crown of wild olives. He tells about a pillar he saw, one of the many the Great King set up to mark his approbation when he passed a place that pleased him. It was inscribed: "These springs are the best and most beautiful of waters. They were visited by Darius, the best and most beautiful of men." By sheer force of contrast the words recall the epitaph on the dead at Thermopylæ: "Stranger, tell the Spartans that we lie here in obedience to their words."

WONDERS OF THE ANCIENT WORLD

by Herodotus

T HE Persians offer sacrifice in the following manner: they raise no altar, light no fire, pour no libations; there is no sound of the flute, no putting on of chaplets, no consecrated barley cake; but the man who wishes to sacrifice brings his victim to a spot of ground which is pure from pollution, and there calls upon the name of the god to whom he intends to offer. It is usual to have the turban encircled with a wreath, most commonly of myrtle. The sacrificer is not allowed to pray for blessings on himself alone, but he prays for the welfare of the king, and of the whole Persian people, among whom he is of necessity included. He cuts the victim

From *The History of Herodotus*, translated by Sir Henry Rawlinson.

in pieces, and having boiled the flesh, he lays it out upon the tenderest herbage that he can find, trefoil especially. When all is ready, one of the Magi comes forward and chants a hymn, which they say recounts the origin of the gods. It is not lawful to offer sacrifice unless there is a Magus present. After waiting a short time the sacrificer carries the flesh of the victim away with him, and makes whatever use of it he may please.

Of all the days in the year, the one which they celebrate most is their birthday. It is customary to have the board furnished on that day with an ampler supply than common. The richer Persians cause an ox, a horse, a camel, and an ass to be baked whole and so served up to them: the poorer classes use instead the smaller kinds of cattle. They eat little solid food but abundance of dessert, which is set on table a few dishes at a time; this it is which makes them say that "the Greeks, when they eat, leave off hungry, having nothing worth mention served up to them after the meats; whereas, if they had more put before them, they would not stop eating." They are very fond of wine, and drink it in large quantities. To vomit or obey natural calls in the presence of another, is forbidden among them. Such are their customs in these matters.

It is also their general practice to deliberate upon affairs of weight when they are drunk; and then on the morrow, when they are sober, the decision to which they came the night before is put before them by the master of the house in which it was made; and if it is then approved of, they act on it; if not, they set it aside. Sometimes, however, they are sober at their first deliberation, but in this case they always reconsider the matter under the influence of wine.

Next to prowess in arms, it is regarded as the greatest proof of manly excellence, to be the father of many sons. Every year the king sends rich gifts to the man who can show the largest number: for they hold that number is strength. Their sons are carefully instructed from their fifth to their twentieth year, in three things alone—to ride, to draw the bow, and to speak the truth. Until their fifth year they are not allowed to come into the sight of their father, but pass their lives with the women. This is done that, if the child die young, the father may not be afflicted by its loss.

The Persians maintain that never yet did anyone kill his own father or mother; but in all such cases they are quite sure that, if matters were sifted to the bottom, it would be found that the child was either a changeling or else the fruit of adultery; for it is not likely they say that the real father should perish by the hands of his child.

Thus much I can declare of the Persians with entire certainty, from my own actual knowledge. There is another custom which is spoken of with reserve, and not openly, concerning their dead. It is said that the body of a male Persian is never buried, until it has been torn either by a dog or a bird of prey. That the Magi have this custom is beyond a doubt, for they practice it without any concealment. The dead bodies are covered with wax, and then buried in the ground.

Concerning Egypt, there is no country that possesses so many wonders, nor any that has such a number of works which defy description. Not only is the climate different from that of the rest of the world, and the rivers unlike any other rivers, but the people also, in most of their manners and customs, exactly reverse the common practice of mankind. The women attend the markets and trade, while the men sit at home at the loom; and here, while the rest of the world works the woof up the warp, the Egyptians work it down; the women likewise carry burthens upon their shoulders, while the men carry them upon their heads. They eat their food out of doors in the streets, but retire for private purposes to their houses, giving as a reason that what is unseemly, but necessary, ought to be done in secret, but what has nothing unseemly about it, should be done openly. A woman cannot serve the priestly office, either for god or goddess, but men are priests to both; sons need not support their parents unless they choose, but daughters must, whether they choose or no.

In other countries the priests have long hair, in Egypt their heads are shaven; elsewhere it is customary, in mourning, for near relations to cut their hair close: the Egyptians, who wear no hair at any other time, when they lose a relative, let their beards and the hair of their heads grow long. All other men pass their lives separate from animals, the Egyptians have animals always living with them; others make barley and wheat their food; it is a disgrace to do so in Egypt, where the grain they live on is spelt, which some call *zea*. Dough they knead with their feet; but they mix mud, and even take up dirt, with their hands. They are the only people in the world— they at least, and such as have learnt the practice from them—who use circumcision. Their men wear two garments apiece, their women but one. They put on the rings and fasten the ropes to sails inside; others put them outside. When they write or calculate, instead of going, like the Greeks, from left to right, they move their hand from right to left; and they insist, notwithstanding, that it is they who go to the right, and the Greeks who go to the left. They have two quite different kinds of writing, one of which is called sacred, the other common.

They are religious to excess, far beyond any other race of men, and use the following ceremonies: They drink out of brazen cups, which they scour every day: there is no exception to this practice. They wear linen garments, which they are specially careful to have always fresh washed. They practice circumcision for the sake of cleanliness, considering it better to be cleanly than comely. The priests shave their whole body every other day, that no lice or other impure thing may adhere to them when they are engaged in the service of the gods. Their dress is entirely of linen, and their shoes of the papyrus plant: it is not lawful for them to wear either dress or shoes of any other material. They bathe twice every day in cold water, and twice each night; besides which they observe, so to speak, thousands of ceremonies.

The following is their manner of sacrifice: They lead the victim, marked with their signet, to the altar where they are about to offer it, and setting the wood alight, pour a libation of wine upon the altar in front of the victim, and at the same time invoke the god. Then they slay the animal, and cutting off his head, proceed to flay the body. Next they take the head, and heaping imprecations on it, if there is a market place and a body of Greek traders in the city, they carry it there and sell it instantly; if, however, there are no Greeks among them, they throw the head into the river. The imprecation is to this effect: They pray that if any evil is impending either over those who sacrifice, or over universal Egypt, it may be made to fall upon that head. These practices, the imprecations upon the heads, and the libations of wine, prevail all over Egypt, and extend to victims of all sorts; and hence the Egyptians will never eat the head of any animal.

The disemboweling and burning are, however, different in different sacrifices. I will mention the mode in use with respect to the goddess whom they regard as the greatest, and honor with the chiefest festival. When they have flayed their steer they pray, and when their prayer is ended they take the paunch of the animal out entire, leaving the intestines and the fat inside the body; they then cut off the legs, the ends of the loins, the shoulders, and the neck; and having so done, they fill the body of the steer with clean bread, honey, raisins, figs, frankincense, myrrh, and other aromatics. Thus, filled, they burn the body, pouring over it great quantities of oil. Before offering the sacrifice they fast, and while the bodies of the victims are being consumed they beat themselves. Afterward, when they have concluded this part of the ceremony, they have the other parts of the victim served up to them for a repast.

The way in which the Indians get the plentiful supply of gold, which enables them to furnish year by year so vast an amount of gold dust to the king, is the following: Eastward of India lies a tract which is entirely sand. Indeed of all the inhabitants of Asia, concerning whom anything certain is known, the Indians dwell the nearest to the east, and the rising of the sun. Beyond them the whole country is desert on account of the sand. The tribes of Indians are numerous, and do not all speak the same language—some are wandering tribes, others not. They who dwell in the marshes along the river live on raw fish, which they take in boats made of reeds, each formed out of a single joint. These Indians wear a dress of sedge, which they cut in the river and bruise; afterward they weave it into mats, and wear it as we wear a breast plate.

Eastward of these Indians are another tribe, called Padæans, who are wanderers, and live on raw flesh. This tribe is said to have the following customs: If one of their number be ill, man or woman, they take the sick person, and if he be a man, the men of his acquaintance proceed to put him to death, because, they say, his flesh would be spoilt for them if he pined and wasted away with sickness. The man protests he is not ill in the least; but his friends will not accept his denial—in spite of all he can say, they kill him, and feast themselves on his body. So also if a women be sick, the women, who are her friends, take her and do with her exactly the same as the men. If one of them reaches to old age, about which there is seldom any question, as commonly before that time they have had some disease or other, and so have been put to death—but if a man, notwithstanding, comes to be old, then they offer him in sacrifice to their gods, and afterward eat his flesh.

There is another set of Indians whose customs are very different. They refuse to put any live animal to death, they sow no corn, and have no dwelling houses. Vegetables are their only food. There is a plant which grows wild in their country, bearing seed, about the size of millet seed, in a calyx: their wont is to gather this seed and having boiled it, calyx and all, to use it for food. If one of them is attacked with sickness, he goes forth into the wilderness, and lies down to die; no one has the least concern either for the sick or for the dead.

Besides these, there are Indians of another tribe, who border on the city of Caspatyrus, and the country of Pactyïca; these people dwell northward of all the rest of the Indians, and follow nearly the same mode of life as the Bactrians. They are more warlike than any of the other tribes, and from them the men are sent forth who go to procure the gold. For it is in this part of India that the sandy desert lies. Here, in this desert, there live amid the sand great ants, in size somewhat less than dogs, but bigger than foxes. The Persian king has a number of them, which have been caught by the hunters in the land whereof we are speaking. Those ants make their dwellings under ground, and like the Greek ants, which they very much resemble in shape, throw up sand heaps as they burrow. Now the sand which they throw up is full of gold. The Indians, when they go into the desert to collect this sand, take three camels and harness them together, a female in the middle and a male on either side, in a leading rein. The rider sits on the female, and they are particular to choose for the purpose one that has but just dropped her young; for their female camels can run as fast as horses, while they bear burthens very much better.

As the Greeks are well acquainted with the shape of the camel, I shall not trouble to describe it; but I shall mention what seems to have escaped their notice. The camel has in its hind legs four thigh bones and four knee joints.

When the Indians therefore have thus equipped themselves they set off in quest of the gold, calculating the time so that they may be engaged in seizing it during the most sultry part of the day, when the ants hide themselves to escape the heat.

When the Indians reach the place where the gold is, they fill their bags with the sand, and ride away at their best speed: the ants, however, scenting them, as the Persians say, rush forth in pursuit. Now these animals are, they declare, so swift, that there is nothing in the world like them: if it were not, therefore, that the Indians get a start while the ants are mustering, not a single gold gatherer could escape. During the flight the male camels, which are not so fleet as the females, grow tired, and begin to drag, first one, and then the other; but the females recollect the young which they have left behind, and never give way or flag. Such, according to the Persians, is the manner in which the Indians get the greater part of their gold; some is dug out of the earth, but of this the supply is more scanty.

Arabia is the last of inhabited lands toward the south, and it is the only country which produces frankincense, myrrh, cassia, cinnamon, and ladanum. The Arabians do not get any of these, except the myrrh, without trouble. The frankincense they procure by means of the gum styrax, which the Greeks obtain from the Phœnicians; this they burn, and thereby obtain the spice. For the trees which bear the frankincense are guarded by winged serpents, small in size, and of varied colors, whereof vast numbers hang about every tree. They are of the same kind as the serpents that invade

Egypt; and there is nothing but the smoke of the styrax which will drive them from the trees.

The Arabians say that the whole world would swarm with these serpents, if they were not kept in check in the way in which I know that vipers are. Of a truth Divine Providence does appear to be, as indeed one might expect beforehand, a wise contriver. For timid animals which are a prey to others are all made to produce young abundantly, that so the species may not be entirely eaten up and lost; while savage and noxious creatures are made very unfruitful. The hare, for instance, which is hunted alike by beasts, birds, and men breeds so abundantly as even to superfetate, a thing which is true of no other animal. You find in a hares belly, at one and the same time, some of the young all covered with fur, others quite naked, others again just fully formed in the womb, while the hare perhaps has lately conceived afresh. The lioness, on the other hand, which is one of the strongest and boldest of brutes, brings forth young but once in her lifetime, and then a single cub; she cannot possibly conceive again, since she loses her womb at the same time that she drops her young. The reason of this is, that as soon as the cub begins to stir inside the dam, his claws, which are sharper than those of any other animal, scratch the womb; as the time goes on, and he grows bigger, he tears it ever more and more; so that at last, when the birth comes, there is not a morsel in the whole womb that is sound.

Now with respect to the vipers and the winged snakes of Arabia, if they increased as fast as their nature would allow, impossible were it for man to maintain himself upon the earth. Accordingly it is found that when the male and female come together, at the very moment of impregnation, the female seizes the male by the neck, and having once fastened, cannot be brought to leave go till she has bit the neck entirely through. And so the male perishes; but after a while he is revenged upon the female by means of the young, which, while still unborn, gnaw a passage through the womb, and then through the belly of their mother, and so make their entrance into the world. Contrariwise, other snakes, which are harmless, lay eggs, and hatch a vast number of young. Vipers are found in all parts of the world, but the winged serpents are nowhere seen except in Arabia, where they are all congregated together. This makes them appear so numerous.

Wonderful is the mode in which they collect the cinnamon. Where the wood grows, and what country produces it, they cannot tell—only some, following probability, relate that it comes from the country in which

Bacchus was brought up. Great birds, they say, bring the sticks which we Greeks, taking the word from the Phœnicians, call cinnamon, and carry them up into the air to make their nests. These are fastened with a sort of mud to a sheer face of rock, where no foot of man is able to climb. So the Arabians, to get the cinnamon, use the following artifice. They cut all the oxen and asses and beasts of burthern that die in their land into large pieces, which they carry with them into those regions, and place near the nests: then they withdraw to a distance, and the old birds, swooping down, seize the pieces of meat and fly with them up to their nests; which, not being able to support the weight, break off and fall to the ground. Hereupon the Arabians return and collect the cinnamon, which is afterward carried from Arabia into other countries. . . .

Where the south declines toward the setting sun lies the country called Ethiopia, the last inhabited land in that direction. There gold is obtained in great plenty, huge elephants abound, with wild trees of all sorts, and ebony; and the men are taller, handsomer, and longer lived than anywhere else.

Now these are the furthest regions of the world in Asia and Libya. Of the extreme tracts of Europe toward the west I cannot speak with any certainty; for I do not allow that there is any river, to which the barbarians give the name of Eridanus, emptying itself into the northern sea, whence, as the tale goes, amber is procured; nor do I know of any islands called the Cassiterides [Tin Islands], whence the tin comes which we use. For in the first place the name Eridanus is manifestly not a barbarian word at all, but a Greek name, invented by some poet or other; and secondly, though I have taken vast pains, I have never been able to get an assurance from an eyewitness that there is any sea on the further side of Europe. Nevertheless, tin and amber do certainly come to us from the ends of the earth.

The northern parts of Europe are very much richer in gold than any other region: but how it is procured I have no certain knowledge. The story runs, that the one-eyed Arimaspi purloin it from the griffins; but here too I am incredulous, and cannot persuade myself that there is a race of men born with one eye, who in all else resemble the rest of mankind. Nevertheless it seems to be true that the extreme regions of the earth, which surround and shut up within themselves all other countries, produce the things which are the rarest, and which men reckon the most beautiful.

The Euxine Sea has nations dwelling around it, with the one exception of the Scythians, more unpolished than those of any other region that we know of. For, setting aside Anacharsis and the Scythian people, there is not within this region a single nation which can be put forward as having any claims to wisdom, or which has produced a single person of any high repute.

As Scythia is utterly barren of firewood, a plan has had to be contrived for boiling the flesh, which is the following. After flaying the beasts, they take out all the bones, and, if they possess such gear, put the flesh into boilers made in the country, which are very like the caldrons of the Lesbians, except that they are of a much larger size; then placing the bones of the animals beneath the caldron, they set them alight, and so boil the meat. If they do not happen to possess a caldron, they make the animal's paunch hold the flesh, and pouring in at the same time a little water, lay the bones under and light them. The bones burn beautifully; and the paunch easily contains all the flesh when it is stript from the bones, so that by this plan your ox is made to boil himself, and other victims also to do the like.

In what concerns war, their customs are the following. The Scythian soldier drinks the blood of the first man he overthrows in battle. Whatever number he slays, he cuts off all their heads, and carries them to the king; since he is thus entitled to a share of the booty, whereto he forfeits all claim if he does not produce a head. In order to strip the skull of its covering, he makes a cut round the head above the ears, and, laying hold of the scalp, shakes the skull out; then with the rib of an ox he scrapes the scalp clean of flesh, and softening it by rubbing between the hands, uses it thenceforth as a napkin. The Scyth is proud of these scalps, and hangs them from his bridle rein; the greater the number of such napkins that a man can show, the more highly is he esteemed among them. Many make themselves cloaks, like the capotes of our peasants, by sewing a quantity of these scalps together. Others flay the right arms of their dead enemies, and make of the skin, which is stripped off with the nails hanging to it, a covering for their quivers. Now the skin of a man is thick and glossy, and would in whiteness surpass almost all other hides. Some even flay the entire body of their enemy, and stretching it upon a frame carry it about with them wherever they ride. Such are the Scythian customs with respect to scalps and skins.

The skulls of their enemies, not indeed of all, but of those whom they most detest, they treat as follows. Having sawn off the portion below the eyebrows, and cleaned out the inside, they cover the outside with leather. When a man is poor, this is all that he does; but if he is rich, he also lines the inside with gold: in either case the skull is used as a drinking cup.

They do the same with the skulls of their own kith and kin if they have at feud with them, and have vanquished them in the presence of the king. When strangers whom they deem of any account come to visit them, these skulls are handed round, and the host tells how that these were his relations who made war upon him, and how that he got the better of them; all this being looked upon as proof of bravery.

Once a year the governor of each district, at a set place in his own province, mingles a bowl of wine, of which all Scythians have a right to drink by whom foes have been slain; while they who have slain no enemy are not allowed to taste of the bowl, but sit aloof in disgrace. No greater shame than this can happen to them. Such as have slain a very large number of foes, have two cups instead of one, and drink from both.

Whenever the Scythian king falls sick, he sends for the three soothsayers of most renown at the time, who come and make trial of their art in the mode above described. Generally they say that the king is ill, because such or such a person, mentioning his name, has sworn falsely by the royal hearth. This is the usual oath among the Scythians, when they wish to swear with very great solemnity. Then the man accused of having forsworn himself is arrested and brought before the king. The soothsayers tell him that by their art it is clear he has sworn a false oath by the royal hearth, and so caused the illness of the king—he denies the charge, protests that he has sworn no false oath, and loudly complains of the wrong done to him. Upon this the king sends for six new soothsayers, who try the matter by soothsaying. If they too find the man guilty of the offense, straightway he is beheaded by those who first accused him, and his goods are parted among them: if, on the contrary, they acquit him, other soothsayers, and again others, are sent for, to try the case. Should the greater number decide in favor of the man's innocence, then they who first accused him forfeit their lives.

The mode of their execution is the following: a wagon is loaded with brushwood, and oxen are harnessed to it; the soothsayers, with their feet tied together, their hands bound behind their backs, and their mouths gagged, are thrust into the midst of the brushwood; finally the wood is set alight, and the oxen, being startled, are made to rush off with the wagon. It often happens that the oxen and the soothsayers are both consumed together, but sometimes the pole of the wagon is burnt through, and the oxen escape with a scorching. Diviners—lying diviners, they call them— are burnt in the way described, for other causes besides the one here spoken of. When the king puts one of them to death, he takes care not to let any of his sons survive: all the male offspring are slain with the father, only the females being allowed to live.

Oaths among the Scyths are accompanied with the following ceremonies: a large earthern bowl is filled with wine, and the parties to the oath, wounding themselves slightly with a knife or an awl, drop some of their blood into the wine; then they plunge into the mixture a scimitar, some arrows, a battle-ax, and a javelin, all the while repeating prayers; lastly the two contracting parties drink each a draft from the bowl, as do also the chief men among their followers.

The tombs of their kings are in the land of the Gerrhi, who dwell at the point where the Borysthenes is first navigable. Here, when the king dies, they dig a grave, which is square in shape, and of great size. When it is ready, they take the king's corpse, and, having opened the belly, and cleaned out the inside, fill the cavity with a preparation of chopped cypress, frankincense, parsley seed, and anise seed, after which they sew up the opening, enclose the body in wax, and, placing it on a wagon, carry it about through all the different tribes. On this procession each tribe, when it receives the corpse, imitates the example which is first set by the Royal Scythians; every man chops off a piece of his ear, crops his hair close, and makes a cut all round his arm, lacerates his forehead and his nose, and thrusts an arrow through his left hand. Then they who have the care of the corpse carry it with them to another of the tribes which are under the Scythian rule, followed by those whom they first visited. On completing the circuit of all the tribes under their sway, they find themselves in the country of the Gerrhi, who are the most remote of all, and so they come to the tombs of the kings. There the body of the dead king is laid in the grave prepared for it, stretched upon a mattress; spears are fixed in the ground on either side of the corpse, and beams stretched across above it to form a roof, which is covered with a thatching of osier twigs. In the open space around the body of the king they bury one of his concubines, first killing her by strangling, and also his cupbearer, his cook, his groom, his lackey, his messenger, some of his horses, firstlings of all his other possessions, and some golden cups; for they use neither silver nor brass. After this they set to work, and raise a vast mound above the grave, all of them vying with each other and seeking to make it as tall as possible.

When a year is gone by, further ceremonies take place. Fifty of the best of the late king's attendants are taken, all native Scythians—for as bought slaves are unknown in the country, the Scythian kings choose any of their subjects that they like, to wait on them—fifty of these are taken and strangled, with fifty of the most beautiful horses. When they are dead, their bowels are taken out, and the cavity cleaned, filled full of chaff, and straightway sewn up again. This done, a number of posts are driven into the ground, in sets of two pairs each, and on every pair half the felly of a wheel is placed archwise; then strong stakes are run lengthways through the bodies of the horses from tail to neck, and they are mounted up upon the fellies. The fifty strangled youths are then mounted severally on the fifty horses. To effect this, a second stake is passed through their bodies along the course of the spine to the neck; the lower end of which projects from the body, and is fixed into a socket, made in the stake that runs lengthwise down the horse. The fifty riders are thus ranged in a circle round the tomb, and so left. Such, then, is the mode in which the kings are buried.

MARCO POLO RETURNS

by Henry H. Hart

It is an enormous leap from Herodotus to that other "greatest traveler of all time," Marco Polo, who, seventeen centuries later, set out from Venice and succeeded in reaching fabulous Cathay, which was hardly a whisper in the world from which he had departed. For centuries afterward, explorers were to be inspired by Polo's account of the wonders he had seen.

He was born in Venice in 1245. His father and his uncle were wandering traders who had succeeded in reaching the court of Kublai Khan. They returned as his emissaries to the Pope at Rome, and when they decided to embark on another voyage, young Marco, then seventeen, accompanied them. Never was there another voyage like it. For more than three years they journeyed over deserts and mountains and finally they reached their

Reprinted from *Venetian Adventurer: Being an Account of the Life and Times and the Book of Messer Marco Polo* by Henry H. Hart with the permission of the publishers, Stanford University Press. Copyright 1947 by the Board of Trustees of Leland Stanford Junior University.

goal, the palace of the great Khan near Peking. For seventeen years they lived there in luxury, trusted advisers of the Khan. Again they journeyed, partly by sea, to their homeland. After many hardships they finally arrived, their clothes in tatters, their beards long. Henry Hart here describes that return and the jeering welcome the travelers received.

Marco Polo brought back to Europe more than a tale of jewels and gold and splendor. He brought back the learning of the East, which was to inspire the West for generations to come. And finally he brought back one of the most famous books of all time, The Travels of Marco Polo which was to be printed in innumerable editions and which still exerts a fascination on the modern reader.

SOBER history has recorded nothing of the landing of the Polos in Venice, nor of their reception by their family and fellow citizens. But legend and editors and commentators have preserved some pretty stories to ornament the wondrous tale of the wanderers. If they are not true, well then—as Giordano Bruno has it—*se non è vero, è ben trovato*. So let us recount the incidents. They may have happened. Who knows? . . .

Their legs were stiff and aching from long days in cramped quarters, and the pavement seemed to heave up toward them like the deck of a ship at sea. Once more seated in the familiar gondolas—how unlike the "shoeboats" of old China—they were conveyed swiftly through the dark canals and under the low bridges—how unlike the quaint structures that arched the canals and streams of Soochow and Quinsai the magnificent—to the old family residence.

At last they reached their home, which was, as Ramusio quaintly states,

in the district of San Giovanni Chrisostomo, as today it can still be seen, which at that time was a most beautiful and very high place . . . and when they arrived there the same fate befell them as befell Ulysses, who, when after twenty years he returned from Troy to Ithaca, his native land, was recognized by none.

They knocked at the door, for they had learned that some of their relatives had moved in and were dwelling there comfortably as in their own homes. Those who responded to their summons did not know them. The travelers had been away nearly twenty-six years, and, though vague reports of their wanderings may have drifted back to Venice during the earlier part of their protracted absence, as the years had rolled by and they had never returned they had long been given up as dead.

The Polos found it almost impossible to convince their kinsfolk of their identity. The long duration of their absence, the many hardships and worries that they had suffered, had changed their faces and their appearance entirely. "They had an indescribable something of the Tartar in their aspect and in their way of speech, having almost forgotten the Venetian tongue. Those garments of theirs were much the worse for wear, and were made of coarse cloth, and cut after the fashion of the Tartars." The dwellers in their house refused to believe that these rough men, who in no way resembled the handsome, well-dressed gentlemen who had sailed from Venice to Acre in 1271, were Messer Nicolo Polo, his brother Messer Maffeo, and his son Marco. No, they were too shabby, too down-at-the-heels, and all in all too disreputable to be taken at their word. One of these who met them at the door was most likely Maffeo, the young half-brother of Marco. They had never seen each other, nor did Marco know that Maffeo existed. For Maffeo, like Marco himself, had been born after his father had left Venice. Finally, with much misgiving and doubt, the doors were grudgingly thrown open, and the three adventurers were hesitatingly permitted to set foot once again in their own house.

"And what should I tell you?" For strange tales like unto those of A *Thousand and One Nights* are told of the homecoming of the three. The story has been handed from father to son that the sordid and tattered clothes of Messer Maffeo sorely irked his neat wife—who must after all have recognized and received him as her husband. One day, even though he seemed to treasure and watch over them as something most precious, she gave his Tartar rags in disgust to a beggar who had come to her door and moved her to pity. And when Messer Maffeo asked that evening for his clothes—for you must know that all his jewels were sewn therein, and the seams and under the patches thereof—she confessed that she had given them away to an unknown beggar. Messer Maffeo flew into a towering rage and became as one possessed. He tore his hair and beat his breast and paced the floor for hours, thinking up some stratagem whereby he might recover his lost riches. At last he decided upon a plan. Early the next morning he betook himself to the Bridge of the Rialto, where the stream of Venetian life pulsed back and forth at every hour and where one could, if one waited long enough, be sure of finding his man. Messer Maffeo carried a wheel with him, and sat him down in a corner and set about spinning the wheel aimlessly, like unto one whose brain is addled. And all the while the crowd milled around him and men cried, "What do you thus, and why?" and his only reply seemed inane and meaningless, the echo of an empty brain. "He will come, God willing," he answered unto each of his questioners—only that. And from mouth to mouth and ear to ear the word flew through the canals of Venice, and into the market places and the churches, and wherever men and women gathered to talk one to the other. For Venetians have been wont of old to gossip, and scandal and tittle-tattle are the life breath of idle folk. And all the city flocked to see the strange sight at the Rialto. But Messer Maffeo was neither dolt nor idiot. On the third day one came in his turn to see the foolery of the madman spinning his wheel; and, behold, it was the same beggar to whom Messer Maffeo's wife had shown charity, and on his back were the very Tartar garments that she had given him! With a cry of triumph Messer Maffeo leaped up and seized the hapless man, and so recovered his coat still intact, with the treasures it contained all untouched. Then indeed did Venice learn that in Messer Maffeo they had no mad fellow citizen but one well versed in the ways of men and in wiles to ensnare them.

Of all the fascinating tales of the return of the Polos, the best known is that told so delightfully by Ramusio.

The kinsfolk of the Polos were, it would seem, still skeptical of the identity of the returned travelers and, even if no longer in doubt as to who they were, appeared to be in no way proud of their seedy, sorry-looking relatives. So the two elder Polos and Marco contrived a stratagem whereby they would secure immediate and unequivocal recognition from the family and at the same time win "the honor" (i.e., the honorable notice) of all the city—in a word, properly and profoundly impress their fellow Venetians.

They sent out invitations to their kinsmen—the most important, we may be sure—requesting them to honor the three returned travelers with their company at a banquet and an entertainment. In all this they were most particular, and all was prepared with great care and splendor, in fact "in most honorable fashion, and with much magnificence in that aforesaid house of theirs." At the appointed hour the canals about the house of the Polos were crowded with gondolas, filled with invited guests in their best finery. They were received with due ceremony, and each was assigned his place for the coming feast. All were curious and expectant, for perhaps the Polos were going to show some of the precious goods which they had brought back with them, or perhaps—who knows?—they were going to distribute gifts of value to their invited guests. You may be sure that none failed to come and greet the two elder Polos and Marco, who were in the great hall to welcome each guest as he arrived. Then they vanished.

When the hour for seating themselves at the table was come, the three came forth from their chamber each clad in long satin robes of crimson hue, reaching even to the ground as was the custom in the Venice of those days. And when the perfumed water had been brought for rinsing the hands, and the guests were all in their proper places at the table, Messer Nicolo and Messer Maffeo and Messer Marco rose from their chairs, retired, divested themselves of the costly satin robes, donned others, of similar cut but of crimson damask, and reappeared. Then, to the horror and dismay of the invited kinsfolk—what wanton waste, with deserving relatives so close at hand!—they gave the order that the costly robes which they had just removed should be cut in pieces and the pieces distributed among the servants. And this was forthwith done.

A short time later, after some of the viands under which the well-set table groaned had been consumed and the guests had tossed the bones under the table and wiped their hands on the fine tablecloth, and after much wine had been drunk, the three rose once more and retired to their chamber. They emerged after a few moments, this time clad in expensive robes of crimson velvet. And when they had seated themselves once more at the table among their guests they ordered the damask robes which they had just removed to be brought out and cut to pieces before the whole company and the pieces given to the servants. More indignation and shocked and protesting murmurs, more meaningful glances—for kinsfolk are thus everywhere and in every age. But the order was forthwith obeyed, and each servitor received his piece of precious cloth.

The meal proceeded; but by now the family was full of wonderment as to what might happen next. A buzz of conversation filled the room from end to end: It must be so. These three men rich enough to throw away a fortune in clothes in a few short hours must be their long-lost relatives. There was no doubt about it. The kinsfolk were convinced, and hailed the three by their names and tried to revive talk of old times and ancient reminiscences. The Polos smiled in their beards, looked grave, but said nothing. The dinner drew near its close, and it came time to set forth the sweets and pastries on the tables. Whereupon uprose the three men and retired once again to their chamber. There their servants removed the velvet robes, and the Polos re-entered the banquet hall dressed in the same kind of clothes as were worn by their invited guests. Again the order was given to cut up and distribute the costly velvet fabrics, and again the order was obeyed. "This thing made [all] marvel, and all the invited guests were as though struck by lightning." The cloths were then removed and the servants were ordered to leave the banquet hall.

As soon as they retired and the doors were closed, Messer Marco again rose from the table and entered his chamber. He returned without delay, bearing the well-worn garments of coarse cloth in which the three had been clad on the day when they had landed in Venice and sought admission to their home. All present held their breath, for none knew what these eccentric men might do next. Forthwith the three seized sharp knives and without more ado started to rip seams and linings,

> and to bring forth from them enormous quantities of most precious gems such as rubies, sapphires, carbuncles, diamonds, and emeralds which had been sewn up in each of the said garments with much cunning and in such fashion that none would have been able to imagine that they were there. For when they took their departure from the Great Khan, they changed all the riches which he had given them into so many rubies, emeralds, and other precious stones, knowing well that had they done otherwise it would never have been possible for them to carry so much gold with them over such a long, difficult, and far-reaching road.

This magnificent and wholly unexpected display of a seemingly inexhaustible amount of precious stones spread so carelessly on the table caused more stir and excitement than ever, and the guests stood about dumbfounded and seemingly bereft of their senses. The tale ends on a sarcastic note, for Messer Giovanni Battista Ramusio appears to have had a rare sense of humor and to have known human frailties full well. His own words are best:

> And now they [the kinsmen] knew in truth that those whom they had formerly doubted were indeed those honored and valorous gentlemen of the House of Polo, and they did them great honor and reverence. And when this thing became known throughout Venice, straightway did the whole city, the gentry as well as the common folk, flock to their house, to embrace them and to shower them with caresses and show demonstrations of affection and reverence, as great as you can possibly imagine.

Now that the city folk realized how rich the three returned merchants really were, they outdid themselves in bestowing upon them public dignities and civic offices. They created Maffeo, who according to Ramusio was the oldest, a greatly honored magistrate. What was done for Nicolo we know not. As for Marco, we are told that "all the young men went every day continuously to visit and to converse with Messer Marco, who was most charming and gracious, and to ask of him matters concerning Cathay, and the Great Khan, and he responded with so much kindness that all felt themselves to be in a certain manner indebted to him."

But a little time and the hubbub and excitement and stir that had been caused by the return of the Polos and by their extravagant and impressive banquet with its dramatic climax gradually died away. Their fellow citizens went about their business, and no longer did passers-by in gondolas or on the bridges or *fondamenta* nudge each other and whisper about them or point them out to strangers. Life settled down again to its normal routine.

To the young Marco St. Mark's had all seemed glorious and spacious and brilliant, the most marvelous building in all the world. Now it appeared cramped and low-ceiled and tawdry, and within there was no peace or quiet for the worshiper. He recalled his visits to the high-vaulted Buddhist temples, dark and cool, enwrapped in a silence which became even deeper at the booming of a distant bell.

And the Piazza which had seemed so vast when he played in it as a boy had shrunk and diminished in comparison with the great spaces of the courts of the Mongol Emperor. Marco had often climbed the steep steps of the Bell Tower and the Drum Tower of Kublai's capital. He had seen the sun rise and set over the miles of upturned roofs and glistening tiles and great parks and gardens of Cambaluc. How small—just a handful of houses surrounded by the sea—seemed Venice.

He would roam the streets alone at night, and look up at the moon, swinging in the sky like a lantern, and at the stars, pale silver and gold. And they recalled to him the joy and color of the Feast of Lanterns in Cathay. And when the waters were still and black as velvet, the twinkling reflections of the stars were like the fireflies glowing in the far-off temple camphor trees, or as he had often seen them carried along the streets in tiny cages and boxes by the boys in the hot nights of the Chinese summer. When the rain pattered on the windows and in the canals below, it whispered of those soft rains in Hangchow through which the slender willows and plums and tall bamboos were seen as through gauze, of those hours when life was good, and of whole days passed seated in some sheltered rock garden drinking tea with old friends. And even the canals sometimes became those of Soochow, with their high-arched bridges and their close-crowded boats. . . .

Little by little Marco realized that he must renounce all thought of wandering back to foreign lands if he was to have any peace of mind.

Quiet walks along the quays or in the squares, accepting the clamorous pigeons of St. Mark's in place of those which he used to loose from his windows in Cambaluc with light whistles attached to their feathers—how sweet the sound as they soared high in the air—these were to be his pleasures and his excursions henceforth. His fellow Venetians knew nothing of the refinements of living as he had learned them in China, but he would have to learn to dwell among them on their terms, not his. Gradually he settled down in Venetian life and activities. He was too young to retire, and conditions were not favorable for a return to the Levant. Ever since 1291, when the Saracens had routed the Christians at Acre, commerce at the eastern end of the Mediterranean had become increasingly difficult. But Marco was not the man to sit back and take no part in affairs about him. In a short time he found himself leading the life of a wealthy bachelor of the city, buying, selling, examining goods and samples in the warehouses or on the quays.

THIRST IN THE DESERT

by Sven Hedin

Marco Polo's journey, although by all odds the most important of the pioneering explorations, was by no means unique. Before and after him, indomitable Catholic friars like Giovanni de Carpini had gone out as envoys to the heathen. Frequently they were received by savage peoples in a savage manner, and the roll of martyrs is heavy with their names.

In medieval times also the Arabs had founded a great empire stretching from Morocco on the west to China on the east, and wherever they went, they preached the greatness of Mohammed. They brought news from Canton and from Timbuktu. Many of them journeyed overland. Others, like Sindbad the Sailor, in the Arabian Nights, sailed the seas to the Spice Islands. The greatest of these early Moslems was Ibn Batuta, a Berber born in Tangier around the year 1300. At the age of twenty-two, he set out on a pilgrimage to

Mecca. He traveled to Egypt and Damascus and Iraq. He made a voyage to the trading posts of the east coast of Africa. He crossed the steppes of Central Asia and negotiated the northwest passages to India, becoming a person of consequence in Delhi. Everywhere he attached to himself wealth, wives and children without number. He was the traveler par excellence of his age.

Echoes of the early Arabian expeditions reached Europe, where they excited curiosity. But it was not until the eleventh century that, fired by religious zeal, the Crusaders journeyed into the Near East and Arabia. They brought back knowledge that would lead eventually to a great new era of exploration.

That era came into flower with the sea voyages of the Portuguese and the trip of Vasco da Gama around the Cape of Good Hope to Calicut. It was followed by other expeditions of trade and of conquest which gradually spread fingers of exploration south toward the islands of the Pacific and north to unknown Cipango. One of the few who managed to reach that island fortress was the Portuguese traveler St. Francis Xavier. And it was not indeed until 1853 that the American Captain M. C. Perry opened up trade relations between Japan and the rest of the world.

Journeys across the mainland of Asia were much less frequent and it was not until the sixteenth century that overland travel became at all common. The way was long, the obstacles great and much of the terrain, like the tundra of Siberia, the deserts of Mongolia and Arabia, and the mountains of Tibet, was barren and worthless. Catholic missionaries, anxious to carry the word of Christ to the heathen, were always in the forefront. In the thirteenth century, Giovanni de Monte Corvino, an Italian friar, made the long and hazardous trek across Asia and became Archbishop of Peking. In the nineteenth century, the Abbés Huc and Gabet explored China, Mongolia and Tibet. In all the centuries between, these missionaries journeyed, struggled and often died in regions which had never before seen a white man.

The Russians to the north penetrated past the Urals and on into Siberia in a slow, remorseless march. It was a struggle that may be compared to the American conquest of the land west of the Mississippi, but with a climate and in territories infinitely more difficult. Hundreds of thousands of anonymous frontiersmen advanced into northwest Asia, exacting tribute from the local tribes. Their progress was extremely difficult but they did manage to reach the ocean; and in the early eighteenth century Vitus Bering, a Danish officer in Russian employ, traveled across Siberia, built boats on the shores of the Eastern Sea and provided the final link between the continents of Asia and North America.

Of the later Russian travelers, perhaps the greatest was Nikolai Przhevalski, a man who used scientific methods of exploration. He traveled to the Tsaidam Swamp and the Gobi Desert in his crisscross treks across Central Asia, and opened up vast areas never before mapped.

Large sections of Inner Asia have remained virtually unexplored to the present day. No trade, no wealth, no salubrious climate is there to greet the traveler. Only the urge to be first, to see wonders that no other civilized eye has observed, remains as an incentive. In modern times, one of the foremost explorers to feel this urge has been Sven Hedin. Born in Sweden, he had been inspired as a boy by the exploits of his countryman Otto Nordenskjöld and other polar explorers. His lifework, however, was accomplished in the desert and mountain regions of Persia, Turkistan and Inner Asia. Later in life he was to lead elaborate scientific expeditions fitted out with the most modern equipment. His first journeys, however, were accomplished under conditions as primitive and dangerous as those of the earliest travelers. Rarely has anyone come so close to death from thirst in the desert and yet managed to survive as Hedin in the adventure which he here describes.

ON February 17, 1895, I left Kashgar, and began a journey which proved to be one of the most difficult I ever undertook in Asia.

We had two *arabas*, or carts with two high wheels, drawn by four horses, one of them between the shafts, and the other three in front, harnessed with ropes. Each team was driven by an *arabakesh*, or driver. The carts had arched roofs made of rush mats. I drove in the first one, with part of the luggage, and Islam Baï, with the heavy boxes, in the other. We had two dogs, Yoldash, from Pamir, and Hamra, from Kashgar. They were tied to Islam Baï's cart.

As we were on our way to the large Desert of Takla-makan, the temptation to penetrate to its interior increased day by day, and I could not resist its mysterious lure. Our road led alternately through fields of dense reed, where there were boars in large numbers, and through forests. And on March 19, we pitched camp in the village of Merket, near the right river bank. This became our headquarters for a time.

Islam Baï bought four iron tanks and six goatskins, to carry the water; sesame oil to nourish the camels in the desert; various provisions, such as flour, honey, dried vegetables, macaroni, etc.; spades and kitchen utensils; and many other things indispensable for a caravan. Most important of all, he bought eight splendid camels, at thirty-five dollars apiece. They were all males. All but one were Bactrian, or two-humped camels.

We named them, in Jagatai Turki, the language of the country, as follows: "The White," "Boghra" (the Stallion), "One-Hump," "Old Man," "Big Blackie," "Little Blackie," "Big Fawnie," and "Little Fawnie."

Besides Islam Baï, I hired three new men, to go with me to the interior of the desert. They were Mohammed Shah, an old, white-bearded camel-driver, whose wife and children lived in Yarkand; Kasim, black-bearded, powerful, and dutiful, accustomed to handling camels; and lastly a man who lived in Merket, also named Kasim, but whom we called Yolchi, or "the guide," because he asserted that he was well acquainted with the desert, and could find his way everywhere. At the last moment, our provisions were augmented by two bags of freshly baked bread, three sheep, ten hens, and a rooster to enliven the quiet of our camps in the eternal sand. The iron tanks and the goatskins were filled with 455 liters of water, designed to last us for twenty-five days.

The portion of the large sand desert that I was about to traverse was triangle-shaped. It was bounded on the west by Yarkand-daria, on the east by Khotan-daria (a tributary of the Yarkand), and on the south by the Kunlun Mountains. The distance from Merket to Khotan-daria was 175 miles; but it was made much longer for us by the innumerable bends our route made between the sand dunes. I hoped to cross the desert in less than a month, and move toward the cool heights of northern Tibet during the warm summer months.

On April 10, in the morning, our eight stately camels and their leaders marched out of Merket. The camels were heavily laden, and the bronze bells tolled solemnly, as if for a funeral. The villagers had assembled on the roofs and in the streets. They all looked grave. We heard an old man say, "They will never come back." Another added, "Their camels are too heavily laden." Two Hindu moneychangers threw some copper coins over my head, and shouted, "Happy journey!" About one hundred mounted men accompanied us a short distance. . . .

On the twenty-first of April, our track lay between two isolated mountains and along the western shore of a long lake. To the east, south, and southwest, nothing was to be seen but sterile, yellow sand dunes. The desert sea yawned before us.

Up to this evening, we had a whole lake of water right outside our tents. The men, the camels, and the other animals could drink their fill. Reeds grew abundantly on the banks; so the camels and the surviving sheep could graze without stint. Perhaps the animals, too, dreamt of this camp, during the nights that followed, as a blessed and happy spot. Yolchi, the guide, who was in disfavor with the other men, and kept to himself most of the time, only crawling up to the fire, to revive its embers, when the others had gone to sleep, now declared that it was but a four days' journey eastward to Khotan-daria, and that we would be able to strike water even before reaching the river. But I told the men to take water for ten days, as the distance might be greater than the guide said. If the tanks were half filled, we would be able to water the camels twice in the interior of the desert. The tanks were put in wooden frames, and protected from direct exposure to the sun by bundles of reeds. To the sound of the splashing water, as the men poured it into the tanks, I fell asleep, on the shore of this last lake.

Early in the morning of April 23, the camels were reloaded, and we started off toward the southeast. I wanted to satisfy myself that our last mountain did not extend into the desert.

In two hours, we had passed the wisps of reeds, and the sterile, sandy dunes grew higher. Another hour, and they were sixty feet high; and presently they rose to eighty and ninety feet.

After a while, we saw the last tamarisks, and passed the last spots of level, clay soil. Here I already observed how my men were laboring with their spades, to make the difficult places easier for the camels.

After sixteen miles, marching, we camped, at dusk, on a small spot of even clay ground, entirely surrounded by high sand dunes. Here grew the last two tamarisks, which the camels stripped of their bark in a few bites. Later on, we had to tie the camels, in order to prevent them from fleeing back to the lake, at night. We dug for water; but as the sandy clay proved to be dry as tinder, we gave up the attempt.

Hamra was missing. We went up on the dunes and whistled, but the dog never came back. Plainly, he had been wiser than we, and had returned over the caravan trail. Yoldash, however, had to pay for his fidelity with his life.

On April 25, we were waked by a northeast wind and flying dust. Colors faded, and distances and dimensions became distorted. A near-by dune took on the appearance of a remote, high mountain.

When the tanks came to be reloaded on their three bearers, the sound of the splashing water was such that I examined the supply. To my surprise, I discovered that it was sufficient for only two days. I questioned the men, and reminded them of my order to bring water for ten days. Yolchi, the guide, answered that we were within two days of Khotan-daria. I dared not scold them, for I myself should have watched how much water was taken from the lake. We had traveled only two days, and it would have been wise to retrace our steps. The caravan would have been saved, and no life would have been lost. But I could not bring myself to go back, and I reposed undue confidence in the guide. In the presence of all, I charged Islam Baï with responsibility for the water supply. The water rations were reduced for the men, and the camels had to go without a single drop.

From that moment, I, as well as my men, went on foot. Entire ranges, plateaus, and stretches of sand extended in all directions. I gave up pitching my tent. We slept under the open sky, all of us. The nights were still cold. We were always in higher spirits when settling down for the night, than in the daytime; for then came rest, the distribution of water, and the evening coolness after the heat of the day.

I said to the men: "Let us dig for water." Everyone was inspirited by this. Kasim took a spade, and straightway began to dig. Only Yolchi, the guide, made fun of the others, saying that water might be struck here at thirty fathoms. They asked him where the river was which he had said we would reach in four days. He was put to shame further, when, at a depth of three feet, the sandy ground became moist.

The further down we went, the moister the sand grew. We could now squeeze it into balls that did not crumble. As each digger wearied he was replaced by a fresh one. The upper part of our bodies was bare, and we perspired freely. Now and then we lay down on the cool, moist sand to cool our fevered blood. The camels, Yoldash, and the sheep waited impatiently around the well. They knew that their thirst would eventually be quenched.

It was pitch-dark; so we placed a couple of candle ends in small niches in the sides of the well.

How far down might the water be? If we had to dig all night, and all the next day, we were determined to find water! We worked with the determination of despair. I sat watching Kasim, who, illuminated from above by the candles, looked fantastic at the bottom of the well, ten feet down. I was waiting to see the reflection thrown back by the first drops of water!

Suddenly Kasim stopped abruptly in his work. The spade slid from his hands. With a half-choked cry he collapsed at the bottom of the well. Fearing that he had had a stroke, I shouted down to him: "What has happened?"

"The sand is dry," he answered; and it sounded like a voice from the grave, like the deathknell of our unfortunate caravan.

The sand was as dry as tinder. We had exhausted our strength in vain. We had used up nearly our whole meager supply of water, and had worked up a violent perspiration, all for nothing. Without a word, the men threw themselves on the ground, hoping to forget the sorrows of the day in sleep. I talked with Islam for a while, and did not conceal the danger of our situation. Yet Khotan-daria could not be far away. We had to see the undertaking through. We had water for one day more. It would have to do for three days. That meant two cups a day per man, one bowl for Yoldash, and one for the sheep. The camels had not been watered for three days. They would not get another drop. Our entire supply was less than a tenth of what a camel would need to drink its fill.

As I rolled myself in a blanket, and lay down on my rug, the camels were still lying at the well, waiting in vain for water, patient and resigned, as always.

Having discarded such superfluous belongings as tent rugs, tent cot, stove, etc., we set out early on the twenty-seventh of April. I went on foot, in advance. The dunes were now only thirty feet high. My hopes rose. But again the dunes mounted to double and treble size, and again our situation seemed hopeless.

The "Old Man" and "Big Blackie" were not able to follow us to that evening's camp. Mohammed Shah and the guide, who had been leading them, came to the camp alone. The former told us that the "Old Man" had lain down, his legs and head stretched out on the sand, while "Big Blackie" had stood erect, with trembling legs, unable to take another step. When his six comrades disappeared among the dunes, he had sent a long, wondering glance after them. And then the men had abandoned the two dying camels. A couple of empty water tanks were abandoned at the same time. . . .

Early in the morning of April 28, a sandstorm, the like of which we had never seen, broke over our camp. The wind heaped piles of sand on us, on our belongings, and on our camels; and, when we rose, at dawn, to meet another terrible day, we found we were nearly buried in sand. Everything had sand in it. My boots and my cap, my leather instrument bag, and other articles had disappeared; and we had to dig the things out again with our hands.

The gale grew into a hurricane. The velocity of the wind was fifty-five miles an hour. During the most violent blasts we nearly choked. Sometimes the camels refused to walk, but lay down and stretched their necks along the sand. Then we also threw ourselves down, pressing our faces against their flanks.

One of the younger camels began to stagger during that day's march.

He was being led in the rear of the caravan by Yolchi. As I walked along, I kept my hand on one of our boxes, so as not to lose my way. Yolchi came up and shouted in my ear that the camel had fallen on a steep sand ridge, and could not be induced to get up. At once I ordered a halt, and sent Mohammed Shah and Kasim to save the camel. They returned in a few minutes and reported that the trail had disappeared, and that they had been unable to find the camel in the thick clouds of whirling sand. As it was a question of life and death for all of us, we had to leave him, as well as his load, consisting of two boxes of provisions, ammunition, and furs. He was doomed to die of thirst in the suffocating, murderous desert.

In the evening, when we camped, we got rid of the other boxes, which contained provisions, furs, blankets, rugs, pillows, books, cooking apparatus, kerosene, pots and pans, a set of agateware and china, etc. We kept only enough food for a few days. All the liquid tinned food was distributed among the men. They ate it, first satisfying themselves, however, that it contained no pork. They greedily drank up the oil in the sardine tins. Another pack saddle was emptied of its hay stuffing; but the camels ate the hay without relish, their throats were so parched. In the evening, I drank my last cup of tea. Only two small iron jars of water were now left.

The gale subsided during the night. At sunrise, on the twenty-ninth of April, Islam reported that one of the water jugs had been stolen during the night. Everyone suspected Yolchi, especially as he did not show up until the next morning.

Hardly one cup of water remained. I told the men that at noon I would dip the corner of a handkerchief in it and moisten my lips and theirs, and that the last drops would suffice for a small mouthful for each. At noon I moistened their lips, but in the evening the jug was empty. I do not know who the guilty one was, and it was no use holding a trial. The desert was endless, and we were all headed toward certain death.

That night, I wrote what I supposed were to be my last lines in my diary: "Halted on a high dune, where the camels dropped. We examined the east through the field glasses; mountains of sand in all directions, not a straw, no life. All, men as well as camels, are extremely weak. God help us!"

When, by chance, I found the bottle in which we kept the Chinese spirits for the Primus stove, I could not resist the temptation of drinking some of it. It was a foolish thing to do; but nevertheless I drank half the bottle. Yoldash heard the gurgling sound, and came toward me, wagging his tail. I let him have a sniff. He snorted, and went away sadly. I threw the bottle away, and the rest of the liquid flowed out into the sand.

That treacherous drink finished me. I tried to rise, but my legs would not support me. The caravan broke camp, but I remained behind. Islam Baï led, compass in hand, going due east. The sun was already burning-hot. My men probably thought I would die where I lay. They went on slowly, like snails.

I exerted all my will power, got up, reeled, fell, crawled for a while along the trail, got up again, dragged myself along, and crawled. One hour passed, and then another. From the ridge of a dune, I saw the caravan. It was standing still. The bells had ceased tinkling. By superhuman efforts, I managed to reach it.

Mohammed Shah was lying on his face, sobbingly invoking Allah. Kasim sat in the shadow of a camel, his face covered with his hands. He told me that Mohammed Shah had been raving about water all the way. Yolchi lay on the sand, as if he were dead.

Islam suggested that we continue, and look for a spot of hard clay ground, where we might dig for water. All the camels were lying down. I climbed on the white one. Like the others, he refused to get up. Our plight was desperate. Here we were to die. Mohammed Shah lay babbling, toying with the sand, and raving about water. I realized that we had reached the last act of our desert drama. But I was not yet ready to give in altogether.

The sun was now glowing like an oven. "When the sun has gone down," I said to Islam, "we will break camp and march all night. Up with the tent!" The camels were freed from their burdens, and lay in the blazing sun all day. Islam and Kasim pitched the tent. I crawled in, undressed completely, and lay down on a blanket, my head pillowed on a sack. Islam, Kasim, Yoldash, and the sheep went into the shade, while Mohammed Shah and Yolchi stayed where they had fallen. The hens were the only ones to keep up their spirits.

This death camp was the unhappiest I lived through in all my wanderings in Asia.

About noon, the slack flaps of the tent began to bulge, and a faint southerly breeze moved over the desert. It blew stronger, and after a couple of hours it was so fresh that I rolled myself up in my blanket.

And now a miracle happened! My debility vanished and my strength returned! If ever I longed for the sunset, it was now. I did not want to die: I *would* not die in this miserable, sandy desert! I could run, walk, crawl on my hands and feet. My men might not survive, but I had to find water!

The sun lay like a red-hot cannon ball on a dune in the west. I was in the best of condition. I dressed, and ordered Islam and Kasim to prepare for departure. The sunset glow spread its purple light over the dunes. Mohammed Shah and Yolchi were in the same position as in the morning. The former had already begun his death struggle; and he never regained consciousness. But the latter woke to life in the cool of the evening. With his hands clenched, he crawled up to me, and cried pitifully: "Water! Give us water, sir! Only a drop of water!" Then he crawled away.

"Is there no liquid here, whatever?" I said.

"Why, the rooster!" So they cut off the rooster's head and drank his blood. But that was only a drop in the bucket. Their eyes fell on the sheep, which had followed us as faithfully as a dog, without complaining. Everyone hesitated. It would be murder to kill the sheep to prolong our lives for only one day. But Islam led it away, turned its head toward Mecca, and slashed its carotids. The blood, reddish-brown and ill-smelling, flowed slowly and thickly. It coagulated immediately into a cake, which the men gulped down. I tried it, too; but it was nauseous, and the mucous membrance of my throat was so dry, that it stuck there, and I had to get rid of it quickly.

Mad with thirst, Islam and Yolchi collected camel's urine in a receptacle, mixed it with sugar and vinegar, held their noses, and drank. Kasim and I declined to join in this drinking bout. The two who had drunk this poison were totally incapacitated. They were overcome with violent cramps and vomiting, and lay writhing and groaning on the sand.

Yolchi crawled into the tent to lie down on my blanket. He looked repulsive, soiled as he was with blood from the lungs of the sheep. I tried to brace him up, and advised him to follow our track during the night. He did not answer. Mohammed Shah was already delirious. In his delirium, he muttered the name of Allah. I tried to make his head comfortable, passed my hand over his burning forehead, begged him to crawl along our trail as far as he could, and told him that we would return to rescue him as soon as we found water.

The two men eventually died in the death camp, or near it. They were never heard of; and when, after a year had elapsed, they were still missing, I gave a sum of money to their respective widows and children.

All five camels were induced to get up, and they were tied to one another in single file. Islam led, and Kasim brought up the rear. We did not take the two dying men along, because the camels were too weak to carry them; and, indeed, in their deplorable condition, they could not have kept their seats between the humps. We also cherished the hope that we would find water, in which case we were going to fill the two goatskins that we still carried, and hurry back to save the unfortunate ones.

When it was pitch-dark, I lit the candle in the lantern, and walked ahead, looking for the easiest way. One of the camels collapsed during the march, and lay down immediately, prepared for death, neck and legs stretched out. His bag was placed on "White," the strongest of the four survivors. The dying camel's bronze bell remained with him. Its tinkling was now a thing of the past.

Our progress was desperately slow. Every step was an effort for the camels. Now one, then the other stopped, and had to rest for a while. Islam suffered from fresh attacks of vomiting, and lay writhing on the sand like a worm. In the faint light from the lantern, I lengthened my stride, and went on ahead. I walked thus for two hours. The sound of the bells died away behind me. There was no sound discernible, save the swishing of the sand under my heels.

At eleven o'clock, I struggled up onto a flat, sandy ridge, to listen and to reconnoiter. The Khotan-daria *couldn't* be far away.

Far away, the clanging of the last bell again became audible. There were intervals of quiet, but the sound came nearer. After I had waited for what seemed like eternity, the four camels stood forth like phantoms. They came up to me on the ridge and lay down right away. They probably mistook the lantern for a campfire. Islam staggered along, threw himself on the sand, and whispered laboredly that he could go no farther. He would die where he was. He made no answer when I tried to encourage him to hold out.

Kasim, who still bore up, was happy when I told him to come with me. Hurriedly he took the shovel and pail, but forgot his cap. Later on, he used my handkerchief to protect himself against sunstroke. I bade farewell to Islam, and told him to sacrifice *everything*, but try to save himself by following our track. He looked as if he were going to die, and made no answer.

After a last look at the patient camels, I hurried away from this painful scene, where a man was fighting death, and where the veterans of our erstwhile proud caravan would end their desert journey for good. I caressed Yoldash, and left it to him to decide whether he would stay or go with us. He stayed, and I never saw the faithful dog again. It was midnight. We had been shipwrecked in the middle of the sea, and were now leaving the sinking ship.

The lantern was still burning beside Islam, but its light soon died out behind us.

Thus we walked on through the night and the sand. After two hours of it, we were so exhausted, from fatigue and from lack of sleep, that we flung ourselves headlong on the sand, and dozed off.

From one o'clock until half-past four in the morning, on May 3, we lay inanimate; and not even the cold night air could rouse us to go on. But at dawn we dragged ourselves forward again. We would take a couple of steps intermittently. We managed to get down the sandy slopes fairly well; but climbing the waves of sand was heavy work.

At sunrise, Kasim caught me by the shoulder, stared, and pointed east, without saying a word.

"What is it?" I whispered.

"A tamarisk," he gasped.

A sign of vegetation at last! God be praised! Our hopes, which had been close to extinction, flamed up once more. We walked, dragged ourselves, and staggered for three hours, before we reached that first bush—an olive branch intimating that the sea of the desert had a shore. We thanked God for this blessed gift, as we chewed the bitter, green needles of the tamarisk. Like a water lily, the bush stood on its wave of sand, basking in the sun. But how far below was the water that nourished its roots?

About ten o'clock, we found another tamarisk; and we saw several more in the east. But our strength was gone. We undressed, buried ourselves in the sand, and hung our clothes on the branches of the tamarisk, to make shade.

We lay in silence for nine hours. The hot desert air dried our faces into parchment. At seven o'clock, we dressed, and continued onward. We went more slowly than ever. After three hours' walk in the dark, Kasim stopped short, and whispered: "Poplars!"

Between two dunes there appeared three poplars, standing close together. We sank down at their base, exhausted with fatigue. Their roots, too, must derive nourishment from below. We took hold of the spade, intending to dig a well; but the spade slipped from our hands. We had no strength left. We lay down and scratched the ground with our nails, but gave up the attempt as useless.

I rose at twilight and urged Kasim to come. Hardly audible was his gasp: "I can't go on."

And so I left the last remnant of the caravan behind, and continued on alone. I dragged myself along, and fell. I crawled up slopes, and staggered down the other side. I lay quiet for long periods, listening. Not a sound! The stars shone like electric torches. I wondered whether I was still on earth, or whether this was the valley of the shadow of death. I lit my last cigarette.

Kasim had always received the butts; but now I was alone, and so I smoked this one to the end. It afforded me a little relief and distraction.

Six hours had passed since the beginning of my solitary journey, when, totally overcome with feebleness, I sank down by a new tamarisk, and went off into the doze which I feared, for death might come while I was asleep. As a matter of fact, I hardly slept at all. All the time, in the gravelike silence, I heard the beating of my heart and the ticking of the chronometers. And after a couple of hours, I heard the swish of steps in the sand, and saw a phantom stagger and struggle to my side.

"Is that you, Kasim?" I whispered.

"Yes, sir."

"Come! We have not far to go!"

Heartened by our reunion, we struggled on. We slid down the dunes; we struggled upward. We would lie, motionless, where we fell, in our battle against the insidious desire for sleep. We slackened our pace, and grew more and more indolent. We were like sleepwalkers; but still we fought for our lives.

Suddenly Kasim grabbed my arm and pointed downward at the sand. There were distinct tracks of human beings!

In a twinkling we were wide-awake. It was plain that the river *must* be near! It was possible that some shepherds had noticed our fire and had come to investigate. Or maybe a sheep, astray in the desert, had been searched for by these men who had so recently passed over the sand.

Kasim bent down, examined the prints, and gasped: "It is our own trail!"

In our listless, somnolent state, we had described a circle without knowing it. That was enough for a while; we could not endure any more. We collapsed on the trail and fell asleep. It was half-past two at night.

When the new day dawned, on the fifth of May, we rose heavily, and with difficulty. Kasim looked terrible. His tongue was white and swollen, his lips blue, his cheeks were hollow, and his eyes had a dying, glassy luster. He was tortured by a kind of death hiccup, which shook his whole frame. When the body is so completely dried up that the joints almost creak, every movement is an effort.

It grew lighter. The sun rose. From the top of a dune, where nothing obstructed the view toward the east, we noticed that the horizon, which for two weeks had revealed a row of yellow saw-teeth, now disclosed an absolutely even, dark-green line. We stopped short, as though petrified, and exclaimed simultaneously: "The forest!" And I added: "The Khotan-daria! Water!"

Again we collected what little strength we had left, and struggled along eastward. We came upon a path, showing traces of men, sheep, and horses, and we thought it might lead to the river. After following it for two hours, we collapsed in the shade of a poplar grove.

We were too weak to move. Kasim lay on his back. He looked as if he were going to die. The river *must* be quite near. Again I urged Kasim to accompany me to the river to drink. He signaled with his hand that he could not rise; and he whispered that he would soon die under the poplars.

Alone I pulled myself along through the forest. Thickets of thorny bushes, and dry, fallen branches, obstructed my way. I tore my thin clothes and scratched my hands; but gradually I worked my way through. I rested frequently, crawled part of the way on all fours, and noticed with anxiety how the darkness grew denser in the woods. Finally the new night came—the last one. I could not have survived another day.

The forest ended abruptly, as though burnt by a fire. I found myself on the edge of a six-foot-high terrace, which descended almost perpendicularly to an absolutely level plain, devoid of vegetation. The ground was packed hard. A withered, leafless twig was sticking out of it. I saw that it was a piece of driftwood, and that I was in the river bed of the Khotan-daria. And it was dry, as dry as the sandy desert behind me!

I knew that the course of the river was almost due north. The shortest distance to the right-hand shore would therefore be straight eastward. Although the moon was up, and I watched the compass, I was all the time, and unconsciously, being drawn toward the southeast. There was no use fighting this force. I walked as though led by an invisible hand. Finally I resisted no more, but walked toward the southeast, where the moon was. I frequently sank down and rested. I was then overcome by a terrible desire for sleep. My head sank to the ground, and I had to use all my will-power not to go to sleep. Had I gone to sleep, exhausted as I was, I am sure I should never have waked again.

Like the beds of all desert rivers in Central Asia, that of Khotan-daria is very wide, flat, and shallow. A light haze floated over the desolate landscape. I had gone about one mile, when the outlines of the forest on the eastern shore appeared below the moon. Dense thickets of bushes and reeds grew on the terraced shore. A fallen poplar stretched its dark trunk down toward the river bed. It looked like the body of a crocodile. The bed still remained as dry as before. It was not far to the shore where I must lie down and die. My life hung on a hair.

Suddenly I started, and stopped short. A water bird, a wild duck or goose, rose on whirring wings, and I heard a splash. The next moment, I stood on the edge of a pool, seventy feet long and fifteen feet wide! The water looked as black as ink in the moonlight. The overturned poplar trunk was reflected in its depths.

In the silent night I thanked God for my miraculous deliverance. Had I continued eastward I should have been lost. In fact, if I had touched shore only a hundred yards north or south of the pool, I would have believed the entire river bed to be dry. I knew that the freshets from melting snowfields and glaciers in northern Tibet flowed down through the Khotan-daria bed only in the beginning of June, to dry up in the late summer and autumn, leaving the bed dry during the winter and spring. I had also heard that in certain places, separated sometimes by a day's journey or more, the river forms eddies, which scoop the bed into greater depths, and that the water may remain the year round in these hollows near the terraced shore. And now I had come upon one of these extremely rare bodies of water!

I sat down calmly on the bank, and felt my pulse. It was so weak that it was hardly noticeable—only forty-nine beats. Then I drank, and drank again. I drank without restraint. The water was cold, clear as crystal, and as sweet as the best spring water. And then I drank again. My dried-up body absorbed the moisture like a sponge. All my joints softened, all my movements became easier. My skin, hard as parchment before, now became softened. My forehead grew moist. The pulse increased in strength; and after a few minutes it was fifty-six. The blood flowed more freely in my veins. I had a feeling of well-being and comfort. I drank again, and sat caressing the water in this blessed pool. Later on, I christened this pool Khoda-verdi-kol, or "The Pool of God's Gift."

My thoughts now flew to Kasim, who lay, faint from thirst, on the edge of the wood on the western shore. Of the stately caravan of three weeks ago, I, a European, was the only one that had held out till the moment of rescue. If I did not waste my minutes, perhaps Kasim, too, might be saved. But in what was I to carry the water? Why, in my waterproof boots! There was, in fact, no other receptacle. I filled them to the top, suspended them at either end of the spade handle, and carefully recrossed the river bed. Though the moon was low, my old track was plainly visible. I reached the forest. The moon went down, and dense darkness descended among the trees. I lost my trail, and went astray among thorny bushes and thickets, which would not give under my stockinged feet.

From time to time, I called "Kasim!" at the top of my voice. But the sound died away among the tree trunks; and I got no answer but the "clevitt" of a frightened night owl.

If I lost my way, perhaps I would never again find the trail, and then Kasim would be lost. I stopped at an impenetrable thicket of dry branches and brush, set fire to the whole thing, and enjoyed seeing the flames lick and scorch the nearest poplars. Kasim could not be far away; he was certain both to hear and to see the fire. But he did not come. I had no choice but to await the dawn.

At the foot of a poplar, out of reach of the fire, I lay down and slept for some hours. The fire protected me against any prowling wild beasts.

When dawn came, the night-fire was still glowing, and a black column of smoke was rising above the forest. It was easy now to find my trail, and the place where Kasim lay. He was still in the same position as the night before. Upon seeing me, he whispered: "I am dying!"

"Will you have some water?" I asked, letting him hear the splashing sound. He sat up, dazed and staring. I handed him one of the boots. He lifted it to his lips and emptied it to the last drop. After a short pause he emptied the other one, too.

"Come along now to the pool," said I.

"I can't," Kasim answered.

"Follow my track, then, as soon as you can. I shall go to the pool, first, then southward along the river bed. Good-by!"

I could do no more for Kasim at the moment; and I thought he was now out of danger.

It was five o'clock in the morning of May 6. I drank again at the pool, bathed, and rested awhile. Then I walked south. . . .

On the eighth of May, I set out before the sun was up, and walked nearly the whole day. Before nightfall I made a startling discovery on the shore of a little island. In the hard-packed sand of the river bed, there appeared quite fresh prints of two barefoot men, driving four mules northward! Why had I not met them? Very likely they had passed me during the night, while I was asleep. Now they were far ahead, and it would be useless to turn back and try to overtake them.

I thought I heard an unusual sound from a jutting tongue of land, so I stopped short and listened. But the forest was dead-silent; so, concluding that it must have been some bird's call, I went on.

But no! After a minute, I heard a human voice and a mooing cow! It was no illusion. There were shepherds!

I emptied the water out of my boots, put them on, wet as they were, and hurried into the forest, breaking through thickets and jumping over fallen trees. Presently I heard the bleating of sheep. A herd was grazing in a glen. The shepherds stood as if petrified, when I burst forth from the jungle.

They had just taken the sheep to the pen near by. Now they made a big fire in front of the hut; and when it had burned itself out, all four of us went to sleep.

The shepherds were named Yusup Baï, Togda Baï, and Pasi Ahun. They tended a hundred and seventy sheep and goats, and seventy cows, which belonged to a merchant in Khotan.

At daybreak, on May 9, I found a bowl of milk and a piece of bread beside me; but the shepherds were gone. I ate my breakfast with Lucullian appetite, and then went to inspect my immediate surroundings. The hut lay on a sandy height, from which one could view the dry bed of the Khotan-daria, near the bank of which the shepherds had their well.

Their clothes were worn and ragged. Their feet were covered with plain pieces of sheepskin, laced together; and in their waist belts they carried their supply of tea. Their household utensils, consisting of two crude wooden vessels, lay on the roof of the hut, together with the corn supply and a primitive guitar with three strings. They had also axes for cutting their way through the forest, and a fire steel, for which there was little use, as they had only to blow the glowing coals, underneath the ashes, into life again.

A very strange thing happened that afternoon. The shepherds were in the woods with the sheep. I sat looking out over the river bed, and saw a caravan of a hundred mules, laden with bags, going from south to north, from Khotan to Aksu. Should I hurry down to the leader? No. That would have been of no use, as I did not have even a copper in my pocket! I would certainly have to stay with my shepherds as a hanger-on, get thoroughly rested at their place for a couple of days, and then walk to Khotan. I lay down to sleep under the brushwood roof.

Awakened suddenly by voices and the clattering of horses, I sat up, and saw three merchants, in white turbans, ride up to the hut, dismount, and approach me, bowing humbly. Two of my shepherd friends had shown them the way, and were now holding their horses.

Seating themselves on the sand, they told of having ridden in the river bed the day before, on their way from Aksu to Khotan, brushing past the wooded terrace on the left shore, when they saw a man, apparently dead, lying at the foot of the terrace. A white camel was grazing among the trees.

Like the Good Samaritan, they had stopped to ask what ailed him. He had whispered, "Su, su" (Water, water). They sent their servant with a jug to the nearest pool, probably the same one that had saved my life. Afterward they gave the man bread and nuts.

I realized at once that it was Islam Baï. He had told them the story of our journey, and had asked them to look for me, although he really believed I was dead. Yusup, the chief of the merchants, offered me one of his horses, and asked me to accompany them to Khotan, to seek rest and quiet.

But I did not want that at all! Their news instantly changed my situation, which had been so gloomy a moment before. Perhaps we might be able to go back to the death camp and find out if the men we left there were still alive. Maybe we could save the baggage, and equip a new caravan. Perhaps my money could be found. The future seemed bright once more.

The three merchants said good-by, and continued their journey, after lending me eighteen small silver coins, worth two dollars, and giving me a bag of white bread.

The shepherds were abashed when they realized that I had told them the truth.

On the tenth of May, I slept all day. I felt like a convalescent after a long illness. At sunset I heard a camel roar, and went out. There was one of the shepherds leading the white camel, with Islam and Kasim staggering behind them!

Islam threw himself at my feet, weeping. He had thought we would never meet again.

THE FORBIDDEN CITY

by Heinrich Harrer

For many readers, the two most fascinating corners of Asia are the deserts of Arabia and the "forbidden" uplands of Tibet. A scientific knowledge of the former country began to develop only in the nineteenth century.

Men of various nationalities made contributions, but partly because of their articulateness, it is the British who hold the center of the stage. The first and greatest of these was Charles M. Doughty, author of that amazing book Travels in Arabia Deserta, who lived with the Bedouins in their tents and described the Arabian scene and the character of the Arabs themselves in a manner utterly unique. Doughty set the pattern for a group of extraordinary Englishmen who were also gifted writers. Among them were Richard Burton, Gertrude Bell and T. E. Lawrence. In the last few decades, with the travels of St. J. Philby and Bertram Thomas, the final traces of ignorance have been removed from our broad knowledge of Arabia's geography.

"Inaccessible Tibet" and the "forbidden city of Lhasa" have in fact been visited sporadically for many centuries. The earliest known traveler there was Friar Odoric of Prodenone, who journeyed through the country in 1330. Several dozen others are known to have arrived there in the centuries that followed. In 1904 Sir Francis Younghusband made his famous military march on Lhasa, and his account of his expedition added greatly to our understanding of the country. A German prisoner of World War II who escaped from a British internment camp in India and who accomplished the journey to Lhasa under extremely adverse circumstances, has written the most recent and certainly one of the most interesting of all the chronicles of Tibet. Here is a selection from Heinrich Harrer's own story in which he tells how he reached Lhasa penniless and in rags, to become a person of importance in the country, an intimate and tutor of the Dalai Lama himself.

W E HAD been some time on the way when a man came toward us wearing clothes which struck us as unusual. He spoke a dialect different from that of the local nomads. He asked us curiously whence? and whither? and we told him our pilgrimage story. He left us unmolested and went on his way. It was clear to us that we had made the acquaintance of our first Khampa.[1]

A few hours later we saw in the distance two men on small ponies, wearing the same sort of clothes. We slowly began to feel uncomfortable and went on without waiting for them. Long after dark we came across a tent. Here we were lucky as it was inhabited by a pleasant nomad family, who hospitably invited us to come in and gave us a special fireplace for ourselves.

In the evening we got talking about the robbers. They were, it seems, a regular plague. Our host had lived long enough in the district to make an

[1] Robber.—Eds.

epic about them. He proudly showed us a Mannlicher rifle for which he had paid a fortune to a Khampa—five hundred sheep, no less! But the robber bands in the neighborhood considered this payment as a sort of tribute and had left him in peace ever since.

He told us something about the life of the robbers. They live in groups in three or four tents which serve as headquarters for their campaigns. These are conducted as follows: heavily armed with rifles and swords they force their way into a nomad's tent and insist on hospitable entertainment on the most lavish scale available. The nomad in terror brings out everything he has. The Khampas fill their bellies and their pockets and, taking a few cattle with them for good measure, disappear into the wide-open spaces. They repeat the performance at another tent every day till the whole region has been skinned. Then they move their headquarters and begin again somewhere else.

Next morning we went on our way, not without misgivings; which increased when we saw a man with a gun, who seemed to be stalking us from the hillside. Nevertheless we kept straight on our course, and the man eventually disappeared. In the evening we found more tents—first a single one and then a cluster of others.

We called to the people in the first tent. A family of nomads came out. They refused with expressions of horror to admit us and pointed distractedly to the other tents. There was nothing for it but to go on. We were no little surprised to receive a friendly welcome at the next tent. Everyone came out. They fingered our things and helped us to unload—a thing which no nomads had ever done—and suddenly it dawned on us that they were Khampas. We had walked like mice into the trap. The inhabitants of the tent were two men, a woman and a half-grown youngster. We had to put a good face on a poor situation. At least we were on our guard and hoped that politeness, foresight and diplomacy would help us to find a way out of the mess.

We had hardy sat down by the fire when the tent began to fill with visitors from the neighboring tents, come to see the strangers. We had our hands full trying to keep our baggage together. The people were as pressing and inquisitive as gypsies.

The visitors from the other tents gradually drifted away and we prepared to go to bed. One of our two hosts insisted on using my rucksack as a pillow and I had the utmost difficulty in keeping it by me. They probably thought that it contained a pistol. If they did, that suited our book and I hoped to increase their suspicion by my behavior. At last he stopped bothering me. We remained awake and on our guard all through the night. That was not very difficult, though we were very weary, because the woman muttered prayers without ceasing. It occurred to me that she was praying in advance for forgiveness for the crime her husband intended to commit against us the next day. We were glad when day broke. At first everything seemed peaceful. I exchanged a pocket mirror for some yak's brains, which we cooked for breakfast. Then we began to get ready to go. Our hosts followed our movements with glowering faces and looked like attacking me when I handed our packs out of the tent to Aufschnaiter. However, we shook them off and loaded our yak. We started off in all haste.

We had gone a few hundred yards when I noticed that my dog was not there. He usually came running after us without being called. As we looked round we saw three men coming after us. They soon caught us up and told us that they too were on the way to the tents of the nomad pilgrims and pointed to a distant pillar of smoke. That looked to us very suspicious as we had never seen such smoke pillars over the nomad tents. When we asked about the dog they said that he had stayed behind in the tent. One of us could go and fetch him. Now we saw their plan. Our lives were at stake. They had kept the dog back in order to have a chance of separating Aufschnaiter and me, as they lacked the courage to attack us both at the same time. And probably they had companions waiting where the smoke was rising. If we went there we would be heavily outnumbered and they could dispose of us with ease. No one would ever know anything about our disappearance. We were now very sorry not to have listened to the well-meant warnings of the nomads.

As though we suspected nothing we went on a short way in the same direction, talking rapidly to one another. The two men were now on either side of us while the boy walked behind. Stealing a glance to right and left we estimated our chances, if it came to a fight. The two men wore double sheepskin cloaks, as the robbers do, to protect them against knife thrusts, and long swords were stuck in their belts. Their faces had an expression of lamblike innocence.

Something had to happen. Aufschnaiter thought we ought first to change our direction, so as not to walk blindly into a trap. No sooner said than done. Still speaking, we abruptly turned away.

The Khampas stopped for a moment in surprise; but in a moment rejoined us and barred our way, asking us, in none too friendly tones, where we were going. "To fetch the dog," we answered curtly. Our manner of speaking seemed to intimidate them. They saw that we were prepared to go to any lengths, so they let us go and after staring after us for a while they hurriedly went on their way, probably to inform their accomplices.

When we got near the tents, the woman came to meet us leading the dog on a leash. After a friendly greeting we went on, but this time we followed the road by which we had come to the robber camp. There was now no question of going forward—we had to retrace our steps. Unarmed as we were, to continue would have meant certain death. After a forced march we arrived in the evening at the home of the friendly family with whom we had stayed two nights before. They were not surprised to hear of our experiences and told us that the Khampas' encampment was called Gyak Bongra, a name which inspired fear throughout the countryside. After this adventure it was a blessing to be able to spend a peaceful night with friendly people.

Next morning we worked out our new travel plan. There was nothing for it but to take the hard road which led through uninhabited country. We bought more meat from the nomads, as we should probably be a week before seeing a soul.

To avoid going back to Labrang Trova we took a short cut entailing a laborious and steep ascent but leading, as we hoped, to the route we meant to follow. Halfway up the steep slope we turned to look at the view and saw, to our horror, two men following us in the distance. No doubt they were Khampas. They had probably visited the nomads and been told which direction we had taken.

What were we to do? We said nothing, but later confessed to one another that we had silently made up our minds to sell our lives as dearly as possible. We tried at first to speed up our pace, but we could not go faster than our yak, who seemed to us to be moving at a snail's pace. We kept on looking back, but could not be sure whether our pursuers were coming up on us or not. We fully realized how heavily handicapped we were by our lack of arms. We had only tent poles and stones to defend ourselves with against their sharp swords. To have a chance we must depend on our wits. . . . So we marched on for an hour which seemed endless, panting with exertion and constantly turning round. Then we saw that the two men had sat down. We hurried on toward the top of the ridge, looking as we went for a place which would, if need be, serve as good fighting ground. The two men got up, seemed to be taking counsel together and then we saw them turn round and go back. We breathed again and drove our yak on so that we might soon be out of sight over the far side of the mountain.

When we reached the crest of the ridge we understood why our two pursuers had preferred to turn back. Before us lay the loneliest landscape I had ever seen. A sea of snowy mountain heights stretched onward endlessly. In the far distance were the Transhimalayas and like a gap in a row of teeth was the pass which we calculated would lead us to the road we aimed at. First put on the map by Sven Hedin, this pass—the Selala—leads to Shigatse. Being uncertain whether the Khampas had really given up the pursuit, we went on marching even after nightfall. Luckily the moon was high and, with the snow, gave us plenty of light. We could even see the distant ranges.

I shall never forget that night march. I have never been through an experience which placed such a strain on the body and the spirit. Our escape from the Khampas was due to the desolation of the region, the nature of which brought us new obstacles to surmount. It was a good thing that I had long ago thrown away my thermometer. Here it would have certainly marked minus thirty degrees as that was the lowest it could record. But that was certainly more than the reality. Sven Hedin registered minus forty degrees hereabouts at this season of the year.

Next day we toiled on painfully, trudging along in the footprints of our gallant yak and hardly looking up. In the afternoon we suddenly thought we were seeing the fata morgana; for, far away on the horizon, yet very clearly outlined, appeared three caravans of yaks moving through the snowy scene. They were moving very slowly forward; and then they seemed to come to a stop—but they did not vanish. So it was no mirage. The sight gave us new courage. We summoned up all our strength, drove our yak on, and after three hours' march reached the spot where the caravans were laagered. There were some fifteen persons in the caravan—men and women —and when we arrived their tents were already pitched. They were astonished to see us, but greeted us kindly and brought us in to get warm by the fire. We found out that they were returning from a combined pilgrimage and trading voyage to Mount Kailas to their homes by Lake Namtso.

What a pleasure it was to be once more sitting by a fire and ladling down hot soup. We felt that this meeting had been ordained by Providence. We did not forget our brave Armin, for we knew how much we owed him, and we asked the caravan leader to let us load our baggage on one of their free yaks, for which we would pay a day's hire. So our beast was able to enjoy a little rest.

Day after day we wandered on with the caravans and pitched our little mountaineer's tent alongside theirs. We suffered very much from the difficulty of pitching our tent during the hurricanes that often blew in these regions. Unlike the heavy yak-hair tents which could resist the wind, our light canvas hut would not stand up in rough weather and we sometimes had to bivouac in the open air. We swore that if we ever again came on an expedition to Tibet we should have with us three yaks, a driver, a nomad's tent and a rifle!

We thought ourselves very lucky to be allowed to join the caravans. The only thing which disturbed us was the extreme slowness of our progress. Compared with our previous marches we seemed to be gently strolling along. The nomads start early, and after covering three or four miles pitch their tents again and send their animals out to graze. Before nightfall they bring them in and fold them near the tents where they are safe from wolves and can ruminate in peace.

We agreed that we could not go on spending our life taking short walks. We must leave the caravan in the near future. We took leave of our friends on Christmas Eve and started off again alone. We felt fresh and rested and covered more than fourteen miles on the first day. Late in the evening we came to a wide plain on which were some isolated tents. Their inmates seemed to be very much on their guard, for as we approached a couple of wild-looking men, heavily armed came up to us. They shouted at us rudely and told us to go to the devil. We did not budge, but put up our hands to show we were not armed and explained to them that we were harmless pilgrims. In spite of our rest days with the caravan, we must have presented a pitiful appearance. After a short colloquy the owner of the larger tent asked us in to spend the night. We warmed ourselves by the fire and were given butter tea and a rare delicacy—a piece of white bread each. It was stale and hard as stone but this little present on Christmas Eve in the wilds of Tibet meant more to us than a well-cooked Christmas dinner had ever done at home.

Our host treated us roughly at first. When we told him by what route we aimed at reaching Lhasa he said dryly that if we had not been killed up to now, we certainly would be in the next few days. The country was full of Khampas. Without arms we would be an easy prey for them. He said this in a fatalistic tone, as one utters a self-evident truth. We felt very disheartened and asked for his advice. He recommended us to take the road to Shigatse which we could reach in a week. We would not hear of that. He thought for a while and then advised us to apply to the district officer of this region, whose tent was only a few miles distant. This officer would be able to give us an escort, if we absolutely insisted on going through the robbers' country.

That evening we had so much to discuss that we hardly gave a thought to Christmas in our own homes. At last we agreed to take a chance and visit the Pönpo. It only took us a few hours to reach his tent and we found it a good omen that he greeted us in a friendly way and placed a tent at our disposal. He then called his colleague and we all four sat down in conference. This time we discarded our story about being Indian pilgrims. We gave ourselves out as Europeans and demanded protection against the bandits. Naturally we were traveling with the permission of the government. This satisfied the Pönpos who promised us an escort; they would be relieved at different stages by fresh men, who would conduct us as far as the northern main road.

That was a real Christmas greeting for us! And now at last we felt like keeping the feast. We had stored up a little rice at Kyirong especially for the occasion. This we prepared and invited the two Pönpos to come and share it. They came bringing all sort of good things with them and we passed a happy, friendly evening together.

On the following day a nomad accompanied us to the next encampment and "delivered" us there. It was something like a relay race with us as the baton. Our guide went back after handing us over. With our next guide we made wonderful progress and we realized how useful it was to have a companion who really knew the way, even though he did not provide absolute security against robbers.

We often saw, happily in the far distance, men on horseback, whom we knew to be Khampas from the unusual type of dogs which accompanied them. These creatures are less hairy than ordinary Tibetan dogs, lean, swift as the wind and indescribably ugly. We thanked God we had no occasion to meet them and their masters at close quarters.

After five days' march we reached the famous Tasam road. We had always imagined this to be a regular highway which, once reached, would put an end to all the miseries of our march. Imagine our disappointment when we could not find even the trace of a track! The country was in no way different from that through which we had been wandering for weeks. There were, it is true, a few empty tents at which caravans could halt, but no other signs of an organized route.

For the last stage we had been accompanied by a couple of sturdy women, who now handed us over to the Tasam road after a touching farewell. We quartered ourselves in one of the empty tents and lit a fire, after which we took stock of our position. We really had some ground for satisfaction. The most difficult part of our journey lay behind us and we were now on a frequented route, which led straight to Lhasa, fifteen days' march ahead. We ought to have been happy in the knowledge that we were so near our goal. But, as a matter of fact, our terrific exertions had got us down to such an extent that we were no longer capable of enjoyment. What with frostbite and lack of money and food, we felt nothing but anxiety. We worried most of all about our animals. My faithful dog was reduced to skin and bones. We had hardly enough food to keep ourselves alive and could spare very little for him. His feet were in such a dreadful state that he could not keep up with us and often we had to wait for hours in our camp before he arrived. The plight of the yak was little better. He had not had enough grass to eat for weeks and was fearfully emaciated. It is true that we had left the snow behind us after leaving Lake Yöchabtso; but the grass was scanty and dry and there was little time for grazing.

All the same we had to go forward next day; and the fact that we were now a caravan route, and had no longer to think ourselves as Marco Polos in the unknown, gave a spur to our morale.

Our first day on the Tasam route differed very little from our worst stage in uninhabited country. We did not meet a soul. A raging storm, driving snow and swathes of mist made our journey a hell. Fortunately the wind was at our backs and drove us onward. If it had been in our faces, we could not have moved a step forward. All four of us were glad when we saw the roadside tents in the evening.

We took it easy and slept late. As we were breakfasting somewhat before noon, there was a stir before the tents. The cook of a Pönpo, wearing a foxskin hat, had arrived to announce the coming of his master and make preparations for him. He ran around and threw his weight about properly.

The arrival of a high official might be of importance for us, but we had been long enough in Asia to know that "high" official status is a relative conception. For the moment we did not excite ourselves. But things turned out well. The Pönpo soon arrived on horseback surrounded by a swarm of servants. He was a merchant in the service of the government and was at present engaged in bringing several hundred loads of sugar and cotton to Lhasa. Hearing about us, he naturally wanted to ask questions. Putting on a virtuous expression, I handed him our travel paper, which had the usual good effect. No longer acting the stern official, he invited us to travel with his convoy. That sounded well, so we gave up the rest day and began to pack our baggage as the caravan was to move on in the afternoon. One of the drivers shook his head as he looked at Armin, a veritable skeleton, and finally offered for a small sum to load our baggage on one of the Tasam yaks and let our beast run loose with us. We gladly agreed. Then off we started in haste. We had to go on with the caravan on foot, while the Pönpo and his servants, who had changed horses at the stage, started later. They caught us up before long. . . .

We had already been marching for some days toward a huge chain of mountains. We knew they were the Nyenchenthanglha Range. There was only one way through them and that was the pass which led direct to Lhasa. On our way to the mountains we passed through low hills. The country was completely deserted and we did not even see wild asses. The weather had improved greatly and the visibility was so good that, at a distance of six miles, our next stopping place appeared to be just in front of us.

The next halt was a place called Tokar. From here we began the ascent into the mountains, and the next regular station was five days away. We did not dare to think how we could hold out till then. In any case we did what we could to keep up our strength and bought a lot of meat to keep us going.

The days seemed endless and the nights even longer. We traveled through an improbably beautiful landscape and came to one of the largest of the world's lakes—Nam Tso or Tengri Nor. But we hardly looked at it, though we had for long looked forward to seeing this mighty inland sea. The once-longed-for sight could not shake us out of our apathy. The climb through the rarefied air had left us breathless, and the prospect of an ascent to nearly twenty thousand feet was paralyzing. From time to time we looked with wonder at the still higher peaks visible from our route. At last we reached the summit of our pass, Guring La. Before us this pass had only once been crossed by a European. This was Littledale, an Englishman, who came over it in 1895. Sven Hedin had estimated it at nearly twenty thousand feet and described it as the highest of the passes in the Transhimalaya region. I think I am right in saying that it is the world's highest pass traversable all the year round.

Here we again found the typical cairns, and fluttering over them the brightest-colored prayer flags I had yet seen. Near them was a row of stone tables with prayers inscribed on them—an imperishable expression of the joy felt by thousands of pilgrims when, after their long and weary march, they saw the pass opening to them the road to the holiest of cities.

Here, too, we met an astonishing throng of pilgrims returning to their distant homes. How often has this road echoed to the words *"Om mani padme hum,"* the time-honored formula of prayer that all Buddhists use and the pilgrims murmur ceaselessly, hoping, among other things, that it will protect them against what they believe is poison gas and we know to be lack of oxygen. They would do better to keep their mouths closed! From time to time we saw on the slopes below us skeletons of animals, bearing witness to the dangerous nature of the road. Our drivers told us that almost every winter pilgrims lost their lives in snowstorms in this mountain crossing. We thanked God for the good weather which had favored us during our climb of four thousand feet.

The first part of our descent led over a glacier. I had fresh cause to wonder at the extraordinary sure-footedness of the yaks in finding their way across the ice. As we stumbled along I couldn't help thinking how much easier it would be to glide over these smooth, uncreviced surfaces on skis. I suppose Aufschnaiter and I were the only people who had ever talked about skiing on the Pilgrims' Road to Lhasa.

In the evening of the fourth day after crossing the pass we reached Samsar, where there was a road station. At last we were in an inhabited place with built houses, monasteries and a castle. This is one of the most important road junctions in Tibet. Five routes meet here and there is a lively caravan traffic. The roadhouses are crowded, and animals are changed in the relay stables. Our Pönpo had already been here for two days, but though on a government mission he had to wait five days for fresh yaks. He procured us a room, fuel and a servant. For the moment the traffic was, so to speak, intense and we had to make up our minds for a long wait, for we could not go on alone.

We used our leisure to go on a day's excursion to some hot springs which we had seen steaming in the distance. These turned out to be a unique natural phenomenon. We came to a regular lake whose black bubbling waters flowed off into a clear burn. Of course we decided to bathe, and walked into the water at a point where it was pleasantly warm. As we walked upstream toward the lake it grew hotter and hotter. Aufschnaiter gave up first, but I kept on, hoping that the heat would be good for my sciatica. I wallowed in the hot water. I had brought with me my last piece of soap from Kyirong, and put it on the bank beside me, looking forward to a thorough soaping as the climax of my bath. Unluckily I had not noticed that a crow was observing me with interest. He suddenly swooped and carried off my treasure. I sprang onto the bank with an oath, but in a moment was back in the hot water, my teeth chattering with cold. In Tibet the crows are as thievish as magpies are with us.

On our way back we saw for the first time a Tibetan regiment—five hundred soldiers on maneuvers. The population is not very enthusiastic about these military exercises, as the soldiers have the right to requisition what they want. They camp in their own tents, which are pitched in very orderly fashion, and there is therefore no billeting; but the local people have to supply them with transport and even riding horses.

When we came back to our lodging a surprise was awaiting us. They had given us as roommate a man wearing fetters on his ankles and only able to take very short steps. He told us smilingly, and as if it was a perfectly normal thing, that he was a murderer and a robber and had been condemned first to receive two hundred lashes and afterward to wear fetters for the rest of his life. This made my flesh creep. Were we already classed with murderers? However, we soon learned that in Tibet a convicted criminal is not necessarily looked down on. Our man had no social disadvantages: he joined in conversation with everybody and lived on alms. And he didn't do so badly.

It had got round that we were Europeans, and curious persons were always coming to see us. Among them was a nice young monk, who was bringing some goods to the monastery of Drebung and had to be off the next day. When he heard that we only had one load of baggage and were very keen to continue our journey, he offered us a free yak in his caravan. He asked no questions about our travel permit. As we had previously reckoned, the nearer we came to the capital, the less trouble we had—the argument being that foreigners who had already traveled so far into Tibet must obviously possess a permit. Nevertheless we thought it wise not to stay too long in any one place, so as not to invite curiosity.

We accepted the monk's offer at once and bade farewell to our Pönpo with many expressions of gratitude. We started in pitch darkness, not long after midnight. After crossing the district of Yangpachen we entered a valley which debouched into the plain of Lhasa.

So near to Lhasa! The name had always given us a thrill. On our painful marches and during icy nights, we had clung to it and drawn new strength from it. No pilgrim from the most distant province could ever have yearned for the Holy City more than we did. We had already got much nearer to Lhasa than Sven Hedin. He had made two attempts to get through from the region through which we had come, but had always been held up in Changthang by the escarpment of Nyenchenthanglha. We two poor wanderers were naturally less conspicuous than his caravan and we had our knowledge of Tibetan to help us, in addition to the stratagems we had been compelled to use; so we had some things in our favor.

In the early morning we arrived at the next locality, Dechen, where we were to spend the day. We did not like the idea. There were two district officers in residence and we did not expect them to be taken in by any travel document.

Our friend the monk had not yet arrived. He had been able to allow himself a proper night's sleep, as he traveled on horseback, and no doubt he started about the time when we arrived at Dechen.

We cautiously started looking for a lodging and had a wonderful break. We made the acquaintance of a young lieutenant who very obligingly offered us his room as he had to leave about midday. He had been collecting in the neighborhood the money contributions payable in lieu of military service. We ventured to ask him whether he could not take our baggage in his convoy. Of course we would pay for it. He agreed at once and a few hours later we were marching with light hearts out of the village behind the caravan.

Our satisfaction was premature. As we passed the last houses someone called to us and when we turned round we found ourselves facing a distinguished-looking gentleman in rich silk garments. Unmistakably the Pönpo. He asked politely but in an authoritative tone where we had come from and where we were going. Only presence of mind could save us. Bowing and scraping, we said we were going on a short walk and had left our papers behind. On our return we would give ourselves the pleasure of waiting on his lordship. The trick succeeded, and we cleared off.

We found ourselves marching into spring scenery. The pasturelands grew greener as we went on. Birds twittered in the plantations and we felt too warm in our sheepskin cloaks, though it was only mid-January.

Lhasa was only three days away. All day Aufschnaiter and I tramped on alone and only caught up with the lieutenant and his little caravan in the evening. In this region all sorts of animals were used for transport—donkeys, horses, cows and bullocks. One saw only yaks in the caravans, as the peasants had not enough pasture to feed herds of them. Everywhere we saw the villagers irrigating their fields. The spring gales would come later, and if the soil were too dry it would all be blown away in dust. It often took generations before constant watering made the soil fertile. Here there is very little snow to protect the winter seed and the peasants cannot grow more than one crop. The altitude has naturally a great influence on agriculture. At 16,000 feet only barley will thrive and the peasants are half-nomads. In some regions the barley ripens in sixty days. The Tölung Valley through which we were now passing is 12,300 feet above sea level, and here they also grow roots, potatoes and mustard.

We spent the last night before coming to Lhasa in a peasant's house. It was nothing like so attractive as the stylish wooden houses in Kyirong. In these parts wood is rare. With the exception of small tables and wooden bedsteads there is practically no furniture. The houses, built of mud bricks, have no windows; light comes in only through the door or the smoke hole in the ceiling.

Our hosts belonged to a well-to-do peasant family. As is usual in a feudally organized country the peasant manages the property for his landlord, and must produce so much for him before making any profit for himself. In our household there were three sons, two of whom worked on the property whilst the third was preparing to become a monk. The family kept cows, horses, and a few fowls and pigs—the first I had seen in Tibet. These are not fed but live on offal and whatever they can grout up in the fields.

We passed a restless night thinking of the next day, which would decide our future. Now came the great question: even if we managed to smuggle ourselves into the town, would we be able to stay there? We had no money left. How, then, were we going to live? And our appearance! We looked more like brigands from the Changthang than Europeans. Over our stained woolen trousers and torn shirts we wore greasy sheepskin cloaks, which showed, even at a distance, how we had knocked about in them. Aufschnaiter wore the remains of a pair of Indian Army boots on his feet, and my shoes were in fragments. Both of us were more barefoot than shod. No, our appearance was certainly not in our favor. Our beards were perhaps our most striking feature. Like all Mongols, the Tibetans have almost no hair on their faces or bodies; whereas we had long, tangled, luxuriant beards. For this reason we were often taken for Kazaks, a Central Asian tribe whose members migrated in swarms during the war from Soviet Russia to Tibet. They marched in with their families and flocks and plundered right and left, and the Tibetan Army was at pains to drive them on into India. The Kazaks are often fair-skinned and blue-eyed and their beards grow normally. It is not surprising that we were mistaken for them, and met with a cold reception from so many nomads.

There was nothing to be done about our appearance. We could not

238 *The Great Explorers*

spruce ourselves up before going to Lhasa. Even if we had had money, where could we buy clothes?

Since leaving Nangtse—the name of the last village—we had been left to our own devices. The lieutenant had ridden on into Lhasa and we had to bargain with our host about transport for our baggage. He lent us a cow and a servant and when we had paid we had a rupee and a half left and a gold piece sewn up in a piece of cloth. We had decided that if we could not find any transport, we would just leave our stuff behind. Barring our diaries, notes and maps, we had nothing of value. Nothing was going to hold us back.

It was January 15, 1946, when we set out on our last march. From Tölung we came into the broad valley of Kyichu. We turned a corner and saw, gleaming in the distance, the golden roofs of the Potala, the winter residence of the Dalai Lama and the most famous landmark of Lhasa. This moment compensated us for much. We felt inclined to go down on our knees like the pilgrims and touch the ground with our foreheads. Since leaving Kyirong we had covered over six hundred miles with the vision of this fabulous city ever in our mind's eye. We had marched for seventy days and only rested during five. That meant a daily average of almost ten miles. Forty-five days of our journey had been spent in crossing the Changthang—days full of hardship and unceasing struggle against cold, hunger and danger. Now all that was forgotten as we gazed at the golden pinnacles—six miles more and we had reached our goal.

We sat down near the cairns which the pilgrims put up to mark their first sight of the Holy City. Our driver, meanwhile, performed his devotions. Going on, we soon came to Shingdongka, the last village before Lhasa. The cowman refused to come any farther, but nothing could discourage us now. We went to find the Pönpo and coolly informed him that we were the advance party of a powerful foreign personage on his way to Lhasa and that we had to reach the city as quickly as possible in order to find quarters for our master. The Pönpo swallowed our tale and gave us an ass and a driver. Years later this story used still to set people laughing at parties in Lhasa, even the houses of ministers. The fact is the Tibetans are very proud of their organization for keeping foreigners out of the country, and they found the manner in which we had broken through the barriers not only deserving of attention but highly humorous. That was all to our advantage, for the Tibetans are a laughter-loving folk.

During the last six miles of the road we mixed with a stream of pilgrims and caravans. From time to time we passed stalls displaying all sorts of delicacies—sweets, white bread and what-not—which almost brought the tears to our eyes. But we had no money. Our last rupee belonged to our driver.

We soon began to recognize the landmarks of the town about which we had read so often. Over there must be Chagpori, the hill on which stands one of the two famous Schools of Medicine. And here in front of us was Drebung, the greatest monastery in the world, which houses ten thousand monks and is a city in itself, with its multitude of stone houses and hundreds of gilded pinnacles pointing upward above the shrines. Somewhat lower down lay the terraces of Nechung, another monastery, which has for centuries been the home of the greatest mystery of Tibet. Here is made manifest the presence of a protective deity, whose secret oracle guides the destinies of Tibet and is consulted by the government before any important decision is taken. We had still five miles to go and every few steps there was something fresh to look at. We passed through broad well-tended meadows surmounted by willows where the Dalai Lama pastures his horses.

For nearly an hour a long stone wall flanked our road and we were told that the summer palace of the God-King lay behind it. Next we passed the British Legation, situated just outside the town, half-hidden by willow trees. Our driver turned to go toward it thinking it must be our destination and we had some trouble in persuading him to go straight on. In fact for a moment we hesitated about going there ourselves, but the memory of the internment camp was still present in our minds and we thought that, after all, we were in Tibet and that it was the Tibetans we should ask for hospitality.

Nobody stopped us or bothered about us. We could not understand it, but finally realized that no one, not even a European, was suspect, because no one had ever come to Lhasa without a pass.

As we approached, the Potala towered ever higher before us. As yet we could see nothing of the town itself, which lay behind the hills on which the palace and the School of Medicine stood. Then we saw a great gate crowned with three *chörten*, which spans the gap between the two hills and forms the entrance to the city. Our excitement was intense. Now we should know our fate for certain. Almost every book about Lhasa says that sentries are posted here to guard the Holy City. We approached with beating hearts. But there was nothing. No soldiers, no control post, only a few beggars holding out their hands for alms. We mingled with a group of people and walked unhindered through the gateway into the town. Our driver told us that the group of houses on our left was only a sort of suburb and so we went on through an unbuilt area coming ever nearer to the middle of the town. We spoke no word, and to this day I can find no terms to express how overwhelming were our sensations. Our minds, exhausted by hardships, could not absorb the shock of so many and such powerful impressions.

We were soon in front of the turquoise-roofed bridge and saw for the first time the spires of the Cathedral of Lhasa. The sun set and bathed the scene in an unearthly light. Shivering with cold we had to find a lodging, but in Lhasa it is not so simple to walk into a house as into a tent in the Changthang. We should probably be at once reported to the authorities. But we had to try. In the first house we found a dumb servant, who would not listen to us. Next door there was only a maid who screamed for help till her mistress came and begged us to go somewhere else. She said she would be driven out of the quarter if she received us. We did not believe that the government could be as strict as all that, but we did not want to cause her unpleasantness and so went out again. We walked through some narrow streets and found ourselves already at the other side of the town. There we came to a house much larger and finer-looking than any we had yet seen, with stables in the courtyard. We hurried in to find ourselves confronted by servants, who abused us and told us to go away. We were not to be moved and unloaded our donkey. Our driver had already been pressing us to let him go home. He had noticed that everything was not in order. We gave him his money and he went off with a sigh of relief.

The servants were in despair when they saw that we had come to stay. They begged and implored us to go and pointed out that they would get into fearful trouble when their master returned. We, too, felt far from comfortable at the idea of exacting hospitality by force, but we did not move. More and more people were attracted by the din, and the scene reminded me of my departure from Kyirong. We remained deaf to all protestations. Dead-tired and half-starved we sat on the ground by our bundles, indifferent to what might befall us. We only wanted to sit, to rest, to sleep.

The angry cries of the crowd suddenly ceased. They had seen our swollen and blistered feet, and, open-hearted, simple folk as they were, they felt pity for us. A woman began it. She was the one who had implored us to leave her house. Now she brought us butter tea. And now they brought us all sorts of things—*tsampa*, provisions and even fuel. The people wanted to atone for their inhospitable reception. We fell hungrily on the food and for the moment forgot everything else.

Suddenly we heard ourselves addressed in perfect English. We looked up, and though there was not much light to see by, we recognized that the richly clad Tibetan who had spoken to us must be a person of the highest standing. Astonished and happy we asked him if he was not, perchance, one of the four young nobles who had been sent to school at Rugby. He said he was not but that he had passed many years in India. We told him shortly what had happened to us, saying we were Germans, and begging to be taken in. He thought for a moment and then said that he could not admit us to his house without the approval of the town magistrate, but he would go to that official and ask for permission.

When he had gone the other people told us that he was an important official and was in charge of the electricity works. We did not dare to set too much store by what he had said, but nevertheless began to settle down for the night. Meanwhile we sat by the fire and talked to the people, who kept coming and going. Then a servant came to us and asked us to follow him saying that Mr. Thangme, the Master of Electricity, invited us into his house. They called him respectfully "Ku-ngö," equivalent to "Highness," and we followed suit.

Thangme and his young wife received us very cordially. Their five children stood around and looked at us open-mouthed. Their father had good news for us. The magistrate had allowed him to take us in for one night, but future arrangements would have to be decided by the Cabinet. We did not worry our heads about the future. After all we were in Lhasa and were the guests of a noble family. A nice, comfortable room was already prepared for us with a small iron stove which warmed us well. It was seven years since we had seen a stove! The fuel used was juniper wood, which smelt very good and was a real luxury, for it needed weeks of travel on the backs of yaks to bring it into Lhasa. We hardly dared, in our ragged garments, to sit on our clean carpet-covered beds. They brought us a splendid Chinese supper, and as we ate they all stood round and talked to us without ceasing. What we must have been through! They could hardly believe that we had crossed the Changthang in winter and climbed over the Nyenchenthanglha Range. Our knowledge of Tibetan astonished them. But how ugly and shabby we seemed to ourselves in these civilized surroundings. Our possessions, indispensable to our journey, suddenly lost all their attraction and we felt we would be glad to be rid of them.

Dead-tired and confused in mind we went at last to bed, but we could

242   *The Great Explorers*

not go to sleep. We had spent too many nights on the hard ground with nothing but our sheepskin cloaks and a torn blanket to cover us. Now we had soft beds and a well-warmed room, but our bodies could not quickly accustom themselves to the change and our thoughts revolved like mill-wheels in our heads. All we had gone through crowded into our minds—the internment camp and the adventures and hardships of the twenty-one months since our escape. And we thought of our comrades and the un-broken monotony of their lives, for though the war had long been over the prisoners were still in captivity. But, for that matter, were *we* now free?

Before we were properly awake we found a servant with sweet tea and cakes standing by our beds. Then they brought us hot water and we at-tacked our long beards with our razors. After shaving we looked more respectable but our long hair was a grave problem. A Moslem barber was called in to get busy on our manes. The result was somewhat exotic, but provoked lively admiration. Tibetans have no trouble with their coiffure. Either they have pigtails or shaven heads.

We did not see Thangme till noon, when he came home much relieved after a visit to the Foreign Minister. He brought us good news and told us we would not be handed over to the English. For the time being we might remain in Lhasa but were politely requested to stay indoors until the Regent, who was in retreat at Taglung Tra, decided about our future. We were given to understand that this was a precautionary measure made advisable by previous incidents in which fanatical monks had been involved. The government was willing to feed and clothe us.

We were highly delighted. A few days' rest was just what we needed. We attacked a mountain of old newspapers with enthusiasm, though the news we gathered was not precisely exhilarating. The whole world was still simmering and our country was going through hard times.

On the same day we received a visit from an official sent by the town magistrate. He was accompanied by six policemen, who looked dirty and untrustworthy. But our visitor was most polite and asked leave to inspect our baggage. We were were astonished that he should be doing his job with such exactness. He had with him a report from Kyirong which he compared with the dates of our itinerary. We ventured to ask him if all the officials through whose districts we had passed would really be punished. "The whole matter will come before the Cabinet," he said thoughtfully, "and the officials must expect to be punished." This upset us very much, and to his amuse-ment we told him how we had dodged the district officers and how often we had deceived them. It was our turn to laugh when he then announced to us that the evening before he had been expecting a German invasion of Lhasa. It seems that everyone with whom we had spoken had rushed off to report to the magistrate. They had the impression that German troops were marching into the city!

In any case we were the talk of the town. Everyone wanted to see us and to hear the story of our adventures with his own ears, and as we were not allowed out people came to visit us. Mrs. Thangme had her hands full and prepared her best tea service to receive guests. We were initiated into the ceremonial of tea parties. Respect for guests is shown by the value and beauty of the tea service. The teacups consist of three parts: a stand, a porcelain cup and a cover. The stand and the cover are often of silver or gold.

Every day important guests came to Thangme's house. He himself was a noble of the fifth class, and since etiquette is very closely observed here, he had hitherto only received the visits of persons of equal or inferior rank. But now it was the most highly placed personages who wanted to see us. Foremost among them was the son of the celebrated Minister Tsarong and his wife. We had already read much about his father. Born in humble circumstances, he became the favorite of the thirteenth Dalai Lama, rose to a highly honorable position and acquired a great fortune by his industry and intelligence. Forty years ago the Dalai Lama was obliged to flee before the Chinese into India, and Tsarong then rendered his master valuable service. He was for many years a Cabinet Minister and as first favorite of the Lama had virtually the powers of a Regent. Subsequently a new favorite named Khünpela dislodged Tsarong from his position of authority. He was, however, able to retain his rank and dignities. Tsarong was now in the third order of the nobility and was Master of the Mint.

His son was twenty-six years old. He had been brought up in India and spoke fluent English. Conscious of his own importance he wore a golden amulet in his pigtail, as the son of a minister had the right to do.

When this young noble came to call, servants handed tea and soon the conversation became lively. The Minister's son was an incredibly versatile young man with a special interest in technical matters. He asked us about the latest discoveries, and told us that he had put together his own radio receiving set and fixed a wind-driven generator on the roof of his house.

We were in the middle of a technical discussion in English, when his wife interrupted us laughingly and said she wanted to ask us some questions. Yangchenla, as she was called, was one of the beauties of Lhasa; she was well dressed and very *soignée,* and clearly acquainted with the use of powder, rouge and lipstick. She was not at all shy, as was obvious from the lively manner in which she questioned us in Tibetan about our journey. Now and again she broke into our explanations with swift gestures and bursts of laughter. She was particularly amused by our account of how we had imposed on the officials with our expired travel permit. She seemed to be astonished at our fluency in Tibetan, but we noticed that neither she nor even the most staid of our visitors could forbear from laughing at us from time to time. Later our friends told us that we spoke the commonest kind of peasant dialect that one could imagine. It was rather like a backwoodsman from the remotest Alpine valley talking his own lingo in a Viennese drawing room. Our visitors were immensely amused but much too polite to correct us.

By the time this young couple left us we had made friends with them. They had brought with them some very welcome gifts—linen, pull-overs and cigarettes, and they begged us to tell them frankly when we wanted anything. The Minister's son promised to help us and later delivered a message from his father inviting us to go and stay with him, if the government gave us their approbation. That all sounded very consoling.

More visitors came trooping in. Our next was a general of the Tibetan Army, who was desperately anxious to learn everything possible about Rommel. He spoke with enthusiasm of the German general and said that with his smattering of English he had read everything available about him in the newspapers. In this respect Lhasa is not at all isolated. Newspapers come in from all over the world via India. There are even a few persons in the town who take in *Life*. The Indian daily papers arrive regularly a week after publication.

The procession of visitors continued. Among them were highly placed monks, who courteously brought us gifts. Some of them became my good friends later on. Then there was a representative of the Chinese Legation and after him an official belonging to the British Agency in Sikkim.

We were particularly honored by the visit of the Commander-in-Chief of the Tibetan Army, General Künsangtse, who insisted on seeing us before leaving for China and India on a friendly mission. He was the younger brother of the Foreign Minister and an unusally well-informed man. It took a load off our minds when he assured us that our request for permission to stay in Tibet would certainly be approved.

We gradually began to feel at home. Our relations with Thangme and his wife developed into a cordial friendship. We were mothered and well fed and everyone was pleased to see that we had such good appetites. However, doubtless as a reaction from hardship and overstrain, we suffered from all sorts of minor complaints. Aufschnaiter had an attack of fever and my sciatica gave me a lot of trouble. Thangme sent for the doctor of the Chinese Legation who had studied in Berlin and Bordeaux. He examined us in approved European style and prescribed various medicines.

It is probable that no other country in the world would welcome two poor fugitives as Tibet welcomed us. Our parcel of clothes, the gift of the government, had arrived with apologies for delay caused by the fact that we were taller than the average Tibetan and there were no ready-made clothes to fit us. So our suits and shoes were made to measure. We were as pleased as children. At last we were able to throw away our lousy old rags. Our new suits, though not up to the highest sartorial standards, were recent and tidy and quite good enough for us.

In the intervals between our numerous visits we worked at our notebooks and diaries. And we soon made friends with the Thangmes' children, who usually had already gone off to school before we got up. In the evening they showed us their homework which interested me very much as I was taking some trouble to learn the written language. Aufschnaiter had long been studying this and during our wanderings had taught me something, but it took me years to learn to write Tibetan more or less fluently. The individual letters present no difficulty, but their arrangement into syllables is no easy task. Many of the characters are taken from the ancient Indian scripts, and Tibetan writing looks more like Hindi than Chinese. Fine, durable parchment-like paper is used and Chinese ink. There are in Tibet several high-class mills, where the paper is made from juniper wood. In addition thousands of loads of paper are imported yearly from Nepal and Bhutan, where the stuff is manufactured in the same way as in Tibet. I have often watched the process of paper-making on the banks of the Kyichu River. The chief drawback of Tibetan paper is that the surface is not smooth enough, which makes writing difficult. Children are usually given wooden tablets for their exercises and use watered ink and bamboo pens. The writing can afterward be wiped out with a wet cloth. Thangme's children often had to rub out their exercises twenty times before getting them right.

Soon we were treated like members of the family. Mrs. Thangme talked over her problems with us, and was delighted when we paid her compliments on her good looks and good taste. Once she invited us to come into her room and look at her jewels. These she kept in a great chest in which her treasures were stored either in small jewel cases or in fine silk wrappings. Her treasures were worth looking at. She had a glorious tiara of corals, turquoise and pearls, and many rings as well as diamond earrings and some little Tibetan amulet-lockets which are hung round the neck by a coral chain. Many women never take these lockets off. The amulet they contain acts as a talisman which, they believe, protects them from evil.

Our hostess was flattered by our admiration of her treasures. She told us that every man was obliged to present his wife with the jewels corresponding to his rank. Promotion in rank entailed promotion in jewelry! But to be merely rich was not enough, for wealth did not confer the right to wear costly jewels. Of course the men grumble about their wives' pretensions, for here, as in the West, every woman seeks to outshine her rivals. Mrs. Thangme, whose jewels must have been worth several thousand pounds, told us that she never went out unaccompanied by a servant, as attacks by thieves on society women were common.

Eight days passed, during which we had dutifully kept indoors. It was a great surprise to us when one day servants came bringing an invitation to visit the home of the Dalai Lama's parents, and telling us to come at once. As we felt ourselves bound by our promise not to leave the house, we consulted our host. He was horrified that we should have any misgivings; such an invitation overrode everything else. A summons from the Dalai Lama or the Regent had precedence over all other considerations. No one would dare to detain us or later to call us to account. On the contrary, hesitation to comply would be a serious offense.

We were glad to learn his opinion, but then began to be nervous about the reason for our summons. Was it a good omen for our future? Anyhow we hurriedly prepared ourselves for the visit, dressing ourselves in our new clothes and Tibetan boots for the first time. We looked quite presentable. Thangme then gave us each a pair of white silk scarves and impressed on us that we must present them when we were received in audience. We had already witnessed this custom in Kyirong and had noticed that it was observed by quite simple people. When paying visits or presenting a petition to a person of higher standing, or at the great festivals, one is supposed to give presents of scarves. These scarves are found in all sorts of qualities and the kind of scarf offered should be consistent with the rank of the giver.

The house of the parents of the Dalai Lama was not far away. We soon found ourselves standing before a great gate, near which the gatekeeper was already on the lookout for us. When he approached he bowed respectfully. We were led through a large garden full of vegetable plots and clusters of splendid willows till we came to the palace. We were taken up to the first floor: a door was opened and we found ourselves in the presence of the mother of the God-King, to whom we bowed in reverence. She was sitting on a small throne in a large, bright room surrounded by servants. She looked the picture of aristocratic dignity. The humble awe which the Tibetans feel for the Great Mother is something strange to us, but we found the moment a solemn one.

The Great Mother smiled at us and was visibly pleased when we handed her the scarves with deep obeisances and stretching out our arms to the fullest extent as Thangme had instructed us. She took them from us and handed them at once to the servants. Then with a beaming countenance she shook our hands, contrary to Tibetan custom. At that moment in came the father of the Dalai Lama, a dignified elderly man. We bowed low again and handed him scarves with due ceremony, after which he shook our hands most unaffectedly. Now and then Europeans came to the house, and the host and hostess were to some degree familiar with European customs and not a little proud of the fact.

Then we all sat down to tea. The tea we drank had a strange flavor, and was made differently from the usual Tibetan brew. We asked about it, and the question broke the ice, for it led our hosts to tell us about their former home. They had lived in Amdo as simple peasants until their son was recognized as the Incarnation of the Dalai Lama. Amdo is in China, in the province of Chinghai, but its inhabitants are almost all Tibetan. They had brought their tea with them to Lhasa and now made it, not as the Tibetans do with butter, but adding milk and salt. They brought something else from their old home—the dialect they spoke. They both used a patois similar to that of the central provinces, but not the same. The fourteen-year-old brother of the Dalai Lama interpreted for them. He had come as a child to Lhasa and had quickly learnt to speak pure Tibetan. He now spoke the Amdo dialect only with his parents.

While we were conversing with them we took occasion to observe our hosts. Each of them made a very good impression. Their humble origin expressed itself in an attractive simplicity, but their bearing and demeanor were aristocratic. It was a big step from a small peasant's house in a distant province to a dukedom in the capital. They now owned the palace they lived in and large properties in the country. But they seemed to have survived the sudden revolution in their lives without deterioration.

The boy whom we met, Lobsang Samten, was lively and wide-awake. He was full of curiosity about us and asked us all manner of questions about our experiences. He told us that his "divine" younger brother had charged him to report on us exactly. We felt pleasantly excited by the news that the Dalai Lama was interested in us, and would have liked to learn more of him. We were told that the name Dalai Lama is not used in Tibet at all. It is a Mongolian expression meaning "Broad Ocean." Normally the Dalai Lama is referred to as the "Gyalpo Rimpoche," which means "Precious King." His parents and brothers use another title in speaking of him. They call him "Kundün," which simply means "Presence."

The Great Parents had in all six children. The eldest son, long before the discovery of the Dalai Lama, had been recognized as an Incarnation of Buddha and invested with the dignity of a Lama in the monastery of Tagtsel. He too was styled "Rimpoche," the form of address applied to all Lamas. The second son, Gyalo Töndrup, was at school in China. Our young acquaintance Lobsang himself was destined for a monastic life. The Dalai Lama himself was now eleven years old. Besides his brothers he had two sisters. Subsequently the Great Mother gave birth to another "Incarnation," Ngari Rimpoche. As the mother of three Incarnations she held the record for the Buddhist world.

Our visit led to cordial relations with this adaptable, clever woman, which were to continue until she fled before the invasion of the Reds from China. Our friendship had nothing to do with the transcendental worship which the Great Mother received from others. But though I have a fairly skeptical attitude toward metaphysical matters, I could not but recognize the power of personality and faith with which she was invested.

It gradually became clear to us what a distinction this invitation was. One must not forget that, with the exception of his family and a few personal servants holding the rank of abbot, no one has the right to address the God-King. Nevertheless, in his isolation from the world he had deigned to take an interest in our fate. When we rose to leave we were asked if we needed anything. We thanked our hosts, but preferred modestly to ask for nothing; in spite of which a line of servants marched up with sacks of meal and *tsampa*, a load of butter and some beautiful soft woolen blankets. "By the personal desire of the Kundün," said the Great Mother, smiling, and pressed into our hands a hundred-sang note. This was done so naturally and as if it was a matter of course that we felt no shame about accepting.

After many expressions of thanks and deep obeisances, we left the room in some embarrassment. As a final proof of friendliness Lobsang, on behalf of his parents, laid the scarves on our necks as we bowed to him. He then took us into the garden and showed us the grounds and the stables, where we saw some splendid horses from Siling and Ili, the pride of his father. In the course of conversation he let drop the suggestion that I might give him lessons in some branches of Western knowledge. That chimed in with my own secret wishes. I had often thought that I could manage to keep myself by giving lessons to the children of noble families.

Loaded with gifts and escorted by servants we returned to Thangme's house. We were in high spirits and felt that now our fortunes were on the mend. Our hosts awaited us with impatient excitement. We had to tell them everything that had happened, and our next visitors were informed in detail of the honor that had been done to us. Our shares rose steeply!

Next day, when the brothers of the Dalai Lama came to visit us, our hostess at first concealed herself out of reverence and appeared only when the whole household had been mustered to greet them. The young Rimpoche, now five and twenty years old, had actually come from his monastery to see us. He laid his hand in blessing on each member of the household. He was the first Incarnated Lama whom we came to know.

SILENT UPON A PEAK IN DARIEN— BALBOA DISCOVERS THE PACIFIC

by Jeannette Mirsky

In all human history, there has rarely been a page so filled with bloodshed and melodrama as that which records the doings of the conquistadors, who were to take possession of all that territory now known as Latin America. As a result of their conquests, Spain was to annex land as far north as California and, excluding Portuguese Brazil, as far south as Tierra del Fuego. The story began with the epic voyages of Columbus. He was succeeded in a matter of years by dozens of expeditions which discovered countless new islands and sailed south and then north along both coasts of South America. In 1500, Vicente Pinzón, who had been captain of the Nina, discovered Brazil and first entered the Amazon, which he called the Freshwater Sea. And Ponce de León, who governed Puerto Rico so savagely that even the Spaniards removed him from power, sailed north to Florida, the land of eternal youth.

Almost at the same time, a Spanish adventurer named Vasco Núñez de Balboa made a discovery which was to rank him among the immortals of exploration. He set out for the New World as a gentleman adventurer, but was shipwrecked on the coast of Española. Clad in rusty mail, his only possession a sword and a dog, he stowed away aboard another expedition, and was allowed to join the company. By superior knowledge, bravery and judgment, he worked his way to leadership of a new settlement in Darien, but in doing so incurred the enmity of Ensico, the former leader, who being forced to return to Spain, so plotted and connived that he destroyed Balboa in the end.

It was in Darien that Balboa heard rumors of a Western ocean, and in a trip across the isthmus made his great discovery. The stirring account by Jeannette Mirsky which follows tells how his journey was accomplished.

It is noteworthy that almost alone among the Spanish conquerors, Balboa showed some sympathy and understanding for the Indians whom he encountered. He accepted as wife the daughter of an Indian chieftain. He treated the tribes he met with respect and kindness and his way was greatly smoothed thereby. His record is one of the few bright spots in a black picture; but it did not avail him against the intrigues of his rivals, who finally did him to death.

IN MINIATURE, the expedition of Balboa is a true picture of what Spanish expeditions were to be: the small insecure footing along the coasts, the advance into unknown and hostile territory, the daily problems of food, health, and transportation, the conquest of nature and natives, the inevitability of the triumph of steel and gunpowder, the sad slaughter as two antithetical civilizations met and tested their unequal strengths, the unbelievable energy that drove the invaders, the singleness of purpose, the final victory. Sometimes one element becomes the dominant note in a particular saga, sometimes another; but always all the elements are there. Other conquistadors, Soto and Cabeza de Vaca, were to have longer and more dramatic odysseys; Cortés and Pizarro and Belalcázar were to conquer far greater and richer kingdoms; but all of them came after Vasco Núñez. His was the first, daring step into the unknown interior. As Columbus had been a pioneer in opening the gates of the Atlantic, so Balboa was the pioneer who ventured still farther into the unknown, into the land of the New World. This, then, and not the number of days or miles, or millions, is the measure of his greatness. Unlike Cortés he had no legend of the returning god, Quetzalcoatl[1], to smooth his path and paralyze his enemies; he had no long-remembering, nostalgic Bernal Díaz to record his

[1] Among the Mexicans there was a prophecy that their god Quetzalcoatl, the Feathered Serpent, would return in the guise of a white, bearded conqueror from the East. Cortés fitted this ancient prediction so well that Montezuma was not sure, until too late, whether he should welcome the god or fight an intruder. Cortés, in his conquest of Mexico, certainly the most famous of all the Spanish assaults on the New World, invites comparison with Balboa. My own feeling is that had Balboa escaped execution—as Cortés did—he would have rivaled him in stature and achievement.

deeds and thoughts and stratagems for posterity. Balboa, the man, rising to greatness and vision, flashed upon the world and vanished in a cloud of blood.

Leaving the steaming, swampy lowlands, Balboa and his men headed for the mountains. Immediately the jungle swallowed them, that massed green that majestically swept almost to the top of the cordilleras. For two days they worked their way over jagged, mountainous country until they arrived at a cluster of leaf-roofed houses, the land and village of Ponca, who had fled before the intruders. But Balboa, marching away from his base, was not content to leave an enemy between himself and the coast.

Occupying the village, Balboa sent to Ponca messengers promising friendship and offering protection against his enemies. Ponca grabbed at this invitation and quickly returned from his hiding place. The two leaders greeted one another warmly and then exchanged presents. Ponca showered Balboa with gold, knowing the surest way to the white man's heart was by such offerings, and excused its modest amount by reminding Balboa that the Spaniards had taken all his gold on their previous visit. Not to be outdone, Balboa presented him with necklaces of glass beads, mirrors, copper bells, and other trifles that the Indians prized highly, and then secured his friendship firmly with a special gift of iron hatchets, the article most valued by the natives. Until the Europeans brought the Indians iron, stones wrought to a razor edge were laboriously used to fell great trees, to build houses, and to shape canoes. Delighted with this princely present, Ponca offered his new friend guides and bearers. Careta's[2] men, who had served in these capacities, were dismissed with presents and sent home well satisfied with Balboa's generosity. Twelve men who were too ill to proceed were left behind for Ponca to care for and, on their recovery, to be helped back to Puerto Careta.

On September 20, Balboa left his good friend Ponca and pushed on. He faced the sudden, sharp lift of the mountains as they stretched up to their full height. During the next four days the party struggled step by step up slippery cliffs, up tree-tangled slopes; thunderous cascades caused long detours; boiling, foaming streams were perilously crossed on bridges improvised by the natives; they scrambled up and on in the darkness of the matted forest.[3] They spent four sweating, puffing days before they reached the territory ruled by the chief Quarequá, powerful, rich, warlike, and so

---

[2] An Indian chieftain whose daughter Balboa had married.—Eds.

[3] Prevost in 1853 found the forest so dense that for eleven days he did not see the clear sky.

secure in his remote mountain fastness that no one had thought to warn him of the white men who had newly come to the coast. Quarequá, the invincible, held the key to transit across the isthmus; here would be decided the outcome of their quest. Balboa first saw the redoubtable chief when the latter, surrounded by his war chiefs and backed by his thousand warriors, advanced, as was his custom, to challenge intruders. "Retrace your steps if you do not wish to be killed to the last man."

So for a moment they faced one another, the small band of Spaniards wearing metal helmets and corselets, their swords drawn, the crossbows fixed, the harquebuses primed; crouched at their feet, their trained dogs waited the signal to jump at the throats of the two-legged game. Their guides and bearers, men of Ponca's tribe, hung back wondering if their powerful new friends could overcome Quarequá, the undisputed master of that region, whose name spelled terror, whose men had never known defeat. The Spaniards looked at the large force opposing them, blocking their path. Quarequá and his war chiefs wore plates of gold on their chests and arms, massive pieces beautifully worked that served as armor and as insignia of rank, resplendent against their copper skins; their breechclouts flaunted golden codpieces or bright seashells to cover their nakedness; they carried shields made of wood and covered with animal skins, heavy two-handed wooden swords, bows and arrows, and fire-hardened, sharp-pointed wooden lances that, hurled from a throwing stick, could go clean through a naked enemy. They relied on these deadly javelins, on their vast superiority of numbers, on supernatural aid invoked by beaten drums and blown conch shells. For a moment the two sides were poised for battle, the Indians disdainful of this small intrusive party, the Spaniards confident of their firearms. Then the slaughter began.

Shouting their battle cries, seeking to drown the small band under waves of warriors, the Indians, led by Quarequá, threw themselves on the Spaniards, who, not yielding an inch, fired their weapons. At this point-blank discharge, the natives stopped. What gods were these that could vomit fire and thunder and kill and wound men they had not even touched? And as they stood, the archers loosed their crossbows and killed and wounded more. Stunned, for a moment the Indians wavered; and, before they could turn to flee, the Spaniards were among them, wielding their sharp steel swords, hacking off arms, legs, cutting through a thigh, severing a head; like butchers cutting up beef and mutton for market, they hacked and cut until Quarequá and six hundred were slain. The dogs pursued the naked, terror-stricken natives and brought them down as though they were wild boars or timid deer. Those who were left alive looked with horror on the battle-field strewn, not with corpses decently slain, but with a mass of arms, legs, torsos, and heads, separate and terrible. Not a Spaniard was killed, and only a few had received slight wounds.

Among the prisoners taken were Quarequá's brother and other chiefs who, dressed in long cotton shirts, were accused by the interpreter of wearing women's clothes because they shared the same passion. To the Spaniards such abnormality was abhorrent and a sign of the Devil, and Balboa right-eously ordered forty of these perverts to be torn to pieces by the dogs. Peter Martyr comments approvingly:

> When the natives saw how severely Vasco had treated these shameless men, they pressed about him as though he were Hercules, and spitting upon those whom they suspected of being guilty of this vice, they begged him to exterminate them, for the contagion was confined to the courtiers and had not yet spread to the people. They gave it to be understood that this sin was the cause of famine and sickness.

When the dogs had finished their terrible task, the bodies were burned.

Surrounded by the broken, fearful natives, who in a few hours had seen their chief, all their nobles, and most of their warriors killed, the Spaniards entered their village. The houses were systematically searched for loot; the golden breastplates and armbands, the golden, polished, mirrorlike discs, and the fantastic nose plugs were stripped from the dead; that was done before Balboa and his men ate and rested in the village of the dead chief. Night came swiftly, and in this mountain country it was cold.

So thorough had been the defeat of Quarequá that Balboa felt free to leave his sick and wounded men in the village to recuperate. Dismissing the guides and bearers furnished him by Ponca, he sent them back with presents. The stunning news of the great victory traveled back with them.

Early in the morning Balboa would take the trail and, with some newly made captives as guides, would lead his seventy men to the mountain peak from which he had been promised a view of the Southern Sea, that sea which he had staked so much, had struggled and fought so hard, to reach. So near he was, so very near, the promise so imminent, that he forgot that he was tired, forgot the cold that made his weary muscles stiff, and knew only that the cold night was long and never-ending. Doubt haunted him, and he wondered if he had been told legend or lies. Would he find the sea as the Indian youth had promised; or had he spent his men, his time and strength, in following false words cunningly spoken? Tomorrow he would stand on his peak and feed his eyes on the blue of the distant sea; but until then he must wait in the awful loneliness of his purpose.

A slight wind came with the morning, and with the dawn they were on the trail. That morning, September 25, a guide, pointing to a near-by mountain, told Balboa that from its summit the Southern Sea was visible. Longingly, he looked where the man pointed. He bade his men wait, and taking only his dog, Leoncico, climbed the peak. With each step forward his tension eased. A moment more, a few more steps, he was at the last rise; he would know whether his venture was to be crowned with success. He was at the bare open summit. He looked, and there was the sight never seen before by any man coming out of his world; and the sight he saw brought him to his knees. There was the sea! a pellucid blue, shot with the gold and silver of the midmorning sun, a mighty sea that thrust an arm deep into the land. He raised his hand to Heaven and saluted the Southern Sea! And its presence proclaimed his success, his firm reconciliation with the King, his fame, his fortune. From his wildly beating heart he poured forth his boundless gratitude to God—thanking Him and all the heavenly host who had reserved this glory for him, a man of but small wit and knowledge, of little experience and lowly parentage.

When Balboa's first wave of relief and thanksgiving was spent he waved his hand to his companions and when they had come up to him he showed them the great sea heretofore unknown to the inhabitants of Europe, Africa, and Asia. Prouder than Hannibal showing Italy and the Alps to his soldiers, Balboa promised great riches to them: "Behold the much-desired ocean! Behold, all you men who have shared such efforts, behold the country of which the son of Comogre and all the others told us such wonders!" And the Spaniards knelt and sang a Te Deum, and their song of thankfulness, of success, of praise, filled the thin mountain air.

To mark this spot stones were piled in the form of an altar and on its top a cross was planted into which the letters "F" and "J" were carved. In the name of Castile and Aragon, of Ferdinand who was regent for his mad daughter, Juana, they dedicated the peak where Balboa first glimpsed the new sea. Balboa thus gave to Charles, who was soon to reign as King of Spain and Emperor, dominion over the vast Pacific.

As was customary, all this was officially written down and the notary who certified to the discovery of the Sea of the South listed the sixty-seven men who stood beside the altar. One of them was Francisco Pizarro, to whom this was the first step in his twenty-year search for the gold of Peru.

The noon sun stood in the sky as Balboa took a last look and then started down the escarpment, eager to have done with the mountains and forests and stand beside his sea.

His path led straight into the territory of a warlike chief, Chiapes, who, like Quarequá, stood at the head of his warriors and scorned the small, straggling band of tired men who sought passage through his country. Again the harquebuses blazed with supernatural lightning and thunder, again the dogs were unleashed to leap and tear, again the chief and his lieutenants fled while the people fell to the earth too frightened to stand up before such potent mysteries. In a few moments the encounter had been settled, and Balboa commanded his men not to kill: he did not want dead Indians—he wanted friends and allies. As he had won over Ponca so now he won Chiapes. Messengers were sent after the terrified chief and he returned with them; mutually acceptable presents—this time the Spaniards received pearls—were exchanged; Balboa had made another ally. . . .

Through the great forest he marched, through the forest that without a break reached to the very limit of the land. Suddenly the trees stopped and he stepped out into the hot sun. He looked at the dry, tree-ringed bay and then, returning to the shade, lay down to wait for the tide to bring the sea to his feet. He had not long to wait: impetuously the water came in and took possession of the bay.

Balboa unfurled the banner that he had carried with him for this solemn act, a precious banner on which the Virgin and Child smiled above the arms of Castile and Aragon; he drew his sword and fastened his buckler and, conscious of the moment and deed, walked into the sea until his knees were covered.

"Long live the high and mighty monarchs, Don Ferdinand and Dona Juana, sovereigns of Castile, of León, of Aragon, in whose name, and for the royal crown of Castile, I take real and corporal and actual possession of these seas and land and coasts and ports and islands of the south, and all thereunto annexed; and of the kingdoms and provinces which do or may appertain to them, in whatever manner, or by whatever right or title, ancient or modern, in times past, present, or to come, without any contradiction. . . ."

Balboa had stood on his peak, and now he gazed at his ocean. Was it, as Columbus had deduced without ever having seen it, a narrow body of water with the River Ganges but ten days' sail from its shore? Did the bits of coral come from Cochin China, the chili pepper from the Spice Islands; was China almost within reach; was he close to the Malay Peninsula, toward which Portugal and Spain were racing?

A lesser man might have made a safe, quick, easy return over the path he had opened so valiantly on his outward journey, but Balboa decided to return by another route so that he could expose more of this rich New World. New trails, new tribes, new treasures beckoned; and to explore and exploit he was ready to face the unknown with its enemies, its hardships, its dangers. Chiapes and Tumaco[4] provided him with salt fish and maize and other foodstuffs, with canoes and paddlers to take him far up the river that knifed through the forests into the country of the neighboring chief, Teoca. Tumaco's son and Chiapes accompanied him as guides, and thus supplied, equipped, and directed by his Indian friends, Balboa started on a roundabout road to his starting point.

On the way they were met by four Spaniards whom Careta, Balboa's father-in-law, had sent out to meet him. The messengers brought the welcome news that four well-laden ships had just reached Darien from Hispaniola. With this to speed his tired steps, Balboa hastened toward the port from which he had started on his overland expedition and reached it on January 17. The next day, with twenty men, he sailed on the brigantine he had left there, and with a fresh breeze and a fair sea reached Darien. Four and a half months after he had started out on a desperate venture, he returned successful, without the loss of a single man, to the seat of his first triumph. To the jubilant colonists he announced the discovery of the Southern Sea.

Unknown to anyone in Darien, Ferdinand had sent a trusted observer to get a true picture of conditions in this, his farthest outpost. Ostensibly in charge of the ships that brought food from Hispaniola came Pedro de Arbolancha with secret orders to ascertain the real state of affairs: had Balboa usurped the royal power and would he prevent the landing of a governor appointed to replace him; was he a tyrant and were the colonists fearful of his rule; what had been done to promote the welfare of the colony? Behind Arbolancha's mission lay all these doubts and fears about Balboa. Enciso had calumniated and discredited him, but Ferdinand was too wary a sovereign not to discount personal jealousies and frustrations; he wanted to know for himself what kind of man was this that the colonists had chosen, what qualities they had recognized and rewarded. Arbolancha's arrival found Balboa and all his friends absent on their great venture, yet even Balboa's enemies who remained behind had only praise for what he had accomplished: for the gardens that had been planted, the slaves and women who had been put at their disposal, the harmony that prevailed.

[4] A conquered chief with whom Balboa had made friends.—Eds.

Arbolancha saw the spontaneous outpouring of affection that greeted Balboa on his arrival; he watched the division of the spoils, he observed the manner in which Balboa carried himself and attended to the affairs of the colony. Here was no lawless ruffian, no dangerous rebel; Balboa was the truest representative of the vigor and power of Spain, a leader who wielded authority and respected it. Arbolancha, an honest and discerning man, became Balboa's firmest friend, his most zealous partisan. He was ready to return to Spain and report fully and faithfully to the King, urging that Balboa be retained as governor of Darien.

Tragedy and disaster were in the making. Arbolancha delayed his leaving two months—for what reasons it is impossible to tell—until the latter part of March. By the time he arrived with his report and his recommendation, Pedrarias Dávila, newly appointed as governor, had just left the Canaries on his way to the New World. This narrow margin of time was to be fatal.

This expedition, the last sent out by the aged Ferdinand of Spain and the first organized by the newly created Casa de Contratación, Spain's India House, was impressive and many-purposed. Applicants for the glittering adventure—for Balboa had mentioned the need of a thousand men if they were to reach the Southern Sea—swamped the India House. Their number was raised from twelve hundred to two thousand. For most of these men this adventure came at a most opportune moment. Many of them, of noble family, were splendidly dressed, for they had equipped their wardrobes lavishly to serve under *el Gran Capitán*, as Spain's too-popular military chief, Gonzalo de Córdoba, was called; he had been nominated to lead an army to protect Ferdinand's kingdom of Naples against the French. The recruits for Italy were left at loose ends when the King suddenly changed his mind. These men, ripe for danger, and having invested their last cent in rich armor and silken finery to make a magnificent appearance in the Italian campaign, clamored for the chance to serve their king in the New World, where, it was rumored, gold was caught in nets like fish. So intense was the fever to join that to a contemporary it seemed as though all the men would leave Seville, which would become a city of women.

The armada sailed on April 11, 1514, and, as Bernal Díaz says, "sometimes with good weather and other times with bad weather," arrived off the town of Darien on June 29.

On the way they had passed the ship in which Arbolancha was returning to Spain after his secret mission. It is tempting to imagine what might have happened had Pedrarias delayed long enough for Arbolancha to have arrived *before* the armada sailed: the King, trusting the report of his special investigator and delighted with his gold and pearls, would not have hesitated to be as ungracious to Pedrarias as he had been to *el Gran Capitán*, to change his mind about the armada as he had about the Neapolitan campaign. In his first joy he might have allowed Balboa to remain in office as governor and continue his friendly relations with the Indians. Had Balboa been allowed to live, he would have followed the clues that led to Peru, of which he had twice been told; and, unlike the murderous Pizarro, would not have viciously broken to useless bits the great civilization of the Incas. Had Balboa lived, Bourne said, "the history of the mainland of South America might have been very different."

Under the thick, syrupy molasses of Pedrarias's fine manners was a sour, irritated conceit. He had expected and been prepared to have to conquer a surly, recalcitrant rebel; instead Balboa, at the head of the town council, knelt and promised for himself and the men of Darien proper obedience, and then graciously offered to Pedrarias the use of his own house. Because Balboa's action had deprived him of a martial entrance, Pedrarias had to be satisfied with a solemn, stately procession: flanked by Bishop Quevedo resplendent in his episcopal robes, the new governor advanced at the head of his fully armed, elegantly clad officials and cavaliers; behind them came chanting, brown-robed friars carrying crosses, swinging censers; and lastly the sailors, artisans, colonists, and men and women who made up the full number of the armada. Wide-eyed, the Indians watched this rich show; pityingly the old colonists, poorly dressed in cotton shirt and drawers and wearing hempen sandals, their lean, sallow faces showing the hardships and fevers of the New World, watched this display of silks and brocades, of fair white skins, and knew that for most of these men and women the New World would prove to be but one step from the next world.

Within a month after they had arrived, seven hundred of the gay, exquisitely dressed young men who had marched so splendidly through the streets of Seville were dead. Most were quickly killed by yellow fever, while the rest starved as their provisions were exhausted. Many a fine wardrobe was bartered bit by bit for cassava bread in a vain effort to postpone death. As hidalgos—younger sons or poor aspiring relatives of the nobility—they clung tenaciously to the work they deemed suitable to their rank; they were fitted only for war or conquest—this had been their calling and tradition in Spain; and unable to adjust to the New World, they rotted and perished. Pedrarias sent a boatload back to Cuba, where some enlisted under the governor: a few pitiable remnants returned to Spain, having spent their fortunes, having lost their health and their hopes.

Pedrarias could have overcome his disappointment at the courteous welcome he received; he could reconcile himself to Darien as it was instead of Castilla del Oro as he had imagined it; but he could not forgive Balboa for having already crossed the isthmus and discovered the Southern Sea. His arrogance, his conceit, his irritability, were transformed into a terrible, unappeasable hate.

The exact date of Balboa's execution is not known; both 1517 and 1519 are mentioned by the historians. The exact date is not important; what matters is that Pedrarias finally satisfied his lacerated pride by a desperate, obscene act. The record of those years leaves a sharp image: Balboa caught and held fast in the silky, sticky meshes of a web that was fashioned out of the frustrations and spewed out of the envy of his enemy, Pedrarias.

Balboa's last enterprise is proof of the energy, the fortitude, the vision and purpose of the man. He was the first to build ships in the New World. In them he set sail over the sea he had discovered toward the great kingdom of which he had twice been told.

When the first two ships were ready, Balboa sailed them to the Pearl Islands, where he had decided to make his base; and while the other brigantines were being finished and additional supplies were on their way from Acla, he sailed off in the direction of Peru. The ships had gone about a hundred miles when the men were terrified to find themselves in a sea of spouting whales, monsters as large as their tiny ships, bloodcurdling creatures that churned the sea into foam. No one had ever seen them before, no one had even heard of them; terror-stricken, the mariners threw out their anchors. When at last the sea was empty, the wind had changed and they sailed back to the Pearl Islands.

That was Balboa's farthest. On his return he found disturbing news. A new governor, Lope de Sosa, was due to arrive at Darien to succeed Pedrarias. What sort of man was he? Would he interfere with this new venture, which, after so much labor, should soon yield rewards? A thousand doubts and questions arose to worry and perplex Balboa. After some discussion with his friends he decided to send one of them back to Acla to ascertain how matters stood. Balboa chose for this mission Andrés Garabito, a man who had served him often and well. Unwittingly, he thus put his life in the hands of a man who for very personal reasons wanted his death: Garabito for a long time had coveted Careta's daughter, Balboa's mistress. She had repulsed him in faithfulness to Balboa. Passion coupled with perfidy possessed Garabito, made him cunning and deadly. From Acla he sent a letter to the jealous and ever-suspicious Pedrarias to the effect that Balboa had four ships ready and fitted for a long voyage, three hundred men, and nothing but the sea between him and the fabulous Peru; that Balboa thus planned to escape from Pedrarias's jurisdiction and seek new lands where he would be free of all legal restraints. Garabito chose his poison well. This time Pedrarias determined that Balboa would not escape alive.

Pedrarias sent a letter, friendly and disarming, asking Balboa to meet him in Acla to discuss supplies for the ships, and thither he himself removed with his officials. He ordered Pizarro, with some armed men, to await Balboa at the rest house atop the mountains and bring the leader to him a prisoner. And as Pedrarias planned it, it happened. At the rest house the unsuspecting Balboa met Pizarro and his men. Pizarro demanded his sword of him and told him he was under arrest. "How is this, Francisco?" Balboa asked him. "Is this the way you have been accustomed to receiving me?" And so certain was he of his innocence that he offered no struggle and allowed himself to be taken prisoner.

The trial was swift, secret, and one-sided. The judge was also the prosecutor. Even the judge, warped by his subservience to Pedrarias, shrank from the penalty his master sought. But the unrelenting governor had his way: Balboa was sentenced to be beheaded the next day. Unspoken, unmentioned had been the real case against Balboa: by building and equipping four ships on the Southern Sea, Balboa had doomed himself. Only his death assured Pedrarias of possessing those ships, which could carry him to gold and glory.

The men at Acla awoke to a dark day of dreadfulness. The man who had given them hope and life, had brought success to them all, who had worn his honors and deeds with modest dignity, the man who was the light and life of Darien, was to be executed.

Such were the life and achievements of Vasco Núñez de Balboa, "conqueror of the mountains, pacifier of the Isthmus, and discoverer of the Austral Sea." Such was his brutal, senseless death.

THE
NOCHE TRISTE
OF CORTÉS

by C. W. Ceram

In all the spectacular annals of the conquistadors, the most spectacular is the conquest of Mexico by Hernán Cortés. Like many another young Spanish gallant, Cortés, fascinated by the stories of gold and conquest which he had heard, sailed for the new world to make his fortune. He first became a planter in Hispaniola and later took part in an expedition to Cuba under Velásquez. Mexico had been discovered by Córdoba in 1517 and by Grijalva in 1518, and Cortés managed to have himself appointed to lead the expedition of conquest. He landed in Yucatán in 1519 with less than a thousand men in his party, and then proceeded along the coast to what is now Vera Cruz. It was here that he first made contact with the Emperor Moctezuma, who lived in a palace on the site which was to become Mexico City. In the Spanish camp there was dissension and conspiracy, but Cortés, determined to win the wealth which the Emperor had been foolish enough to expose, determined on a bold stroke and burned his fleet. There was now no choice but to go forward, and in August of 1519 the party advanced on the capital. In Prescott's Conquest of Mexico we can read in detail the incredible story of intrigue and violence which followed. Beset by revolt among his own followers and faced with hundreds of thousands of hostile warriors, Cortés managed to make Moctezuma his prisoner. The lowest ebb of his fortunes occurred during the famous Noche Triste, one of the great moments in Spanish-American history. It is the story of this night of sadness which C. W. Ceram relates.

Reprinted from *Gods, Graves and Scholars* by C. W. Ceram, translated from the German by E. B. Garside, by permission of Alfred A. Knopf, Inc. Copyright 1951 Alfred A. Knopf, Inc.

THE Spaniards of the age of conquest marched behind the banner of the cross and shouted the battle cry of *"Espiritu Santo"* during the heat of battle. Wherever they carved out a foothold they planted crosses, then built churches as speedily as they could. Before taking to the field they were confessed by their priests, and their victories were celebrated with a ceremonial Mass. And so it was perfectly natural that they should try to convert the Aztec people.

Before entering the Aztec kingdom, the Spaniards had been dealing with savages, whose religion was a barbaric animism in which natural forces and ghosts were revered. The rites and customs of this elemental religious complex were easily shaken. With the Aztecs, however, the situation was quite different. Their religion was of a higher order, a "culture religion." The whole culture acquired a stamp as distinctive as any exhibited by the universalist or redemptive religions.

The mistake of the Spanish conquistadors and their priests was that they recognized this fact too late. The outlook of sixteenth-century Europeans strongly hindered any concessions to civilizations different from their own. This narrow attitude, which recognized highs and lows only on its own scale, and on no other, was not in the least modified when the conquistadors saw in Mexico unmistakable signs of a clearly differentiated and highly developed social life. They became acquainted with educational methods in some respects superior to their own and were not impressed. Nor did the discovery that the Aztec priests were amazingly learned in astronomy have any effect on them. They saw nothing but the devil's handiwork in the rich city of Mexico, with its lagoons, dikes, streets, and floating islands of flowers.

Unfortunately the Aztec religion had one feature that repelled everyone who encountered it and inevitably fostered belief in Aztec diabolism. This was the practice of human sacrifice on an incredibly large scale, a rite culminating in the priest's tearing the living heart out of the victim's breast. And only we moderns, perhaps, have the right to remind the Spaniards, who were roused to anger by the Aztec practice, that their own Inquisition slowly roasted Spanish flesh during the autos-da-fé. At the same time it is true enough that this Aztec ritual was cruel beyond anything of the kind ever known in the world.

In actual fact a highly developed morality was mingled with barbaric amorality in the Aztec civilization. To accept both strains was beyond zealot capacity. In consequence the Spaniards overlooked the fact that the

Aztec people, unlike the Indians encountered by Columbus, Vespucci, and Cabral, could be humbled only up to that point at which their religion was involved. This critical point was reached when the Spaniards began to desecrate the temples and the gods. Nevertheless, they laid on with a ruthless hand. The essential incompatibility of Spaniard and Aztec set the stage for a series of violent acts that nearly destroyed the fruits of Cortés's military and political conquests.

It is worthy of remark that among the members of the Cortés expedition it was not the priests who were the worst bigots. Father Juan Díaz and Father Bartolomé Olmedo, particularly the latter, tempered the conduct of their religious office with political understanding.

According to all reports, it was Cortés himself, perhaps yielding to a subconscious impulse to justify his own deeds, who first attempted to convert Moctezuma. The Emperor politely heard out the Spaniard's language. When the great conquistador invidiously compared the pure and simple rite of the Catholic Mass with the hideous Aztec practice of human sacrifice, however, Moctezuma put in a word. It was much less revolting to him, he explained, to sacrifice human beings than it was to eat the flesh and blood of God himself. We do not know whether Cortés was quite able to counter this dialectic.

Cortés went even further. He asked for permission to examine one of the large temples, and after Moctezuma had consulted with his priests, this permission was reluctantly granted. At once Cortés climbed up the great stairs of the teocalli, which was located in the middle of the capital, not far from the Spanish headquarters. When he suggested to Father Olmedo that the teocalli would be the most appropriate place to house the cross, the priest advised against this. They went in to look at the jasper block on which the sacrificial victims were slaughtered with an obsidian knife. They saw the image of the god Huitzilopochtli, terrifying of visage, identical, in Spanish eyes, with the very devil himself as described by their priests. The hideous idol was embraced within the thick folds of a serpent studded with pearls and precious stones. Bernal Díaz, also present during this visit, was the first to become aware of an even more gruesome sight. The walls of the whole room were plastered thickly with dried human blood. "The evil stench," writes Díaz, "was less tolerable than that of the slaughterhouses in Castile." Then he looked closely at the altar stone. There lay three human hearts, which he fancied were still smoking and bleeding.

Having descended by way of the long teocalli stairs, the Spaniards, a little later, caught sight of a large framework building on a mound, which they were moved to explore. Within, neatly piled up to the rafters, they found the skulls of Huitzilopochtli's victims. A soldier estimated that there were 136,000 of them.

Soon after, when the phase of request had been succeeded by the phase of curt command backed by threats, Cortés moved his headquarters into one of the towers of the teocalli. After his first visit to the sacred Aztec hill he had used abusive language to Moctezuma, who had been taken aback, but had made no protest. But Moctezuma's reaction to Cortés's second invasion of the sacred precincts was more positive. He became greatly excited and informed the Spaniard that his people would not endure such an intrusion. Cortés, in recalcitrant language, ordered the temple to be cleaned. This having been done, he had an altar set up, and equipped it with the cross and an image of the Virgin Mary. The Aztec gold and jewels were removed and the walls decorated with flowers. The Spaniards then gathered on the long stairway and the upper platform of the teocalli to hear the first *Te Deum.* Joyous tears, we are told, streamed down their cheeks, so greatly were they moved by this victory of the faith.

The deed that was to exhaust the Aztecs' patience was but one step away.

The story can be told briefly. When Cortés was away from the capital— on a punitive expedition against Narváez, a rival Spanish captain—a delegation of Aztec priests consulted with Alvarado, Cortés's second-in-command, and asked leave to celebrate the "incensing of Huitzilopochtli" with the customary religious songs and dances. Part of the Aztec temple, of course, had already been converted into a Catholic chapel, and the feast was to take place in the court of the teocalli.

Alvarado gave his consent, but under two conditions: the Aztecs were not to make any human sacrifices; they must come without weapons.

On the feast day about six hundred Aztecs, mostly members of the nobility, appeared—reports differ as to the exact number—and none of them armed. They were decked out in their most magnificent costumes and ornaments. The ceremony was approaching its climax when a number of Spaniards in full armor who had been mingling with the crowd fell on the defenseless worshipers at a prearranged signal and killed them all.

This deed, even within its context, is incomprehensible and to this day has never been fully explained. The ferocity of the Spaniards was utterly senseless. An eyewitness remarked that "the blood flowed in streams like water in a heavy shower."

When Cortés, accompanied by a strong force, returned to Mexico City after his victory over Narváez, the capital had completely changed. Shortly after this frightful piece of treachery the Aztecs had to a man risen in revolt. They had chosen Moctezuma's brother, Cuitlahuac, as leader in place of the imprisoned Emperor and were blockading the palace where Alvarado had barricaded himself. When Cortés drew into Mexico City, Alvarado was in desperate need of relief. But to raise the Aztec siege meant running the risk of falling into the same sort of trap that held Alvarado. And more besides.

Every sortie now launched by Cortés became a Pyrrhic victory. When he destroyed three hundred houses, the Aztecs destroyed the bridges and dikes over which he would have to retreat if he withdrew from the city. When he burned down the great teocalli, the Aztecs stormed his fortifications with redoubled fury.

Moctezuma's behavior in this situation is hard to understand. His past military record was indisputably good. So far as is known, he had taken active part in nine battles. Under his rule the Aztec kingdom had reached a peak of might and splendor. Yet after the arrival of the Spaniards this great ruler seemed steadily to lose his grip. He now came to the Spaniards and offered to mediate with his people. Wearing the full insignia of his imperial office, he went onto the walls and began to speak, but was stoned by the crowd, receiving wounds that brought about his death. On June 30, 1520 died Moctezuma II, the once great Emperor of the Aztecs, to the last a Spanish prisoner.

Now that the Spaniards no longer held the person of Moctezuma as a trump card in the play for Mexico, their predicament had become serious indeed. Cortés was now to experience a most nerve-racking adventure, the *noche triste*, as the history books call it.

As the "sad night" loomed, Cortés issued orders for a breakout. This was a counsel of despair, in view of the fact that a mere handful of men would have to fight their way through ten thousand bloodthirsty Aztec warriors. Before making this final move, Cortés had the Aztec treasure spread out, saying disdainfully: "Take what you will of it. But beware not to overload yourselves. He travels safest in the dark who travels lightest." A fifth part of the treasure was reserved for the Spanish King so as to ensure royal clemency should Cortés suffer defeat, yet live. This fifth was carried in the middle of the retreating column, in that section called the "battle."

Cortés's veterans took their leader's advice to heart and burdened themselves with only a little gold, but Narváez's troops loaded themselves down with valuables. They stuck gold ingots in their belts and boot tops, they bound jeweled implements to their bodies, and so weighted themselves that after the first half-hour they had fallen back, all out of wind, as far as the rear guard.

In this first half-hour of the night of July 1, 1520 the Spaniards succeeded in withdrawing, unseen by the Aztecs, through the sleeping city and out on the causeway. At this juncture the cries of the Aztec sentinels rang out, and the priests began to sound the great drum in the temple of the war god. Hell broke loose.

By laying down a portable bridge that had been especially carpentered for this purpose, the Spaniards managed to cross the first breach cut in the causeway by the Aztecs. There was a sound like that of trees soughing in a rainy wind. Then the heavens were rent by war cries, a sound that mingled with the frantic splashing of canoe paddles. Showers of arrows and stones rained down on the Spaniards. The shrieks of their wounded were answered by the yells of the Aztecs. Warriors began to climb out of the darkness up onto the causeway, where they engaged in hand-to-hand combat with the Spaniards, using clubs furnished with iron-hard cutting edges of obsidian.

Where was the portable bridge when the Spanish van reached the second breach let into the causeway to hinder their retreat? Frantic calls to the rear elicited the alarming information that under the weight of so many men and horses the supports of the improvised bridge had sunk into the soft earth and could not be budged. What up to now had been an organized retreat degenerated quickly into a rout. The troops became a mob; each man fought aimlessly for his own life. On foot and horseback the Spaniards plunged into the waters of the lake in their frantic efforts to gain the farther shore. Packs, weapons, and finally the gold were all sloughed off and lost in the darkness of the night.

There is no point in dwelling too long on the particulars of this battle. Not one Spaniard, not even Cortés—who, according to all reports, wrought miracles of courage—came off unwounded. When the morning grayed and the remnants of the Spanish force had crossed the dike, the Aztecs meanwhile having been diverted from their harassment of the enemy by the rich spoil, the commander took stock of the situation. Contemporary accounts of the losses suffered during the *noche triste* do not agree. By conservative estimate the Spaniards lost about a third, their Tlascalan allies a fourth or fifth, of their combined forces. All the muskets and cannon had been lost, a part of the crossbows, and most of the horses. Cortés's band had been reduced to a ghostly shadow of the proud column that had entered the capital nine months earlier.

But the Spaniards' Via Dolorosa was still not at an end. For eight days after the *noche triste* there was constant skirmishing as the Spaniards struggled to save themselves by retreating into Tlascalan territory. The Tlascalans, their allies, were the traditional enemies of the Aztecs. They retreated very slowly, being weakened by exhaustion and hunger. Then, on July 8, 1520, the crippled band, having toiled up the steeps enclosing the valley of Otumba, were greeted by a spectacle that seemed to seal their fate.

As far as the eye could see, the valley, the only avenue of escape, was filled with Aztec warriors arrayed in better battle order than anything the Spaniards had yet seen in Mexico. At the head of the methodically disposed battle columns the Spaniards could make out the chiefs, standing out from the rest. In their shimmering feather cloaks they looked like bright birds against the snow of the white cotton mail worn by the common warriors.

The situation was hopeless, but the Spaniards did not hang back. They had no choice but to press forward and take their chances or to become sacrificial victims for the Aztec gods. Prisoners of war taken by the Aztecs were commonly left to rot in wooden cages until a sufficient number had been collected to make their immolation interesting. The only thing to do, therefore, was face almost certain death and try to force a path through the Aztec horde. There was no other way.

And now, at the moment of complete hopelessness—the Aztecs were later estimated to have numbered 200,000 men, and the Spaniards were attacking without benefit of the firearms that had won them their initial victories—a miracle occurred.

Cortés's men broke into the sea of Aztecs in three groups: a large striking force at the center; on either wing the remaining handful of cavalry, totaling some twenty men. At once the Spaniards and their Tlascalan allies were swallowed up. The lanes that the twenty riders plowed through the enemy closed in behind as the Aztecs sprang back like grass in a plowed furrow. Cortés, who fought in the front line, lost his horse, mounted another, was wounded on the head, but hacked his way on. Still, the Aztecs were legion. Between cut and thrust he chanced to see, from a slight elevation, a cluster of strikingly ornamented warriors, and in their midst a litter. On the litter he recognized the cacique in command of the whole Aztec force, a certain Cihuacu, distinguished by his staff with a golden net for a banner, and the field badge attached to his back. Then the miracle came to pass, not one worked by the Virgin Mary or the saints, but the miracle of Hernán Cortés, a deed worthy of being sung about any warrior's campfire. The wounded Cortés spurred his steed forward, hardly waiting for the two or three tried and trusted cavaliers who swept along in his wake. Together they pressed on, with thrust of lance and sword, riding down the Aztecs, sticking and cutting, always hammering their way diagonally through the warrior phalanx. The enemy gave way before their savage onslaught. In a few minutes Cortés's mad ride had brought him up to the Aztec cacique. Murderously he thrust him through with his lance. Tearing loose the cacique's badge, he waved it aloft over the seething battle.

Like magic the tide turned. The Aztecs, seeing their victory emblem in the hands of the conquistador, who to them seemed stronger than their gods, precipitately fled the field. This was a supreme moment. When Hernán Cortés seized the Aztec banner, Indian Mexico was doomed and the kingdom of the last Moctezuma had died. The historian Prescott sums up the Spanish conquest in these words:

Whatever may be thought of the Conquest in a moral view, regarded as a military achievement it must fill us with astonishment. That a handful of adventurers, indifferently armed and equipped, should have landed on the shores of a powerful empire inhabited by a fierce and warlike race, and, in defiance of the reiterated prohibitions of its sovereign, have forced their way into the interior;—that they should have done this, without knowledge of the language or of the land, without chart or compass to guide them, without any idea of the difficulties they were to encounter, totally uncertain whether the next step might bring them on a hostile nation, or on a desert, feeling their way along in the dark, as it were;—that, though nearly overwhelmed by their first encounter with the inhabitants, they should have still pressed on to the capital of the empire, and, having reached it, thrown themselves unhesitatingly into the midst of their enemies;—that, so far from being daunted by the extraordinary spectacle there exhibited of power and civilization, they should have been but the more confirmed in their original design; —that they should have seized the monarch, have executed his ministers before the eyes of his subjects, and, when driven forth with ruin from the gates, have gathered their scattered wreck together, and, after a system of operations, pursued with consummate policy and daring, have succeeded in overturning the capital, and establishing their sway over the country;—that all this should have been so effected by a mere handful of indigent adventurers, is a fact little short of the miraculous,—too startling for the probabilities demanded by fiction, and without a parallel in the pages of history.

For the sake of the record it should be mentioned that in the months immediately following the Battle of Otumba, prior to their final dissolution, the Aztec people rose to heights befitting their tradition as "Roman Americans." After Cuitlahuac, who died of smallpox after ruling for four months, came Cuauhtemoc, an Emperor in his twenty-fifth year. So vigorously did he defend his country's capital against Cortés, who meanwhile had added strong reinforcements to his army, that the Spaniards suffered greater losses at his hands than from any previous Aztec commander. Yet the end was inevitable. Cuauhtemoc was taken prisoner, tortured, and hanged. The capital was destroyed, its houses burned to the ground, its idols overturned, its canals filled in.

Mexico made a new start with the Christianization and colonization of the land by the Spaniards. During the last siege the Spaniards from the teocalli height had watched Aztec priests in the plaza below rip the hearts from the breasts of fallen compatriots. Now they built a gleaming collegiate church on the same site and dedicated it to St. Francis. The houses of the city were rebuilt. After a few years two hundred Spanish families lived in Mexico City, and some thirty thousand pure-blooded Indians. The land round about the city was divided up according to the *repartimiento* system, which in effect imposed slavery on all the peoples who had once made up the Aztec realm—and of course on all the tribes who fell prey to later conquests. None but the Tlascalans, to whose aid Cortés was so deeply indebted, were exempted from the rule, and even they only for a time.

This sudden Spanish ascendancy, otherwise of such dazzling benefit to the motherland, was marred by only one defect: the destruction of the treasure of Moctezuma. The booty lost during the *noche triste* the Spaniards had hoped to retrieve when they retook Mexico City, but it had all vanished and has never to this day been recovered. Cortés had Cuauhtemoc tortured before hanging him, but he would not sing to the Spanish tune. Cortés also had all the ditches and lagoons searched by divers, who explored the bottom with their feet. But nothing was gained from this effort except a great many cut toes and a few scattered pieces that the Aztecs had overlooked. The total value of the treasure recovered from the lake did not amount to more than 130,000 gold castellanos, or about one-fifth of the value of the share labeled originally for delivery to the Spanish government.

The conquistadors themselves must have felt a certain grim satisfaction when the news came to Cortés, in a letter postmarked May 15, 1522, from the captain entrusted with the transport of the treasure to Spain, that his vessel had been captured by a French privateer. In the end it was not Charles I of Spain, but Francis I of France who, to his genuine surprise, came into possession of the Aztec treasure.

FIRST DOWN THE AMAZON

by William H. Prescott

One of Balboa's company when he discovered the Pacific had been another adventurer named Francisco Pizarro. Intrigued by the stories of wealth and conquest which were presumably to be found on the western coast of South America, Pizarro joined with others in outfitting an expedition and in 1524 set sail on the Great South Sea. He finally arrived at Tumbes, where he saw his first Peruvian city, a town rich with gold and silver and blazing with color. Here he was informed that there were far richer and more important cities in the interior. He returned to Panama and then to Spain, where the King appointed him Governor of Peru. On his second voyage, he carried with him his brother Gonzalo.

From Indians whom he had tortured, Gonzalo learned of a great country toward the east called "the land of cinnamon trees" and the even more fabulous realm of El Dorado. Inflamed with greed, he decided on an expedition and Francisco de Orellana volunteered to join him. They crossed the Andes, where the wealth they had come for proved a delusion. In the selection that follows, Prescott tells how, after an interval in which they were faced with starvation, it was agreed that Orellana should go downstream with part of the company in search of food, and how when they did not return, Orellana was accused of treason and cowardice. Actually, there is considerable doubt whether it would have been possible for him to go back upstream.

From *The Conquest of Peru*.

Orellana *navigated the entire length of the Amazon, becoming the first person to cross the South American Continent. The journey involved navigation of thousands of miles never before seen, imminent danger of starvation and constant running battles with hostile Indians. For this feat Orellana's name deserves a place in any roster of the great explorers. Curiously, it was his account of the Amazons, the women warriors of whom he heard, rather than the importance of the exploit itself, which brought notoriety to the expedition, and gave the river its name.*

GONZALO PIZARRO received the news of his appointment to the government of Quito with undisguised pleasure—not so much for the possession that it gave him of this ancient Indian province as for the field that it opened for discovery toward the East, the fabled land for Oriental spices, which had long captivated the imagination of the conquerors. He repaired to his government without delay, and found no difficulty in awakening a kindred enthusiasm to his own in the bosoms of his followers. In a short time he mustered three hundred and fifty Spaniards and four thousand Indians. One hundred and fifty of his company were mounted, and all were equipped in the most thorough manner for the undertaking. He provided, moreover, against famine by a large stock of provisions and an immense drove of swine which followed in the rear.

It was the beginning of 1540 when he set out on this celebrated expedition. The first part of the journey was attended with comparatively little difficulty while the Spaniards were yet in the land of the Incas; for the distractions of Peru had not been felt in this distant province, where the simple people still lived as under the primitive sway of the Children of the Sun. But the scene changed as they entered the territory of Quixos, where the character of the inhabitants, as well as of the climate, seemed to be of another description. The country was traversed by lofty ranges of the Andes, and the adventurers were soon entangled in their deep and intricate passes. As they rose into the more elevated regions, the icy winds that swept down the sides of the Cordilleras benumbed their limbs, and many of the natives found a wintry grave in the wilderness. While crossing this formidable barrier, they experienced one of those tremendous earthquakes which in these volcanic regions so often shake the mountains to their base. In one place, the earth was rent asunder by the terrible throes of Nature, while streams of sulphurous vapor issued from the cavity, and a village with some hundreds of houses was precipitated into the frightful abyss.

On descending the eastern slopes, the climate changed. As they came on the lower level the fierce cold was succeeded by a suffocating heat, while tempests of thunder and lightning, rushing from out the gorges of the sierra, poured on their heads with scarcely any intermission day or night, as if the offended deities of the place were willing to take vengeance on the invaders of their mountain solitudes. For more than six weeks the deluge continued unabated, and the forlorn wanderers, wet, and weary with incessant toil, were scarcely able to drag their limbs along the soil broken up and saturated with the moisture. After some months of toilsome travel, in which they had to cross many a morass and mountain stream, they at length reached Canelas, the Land of Cinnamon. They saw the trees bearing the precious bark, spreading out into broad forests, yet however valuable an article for commerce it might have proved in accessible situations, in these remote regions it was of little worth to them. From the wandering tribes of savages whom they had occasionally met in their path they learned that at ten days' distance was a rich and fruitful land, abounding with gold and inhabited by populous nations. Gonzalo Pizarro had already reached the limits originally proposed for the expedition. But this intelligence renewed his hopes, and he resolved to push the adventure farther. It would have been well for him and his followers had they been content to return on their footsteps.

At length the way-worn company came on a broad expanse of water formed by the Napo, one of the great tributaries of the Amazon, and which, though only a third- or fourth-rate river in America, would pass for one of the first magnitude in the Old World. The sight gladdened their hearts, as by winding along its banks they hoped to find a safer and more practicable route. After traversing its borders for a considerable distance, closely beset with thickets which it taxed their strength to the utmost to overcome, Gonzalo and his party came within hearing of a rushing noise that sounded like subterranean thunder. The river, lashed into fury, tumbled along over rapids with frightful velocity, and conducted them to the brink of a magnificent cataract, which, to their wondering fancies, rushed down in one vast volume of foam to the depth of twelve hundred feet!

For some distance above and below the falls, the bed of the river contracted so that its width did not exceed twenty feet. Sorely pressed by hunger, the adventurers determined, at all hazards, to cross to the opposite side, in hopes of finding a country that might afford them sustenance. A frail bridge was constructed by throwing the huge trunks of trees across the chasm, where the cliffs, as if split asunder by some convulsion of nature, descended sheer down a perpendicular depth of several hundred feet. Over this airy causeway the men and horses succeeded in effecting their passage, with the loss of a single Spaniard, who, made giddy by heedlessly looking down, lost his footing and fell into the boiling surges below.

Yet they gained little by the exchange. The country wore the same unpromising aspect, and the river banks were studded with gigantic trees or fringed with impenetrable thickets. The tribes of Indians whom they occasionally met in the pathless wilderness were fierce and unfriendly, and they were engaged in perpetual skirmishes with them. From these they learned that a fruitful country was to be found down the river at the distance of only a few days' journey, and the Spaniards held on their weary way, still hoping and still deceived, as the promised land flitted before them, like the rainbow, receding as they advanced.

At length, spent with toil and suffering, Gonzalo resolved to construct a bark large enough to transport the weaker part of his company and his baggage. The forests furnished him with timber; the shoes of the horses which had died on the road or been slaughtered for food were converted into nails; gum distilled from the trees took the place of pitch; and the tattered garments of the soldiers supplied a substitute for oakum. It was a work of difficulty, but Gonzalo cheered his men in the task, and set an example by taking part in their labors. At the end of two months a brigantine was completed, rudely put together, but strong and of sufficient burden to carry half the company—the first vessel constructed by Europeans that ever floated on these inland waters.

Gonzalo gave the command to Francisco de Orellana, a cavalier from Truxillo, on whose courage and devotion to himself he thought he could rely. The troops now moved forward, still following the descending course of the river, while the brigantine kept alongside. When a bold promontory or more impracticable country intervened, it furnished timely aid by the transportation of the feebler soldiers. In this way they journeyed for many a wearisome week through the dreary wilderness on the borders of the Napo. Every scrap of provisions had been long since consumed. The last of their horses had been devoured. To appease the gnawings of hunger, they were fain to eat the leather of their saddles and belts. The woods supplied them with scanty sustenance, and they greedily fed upon toads, serpents, and such other reptiles as they occasionally found.

They were now told of a rich district, inhabited by a populous nation, where the Napo emptied into a still greater river that flowed toward the east. It was, as usual, at the distance of several days' journey, and Gonzalo Pizarro resolved to halt where he was and send Orellana down in his brigantine to the confluence of the waters to procure a stock of provisions, with which he might return and put them in condition to resume their march. That cavalier, accordingly, taking with him fifty of the adventurers, pushed off into the middle of the river, where the stream ran swiftly, and his bark, taken by the current, shot forward with the speed of an arrow and was soon out of sight.

Days and weeks passed away, yet the vessel did not return. No speck was to be seen on the waters as the Spaniards strained their eyes to the farthest point, where the line of light faded away in the dark shadows of the foliage on the borders. Detachments were sent out, and came back without intelligence of their comrades. Unable longer to endure this suspense, or indeed to maintain themselves in their present quarters, Gonzalo and his famishing followers now determined to proceed toward the junction of the rivers. Two months elapsed before they accomplished this terrible journey—those of them who did not perish on the way—although the distance probably did not exceed two hundred leagues. They at length reached the spot so long desired, where the Napo pours its tide into the Amazon, that mighty stream which, fed by its thousand tributaries, rolls on toward the ocean for many hundred miles through the heart of the great continent—the most majestic of American rivers.

But the Spaniards gathered no tidings of Orellana, while the country, though more populous than the region they had left, was as little inviting in its aspect and was tenanted by a race yet more ferocious. They now abandoned the hope of recovering their comrades, who they supposed must have miserably perished by famine or by the hands of the natives. But their doubts were at length dispelled by the appearance of a white man wandering half-naked in the woods, in whose famine-stricken countenance they recognized the features of one of their countrymen. It was Sanchez de Vargas, a cavalier of good descent, and much esteemed in the army. He had a dismal tale to tell.

Orellana, borne swiftly down the current of the Napo, had reached the point of its confluence with the Amazon in less than three days—accomplishing in this brief space of time what had cost Pizarro and his company two months. He had found the country altogether different from what had been represented, and, so far from supplies for his countrymen, he could barely obtain sustenance for himself. Nor was it possible for him to return as he had come and make head against the current of the river; the attempt to journey by land was an alternative scarcely less formidable. In this dilemma an idea flashed across his mind. It was to launch his bark at once on the bosom of the Amazon and descend its waters to its mouth. He would then visit the rich and populous nations that, as report said, lined its borders, sail out on the great ocean, cross to the neighboring isles, and return to Spain to claim the glory and the guerdon of discovery. The suggestion was eagerly taken up by his reckless companions, welcoming any course that would rescue them from the wretchedness of their present existence, and fired with the prospect of new and stirring adventure— for the love of adventure was the last feeling to become extinct in the bosom of the Castilian cavalier. They heeded little their unfortunate comrades whom they were to abandon in the wilderness.

Orellana succeeded in his enterprise. But it is marvelous that he should have escaped shipwreck in the perilous and unknown navigation of that river. Many times his vessel was nearly dashed to pieces on its rocks and in its furious rapids. He was in still greater peril from the warlike tribes on its borders, who fell on his little troop whenever he attempted to land, and followed in his wake for miles in their canoes. He at length emerged from the great river. Once upon the sea, Orellana made for the isle of Cubagua, thence, passing over to Spain, he repaired to Court and told the circumstances of his voyage—of the nations of Amazons whom he had found on the banks of the river, the El Dorado which report assured him existed in the neighborhood, and other marvels—the exaggeration rather than the coinage of a credulous fancy. His audience listened with willing ears to the tales of the traveler, and in an age of wonders, when the mysteries of the East and the West were hourly coming to light, they might be excused for not discerning the true line between romance and reality.

He found no difficulty in obtaining a commission to conquer and colonize the realms he had discovered. He soon saw himself at the head of five hundred followers, prepared to share the perils and the profits of his expedition. But neither he nor his country was destined to realize these profits. He died on his outward passage, and the lands washed by the Amazon fell within the territories of Portugal. The unfortunate navigator did not even enjoy the undivided honor of giving his name to the waters he had discovered. He enjoyed only the barren glory of the discovery, surely not balanced by the iniquitous circumstances which attended it.

One of Orellana's party maintained a stout opposition to his proceedings, as repugnant both to humanity and honor. This was Sanchez de Vargas, and the cruel commander was revenged on him by abandoning him to his fate in the desolate region where he was now found by his countrymen.

The Spaniards listened with horror to the recital of Vargas, and their blood almost froze in their veins as they saw themselves thus deserted in the heart of this remote wilderness and deprived of their only means of escape from it. They made an effort to prosecute their journey along the banks, but after some toilsome days, strength and spirits failed, and they gave up in despair.

Then it was that the qualities of Gonzalo Pizarro as a fit leader in the hour of despondency and danger shone out conspicuous. To advance farther was hopeless. To stay where they were, without food or raiment, without defense from the fierce animals of the forest and the fiercer natives, was impossible. One only course remained: it was to return to Quito. But this brought with it the recollection of the past, of sufferings which they could too well estimate—hardly to be endured even in imagination. They were now at least four hundred leagues from Quito, and more than a year had elapsed since they had set out on their painful pilgrimage. How could they encounter these perils again?

Yet there was no alternative. Gonzalo endeavored to reassure his followers by dwelling on the invincible constancy they had hitherto displayed, adjuring them to show themselves still worthy of the name of Castilians. He reminded them of the glory they would forever acquire by their heroic achievement, when they should reach their own country. He would lead them back, he said, by another route, and it could not be but that they should meet somewhere with those fruitful regions of which they had so often heard. It was something, at least, that every step would take them nearer home. It was clearly the only course now left; they should prepare to meet it like men. The spirit would sustain the body, and difficulties encountered in the right spirit were half vanquished already.

The soldiers listened eagerly to his words of promise and encouragement. The confidence of their leader gave life to the desponding. They felt the force of his reasoning, and as they lent a willing ear to his assurances the pride of the old Castilian honor revived in their bosoms and everyone caught somewhat of the generous enthusiasm of their commander. He was, in truth, entitled to their devotion. From the first hour of the expedition he had freely borne his part in its privations. Far from claiming the advantage of his position, he had taken his lot with the poorest soldier, ministering to the wants of the sick, cheering up the spirits of the desponding, sharing his stinted allowance with his famished followers, bearing his full part in the toil and burden of the march, ever showing himself their faithful comrade no less than their captain. He found the benefit of this conduct in a trying hour like the present.

I will spare the reader the recapitulation of the sufferings endured by the Spaniards on their retrograde march to Quito.

They took a more northerly route than that by which they had approached the Amazon, and if it was attended with fewer difficulties, they experienced yet greater distresses from their greater inability to overcome them. Their only nourishment was such scanty fare as they could pick up in the forest, or happily meet with in some forsaken Indian settlement, or wring by violence from the natives. Some sickened and sank down by the way, for there was none to help them. Intense misery had made them selfish. Many a poor wretch was abandoned to his fate to die alone in the wilderness, or to be devoured while living by the wild animals which roamed over it.

At length, in June, 1542, after somewhat more than a year consumed in their homeward march, the wayworn company came on the elevated plains in the neighborhood of Quito. But how different their aspect from that which they had exhibited on issuing from the gates of the same capital two years and a half before, with high romantic hope and in all the pride of military array! Their horses gone, their arms broken and rusted, the skins of wild animals instead of clothes hanging loosely about their limbs, their long and matted locks streaming wildly down their shoulders, their faces burned and blackened by the tropical sun, their bodies wasted by famine and sorely disfigured by scars—it seemed as if the charnel house had given up its dead as, with uncertain step, they glided slowly onward, like a troop of dismal specters. More than half of the four thousand Indians who had accompanied the expedition had perished, and of the Spaniards only eighty, and many of these irretrievably broken in constitution, returned to Quito.

The few Christian inhabitants of the place with their wives and children came out to welcome their countrymen. They ministered to them all the relief and refreshment in their power, and as they listened to the sad recital of their sufferings they mingled their tears with those of the wanderers. The whole company entered the capital, where their first act—to their credit be it mentioned—was to go in a body to the church and offer up thanksgivings to the Almighty for their miraculous preservation through their long and perilous pilgrimage. Such was the end of the expedition to the Amazon—an expedition which, for its dangers and hardships, the length of their duration, and the constancy with which they were endured, stands perhaps unmatched in the annals of American discovery.

EARTHQUAKE
IN THE ANDES—
CHARLES DARWIN

by Ruth Moore

So far in our selections on Latin America, our saga has been one of conquest and bloodshed in the name of religion but with a basic interest in loot. But another spirit was awakening in the world, the spirit of scientific discovery. Men were coming to realize that knowledge was more lasting and important than nuggets. By the nineteenth century this spirit was leading men to distant parts of the globe in search of new species of birds and animals, and tribes that lived in more interesting ways than the so-called civilized races. One of their most fertile fields was South America, and many great naturalist scientists made important discoveries there.

One of the first was Alexander von Humboldt, who in 1799 landed in Cumaná to begin the journeys in which he examined new species of plants and animals. He had been inspired by the travels of his friend, George Forster, who had sailed on Captain Cook's second voyage. During his extensive travels, he made a detailed study of the Orinoco, and on one expedition, while studying the headstreams of the Amazon, crossed the Andes five times. He wrote of everything he saw with such skill and vision that young Charles Darwin, on reading his accounts, was in his turn inspired to follow the great man's example. So it came about that he agreed to go on the celebrated "Voyage of the Beagle."

As Ruth Moore points out in her excellent short biography, from which the following selection is taken, this voyage was to plant in Darwin's mind seeds which were to revolutionize the entire world of science. As we follow Darwin in his journey over the Andes, we see again and again his amazing powers of observation, in particular his ability to go from the particular to the general. On the surface, the account may appear less exciting than the exploits of the conquistadors. Actually, its implications are far more stirring and important.

IT WAS in June, 1834, in the depths of winter, that the *Beagle* at long last sailed into the desolate Strait of Magellan and headed for the Pacific. There was no comfort to be found anywhere at this end of the Continent. The water was so deep they were unable to obtain an anchorage, and during a pitch-dark night of fourteen hours the *Beagle* was forced to stand off in the narrow channel. Once she came very near to the rocks.

Ahead lay numberless rocks and islets, on which the long swell of the open Pacific broke with an incessant and deafening roar. It was enough, Darwin noted, to make a landsman dream for a week about death, peril, and shipwreck. As they entered the Pacific through this formidable door, northerly gales swept down upon them. The *Beagle* rode them out with close-reefed topsail, fore trysail, and staysail, but even after the wind had ceased the great sea prevented their making any headway. In the midst of the tumult, death came to the *Beagle's* purser, who had long been sinking under a complication of disorders. A solemn funeral service was read on the quarter-deck and his body was lowered into the sea. Darwin, already desperately seasick, listened with the deepest gloom and sorrow to that "aweful and solemn sound, the splash of waters over the body of an old ship-mate."

But tragedy and storm were now over. In July they were at Valparaiso, Chile, where the climate "felt quite delicious," the sky was "so clear & blue, the air so dry, & the sun so bright." Added to these boons there were good fresh beef to eat, and an old school friend, Richard Corfield, who invited Darwin to stay in his very comfortable house.

Just beyond Valparaiso loomed the Andes, that omnipresent, divisive backbone of the Continent toward which Darwin had looked for so long from the Atlantic coast and from the south. In August snow had closed all the mountains except the "basal parts." A crossing was impossible at that season, but Darwin set out with a guide and a string of mules for the lower slopes.

They made a camp on a height looking down on the Bay of Valparaiso. As the sun set and the deep black shadows of the night enveloped the valleys below, the snowy peaks above them still caught the sun's last rays and turned a glowing ruby-red. Not until this "glorious sunset" had faded did they light a fire in their little arbor of bamboo trees and fry their *charqui*—slips of dried beef. Sipping his *maté* and listening to the occasional cry of the goatsucker and the shrill of the mountain viscacha, almost the only sounds that broke the stillness, Darwin reveled again as he often had on the pampas in "the inexpressible charm of living in the open air."

Darwin made several trips to the gold and copper mines of the region. On one of them he drank some *"chichi,"* a weak, sour Chilean wine, which he said "half poisoned me." One night he considered himself extremely lucky to find some clean straw for a bed—a success that later amused him with the relativity of all things. He laughed to think what he would have said to a bed of straw and "stinking horse cloths" if he had been in England and unwell.

When he finally reached Corfield's house he was seriously ill for more than a month. The ship's doctor prescribed "a lot of calomel and rest," and it seemed to work. Later Darwin sometimes felt that this sickness may have been a factor in his lifelong ill-health, but at the time he was principally concerned about the "grievous loss of time" and the loss of the animals he had hoped to collect.

As soon as Darwin was able to travel, the *Beagle* left for a curtailed survey of southern Chile, and of the island of Chiloé and the Chonos Archipelago, which lay just off the Chilean coast.

One day as Charles was wandering in the Chiloé woods, he stretched out on the ground for a little rest and felt the ground rock under him. The motion almost made him giddy, it was so like that of a vessel in a cross-ripple. The swaying motion that jarred him so lightly was the famous earthquake of February 20, 1835, one of the most severe in the region's long history of quakes. Hardly a house was left standing in the town of Concepción, and gaping rents traversed the ground. Even greater damage had been done by a huge tidal wave that swept across the sea. As it broke at the head of the bay, it tore loose a four-ton cannon and tossed it and a schooner ashore as though they had been the lightest pieces of driftwood.

For almost three years Darwin had been studying the elevation and subsidence of the land around the coast of South America. Here, almost before his eyes, the actual process was happening. By careful measurement he established that the big quake had raised the land around Concepción Bay between two and three feet, and on an island about thirty miles away Captain Fitzroy found putrid mussels adhering to rocks ten feet above the high-water mark. The inhabitants formerly had dived at low spring tide for these very shells. Darwin could understand with new clarity why he had found seashells scattered over the land of the region at heights of as much as thirteen hundred feet above the water.

"It is hardly possible to doubt," he recorded in his journal, "that this great elevation has been effected by successive small uprisings, such as that which accompanied the earthquake of this year, and likewise by an insensibly slow rise which is certainly in progress on some parts of this coast."

Along the *Beagle's* route Darwin had received and eagerly read the second and third volumes of Lyell's geology. He had not only found Lyell right in his theory that the earth had been shaped by forces similar to those acting in his time, but in a letter to a cousin added: "I am tempted to carry parts to a greater extent even than he does." To see was to be convinced.

The mighty climax to which these workings of nature could rise lay ahead—the Andes. Darwin returned to Chile to make his long-anticipated crossing of the great walled mountains. For the journey he hired his guide of the earlier expedition and an *arriero* with ten mules and a *madrina*. The *madrina*, a little mare with a tinkling bell around her neck, acted, as Darwin explained it, as a "sort of stepmother to the mules"; they would follow her and her bell anywhere.

They soon had to cross some of the mountain torrents that rushed down boulder-strewn courses with a roar like that of the sea. On the other side of the Andes, Darwin often had studied the vast plains of sand, shingle, and mud, and had questioned if he could be right in thinking that the rivers had deposited such immeasurable masses. But listening at night to the thunder of the Andes torrents and remembering that they had been running while whole races of animals disappeared from the earth, he could understand where the material of the plains had come from. He could understand how even mountains as immense as these could be worn down and their boundless substance be swept down to the plains, where he had seen it spread out, smooth, graded, and deep over miles without end.

They climbed higher and higher until the well-marked road turned into a zigzag track near the top of the Peuquenes Range, which is the main western ridge of the Cordillera. At twelve thousand feet there was a transparency of the air, a confusion of distances, that gave one a sense of another world. The mules would halt every fifty yards, and the breath came lightly. The *Chilenos* called this difficulty in breathing the *puna*— "All the waters up here have *puna*," they would say; or "Where there is snow there is *puna*." Darwin experienced a slight tightness across the head and chest, but suddenly at about thirteen thousand feet he saw a strata of shells. The *puna* was forgotten.

Shells at thirteen thousand feet, shells which must once have lain in the matrix that still held them at the very bottom of the sea! Darwin could identify many of them: *Gryphœa, Ostrea, Turratella,* ammonites, and small bivalves. He collected as many as time allowed. If the ever present danger of snow had not made further delay inadvisable, he would have "reaped a grand harvest."

Startling as it was to discover shells near the crest of one of the world's highest mountain ranges, Darwin was not unprepared for the find. As he climbed he had seen with increasing astonishment that the upper reaches of these towering mountains were made up of layer after layer of sedimentary rocks, rocks that had been formed in the sea by the unending downward drift of the skeletons and shells of living water organisms and the sediments of the earth. The upper parts of the Andes were not, as science then thought, the once-molten outpouring of a volcano or of a series of volcanoes.

Darwin knew that such findings would sound incredible to older geologists. In writing to Henslow he cautiously began: "I know some of the facts, of the truth of which I in my own mind feel fully convinced, will appear to you quite absurd and incredible," and then he told him of his discovery of the ocean-bottom origin of the peaks of the Peuquenes and of their uplifting.

Pushing on, they descended into the high mountainous country that lay between the Peuquenes and the Portillo chain, the other main ridge of the Andes. At the eleven-thousand-foot elevation where they camped, the miserable little fire that was all they could coax from a few scrubby roots did not begin to offset the piercing cold of the wind. Nor would it boil potatoes; after several hours they were as hard as ever, and even after they had remained on the fire all night they were uncooked. The next morning, following a potatoless breakfast, Darwin heard his two men talking about what had caused the trouble—"that cursed pot [a new one] did not choose to boil the potatoes."

There was another climb over the still higher though, Darwin was convinced, younger Portillo range. At its fourteen-thousand-foot crest the air was so clear and dry that the moon and stars took on a brilliancy Darwin had never seen matched. Electricity crackled at the least touch. When Darwin chanced to rub his waistcoat in the dark, it glowed as though it had been washed with phosphorus.

The descent to the Argentine pampas was short and steep, for on the

Atlantic side the mountains rose abruptly from the plain. For a while a level, gleamingly white sea of clouds blocked out the view below, but once they were through this horizontal screen, the great Argentine plain stretched out below them as Darwin had long wanted to see it, from the west. And at first he was disappointed; it was like looking out across the sea. Then he made out some small irregularities to the north, and in the rising sun the rivers began to glitter like silver threads until they were lost in the immensity of distance.

Darwin swung a little northward in order to recross the Andes through the Uspallata Pass. The mountains there, a continuation of the grand eastern chain, were as amazing as those to the south. Darwin soon found that they were made up of alternating layers of lava and sedimentary rocks.

During his first two days of studying the formations and chipping off specimens, Darwin said to himself fifty times over that they looked exactly like the sandstone-lava formations he had seen in Patagonia and Chiloé. No shells, of course, would be found in such sandstone, but in the similar formations he had often come upon small pieces of silicified wood. Could there be such wood in these formations too? Almost without meaning to, he began what he was sure would be a "forlorn hunt."

He had gone only a short distance when at an elevation of seven thousand feet he saw some snow-white projecting columns standing alone in a little group on a bare mountain slope. Darwin hurried over to them. To his amazement and delight they proved to be petrified trees! Eleven were silicified and between thirty and forty had been crystallized into white spar. The stumps measured from three to five feet in circumference.

It was not difficult for Darwin to interpret the "marvellous story this scene unfolded," though he continued to feel that he scarcely dared to believe such perfect evidence.

Once upon a time the stone stumps had stood green and budding on the shores of the Atlantic. The ocean, which in the 1830's was more than seven hundred miles distant, had then rolled up to the very foot of the Andes. As had happened many times before, this shore began to sink, and as it slowly went down, the tree stumps, firmly anchored by their roots, went down with it. Water flowed around them and sand drifted over them, completely encasing the wood—some of the stone lay there on the mountainside still bearing the true markings of the bark. This quiet history of subsidence changed abruptly when an underwater volcano erupted and sent a great mass of black lava rolling over the trees and the sand that had enveloped them. At places the molten mass piled up to a depth of a thousand feet. In time quiet reigned again and the sand once more drifted in, and then there was another explosion. Five times this story was repeated, sand and lava and sand and lava again. The ocean that received such masses must have been profoundly deep, but again the subterranean forces exerted themselves and the bed of the sea was slowly but relentlessly uplifted into a mountain range more than seven thousand feet high. It was then that the winds and the rains and the snows began their work; over another great length of time they eroded away the upper layers of sandstone and lava until at last the petrified stumps stood forth bare and uncovered on the gaunt mountain slope where Charles Darwin found them.

"Vast and scarcely comprehensible as such changes must appear," Darwin wrote in his journal, "yet they have all occurred within a period recent when compared with the history of the Cordillera, and the Cordillera itself is absolutely modern as compared with many of the fossiliferous strata of Europe and America."

Darwin's twenty-four-day crossing of the Andes ended with a pleasant ride south along the coastal plain to Santiago. It was April, the Chilean autumn; figs and peaches were spread out on cottage roofs to dry, and the men, women, and children were working in the vineyards. The scene was a "pretty one," but Darwin's thoughts were turning increasingly to England and it only made him miss the "pensive stillness" of the English autumn.

The *Beagle* lingered on the west coast of South America for another four months, making additional surveys in northern Chile and Peru. Darwin traveled into the northern Chilean mountains several times, but they were "tame" in comparison to the grandeur he had seen, and he tired of noting that the lowland country was "barren and sterile."

AMONG THE CANNIBAL MANGEROMAS

by Algot Lange

The following selection is taken from the account by Algot Lange of his remarkable experiences as an ethnologist In the Amazon Jungle. In the introduction Frederick S. Dellenbaugh, the noted explorer, writes of Lange's journey to the headwaters of the Amazon: "I knew he would encounter many set-backs, but I never would have predicted the adventures he actually passed through alive.

"He started in fine spirits: buoyant, strong, vigorous. When I saw him again in New York, on his return, he was an emaciated fever wreck, placing one foot before the other only with much exertion and indeed barely able to hold himself erect."

One of the most interesting and harrowing of Lange's adventures began when he started out with a group of native workers to find sources of rubber in hitherto uninvestigated territory. The expedition was disastrous, resulting in starvation and death. Lange himself managed to reach a place inhabited by a tribe of cannibal Mangeromas who looked after him when he was ill and treated him kindly. Fortunately for him, the Mangeromas never eat their friends, only their enemies. As a result he was spared to make valuable contributions to our understanding of the ethnology of the western Amazon, a formidable region until then largely unknown to the white man. His story of his adventures was published in 1912.

I HAVE a vague recollection of hearing the barking of dogs, of changing my crawling direction to head for the sound, and then, suddenly, seeing in front of me a sight which had the same effect as a rescuing steamer on the shipwrecked.

From In the Amazon Jungle by Algot Lange. Reprinted by permission of G. P. Putnam's Sons.

To my confused vision it seemed that I saw many men and women and children, and a large, round house; I saw parrots fly across the open space in brilliant, flashing plumage and heard their shrill screaming. I cried aloud and fell forward when a little curly-haired dog jumped up and commenced licking my face, and then I knew no more.

When I came to I was lying in a comfortable hammock in a large, dark room. I heard the murmur of many voices and presently a man came over and looked at me. I did not understand where I was, but thought that I, finally, had gone mad. I fell asleep again. The next time I woke up I saw an old woman leaning over me and holding in her hand a gourd containing some chicken broth which I swallowed slowly, not feeling the cravings of hunger, in fact not knowing whether I was dead or alive. The old woman had a peculiar piece of wood through her lip and looked very unreal to me, and I soon fell asleep again.

On the fifth day, so I learned later, I began to feel my senses return, my fever commenced to abate, and I was able to grasp the fact that I had crawled into the *maloca*, or communal village, of the Mangeromas. I was as weak as a kitten, and, indeed, it has been a marvel to me ever since that I succeeded at all in coming out of the Shadow. The savages, by tender care, with strengthening drinks prepared in their own primitive method, wrought the miracle, and returned to life a man who was as near death as anyone could be, and not complete the transition. They fed me at regular intervals, thus checking my sickness, and when I could make out their meaning, I understood that I could stay with them as long as I desired.

Luckily I had kept my spectacles on my nose (they were the kind that fasten back of the ears) during the previous hardships, and I found these sticking in their position when I awoke. My khaki coat was on the ground under my hammock, and the first thing was to ascertain if the precious contents of its large pockets had been disturbed, but I found everything safe. The exposed plates were there in their closed boxes, the gold dust was also there and mocked me with its yellow glare, and my hypodermic outfit was intact and was used without delay, much to the astonishment of some of the men, standing around my hammock.

When my head was clear and strong enough to raise, I turned and began my first visual exploration of my immediate surroundings. The big room I found to be a colossal house, forty feet high and one hundred and fifty feet in diameter, thatched with palm leaves and with sides formed of the stems of the *pachiuba* tree. It was the communal residence of this entire tribe, consisting, as I learned later, of two hundred and fifty-eight souls. A single door and a circular opening in the roof were the only apertures of this enormous structure. The door was very low, not more than four feet, so that it was necessary to creep on one's knees to enter the place, and this opening was closed at night, that is to say, about six o'clock, by a sliding door which fitted so snugly that I never noticed any mosquitoes or *piums* in the dark, cool room.

The next day I could get out of my hammock, though I could not stand or walk without the aid of two women, who took me over to a man I later found to be the chief of the tribe. He was well fed, and by his elaborate dress was distinguished from the rest of the men. He had a very pleasant, good-natured smile, and almost constantly displayed a row of white, sharp-filed teeth. This smile gave me some confidence, but I very well knew that I was now living among cannibal Indians, whose reputation in this part of the Amazon is anything but flattering. I prepared for the new ordeal without any special fear—my feelings seemed by this time to have been pretty well exhausted and any appreciation of actual danger was considerably reduced as a result of the gamut of the terrors which I had run.

I addressed the Chief in the Portuguese language, and also in Spanish, but he only shook his head; all my efforts were useless. He let me know in a friendly manner that my hammock was to be my resting place and that I would not be molested. His tribe was one that occupied an almost unknown region and had no connection with white men or Brazilians or people near the river. I tried in the course of the mimical conversation to make him understand that, with six companions from a big Chief's *maloca* (meaning Coronel da Silva and the Floresta headquarters), I had penetrated into the woods near this mighty Chief's *maloca*—here I pointed at the Chief—that the men had died from fever and I was left alone and that luckily, I had found my way to the free men of the forest (here I made a sweeping movement with my hands). He nodded and the audience was over. I was led back to my hammock to dream and eat, and dream again.

The hospitality of my friends proved unbounded. The Chief appointed two young girls to care for me, and though they were not startling from any point of view, especially when remembering their labial ornaments and their early developed abdominal hypertrophies, they were as kind as anyone could have been, watching me when I tried to walk and supporting me when I became too weak. There was a certain broth they prepared, which was delicious, but there were others which were nauseating and which I had to force myself to eat. I soon learned that it was impolite to refuse any dish that was put in front of me, no matter how repugnant. One day the Chief ordered me to come over to his family triangle and have dinner with him. The meal consisted of some very tender fried fish which were really delicious; then followed three broiled parrots with fried bananas which were equally good; but then came a soup which I could not swallow. The first mouthful almost choked me—the meat which was one of the ingredients tasted and smelled as if it had been kept for weeks, the herbs which were used were so bitter and gave out such a rank odor that my mouth puckered and the muscles of my throat refused to swallow. The Chief looked at me and frowned, and then I remembered the forest from which I had lately arrived and the starvation and the terrors; I closed my eyes and swallowed the dish, seeking what mental relief I could find in the so-called autosuggestion.

But I had the greatest respect for the impulsive, unreasoning nature of these sons of the forest. Easily insulted, they are well-nigh implacable. This incident shows upon what a slender thread my life hung. The friends of one moment might become vindictive foes of the next.

The chiefs had several wives, but the tribesmen were never allowed to take more than one. Whenever a particularly pretty girl desired to join the household of the Great Chief or of a subchief, she set to work and for months and months she made necklaces of alligator teeth, peccary teeth, and finely carved ivory nuts and colored pieces of wood. She also would weave some elaborate hammock and fringe this with the bushy tails of the squirrels and the forest cats, and when these articles were done, she would present them to the Chief, who, in return for these favors, would bestow upon her the great honor of accepting her as a wife.

The men were good hunters and were experts in the use of bow and arrow and also the blowgun, and never failed to bring home a fresh supply of game for the village. This supply was always divided equally, so that no one should receive more than he needed for the day. At first glance the men might appear lazy, but why should they hurry and worry when they have no landlord, and no grocer's bills to pay; in fact, the value of money is entirely unknown to them.

I was allowed to walk around as I pleased, everybody showing me a kindness for which I shall ever gratefully remember these "savages." I frequently spent my forenoons on a tree trunk outside the *maloca* with the Chief, who took a particular interest in my welfare. We would sit for hours and talk, he sometimes pointing at an object and giving its Indian name, which I would repeat until I got the right pronunciation. Thus, gradually instructed, and by watching the men and women as they came and went, day after day, I was able to understand some of their language and learned to answer questions fairly well. They never laughed at my mistakes, but repeated a word until I had it right.

My life among the Mangeromas was, for the greater part, free from adventure, at least as compared with former experiences, and yet I was more than once within an inch of meeting death. In fact, I think that I looked more squarely in the eyes of death in that peaceful little community than ever I did out in the wilds of the jungle or in my most perilous adventures. The creek that ran near the *maloca* supplied the Indians with what water they needed for drinking purposes. Besides this the creek gave them an abundant supply of fish, a dish that made its appearance at every meal. Whatever washing was to be done—the natives took a bath at least twice a day—was done at some distance down the creek so as not to spoil the water for drinking and culinary purposes. Whenever I was thirsty I was in the habit of stooping down at the water's edge to scoop the fluid up in my curved hands. One morning I had been tramping through the jungle with two companions who were in search of game, and I was very tired and hot when we came to a little stream which I took to be the same that ran past the *maloca*. My friends were at a short distance from me, beating their way through the underbrush, when I stooped to quench my thirst. The cool water looked to me like the very Elixir of Life. At that moment, literally speaking, I was only two inches from death. Hearing a sharp cry behind me I turned slightly to feel a rough hand upon my shoulders and found myself flung backward on the ground.

"Poison," was the reply to my angry question. Then my friend explained, and as he talked my knees wobbled and I turned pale. It seems that the Mangeromas often poison the streams below the drinking places in order to get rid of their enemies. In the present case there had been a rumor that a party of Peruvian rubber workers might be coming up the creek, and this is always a signal of trouble among these Indians. Although you cannot induce a Brazilian to go into the Indian settlements or *malocas*, the Peruvians are more than willing to go there, because of the chance of abducting girls. To accomplish this, a few Peruvians sneak close to the *maloca* at night, force the door, which is always bolted to keep out the Evil Spirit, but which without difficulty can be cut open, and fire a volley of shots into the hut. The Indians sleep with the blowguns and arrows suspended from the rafters, and before they can collect their sleepy senses and procure the weapons the Peruvians, in the general confusion, have carried off some of the girls. The Mangeromas, therefore, hate the Peruvians and will go to any extreme to compass their death. The poisoning of the rivers is effected by the root of a plant that is found throughout the Amazon valley; the plant belongs to the genus *Lonchocarpus*.

Thinking to amuse some of my friends, I one day kindled a flame by means of my magnifying glass and a few dry twigs. A group of ten or twelve Indians had gathered squatting in a circle about me, to see the wonder that I was to exhibit, but at the sight of smoke followed by flame they were badly scared and ran for the house, where they called the Chief. He arrived on the scene with his usual smile.

He asked me to show him what I had done. I applied the focused rays of the sun to some more dry leaves and twigs and, finally, the flames broke out again. The Chief was delighted and begged me to make him a present of the magnifier. As I did not dare to refuse, I showed him how to use it and then presented it with as good grace as I could.

Some time after this, I learned that two Peruvians had been caught in a trap set for the purpose. The unfortunate men had spent a whole night in a pit, nine feet deep, and were discovered the next forenoon by a party of hunters, who immediately killed them with unpoisoned, big-game arrows. In contrast to the North American Indians they never torture captives, but kill them as quickly as possible. On such occasions a day of feasting always follows and an obscure religious rite is performed.

It is true that the Mangeromas are cannibals, but at the same time their habits and morals are otherwise remarkably clean. Without their good care and excellent treatment, I have no doubt I would now be with my brave companions out in that dark, green jungle.

But to return to my story of the two Peruvians caught in the pit trap: the warriors cut off the hands and feet of both corpses, pulled the big game arrows out of the bodies, and had an audience with the Chief. He seemed to be well satisfied, but spoke little, just nodding his head and smiling. Shortly after the village prepared for a grand feast. The fires were rebuilt, the pots and jars were cleaned, and a scene followed which to me was frightful. Had it not happened, I should always have believed this little world out in the wild forest an ideal, pure, and morally clean community. But now I could only hasten to my hammock and simulate sleep, for I well knew, from previous experience, that otherwise I would have to partake of the meal in preparation: a horrible meal of human flesh! It was enough for me to see them strip the flesh from the palms of the hands and the soles of the feet and fry these delicacies in the lard of tapir. I hoped to see no more.

An awful thought coursed through my brain when I beheld the men bend eagerly over the pans to see if the meat were done. How long would it be, I said to myself, before they would forget themselves and place my own extremities in the same pots and pans. Such a possibility was not pleasant to contemplate, but as I had found the word of these Indians to be always good, I believed I was safe. They were never false and they hated falsehood. True, they were cunning, but once their friend always their friend, through thick and thin. And the Chief had promised that I should not be eaten, either fried or stewed! Therefore I slept in peace.

I was sitting outside the *maloca* writing my observations in the notebook which I always carried in my hunting coat, when two young hunters hurried toward the Chief, who was reclining in the shade of a banana tree near the other end of the large house. It was early afternoon, when most of the men of the Mangeromas were off hunting in the near-by forests, while the women and children attended to various duties around the village. Probably not more than eight or ten men remained about the *maloca*.

I had recovered from my sickness and was not entirely devoid of a desire for excitement—the best tonic of the explorer. The two young hunters with bows and arrows halted before the Chief. They were gesticulating wildly; and although I could not understand what they were talking about, I judged from the frown of the Chief that something serious was the matter.

He arose with unusual agility for a man of his size, and shouted something toward the opening of the *maloca*, whence the men were soon seen coming with leaps and bounds. Anticipating trouble, I also ran over to the Chief, and, in my defective Mangeroma lingo, inquired the cause of the excitement. He did not answer me, but, in a greater state of agitation than I had previously observed in him, he gave orders to his men. It did not take me long to understand that we were in danger from some Peruvian *caboclos*. The two young men who had brought the news to the Chief had spied a detachment of Peruvian half-breeds. There were about a score of them, all ugly *caboclos*, or half-breed *caucheros*, hunting rubber and no doubt out also for prey in the shape of young Mangeroma girls, as was their custom.

The enemy had been observed more than ten miles off, in an easterly direction, when our two hunters were on the trail of a large herd of peccaries, or wild boars, they had sighted in the early morning. The Peruvians were believed to be heading for the *maloca* of the Mangeromas, as there were no other settlements in this region excepting the up-creek tribe, but this numbered at least five hundred souls, and would be no easy prey for them.

I now had a remarkable opportunity to watch the war preparations of these savage, cannibal people, my friends, the Mangeromas. Their army consisted of twelve able-bodied men, all fine muscular fellows, about five feet ten in height, and bearing an array of vicious-looking weapons such as few white men have seen. First of all were three clubmen, armed with strong, slender clubs, of hard and extremely tough Caripari wood. The handle, which was very slim, was provided with a knob at the end to prevent the club from slipping out of the hand when in action. The heavy end was furnished with six bicuspid teeth of the black jaguar, embedded in the wood and projecting about two inches beyond the surface. The club had a total length of five feet and weighed about eight pounds. The second division of the wild-looking band consisted of three spearmen, each provided with the three-pronged spears, a horrible weapon which always proves fatal in the hands of these savages. It is a long straight shaft of Caripari wood, about one inch in thickness, divided into three parts at the end, each division being tipped with a barbed bone of the sting ray. These bones, about three and a half inches long, were smeared with wourali poison, and thus rendered absolutely fatal even when inflicting only a superficial wound. Each man carried two of these spears, the points being protected by grass sheaths. The third division was composed of three bow-and-arrow men, the youngest men in the tribe, boys of sixteen and seventeen. They were armed with bows of great length, from six to seven feet, and each bore, at his left side, a quiver, containing a dozen big-game arrows fully five feet long. These arrows, as far as I could ascertain, were not poisoned, but their shock-giving and rending powers were extraordinary. The arrowheads were all made of the bones of the sting ray, in themselves formidable weapons, because of the many jagged barbs that prevent extraction from a wound except by the use of great force, resulting in ugly laceration.

The fourth and last division consisted of three blowgun men, the most effective and cunning of this deadly and imposing array. As so much depended upon the success of a first attack on the Peruvians, who not only outnumbered us, but also were armed with Winchesters, the blowguns were in the hands of the older and more experienced men.

The Chief gave the order for the bow-and-arrow men to start in single file, the others to follow after, in close succession. The Chief and I fell in at the rear. In the meantime I had examined my Luger automatic pistol to make sure of the smooth action of the mechanism, and found besides that I had in all thirty-seven soft-nose bullets. This was my only weapon, but previous narrow escapes from death and many close contacts with danger had hardened me, so I was willing to depend entirely upon my pistol. The women and children of the *maloca* stood around, as we disappeared in the jungle, and, while they showed some interest in the proceeding, they displayed little or no emotion. A couple of sweethearts exchanged kisses as composedly as if they had been bluecoats parting with the ladies of their choice before going to the annual parade.

For an hour we traveled in a straight line, pushing our way as noiselessly as possible through the thick mass of creepers and lianas. About three o'clock, one of the scouts sighted the Peruvians, and our Chief decided that an attack should be made as soon as possible, before darkness could set in. We stopped and sent out two bow-and-arrow men to reconnoiter. An anxious half-hour passed before one of them returned with the report that the Peruvians were now coming toward us and would probably reach our position in a few minutes. I could almost hear my heart thump; my knees grew weak, and for a moment I almost wished that I had stayed in the *maloca*.

The Chief immediately directed certain strategic movements which, in ingenuity and foresight, would have been worthy of a Napoleon.

We were between two low hills, covered with the usual dense vegetation, which made it impossible to see an advancing enemy at a distance of more than five yards. The three blowgun men were now ordered to ascend the hills on each side of the valley and conceal themselves about halfway up the slopes, and toward the enemy. They were to insert the poisoned arrows in their guns and draw a bead on the Peruvians as they came on cutting their way through the underbrush. The bow-and-arrow men posted themselves farther on, about five yards behind the blowgun men, with big-game arrows fitted to the bowstrings, ready to shoot when the first volley of the deadly and silent poisoned arrows had been fired. Farther back were the spearmen with spears unsheathed, and finally came the three brave and ferocious clubmen. Of these last warriors, a tall athlete was visibly nervous, not from fear but from anticipation. The veins of his forehead stood out, pulsating with every throb of his heart. He clutched the heavy club and continually gritted his white, sharp-filed teeth in concentrated rage. It was wisely calculated that the Peruvians would unconsciously wedge themselves into this trap, and by the time they could realize their danger their return would be cut off by our bow-and-arrow men in their rear.

After a pause that seemed an eternity to most of us no doubt, for the savage heart beats as the white man's in time of danger and action, we heard the talking and shouting of the enemy as they advanced, following the natural and easiest route between the hills and cutting their way through the brush. I stood near the Chief and the young clubman Arara, who, on account of his bravery and great ability in handling his club, had been detailed to remain near us.

Before I could see any of the approaching foe, I heard great shouts of anger and pain from them. It was easy for me to understand their cries as they spoke Spanish and their cursings sounded loud through the forest.

The blowgun men, perceiving the Peruvians at the foot of the hill only some twenty feet away, had prudently waited until at least half a dozen were visible, before they fired a volley of poisoned arrows. The three arrows fired in this first volley all hit their mark. Hardly had they gone forth, when other arrows were dexterously inserted in the tubes. The work of the blowgun men was soon restricted to the picking out of any stray enemy, their long, delicate, and cumbersome blowguns preventing them from taking an active part in the melee. Now the conflict was at its height and it was a most remarkable one, on account of its swiftness and fierceness. The bow-and-arrow men charging with their sting ray arrows poisoned with the wourali took the place of the cautiously retreating blowgun men. At the same instant the spearmen rushed down, dashing through the underbrush at the foot of the hill, like breakers on a stormy night.

The rear guard of the Peruvians now came into action, having had a chance to view the situation. Several of them filed to the right and managed to fire their large-caliber bullets into the backs of our charging bow-and-arrow men, but, in their turn, they were picked off by the blowgun men, who kept firing their poisoned darts from a safe distance. The fearful yells of our men, mingled with the cursing of the Peruvians, and the sharp reports of their heavy rifles, so plainly heard, proved that the center of battle was not many yards from the spot where I was standing.

The clubmen now broke into action; they could not be kept back any longer. The tension had already been too painful for these brave fellows, and with fierce war cries of "Yob—hee—hee" they launched themselves into the fight, swinging their strong clubs above their heads and crushing skulls from left to right. By this time the Peruvians had lost many men, but the slaughter went on. The huge black clubs of the Mangeromas fell again and again, with sickening thuds, piercing the heads and brains of the enemy with the pointed jaguar teeth.

Suddenly two Peruvians came into view not more than twelve feet from where the Chief, Arara the big clubman, and I were standing. One of these was a Spaniard, evidently the captain of this band of marauders (or, to use their correct name, *caucheros*). His face was of a sickly, yellowish hue, and a big, black mustache hid the lower part of his cruel and narrow chin. He took a quick aim as he saw us in his path, but before he could pull the trigger, Arara, with a mighty side swing of his club literally tore the Spaniard's head off. Now, at last, the bonds of restraint were broken for this handsome devil Arara, and yelling himself hoarse, and with his strong but cruel face contracted to a fiendish grin, he charged the enemy; I saw him crush the life out of three.

The Chief took no active part in the fight whatever, but added to the excitement by bellowing with all his might an encouraging "Aa—oo—ah." No doubt, this had a highly beneficial effect upon the tribesmen, for they never for an instant ceased their furious fighting until the last Peruvian was killed. During the final moments of the battle, several bullets whirred by me at close range, but during the whole affair I had had neither opportunity nor necessity for using my pistol. Now, however, a *caboclo*, with a large, bloody machete in his hand, sprang from behind a tree and made straight for me. I dodged behind another tree and saw how the branches were swept aside as he rushed toward me.

Then I fired point-blank, sending three bullets into his head. He fell on his face at my feet. As I bent over him, I saw that he had a blowgun arrow in his left thigh; he was therefore a doomed man before he attacked me. This was my first and only victim, during this brief but horrible slaughter. As I was already thoroughly sick from the noise of cracking rifles and the thumping of clubs smashing their way into the brains of the Peruvians, I rushed toward the center of the valley where the first attack on the advance guard of the enemy had taken place, but even more revolting was the sight that revealed itself. Here and there bushes were shaking as some *caboclo* crawled along on all fours in his death agony. Those who were struck by the blowgun arrows seemed simply to fall asleep without much pain or struggle, but the victims of the clubmen and the bow-and-arrow men had a terrible death. They could not die by the merciful wourali poison, like those shot by the blowgun, but expired from hemorrhages caused by the injuries of the ruder weapons. One poor fellow was groaning most pitifully. He had received a well-directed big-game arrow in the upper part of the abdomen, the arrow having been shot with such terrible force that about a foot of the shaft projected from the man's back. The arrowhead had been broken off by striking a vertebra.

The battle was over. Soon the *urubus*, or vultures, were hanging over the treetops waiting for their share of the spoils. The men assembled in front of the Chief for roll call. Four of our men were killed outright by rifle bullets, and it was typical of these brave men that none were killed by machete stabs. The entire marauding expedition of twenty Peruvians was completely wiped out, not a single one escaping the deadly aim of the Mangeromas. Thus was avoided the danger of being attacked in the near future by a greater force of Peruvians, called to this place from the distant frontier by some returning survivor.

It is true that the Mangeromas lay in ambush for their enemy and killed them, for the greater part, with poisoned arrows and spears, but the odds were against the Indians, not only because the *caboclos* were attacking them in larger numbers, but because they came with modern, repeating firearms against the hand weapons of the Mangeromas. These marauders, too, came with murder and girl robbery in their black hearts, while the Mangeromas were defending their homes and families. But it is true that after the battle, so bravely fought, the Indians cut off the hands and feet of their enemies, dead or dying, and carried them home.

The fight lasted only some twenty minutes, but it was after sunset when we reached the *maloca*. The women and children received us with great demonstrations of joy. Soon the pots and pans were boiling inside the great house. I have previously observed how the Mangeromas would partake of parts of the human body as a sort of religious rite, whenever they had been successful with their man traps; now they feasted upon the hands and feet of the slain, these parts having been distributed among the different families.

I crept into my hammock and lit my pipe, watching the great mass of naked humanity. All the men had laid aside their feather dresses and squirrel tails, and were moving around among the many fires on the floor of the hut. Some were sitting in groups discussing the battle, while women bent over the pots to examine the ghastly contents. Here, a woman was engaged in stripping the flesh from the palm of a hand and the sole of a foot, which operation finished, she threw both into a large earthen pot to boil; there, another woman was applying an herb poultice to her husband's wounds.

Over it all hung a thick, odoriferous smoke, gradually finding its way out through the central opening in the roof.

This was a feast, indeed, such as few white men, I believe, have witnessed.

That night and the next day, and the following four days, great quantities of *chicha* were drunk and much meat was consumed to celebrate the great victory, the greatest in the annals of the Mangeromas of Rio Branco.

The supply of wourali poison had run low and three wourali men were to go out in the forest to collect poison plants, a journey which would require several days to complete. This occasion was set as the time of my departure.

It was a rainy morning when I wrapped my few belongings in a leaf, tied some grass fibers around them, and inserted them in the large pocket of my khaki coat. The box with the gold dust was there, also the boxes with the exposed photographic plates. Most of the gold had filtered out of the box, but a neat quantity still remained. One of my servants—a handsome girl—who, excepting for the labial ornaments, could have been transformed into an individual of quite a civilized appearance by opportunity, gave me a beautiful black necklace as a souvenir. It was composed of several hundred pieces, all carved out of ebony nuts. It had cost her three weeks of constant work. I embraced and was embraced by almost everybody in the *maloca*, after which ceremony we went in procession to the canoe that was to take me down to the Branco River. The Chief bade me a fond farewell, that forever shall be implanted in my heart. I had lived here weeks among these cannibal Indians, had enjoyed their kindness and generosity without charge; I could give them nothing in return and they asked nothing. I could have stayed here for the rest of my natural life if I had so desired, but now I was to say good-by forever. How wonderful was this farewell! It was my opportunity for acknowledging that the savage heart is by no means devoid of the feelings and sentiments that characterize more elevated, so-called civilized individuals.

For the last time I heard the little dog bark, the same that had licked my face when I fainted in front of the *maloca* upon my first arrival; and the large *arara* screamed in the treetops as I turned once more toward the world of the white man.

The journey was without incident. The wourali men set me off near the mouth of the Branco River, at a distance which I covered in less than five hours by following the banks. I was greeted by Coronel Maya of the Compagnie Transatlantique de Caoutchouc, who sent me by canoe down the old Itecoahy, until we reached the Floresta headquarters.

THE MARTYRDOM OF
ISAAC JOGUES

by Francis Parkman

While the Spaniards and the Portuguese were exploring and conquering
South America and even entering the south and west of the North American
Continent, the French were penetrating the lands far to the north in Canada.
One of the greatest of these French explorers was *Jacques Cartier*, who in
1534 placed a cross on the forbidding shores of the Gaspé and claimed it
in the name of France. In a second expedition the following year he discovered the mighty St. Lawrence and sailed down it in the belief that he
had found the passage to Cathay. Instead, of course, he had discovered
Canada.

Over seventy years later *Samuel Champlain*, after exploring the West
Indies and Mexico, appeared on these same shores. He was, as the great
historian, Francis Parkman, calls him, the "Aeneas of a destined people."
Like so many who would follow him into the Canadian forests, he longed
to "unveil the mystery of that boundless wilderness, and plant the Catholic
faith and the power of France amid its ancient barbarism." He became the
"pioneer" of that "advancing host" to which the Jesuit, *Isaac Jogues*, whose
tragic tale Parkman here tells, also belonged, and with La Salle, Marquette
and Jolliet, helped to open up the vast unknown Canadian territories.

Champlain, with his companions on his first expedition, set up the first
wooden buildings on the future site of the city of Quebec and somehow
with his men weathered that first "wintry purgatory" in this inhospitable
land. As rugged as the weather that first winter, as difficult to face, were the
bands of hostile Indians which surrounded the little settlement. Later
Champlain clashed with them on his voyage to the lake which bears his
name. And Isaac Jogues was to pay the ultimate price for falling into
their hands.

From *Pioneers of France in the New World*.

THE waters of the St. Lawrence rolled through a virgin wilderness, where, in the vastness of the lonely woodlands, civilized man found a precarious harborage at three points only—at Quebec, at Montreal, and at Three Rivers. Here and in the scattered missions was the whole of New France—a population of some three hundred souls in all. And now, over these miserable settlements, rose a war cloud of frightful portent.

It was thirty-two years since Champlain had first attacked the Iroquois. They had nursed their wrath for more than a generation, and at length their hour was come. The Dutch traders at Fort Orange, now Albany, had supplied them with firearms. The Mohawks, the most easterly of the Iroquois nations, had, among their seven or eight hundred warriors, no less than three hundred armed with the harquebus, a weapon somewhat like the modern carbine. They were masters of the thunderbolts which, in the hands of Champlain, had struck terror into their hearts.

We have surveyed the character and organization of this ferocious people, —their confederacy of five nations, bound together by a peculiar tie of clanship; their chiefs, half hereditary, half elective; their government, an oligarchy in form and a democracy in spirit; their minds, thoroughly savage, yet marked here and there with traits of a vigorous development. The war which they had long waged with the Hurons was carried on by the Senecas and the other Western nations of their league; while the conduct of hostilities against the French and their Indian allies in Lower Canada was left to the Mohawks. In parties of from ten to a hundred or more, they would leave their towns on the river Mohawk, descend Lake Champlain and the river Richelieu, lie in ambush on the banks of the St. Lawrence, and attack the passing boats or canoes. Sometimes they hovered about the fortifications of Quebec and Three Rivers, killing stragglers, or luring armed parties into ambuscades. They followed like hounds on the trail of travelers and hunters; broke in upon unguarded camps at midnight; and lay in wait, for days and weeks, to intercept the Huron traders on their yearly descent to Quebec. Had they joined to their ferocious courage the discipline and the military knowledge that belong to civilization, they could easily have blotted out New France from the map, and made the banks of the St. Lawrence once more a solitude; but though the most formidable of savages, they were savages only.

In the early morning of the second of August, 1642, twelve Huron canoes were moving slowly along the northern shore of the expansion of the St. Lawrence known as the Lake of St. Peter. There were on board about forty persons, including four Frenchmen, one of them being the Jesuit, Isaac Jogues. During the last autumn (1641) he, with Father Charles Raymbault, had passed along the shore of Lake Huron northward, entered the strait through which Lake Superior discharges itself, pushed on as far as the Sault Ste Marie, and preached the Faith to two thousand Ojibways and other Algonquins there assembled. He was now on his return from a far more perilous errand. The Huron mission was in a state of destitution. There was need of clothing for the priests, of vessels for the altars, of bread and wine for the eucharist, of writing materials—in short, of everything; and early in the summer of the present year Jogues had descended to Three Rivers and Quebec, with the Huron traders, to procure the necessary supplies. He had accomplished his task, and was on his way back to the mission. With him were a few Huron converts, and among them a noted Christian chief, Eustache Ahatsistari. Others of the party were in course of instruction for baptism; but the greater part were heathen, whose canoes were deeply laden with the proceeds of their bargains with the French fur traders.

Jogues sat in one of the leading canoes. He was born at Orleans in 1607, and was thirty-five years of age. His oval face and the delicate mold of his features indicated a modest, thoughtful, and refined nature. He was constitutionally timid, with a sensitive conscience and great religious susceptibilities. He was a finished scholar, and might have gained a literary reputation; but he had chosen another career, and one for which he seemed but ill fitted. Physically, however, he was well matched with his work; for, though his frame was slight, he was so active that none of the Indians could surpass him in running.

With him were two young men, René Goupil and Guillaume Couture, *donnés* of the mission—that is to say, laymen who, from a religious motive and without pay, had attached themselves to the service of the Jesuits. Goupil had formerly entered upon the Jesuit novitiate at Paris, but failing health had obliged him to leave it. As soon as he was able, he came to Canada, offered his services to the Superior of the mission, was employed for a time in the humblest offices, and afterward became an attendant at the hospital. At length, to his delight, he received permission to go up to the Hurons, where the surgical skill which he had acquired was greatly needed; and he was now on his way thither. His companion, Couture, was a man of intelligence and vigor, and of a character equally disinterested. Both were, like Jogues, in the foremost canoes; while the fourth Frenchman was with the unconverted Hurons, in the rear.

The twelve canoes had reached the western end of the Lake of St. Peter, where it is filled with innumerable islands. The forest was close on their right; they kept near the shore to avoid the current, and the shallow water before them was covered with a dense growth of tall bulrushes. Suddenly the silence was frightfully broken. The war whoop rose from among the rushes, mingled with the reports of guns and the whistling of bullets; and several Iroquois canoes, filled with warriors, pushed out from their concealment, and bore down upon Jogues and his companions. The Hurons in the rear were seized with a shameful panic. They leaped ashore; left canoes, baggage, and weapons, and fled into the woods. The French and the Christian Hurons made fight for a time; but when they saw another fleet of canoes approaching from the opposite shores or islands, they lost heart, and those escaped who could. Goupil was seized amid triumphant yells, as were also several of the Huron converts. Jogues sprang into the bulrushes, and might have escaped; but when he saw Goupil and the neophytes in the clutches of the Iroquois, he had no heart to abandon them, but came out from his hiding place, and gave himself up to the astonished victors. A few of them had remained to guard the prisoners; the rest were chasing the fugitives. Jogues mastered his agony, and began to baptize those of the captive converts who needed baptism.

Couture had eluded pursuit; but when he thought of Jogues and of what perhaps awaited him, he resolved to share his fate, and, turning, retraced his steps. As he approached, five Iroquois ran forward to meet him; and one of them snapped his gun at his breast, but it missed fire. In his confusion and excitement, Couture fired his own piece, and laid the savage dead. The remaining four sprang upon him, stripped off all his clothing, tore away his finger nails with their teeth, gnawed his fingers with the fury of famished dogs, and thrust a sword through one of his hands. Jogues broke from his guards, and, rushing to his friend, threw his arms about his neck. The Iroquois dragged him away, beat him with their fists and war clubs till he was senseless, and, when he revived, lacerated his fingers with their teeth, as they had done those of Couture. Then they turned upon Goupil, and treated him with the same ferocity. The Huron prisoners were left for the present unharmed. More of them were brought in every moment, till at length the number of captives amounted in all to twenty-two, while three Hurons had been killed in the fight and pursuit. The Iroquois, about seventy in number, now embarked with their prey; but not until they had knocked on the head an old Huron, whom Jogues, with his mangled hands, had just baptized, and who refused to leave the place. Then, under a burning sun, they crossed to the spot on which the town of Sorel now stands, at the mouth of the river Richelieu, where they encamped.

Their course was southward, up the river Richelieu and Lake Champlain; thence, by way of Lake George, to the Mohawk towns. The pain and fever of their wounds, and the clouds of mosquitoes, which they could not drive off, left the prisoners no peace by day nor sleep by night. On the eighth day, they learned that a large Iroquois war party, on their way to Canada, was near at hand; and they soon approached their camp, on a small island near the southern end of Lake Champlain. The warriors, two hundred in number, saluted their victorious countrymen with volleys from their guns; then, armed with clubs and thorny sticks, ranged themselves in two lines, between which the captives were compelled to pass up the side of a rocky hill. On the way, they were beaten with such fury that Jogues, who was last in the line, fell powerless, drenched in blood and half dead. As the chief man among the French captives, he fared the worst. His hands were again mangled, and fire applied to his body; while the Huron chief, Eustache, was subjected to tortures even more atrocious. When, at night, the exhausted sufferers tried to rest, the young warriors came to lacerate their wounds and pull out their hair and beards.

In the morning they resumed their journey. And now the lake narrowed to the semblance of a tranquil river. Before them was a woody mountain, close on their right a rocky promontory, and between these flowed a stream, the outlet of Lake George. On those rocks, more than a hundred years after, rose the ramparts of Ticonderoga. First of white men, Jogues and his companions gazed on the romantic lake that bears the name, not of its gentle discoverer, but of the dull Hanoverian king. Like a fair Naiad of the wilderness, it slumbered between the guardian mountains that breathe from crag and forest the stern poetry of war. But all then was solitude; and the clang of trumpets, the roar of cannon, and the deadly crack of the rifle had never as yet awakened their angry echoes.

Again the canoes were launched, and the wild flotilla glided on its way—now in the shadow of the heights, now on the broad expanse, now among the devious channels of the narrows, beset with woody islets, where the hot air was redolent of the pine, the spruce, and the cedar.

The Iroquois landed at or near the future site of Fort William Henry, left their canoes, and, with their prisoners, began their march for the nearest Mohawk town. Each bore his share of the plunder. Even Jogues, though his lacerated hands were in a frightful condition and his body covered with bruises, was forced to stagger on with the rest under a heavy load. He with his fellow prisoners, and indeed the whole party, were half starved, subsisting chiefly on wild berries. They crossed the upper Hudson, and in thirteen days after leaving the St. Lawrence neared the wretched goal of their pilgrimage—a palisaded town, standing on a hill by the banks of the river Mohawk.

The whoops of the victors announced their approach, and the savage hive sent forth its swarms. They thronged the side of the hill, the old and the young, each with a stick, or a slender iron rod, bought from the Dutchmen on the Hudson. They ranged themselves in a double line, reaching upward to the entrance of the town; and through this "narrow road of Paradise," as Jogues calls it, the captives were led in single file—Couture in front, after him a half-score of Hurons, then Goupil, then the remaining Hurons, and at last Jogues. As they passed, they were saluted with yells, screeches, and a tempest of blows. One, heavier than the others, knocked Jogues's breath from his body, and stretched him on the ground; but it was death to lie there, and, regaining his feet, he staggered on with the rest. When they reached the town, the blows ceased, and they were all placed on a scaffold, or high platform, in the middle of the place. The three Frenchmen had fared the worst, and were frightfully disfigured. Goupil, especially, was streaming with blood, and livid with bruises from head to foot.

They were allowed a few minutes to recover their breath, undisturbed, except by the hootings and gibes of the mob below. Then a chief called out, "Come, let us caress these Frenchmen!"—and the crowd, knife in hand, began to mount the scaffold. They ordered a Christian Algonquin woman, a prisoner among them, to cut off Jogues's left thumb, which she did; and a thumb of Goupil was also severed, a clamshell being used as the instrument, in order to increase the pain. It is needless to specify further the tortures to which they were subjected, all designed to cause the greatest possible suffering without endangering life. At night, they were removed from the scaffold and placed in one of the houses, each stretched on his back, with his limbs extended, and his ankles and wrists bound fast to stakes driven into the earthen floor. The children now profited by the examples of their parents, and amused themselves by placing live coals and red-hot ashes on the naked bodies of the prisoners, who, bound fast, and covered with wounds and bruises which made every movement a torture, were sometimes unable to shake them off.

In the morning, they were again placed on the scaffold, where, during this and the two following days, they remained exposed to the taunts of the crowd. Then they were led in triumph to the second Mohawk town, and afterward to the third, suffering at each a repetition of cruelties, the detail of which would be as monotonous as revolting.

In a house in the town of Teonontogen, Jogues was hung by the wrists between two of the upright poles which supported the structure, in such a manner that his feet could not touch the ground; and thus he remained for some fifteen minutes, in extreme torture, until, as he was on the point of swooning, an Indian, with an impulse of pity, cut the cords and released him. While they were in this town, four fresh Huron prisoners, just taken, were brought in, and placed on the scaffold with the rest. Jogues, in the midst of his pain and exhaustion, took the opportunity to convert them. An ear of green corn was thrown to him for food, and he discovered a few raindrops clinging to the husks. With these he baptized two of the Hurons. The remaining two received baptism soon after from a brook which the prisoners crossed on the way to another town.

Couture, though he had incensed the Indians by killing one of their warriors, had gained their admiration by his bravery; and, after torturing him most savagely, they adopted him into one of their families, in place of a dead relative. Thenceforth he was comparatively safe. Jogues and Goupil were less fortunate. Three of the Hurons had been burned to death, and they expected to share their fate. A council was held to pronounce their doom; but dissensions arose, and no result was reached. They were led back to the first village, where they remained, racked with suspense and half dead with exhaustion. Jogues, however, lost no opportunity to baptize dying infants, while Goupil taught children to make the sign of the cross. On one occasion, he made the sign on the forehead of a child, grandson of an Indian in whose lodge they lived. The superstition of the old savage was aroused. Some Dutchmen had told him that the sign of the cross came from the Devil, and would cause mischief. He thought that Goupil was bewitching the child; and, resolving to rid himself of so dangerous a guest, applied for aid to two young braves. Jogues and Goupil, clad in their squalid garb of tattered skins, were soon after walking together in the forest that adjoined the town, consoling themselves with prayer, and mutually exhorting each other to suffer patiently for the sake of Christ and the Virgin, when, as they were returning, reciting their rosaries, they met the two young Indians, and read in their sullen visages an augury of ill. The Indians joined them, and accompanied them to the entrance of the town, where one of the two, suddenly drawing a hatchet from beneath his blanket, struck it into the head of Goupil, who fell, murmuring the name of Christ. Jogues dropped on his knees, and, bowing his head in prayer, awaited the blow, when the murderer ordered him to get up and go home. He obeyed, but not until he had given absolution to his still breathing friend, and presently saw the lifeless body dragged through the town amid hootings and rejoicings.

Jogues passed a night of anguish and desolation, and in the morning, reckless of life, set forth in search of Goupil's remains. "Where are you going so fast?" demanded the old Indian, his master. "Do you not see those fierce young braves, who are watching to kill you?" Jogues persisted, and the old man asked another Indian to go with him as a protector. The corpse had been flung into a neighboring ravine, at the bottom of which ran a torrent; and here, with the Indian's help, Jogues found it, stripped naked, and gnawed by dogs. He dragged it into the water, and covered it with stones to save it from further mutilation, resolving to return alone on the following day and secretly bury it. But with the night there came a storm; and when, in the gray of the morning, Jogues descended to the brink of the stream, he found it a rolling, turbid flood, and the body was nowhere to be seen. Had the Indians or the torrent borne it away? Jogues waded into the cold current: it was the first of October; he sounded it with his feet and with his stick; he searched the rocks, the thicket, the forest; but all in vain. Then, crouched by the pitiless stream, he mingled his tears with its waters, and, in a voice broken with groans, chanted the service of the dead.

The Indians, it proved, and not the flood, had robbed him of the remains of his friend. Early in the spring, when the snows were melting in the woods, he was told by Mohawk children that the body was lying, where it had been flung, in a lonely spot lower down the stream. He went to seek it, found the scattered bones, stripped by the foxes and the birds; and, tenderly gathering them up, hid them in a hollow tree, hoping that a day might come when he could give them a Christian burial in consecrated ground.

After the murder of Goupil, Jogues's life hung by a hair. He lived in hourly expectation of the tomahawk, and would have welcomed it as a boon. By signs and words, he was warned that his hour was near; but, as he never shunned his fate, it fled from him, and each day, with renewed astonishment, he found himself still among the living.

Late in the autumn, a party of the Indians set forth on their yearly deer hunt, and Jogues was ordered to go with them. Shivering and half famished, he followed them through the chill November forest, and shared their wild bivouac in the depths of the wintry desolation. The game they took was devoted to Areskoui, their god, and eaten in his honor. Jogues would not taste the meat offered to a demon; and thus he starved in the midst of plenty. At night, when the kettle was slung, and the savage crew made merry around their fire, he crouched in a corner of the hut, gnawed by hunger, and pierced to the bone with cold. They thought his presence unpropitious to their hunting, and the women especially hated him. His demeanor at once astonished and incensed his masters. He brought them firewood, like a squaw; he did their bidding without a murmur, and patiently bore their abuse; but when they mocked at his God, and laughed at his devotions, their slave assumed an air and tone of authority, and sternly rebuked them.

He would sometimes escape from "this Babylon," as he calls the hut, and wander in the forest, telling his beads and repeating passages of Scripture. In a remote and lonely spot, he cut the bark in the form of a cross from the trunk of a great tree; and here he made his prayers. This living martyr, half clad in shaggy furs, kneeling on the snow among the icicled rocks and beneath the gloomy pines, bowing in adoration before the emblem of the faith in which was his only consolation and his only hope, is alike a theme for the pen and a subject for the pencil.

The Indians at last grew tired of him, and sent him back to the village. Here he remained till the middle of March, baptizing infants and trying to convert adults. He told them of the sun, moon, planets, and stars. They listened with interest; but when from astronomy he passed to theology, he spent his breath in vain. In March, the old man with whom he lived set forth for his spring fishing, taking with him his squaw and several children. Jogues also was of the party. They repaired to a lake, perhaps Lake Saratoga, four days distant. Here they subsisted for some time on frogs, the entrails of fish, and other garbage. Jogues passed his days in the forest, repeating his prayers, and carving the name of Jesus on trees, as a terror to the demons of the wilderness. A messenger at length arrived from the town; and on the following day, under the pretense that signs of an enemy had been seen, the party broke up their camp, and returned home in hot haste. The messenger had brought tidings that a war party, which had gone out against the French, had been defeated and destroyed, and that the whole population were clamoring to appease their grief by torturing Jogues to death. This was the true cause of the sudden and mysterious return; but when they reached the town, other tidings had arrived. The missing warriors were safe, and on their way home in triumph with a large number of prisoners. Again Jogues's life was spared; but he was forced to witness the torture and butchery of the converts and allies of the French. Existence became unendurable to him, and he longed to die. War parties were continually going out. Should they be defeated and cut off, he would pay the forfeit at the stake; and if they came back, as they usually did, with booty and prisoners, he was doomed to see his countrymen and their Indian friends mangled, burned, and devoured.

Jogues had shown no disposition to escape, and great liberty was therefore allowed him. He went from town to town, giving absolution to the

Christian captives, and converting and baptizing the heathen. On one occasion, he baptized a woman in the midst of the fire, under pretense of lifting a cup of water to her parched lips. There was no lack of objects for his zeal. A single war party returned from the Huron country with nearly a hundred prisoners, who were distributed among the Iroquois towns, and the greater part burned. Of the children of the Mohawks and their neighbors, he had baptized, before August, about seventy; insomuch that he began to regard his captivity as a Providential interposition for the saving of souls.

At the end of July, he went with a party of Indians to a fishing place on the Hudson, about twenty miles below Fort Orange. While here, he learned that another war party had lately returned with prisoners, two of whom had been burned to death at Osseruenon. On this, his conscience smote him that he had not remained in the town to give the sufferers absolution or baptism; and he begged leave of the old woman who had him in charge to return at the first opportunity. A canoe soon after went up the river with some of the Iroquois, and he was allowed to go in it. When they reached Rensselaerswyck, the Indians landed to trade with the Dutch, and took Jogues with them.

The center of this rude little settlement was Fort Orange, a miserable structure of logs, standing on a spot now within the limits of the city of Albany. It contained several houses and other buildings; and behind it was a small church, recently erected, and serving as the abode of the pastor, Dominie Megapolensis, known in our day as the writer of an interesting though short account of the Mohawks. Some twenty-five or thirty houses, roughly built of boards and roofed with thatch, were scattered at intervals on or near the borders of the Hudson, above and below the fort. Their inhabitants, about a hundred in number, were for the most part rude Dutch farmers, tenants of Van Renesselaer, the patroon, or lord of the manor. They raised wheat, of which they made beer, and oats, with which they fed their numerous horses. They traded, too, with the Indians, who profited greatly by the competition among them, receiving guns, knives, axes, kettles, cloth, and beads, at moderate rates, in exchange for their furs. The Dutch were on excellent terms with their red neighbors, met them in the forest without the least fear, and sometimes intermarried with them. They had known of Jogues's captivity, and, to their great honor, had made efforts for his release, offering for that purpose goods to a considerable value, but without effect.

At Fort Orange, Jogues heard startling news. The Indians of the village where he lived were, he was told, enraged against him, and determined to burn him. About the first of July, a war party had set out for Canada, and one of the warriors had offered to Jogues to be the bearer of a letter from him to the French commander at Three Rivers, thinking probably to gain some advantage under cover of a parley. Jogues knew that the French would be on their guard; and he felt it his duty to lose no opportunity of informing them as to the state of affairs among the Iroquois. A Dutchman gave him a piece of paper; and he wrote a letter, in a jargon of Latin, French, and Huron, warning his countrymen to be on their guard, as war parties were constantly going out, and they could hope for no respite from attack until late in the autumn. When the Iroquois reached the mouth of the river Richelieu, where a small fort had been built by the French the preceding summer, the messenger asked for a parley, and gave Jogues's letter to the commander of the post, who, after reading it, turned his cannon on the savages. They fled in dismay, leaving behind them their baggage and some of their guns; and returning home in a fury, charged Jogues with having caused their discomfiture. Jogues had expected this result, and was prepared to meet it; but several of the principal Dutch settlers, and among them Van Curler, who had made the previous attempt to rescue him, urged that his death was certain if he returned to the Indian town, and advised him to make his escape. In the Hudson, opposite the settlement, lay a small Dutch vessel nearly ready to sail. Van Curler offered him a passage in her to Bordeaux or Rochelle—representing that the opportunity was too good to be lost, and making light of the prisoner's objection that a connivance in his escape on the part of the Dutch would excite the resentment of the Indians against them. Jogues thanked him warmly; but, to his amazement, asked for a night to consider the matter, and take counsel of God in prayer.

He spent the night in great agitation, tossed by doubt, and full of anxiety lest his self-love should beguile him from his duty. Was it not possible that the Indians might spare his life, and that, by a timely drop of water, he might still rescue souls from torturing devils and eternal fires of perdition? On the other hand, would he not, by remaining to meet a fate almost inevitable, incur the guilt of suicide? And even should he escape torture and death, could he hope that the Indians would again permit him to instruct and baptize their prisoners? Of his French companions, one, Goupil, was dead; while Couture had urged Jogues to flight, saying that he would then follow his example, but that, so long as the Father remained a prisoner, he, Couture, would share his fate. Before morning, Jogues had made his decision. God, he thought, would be better pleased should he embrace the opportunity given him. He went to find his Dutch friends, and, with a profusion of thanks, accepted their offer. They told him that a boat should be left for him on the shore, and that he must watch his time, and escape in it to the vessel, where he would be safe.

He and his Indian masters were lodged together in a large building, like a barn, belonging to a Dutch farmer. It was a hundred feet long, and had no partition of any kind. At one end the farmer kept his cattle; at the other he slept with his wife, a Mohawk squaw, and his children, while his Indian guests lay on the floor in the middle. As he is described as one of the principal persons of the colony, it is clear that the civilization of Rensselaers-wyck was not high.

In the evening, Jogues, in such a manner as not to excite the suspicion of the Indians, went out to reconnoiter. There was a fence around the house, and, as he was passing it, a large dog belonging to the farmer flew at him, and bit him very severely in the leg. The Dutchman, hearing the noise, came out with a light, led Jogues back into the building, and bandaged his wound. He seemed to have some suspicion of the prisoner's design; for, fearful perhaps that his escape might exasperate the Indians, he made fast the door in such a manner that it could not readily be opened. Jogues now lay down among the Indians, who, rolled in their blankets, were stretched around him. He was fevered with excitement; and the agitation of his mind, joined to the pain of his wound, kept him awake all night. About dawn, while the Indians were still asleep, a laborer in the employ of the farmer came in with a lantern, and Jogues, who spoke no Dutch, gave him to understand by signs that he needed his help and guidance. The man was disposed to aid him, silently led the way out, quieted the dogs, and showed him the path to the river. It was more than half a mile distant, and the way was rough and broken. Jogues was greatly exhausted, and his wounded limb gave him such pain that he walked with the utmost difficulty. When he reached the shore, the day was breaking, and he found, to his dismay, that the ebb of the tide had left the boat high and dry. He shouted to the vessel, but no one heard him. His desperation gave him strength; and, by working the boat to and fro, he pushed it at length, little by little, into the water, entered it, and rowed to the vessel. The Dutch sailors received him kindly, and hid him in the bottom of the hold, placing a large box over the hatchway.

He remained two days, half stifled, in this foul lurking place, while the Indians, furious at his escape, ransacked the settlement in vain to find him. They came off to the vessel, and so terrified the officers that Jogues was sent on shore at night, and led to the fort. Here he was hidden in the garret of a house occupied by a miserly old man, to whose charge he was consigned. Food was sent to him; but, as his host appropriated the larger part to himself, Jogues was nearly starved. There was a compartment of his garret, separated from the rest by a partition of boards. Here the old Dutchman, who, like many others of the settlers, carried on a trade with the Mohawks, kept a quantity of goods for that purpose; and hither he often brought his customers. The boards of the partition had shrunk, leaving wide crevices; and Jogues could plainly see the Indians, as they passed between him and the light. They, on their part, might as easily have seen him, if he had not, when he heard them entering the house, hidden himself behind some barrels in the corner; where he would sometimes remain crouched for hours, in a constrained and painful posture, half-suffocated with heat, and afraid to move a limb. His wounded leg began to show dangerous symptoms; but he was relieved by the care of a Dutch surgeon of the fort. The minister, Megapolensis, also visited him, and did all in his power for the comfort of his Catholic brother, with whom he seems to have been well pleased, and whom he calls "a very learned scholar."

When Jogues had remained for six weeks in this hiding place, his Dutch friends succeeded in satisfying his Indian masters by the payment of a large ransom. A vessel from Manhattan, now New York, soon after brought up an order from the Director General, Kieft, that he should be sent to him. Accordingly he was placed in a small vessel, which carried him down the Hudson. The Dutch on board treated him with great kindness; and, to do him honor, they named after him one of the islands in the river. At Manhattan he found a dilapidated fort, garrisoned by sixty soldiers, and containing a stone church and the Director General's house, together with storehouses and barracks. Near it were ranges of small houses, occupied chiefly by mechanics and laborers; while the dwellings of the remaining colonists, numbering in all four or five hundred, were scattered here and there on the island and the neighboring shores. The settlers were of different sects and nations, but chiefly Dutch Calvinists. Kieft told his guest that eighteen different languages were spoken at Manhattan. The colonists were in the midst of a bloody Indian war, brought on by their own besotted cruelty; and while Jogues was at the fort, some forty of the Dutchmen were killed on the neighboring farms, and many barns and houses burned.

The Director General, with a humanity that was far from usual with him, exchanged Jogues's squalid and savage dress for a suit of Dutch cloth, and gave him passage on a small vessel which was then about to sail. The voyage was rough and tedious; and the passenger slept on deck or on a coil of ropes, suffering greatly from cold, and often drenched by the waves that broke over the vessel's side. At length she reached Falmouth, on the southern coast of England, when all the crew went ashore for a carouse, leaving Jogues alone on board. A boat presently came alongside with a gang of desperadoes, who boarded her, and rifled her of everything valuable, threatened Jogues with a pistol, and robbed him of his hat and coat. He obtained some assistance from the crew of a French ship in the harbor, and, on the day before Christmas, took passage in a small coal vessel for the neighboring coast of Brittany. In the following afternoon he was set on shore a little to the north of Brest, and, seeing a peasant's cottage not far off, he approached it, and asked the way to the nearest church. The peasant and his wife, as the narrative gravely tells us, mistook him, by reason of his modest deportment, for some poor but pious Irishman, and asked him to share their supper, after finishing his devotions,—an invitation which Jogues, half famished as he was, gladly accepted. He reached the church in time for the early Mass, and with an unutterable joy knelt before the altar, and renewed the Communion of which he had been deprived so long. When he returned to the cottage, the attention of his hosts was at once attracted to his mutilated and distorted hands. They asked with amazement how he could have received such injuries; and when they heard the story of his tortures, their surprise and veneration knew no bounds. Two young girls, their daughters, begged him to accept all they had to give—a handful of sous; while the peasant made known the character of his new guest to his neighbors. A trader from Rennes brought a horse to the door, and offered the use of it to Jogues, to carry him to the Jesuit college in that town. He gratefully accepted it; and, on the morning of the fifth of January, 1644, reached his destination.

He dismounted, and knocked at the door of the college. The porter opened it, and saw a man wearing on his head an old woolen nightcap, and in an attire little better than that of a beggar. Jogues asked to see the Rector; but the porter answered, coldly, that the Rector was busied in the sacristy. Jogues begged him to say that a man was at the door with news from Canada. The missions of Canada were at this time an object of primal interest to the Jesuits and above all to the Jesuits of France. A letter from Jogues, written during his captivity, had already reached France, as had also the Jesuit *Relation* of 1643, which contained a long account of his capture; and he had no doubt been an engrossing theme of conversation in every house of the French Jesuits. The Father Rector was putting on his vestments to say Mass; but when he heard that a poor man from Canada had asked for him at the door, he postponed the service, and went to meet him.

Jogues, without discovering himself, gave him a letter from the Dutch Director General attesting his character. The Rector, without reading it, began to question him as to the affairs of Canada, and at length asked him if he knew Father Jogues.

"I knew him very well," was the reply.

"The Iroquois have taken him," pursued the Rector. "Is he dead? Have they murdered him?"

"No," answered Jogues; "he is alive and at liberty, and I am he." And he fell on his knees to ask his Superior's blessing.

That night was a night of jubilation and thanksgiving in the college of Rennes.

Jogues became a center of curiosity and reverence. He was summoned to Paris. The Queen, Anne of Austria, wished to see him; and when the persecuted slave of the Mohawks was conducted into her presence, she kissed his mutilated hands, while the ladies of the Court thronged around to do him homage. We are told, and no doubt with truth, that these honors were unwelcome to the modest and singlehearted missionary, who thought only of returning to his work of converting the Indians. A priest with any deformity of body is debarred from saying Mass. The teeth and knives of the Iroquois had inflicted an injury worse than the torturers imagined, for they had robbed Jogues of the privilege which was the chief consolation of his life; but the Pope, by a special dispensation, restored it to him, and with the opening spring he sailed again for Canada.

It was to hold the Mohawks to their faith that Father Isaac Jogues was chosen. No white man, Couture excepted, knew their language and their character so well. His errand was half political, half religious; for not only was he to be the bearer of gifts, wampum belts, and messages from the Governor, but he was also to found a new mission, christened in advance with a prophetic name—*the Mission of the Martyrs.*

For two years past, Jogues had been at Montreal; and it was here that he received the order of his Superior to proceed to the Mohawk town. At first, nature asserted itself, and he recoiled involuntarily at the thought of the horrors of which his scarred body and his mutilated hands were a living memento. It was a transient weakness; and he prepared to depart with more than willingness, giving thanks to Heaven that he had been found worthy to suffer and to die for the saving of souls and the greater glory of God.

He felt a presentiment that his death was near, and wrote to a friend,

"I shall go, and shall not return." An Algonquin convert gave him sage advice. "Say nothing about the Faith at first, for there is nothing so repulsive, in the beginning, as our doctrine, which seems to destroy everything that men hold dear; and as your long cassock preaches, as well as your lips, you had better put on a short coat." Jogues, therefore, exchanged the uniform of Loyola for a civilian's doublet and hose; "for," observes his Superior, "one should be all things to all men, that he may gain them all to Jesus Christ." It would be well if the application of the maxim had always been as harmless.

Jogues left Three Rivers about the middle of May, with the Sieur Bourdon, engineer to the Governor, two Algonquins with gifts to confirm the peace, and four Mohawks as guides and escort. He passed the Richelieu and Lake Champlain, well-remembered scenes of former miseries, and reached the foot of Lake George on the eve of Corpus Christi. Hence he called the lake "Lac St. Sacrement"; and this name it preserved, until, a century after, an ambitious Irishman, in compliment to the sovereign from whom he sought advancement, gave it the name it bears.

From Lake George they crossed on foot to the Hudson, where, being greatly fatigued by their heavy loads of gifts, they borrowed canoes at an Iroquois fishing station, and descended to Fort Orange. Here Jogues met the Dutch friends to whom he owed his life, and who now kindly welcomed and entertained him. After a few days he left them and ascended the river Mohawk to the first Mohawk town. Crowds gathered from the neighboring towns to gaze on the man whom they had known as a scorned and abused slave, and who now appeared among them as the ambassador of a power which hitherto, indeed, they had despised, but which in their present mood they were willing to propitiate.

There was a council in one of the lodges; and while his crowded auditory smoked their pipes, Jogues stood in the midst, and harangued them. He offered in due form the gifts of the Governor, with the wampum belts and their messages of peace, while at every pause his words were echoed by a unanimous grunt of applause from the attentive concourse. Peace speeches were made in return; and all was harmony. When, however, the Algonquin deputies stood before the council, they and their gifts were coldly received. The old hate, maintained by traditions of mutual atrocity, burned fiercely under a thin semblance of peace; and though no outbreak took place, the prospect of the future was very ominous.

The business of the embassy was scarcely finished, when the Mohawks counseled Jogues and his companions to go home with all dispatch, saying that if they waited longer, they might meet on the way warriors of the four upper nations, who would inevitably kill the two Algonquin deputies, if not the French also. Jogues, therefore, set out on his return; but not until, despite the advice of the Indian convert, he had made the round of the houses, confessed and instructed a few Christian prisoners still remaining here, and baptized several dying Mohawks. Then he and his party crossed through the forest to the southern extremity of Lake George, made bark canoes, and descended to Fort Richelieu, where they arrived on the twenty-seventh of June.

His political errand was accomplished. Now, should he return to the Mohawks, or should the Mission of the Martyrs be for a time abandoned? Lalemant, who had succeeded Vimont as Superior of the missions, held a council at Quebec with three other Jesuits, of whom Jogues was one, and it was determined, that, unless some new contingency should arise, he should remain for the winter at Montreal. This was in July. Soon after, the plan was changed, for reasons which do not appear, and Jogues received orders to repair to his dangerous post. He set out on the twenty-fourth of August, accompanied by a young Frenchman named Lalande, and three or four Hurons. On the way they met Indians who warned them of a change of feeling in the Mohawk towns, and the Hurons, alarmed, refused to go farther. Jogues, naturally perhaps the most timid man of the party, had no thought of drawing back, and pursued his journey with his young companion, who, like other *donnés* of the missions, was scarcely behind the Jesuits themselves in devoted enthusiasm.

The reported change of feeling had indeed taken place; and the occasion of it was characteristic. On his previous visit to the Mohawks, Jogues, meaning to return, had left in their charge a small chest or box. From the first they were distrustful, suspecting that it contained some secret mischief. He therefore opened it, and showed them the contents, which were a few personal necessaries; and having thus, as he thought, reassured them, locked the box, and left it in their keeping. The Huron prisoners in the town attempted to make favor with their Iroquois enemies by abusing their French friends—declaring them to be sorcerers, who had bewitched, by their charms and mummeries, the whole Huron nation, and caused drought, famine, pestilence, and a host of insupportable miseries. Thereupon, the suspicions of the Mohawks against the box revived with double force; and they were convinced that famine, the pest, or some malignant spirit was shut up in it, waiting the moment to issue forth and destroy them. There was sickness in the town, and caterpillars were eating their corn: this was ascribed to the sorceries of the Jesuit. Still they were divided in opinion. Some stood firm for the French; others were furious against them. Among the Mohawks, three clans or families were predominant, if indeed they did not compose the entire nation—the clans of the Bear, the Tortoise, and the Wolf. Though, by the nature of their constitution, it was scarcely possible that these clans should come to blows, so intimately were they bound together by ties of blood, yet they were often divided on points of interest or policy; and on this occasion the Bear raged against the French, and howled for war, while the Tortoise and the Wolf still clung to the treaty. Among savages, with no government except the intermittent one of councils, the party of action and violence must always prevail. The Bear chiefs sang their war songs, and, followed by the young men of their own clan, and by such others as they had infected with their frenzy, set forth, in two bands, on the warpath.

The warriors of one of these bands were making their way through the forests between the Mohawk and Lake George, when they met Jogues and Lalande. They seized them, stripped them, and led them in triumph to their town. Here a savage crowd surrounded them, beating them with sticks and with their fists. One of them cut thin strips of flesh from the back and arms of Jogues, saying, as he did so, "Let us see if this white flesh is the flesh of an oki." "I am a man like yourselves," replied Jogues; "but I do not fear death or torture. I do not know why you would kill me. I come here to confirm the peace and show you the way to heaven, and you treat me like a dog." "You shall die tomorrow," cried the rabble. "Take courage, we shall not burn you. We shall strike you both with a hatchet, and place your heads on the palisade, that your brothers may see you when we take them prisoners." The clans of the Wolf and the Tortoise still raised their voices in behalf of the captive Frenchmen; but the fury of the minority swept all before it.

In the evening—it was the eighteenth of October,—Jogues, smarting with his wounds and bruises, was sitting in one of the lodges, when an Indian entered, and asked him to a feast. To refuse would have been an offense. He arose and followed the savage, who led him to the lodge of the Bear chief. Jogues bent his head to enter, when another Indian, standing concealed within, at the side of the doorway, struck at him with a hatchet. An Iroquois, called by the French Le Berger, who seems to have followed in order to defend him, bravely held out his arm to ward off the blow; but the hatchet cut through it, and sank into the missionary's brain. He fell at the feet of his murderer, who at once finished the work by hacking off his head.

Lalande was left in suspense all night, and in the morning was killed in a similar manner. The bodies of the two Frenchmen were then thrown into the Mohawk, and their heads displayed on the points of the palisade which enclosed the town.

CAPTAIN SMITH AND POCAHONTAS

by E. Keble Chatterton

The Spaniards had taken possession of Latin America, and the French had established a foothold in Canada. It was not to be dreamed that the England of Elizabeth, whose sea captains numbered such men as Drake, Frobisher and Hawkins, would stand idly by and permit the richest prizes to be snatched from them. Gloriana gave aid to the would-be colonizers, but the plans of Gilbert, Raleigh and Grenville came to nothing. There was a change of fortune during the reign of James I. James granted a royal charter to a company for Virginia, and in 1607, a settlement was founded in Jamestown. It was plagued by disaster and during the following winter, half the population died from disease and hunger. Luckily, the colony contained one individual of resource and determination—Captain John Smith, a veteran of the Turkish wars. He took command and helped the colonizers survive. One episode from Smith's biography, his rescue from death by Pocahontas, considered mythical by some historians, is famous but few of us understand its background, which is explained by E. Keble Chatterton in the selection which follows.

The Jamestown settlement was one of a number which sprang up during a short period. In 1620, a group of about a hundred souls set forth on the Mayflower, and after two and one-half months of voyaging landed on Plymouth Rock. About a decade later, the Massachusetts Bay Colony in New England, under the governorship of John Winthrop, settled in Salem. From the latter colony spread offshoots in Connecticut and Rhode Island. These five settlements, pinned against the Atlantic shore by a hostile wilderness, were the first English seeds from which the Thirteen Colonies developed.

SMITH'S energetic brain and body got to work, and if he were not yet the nominal head of the settlement he was in fact the moving spirit and actual leader. The position had to be faced and stock taken. What was to be done? It were useless complaining that the London Company had sent them out inadequately equipped: for the coming had been quite voluntary, the passage out was expected to take not five months but two, and thus they should by schedule have arrived with far more victuals and with the advantage of the right time to plant their seeds. The only thing now was to get busy and see that others did the same.

The new President,[1] it may be stated at once, was not a success. The planters neither loved this commanding officer of the pinnace nor respected his judgment: it was therefore fortunate that he had entrusted to John Smith the management of all out-of-door matters. By personal example, encouragement, kind words and always working hardest of all, Smith was thus able to make even idlers work. Some he set mowing, others binding thatch for the roofs, others to build houses, so that, within a short time, though he had no lodging for himself he had provided it for most of the others. This was a first and most excellent step toward a real settling down; and the next was to institute some sort of trade with the natives for the colony's very existence.

Thus, like a salesman who goes out seeking for his firm's commerce, Smith had now to become adventurer in quite a new department of life. Since the head of the firm was allowing the affair to die of neglect, it must be Smith who should set forth and save the whole undertaking. He was further encouraged by the fact that the natives' previous hostility had begun to decrease. Therefore we see him selecting some half-dozen of his workmen and going off in the shallop to Kecoughtan, an Indian village at the mouth of the James River, to barter corn and to get fish from the river. Owing to the autumn gales it was not possible to fish, but by bartering hatchets, beads and copper, and the employment of tact, Smith was able to obtain and bring back fish, oysters, bread, deer, turkeys, fowls and nearly thirty bushels of corn. This caused great comfort to a lot of starving men at Jamestown who were rotting with idleness and despair.

That successful expedition had not been easy, for there was the language

[1] Captain Ratcliffe, who was elected to succeed Captain Wingfield as head of the colony.—Eds.

difficulty, the men's clothes were in bad condition, and for some reason there were now no sails to the boat. It had also been necessary to use their muskets and make a demonstration of force that the Indians might know the visitors were determined to get what they wanted. A short assault, however, soon settled matters, peace was made, and trade established. And yet this visit had no permanent good, for the community at Jamestown seemed to be going to the bad as long as Smith was away from it. Some had died of "the bloudie Flixe," swellings, "Burning Feuers"; "some departed suddenly," but some of them had perished from sheer hunger. That malarial peninsula, stockaded from the mainland, with the James River for drinking water salty on the flood and covered with slime at low tide; the bare cold ground used by some as a bed; the company living from hand to mouth and hardly daring to consider the future—all this was to cause the gravest anxiety. The heat from June to September had been found as fierce as in Spain; but the winter cold from December to March was to try them severely. During this winter of 1607-8 it happened that the frost in Europe was particularly keen, and the same condition occurred in Virginia. But, still, not all this could prevent Smith from going ahead in his energetic manner and trying to get order out of chaos.

He was thinking of the future and the need of provisions, so he caused the pinnace to be fitted out for a longer journey, and in the meantime made three or four trips in the shallop; yet what he brought back the settlers squandered carelessly. Some of them were a hopeless lot and quite unworthy of sympathy or assistance, and Smith refers to them in one scathing passage thus:

> "Being for most part of such tender educations and small experience in martiall accidents: because they found not English cities, nor such faire houses, nor at their owne wishes any of their accustomed dainties, with feather beds and downe pillowes, Tavernes and alehouses in every breathing place, neither such plenty of gold and siluer and dissolute liberty as they expected, [they] had little or no care of any thing, but to pamper their bellies, to fly away with our Pinnaces, or procure their means to returne for England. For the Country was to them a miserie, a ruine, a death, a hell; and their reports here, and their owne actions there according.

To him who had been through such strenuous times in Europe and Asia, all this slovenliness and idle indulgence, all this ineptitude and crass stupidity were most infuriating. It was whilst Smith was away on one of these trips that some of the Jamestown people arranged with the sailors in the pinnace to take them across to England; but Smith's unexpected return revealed this plot. It was no easy matter to prevent the pinnace getting away, but by firing at her with falcon balls and musket shot he gave her the opportunity of either remaining or being sunk in the river. Thus by his strong, quick action this young man at the right moment again saved the situation. Kendal was presently tried by jury, convicted and executed as having been the chief instigator. That settled conspiracy of a kind, but a little later on during this same autumn, when the colony's provisions could not last more than another fortnight, Captains Ratcliffe and Archer planned to sail away to England and obtain supplies; but John Smith was able to suppress this mean plot also. By this time the latter was able to get on with his exploration of the country and rivers with a view to bartering food from the natives. There can be no doubt but that this work of discovery, with all its risks, was most congenial to his love of geographical knowledge; and all those brawls, underhand schemes and conspiracies were not less abhorrent. Smith dealt with life and men on the square, and he hated that which was mean or petty or false; so these various river journeys in the neighborhood of Chesapeake Bay did much to maintain his own spirits away from the Jamestown worries and jealousies.

In this manner he explored the river Chickahominy, which flows into the Powhatan from the north about nine miles above Jamestown. On November 9 with eight men he took the barge and started upstream, leaving the pinnace to follow on the next tide; and having got far enough he found the Indians, bought their corn, came back by midnight with the ebb and unloaded seven hogsheads of the corn into the colony. The pinnace had made a mess of her duty and got aground. On the next day Smith again went up the river and such was the good will established that the Indians were there already waiting with their baskets to load up the barge; in this manner he was able to add another seven hogsheads to the colony's store. . . .

Proceeding up the Powhatan River in the barge, he turned to starboard into the Chickahominy (which is ninety miles long) and went for forty miles till he reached an Indian village named Apocant, which was the farthest in habitation up this tributary. After another ten miles the river narrowed, so he hired a canoe with a couple of Indians and took back the barge to Apocant, leaving her to ride in a broad bay with instructions that no one of the seven men in her was to go ashore until Smith's return.

Within fifteen minutes Smith suddenly heard a loud cry and a shouting of the Redskins, but no sound of a musket. Quick to take in a situation, and quick to act, he now guessed that the Indians had betrayed them, so bound his Indian guide's arm fast "to my hand in a garter," at the same time having a pistol ready. The Indian seemed surprised at the sudden turn of events and advised flight, but just then an arrow came hurtling along and struck Smith on the right thigh, yet miraculously doing no harm. Two Indians were then seen drawing their bows, but the Englishman's discharge of his pistol stopped them. And now more arrows began to come flying, so, instead of digging himself in, Smith made the Indian's body serve as protective armor.

The next incident was that an Indian chief named Opechancanough with two hundred men surrounded our pioneer, so here he was in one of those tight corners with death uncommonly close at hand.

Smith decided that the only thing was to appeal to their mercy, but not one of them dared to approach until the explorer had thrown away his arms, whereupon they seized him and led him away to the chief. Here he was able to meet violence with mental cleverness. Nor can we help smiling at the plausible manner of his method. Just as in dealing with an infant or a lunatic one would seek first to side-track his interest with some toy, so did Smith work on the uncivilized chief's childlike simplicity. "I presented him with a compasse diall," he wrote less than two years later, "describing by my best meanes the vse therof: whereat he so amazedly admired, as he suffered me to proceed in a discourse of the roundnes of the earth, the course of the sunne, moone, starres, and plannets."

Could anything be more ludicrously brilliant than in the hour of death to engage an enemy's attention in a geographical discussion? It was nonetheless just the kind of surprising thing that this ingenious young warrior, who had extricated armies and escaped from slavery, would perform. And, if he were taking advantage of the savage mind, Smith felt the objective justified it. The result was that the chief became quite friendly, "with kinde speeches and bread requited me, conducting me where" the canoe lay—but in that canoe was Robinson dead, with a score of arrows in him. Emry, too, was gone yet whither Smith just then knew not; and as they went on the march Smith expected that his own execution would occur at any stopping place, but he was taken to the chief's village as an interesting prisoner. He was well fed: "my gowne, points and garters, my compas and my tablet they gaue me again."

What had happened to the barge party who had been left at Apocant farther down the river? Smith had departed from them "with expresse charge not any to go ashore till my returne." This order was disobeyed; for "hee was not long absent, but his men went a shore, whose want of government gaue both occasion and opportunity to the Salvages to surprise one George Cassen, whom they slew, and much failed not to haue cut off the boat and all the rest." Cassen's disobedience, with that of his shipmates, had created the crisis and caused the death of Robinson and Emry; for the Indians extracted from Cassen the information as to where Smith had gone, and forthwith began to search the bends of the river.

The manner of Cassen's execution, in accordance with the native savagery, had been revolting. He had been tied to a tree, the executioner with mussel shells had then cut off his joints one by one and burnt them; the head had then been flayed of its skin also by mussel shells, and after further atrocity he and tree were burnt together. Having regard to the innate ferociousness of these "naturals," it is really surprising that the English pioneers going up and down those rivers, exploring the land and coming in contact as strangers with the Indians, did not have far more numerous fatal incidents among their adventures.

When the barge brought the news to Jamestown great sorrow filled the planters. Smith had been captured about December 16, and for the next three weeks he was in daily expectation of death.

And now Smith, in spite of his captivity and expectant death, was to do a good turn to his fellow colonists. The Redskins began preparations to attack Jamestown and sought his advice as how best this could be done, promising him in return life, liberty, land and women. Smith's cunning brain, however, invented a plan for getting information through to warn the planters at Jamestown, which was in the area known to the natives as Paspahegh: the colony must be saved at all costs, and he was resourceful enough, plucky enough, to contrive the following risk. He begged that a messenger might take to Jamestown a letter which Smith would write. For what purpose? That his compatriots might know that he was well, being kindly treated, and thus they would not come forth and avenge his death. That idea appealed to these primitives when their prisoner had impressed on them how powerful were the Jamestown guns, how well mined were the surrounding fields, and how assuredly Captain Newport on his return from England would punish the Indians for any damage done to Jamestown. He wrote down "in part of a table booke" the Indians' intentions to attack the fort, and requested that the colonists would send him certain articles in an accompanying list.

One day later the three messengers returned from Jamestown; the effect on their untutored minds of writing and reading was like some wizardry.

For everything had happened exactly as Smith had foretold them. He had written requesting the planters to sally forth to frighten the messengers, and they had done so. He had told these messengers that if they returned to the same place by Jamestown at night an answer and certain articles should there be waiting them: they came back to that spot and found everything as he had promised. Thus they went hurrying thence to where their master detained Smith, themselves and their companions marveling that Smith had the power of divination or that the paper could speak!

But now he was to be carried about the country, from one tribe to another, on exhibition, and in this manner was to visit the Rappahannock and Potomac rivers which flow out into the Chesapeake Bay. And during this period he was to witness strange, weird ceremonies which were not comforting to a man in the hands of savage people. Thus with fearful incantations, his body painted all over, his head covered with the skins of snakes and weasels, some grim fellow would come dancing forth making extraordinary gestures. It was all like some hideous dream, with grotesque cacophonous noises, such as when the mind is delirious and the ear not attuned.

But at last after all this wandering about Virginia they brought him to Werowocomoco on the Pamunkey (or York) River on the fifth of January, 1608, to the Great Powhatan who ruled over the territory which included the region where the lesser Powhatan lived near the falls of the river similarly named. Here in the royal wigwam the big chief received him in state, sitting amidst his two hundred subjects on a matted platform with a fire burning in front of him. Smith was struck by the grave and majestic demeanor of this seminaked savage. Of this great ruler the English planters had never yet heard, and Smith was "the first Christian this proud King and his grim attendants euer saw."

Powhatan welcomed the White Man with kindly words "and great Platters of sundrie victuals." "So fat they fed mee," Smith reasoned, "that I much doubted they intended to haue sacrificed mee."

But, with alarming contrast, kindly entertainment was to precede tragedy: for now a long consultation was held, two great stones were brought before Powhatan which were to form the executioners' block. Smith was seized, his head laid on the stones and the men with their clubs were just about to beat out his brains when Pocahontas, the young daughter of Powhatan, rushed forward and laying her own head upon Smith's thus saved him from death. The appeal of this child, so dear to the chief, prevailed: the White Man's life should be spared and he should live to make hatchets for the chief; bells, beads and copper for her. This dramatic incident is of course known to every school in England and America: it has been used as a one-act play, and as the foundation for romances in fiction. "La Belle Sauvage" has given her name to legends and taverns and even localities, yet the truth of her saving Smith's life has been quite unreasonably doubted.

Let us clear the ground a little. In the first place we can rule out all sentimental, sexual romance from the incident. It was rather a case where that natural human pity and abhorrence of death, which are characteristic of womanhood and girlhood, entered to stop the painful sight of suffering: and, further, as Mr. A. G. Bradley in his critical introduction to Smith's works long since pointed out, Pocahontas "merely exercised the right common to the women of Indian tribes, old or young, and claimed his person and his life as her own property and for adoption into the tribe." There may, it is true, have been something in feminine curiosity. This was the first white male specimen she had ever seen: so why kill him, and why not preserve him as the unusual?

PEG-LEG SMITH, MOUNTAIN MAN

by David Lavender

The exploits of the intrepid band who have come to be known as the "mountain men" bulk large in American legend.

As Boone and Gerty of an earlier day had roamed the forests that stretched from the Eastern seaboard to the Mississippi, these nineteenth-century explorers were forced west of the Father of Waters, beyond the great plains and up the majestic slopes of the Rockies to find the solitude in which they could hunt the furs which were their livelihood and live the untrammeled lives their souls desired. They developed an uncanny sense of terrain—Jim Bridger, for example, had a photographic memory of river systems, trails

From *Bent's Fort* by David Lavender. Copyright © 1954 by David Lavender, reprinted by permission of Doubleday & Company, Inc.

and mountains. Sometimes in organized bands of trappers, sometimes on solitary expeditions, they combed the little-known corners of the wilderness. Some were to act as guides for the trains of immigrants which followed. They were uncouth, lawless and violent men but their contribution to the exploration of the West was enormous and their individual exploits heroic. Peg-leg Smith was one of the great ones, as witness the story of how he lost his leg and managed to survive.

LYING along a north-south axis in central Colorado are four huge, mountain-cupped bowls. Grass-filled, softly rolling, almost treeless, they derive from their circling whale-backed peaks an austerity that makes the word "lovely" too gentle for describing them. The southernmost is called San Luis Valley; the others by the mountain name of park—North, Middle, and South parks, the latter the famed Bayou Salade of the fur hunters.

It was in North Park, called Park Kyack by the French fur trappers, that Sylvestre Pratte fell seriously ill in the fall of 1827. After an anxious time of rude nursing, he died. Solemnly the trappers buried him and then took counsel among themselves. The result was a serious decision for Pratte's clerk and second-in-command.

The men were uneasy about their status. They had been out for some time now, had already caught about three hundred pounds of beaver. Some among them thought that in order to secure their wages they should seize the fur, together with personal property, belonging to Sylvestre—his rifle, pistol, gloves, the cloth he had brought along for Indian trade, his seventeen traps, seven mules, eight horses. Then what? Should the party disintegrate into competitive groups, trying to beat each other to the best streams during what remained of the fall season? Should they then return to Taos and face the winter with whatever they had managed to garner and hope for a new bourgeois to sign them up in the spring?

Wiser heads said no. It was better to stick together.

But suppose the winter-long effort ended in failure? Who, then, would guarantee their wages?

They turned to Ceran St. Vrain, a veteran of twenty-five. Would he assume command—and responsibility?

The safe thing was to refuse. Keeping the men out through the winter would cost six or seven thousand dollars in wages. If the trip failed to net that amount, what was to prevent the St. Louis executors of Pratte's estate from disclaiming the account on the grounds that the expedition could have, and should have, disbanded after Sylvestre's death? Yet Ceran returned the trust which his men held for him. They were good hunters. They would stick to their jobs and the venture might pull through. He decided to take the chance.

Trapping as they went, the party moved along the sources of the North Platte toward the present Colorado-Wyoming border. By now they were shaken into trail shape. On a pack horse each man carried the furs he had caught, his buffalo bed robes, and a heavy skin sack (which could be boiled and eaten in emergency) loaded with six five-pound traps costing from twelve to sixteen dollars in St. Louis, the traps' three-pound chains, spare springs, and tools for repair. On the rider's own mount was a "possible sack" bulky with powder, galena lead, flints, tobacco, sewing materials, occasionally a book or two, and dressed deerskin for replacing his moccasins, which wore out rapidly. About his person hung a skinning knife, whetstone, pipe case, awl holder, perhaps a tomahawk, scent container, bullet pouch, and a powder carrier of black buffalo horn scraped as thin as isinglass and stoppered with a wooden plug. Always in hand was his gun—generally a heavy one, eleven to twelve pounds, with a forty-inch barrel, .50-caliber, firing a half-ounce slug with impact enough to drop a grizzly or buffalo. A man loved his gun, named it (Ceran called his Silver Heels), and had it rebored again and again to repair damage from water and dust, until it looked as huge as a tunnel. His wiping stick was carried in the bore and served, in addition to its intended function, as a rest on which the hunter could lean the ponderous muzzle when he knelt to take aim. In spite of affection for the gun, however, the men were not above using bows and arrows; the weapons conserved ammunition, gave no telltale report, and in the sightless night could be aimed by hunch better than a rifle.

Down to his shoulders hung the hunter's long hair, covered with a felt hat or perhaps the hood of a capote. He liked wool clothing, for it would not shrink as it dried and wake him, when he dozed beside the fire, by agonizingly squeezing his limbs. But wool soon wore out, and he then clad himself in leather, burdensomely heavy to wear, fringed on the seams with the familiar thongs which were partly decorative but mostly utilitarian, to let rain drip off the garment rather than soak in, and to furnish material for mending. Further waterproofing was added by wiping butcher and eating knives on the garments until they were black and shiny with grease. Upper garments might be of the pull-over type or cut like a coat, the buttonless edges folded over and cinched into place with a belt. No underclothing was worn, just a breechclout. "Trousers" were often nothing more than Indian-style, thigh-length leggings, the lower parts perhaps made of nonshrinkable strips of blanket. In extreme cold a Hudson's Bay blanket or a buffalo robe was draped Indian-wise over the entire costume.

Much of the hunter's life was spent in water. In the evening twilight he waded cautiously upstream, searching out good sets for his traps. These he placed under the icy water in the beaver's natural runway, chaining each trap in such fashion that the caught animal would be drowned before it could reach land and gnaw off its paw. Over each set he bent a twig baited with evil-smelling castoreum. The next dawn he examined his line, often having to reach deep to retrieve his prey, skinned the corpses, and packed the hides back to camp. There they were "grained" (the clinging bits of flesh removed) on slant-topped wooden blocks and then stretched on oval willow frames to dry, a process sometimes hastened by burning punky wood in a pit beneath them. In big-company brigades the handling of the skins was the work of the camp tenders; free trappers did it themselves. In either case there was little leisure. A thirty-man company could skim the cream off a circle of considerable radius during a single night, and therefore camp sites were moved every day or so.

When setting their traps the men split into twos or threes. Some individualists worked singly and jealously—Old Bill Williams for one, and evidently Tom Smith also, at least on Ceran's 1827-28 expedition. Indians found this habit an invitation to attack from ambush, and St. Vrain's party had already had a skirmish or two along the North Platte. A frontier maxim rightly held that the best Indian fighter was the one who avoided the most battles. Ceran was worried. When Tom Smith kept brazenly exposing himself, the captain rode out to the stream one day to tell him for God's sake to quit taking so many chances. As they were arguing about it, a discharge came from the brush—a gun, according to some accounts; an arrow, according to others. Probably it was a gun, because whatever struck Tom just below the knee had power enough to break both the leg bones.

Ceran flopped down to meet a charge, but the shot had been a typical skulking strike from ambush with no follow-up. He looked for Tom. The man had tried to jump to his rifle leaning against a nearby tree, but his leg had caved in. Now he was writhing on the ground.

They got him back to camp, choked down some of his cursing with a bolt of Taos Lightning, and cut away the legging. Splintered ends of the bones protruded through the flesh. The men glanced sideways at each other. They had seen enough mangled beaver limbs to know that Tom's lower leg would never be any good again. So had Tom.

"Cut it off," he said.

Amputating a beaver's leg and a man's are two different things. The group stood there hang-handed. Tom roared for Basil, the cook, to bring him a sharp knife. Reluctantly it was produced, and with his own hands Tom began slicing at the bloody flesh. His snarls brought the watchers hopping out of their trance for such accessories as they had—water, horsehair or perhaps buffalo sinews for ligatures, a tourniquet, more whisky. The bone was a problem. Some stories have it that the camp possessed a keyhole saw which was pressed into service; others say that teeth were filed into a knife blade. But perhaps, if both tibia and fibula were shattered badly enough, no saw was necessary. At any rate, before the job was completed, Tom slid toward unconsciousness. Milton Sublette took the knife and finished.

There had been preparations to stop the gush of blood by searing the stump with a hot iron. But the sight of the glowing bar had made Tom bellow protest. Well, they thought, it wouldn't matter much what they did. Humor him along. Abandoning the projected searing, they tied up the arteries as well as they could, wrapped the stump in a dirty shirt, and swaddled Tom in a buffalo robe. After promising not to abandon him until they were sure he was dead (as young Jim Bridger, green to the trade, had abandoned Old Hugh Glass after Hugh was mangled by a grizzly), they went on about their work. Poor old Tom. He was as strident as a bull elk, as obstreperous a drunk as ever had cleaned out a Taos fandago. But he was a gone beaver now.

The weather was icy, the night a knife-edged glitter under the frozen stars. The cold seeped into Tom's bed. Perhaps that was what coagulated the blood. When Ceran and big Milton Sublette came the next morning to look at his corpse, the bleeding had ceased and Tom was perky enough to curse them soundly. Amazed, they stayed in camp another day, waiting for him to get his dying over with. When he strengthened instead, they stitched him up in a wrapper and a sugar-loaf hat made from red flannel trade cloth. Then they slung a litter tandem between two horses and loaded him in. Ceran appointed two men as his special attendants, and on they went. After all, business was business.

They turned west from the North Platte across the Park Mountains, their horses floundering in the soft, still snow as they searched for openings through thick forests of spruce and among some of the most gigantic aspen trees on the continent. The rough going grew rougher when they dropped down through dense scrub oak into the narrow valley of the Little Snake, aptly named from its looping progress along the present Colorado-Wyoming border. The willows were thick, the hillsides rocky. In sleety weather the litter horses lost footing. Down the bank they rolled. Out of the tangle flew Smith, to land sitting in an ice-scummed pool. His nurses yelled for help. This time he was killed for certain. But no, there he sat in his red wrapper, his red hat askew and dripping as he bawled out his opinion of matters in general. The men began to laugh, and gradually Tom did too.

Leaving the Little Snake where it swung south toward the huge canyon of the Yampa, the party struck across southern Wyoming into the valley of the Green. There winter caught them—cruel, merciless, snow-heaped, the most rigorous, St. Vrain later wrote Bernard Pratte, that he had ever experienced. Either now or perhaps a little earlier Tom discovered that the bone ends left protruding by his shrinking flesh were loose. He had Sublette pull them out with a bullet mold used as pincers. Further cure was applied by a band of Ute Indians who moved in to share winter quarters with the trappers. Men, women, children—the whole howling, chanting, singing lot—chewed up roots and spat them on the stump. Obviously it was the proper remedy, for the flesh healed, and as Tom lay snugly in one of the lodges he began whittling out a wooden substitute. From now on he would be Peg-leg Smith, growing in time beyond the cramped confines of reality into a myth of a nation's youth. Youth propping itself against frontier bars, unstrapping a wooden leg, and with its very symbol of defeat joyously pounding its assailants into submission. Youth picking up, one summer in the desert, gold nuggets whose source could never be located again, and by the failure preserving the dream that took men west—everyman's dream of a lost Peg-leg mine, never quite found and so never quite pinching down and growing thin with truth. Tomorrow, always tomorrow, it would be there, gloriously waiting.

FRÉMONT,
PATHMARKER
OF THE WEST

by Allan Nevins

Westward expansion across the American Continent was a laborious process. From the time of the first settlements to the Revolution, the colonies occupied a tiny area, hugging the Atlantic coast. There was a slow push west by those who needed land, and occasional frontiersmen penetrated the virgin forests. As always, a war and its military necessities stimulated new activity. Something about this activity and about a soldier and his friends who played a part in it, is related in "The Old Frontiersman" by Walter Havighurst, which appears in the first section of this book. These were the men who blazed the trail to the Mississippi.

With the opening of the nineteenth century, the new nation was just beginning to feel its muscles. A capable and far-sighted President was planning the Louisiana Purchase. He was watching with concern the encroachments of the Canadian fur traders in the Far West, and determined that the United States should have a stake in the unknown land. As leader of an expedition to "trace the Missouri to its source, to cross the Highlands, and follow the best water-communication which offered itself from thence to the Pacific Ocean," Jefferson chose his secretary Meriwether Lewis, and Lewis selected as his companion William Clark, the brother of George Rogers Clark, with whom he had served in the Army. They wintered in St. Louis in 1803-4, and on May 14, 1804, broke camp and began to make their way up the Missouri. There were in the expedition forty-five men, including an Indian interpreter and guide. By the end of April they had passed the junction of the Yellowstone and the Missouri, and in July the headwaters of the latter river. Half-starved, they struggled through the mountains and it was not until mid-October that they reached the Columbia. On November 7 they caught a glimpse of the Pacific and heard the roar of breakers. It took them until September 23 of the next year to return to St. Louis where they were greeted by an ovation. Their journey had been an amazing success. They had covered thousands of miles of unexplored territory and won the gratitude of the nation.

Theirs was the first and greatest expedition that explored the Western half of the continent, but their descriptions of their explorations were dull, lacking the appeal of a lesser man like Frémont. Allan Nevins the historian has quite properly called Frémont the "pathmarker of the West." He went where others had been before him, but he had as a guide one of the most famous of Western scouts, Kit Carson, and he was assisted by a trained geographer and skillful map maker, Charles Preuss. The colorful reports and excellent maps which resulted from his expeditions had great influence on the wave of immigraton that followed. Brigham Young, for example, followed his reports carefully.

The first expedition in which Frémont took part was commanded by Joseph Nicolas Nicollet, a first-rate scientist who taught Frémont the elements of surveying and topography. They spent a year mapping the Missouri-Mississippi region. Next Frémont led an expedition of his own westward to the Rockies and the South Pass across the Continental Divide. It is this expedition which Allan Nevins describes in the selection that follows. Frémont's report led to a wave of popularity that delighted him. It led also to his third expedition, in which he went west to the Columbia, then down into the Sacramento Valley. In his report of this expedition, he described also the Great Salt Lake, the Great Basin, the California River valleys and the Southwestern deserts.

Frémont was the first to make a complete circuit of the West. He knew the Oregon Trail and the frontier between Mexico and California. He was unquestionably a great explorer, but he was also a person whose character many solider men thought of with suspicion. He was constantly under fire from his enemies and during the Presidency of Polk was court-martialed and forced to resign from the Army. But more than any other person, he showed how the American West could be made available to the settlers who followed.

PROBABLY there was no happier young man in the country on May 2, 1842, than John C. Frémont. We can imagine him taking leave of his wife of six months in the Benton home; kissing Mrs. Benton; receiving some pompous, fatherly admonitions from the Senator; and, spruce in his blue and gold uniform, running down the steps in the warm spring sunshine to the carriage that was to take him to the railway station. He was but twenty-nine years old. Yet he was at last in full command of his own expedition, with a long summer of outdoor life and adventure ahead of him, and an opportunity to achieve new distinction as an explorer. The poor half-orphan of the Charleston streets, the youth brought into the backdoor of the Army by Poinsett's influence, had achieved a position that any West Pointer might envy: the son-in-law of Senator Benton, the husband of the most charming girl in the capital, the successor of the famous Nicollet.

Could he have foreseen what a pleasant and profitable expedition lay before him, his feeling of elation would have been heightened. Frémont within the next decade was to pass through harrowing physical hardship, but this first expedition included few days that he could not remember with pleasure. It was a summer's tour in the kindliest of weather. It was not too ambitious; going only as far as the South Pass and Wind River Mountains, he penetrated no dangerous country. Yet it was sufficiently full of contacts with Indians, buffalo, and frontiersmen, of adventures on plain, mountain precipice, and river rapids. At the end he was to receive not only the congratulations of Lieutenant Colonel Abert and Senator Benton, but a public interest and recognition which surpassed his best hopes.

It took twenty days for the Lieutenant, accompanied by Jessie's brother Randolph, to reach the Missouri.

Men who made such a journey in 1842 found the tide of Western travel mounting to a torrent. The boats were crowded with land speculators, talking of fortunes in the new Illinois and Iowa townships; surveyors; Louisville and Cincinnati drummers; an occasional hunter and trapper, conspicuous in leather garments and coonskin cap; frontiersmen who found their old homes too crowded and were seeking new; and above all, a motley throng, mechanics from the East, Englishmen with capital, Irishmen without, and guttural Germans, hunting cheap land and free opportunities. Their talk was of the great new Mormon community growing up at Nauvoo, Illinois; of the money which Kentuckians made by taking droves of mules and horses to market through Cumberland Gap; of the latest lynching in Arkansas or Missouri; of the work the government was doing for the Chicago harbor, and the huge lake trade; of new river cities like Hannibal, Quincy, and Keokuk; and of the trade the Magoffin brothers were carrying on with caravans of goods to Santa Fe.

Frémont's imagination must have responded to it. He knew that every turnpike, every canal and lake route from East to West, was adding its share to the volume of emigrant travel. He recalled Benton's prediction that within a century the population west of the Rockies would exceed the whole population of the nation in 1820. And here he was, avant-courier and pathmarker for this human stream so rapidly remaking America!

Reaching St. Louis, Frémont was received at one of its finest mansions —the home of Mrs. Sarah Benton Brant, Mrs. Benton's favorite niece and the wife of an old friend and army officer. Here he had not only a room, but an introduction to the best St. Louis society, curious to see Colonel Benton's son-in-law. Yet he tarried only a few days. He or Benton had doubtless written ahead to the Chouteaus[1] in St. Louis to assemble men and material, which they could easily do; and Cyprian Chouteau now gave his entire time to Frémont's needs. Preparations were quickly completed. Frémont records an observation of latitude and longitude at the Brant house on May 27, and certainly within a few days thereafter he was on his way up the river.

The personnel and equipment of this party were to a considerable extent typical of his later ventures. One man had been hired before leaving Washington—Charles Preuss, a skilled German topographer. He had called one evening on Frémont, his face so red, his voice so incoherent from nervousness, that they had at first thought him drunk. A failure of appropriations had thrown him out of employment, and Frémont saw to it that his family, then in need, were provided with a Christmas dinner. He did more; he found a job for Preuss in reducing astronomical observations, and since Preuss knew nothing of such tasks, himself performed the work at night. Thus he kept the man on a payroll until the expedition started. This service Preuss repaid by years of devoted and much-enduring service as topographer. In St. Louis Frémont hired as hunter the frontiersman Lucien B. Maxwell, son-in-law of a wealthy New Mexican merchant, and himself in later years owner of the vast Maxwell grant. Henry Brant, young son of Frémont's host, was taken along as general aide. In addition to these and the boy Randolph, there were nineteen voyageurs, most of them French Creoles of long experience in the fur trade; the most notable being Basil Lajeunesse, of the Santa Fe Trail, Taos, and Bent's Fort, who later lost his life in Frémont's service. All were well armed, and all but eight mounted on good horses. These eight drove as many mule carts, packed with baggage, instruments, and food. Some loose horses and four oxen for slaughtering completed the train.

What the party at first lacked was a frontiersman of thorough acquaint-

[1] Rich fur traders interested in exploration of the Indian country.—Eds.

ance with the plains and mountains to serve as guide. For a time Frémont had thought of employing an old experienced "mountain man," Major Andrew Drips, who had trapped through much of the Rockies for the American Fur Company, and Pierre Chouteau wrote to Drips in Frémont's behalf; but a much better man unexpectedly became available. A rare stroke of luck threw Frémont into contact with one of the most efficient, and certainly the most picturesque, of Western scouts, Kit Carson. In his autobiography Carson says simply that he met with Frémont, informed him that he had spent some time in the mountains and believed that he could guide the party to any point it wished to go, and after some inquiry, was employed. Frémont's story is fuller. He writes that as his party was ascending the Missouri by steamboat from St. Louis to Chouteau's Post, or Kansas Landing, near the present site of Kansas City, his attention was drawn to a man of medium height, broad-shouldered, deep-chested, of clear, steady eye and frank, modest speech. It was Carson, and the Lieutenant was so much pleased with his personality and qualifications that he was glad to accept his services. Perhaps the fact that Carson and Lucien Maxwell were old companions and close friends had something to do with the arrangement.

The attraction between Carson and Frémont, which gave birth to a deep and lifelong attachment, was largely the magnetism of opposites. Carson showed his Scotch-Irish ancestry as clearly as Frémont did his French blood; he was cool, quiet, observant, and determined, while Frémont was quick, sensitive, passionate, and impetuous. His rugged honesty, his transparent sincerity, his gentleness and kindliness (save to Indians and Mexicans, whom he regarded as most frontiersmen did), his loyalty and reliability, made him unusual among mountain men. Possessing no high intellectual qualities, probably inferior in mental grasp to such a frontiersman as Thomas Fitzpatrick ("Broken Hand"), and no better acquainted with Western wilds than Jim Bridger, Fitzpatrick, or several other contemporaries, he owed his pre-eminence chiefly to the solidity and wholesomeness of his character. It was precisely in solidity and balance that Frémont was most deficient. Both were young men, Carson being thirty-three; but Carson, who was a widower and father—he had visited St. Louis to place his young daughter with relatives or in a Catholic school—was much the more mature. Both might be called well educated, but in very different senses. Frémont's education was almost all scientific, Carson's was almost all the practical education of that frontier to which he had been an apprentice since the age of fifteen. He possessed no book knowledge, he was as yet unable to read and write, and he spoke an ungrammatical lingo of the Southwest, something like the "Pike" dialect that later found its way into print. But his mind was broader, and more thorough, if less superficially brilliant, than Frémont's, and he had made the utmost of his opportunities for learning what is not in books. He had a serviceable command of French, Spanish, and several Indian tongues, could carry on a conversation with unfamiliar tribes by signs, and had fully mastered the lore of plains and mountains.

Since Frémont was to see much not only of Carson but of other mountain men, we may pause briefly to examine the ways of this picturesque and useful breed of men. Many of the principal figures led lives that were stamped by a remarkable similarity, for as a group they passed through three well-defined phases. The mountain men appeared early in the century as trappers, threading the snow-crowned ranges and following the rushing streams through dark fir-clad valleys or cañons of red rock for beaver pelts. By 1842 the beaver, forerunners of the buffalo, were so nearly exterminated that trapping became unprofitable, while the tides of conquest and settlement were about to flow over the Far West. Some mountain men, therefore, as masters of topography, veritable walking maps, turned aside to guide exploring expeditions like Frémont's, parties of emigrants, and military columns; others turned to supplying emigrant trains with meat and other necessities. But that phase proved even more transient than the day of the trapper. Within another fifteen years the West had become so well mapped and so largely settled that guides lagged superfluous on the stage. Some adventurous frontiersmen, like Hawkeye in *The Prairie*, turned at last into prosaic farmers, some to trade, and some to government appointments as Indian agents.

Nothing better demonstrates the general similarity of their careers than the striking parallelism in the lives of Carson, Fitzpatrick, and James Bridger; men representing three different blood strains, hailing from three widely separated points, and wholly unlike in character and gifts. Carson, of Scottish blood, was born in Kentucky, Fitzpatrick, of Irish, in County Cavan, and Bridger, of English, in Virginia. Yet their lives were molded by social and geographical forces into much the same pattern. All three, carried by the westward movement to Missouri, began their careers from that state within a half-dozen years of its admission into the Union. Bridger at St. Louis in 1822 joined General William Ashley's first expedition up the Missouri to trap furs—that famous undertaking in which the general advertised for "one hundred enterprising young men." A year later Fitzpatrick, having drifted westward from his emigrant ship, joined Ashley's second expedition up the Missouri. In 1826 Kit Carson, his father dead, apprenticed to a harsh Missouri saddler, ran away to join an expedition to Santa Fe, and was soon trapping with Ewing Young's party in the Southwest. All three spent fewer than twenty years as trappers and hunters, when the depletion of the beaver colonies brought their calling to an end. Fitzpatrick quit the mountains in 1841 to guide the first emigrant train, the Bidwell-Bartleson party, from the Missouri to Fort Hall. Carson quit in 1842 to join Frémont. Bridger quit in 1842 to establish the first important supply station on the Oregon Trail, Fort Bridger. The days of the old-time trapper were gone forever. Then, after a few years, the curtain rose on the third and quietest phase in the lives of the three men. They must perforce adjust themselves to an increasingly settled and workaday West. The government in 1846 appointed Fitzpatrick as Indian agent for the Cheyenne, Arapahoe, and part of the Sioux on the upper Platte and Arkansas. In 1853 it appointed Carson as Indian agent at Taos in charge of two tribes of Utes. Bridger, driven out of his way-station business in 1853 by the Mormons, thereafter divided his time between farming and government positions, repeatedly acting as official interpreter and intermediary with the Indians, and as an army guide.

Naturally it is the first phase in the lives of these rovers which has chiefly appealed to students of the West. They were as distinct a group, these mountain men, as the cowboys who came later; a hard, practical race, who dealt in the unknown, and without compass, often without companion, wrested a living from its perils. Then French *coureurs*, a daring set of adventurers, had been the first to penetrate the West, but the cooler, longer-headed, deadly shooting Missourians, born woodsmen all, easily surpassed them. The trappers were of course rude and ignorant, with frontier manners; so wild that, like Kit, they were glad to marry Indian women; many of them with records as killers. A streak of pride, a wild vanity often entered into their composition, and they liked to be called "white Injuns," but off of the trail and away from the rendezvous they were essentially modest. After all, the pride was chiefly in their stoic endurance of exertions, toils, and privations, their prowess with trap, knife, and ax, their deadliness with their trusted guns—Old Bullthrower; Knock-Him-Stiff; Old Straightener. A trapper might take many wives, but he was monogamous in his devotion to his rifle. They were hard workers, hard players, hard fighters, hard drinkers—even Kit, in his early days; they were inured to excess. Leading lives of perfect liberty in the wilderness, in society they often turned to perfect license; and in his autobiography even the quiet Kit speaks of his wild early courses when fresh in Taos from the lonely trail with money burning in his pocket and the barroom and fandango to allure him.

Their roving mountain life, for all its hardships, grime, and peril, was sweet at the bottom of the cup; its wild intoxication, like that of the sea, gradually entering the veins. Ashley said after he entered Congress that his best days had been his mountain days, his best friends his trapper friends. That adventurous Briton, Lieutenant George F. Ruxton, on his last trip to the Far West wrote his New York publisher that he was "half froze for buffler meat and mountain doin's," and died seeking his favorite spot beyond the Park Range, "my solitary camp in the Bayou Salade." Kit Carson, for twenty years a tireless wanderer, ever courting new adventures, felt this fascination as much as the others. He even more than others was absolutely fearless, for death rode close by each trapper as by Dürer's knight. It was death in a dozen forms—by famine; by sudden blizzard in the savage mountains; from wild beasts; from still wilder savages; "anything possible and nothing permanent except death." Three great preoccupations ever filled the trapper's mind—beaver, buffalo, and Indians; fur, meat, and peril; money, food, and war. Carson knew as well as anyone how to set his line of Newhouse beaver traps, to bait them with the medicine of pungent oils used by the mountain men, to skin, grain, and stretch the pelts for dry-curing in the sun, to pack them into bales for carriage to market. He was as expert as the best in detecting beaver sign on apparently deserted streams and in reaping a rich harvest up solitary valleys. Sometimes hundreds of pelts, worth eight dollars or more apiece, would be taken on a single small river. Like other mountain men, he became a remarkable horseman. He was "the most daring and reckless of riders," avers his Taos friend Oliver Wiggins, adding that he could "with ease pick up a silver dollar from the ground, when going at full speed, mounted on the swiftest pony." At one time he delighted to take a heavy American horse and "dash down steep hills at full gallop." Hardihood, nerve, perfect health, and a delight in reckless feats, made trapping and guiding an ideal occupation for half his lifetime.

As the years passed, Carson had extended his activities until few men knew the great West so well, or could be trusted to meet every wilderness contingency so expertly. He had won his first spurs as member of a singularly daring expedition. With Ewing Young's trapping party, he had crossed upper Arizona and the Mojave, gone west to Los Angeles, and then, turning north, had traversed California to the Sacramento River, there lingering for some time. This acquaintance with interior California was later to serve Frémont well. Then entering the service of the Rocky Mountain Fur Company, a number of years before he met Frémont he carried a zigzag line through the Rockies north from Taos almost to the Canadian boundary. He and his companions on this remarkable trip first struck into the interior of Colorado, then crossed the Continental Divide at South Pass, and continuing through western Wyoming, finally reached the Salmon River in northern Idaho, where they spent the winter with the friendly Nez Percé. Thereafter, in one employ or another, Carson was found in successive years at widely scattered points in the West, his trails making an intricate network. He was in the Three Forks country, part of the sources of the Missouri; along the valley of the Green; with an expedition which went down the Humboldt in northern Nevada; at Fort Hall on the Snake; and with James Bridger on the Yellowstone. Incessantly moving, incessantly observant, he was accumulating an unsurpassed fund of information upon all parts of the West, from the Gila to the Columbia, from the Sacramento to the Platte.

By the time Carson met Frémont, no one was better skilled in Indian customs, ways, and mental habits, and no one knew more of the craft of mountains and plains. His sagacity, caution, and quick intuition had become famous. Place him in a situation of imminent danger from Indians, wild beasts, or prairie fire, and he would instantly devise the best means of extricating himself. Once in 1833, while his party were trapping on the Arkansas, some Crow Indians stole nine horses from them, and Carson and others went in pursuit. Creeping at night upon the Indian encampment, they succeeded in leading the horses off while the Indians slept. Most of the party favored immediate flight with their recovered property, for they would have a start of several hours. But Carson demurred because he desired revenge. Moreover, he grasped the dangerous elements in the situation: the horses were exhausted; they would assuredly be followed; the Indians outnumbered them three to one and could surround them at pleasure, when they would certainly be shot from ambush without mercy. Their proper course, he thought, was to attack the savages. In the battle which followed Carson's men, profiting by surprise, won an easy and bloody victory. One of his undoubted faults at this period was his implacable harshness toward Indians. But we must remember that throughout much of the West hostilities were almost incessant. Lieutenant G. Douglas

Brewerton in his fine narrative of a ride with Kit Carson has described his ingrained caution whenever in hostile country:

> During this journey I have often watched Carson's preparation for the night. A braver man than Kit perhaps never lived. In fact, I doubt if he ever knew what fear was. But with all this he exercised great caution. While arranging his bed, his saddle, which he always used as a pillow, was disposed in such a manner as to form a barricade for his head. His pistols, half-cocked, were placed above it, and his trusty rifle reposed beneath the blanket by his side, where it was not only ready for instant use, but perfectly protected from the damp. Except now and then to light his pipe, you never caught Kit at night exposing himself to the full glare of the campfire.

Though Carson had been doing fairly well as one of the best trappers alive, as trader, and as hunter for Bent's Fort, he knew that the days of profitable beaver-taking in the West were numbered, and was glad to accept a fixed salary. Frémont offered him one hundred dollars a month. Moreover, Carson's visit to Missouri had left him restless and in the mood for a roving summer trip. He had spent only ten days in St. Louis, for though he was curious as to the sights of the town, the noise, crowds, and heat wearied him; "for many consecutive years," he said later, "I never slept under the roof of a house, or gazed upon the face of a white woman." He longed for new scenes in the open. The friendship begun on the little Missouri steamboat struggling upstream in the June sunshine of 1842 was to last until Carson's death in 1868, and throughout two expeditions was to be the happiest of partnerships. Carson could truthfully inform a Senate committee six years later that he was "under more obligations to Frémont than to any other man alive." Until now, his name had seldom if ever appeared in print, and he was totally unknown outside his own trapper circles; but Frémont was to give him a generous publicity which would make him famous throughout the land. This service he was to repay by unremitting loyalty and unselfish effort. "With me," testified Frémont in a letter of 1847, "Carson and Truth mean the same thing. He is always the same—gallant and disinterested."

At the Cyprian Chouteau post, about ten miles up from the mouth of the Kansas, Carson hurried two Delaware runners off down the Santa Fe Trail to Taos, with instructions for about fifteen of his own men to meet him, with equipment, at Fort Laramie. The final parcels were placed in the carts. On Friday, June 10, the column lengthened out from the belt of woods bordering the Kansas, past several well-kept Indian farms, and on to the open prairie. The routine of the march was at once established, and, as it was typical of later expeditions, we may glance at it in some detail.

Frémont and Carson planned their discipline, like that of all emigrant trains, freight caravans, and trapping bands, in a way to give them constant protection against a surprise attack. They did not wait until dusk to camp, but chose a suitable spot a good hour or two before nightfall. By sunset they had the carts wheeled into a compact circle. Within this effective barricade the tents were pitched, with a merry din of stake-driving; saddles, blankets, and eating utensils were thrown down; four fires were kindled and kettles slung for as many different messes; and a homelike scene soon presented itself. Meanwhile, the horses and mules had been hobbled and turned loose, under a guard, to graze. While it was yet broad daylight, the men ate supper, and the fires were allowed to die down so that they would throw no dangerous illumination over the camp. When darkness fell, the animals were driven close to the wagons, and picketed by a twenty- or thirty-foot halter, which permitted them to get a little grass. Camp guard was mounted at eight, and the three sentries were relieved every two hours, the last or morning watch constituting the horse guard for the day.

By nine o'clock, the tired men were usually wrapped in slumber; by half past four, they were aroused. The horses and mules were again turned loose with hobbles, breakfast was eaten, and by six-thirty they were on the march again. At noon, they would halt for one, or sometimes two, hours, rather to rest the animals than the men. Such was the regular daily procedure, disturbed only by accident or unexpected physical obstacles. A stormy night was at first their chief hardship, for it meant sleeping in muddy puddles. Twenty-eight miles over the open prairie seems to have been regarded as "a hard day's march," and twenty-four miles was more usual.

The provisions of the camp were substantial and not altogether Spartanly simple. The party carried sugar, and great were the lamentations of one of the messes when, in crossing the swollen Kansas at the usual ford, it lost its supply in the muddy waters. Greater still was the regret of the whole expedition when, at the same crossing, almost all its coffee disappeared under the swirling current. They purchased some twenty pounds from a half-breed, but this did not go far. Later they fell back upon a tea brewed from the roots of the wild cherry. In the early stages they were able to buy from the Indians vegetables—pumpkins, onions, beans, and lettuce. Later, when they came up with the herds of buffalo, the men were jubilant over the supply of tender meat. Shouts and songs resounded from every part of the line, and the evening campfires signaled a feast which ended only with the break-up of the encampment the following morning; at any time of the night, men might be seen roasting the choicest bits—the hump, the tenderloin, the tongue, the sirloin steaks—*en appolas* (that is, on sticks) over the fire. There was no scarcity of tobacco, and at first enough bread, though later it became a coveted luxury. Of course the garb of the men, as the journey lengthened, grew steadily more ragged. A dozen days out they met a party of trappers coming from a long sojourn in the interior; "we laughed then at their forlorn and vagabond appearance," says Frémont, "and in our turn, a month or two afterward, furnished the same occasion for merriment to others."

Frémont was busy from morning to midnight. He maintained discipline with an iron hand under a glove of unvarying tact. He occupied himself evening and noon, when the weather permitted, in taking astronomical observations; he carefully observed botanical and geological features of the country, and wrote a detailed daily journal. The map of the expedition was kept complete from day to day, and Preuss was assigned the task of sketching any scene or position of unusual importance. At various halts, the men were trained in firing at a mark and in repelling attacks.

This first expedition, thus led by Frémont and guided by Carson, was absent from June 15, 1842, the date when they left the ford of the Kansas, until October 1, when, marching down the Missouri, the men at daybreak heard the cowbells on the first border farms. In three and a half months it accomplished all the objects expected by the government, and still others expected only by Benton and his fellow expansionists. Nominally, the expedition was intended to acquaint the government with the nature of the "rivers and country between the frontiers of Missouri and the base of the Rocky Mountains; and especially to examine the character, and ascertain the latitude and longitude of the South Pass, the great crossing-place to these mountains on the way to Oregon." Actually, as Benton's before-quoted statement upon the government's ignorance of its main conception indicates, it had far larger objects in view. Senator Linn intended to bring into the next session of Congress (1842-43) another bill for the occupation of Oregon; and Frémont's expedition was a preparatory measure. As he himself writes, it was "auxiliary to and in aid to the emigration to the Lower Columbia," already in full swing; and it was intended not only to advertise the easiness of the Platte River–South Pass route, but to "indicate and describe the line of travel, and the best positions for military posts."

The party first proceeded up the Kansas to observe the general character of its valley, and then crossed to the Platte, which it followed to the foot-hills of the Rockies. It was a great moment when, on July 9, they caught their first glimpse of the snowy summit of Long's Peak. Next day they halted at St. Vrain's Fort, a trading post about forty miles north of present-day Denver, where the courtly Ceran St. Vrain, of the St. Louis trading firm of Bent, St. Vrain & Co., himself welcomed them. Struggling up the Sweetwater Valley, the party on August 8 reached South Pass. This was not, as Frémont, in spite of all that Carson had told him, was surprised to find, an abrupt break in the mountain wall, but a broad open-ing reached by such a gradual ascent that he had difficulty in fixing the precise point of the Continental Divide, where the waters flowing east parted from those flowing to the Pacific. There was no gorge, like the Allegheny gaps or Alpine passes. Instead, a wide sandy road lifted by a slow and regular grade to the summit, about seven thousand feet above the sea.

The party, now 950 miles from the mouth of the Kansas, continued its march to the headwaters of the Green River, which flows into the Colorado. This reached, Frémont set out to explore the Wind River chain, a magnifi-cent group of snow-capped mountains, the highest in Wyoming, which rose before them, pile upon pile, their icy caps glittering in the bright light of the August day.

The spectacular feat of the expedition, whose leader always delighted in the spectacular, was the ascent of what Frémont mistakenly considered the highest peak of the Central Rockies, Frémont's Peak, which is 13,730 feet high. One other summit in the Wind River chain, Gannett Peak, five miles north, is actually some fifty or sixty feet higher, while Colorado has almost thirty peaks of fourteen thousand feet or more. Nor is Frémont's Peak difficult of access or dangerous to the climber. Frémont and five companions set out early on the morning of August 15; they found them-selves, after some rough ascents, riding beneath a nearly perpendicular wall of granite, terminating from two to three thousand feet above their heads in a serrated line of broken, jagged cones. At what seemed the best point they undertook to mount this wall, climbing leisurely. Three little lakes of dark emerald, apparently deep, lay in a chasm below. Above the snow line, they had to use thin moccasins of buffalo skin, and at one point Frémont worked his way across a vertical precipice by clinging to the crevices; but from the ledge thus gained it was an easy matter to reach the crest.

"I sprung upon the summit," writes Frémont, "and another step would have precipitated me into an immense snow field five hundred feet below. To the edge of this field was a sheer icy precipice; and then, with a gradual fall, the field sloped off for about a mile until it struck the foot of another ridge." Though the day was sunny and bright, a slight shining mist obscured the view over the surrounding country. Nevertheless, the prospect was inspiring. To the west, they descried a vast shining network of lakes and streams, the waters from which fed the Colorado; and on the other side, the deep-forested trough of the Wind River Valley, with the faint gleam of streams which flowed into the Yellowstone and down to the Missouri. Far northwestward, bright in the haze, they could pick out the snowy peaks of the Three Tetons, which marked the sources of the Snake and the Columbia. Frémont's breast expanded as he surveyed this immense land-scape. Fixing a ramrod in the gneiss, he unfurled a special flag, carrying the regulation thirteen stripes, but bearing in the corner a white field with a blue eagle perched upon an Indian pipe of peace, and blue stars. They lingered till midafternoon, when they returned to their cache of dried coffee and meat at the foot of the peak, and slept that night on the rocks.

The principal adventure of the party occurred on its return. Frémont's orders were to survey the Platte, and he wished to save time by making as much use of waterways as possible. While still on the Sweetwater, he had his men inflate the collapsible rubber boat which he had brought from the East, and load it with the instruments and equipment he carried. The shallowness of the stream made progress impossible, and they took to the land again. But when the Platte was reached, they found it flowing broad and deep, swollen beyond its usual size. Frémont therefore divided his party. The larger group he directed to proceed across country on foot to a point named Goat Island, an unmistakable mark; while he, Preuss, and five others provisioned the rubber boat for a dozen days, and began the descent by water. After a few hours, a hollow roar announced that a series of falls was before them. Frémont reconnoitered, and then, thinking of the heavy labor of unloading his apparatus and other baggage, recklessly determined to run the rapids. He did not know until afterward that some eighteen years earlier Fitzpatrick had lost a valuable cargo of beaver pelts at this point.

One series of little cataracts was traversed successfully, the elastic boat bending to every shock. A steeper and fiercer channel lay just ahead, shut in by high rocky walls; but emboldened by their previous success they decided to risk its descent also. Everything was tied securely; the men threw off most of their clothing, and pushed into the stream. To save the valuable chronometer, Preuss took it and attempted to walk along the stream on rocks which were piled up on either side, but shortly found that the shore disappeared and the walls fell vertically into the torrent. He therefore clambered back into the boat, which moved more and more swiftly.

At once it became plain that their position was perilous. They had attached a rope about fifty feet long to the stern of the boat, and three men had been left to clamber along the rocks with it, trying to lessen its speed. All in vain; after a few hundred feet they realized that their Bucephalus was too much for them: "To go back was impossible; the torrent before us was a sheet of foam; and, shut up in the chasm by the rocks, which in some places seemed almost to meet overhead, the roar of the waters was deafening." The force of the torrent became too great for the men on shore to withstand. Two of them loosed their hold, but Basil Lajeunesse hung on an instant too long, and was jerked head foremost from a twelve-foot ledge into the boiling water. The boat shot downstream like an arrow, Lajeunesse being carried down after it in the rapid waters and needing all his strength as a swimmer to keep from being dashed against the rocky shore. His head could be seen at momentary intervals as a black spot bobbing in the foam. Fortunately, the boat was soon brought into an eddy below and held stationary long enough to allow the half-drowned man to be dragged over its gunwale, cursing. Then, after catching breath, they went on, and in another moment met disaster:

> We cleared rock after rock, and shot past fall after fall, our little boat seeming to play with the cataract. We became flushed with success and familiar with the danger; and, yielding to the excitement of the occasion, broke forth together into a Canadian boatsong. Singing, or rather shouting, we dashed along; and were, I believe, in the midst of a chorus when the boat struck a concealed rock immediately at the foot of the fall, which whirled her over in an instant. Three of my men could not swim, and my first feeling was to assist them, and save some of our effects; but a sharp concussion or two convinced me that I had not yet saved myself. A few strokes brought me into an eddy, and I landed on a pile of rocks on the left side. Looking around, I saw that Preuss had gained the same shore on the same side, about twenty yards below; and a little climbing and swimming soon brought him to my side. On the opposite side, against the wall, lay the boat, bottom up; and Lambert was in the act of saving Descoteaux, whom he had grasped by the hair, and who could not swim. . . . For a hundred yards below, the current was covered with floating books and boxes, bales of blankets, and scattered articles of clothing; and so strong and boiling was the stream that even

our heavy instruments, which were all in cases, kept on the surface, and the sextant, circle, and the long black box of the telescope were in view at once.

Yet the party extricated itself better than it might have expected. The boat was righted and taken downstream a mile and a half, where a broad expanse of rock offered a resting place. For this distance, the banks and shallows were searched, and much of the baggage was recovered. One of the men had clung to Frémont's double-barreled gun. All the registers were found with the exception of one of Frémont's journals, containing his notes upon incidents of travel, topographical descriptions, some scattered astronomical observations, and the barometrical register west of Laramie. Happily, duplicates of his most important barometrical observations were preserved in the other journals. The circle was saved, and a number of blankets. But all the heavier articles—the sextant, telescope, and remaining guns—had sunk beyond recovery; the party was left stripped of every morsel of food, ammunition, and arms, at the mercy of savages and in danger of starvation. It was necessary to push on at once to the men who had gone by land to Goat Island.

The battered boat had to be left behind, for the rocky pass was too narrow to allow egress from the cañon; while the recovered baggage was deposited in a safe spot and left. Climbing slowly to the top of the cañon, the half-naked explorers hurried forward over the rocky ground. Frémont hobbled along on one moccasin, his unprotected food cut by sharp rocks. The party had to cross the winding river repeatedly, sometimes fording it and sometimes swimming, and to climb the ridges of two more cañons before, late in the evening, they came within sight of Goat Island. They were soon sitting about a hot fire, eating pieces of buffalo steak roasted at the coals, and telling the story of their adventures.

This catastrophe was a forcible lesson upon the folly of Frémont's precipitancy. The cautious Nicollet would never have permitted him to take such a risk. His impetuosity might have destroyed completely the records of his expedition and given a disastrous check to his career; it might have cost several lives, and, if his group had failed to join the other members of the expedition, would certainly have done so. This instance of rashness was all too characteristic of the man; but fortunately his character had another side, which was amply demonstrated in these three months.

On the whole, Frémont in this expedition showed coolness, sagacity, and more than once a really remarkable resourcefulness in meeting emergencies. A test of his ingenuity occurred as they were just entering the Wind River

Range. In crossing a broad stream, pouring rapidly over a slippery bed of boulders and quartz slabs, where the pack animals fell repeatedly, the horse bearing the barometer struck it against a rock and broke it. It was the only barometer the expedition owned. Since it was indispensable for an accurate measurement of altitudes, its loss seemed a heavy blow. They had brought it a thousand miles, watching over it with anxious solicitude day and night, and now, just as they reached the high Rockies, it was smashed. The men were as dejected as Frémont himself. But they no sooner made camp than he set about trying to repair the catastrophe.

He discovered that while the glass cistern had been broken about midway, no air had found its way into the tube. He had a number of vials of rather thick glass, some of them of the same diameter as the cistern, and, with a rough file from the tool chest, he spent the day slowly endeavoring to cut them to the requisite length. Unfortunately, they all broke. Next morning, having placed the barometer at night out of harm's way in a groove in one of the trees, he began to work upon a different device. Taking a powder-horn which happened to be remarkably translucent, he boiled it, stretched it on a piece of wood to the requisite diameter, and scraped it very thin, until it was almost as clear as glass. Then using some strong glue made from a buffalo's tendons, he fastened the horn firmly in its place on the instrument, and filled it with mercury, properly heated. A piece of skin, secured with thread and glue, furnished a suitable pocket, and the brass cover was screwed into place. After the instrument had been left some hours to dry, Frémont and his companions anxiously tested it. When it was reversed, they had the joy of finding it in perfect order, its indications being almost identical with those it had marked before it was broken. The day was saved.

Frémont also proved his ability to secure a firm hold upon the confidence of his men. On its outward march the party had divided at the forks of the Platte, the main body under Clement Lambert and Carson going by the regular Oregon Trail route to Fort Laramie, while Frémont with four others proceeded toward the same point by the before-mentioned Fort St. Vrain. When the two detachments joined hands at Fort Laramie they were met by alarming news. This fort, strongly built of adobe and wooden palisades, was maintained by the American Fur Company for its traders and the protection of emigrants along the Oregon Trail. The famous frontiersman, Jim Bridger, had just come down the North Platte trail with a company of traders. He brought word that the Sioux, Blackfeet, and Cheyenne had combined and were on the warpath, and that the route from Laramie to South Pass was very perilous. This news was received with alarm by the *voyageurs,* and even Carson was so much affected that he made an oral will, which trappers seldom did save in extremity. Less than a year earlier the Sioux and Cheyenne had fallen upon a party of about sixty whites on the Little Snake, and in the ensuing encounter had killed five, including the leader. These tribes had recently let a party of emigrants led by Fitz-patrick through their country, but had served notice that the path was no longer open, and that any new group found upon it would be destroyed. From all that Frémont could learn, the country ahead was swarming with scattered groups of warriors.

Yet the Lieutenant, though Carson believed that the party would almost certainly have a clash if they pushed forward, did not hesitate. Both traders and Indians advised him to wait until the war parties had completed their raids and returned home; but he knew that to stop was in fact almost impossible. It was he who had insisted that the orders for the expedition include South Pass, and he felt he had to go thither. A main purpose of the reconnaissance was to determine the best points at which to plant forts for protection against Indians, and it would hardly do to refuse to face the Indians in the field. There was an Oregon caravan not far ahead of Frémont, and if it was in trouble his duty was to follow at once. Moreover, Frémont well knew with what sneers he would be greeted in the East by West Point men if he returned confessing that an Indian scare had forced him to abbreviate his plans. He was a newcomer in the Army, and very decidedly upon his mettle. If he flinched, the regular officers would never cease reminding him that he had allowed a trail—a settler's trail at that—to be closed in his face.

As a measure of precaution, Frémont engaged an interpreter, one of the fur traders of the region, named Joseph Bissonette, who, if they came in contact with the Indians, would be able to explain that the purposes of the expedition were purely scientific. Bissonette told him that the chief danger would lie in being attacked before the savages knew who they really were. Then, the equipment repaired and everything ready for a start, the Lieuten-ant called his men about him at evening and told them he was determined to push forward at dawn the next day; that they were well armed and accustomed to the country; and that they had known on the Missouri that the Indians were restless, and ought not to object now to the peril. How-ever, he wanted no undependable followers, and those who were apprehen-sive might drop out. A few days before, the *voyageurs* had been complaining of the lack of excitement: *"Il n'y aura pas de vie pour nous."* Now only one man had the effrontery to come forward and accept the permission to retreat, and Frémont, after asking some questions to expose him to the ridicule of the others, let him go.

The two youths, Randolph Benton and Henry Brant, were reluctantly left at the fort—Randolph's high spirits had made him a general favorite—for it was unjustifiable to risk their lives. As it turned out, the party sighted few Indians on the Sweetwater Trail, and none hostile enough to contest their passage. The episode gave Frémont added prestige. Carson's biographer has aptly characterized him as he must have appeared at this time to the mountain men:

> A states-bred man but a man who showed trail experience; something of the dandy but nothing of the popinjay; a captain in command but prompt to fall to with the best of them; a captain and a comrade in one —a leader with the enthusiasm of a greenhorn, but without the greenhorn's blatant ignorance.

The final stages of Frémont's return trip exhibited his tenacity and his skillful use of the experience gained with Nicollet and Sibley. Even after the wreck of the rubber boat he did not give up his wish to descend the Platte by water. There was little wood, but he did not need it. Several buffalo bulls were killed and skinned; the four best hides were sewn together with buffalo sinews, and this tough fabric was stretched over a framework of river willows. Then the seams were calked with a glue made of ashes and tallow, and the vessel was left in the hot sun till the drying skins drew taut. The result was a broad shallow "bull boat," such as trappers often used, eight feet long and almost wide enough for a man to lie down in. It drew, when Frémont, Preuss, and two others took up the paddles, only four inches. Unfortunately, the Platte did not offer four inches. For three or four miles the men tugged and pushed their ungainly craft over sandy shallows, and finally in discouragement left it on a sand bar. They continued afoot, and on September 18 reached the Grand Island; four days later, they bought some green vegetables from friendly Pawnees engaged in harvesting their gardens. On September 30, they sighted the yellow Missouri; and on October 1, Frémont, rising long before daybreak, heard with a feeling of inexpressible pleasure the mellow tinkle of cowbells from farms on the opposite side of the river. He was back on the edge of civilization.

What Frémont had accomplished was best summarized by his friend Linn a little later in a speech to the Senate. After describing how he had followed the Platte and Sweetwater, the Missourian remarked:

He reached the [South] Pass on the 8th of August, and describes it as a low and wide depression of the mountains, where the ascent is as easy as the hill on which this Capitol stands, and where a plainly beaten wagon road leads to the Oregon through the valley of Lewis's River, a fork of the Columbia. He went through the Pass, and saw the headwaters of the Colorado, of the Gulf of California. . . .

Linn, accepting the story of the "loftiest peak" of the Rockies, briefly dilated on it, and then proceeded:

From that ultimate point he returned by the valley of the Great Platte, following the stream in its whole course, and solving all questions in relation to its navigability, and the character of the country through which it flows.

He added that the use of the eight mule-drawn carts proved the facility of traveling in this region; that herds of buffalo had given food to the men, the short grass to the horses and mules; and that the fact that two boys, one only twelve, accompanied the expedition, proved that whole families could traverse the country without risk. The expedition had done something to encourage Oregon migration; it would do still more when Frémont's report was published.

DEATH AT DONNER LAKE

by *Virginia Reed Murphy*

Among the settlers who followed in the path that Frémont had plotted, were five hundred Americans who entered California in 1846. One party has become legendary in the history of the American frontier. They reached the Sierras at the beginning of winter and by failing to push on when the road was relatively clear, they were trapped by drifting snow. The rest of the story had a nightmare quality. Cold and shelterless, part of the party fought for survival while a few went on to summon help. Starvation was to lead

From A *Happy Issue*, a letter written in 1847.

to cannibalism and of the original group of eighty-seven, forty-eight survived. One of these survivors was a young girl who later wrote the story of her adventures in the selection which follows.

SNOW was already falling, although it was only the last week in October. Winter had set in a month earlier than usual. All trails and roads were covered, and our only guide was the summit which it seemed we would never reach. Despair drove many nearly frantic. Each family tried to cross the mountains but found it impossible. When it was seen that the wagons could not be dragged through the snow, their goods and provisions were packed on oxen and another start was made, men and women walking in snow up to their waists, carrying their children in their arms and trying to drive their cattle. The Indians said they could find no road; so a halt was called, and Stanton went ahead with the guides and came back and reported that we could get across if we kept right on, but that it would be impossible if snow fell. He was in favor of a forced march until the other side of the summit should be reached, but some of our party were so tired and exhausted with the day's labor that they declared they could not take another step; so the few who knew the danger that the night might bring yielded to the many, and we camped within three miles of the summit.

That night came the dreaded snow. Around the campfires under the trees great feathery flakes came whirling down. The air was so full of them that one could see objects only a few feet away. The Indians knew we were doomed, and one of them wrapped his blanket about him and stood all night under a tree. We children slept soundly on our cold bed of snow with a soft white mantle falling over us so thickly that every few moments my mother would have to shake the shawl—our only covering—to keep us from being buried alive. In the morning the snow lay deep on mountain and valley. With heavy hearts we turned back to a cabin that had been built by the Murphy-Schallenberger party two years before. We built more cabins and prepared as best we could for the winter. That camp, which proved the camp of death to many in our company, was made on the shore of a lake, since known as Donner Lake. The Donners were camped in Alder Creek Valley below the lake, and were, if possible, in a worse condition than ourselves. The snow came on so suddenly that they had no time to build cabins, but hastily put up brush sheds, covering them with pine boughs.

Three double cabins were built at Donner Lake, which were known as the Breen Cabin, the Murphy Cabin, and the Reed-Graves Cabin. The cattle were all killed, and the meat was placed in snow for preservation. My mother had no cattle to kill, but she made arrangements for some, promising to give two for one in California. Stanton and the Indians made their home in my mother's cabin.

Many attempts were made to cross the mountains, but all who tried were driven back by the pitiless storms. Finally a party was organized, since known as the Forlorn Hope. They made snowshoes, and fifteen started—ten men and five women—but only seven lived to reach California; eight men perished. They were over a month on the way, and the horrors endured by that Forlorn Hope no pen can describe nor imagination conceive. The noble Stanton was one of the party, and perished the sixth day out, thus sacrificing his life for strangers. I can find no words in which to express a fitting tribute to the memory of Stanton.

The misery endured during those four months at Donner Lake in our little dark cabins under the snow would fill pages and make the coldest heart ache. Christmas was near, but to the starving its memory gave no comfort. It came and passed without observance, but my mother had determined weeks before that her children should have a treat on this one day. She had laid away a few dried apples, some beans, a bit of tripe, and a small piece of bacon. When this hoarded store was brought out, the delight of the little ones knew no bounds. The cooking was watched carefully, and when we sat down to our Christmas dinner, Mother said, "Children, eat slowly, for this one day you can have all you wish." So bitter was the misery relieved by that one bright day that I have never since sat down to a Christmas dinner without my thoughts going back to Donner Lake.

The storms would often last ten days at a time, and we would have to cut chips from the logs inside which formed our cabins in order to start a fire. We could scarcely walk, and the men had hardly strength to procure wood. We would drag ourselves through the snow from one cabin to another, and some mornings snow would have to be shoveled out of the fireplace before a fire could be made. Poor little children were crying with hunger, and mothers were crying because they had so little to give their children. We seldom thought of bread, we had been without it so long. Four months of such suffering would fill the bravest hearts with despair. . . .

Time dragged slowly along till we were no longer on short allowance but were simply starving. Mother determined to make an effort to cross the mountains. She could not see her children die without trying to get them food. It was hard to leave them, but she felt that it must be done. She told them she would bring them bread, so they were willing to stay, and with no guide but a compass we started—my mother, Eliza, Milt Elliott, and myself. Milt wore snowshoes, and we followed in his tracks. We were five days in the mountains; Eliza gave out the first day and had to return, but we kept on and climbed one high mountain after another only to see others higher still ahead. Often I would have to crawl up the mountains, being too tired to walk. The nights were made hideous by the screams of wild beasts heard in the distance. Again, we would be lulled to sleep by the moan of the pine trees, which seemed to sympathize with our loneliness. One morning we awoke to find ourselves in a well of snow. During the night, while in the deep sleep of exhaustion, the heat of the fire had melted the snow and our little camp had gradually sunk many feet below the surface until we were literally buried in a well of snow. The danger was that any attempt to get out might bring an avalanche upon us, but finally steps were carefully made and we reached the surface. My foot was badly frozen, so we were compelled to return, and just in time, for that night a storm came on, the most fearful of the winter, and we should have perished had we not been in the cabins.

We now had nothing to eat but raw hides, and they were on the roof of the cabin to keep out the snow; when prepared for cooking and boiled they were simply a pot of glue. When the hides were taken off our cabin and we were left without shelter, Mr. Breen gave us a home with his family, and Mrs. Breen prolonged my life by slipping me little bits of meat now and then when she discovered that I could not eat the hide. Death had already claimed many in our party, and it seemed as though relief never would reach us. Baylis Williams, who had been in delicate health before we left Springfield, was the first to die; he passed away before starvation had really set in. . . .

On his arrival at Sutter's Fort my father made known the situation of the emigrants, and Captain Sutter offered at once to do everything possible for their relief. He furnished horses and provisions, and my father and Mr. McClutchen started for the mountains, coming as far as possible with horses and then with packs on their backs proceeding on foot; but they were finally compelled to return. Captain Sutter was not surprised at their defeat. He stated that there were no able-bodied men in that vicinity, all having gone down the country with Frémont to fight the Mexicans. He advised my father to go to Yerba Buena, now San Francisco, and make his case known to the naval officer in command. My father was in fact conducting parties there—when the seven members of the Forlorn Hope arrived from across the mountains. Their famished faces told the story. Cattle were killed and men were up all night, drying beef and making flour by hand mills, nearly two hundred pounds being made in one night, and a party of seven, commanded by Captain Reasen P. Tucker, were sent to our relief by Captain Sutter and the alcalde, Mr. Sinclair. On the evening of February 19, 1847, they reached our cabins, where all were starving. They shouted to attract attention. Mr. Breen clambered up the icy steps from our cabin, and soon we heard the blessed words, "Relief, thank God, relief!" There was joy at Donner Lake that night, for we did not know the fate of the Forlorn Hope; and we were told that relief parties would come and go until all were across the mountains. But with the joy sorrow was strangely blended. There were tears in other eyes than those of children; strong men sat down and wept. For the dead were lying about on the snow, some even unburied, since the living had not had strength to bury their dead. When Milt Elliott died—our faithful friend who seemed so like a brother—my mother and I dragged him up out of the cabin and covered him with snow. Commencing at his feet, I patted the pure white snow down softly until I reached his face. Poor Milt! it was hard to cover that face from sight forever, for with his death our best friend was gone.

On the twenty-second of February the first relief started with a party of twenty-three—men, women, and children. My mother and her family were among the number. It was a bright, sunny morning, and we felt happy; but we had not gone far when Patty and Tommy gave out. They were not able to stand the fatigue, and it was not thought safe to allow them to proceed; so Mr. Glover informed Mama that they would have to be sent back to the cabins to await the next expedition. What language can express our feelings? My mother said that she would go back with her children— that we would all go back together. This the relief party would not permit, and Mr. Glover promised Mama that as soon as they reached Bear Valley he himself would return for her children. . . . Mr. Glover returned with the children and, providing them with food, left them in the care of Mr. Breen.

With sorrowful hearts we traveled on, walking through the snow in single file. The men wearing snowshoes broke the way, and we followed in their tracks. At night we lay down on the snow to sleep, to awake to find our clothing all frozen, even to our shoestrings. At break of day we were again on the road, owing to the fact that we could make better time over the frozen snow. The sunshine, which it would seem would have been welcome, only added to our misery. The dazzling reflection of the snow was very trying to the eyes, while its heat melted our frozen clothing, making [it] cling to our bodies. My brother was too small to step in the tracks made by the men, and in order to travel he had to place his knee on the little hill of snow after each step and climb over. Mother coaxed him along, telling him that every step he took he was getting nearer Papa and nearer something to eat. He was the youngest child that walked over the Sierra Nevada. On our second day's journey John Denton gave out and declared it would be impossible for him to travel, but he begged his companions to continue their journey. A fire was built and he was left lying on a bed of freshly-cut pine boughs, peacefully smoking. He looked so comfortable that my little brother wanted to stay with him, but when the second relief party reached him, poor Denton was past waking. His last thoughts seemed to have gone back to his childhood's home, as a little poem was found by his side, the pencil apparently just dropped from his hand.

Captain Tucker's party on their way to the cabins had lightened their packs of a sufficient quantity of provisions to supply the sufferers on their way out. But when we reached the place where the cache had been made by hanging the food on a tree, we were horrified to find that wild animals had destroyed it; and again starvation stared us in the face. But my father was hurrying over the mountains and met us in our hour of need with his hands full of bread. He had expected to meet us on this day and had stayed up all night, baking bread to give us. He brought with him fourteen men. Some of his party were ahead, and when they saw us coming they called out: "Is Mrs. Reed with you? If she is, tell her Mr. Reed is here." We heard the call; Mother knelt on the snow, while I tried to run to meet Papa.

When my father learned that two of his children were still at the cabins, he hurried on, so fearful was he that they might perish before he reached them. He seemed to fly over the snow, and made in two days the distance we had been five in traveling, and was overjoyed to find Patty and Tommy alive. He reached Donner Lake on the first of March and what a sight met his gaze! The famished little children and the deathlike look of all made his heart ache. He filled Patty's apron with biscuits which she carried around, giving one to each person. He had soup made for the infirm and rendered every assistance possible to the sufferers. Leaving them with about seven days' provisions, he started out with a party of seventeen, all that were able to travel. Three of his men were left at the cabins to procure wood and assist the helpless. My father's party (the second relief) had not traveled many miles when a storm broke upon them. With the snow came a perfect hurricane. The crying of half-frozen children, the lamenting of the mothers, and the suffering of the whole party was heart-rending; and above all could be heard the shrieking of the storm king. One who has never witnessed a blizzard in the Sierra can form no idea of the situation. All night my father and his men worked unceasingly through the raging storm, trying to erect shelter for the dying women and children. At times the hurricane would burst forth with such violence that he felt alarmed on account of the tall timber surrounding the camp. The party were destitute of food, all supplies that could be spared having been left with those at the cabins. The relief party had cached provisions on their way over to the cabins, and my father had sent three of the men forward for food before the storm set in, but they could not return. Thus, again, death stared all in the face. At one time the fire was nearly gone; had it been lost, all would have perished. Three days and nights they were exposed to the fury of the elements. Finally my father became snow-blind and could do no more, and he would have died but for the exertions of William McClutchen and Hiram Miller, who worked over him all night. From this time forward the toil and responsibility rested upon McClutchen and Miller.

The storm at last ceased, and these two determined to set out over the snow and send back relief to those not able to travel. Hiram Miller picked up Tommy and started. Patty thought she could walk, but gradually everything faded from her sight, and she too seemed to be dying. All other sufferings were now forgotten, and everything was done to revive the child. My father found some crumbs in the thumb of his woolen mitten; warming and moistening them between his own lips, he gave them to her and thus saved her life, and afterward she was carried along by different ones in the company. Patty was not alone in her travels. Hidden away in her bosom was a tiny doll which she had carried day and night through all of our trials. Sitting before a nice, bright fire at Woodworth's Camp, she took dolly out to have a talk, and told her of all her new happiness.

TIPPU TIB OF
ZANZIBAR

by Daniel P. Mannix

For many years after large areas of the other continents had been opened up Africa remained the mysterious "Dark Continent." Its coasts had been explored, but its vast interior was virtually unknown. It seemed to offer none of the enticements of gold and spices that had lured adventurers to the Orient and the "New World." It contained ferocious tribes, dangerous animals and the dreaded tsetse fly. Only Arab slave traders dared venture into its jungles.

Soon, however, the British and particularly the Scots, urged on by their hunger for new lands, began to penetrate the unknown. In the vanguard was James Bruce, the first great scientific explorer of Africa. In 1768 he set out to solve the problem of the headwaters of the Nile. Like Humboldt and Darwin, Bates and Wallace, he was driven by scientific curiosity. He found the source of the Blue Nile which had been seen a hundred and fifty years before by the Portuguese Jesuits. While his basic discovery was not new, his detailed information about the country and the people had never before been recorded. The book he wrote aroused intense feeling about the slave trade and helped to awaken a new interest in Africa.

In 1788 the African Association was founded in England. Under its auspices four explorers were sent to the still-dark continent to investigate the mysterious Niger. Three of them died and the fourth returned to England unsuccessful. Then, in 1795, the Association chose a Scottish physician who was destined to become one of the most famous explorers in African history. His name was Mungo Park. He set out for the interior accompanied by a Negro servant, two asses and a horse. On his way to the Niger he was robbed, captured and held prisoner by a "Moorish" chief. Finally, after three months, he escaped to continue his exploration of the great river which, as he discovered, flows eastward. But still no one knew where it rose or even where it emptied into the sea. In an effort to find the answers, Park set out on a second expedition. He sailed over half its length, but before he could go further he was attacked by hostile natives and killed. It remained for later explorers to solve the secrets he investigated. But Mungo Park's example and the book he wrote about his journeys led to the great era of exploration in which the names of Livingstone and Stanley, Burton, Speke and Grant were to become world-famous.

The accomplishments of the British would frequently have been impossible without the experience and assistance of pioneers of other races. Such a pioneer was Tippu Tib, the legendary slave trader of Zanzibar. He drove his slave gangs, yoked together with forked sticks, from the central lakes to the coast and in the pursuit of his profession explored large sections of Africa. Later he was of assistance to the British of the great period, who opened Africa to the dubious benefits of civilization.

Tippu Tib's story is told in a selection from Tales of the African Frontier by John A. Hunter and Daniel P. Mannix. Mannix traveled from Lake Victoria to Zanzibar to gather his material. He talked to pioneers who remembered this last great frontier, and who told him stories of Kenya in the days when it was "as remote from the rest of the world as though it were on another planet." The selection which follows recreates that incredible period.

IN THE 1870's, visitors to the exotic island of Zanzibar, which lies a few miles off the coast of East Africa, often commented on the great numbers of white shells that covered the bottom of the bay. These objects were not shells. They were bones of dead slaves, who had been dumped over the sides of the Arab vessels that brought twenty thousands of these wretches every year to the great Zanzibar slave market, the largest institution of its kind in the world. The man who was responsible for a goodly number of these bones was Hamed bin Muhammed, called by the natives Tippu Tib, an onomatopoeic term meant to imitate the sound of his rapidly firing guns. Tippu Tib was probably the greatest slaver in history. He was also an outstanding explorer, an excellent administrator, an ardent patriot, and the man who, by his generous assistance, made possible the work of Livingstone, Stanley, and the explorers, Speke, Cameron and Wissmann.

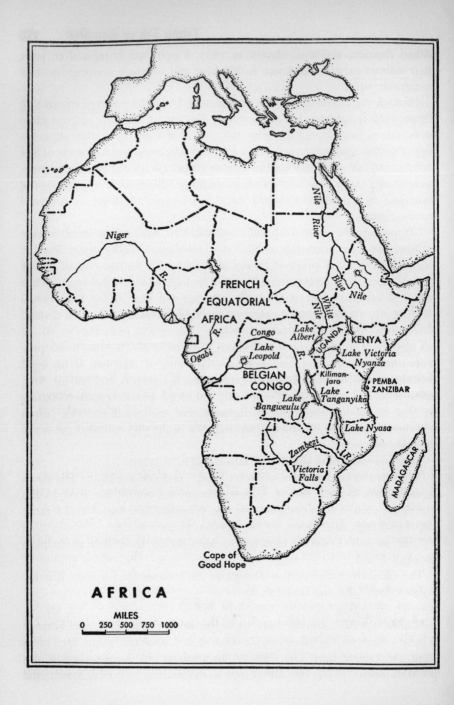

Niger

Nile River

Blue Nile

White Nile

FRENCH
EQUATORIAL
AFRICA

R.

Congo

R.

Ogabi

Lake
Albert

UGANDA

KENYA

Lake Victoria
Nyanza

Lake
Leopold

BELGIAN
CONGO

Kiliman-
jaro

Lake
Tanganyika

PEMBA
ZANZIBAR

Lake
Bangweulu

Lake Nyasa

Zambezi

R.

MADAGASCAR

Victoria
Falls

Cape of
Good Hope

AFRICA

MILES

0   250 500 750 1000

2

When Zanzibar abolished slavery in 1897, Tippu's slaves refused to leave their beloved master. His house in Zanzibar still stands, a memento to this remarkable man.

Through the kindness of some Arab friends, I had the privilege of meeting Tippu Tib's daughter-in-law in Zanzibar. She was an old lady of great character, rather thickset, with a firm jaw and alert black eyes who sat cross-legged on the couch of our friend's house as modern custom prevented her from taking her usual seat on the Persian carpet. With our friends as interpreters, she answered my questions with decision and authority—not unnatural in a woman who had once had complete control over several hundred slaves.

"Tippu was the man who really opened East Africa, not these foreign explorers who are given the credit," she said firmly. "Livingstone, Stanley, Burton—all of them simply followed along the trails he had opened. None of them would ever have gotten through if he hadn't broken the power of the native chiefs first. He civilized the country and was ruling there when the Belgians, Germans and English intimidated our sultan and then divided the country among themselves. And now look at the mess they're all in! It's the result of their racial prejudice. We had slaves, but no racial prejudice. An Arab would marry a Negro slave girl, or take her as his legal concubine, and her children had just as much rights as any by his Arab wife—if he had one. Tippu Tib himself had Negro blood. It meant nothing to him or anyone else. The Europeans have tried to force this 'white supremacy' nonsense on the natives and as a result they're hated far worse than we ever were."

"Tell me something about your father-in-law," I asked.

"He was the kindest man who ever lived," said the old lady. "His slaves regarded him as their father. When he went on one of his trips to the mainland, even if he were gone for five years the household would move about as though in a trance, waiting for him to come back."

"But he was a slaver, reported to have killed thousands of helpless people," I said.

The old lady sniffed. "You foreigners can't understand a man like my father-in-law," she said disdainfully.

Hamed bin Muhammed, later to be known as Tippu Tib, was born in a little village on the island of Zanzibar called Kwarara, about fifty miles from the capital city. The date of his birth is not known, but it was probably about 1850. His father was a moderately successful trader and took his son with him on trips up and down the coast and occasionally on short safaris into East Africa. On these trips, little Hamed would listen to the old traders, sipping their thick brown coffee in a native hut or warming their bones around a brazier on the deck of a dhow, tell of the fabulous villages that lay in the interior. These villages used elephant tusks for stockades, built their chiefs' thrones of ivory, and lined the sides of their huts with the precious stuff as though the tusks were logs of wood. There a man could buy a beautiful girl for a handful of beads and the streams were yellow with gold. Listening to these stories, young Hamed swore that he would someday find these villages and be a great explorer like Ebn Haukal, the famous Arab geographer who discovered Lake Victoria in the tenth century, or Jabl-ul-Qumar who traveled to Uganda and described the Mountains of the Moon.

In 1867, when Hamed was about seventeen years old, he determined to lead an expedition to the central lake district and return rich in ivory and slaves. This was merely a trading-exploration trip, not a punitive expedition. The Arabs at this time did not use force in obtaining slaves. Slavery was common among the African tribes and the Arab traders bought slaves in the villages just as they bought ivory and other merchandise. The relations between the Arabs and the natives were so peaceful that the Arabs proudly boasted, "An Arab can walk across Africa with no weapon except a cane."

To raise money for his trip, Hamed borrowed heavily from the Indian moneylenders in Zanzibar who charged interest running up to 700 per cent. His relations were so proud and confident of the youngster that they put up their property as security. Hamed sailed for Dar-es-Salaam, the port of modern Tanganyika, with a few Arab followers and as soon as he landed, set about hiring porters.

Recognizing that Hamed was an inexperienced boy, the porters demanded the outrageous wage of ten dollars for the trip, which, as it was only to last five years, was ridiculous. The innocent Hamed agreed, and then issued each porter half of the sum to support his family during his absence. The first night out, the porters all quietly deserted, leaving Hamed with his bales of trading goods and his followers alone in the jungle.

When Hamed woke in the morning and found what had happened, his senses nearly deserted him. In his despair, the boy realized that not only he was ruined, but also his trusting family who had mortgaged their homes to the moneylenders. Now Hamed showed the determination that was to make him Tippu Tib. He and his men went back to the village and seized every man they could find. As the Zanzibarians had guns and the natives did not, no resistance was made. Hamed marched his captives to a blacksmith and had them fastened together with chains. Then he set out on his trip, confident that this time his porters wouldn't desert.

Hamed and his caravan reached Tabora, an Arab frontier post near Lake Tanganyika. Tabora was "the end of the line" as far as caravans were concerned. But here were no stockades made of ivory or lovely girls being sold for a few beads. The traders chuckled as they listened to the boy. Yes, thirty years ago that might have been the case but now both ivory and slaves were scarce and expensive.

Unless, of course, Hamed wanted to trade with King Nsama. Nsama, whom Livingstone later described as the "Napoleon of Africa," was a local ruler who had successfully conquered and enslaved all the tribes near his kingdom. He was reputed to have a vast store of ivory. A short time before, an Arab caravan had gone into his kingdom to trade with him. None of them were ever seen again.

Hamed decided to trade with King Nsama. First, he used up the last of his money to buy all the guns he could in Tabora. The guns were old "Brown Bess" muskets, even then regarded as obsolete, but in Tabora, they were worth their weight in gold and gunpowder its weight in silver. Hamed had a handful of Arab followers, all with more or less Negro blood. In addition, he had some fifty Manyemas, a particularly warlike tribe which the Arabs used as mercenaries. Thus equipped, Hamed and his men went off to interview King Nsama.

Nsama lived in a fortified village, surrounded by a high stockade and a deep ditch, the bottom of which was studded with dagger-sharp bamboo stakes. The sides of the stockade were covered with thorn branches that served the same purpose as barbed wire. However, the king received the young Arab most graciously. He had the drawbridge lowered over the moat and asked Hamed and his followers to come in, merely stipulating that they leave their guns behind.

The Zanzibarians obeyed, except that they concealed their guns under their long, white robes. However, there was clearly no cause for alarm. King Nsama received them politely and accepted the gifts Hamed had brought him. Then as his guests turned away, the king shouted an order. Instantly, the drawbridge was raised, armed warriors appeared on all sides and a murderous hail of arrows came from archers concealed in the watchtowers on the stockade.

Two of Hamed's men were killed instantly. Hamed himself received three arrow wounds. In spite of his injuries, Hamed rallied his men. They pulled out their concealed guns and opened fire. The astounded warriors fell back and Hamed and his men fought their way to a hut. Meanwhile, the rest of his party opened fire on the village from across the moat. Under this crossfire, the natives could not hold out. They lowered the drawbridge and fled, the king leading the rout. Hamed and his men were left in possession of the village.

This victory was achieved with twenty guns. That a small body of men, armed only with muskets, could defeat a powerful ruler and his warriors seems incredible but allowance must be made for the psychological effects of the almost unknown firearms. Also, these Central African tribes were simply not the fighting men that the Zulu or the Kenya Masai were.

In the king's storehouse, Hamed found 1,950 frasilahs of ivory (a frasilah was about 35 pounds), worth approximately $50,000. This Hamed appropriated. He returned to Tabora with his spoils, to the astonishment of the Arab traders. The natives gave him the name of Tippu Tib, so impressed were they by his musketry. "I learned that day in Nsama's village that the gun is king of Africa," said Tippu Tib grimly. Certainly, he developed a passion for firearms that lasted all his life.

Tippu Tib invested part of his ivory in more guns and struck out for unopened country. Near Lake Tanganyika, he met Dr. Livingstone. The young Arab was greatly impressed by the missionary's courage and sincerity. "Although he was not of my faith, he was unquestionably a man of God," said Tippu Tib. He gave Livingstone some much-needed supplies and then went on. In his books, Livingstone speaks of Tippu Tib with marked respect although naturally he vehemently condemns the Arab's methods.

In Ugalla, to the northeast of Lake Tanganyika, Tippu Tib took the next step that was to make him king of Central Africa and of the Arab slavers. He and a few of his men entered one of the fortified villages to trade while the rest of his force remained outside in the Arab camp. While Tippu Tib was negotiating with the chief for some ivory, one of his followers purchased a bowl of corn from a woman and started to carry it away. An aggressive young warrior knocked the bowl out of his hands and started scolding the woman. A general altercation followed, in which both Arabs and natives joined. Tippu Tib tried to stop the dispute, but the angry voices had run throughout the village and a number of young warriors rushed up, flourishing their spears and giving their war cries. Spears and arrows began to fly and the chief turned to run. One of the Arabs shouted to him to stop and when the chief kept on, shot him. Instantly the battle was joined.

The Arabs were driven from the town and fell back on their camp. They found it deserted. The war drums of the village were thundering out the alarm and already scores of warriors were pouring in from the outlying areas to avenge the death of their chief. Tippu Tib and his few supporters were in a desperate position. Tippu decided that their only chance was to return to the village, capture it, and entrench themselves behind the stockade. But as they approached the gate, an overwhelming force rushed out to meet them. At the same moment, they were attacked from the rear by the hostile tribesmen.

Tippu Tib knew it was all over. He called on his men to kill as many of the pagans as possible before they died. Then the force pouring out of the village began to fire, not at Tippu and his men, but at the oncoming tribesmen. For a moment, Tippu could not believe his senses. Then he saw the blood-red flag of Zanzibar floating over the group and recognized the faces of the men he had left in the camp. When the fighting started, these men had attacked the village from the rear and had occupied it while Tippu Tib and his party were being driven out the main gate.

For the next two days, the Arabs looted the surrounding villages and enslaved the inhabitants. After a victory, the Manyema mercenaries took for granted that all prisoners were to be used as slaves and Tippu Tib made no attempt to interfere with this custom. It would have been worth his life if he had, as the Manyemas got a percentage on all slaves taken. The captive villagers were loaded with ivory from the chief's store and sent to the coast where both were sold. The resulting profits were tremendous. Under the old system of hiring porters to carry the ivory, only a small profit could be made on each shipment, but this device opened a whole new era in Africa.

Tippu Tib had stumbled, partly by accident and partly by force of circumstances, on the first half of the formula that was to make him famous: capture a village, enslave the people, have them carry their ivory to the coast, and then sell both slaves and ivory. The second half of the formula fell into place a few months later.

While trading near Lake Kissale, part of the chain of Central African lakes, Tippu Tib was invited by a certain tribe to purchase ivory in their villages. This tribe was constantly at war with a rival tribe, and over the years a curious understanding had sprung up between them. After a war, the winning tribe settled on the lake shore while the losers retired to the jungle until they felt themselves strong enough for a return match. If they won, they took the lake area while the defeated group in turn hid in the jungle.

It was the tribe then living in the jungle who had asked Tippu Tib to trade. Tippu set out with his caravan but on the way was attacked by the lake tribe, who refused to allow the Arabs to trade with their enemies. Tippu and his men were driven back. In a rage, the Arabs joined forces with the jungle group and marched against the lake people. The guns of the Arabs naturally decided the already delicate balance between the groups. But this time the defeated lake people were not allowed to escape into the jungle. The victorious tribe, because of the Arab support, was able for the first time to inflict a complete defeat on their enemies. Those who were not killed and eaten by the conquerors were sent to the Zanzibar slave market by the Arabs, so that the beaten tribe was completely exterminated.

Tippu Tib moved on to new regions, but the victorious tribe, no longer afraid of attack by their ancient enemies, now started a series of raids on other neighboring people. Soon they became so arrogant that they demanded Tippu Tib pay tribute on all ivory caravans sent back through their country. Tippu Tib promptly organized the neighboring tribes against them and soon the erstwhile conquerors were themselves headed for Zanzibar with yokes around their necks and laden with their treasury of ivory.

The formula was now complete. From then on, Tippu Tib applied it with almost monotonous regularity. The Arabs would move into a village and offer to buy ivory. As all the native tribes were hostile to each other, jealous neighbors would sooner or later attack the village. Then the Arabs would support their friends. The Arab guns always decided the issue and the winning tribe, confident that the victory was due solely to their own tribal courage and ability, would start on a career of conquest. Eventually they would turn on the Arabs. Then the Arabs would form a confederation against them and soon they would go the same path as their victims. In this way, the power of Tippu Tib continued to grow and a constant stream of ivory and slaves flowed out of Central Africa to Zanzibar.

Tippu Tib always claimed that he was really a man of peace and would have much preferred to conduct business without the constant series of wars caused by the mutual suspicion among the tribes. This may have been more or less true. Certainly whenever possible Tippu Tib used peaceful methods to obtain his ends rather than expend valuable gunpowder. On several occasions, he cemented friendly relations with a tribe by marrying one of the chief's daughters, although from the Arab point of view, he was merely taking her into legal concubinage. He and his men were outnumbered more than a thousand to one and could count on no support from Zanzibar in case of trouble, so he could not rely simply on force. The Arab spent endless weeks and months chatting with the natives, learning to understand their point of view, their prejudices and their traditions. Often the information he received was worth more than all the guns in Africa.

In one village, Tippu talked to a slave girl who had been captured from a country far in the interior. The girl told him that years before the daughter of the chief had been carried off by raiders. The chief was now old and wanted to retire but the only rightful heir to the throne would be the son of the missing "princess." From the girl, Tippu learned the tribe's language, customs, religion and the genealogy of the royal family. Then he traveled to the country and presented himself as the heir to the throne. The Arab's strong admixture of Negro blood made this possible and the simple villagers could not imagine how a complete stranger would know their language and customs unless he was indeed of their people. The old chief joyfully retired and Tippu Tib took over.

Tippu Tib's conquest of Central Africa was not always so simple. The Arabs were constantly being attacked and repeatedly caravans were ambushed and wiped out. On several occasions, things grew so hot that even Tippu's hardened followers begged him to abandon his ivory and escape while he could. Tippu merely retorted, "My ivory is worth more than my life," and time after time led his men to victory over the disorganized tribesmen.

Like any other successful businessman, Tippu Tib soon had many imitators. These men had learned only too well his grim motto, "The gun is the king of Africa," but they did not possess Tippu's knowledge of the natives and his ability to administer a district after he had conquered it. These men deliberately provoked native wars and then reaped a harvest in slaves. "Kill the men and rope the women" was their slogan and they lived up to it. The names given these Arab slavers by the natives are descriptive. There was "The Clean-Sweeper," "The Destroyer," "Bitter as Bile" and many more. The slave trade, always a grisly business, now became a screaming horror. The caravan routes were marked by the lines of white bones scattered on either side of the path. Livingstone believed that only about one slave in five survived to reach Zanzibar but many well-informed men considered the doctor's estimate too conservative. The area around the shipping ports resembled a huge abattoir and worse, for the slaves considered too weak to survive the voyage to Zanzibar were thrown out to die among the corpses of their friends. The stench of the rotting bodies, the moans of the dying and the constant screaming of babies, disregarded after their mothers had died, made the ports hideous. Among the other ghastly sights were scores of little boys with their intestines protruding through wounds caused by the Arabs' crude attempts to castrate them for eunuchs.

These miserable children crawled about the streets until they died. It is thought that only one in twenty survived the operation.

Many of the early missionaries and explorers urged the Arabs to take better care of their slaves if only for motives of self-interest. The historic answer to this plea was given by a British official who remarked, "The Arabs regard it like transporting ice. You know most of it will melt away, but there'll be enough left to show a profit." With an unlimited source of supply in the interior, there was really no reason to worry about the high mortality rate.

But the supply was not unlimited. The Arab slavers were actually beginning to depopulate Central Africa. As soon as the numbers of any species are reduced below a certain point, there is not enough "breeding stock" left to maintain the race. The native wars, savage as they were, had seldom resulted in the complete extermination of a tribe. This now became common. The suffering of the slaves was a comparatively minor matter compared to the fact that whole villages were being wiped out to obtain a handful of women and children. The villagers left behind were so few that they couldn't rebuild their homes, clear their fields or protect themselves from wild animals. Great areas were so desolated that the caravans had trouble getting through them, for there was no food of any kind to be obtained.

What was the man like who had caused this holocaust? Stanley gives the following description:

> He was a tall, black-bearded man of negroid complexion in the prime of life, straight and quick in his movements, a picture of energy and strength. He had a fine, intelligent face with a nervous twitching of the eyes and gleaming white, perfectly formed teeth. He had the air of a well-bred Arab and was courtier-like in his manner. I came to the conclusion that he was a remarkable man, the most remarkable that I had met among the Arabs. He was neat in his person; his clothes were of spotless white, his fez-cap brand new, his waist encircled by a rich dagger-belt, his dagger was splendid with silver filigree and his whole appearance that of an Arab gentleman in very comfortable circumstances.

Tippu Tib was a very devout man. He belonged to a puritanical Mohammedan sect that severely condemns any form of laxness and forbids even the use of tobacco to its adherents. Tippu Tib was deeply shocked and disgusted when he found one of his best lieutenants drunk on native beer in a village and refused to have anything more to do with the man. Although some of the slavers were apt to be free in their relations with native women, Tippu scrupulously observed his religious principles. Although he had a harem of several dozen women who traveled with him, these were all legal concubines and their children were, according to Moslem law, legitimate and entitled to a share in their father's estate. A concubine was not a slave and could not be sold, although she did not have the position of a true wife. Tippu Tib always refused to allow himself to be carried in a litter by slaves or even ride a donkey. "I am a poor Arab whom Allah has raised to greatness," he said. "I walk so that I will not forget my humble origin."

Tippu Tib made many trips back to Zanzibar during this period with a fabulous amount of slaves and ivory. As a young man, he had planned to make only a few trips to Central Africa, collect a huge profit, and then retire to live the life of an Arab gentleman. His first trip had brought him in even greater profits than he had dreamed of, but the sultan levied a heavy tax on both slaves and ivory. By the time Tippu Tib had paid off the moneylenders and the sultan's tax, given his followers a percentage of the loot and settled his other expenses, he had barely enough money left to equip another expedition. Then as his empire grew, his overhead also increased. There is no doubt that Tippu Tib did become enormously rich, but by then his sights were set higher, and what would have seemed like fantastic riches to most Arabs merely provided for the upkeep of his Zanzibar estates. So, in order to increase his fortune, he continued to open fresh country, always counting on the big haul that would enable him to retire in comfort.

The explorers and missionaries whom Tippu Tib helped reads like a roll call of all the great names in early East Africa. Although the Arab perfectly understood that these men had come to destroy the slave trade which was the source of his wealth, he never turned down a request for help. He gave food and guides to Cameron, the first man to cross the continent, and Cameron later said that without Tippu Tib's help he would have died. He helped Speke, who discovered the sources of the Nile; Wissmann, who made the first west-to-east crossing of the country, and many others. When these men tried to draw him into a discussion on the ethics of the slave trade, Tippu Tib would gently reply that Abraham and Jacob had slaves and God favored them. He also pointed out that once the slaves reached their various destinations, they were well treated and most of them far better off than under the cruel rule of the native kings. "Belgium, France, Brazil and Portugal are buying the slaves I supply," he remarked. "Are not these all civilized, Christian countries? Let them stop demanding slaves and I will stop supplying them." If the conversation grew acrimonious, the Arab would say courteously, "On these matters we do not agree, but do not let us quarrel."

In 1870, some of Tippu Tib's lieutenants brought him word that a strange white man was wandering about the country at the head of an enormous safari of armed porters, saying he was looking for the lost Dr. Livingstone. The Arabs had politely assured this curious individual that Dr. Livingstone was not lost at all but living quite comfortably at the prosperous Arab village of Ujiji on Lake Tanganyika. Tippu Tib instructed his men to give this stranger food and take him to Dr. Livingstone.

Tippu Tib was interested in this foreigner, as he was in all Europeans, and arranged a meeting with him after he had found Dr. Livingstone. Thus Tippu Tib met Stanley, a momentous meeting for both of them as events turned out. At first, Tippu was amused by the self-confidence and boastfulness of the American, so unlike the quiet restraint typical of the upper-class Arabs. Stanley exhibited a repeating rifle which he claimed could shoot many times in succession. Tippu, with his great passion for firearms, begged for a demonstration. "No," said Stanley, "the bullets cost too much." "Ah, indeed," said Tippu politely, who was now convinced that this bombastic stranger was a fraud. "By a curious coincidence, I know of a native tribe that has a bow which will shoot twenty arrows at one time and every arrow kills a man. Unfortunately, the arrows are so expensive they never shoot it." Stanley grabbed up his rifle and fired a series of shots into a tree in quick succession. Tippu Tib was greatly impressed. He decided that this stranger, in spite of his loud talk, was able to live up to his claims.

Stanley wanted Tippu Tib's help, as did all the early explorers. Stanley had heard of a great river running westward from the central lakes which he thought might eventually flow into the Atlantic Ocean. This river was the Congo, but neither Tippu Tib nor Stanley knew that at the time. Stanley planned to follow the course of the river and thus cross the continent.

Tippu Tib agreed to help Stanley reach this river. The Arab was always greatly interested in Europeans, who he knew had technical knowledge and power greatly exceeding that of his own people. He also admired Stanley personally. The natives called Stanley "The Stone Breaker" because of his ability to smash his way through all obstacles, and this was a quality Tippu could understand and respect.

After a long and exhausting journey, the river was reached. When the time came for Tippu Tib and his men to return, Stanley gave them a farewell party. One of the events was a foot race. Tippu Tib took this contest very seriously, spending hours trotting up and down the river bank to get into condition. He won the race, beating Pocock, one of Stanley's assistants, by a few yards, to the Arab's great satisfaction. He and Stanley parted with many expressions of mutual friendship and Stanley promised to send Tippu Tib a handsome present when he got back to the United States.

When Tippu Tib returned to his own district, he found a letter awaiting him from the sultan of Zanzibar, ordering him to return immediately. Tippu got together a great caravan of slaves and ivory and started for the coast "at all speed," as he put it. Some impression of an Arab's idea of speed may be gained from the fact that the trip took three years. As he passed through Tanganyika, he was astonished at the changes that had taken place in the last few years. Mission stations dotted the hills, ships were sailing on Lake Tanganyika, European trading posts and forts had sprung up along the old caravan routes. The country was growing.

Tippu Tib had been so long in the interior that for three years little ivory had reached the markets of the world. Ivory cutters in the factories of London, India and Connecticut were starving. When swift clippers brought the news that a big shipment of ivory was headed for the coast, the church bells were rung and people fell on their knees in the streets to give thanks that Tippu Tib had once again won through.

Tippu Tib arrived in Zanzibar a hero. There he found the present Stanley had promised. It was an autographed photograph of the explorer. Instead of being indignant, Tippu Tib considered this most amusing. He told the story as a great joke on himself for many years.

Tippu's meeting with the sultan was less amusing. Years later, Tippu reported his conversation with the sultan to Dr. Heinrich Brode, a German resident of Zanzibar. The sultan, Tippu explained, desperately needed his advice. The German government had laid claim to Tanganyika and enforced their demands by anchoring the German fleet in Zanzibar Harbor. The British government, goaded by the Anti-Slavery Society, was blockading the coast in an effort to stop the slave trade. The Belgians had already announced that the Congo was their property. Tippu was furious. "East Africa belongs to your majesty," he protested. "I took it for you. I was the first man there and these foreigners simply followed in the paths I made. Give me guns and powder, and I'll raise the natives and drive them out." "Do you think I'm worried about the mainland?" cried the sultan. "My only problem is whether it's better to have Germany or Great Britain take over Zanzibar as a protectorate. What do you think?"

"When I heard that, I knew all was lost," said Tippu Tib to Dr. Brode.

Tippu Tib was a patriot, but he was also a man of hard common sense. In the next few weeks, he was convinced beyond all question that the European powers were too strong for the Arabs to resist. Nothing was left except to make the best terms possible. Yet he could not help mourning the loss of East Africa, that great area he had opened with sweat and blood.

While Tippu Tib was still in this despairing mood, Stanley arrived in Zanzibar with a fresh scheme.

Stanley's rescue of Livingstone had been the great journalistic sensation of the day. But now that was all over and some new sensation had to be found that could top it. At first, this seemed impossible, although the newspapers had worked frantically to find someone, somewhere, who had to be rescued. At last, they hit on Emin Pasha.

Emin Pasha, born Edmund Schnitzer, was a scholarly, serious, conscientious German Jew who had accepted a position as governor of the southernmost provinces of Egypt. He had done a magnificent job. Emin Pasha, to give him his Egyptian title, was not only an excellent governor with a deep sympathy for the natives, but also a zoologist, botanist and anthropologist whose papers on these subjects had aroused great interest throughout the world. In 1883, the Mahdi—a half-mad dervish or a great national leader, depending on your point of view—had led an uprising against the pasha of Egypt and the British who had put the pasha in power. Emin had been cut off from Egypt by the Mahdi's forces. Then Kabarega, the great warrior king of Bunyoro in northern Uganda, had also gone on the warpath and cut Emin off from the south. "Who will save Emin Pasha?" cried the newspapers. The anxious people of Europe and America, many of whom had never heard of Emin Pasha a few weeks before, gladly raised $100,000, then a huge sum, to outfit an expedition to rescue him. Stanley was elected to head it.

Stanley was no fool and he knew that he could not possibly get through to Emin without the help of Tippu Tib. He also knew that Tippu would not exactly fall over himself in his efforts to help Stanley a second time. But Stanley held a trump card. After explaining the situation to Tippu Tib, Stanley produced a letter from the king of Belgium, telling Tippu that if he helped Stanley his majesty would make him governor and virtual king of the Congo, which the Belgians had recently seized. How Stanley ever talked the Belgian king into this arrangement is a mystery. It was certainly one of the greatest pieces of salesmanship on record.

The Arab's hands must have shaken as he read the letter. The Congo was his country. He had discovered it, subdued the tribes, built the first trading stations there, knew the people intimately. Now he was being given the chance to return once again as a king. True, he would be theoretically under the Belgians but Tippu Tib knew what that meant. As long as he paid the

Belgians a certain amount of ivory and provided "free labor" for the rubber plantations, he would be a complete ruler. He accepted Stanley's terms.

Rescuing Emin would be simple. Tippu Tib knew the trails and exactly how they should go. But Stanley had other ideas. The rescue of Emin had to be so thrilling that it would even surpass the rescue of Livingstone. He couldn't just walk in and rescue the man. Stanley's idea was to sail south from Zanzibar completely around the continent of Africa by way of the Cape of Good Hope. Then he would outfit an expedition at the mouth of the Congo, sail up the river, and finally go up along Lake Victoria to Emin's rescue. It would be an amazing and highly dramatic feat.

Tippu Tib thought this idea was madness. But Tippu Tib wasn't paying for this trip and the newspapers and the public were. Stanley won.

The first part of the trip went smoothly enough, although it was just as well that Emin Pasha didn't have to hold his breath while the rescue party sailed four thousand miles and then traveled up the Congo against the current. When the expedition reached a point some two hundred miles north of Leopoldville, their boats were in such bad condition that Stanley decided to go on by foot. The trip up the river had taken much longer than expected, so Stanley resolved to press on with a small group and have the rest of the supplies brought up by a rear guard. It was agreed that Tippu Tib was to remain in the Congo as governor but he was to send off the rear guard with five hundred porters as soon as possible.

Stanley went on with his small force as rapidly as possible. He had to pass through districts laid bare by "The Destroyer," "The Clean-Sweeper" and "Bitter as Bile." There was no food to be had by threats or trade goods. His men lived on roots. The porters began to die. Wild tribes attacked them. Stanley sent back desperate messages, imploring the rear guard to hurry but the rear guard did not come. The men finally abandoned their loads and staggered on as best they could. Emin Pasha heard of their coming and sent out a force to meet them. Finally, Stanley and what was left of his force staggered into Emin's camp and collapsed on the ground.

At least, Stanley had finally reached Emin. Now a completely unforeseen problem occurred. Emin positively refused to be rescued. He would not abandon the native tribes who had trusted him, for he knew only too well what would happen to them at the hands of Kabarega, the king of Bunyoro.

This put Stanley in a horrible position. The newspapers of the world were eagerly awaiting the news of how he had rescued Emin Pasha. He argued, pleaded and even threatened the stubborn governor. Fortunately for him, Emin's troops mutinied and Emin was forced to start back for the

Congo with Stanley, although the now almost hysterical governor resisted every step of the way.

The trip north through Uganda to reach Emin had been a living death, but the trip back was far worse. Stanley not only had his own men to feed but also Emin's forces. Time after time he sent messages for the rear guard to bring up supplies but the rear guard still failed to appear. At last, the exhausted group reached the Congo. Stanley considered the failure of the rear guard to come was due solely to Tippu Tib, who had betrayed him. The furious explorer got rid of Emin as soon as possible and left for Zanzibar. There he started a lawsuit against Tippu Tib for not supplying the porters. This lawsuit was one of the *causes célèbres* of its day.

Why hadn't Tippu Tib sent the rear guard? Although I had read many accounts of the unfortunate Emin Pasha mission, I had never found a satisfactory explanation of Tippu Tib's strange conduct. Then while I was in Zanzibar, I was able through the kindness of the curator of the Peace Memorial Museum to see a letter Tippu Tib sent to Zanzibar by runner while Stanley was trying to reach Emin. In the letter, Tippu Tib points out that Stanley had promised to supply him with gunpowder, then a very precious commodity in the Congo, so he could arm the men who were to protect the rear guard. He had reminded Stanley of this promise, but the explorer, who was eagerly rushing off after Emin, told him to get the powder as best he could: "But there is no powder to be had," wrote Tippu Tib to his friend in Zanzibar.

Much against my better judgment, I did send off 500 porters with a few Arab guards. They were attacked by natives, just as Stanley had been. They managed to beat off the natives but by that time had used up their small supply of powder and had to return. Send me powder by the quickest caravan route as Stanley is in a serious situation.

The British had now taken over Zanzibar as a protectorate, partly in an attempt to satisfy the Anti-Slavery Society and partly in response to a plea from the sultan, who feared the growing power of Germany. Tippu Tib received a notice from the British judge in Zanzibar that unless he appeared in court within six months to answer Stanley's charges, all his possessions in Zanzibar would be confiscated. The Arab's traditional calm was not easily disturbed, but this summons threw him into a white-hot fury. His friends urged him not to return to Zanzibar, arguing that he could expect no justice at the hands of the Europeans and would probably find himself thrown in prison. The once invariably courteous Tippu Tib snapped at them, "Mind your own business! I'll have my name cleared if I lose my life doing it."

Tippu Tib sped back toward the coast by a series of forced marches—no leisurely three-year jaunt this time. He was no longer a young man and on the way he collapsed. A mission station of the White Fathers nursed him back to health. As soon as he could raise his head, he ordered his men to put him in a litter and take him on. While crossing Tanganyika, word was brought him that a group of Arabs planned to murder an English missionary named Alfred J. Swann who had been particularly outspoken in his condemnation of the slave trade. "The fools!" snapped Tippu Tib. "What do they hope to accomplish by that? It will only bring the English down on us." He sent some of his men ahead to bring the missionary to Tippu's camp for protection.

Swann gives an almost stenographic account of his meeting with the old slaver in his book *Fighting the Slave-Hunters in Central Africa.* Tippu Tib received him with the usual formal politeness, but the Arab was so seething with his wrongs that soon he burst out into bitter denunciations of Stanley and the European nations that had taken his kingdom. Throwing the judge's summons on the floor of the tent, he exclaimed:

"Look at that! I am ordered to be at the coast two months from now. Stanley says I deliberately tried to hinder him from reaching Emin Pasha. If I had wanted to stop Stanley, I would have had him killed years ago, I do not merely hinder, I destroy! And if I help, I help at all costs."

Counting on his fingers, he went on, "Who helped Cameron, Speke, Livingstone and Gleerup? Who has just saved your life? Haven't I always helped even the missionaries who are trying to destroy my business? I am mad with anger when I think of what I did for Stanley. In order to make a big work out of nothing, he went up the Congo to find Emin Pasha. Why didn't he go straight across from the coast? I didn't want to go that long way around, preferring to take the familiar caravan routes, but he would not be denied, so out of courtesy I went with him. I help foreigners and then they turn on me and seize the country I discovered. You Europeans are very unjust!"

Swann replied, in effect, that the cruelty of the Arabs had caused them to forfeit any rights they had in Africa.

"Is that so?" exclaimed Tippu Tib. "How did you get India?"

"We fought for it."

"Then what you fight for and win belongs to you by right of conquest?"

"Yes, that is European law."

"So it is with us Arabs. I came here as a young man, fought these natives and subdued them, losing both friends and treasure in the struggle. Is it not therefore mine by both your law and ours?"

"It is only yours as long as you govern and use it properly."

"Who is to be my judge?"

"Europe!"

"Ah!" said the Arab, smiling grimly. "Now you speak the truth. Do not let us talk of justice. People are only just when it pays. The white man is stronger than I am. They will eat up my possessions as I ate those of the pagans, and . . ."

He paused and then went on fiercely: "Finally someone will eat up yours! The day is not as far off as you think. I see the clouds gathering in the sky. I hear the thunder!"

These last, terrible words sounded like a curse. Swann never forgot them.

When Tippu Tib arrived in Zanzibar, Stanley had already gone. The explorer had left a bill of indictment against Tippu Tib in the name of "Emin Pasha and his people." Emin indignantly repudiated the use of his name and so the judge dismissed the case. But Tippu Tib was so embittered that he never returned to the mainland. He retired from the slave trade and spent the rest of his life in Zanzibar.

In 1890, the Arab slavers in the Congo rose against the Europeans, calling on Tippu Tib to join them. Tippu Tib refused. He knew that resistance was hopeless. He was right. After a few minor victories, the Arabs were completely crushed. "The Destroyer" was killed and eaten by the Belgians' cannibal native troops. "The Locust" was taken prisoner. "Bitter as Bile" was captured and shot. Only "The Clean-Sweeper" managed to escape. What happened to him, no one knows. Among the others to die were one of Tippu Tib's sons who had joined the uprising and his nephew who was drowned while trying to escape the Belgian troops by swimming a river.

There were also minor revolts against the Germans in Tanganyika and the British in Mombasa. These were both put down. The British fleet shelled Zanzibar and established their own sultan in power. By the end of the century, the Arab empire which Tippu Tib had established was gone. From his home in Zanzibar, the old Arab watched the collapse sadly but philosophically. There was nothing he could do. It was the will of Allah.

Sitting in our Arab friends' comfortable living room and listening to Tippu Tib's daughter-in-law tell of these wild and terrible days, it seemed incredible that within the memory of this old lady the Arabs had once owned East Africa and parceled out areas as big as European countries as their private man-hunting grounds.

"I married into the family of Tippu Tib when I was a young girl of thirteen," the old lady explained in answer to one of my questions. "My home was in Lamu, an island about five hundred miles north of Zanzibar. The old Arab families in Lamu were rich and dignified and had the reputation of bringing up their daughters very strictly. Tippu's son—this wasn't the boy who was killed in the war against the Belgians, but another of his children—was a wild young man. He kept getting married and divorced until finally his father decided to get him a Lamu girl to steady him down. So he and my parents arranged the marriage. I came to Zanzibar in a special dhow with painted sails and the stern covered with brightly colored, hand-carved woodwork. The gunnels of the ship were inlaid with silver and we sat on thick Persian carpets spread over the deck. We sailed into the harbor with drums beating and conch shells blowing. Tippu Tib's son came out to meet us in a barge rowed by slaves in brilliant uniforms, also with drummers and trumpeters. It was the great moment of my life. Girls today can never know what it was like.

"My husband was all right, although he was a typical rich man's son. I got his household straightened out and then as I grew older, men being what they are, I picked out his concubines for him. I made sure that they were good, steady girls with no nonsense about them. But the boy was never the man his father was. Everyone worshipped his father. All the Arabs were generous, but none as generous as he. Every day, forty or fifty poor people would come to our house for food and they were never turned away empty. At a certain hour, the slaves would blow a horn as a signal and within ten minutes the courtyard would be full of people. At the end of Ramadan, our great religious celebration, Tippu provided all the poor in Zanzibar with new clothes. He had hundreds of acres of land, worked by slaves. The slaves worked in the morning for him and then in the afternoon did whatever they pleased. They could till their own fields which he had given them or, if they wanted to work on his estates, they were paid for it. The lucky ones were the household slaves. We had hundreds of them, mostly just for show, and their main duty was to wear lovely clothes and look impressive. Of course, they waited on us. We women never lifted a hand. Anything we wanted was instantly brought to us by the slaves. When I think of how my daughters are living today, in fact how I am living, well . . . let's continue to talk of the past.

"In the autumn [which in Zanzibar corresponds to our spring, as the island is south of the Equator] we would leave the town house and go out to our country estate where it was cooler. That was the big event of the year and there was always great excitement. On the day of departure, everyone was up before dawn. We women rode snow-white mules, with saddles studded with gold and silver. A slave would kneel and you stepped on his back to mount. Of course, we were all veiled in those days and wore our long robes. A slave walked by each of us holding a parasol over our heads and other slaves, on Arabian horses and armed with muskets inlaid with silver, rode on either side as a guard—just for show, of course. Everything was carried on the heads of slaves and we had a line of two or three hundred of them. There was an old slave who acted as major-domo and sometimes we girls would race each other on our donkeys and get ahead of the main party, which always made the old fellow furious with us.

"A party under another old slave had gone on to the country estate several days before, so when we arrived everything was ready for us. We amused ourselves walking under the big mango and fig trees—they've been cut down now to make room for the clove plantations—or playing with our pet animals or using the baths [a system of Turkish baths regarded as a necessity in all big Arab homes]. Mostly we just sat around and gossiped, exactly as we're doing now.

"Tippu Tib was always very courteous to the women but he didn't talk to us very much. In those days, when an Arab went to see a woman, it was for a purpose and there wasn't much conversation involved. He was always most correct in his behavior. He only had one wife, although our religion allows us four, and he made a point of spending the morning with her. The afternoon he spent with the favorite concubines. Then in the evening, he saw the other concubines too."

My wife, who was busily taking notes, asked, "Were those the only women he saw?"

The old lady looked at her in amazement. "Good heavens, for an elderly gentleman, wasn't that enough?

"When the English freed the slaves, there was a terrible period of disorder on the island," she went on. "The slaves were like children with no sense of responsibility. Bands of them wandered around the island, robbing and killing. Finally the English had to send troops here to control them. I remember how disgusted we were when we first saw the English women—utterly indecent and with no sense of hygiene. They went around with naked faces and carrying little dogs. As everyone knows, a dog is an unclean animal. They'd even kiss the creatures on the nose and you know into what sort of things a dog sticks his nose. Of course, we're used to them now.

"They threw us out of Africa and now the natives are going to throw them out, exactly as Tippu Tib said would happen."

After the old lady had left, our friends explained that she was living under very simple circumstances in a small apartment in the town, but even so she was far better off than most of the old Arab aristocracy who had been completely ruined when the slaves were emancipated. She had been shrewd enough to exchange most of her possessions for jewelry and was living on the proceeds from the sale of the ornaments.

Tippu Tib died in Zanzibar on June 13, 1905. All his heirs, both by his wife and his concubines, shared in the distribution of his estate according to Arab law, so his great fortune was quickly dissipated. His house is still standing in Zanzibar, although it has now been cut up into apartments.

It is said that on his deathbed, Tippu Tib became delirious and thought he was once again in the Congo, leading his wild hordes against the stockaded villages and shouting his war cry, "Allah conquers! Kill, kill, kill!" while his guns went "Tip-tip-tib." Thus died this great and terrible man, and modern East Africa began.

LIVINGSTONE'S
LAST JOURNEY

by D. C. Somervell

The most famous name in African exploration is that of a Glasgow missionary. As a boy, David Livingstone worked as a "piecer" in the cotton factory where his father also was employed. He began at six in the morning and continued until eight at night. Then he went to night school and studied until he fell asleep. In his "spare" time, he read everything he could find on science, travel and exploration, despite the remonstrances of his father who felt that such reading was ungodly. Later he took medical and missionary courses in Glasgow. He went to Africa purely as a missionary, with no thought of the passion for exploration which was later to possess him. His biographer, D. C. Somervell, states that during his lifetime he had "travelled

From *Livingstone* by D. C. Somervell. Reprinted by permission of Gerald Duckworth & Co., Ltd.

29,000 miles in Africa and added 1,000,000 square miles to the world maps. He had discovered six lakes—Mgami, Shirwa, Nyassa, Mweru and Benjwede; he had been the first European to traverse the whole length of another, Tanganyika; he had mapped innumerable mountains and rivers, including the biggest waterfall in the world"—*Victoria Falls*.

As an individual, Livingstone was shy and reserved. In dealing with Europeans he was ineffectual, but as a leader of Africans he was ideal—patient, cheerful and firm. Even those who know nothing of the man and what he did have heard of the famous meeting between Livingstone and Stanley, and the latter's greeting, "Dr. Livingstone, I presume?" an episode which is described in the narrative that follows. Two men more different in temperament and upbringing it would be hard to imagine. Stanley was a workhouse boy turned reporter. Brash and arrogant, he was more enamored of publicity than of accomplishment. He traveled in style, as opposed to Livingstone, who traveled light. It is perhaps a measure of Livingstone's greatness that he was able to inspire this self-centered individual with his own passion for knowledge, and Stanley was later to make important discoveries about the river systems of Africa.

The meeting between the two men took place late in Livingstone's career. His death and the incredible voyage which his native followers made with his body are here described.

LIVINGSTONE was off again on his travels. "Now that I am on the point of starting on another trip into Africa I feel quite exhilarated. Whether exchanging the customary civilities on arriving at a village, accepting a night's lodging, purchasing food for the party, asking for information, or answering polite African enquiries as to our objects in traveling, we begin to spread a knowledge of that people by whose agency their land will yet become enlightened and freed from the slave trade. . . . The mere animal pleasure of traveling in a wild unexplored country is very great. We have usually the stimulus of remote chances of danger either from beasts or men. . . . The effect of travel on a man whose heart is in the right place is that the mind is made more self-reliant: it becomes more confident of its own resources. . . . No doubt much toil is involved, and fatigue of which travellers in more temperate climes can form but a faint conception; but the sweat of one's brow is no longer a curse when one works for God: it proves a tonic to the system and is actually a blessing." Such were the reflections with which Livingstone set out on what was to prove a seven years' journey, ending only with his death.

He started up the Rovuma in April, 1866, and, traveling over the watershed above it, reached Lake Nyasa in August. The horrid relics of the slave traders—deserted villages, impaled corpses—were everywhere to be seen, and Livingstone's own party had begun to disintegrate. First the porters from the coast had gone, then the sepoys; the Nassickers and the Johanna men would soon follow them. The hostility of the Arabs cut off his communications with the coast, and prevented him from getting transport across the lake. Livingstone was naïvely surprised by their hostility. "All the Arabs flee from me, the English name in their minds being inseparably connected with recapturing slaves; they cannot conceive that I have any other object in view." So he had to march on foot round the southern end of the lake, whence he struck northwestward toward Tanganyika. The rains came on; heavy going through excessively adhesive mud; fever and dysentery. The entry "Too ill to march" begins to appear in the journal.

Early in January, 1867 one of his boys deserted with the medicine chest. "I felt," he writes, "as if I had received the sentence of death." And so he had, though his amazing constitution secured him a six years' reprieve. But he would not turn back. "It is not too much to say," writes Mr. Coupland, "that Livingstone's decision to go on into the unknown without his medicine chest proved, in the long run, suicidal."

The use of this last word suggests a surmise which cannot but occur to the reader's mind as he follows the records of the remaining years of Livingstone's life. Did he deliberately resolve to go on until he died? Did he, like Gordon in Khartoum a few years later, feel that he had done with England, and that, whatever the future might have in store for him, he would never go back there again? Did he, who so continuously reread his Bible from cover to cover, realize that his martyrdom in Africa might do more for the cause than any conceivable return to civilization?

After the loss of the medicine chest came famine, and, following thereon, rheumatic fever, for which he rested three days. When he started on again, "every step jars the chest, and I am very weak. . . . I have a constant singing in the ears, and can scarcely hear the loud tick of the chronometers." None the less, he reached the southern end of Tanganyika in April, 1867 (just a year after leaving the coast), and, though immobilized there for a month by fever and prostration, he was thrilled and delighted by the beauty of the lake.

On Tanganyika he fell in with Arab traders—slave traders, no doubt, when occasion served—and traveled with them southwestward to Lake Mweru, and then onward alone, with only four faithful porters, to Lake

Bangweolo. He had added two hitherto unknown lakes to European geography, and, though he knew it not, had hit upon the headwaters of the Congo. These lakes, and the mysterious river, the Lualaba, which ran north from them, were to fascinate Livingstone for the remainder of his days. He was determined that they should prove to be the sources of the Nile. It would be most disappointing if they proved to belong to the Congo, a river mouth of West Africa with associations both sordid and Portuguese. How much more glorious was the Nile—the Nile of Moses and Herodotus! He could never accept Speke's theory that the Nile rose in Lake Victoria. It must be further south than that. He must pick up the Lualaba north of Lake Mweru, and see what became of it. Possibly his discoveries might confirm in some important detail the truth of Holy Scripture and confound the infidel.

But first he must go to Ujiji. Ujiji was the principal town on the eastern shore of Lake Tanganyika, and here Livingstone had arranged for the establishment of an advanced base, whither stores, correspondence, etc., were to be forwarded by his agents in Zanzibar. The journeys to Mweru and Bangweolo and the delays which interrupted them had taken well over a year, and on his return to his Arab associates Livingstone had a severe attack of pneumonia. Doubtless he owed his recovery to the services of his hosts. It is a strange association, is it not—Livingstone the honored and grateful guest of Mohamad Bogharib, the notorious paladin of the slave trade? But what else was he to do? He had no trusty Makololo with him now, nor was he traveling, as in those happy old days, through country whose tribes could be relied on, after a little diplomatic management, to speed him on his way. West of Tanganyika he must travel with the Arabs or not at all. And as for Bogharib, what did he think about his guest? He has left no journals, and we do not know, but he probably regarded Livingstone as an entirely harmless old lunatic, whom one should befriend as one should befriend all who are in trouble—unless, of course, it is to one's own manifest disadvantage to do so.

Livingstone, traveling by litter and by canoe, under Arab escort, reached Ujiji in March, 1869, and was bitterly disappointed to find that of the expected stores, very little was to be found, and no letters, papers, or medicines. Either they had never been dispatched, or they had failed to accomplish the formidable eight-hundred-mile journey, or they had been stolen after arrival. It was really nothing to be surprised about. Zanzibar was the coastal base of the slave trade, Ujiji its advanced base upcountry. Livingstone was the declared enemy of that trade. With the best will in the world, African inefficiency was likely to have made a sad mess of any plans as ambitious as were involved in the creation of Livingstone's advanced base. And what ground had he for expecting any good will whatever?

Nonetheless, medicine or no medicine, the incredible man made a rapid recovery. He found "flannel to the skin and tea very beneficial . . . my cough has ceased, I can walk half a mile"; and, after four months at Ujiji, he was off again across the lake and northwestward to solve the problem of the Lualaba. He expected to be back in five months; actually he was away from Ujiji for more than two years.

It is a distressing record, this journey, of physical decline and adverse circumstance. The slave traders had arrived ahead of him, lured by the prospect of exceptionally cheap ivory. In two months he had reached Bambarré, about a hundred miles west of Tanganyika, but the Arab traders would not let him cross the Luamo, a tributary of the great river he was seeking. By New Year's Day, 1870, his prayer is "to finish the work in hand *and retire* before the year is out." But all the journal of 1870 is full of records of sickness—choleraic purging, hemorrhage, "sheer weakness"; though, even so, one encounters such typically indomitable entries as "rest, shelter, and boiling all the water I used, and above all the new species of potato called nyambo, much famed among the natives as restorative, have put me all to rights." In June his porters deserted in a body, and he set off in pursuit of the Lualaba with no more than three—Susi, Chumah, and one with the surprisingly un-African name of Gardner. And then his feet failed him. Foot sores, instead of healing as heretofore, developed into festering ulcers. He "limped back to Bambarré" and remained there eight months.

And yet it would be very wide of the mark to imagine Livingstone's spirit crushed by his misfortunes. Even at this time his journal, and the long letters he wrote with a view to "posting" in a somewhat problematical future, abound with lively comments on things far and near. He deals ironically with the panic occasioned by the Jamaica riots—he had, of course, got some European news at Ujiji—and returns again to a favorite subject—poor Bishop Tozer, "strutting about with his crozier at Zanzibar, and occasionally on a fine clear day getting a distant view of the continent in which he claimed to be bishop."

Early in 1871 ten porters arrived with a letter from Kirk, now Consul at Zanzibar. His ulcers had been healed by an Arab prescription, and he was off again. After a few weeks' journey he stood at last on the banks of the Lualaba at Nyangwe. And now, surely, the worst was passed. He would travel six days down the Lualaba in canoe, then up its western tributary the Lomane, a trifle of three or four hundred miles, to Katanga, where he had convinced himself, on the evidence of reports from Arabs, that he would find the sources of the Nile to be exactly as described by the priest of Sais to Herodotus—the two conical mountains, Crophi and Mophi, and all the rest of it.

But he could not get a canoe. He waited and waited, month after month, amusing himself with watching the native markets. The journals of these months are filled with vivid descriptions of these markets.

The market is a busy scene—everyone is in dead earnest. Each is intensely eager to barter food for relishes, and makes strong assertions as to the goodness or badness of everything: the sweat stands in beads on their faces: cocks crow briskly even when slung over the shoulder with their heads hanging down. . . . A stranger in the market had ten human under-jaw bones hung by a string over his shoulder: on enquiry, he professed to have killed and eaten the owners. . . . I see new faces in the market every day. Two nice girls were trying to sell their venture, which was roasted white ants, called Gumbé.

It is charming, and full of vitality. But it is a distraction from the main theme. Perhaps the iron resolve was faltering at last.

In July came a catastrophe which proved decisive. Livingstone had joined his puny forces with one Dugumbé, an Arab of the type of Bogharib, whom he had called, with a quaint note of apology, a "gentleman slaver," to distinguish this curious Good Samaritan from the viler of his species. Dugumbé, it was hoped, was such another "gentleman," and would launch him on the way to Katanga. Unhappily, Dugumbé's men became involved in a quarrel with the Lualaba natives, and there ensued a dreadful massacre in which several hundred natives were killed in the most revolting circumstances. There was reason to think that the outrage was a piece of calculated "frightfulness," intended to avenge some obscure feud or to strike terror into the population, which was about to be raided for slaves. After this, Livingstone had to part company with Dugumbé, and the only alternative was to return to Ujiji. He started in July, and, after being very nearly murdered by spearmen in the forest, reached his base in October. Once again the stores sent up from Zanzibar had disappeared on the route or after arrival. There was nothing left of them but a small quantity of barter goods, which he calculated would last him one month. His health on this return journey had been worse than ever. He was dead beat. Day after day he sat in his house at Ujiji with no prospect and no hope.

Then, at the end of a dreadful month, occurred the episode which is today, perhaps, the only universally familiar incident in Livingstone's career. The faithful Susi came rushing in to announce the arrival of "an Englishman!"

The American flag at the head of the caravan told of the nationality of the stranger. Bales of goods, baths of tin, huge kettles, cooking-pots, tents, etc., made me think, "This must be a luxurious traveller and not one at his wits' end like me." It was Henry Moreland Stanley,[1] the travelling correspondent of the *New York Herald*, sent by James Gordon Bennett, junior, at the expense of more than £4,000, to obtain accurate information about Dr. Livingstone if living, and if dead to bring home my bones. . . . I really do feel extremely grateful.

Stanley's account must also be given.

As I advanced slowly towards him, I noticed he was pale, looked wearied, had a gray beard, wore a bluish cap with a faded gold band round it, had on a red-sleeved waistcoat and a pair of gray tweed trousers. I would have run to him, only I was a coward in the presence of such a mob—would have embraced him, only, he being an Englishman, I did not know how he would receive me. So I did what cowardice and false pride suggested was the best thing—walked deliberately up to him, took off my hat and said, "Dr. Livingstone, I presume?" "Yes," said he with a kind smile, lifting his cap slightly. I replace my hat on my head, and he puts on his cap, and we both grasp hands, and I then say aloud—"I thank God, Doctor, I have been permitted to see you." He answered, "I feel thankful that I am here to welcome you."

When Livingstone had gone up the Rovuma four and a half years before, he had disappeared from the ken of the civilized world. The first news of him to be received was, indeed, a circumstantial account of his death at the hands of slave-raiding Africans in the country beyond Lake Nyasa. It came from the Johanna men, who realized that if they returned to the coast with an admission that they had deserted their leader, they would not only not receive their arrears of pay, but would probably be punished. So they concocted a spirited tale of encounter and massacre, "and we alone have escaped to tell you." It was somewhat odd that all the Johanna men should have escaped, and no one else; nonetheless, the tale was ingeniously constructed, and its sponsors lied with a consistency and unanimity which would have done credit to scoundrels of a more advanced civilization. The authorities were reluctantly convinced, all except a Mr. E. D. Young,

---

[1] Livingstone mistook his second name, which was Morton.

who had been with Livingstone for a short time on the Zambezi, and now offered to go out and disprove the Johanna story. Funds were forthcoming, and the Young expedition, though it did not attempt to find Livingstone alive, proved that he had been alive and active long after the date of his alleged murder. It is some satisfaction to know that the leader of the Johanna men was incarcerated for eight months in an exceedingly insanitary gaol. . . .

In a Life of Livingstone, the Stanley episode was but a gleam of twilight sunshine before the oncoming dark. Under the stimulus of Stanley's companionship and the comforts Stanley could supply, the old man's vitality once more amazingly reasserted itself. "He is about sixty years old," wrote Stanley,

> though after he was restored to health he looked like a man who had not passed his fiftieth year. His hair has a brownish colour yet, but is here and there streaked with gray lines over the temples; his whiskers and moustache are very gray. He shaves his chin daily. His eyes, which are hazel, are remarkably bright; he has a sight as keen as a hawk. His teeth alone indicate the weakness of age; the hard fare has made havoc of their lines. When walking he takes a firm but heavy tread, like that of an overworked or fatigued man. . . . There is a good-natured *abandon* about him. Whenever he began to laugh, there was a contagion about it that compelled me to imitate him. It was a laugh such as Herr Teufelsdröckh's—a laugh of the whole man from head to heel. If he told a story his face was lit up by the sly fun it contained.

Together they explored by boat the northern shores of Lake Tanganyika to see if its waters ran out toward the north or perhaps the Lualaba, but there was no outlet at all; this lake had to be definitely written off the list of possible Nile sources.

But Stanley was not to be allowed to take his trophy home. Health was restored, and what should prevent Livingstone continuing and completing his program?

One year of life remained for him. Five months of it was spent waiting at Unyanyembe for porters with stores which were to be sent up by Stanley from the coast. He could still enjoy himself watching the birds. "A family of ten whydah birds come to the pomegranate trees in our yard. The eight young ones are fed by the dam as young pigeons are. The food is brought up from the crop without the bowing and bending of the pigeon. They chirrup briskly for food. The dam gives most, while the red-breasted cock gives one or two, and then knocks the rest away." A month later: "Whydahs, though full fledged, still gladly take a feed from their dam, putting down the breast to the ground, cocking up the bill, and chirruping in the most engaging way they know. She gives them a little, but administers a friendly shove too."

Then the porters arrived, and, with blessings on Stanley's head, he set off once more with fifty-six men, round the southern end of Tanganyika to Bangweolo. Thence he would go west to Katanga, find the Herodotean source with its famous conical hills, down the Lomane to its join with the Lualaba, and so back to Ujiji and home. But it could not be. Increasing weakness and internal hemorrhage immobilized him at Chitamba's village of Ilala, near Bangweolo, in April, and there he died early in May. Susi, Chumah, and four others came to the tent door. The Doctor was kneeling by his bed, his face buried in his hands on the pillow—dead.

Susi and Chumah had been faithful to the end, and now they felt a call to a duty which demanded not only faithful service, but initiative and leadership. They would carry their master's body to the coast, and hand it over to his own people, and they prevailed upon the company of porters recently supplied by Stanley to undertake the duty with them. Their proceedings were, from first to last, marked by an astonishing resolution and efficiency. Mere Africans though they were, the spirit of their dead master descended upon them. They embalmed the body, buried the heart at Ilala, made an inventory of all Livingstone's property which they carried with them and set off upon a journey of some fifteen hundred miles. At Unyanyembe they met yet another English expedition in search of Livingstone, and its leader wanted to bury the body at that place, but Susi and Chumah would have none of it. It was not for the faithful disciples of David Livingstone to take orders or accept advice from Lieutenant Cameron, Lieutenant Murphy, and Dr. Dillon. They resumed their journey, and reached the coast at Bagamoio, opposite Zanzibar, in February, 1874. Two months later the body was buried in Westminster Abbey, the leading pallbearers being an African boy and H. M. Stanley.

Livingstone had suffered much at the hands of the African peoples, to whose welfare he had devoted his life. It would be possible to collect, from his books and journals, a truly formidable array of what might be regarded as absolutely damning evidence against the African character, and in favor of the arguments of those who hold that the African is fit for nothing better than either the savagery that must be his lot in isolation, or a life of brutish labor in the service of his betters, which differs from slavery in little but the name. Such evidence was never regarded as damning by the man who so candidly compiled it. Livingstone never stooped to whitewash the black man, but he never lost his faith in him. If nothing else had ever occurred to justify his faith, Susi and Chumah would do so. The disciples of Jesus forsook Him and fled, and did not recover their constancy until they had seen a Risen Lord. It was only a dead body which Susi and Chumah and their fellows carried to the coast.

THE COURT OF THE
KING OF UGANDA

by John Hanning Speke

In the previous selection we traced the last expedition of the great missionary Livingstone. At about that same time and farther north, another famous African traveler, Richard Burton, had made the dangerous journey across Somaliland to the unknown city of Harar. On his next and even more important expedition, he was joined by John H. Speke. Together they traveled inland from the Zanzibar coast. Seven and a half months later, after a rugged march, they reached Lake Tanganyika. And six months later, after the two had quarreled bitterly and separated, Speke discovered the greatest of the three great Central African lakes—Victoria Nyanza—which he concluded was the long-looked-for source of the Nile.

Before he reached that great body of water, he was subjected to a bizarre experience. In the savage court of the King of Uganda, a capricious and absolute monarch who had never before seen a white man, he was first treated with suspicion, then accepted as a friend, and finally and grudgingly sent on his way. Who knows how often his savage host may have considered his destruction; but Speke lived to tell the tale of one of the most extraordinary courts that ever existed.

7TH—Our spirits were now further raised by the arrival of a semi-Hindu-Swahili, named Juma, who had just returned from a visit to the King of Uganda, bringing back with him a large present of ivory and

From *Journal of the Discovery of the Source of the Nile.*

slaves; for he said he had heard from the king of our intention to visit him, and that he had despatched officers to call us immediately. This intelligence delighted Rumanika as much as it did us, and he no sooner heard it than he said, with ecstasies, "I will open Africa, since the white men desire it; for did not Dagara command us to show deference to strangers?" Then, turning to me, he added, "My only regret is, you will not take something as a return for the great expenses you have been put to in coming to visit me." The expense was admitted, for I had now been obliged to purchase from the Arabs upward of four hundred pounds worth of beads, to keep such a store in reserve for my return from Uganda as would enable me to push on to Gondokoro. . . .

8th to 10th—At last we heard the familiar sound of the Uganda drum. Maula, a royal officer, with a large escort of smartly dressed men, women and boys, leading their dogs and playing their reeds, announced to our straining ears the welcome intelligence that their king had sent them to call us. N'yamgundu, who had seen us in Usui, had marched on to inform the king of our advance and desire to see him; and he, intensely delighted at the prospect of having white men for his guests, desired no time should be lost in our coming on. Maula told us that his officers had orders to supply us with everything we wanted whilst passing through his country, and that there would be nothing to pay.

One thing only now embarrassed me—Grant[1] was worse, without hope of recovery for at least one or two months. This large body of Waganda could not be kept waiting. To get on as fast as possible was the only chance of ever bringing the journey to a successful issue; so, unable to help myself, with great remorse at another separation, on the following day I consigned my companion, with several Wanguana, to the care of my friend Rumanika. . . .

This business concluded in camp, I started my men and went to the palace to bid adieu to Rumanika, who appointed Rozaro, one of his officers, to accompany me wherever I went in Uganda, and to bring me back safely again. At Rumanika's request I then gave Mtesa's pages some ammunition to hurry on with to the great King of Uganda, as his majesty had ordered them to bring him, as quickly as possible, some strengthening powder, and also some powder for his gun. Then, finally, to Maula, also under Rumanika's instructions, I gave two copper wires and five bundles of beads; and when all was completed, set out on the march, perfectly sure in my mind that before very long I should settle

[1] Speke's companion on the expedition.—Eds.

the great Nile problem forever; and, with this consciousness, only hoping that Grant would be able to join me before I should have to return again, for it was never supposed for a moment that it was possible I ever could go north from Uganda. Rumanika was the most resolute in this belief, as the kings of Uganda, ever since that country was detached from Unyoro, had been making constant raids, seizing cattle and slaves from the surrounding countries.

[14 Feb., 1862] Here I was also brought to a standstill, for N'yamgundu said I must wait for leave to approach the palace. He wished to have a look at the presents I had brought for Mtesa. I declined to gratify it, taking my stand on my dignity; there was no occasion for any distrust on such a trifling matter as that, for I was not a merchant who sought for gain, but had come at great expense, to see the king of this region. I begged, however, he would go as fast as possible to announce my arrival, explain my motive for coming here, and ask for an early interview, as I had left my brother Grant behind at Karague, and found my position, for want of a friend to talk to, almost intolerable. It was not the custom of my country for great men to consort with servants, and until I saw him, and made friends, I should not be happy. I had a great deal to tell him about as he was the father of the Nile, which river drained the N'yanza down to my country to the northward. With this message N'yamgundu hurried off as fast as possible.

[16 Feb.] I then very much wished to go and see the escape of the Mwerango River, as I still felt a little skeptical as to its origin, whether or not it came off those smaller lakes I had seen on the road the day before I crossed the river; but no one would listen to my project. They all said I must have the King's sanction first, else people, from not knowing my object, would accuse me of practicing witchcraft and would tell their King so. They still all maintained that the river did come out of the lake, and said, if I liked to ask the King's leave to visit the spot, then they would go and show it me. I gave way, thinking it prudent to do so, but resolved in my mind I would get Grant to see it in boats on his voyage from Karague. There were no guinea fowls to be found here, nor a fowl, in any of the huts, so I requested Rozaro to hurry off to Mtesa, and ask him to send me something to eat. He simply laughed at my request, and said I did not know what I was doing. It would be as much as my life was worth to go one yard in advance of this until the King's leave was obtained. I said, rather than be starved to death in this ignominious manner, I would return to Karague; to which he replied, laughing, "Whose leave have you got to do that? Do you suppose you can do as you like in this country?"

[17 Feb.] Next day, in the evening, N'yamgundu returned full of smirks and smiles, dropped on his knees at my feet and, in company with his "children," set to n'yanzigging (a form of giving thanks to great men). In his excitement he was hardly able to say all he had to communicate. Bit by bit, however, I learned that he first went to the palace, and, finding the King had gone off yachting to the Murchison Creek, he followed him there. The King for a long while would not believe his tale that I had come, but being assured he danced with delight, swore he would not taste food until he had seen me. "Oh," he said, over and over again and again, according to my informer, "can this be true? Can the white man have come all this way to see me? What a strong man he must be too, to come so quickly! Here are seven cows, four of them milch ones, as you say he likes milk, which you will give him; and there are three for yourself for having brought him so quickly. Now hurry off as fast as you can, and tell him I am more delighted at the prospect of seeing him than he can be to see me. There is no place here fit for his reception. I was on a pilgrimage which would have kept me here seven days longer; but as I am so impatient to see him, I will go off to my palace at once, and will send word for him to advance as soon as I arrive there."

[18 Feb.] About noon the succeeding day, some pages ran in to say we were to come along without a moment's delay, as their king had ordered it. He would not taste food until he saw me, so that everybody might know what great respect he felt for me. In the meanwhile, however, he wished for some gunpowder. I packed the pages off as fast as I could with some, and then tried myself to follow, but my men were all either sick or out foraging, and therefore we could not get under way until the evening. . . .

[19 Feb.] One march more and we came in sight of the King's kibuga or palace, in the province of Bandawarogo, N. lat. 0° 21′ 19″, and E. long. 32° 44′ 30″. It was a magnificent sight. A whole hill was covered with gigantic huts, such as I had never seen in Africa before. I wished to go up to the palace at once, but the officers said, "No, that would be considered indecent in Uganda; you must draw up your men, and fire your guns off, to let the King know you are here; we will then show you your residence, and tomorrow you will doubtless be sent for, as the King could not now hold a levee whilst it is raining." I made the men fire, and then was shown into a lot of dirty huts, which they said were built expressly for all the King's visitors. The Arabs, when they came on their visits always put up here, and I must do the same. At first I stuck out on my claims as a foreign prince, whose royal blood could not stand such an indignity. The palace was my sphere, and unless I could get a hut there, I would return without seeing the King.

In a terrible fright at my blustering, N'yamgundu fell at my feet, and implored me not to be hasty. The King did not understand who I was, and could not be spoken to then. He implored me to be content with my lot for the present, after which the King, when he knew all about it, would do as I liked, he was sure, though no strangers had ever yet been allowed to reside within the royal enclosures. I gave way to this good man's appeal, and cleaned my hut by firing the ground, for, like all the huts, in this dog country, it was full of fleas. Once ensconced there, the King's pages darted in to see me, bearing a message from their master, who said he was sorry the rain prevented him from holding a levee that day, but the next he would be delighted to see me. Irungu, with all Suwarora's men, then came to a collection of huts near where I was residing, and whilst I lay in bed that night, Irungu with all his wives came in to see me and beg for beads.

[19 Feb.] Today the King sent his pages to announce his intention of holding a levee in my honor. I prepared for my first presentation at court, attired in my best, though in it I cut a poor figure in comparison with the display of the dressy Waganda. They wore neat bark cloaks resembling the best yellow corduroy cloth, crimp and well set, as if stiffened with starch, and over that, as upper cloaks, a patchwork of small antelope skins, which I observed were sewn together as well as any English glovers could have pieced them; whilst their headdresses, generally, were abrus turbans, set off with highly polished boar tusks, stick charms, seeds, beads, or shells; and on their necks, arms and ankles they wore other charms of wood, or small horns stuffed with magic powder, and fastened on by strings generally covered with snakeskin. N'yamgundu and Maula demanded, as their official privilege, a first peep; and this being refused, they tried to persuade me that the articles comprising the present required to be covered with chintz, for it was considered indecorous to offer anything to his majesty in a naked state. This little interruption over, the articles enumerated below[2] were conveyed to the palace in solemn procession thus: With

[2] 1 black tin box, 4 rich silk cloths, 1 rifle (Whitworth's), 1 gold chronometer, 1 revolver pistol, 3 rifled carbines, 3 sword bayonets, 1 box ammunition, 1 box bullets, 1 box gun-caps, 1 telescope, 1 iron chair, 10 bundles best beads, 1 set of table-knives, spoons, and forks. (*Speke's note.*)

N'yamgundu, Maula, the pages, and myself on the flanks, the Union Jack carried by the kirangozi guide led the way followed by twelve men as a guard of honor, dressed in red flannel cloaks, and carrying their arms sloped, with fixed bayonets; whilst in their rear were the rest of my men, each carrying some article as a present.

On the march toward the palace, the admiring courtiers, wonderstruck at such an unusual display, exclaimed in raptures of astonishment, some with both hands at their mouths, and others clasping their heads with their hands "*Irungi! irungi!*" which may be translated "Beautiful! beautiful!" I thought myself everything was going on as well as could be wished; but before entering the royal enclosures, I found, to my disagreeable surprise, that the men with Suwarora's hongo or offering, which consisted of more than a hundred coils of wire, were ordered to lead the procession, and take precedence of me. There was something specially aggravating in this precedence; for these very brass wires which they saw, I had myself intended for Mtesa, that they were taken from me by Suwarora as far back as Usui, and it would never do, without remonstrance, to have them boastfully paraded before my eyes in this fashion. My protests, however, had no effect upon the escorting Wakungu[3]. Resolving to make them catch it, I walked along as if ruminating in anger up the broad highroad into a cleared square, which divides Mtesa's domain on the south from his Kamraviona's or commander-in-chief on the north, and then turned into the court. The palace or entrance quite surprised me by its extraordinary dimensions and the neatness with which it was kept. The whole brow and sides of the hill on which we stood were covered with gigantic grass huts, thatched as neatly as so many heads dressed by a London barber, and fenced all round with the tall yellow reeds of the common Uganda tiger grass; whilst within the enclosure, the lines of huts were joined together, or partitioned off into courts, with walls of the same grass. It is here most of Mtesa's three or four hundred women are kept, the rest being quartered chiefly with his mother, known by the title of N'yamasore, or Queen Dowager. They stood in little groups at the doors, looking at us, and evidently passing their own remarks, and enjoying their own jokes, on the triumphal procession. At each gate as we passed, officers on duty opened and shut it for us, jingling the big bells which are hung upon them, as they sometimes are at shop doors to prevent a silent stealthy entrance.

The first court passed, I was even more surprised to find the unusual ceremonies that awaited me. There courtiers of high dignity stepped for-

[3] Nobles.—Eds.

ward to greet me, dressed in the most scrupulously neat fashions. Men, women, bulls, dogs, and goats, were led about by strings; cocks and hens were carried in men's arms; and little pages, with rope turbans, rushed about, conveying messages, as if their lives depended on their swiftness, everyone holding his skin cloak tightly round him lest his naked legs might by accident be shown.

This, then, was the antereception court; and I might have taken possession of the hut, in which musicians were playing and singing on large nine-stringed harps, like the Nubian tambira, accompanied by harmonicons. By the chief officers-in-waiting, however, who thought fit to treat us like Arab merchants, I was requested to sit on the ground outside in the sun with my servants. Now, I had made up my mind never to sit upon the ground as the natives and Arabs are obliged to do, nor to make my obeisance in any other manner than is customary in England, though the Arabs had told me that from fear they had always complied with the manners of the court. I felt that if I did not stand up for my social position at once, I should be treated with contempt during the remainder of my visit, and thus lose the vantage ground I had assumed of appearing rather as a prince than a trader, for the purpose of better gaining the confidence of the king. To avert overhastiness, however—for my servants began to be alarmed as I demurred against doing as I was bid—I allowed five minutes to the court to give me a proper reception, saying, if it were not conceded I would then walk away.

Nothing, however, was done. My own men, knowing me, feared for me, as they did not know what a "savage" king would do in case I carried out my threat; whilst the Waganda, lost in amazement at what seemed little less than blasphemy, stood still as posts. The affair ended by my walking straight away home, giving Bombay orders to leave the present on the ground and to follow me.

Although the King is said to be unapproachable, excepting when he chooses to attend court—a ceremony which rarely happens—intelligence of my hot wrath and hasty departure reached him in an instant. He first, it seems, thought of leaving his toilet room to follow me, but, finding I was walking fast and had gone far, changed his mind, and sent Wakungu running after me. Poor creatures! they caught me up, fell upon their knees, and implored I would return at once, for the King had not tasted food, and would not until he saw me. I felt grieved at their touching appeals; but, as I did not understand all they said, I simply replied by patting my heart and shaking my head, walking if anything all the faster.

On my arrival at my hut, Bombay and others came in, wet through with perspiration, saying the King had heard of all my grievances. Suwarora's hongo was turned out of court, and, if I desired it, I might bring my own chair with me, for he was very anxious to show me great respect—although such a seat was exclusively the attribute of the King, no one else in Uganda daring to sit on an artificial seat.

My point was gained, so I cooled myself with coffee and a pipe, and returned rejoicing in my victory, especially over Suwarora. After returning to the second tier of huts from which I had retired, everybody appeared to be in a hurried, confused state of excitement, not knowing what to make out of so unprecedented an exhibition of temper. In the most polite manner, the officers-in-waiting begged me to be seated on my iron stool, which I had brought with me, whilst others hurried in to announce my arrival. But for a few minutes only I was kept in suspense, when a band of music, the musicians wearing on their backs long-haired goatskins, passed me, dancing as they went along, like bears in a fair, and playing on reed instruments worked over with pretty beads in various patterns, from which depended leopard-cat skins—the time being regulated by the beating of long hand drums.

The mighty King was now reported to be sitting on his throne in the state hut of the third tier. I advanced, hat in hand, with my guard of honor following, formed in "open ranks," who in their turn were followed by the bearers carrying the present. I did not walk straight up to him as if to shake hands, but went outside the ranks of a three-sided square of squatting Wakungu, all habited in skins, mostly cowskins; some few of whom had, in addition, leopard-cat skins girt round the waist, the sign of royal blood. Here I was desired to halt and sit in the glaring sun; so I donned my hat, mounted my umbrella, a phenomenon which set them all a-wondering and laughing, ordered the guard to close ranks, and sat gazing at the novel spectacle. A more theatrical sight I never saw. The King, a good-looking, well-figured, tall young man of twenty-five, was sitting on a red blanket spread upon a square platform of royal grass, encased in tiger-grass reeds, scrupulously well dressed in a new mbugu[4]. The hair of his head was cut short, excepting on the top, where it was combed up into a high ridge, running from stem to stern like a cockscomb. On his neck was a very neat ornament—a large ring, of beautifully worked small beads, forming elegant patterns by their various colors. On one arm was another bead ornament, prettily devised; and on the other a wooden charm, tied by

[4] Bark cloth.—Eds.

a string covered with snakeskin. On every finger and every toe he had alternate brass and copper rings; and above the ankles, halfway up to the calf, a stocking of very pretty beads. Everything was light, neat and elegant in its way; not a fault could be found with the taste of his "getting up." For a handkerchief he held a well-folded piece of bark, and a piece of gold-embroidered silk, which he constantly employed to hide his large mouth when laughing, or to wipe it after a drink of plantain wine, of which he took constant and copious drafts from neat little gourdcups, administered by his ladies-in-waiting, who were at once his sisters and wives. A white dog, spear, shield and woman—the Uganda cognizance—were by his side, as also a knot of staff officers, with whom he kept up a brisk conversation on one side; and on the other was a band of Wichwezi, or lady sorcerers.

I was now asked to draw nearer within the hollow square of squatters, where leopard skins were strewed upon the ground, and a large copper kettledrum, surmounted with brass bells on arching wires, along with two other smaller drums covered with cowrie shells, and beads of color worked into patterns, were placed. I now longed to open conversation, but knew not the language, and no one near me dared speak, or even lift his head from fear of being accused of eying the women; so the King and myself sat staring at one another for full an hour—I mute, but he pointing and remarking with those around him on the novelty of my guard and general appearance, and even requiring to see my hat lifted, the umbrellas shut and opened, and the guards face about and show off their red cloaks—for such wonders had never been seen in Uganda.

Then, finding the day waning, he sent Maula on an embassy to ask me if I had seen him; and on receiving my reply, "Yes, for full one hour," I was glad to find him rise, spear in hand, lead his dog, and walk unceremoniously away through the enclosure into the fourth tier of huts; for this being a pure levee day, no business was transacted.

The King's gait in retiring was intended to be very majestic, but did not succeed in conveying to me that impression. It was the traditional walk of his race, founded on the step of the lion; but the outward sweep of the legs, intended to represent the stride of the noble beast, appeared to me only to realize a very ludicrous kind of waddle, which made me ask Bombay if anything serious was the matter with the royal person.

I had now to wait for some time, almost as an act of humanity; for I was told the state secret, that the King had retired to break his fast and eat for the first time since hearing of my arrival; but the repast was no sooner over than he prepared for the second act, to show off his splendor, and I was invited in, with all my men, to the exclusion of all his own officers save my two guides. Entering as before, I found him standing on a red blanket, leaning against the right portal of the hut, talking and laughing, handkerchief in hand, to a hundred or more of his admiring wives, who, all squatting on the ground outside, in two groups, were dressed in new mbugus. My men dared not advance upright, nor look upon the women, but, stooping, with lowered heads and averted eyes, came cringing after me. Unconscious myself, I gave loud and impatient orders to my guard, rebuking them for moving like frightened geese, and, with hat in hand, stood gazing on the fair sex till directed to sit and cap.

Mtesa then inquired what messages were brought from Rumanika; to which Maula, delighted with the favor of speaking to royalty, replied by saying, Rumanika had gained intelligence of Englishmen coming up the Nile to Gani and Kidi. The King acknowledged the truthfulness of their story, saying he had heard the same himself; and both Wakungu, as is the custom in Uganda, thanked their lord in a very enthusiastic manner, kneeling on the ground—for no one can stand in the presence of his majesty—in an attitude of prayer, and throwing out their hands as they repeated the words, *"N'yanzig, N'yanzig, ai N'yanzig Mkahma wangi,"* etc., etc., for a considerable time; when thinking they had done enough of this, and heated with the exertion, they threw themselves flat upon their stomachs, and, floundering about like fish on land, repeated the same words over and over again, and rose doing the same, with their faces covered with earth; for majesty in Uganda is never satisfied till subjects have groveled before it like the most abject worms. This conversation over, after gazing at me, and chatting with his women for a considerable time, the second scene ended. The third scene was more easily arranged, for the day was fast declining. He simply moved with his train of women to another hut, where, after seating himself upon his throne, with his women around him, he invited me to approach the nearest limits of propriety, and to sit as before. Again he asked me if I had seen him—evidently desirous of indulging in his regal pride; so I made the most of the opportunity thus afforded me of opening a conversation by telling him of those grand reports I had formerly heard about him, which induced me to come all this way to see him, and the trouble it had cost me to reach the object of my desire; at the same time taking a gold ring from off my finger, and presenting it to him, I said, "This is a small token of friendship; if you will inspect it, it is made after the fashion of a dog collar, and being the king of metals, gold, is in every respect appropriate to your illustrious race."

He said, in return, "If friendship is your desire, what would you say if I showed you a road by which you might reach your home in one month?" Now everything had to be told to Bombay, then to Nasib, my Kiganda interpreter, and then to either Maula, or N'yamgundu, before it was delivered to the King for it was considered indecorous to transmit any message to his majesty excepting through the medium of one of his officers. Hence I could not get an answer put in; for as all Waganda are rapid and impetuous in their conversation, the King probably forgetting he had put a question, hastily changed the conversation and said "What guns have you got? Let me see the one you shoot with." I wished still to answer the first question first, as I knew he referred to the direct line to Zanzibar across the Masai and was anxious without delay to open the subject of Petherick and Grant; but no one dared to deliver my statement. Much disappointed, I then said, "I had brought the best shooting gun in the world —Whitworth's rifle—which I begged he would accept, with a few other trifles; and, with his permission, I would lay them upon a carpet at his feet, as is the custom of my country when visiting sultans." He assented, sent all his women away, and had an mbugu spread for the purpose, on which Bombay, obeying my order, first spread a red blanket and then opened each article one after the other, when Nasib, according to the usage already mentioned, smoothed them down with his dirty hands, or rubbed them against his sooty face, and handed them to the King to show there was no poison or witchcraft in them. Mtesa appeared quite confused with the various wonders as he handled them, made silly remarks, and pondered over them like a perfect child, until it was quite dark. Torches were then lit, and guns, pistols, powder, boxes, tools, beads—the whole collection, in short—were tossed together topsy-turvy, bundled into mbugus, and carried away by the pages. Mtesa now said, "It is late, and time to break up; what provision would you wish to have?" I said, "A little of everything, but no one thing constantly." "And would you like to see me tomorrow?" "Yes, every day." "Then you can't tomorrow for I have business; but the next day come if you like. You can now go away, and here are six pots of plantain wine for you; my men will search for food tomorrow."

[21 Feb.] In the morning, whilst it rained, some pages drove in twenty cows and ten goats, with a polite metaphorical message from their King, to the effect that I had pleased him much, and he hoped I would accept these few "chickens" until he could send more—when both Maula and N'yamgundu, charmed with their success in having brought a welcome guest to Uganda, never ceased showering eulogiums on me for my fortune in having gained the countenance of their King. The rain falling was considered at court a good omen, and everybody declared the king mad with delight. Wishing to have a talk with him about Petherick and Grant, I at once started off the Wakungu to thank him for the present, and to beg pardon for my apparent rudeness of yesterday, at the same time requesting I might have an early interview with his majesty, as I had much of importance to communicate; but the solemn court formalities which these African kings affect as much as Oriental emperors, precluded my message from reaching the King. I heard, however, that he had spent the day receiving Suwarora's hongo of wire, and that the officer who brought them was made to sit in an empty court, whilst the King sat behind a screen, never deigning to show his majestic person. I was told, too, that he opened conversation by demanding to know how it happened that Suwarora became possessed of the wires, for they were made by the white men to be given to himself, and Suwarora must therefore have robbed me of them; and it was by such practices he, Mtesa, never could see any visitors. The officer's reply was, Suwarora would not show the white men any respect, because they were wizards who did not sleep in houses at night, but flew up to the tops of hills, and practiced sorcery of every abominable kind. The King to this retorted, in a truly African fashion, "That's a lie; I can see no harm in this white man; and if he had been a bad man, Rumanika would not have sent him on to me." At night, when in bed, the King sent his pages to say, if I desired his friendship I would lend him one musket to make up six with what I had given him, for he intended visiting his relations the following morning. I sent three, feeling that nothing would be lost by being "open-handed."

[22 Feb.] Today the King went the round of his relations, showing the beautiful things given him by the white man—a clear proof that he was much favored by the "spirits," for neither his father nor any of his forefathers had been so recognized and distinguished by any "sign" as a rightful inheritor to the Uganda throne: an anti-Christian interpretation of omens, as rife in these dark regions now as it was in the time of King Nebuchadnezzar. At midnight the three muskets were returned, and I was so pleased with the young King's promptitude and honesty, I begged he would accept them.

[23 Feb.] At noon Mtesa sent his pages to invite me to his palace. I went, with my guard of honor and my stool, but found I had to sit waiting in an antehut three hours with his commander-in-chief and other high officers before he was ready to see me. During this time Wasoga minstrels, playing on tambira, and accompanied by boys playing on a harmonicon, kept us amused; and a small page, with a large bundle of grass, came to me and said, "The King hopes you won't be offended if required to sit on it before him; for no person in Uganda, however high in office, is ever allowed to sit upon anything raised above the ground, nor can anybody but himself sit upon such grass as this; it is all that his throne is made of. The first day he only allowed you to sit on your stool to appease your wrath."

On consenting to do in "Rome as the Romans do," when my position was so handsomely acknowledged, I was called in, and found the court sitting much as it was on the first day's interview, only that the number of squatting Wakungu was much diminished; and the King, instead of wearing his ten brass and copper rings, had my gold one on his third finger. This day, however, was cut out for business, as, in addition to the assemblage of officers, there were women, cows, goats, fowls, confiscations, baskets of fish, baskets of small antelopes, porcupines, and curious rats caught by his gamekeepers, bundles of mbugu, etc., etc., made by his linen drapers, colored earths and sticks by his magician, all ready for presentation; but, as rain fell, the court broke up, and I had nothing for it but to walk about under my umbrella, indulging in angry reflections against the haughty King for not inviting me into his hut.

When the rain had ceased, and we were again called in, he was found sitting in state as before, but this time with the head of a black bull placed before him, one horn of which, knocked off, was placed alongside, whilst four living cows walked about the court.

I was now requested to shoot the four cows as quickly as possible; but having no bullets for my gun, I borrowed the revolving pistol I had given him, and shot all four in a second of time; but as the last one, only wounded, turned sharply upon me, I gave him the fifth and settled him. Great applause followed this *wonderful* feat, and the cows were given to my men. The King now loaded one of the carbines I had given him with his own hands, and giving it full-cock to a page, told him to go out and shoot a man in the outer court; which was no sooner accomplished than the little urchin returned to announce his success, with a look of glee such as one would see in the face of a boy who had robbed a bird's nest, caught a trout, or done any other boyish trick. The King said to him, "And did you do it well?" "Oh yes, capitally." He spoke the truth, no doubt, for he dared not have trifled with the King; but the affair created hardly any interest. I never heard, and there appeared no curiosity to know, what individual human being the urchin had deprived of life.

[27 Feb.] To call upon the Queen Mother respectfully, as it was the opening visit, I took, besides the medicine chest, a present of eight brass and copper wire, thirty blue-egg beads, one bundle of diminutive beads, and sixteen cubits of chintz, a small guard, and my throne of royal grass. The palace to be visited lay half a mile beyond the King's, but the high road to it was forbidden me, as it is considered uncourteous to pass the King's gate without going in. So after winding through back gardens, the slums of Bandowaroga, I struck upon the highroad close to her majesty's, where everything looked like the royal palace on a miniature scale. A large cleared space divided the Queen's residence from her Kamraviona's. The outer enclosures and courts were fenced with tiger grass; and the huts, though neither so numerous nor so large, were constructed after the same fashion as the King's. Guards also kept the doors, on which large bells were hung to give alarm, and officers-in-waiting watched the throne rooms. All the huts were full of women, save those kept as waiting rooms, where drums and harmonicons were placed for amusement. On first entering, I was required to sit in a waiting hut till my arrival was announced; but that did not take long, as the Queen was prepared to receive me; and being of a more affable disposition than her son, she held rather a levee of amusement than a stiff court of show. I entered the throne hut as the gate of that court was thrown open, with my hat off, but umbrella held over my head, and walked straight toward her till ordered to sit upon my bundle of grass.

Her majesty—fat, fair, and forty-five—was sitting, plainly garbed in mbugu, upon a carpet spread upon the ground within a curtain of mbugu, her elbow resting on a pillow of the same bark material; the only ornaments on her person being an abrus necklace, and a piece of mbugu tied round her head, whilst a folding looking glass, much the worse for wear, stood open by her side. An iron rod like a spit, with a cup on the top, charged with magic powder, and other magic wands, were placed before the entrance; and within the room, four Mabandwa sorceresses or devil drivers, fantastically dressed, as before described, and a mass of other women, formed the company. For a short while we sat at a distance exchanging inquiring glances at one another, when the women were dismissed, and a band of music, with a court full of Wakungu, was ordered in to change the scene. I also got orders to draw near and sit fronting her within the hut. Pombe, the best in Uganda, was then drunk by the Queen, and handed to me and to all the high officers about her, when she smoked her pipe, and bade me smoke mine. The musicians, dressed in long-haired Usoga goatskins, were now ordered to strike up, which they did, with their bodies swaying or dancing like bears in a fair. Different drums were then beat, and I was asked if I could distinguish their different tones.

The Queen, full of mirth, now suddenly rose, leaving me sitting, whilst she went to another hut, changed her mbugu for a deole, and came back again for us to admire her, which was no sooner done to her heart's content, than a second time, by her order, the court was cleared, and, when only three or four confidential Wakungu were left, she took up a small faggot of well-trimmed sticks, and, selecting three, told me she had three complaints. "This stick," she says, "represents my stomach, which gives me much uneasiness; this second stick my liver, which causes shooting pains all over my body; and this third one my heart, for I get constant dreams at night about Sunna, my late husband, and they are not pleasant." The dreams and sleeplessness I told her was a common widow's complaint, and could only be cured by her majesty making up her mind to marry a second time; but before I could advise for the bodily complaints, it would be necessary for me to see her tongue, feel her pulse, and perhaps, also, her sides. Hearing this, the Wakungu said, "Oh, that can never be allowed without the sanction of the King"; but the Queen, rising in her seat, expressed her scorn at the idea of taking advice from a mere stripling, and submitted herself for examination.

I then took out two pills, the powder of which was tasted by the Wakungu to prove that there was no devilry in "the doctor," and gave orders for them to be eaten at night, restricting her pombe and food until I saw her again. My game was now advancing, for I found through her I should get the key to an influence that might bear on the king, and was much pleased to hear her express herself delighted with me for everything I had done except stopping her grog, which, naturally enough in this great pombe-drinking country, she said would be a very trying abstinence.

The doctoring over, her majesty expressed herself ready to inspect the honorarium I had brought for her, and the articles were no sooner presented by Bombay and Nasib, with the usual formalities of stroking to insure their purity, than she, boiling with pleasure, showed them all to her officers, who declared, with a voice of most exquisite triumph, that she was indeed the most favored of queens. Then, in excellent good taste, after saying that nobody had ever given her such treasures, she gave me in return, a beautifully worked pombe sucking pipe, which was acknowledged by everyone to be the greatest honor she could pay me.

Not satisfied with this, she made me select, though against my desire, a number of sambo, called here gundu, rings of giraffe hair wound round with thin iron or copper wire, and worn as anklets; and crowned all with sundry pots of pombe, a cow, and a bundle of dried fish, of the description given in the woodcut, called by my men Samaki Kambari. This business over, she begged me to show her my picture books, and was so amused with them that she ordered her sorceresses and all the other women in again to inspect them with her. Then began a warm and complimentary conversation, which ended by an inspection of my rings and all the contents of my pockets, as well as of my watch, which she called Lubari—a term equivalent to a place of worship, the object of worship itself, or the iron horn or magic pan. Still she said I had not yet satisfied her; I must return again two days hence, for she liked me much—excessively—she could not say how much; but now the day was gone, I might go. With this queer kind of adieu she rose and walked away, leaving me with my servants to carry the royal present home.

[3 March] I told her I had visited all the four quarters of the globe, and had seen all colors of people, but wondered where she got her pipe from, for it was much after the Rumish (Turkish) fashion, with a long stick. Greatly tickled at the flattery, she said, "We hear men like yourself come to Amara from the other side and drive cattle away." "The Gallas, or Abyssinians, who are tall and fair, like Rumanika" I said, "might do so, for they live not far off on the other side of Amara, but we never fight for such paltry objects. If cows fall into our hands when fighting we allow our soldiers to eat them, while we take the government of the country into our own hands." She then said, "We hear you don't like the Unyamuezi route, we will open the Ukori one for you." "Thank your majesty," said I, in a figurative kind of speech to please Waganda ears; and turning the advantage of the project on her side. "You have indeed hit the right nail on the head. I do not like the Unyamuezi route, as you may well imagine, when I tell you I have lost so much property there by mere robbery of the people and their kings. The Waganda do not see me in a true light; but if they have patience for a year or two, until the Ukori road is open, and trade between our respective countries shall commence, they will then see the fruits of my advent; so much so, that every Mganda will say the first Uganda year dates from the arrival of the first Mzungu (white) visitor.

As one coffee seed sown brings forth fruit in plenty, so my coming here may be considered." All appreciated this speech, saying, "The white man, he even speaks beautifully! beautifully! beautifully! beautifully!" and, putting their hands to their mouths, they looked askance at me, nodding their admiring approval.

The Queen and her ministers then plunged into pombe and became uproarious, laughing with all their might and main. Small bugu cups were not enough to keep up the excitement of the time, so a large wooden trough was placed before the Queen and filled with liquor. If any was spilt, the Wakungu instantly fought over it, dabbing their noses on the ground, or grabbing it with their hands, that not one atom of the Queen's favor might be lost; for everything must be adored that comes from royalty, whether by design or accident. The Queen put her head to the trough and drank like a pig from it, and was followed by her ministers. The band, by order, then struck up a tune called the Milele, playing on a dozen reeds, ornamented with beads and cow tips, and five drums of various tones and sizes, keeping time. The musicians dancing with zest, were led by four band masters, also dancing, but with their backs turned to the company to show off their long, shaggy, goatskin jackets, sometimes upright, at other times bending and on their heels, like the hornpipe dancers of Western countries.

It was a merry scene, but soon became tiresome; when Bombay, by way of flattery, and wishing to see what the Queen's wardrobe embraced, told her, any woman, however ugly, would assume a goodly appearance if prettily dressed; upon which her gracious majesty immediately rose, retired to her toilet hut, and soon returned attired in a common check cloth, an abrus tiara, a bead necklace, and with a folding looking glass, when she sat, as before, and was handed a blown-glass cup of pombe, with a cork floating on the liquor, and a napkin mbugu covering the top, by a naked virgin. For her condescension in assuming plain raiment, everybody of course, n'yanzigged. Next, she ordered her slave girls to bring a large number of sambo (anklets) and begged me to select the best, for she liked me much. In vain I tried to refuse them: she had given more than enough for a keepsake before, and I was not hungry for property; still I had to choose some, or I would give offense. She then gave me a basket of tobacco, and a nest of hen eggs for her "son's" breakfast. When this was over, the Mukonderi, another dancing tune with instruments something like clarionets, was ordered; but it had scarcely been struck up, before a drenching rain, with strong wind, set in and spoilt the music, though not the playing—for none dared stop without an order; and the Queen, instead of taking pity, laughed most boisterously over the exercise of her savage power as the unfortunate musicians were nearly beaten down by the violence of the weather.

When the rain ceased, her majesty retired a second time to her toilet hut, and changed her dress for a puce-colored wrapper, when I, ashamed of having robbed her of so many sambo, asked her if she would allow me to present her with a little English "wool" to hang up instead of her mbugu curtain on cold days like this. Of course she could not decline, and a large double scarlet blanket was placed before her. "Oh, wonder of wonders!" exclaimed all the spectators, holding their mouths in both hands at a time—such a "pattern" had never been seen here before. It stretched across the hut, was higher than the men could reach—indeed it was a perfect marvel; and the man must be a good one who brought such a treasure as this to Uddu. "And why not say Uganda?" I asked. "Because all this country is called Uddu. Uganda is personified by Mtesa; and no one can say he has seen Uganda until he has been presented to the King."

As I had them all in a good humor now, I complained I did not see enough of the Waganda—and as everyone dressed so remarkably well, I could not discern the big men from the small; could she not issue some order by which they might call on me, as they did not dare do so without instruction, and then I, in turn, would call on them? Hearing this, she introduced me to her prime minister, chancellor of exchequer, women keepers, hangmen, and cooks as the first nobles in the land, that I might recognize them again if I met them on the road. All n'yanzigged for this great condescension, and said they were delighted with their guest; then producing a strip of common joho to compare it with my blanket, they asked if I could recognize it. Of course, said I, it is made in my country, of the same material, only of coarser quality. Then, indeed, said the whole company, in one voice, we do like you and your cloth too—but you most. I modestly bowed my head, and said their friendship was my chief desire.

This speech also created great hilarity; the Queen and councilors all became uproarious. The Queen began to sing and the councilors to join in a chorus; then all sang and all drank, and drank and sang, till, in their heated excitement, they turned the palace into a pandemonium; still there was not noise enough, so the band and drums were called again, and tomfool —for Uganda, like the old European monarchies, always keeps a jester— was made to sing in the gruff, hoarse, unnatural voice which he ever affects to maintain his character, and furnished with pombe when his throat was dry.

Now all of a sudden, as if a devil had taken possession of the company, the prime minister with all the courtiers jumped upon their legs, seized their sticks, for nobody can carry a spear when visiting, swore the Queen had lost her heart to me, and running into the yard, returned, charging and jabbering at the Queen; retreated and returned again, as if they were going to put an end to her for the guilt of loving me, but really to show their devotion and true love to her. The Queen professed to take this ceremony with calm indifference, but her face showed that she enjoyed it. I was now getting very tired of sitting on my low stool and begged for leave to depart, but N'yamasore would not hear of it; she loved me a great deal too much to let me go away at this time of day, and forthwith ordered in more pombe. The same roistering scene was repeated; cups were too small, so the trough was employed; and the queen graced it by drinking, pig-fashion, first, and then handing it round to the company.

[24 March] Then twenty naked virgins, the daughters of Wakungu, all smeared and shining with grease, each holding a small square of mbugu for a fig leaf, marched in a line before us, as a fresh addition to the harem, whilst the happy fathers floundered n'yanzigging on the ground, delighted to find their darlings appreciated by the King. Seeing this done in such a quiet mild way before all my men who dared not lift their heads to see it, made me burst into a roar of laughter, and the King, catching the infection from me, laughed as well: but the laughing did not end there—for the pages for once giving way to nature, kept bursting—my men chuckled in sudden gusts—while even the women, holding their mouths for fear of detection responded—and we all laughed together. Then a sedate old dame rose from the squatting mass, ordered the virgins to right-about, and marched them off, showing their still more naked reverses.

[25 March] I have now been for some time within the court precincts, and have consequently had an opportunity of witnessing court customs. Among these, nearly every day since I have changed my residence, incredible as it may appear to be, I have seen one, two, or three of the wretched palace women led away to execution, tied by the hand, and dragged along by one of the body guard, crying out, as she went to premature death, "Hai Minange!" ("O my lord!") "Kbakka!" ("My king!") at the top of her voice, in the utmost despair and lamentation; and yet there was not a soul who dared lift hand to save any of them, though many might be heard privately commenting on their beauty. . . .

[27 March] After breakfast I started on a visit to Congow; but finding he had gone to the king as usual, called at Masimbi's and he being absent also, I took advantage of my proximity to the Queen's palace to call on her majesty. For hours I was kept waiting; firstly, because she was at breakfast; secondly, because she was "putting on medicine"; and, thirdly, because the sun was too powerful for her complexion; when I became tired of her nonsense, and said, "If she does not wish to see me, she had better say so at once, else I shall walk away; for the last time I came I saw her but for a minute when she rudely turned her back upon me, and left me sitting by myself." I was told not to be in a hurry—she would see me in the evening. This promise might probably be fulfilled six blessed hours from the time when it was made; but I thought to myself, every place in Uganda is alike when there is no company at home, and so I resolved to sit the time out, like patience on a monument, hoping something funny might turn up after all.

At last her majesty stumps out, squats behind my red blanket, which is converted into a permanent screen, and says hastily, or rather testily, "Can't Bana perceive the angry state of the weather?—clouds flying about, and the wind blowing half a gale? Whenever that is the case, I cannot venture out." Taking her lie without an answer, I said, I had now been fifty days or so doing nothing in Uganda—not one single visitor of my own rank ever came near me, and I could not associate with people far below her condition and mine—in fact, all I had to amuse me at home now was watching a hen lay her eggs upon my spare bed. . . .

The Wakungu then changed the subject by asking, if I married a black woman, would there be any offspring, and what would be their color? The company now became jovial when the queen improved it by making a significant gesture, and with roars of laughter asking me if I would like to be her son-in-law, for she had some beautiful daughters, either of the Wahuma or Waganda breed. Rather staggered at first by this awful proposal, I consulted Bombay what I should do with one if I got her. He, looking more to Number One than my convenience, said, "By all means accept the offer, for if *you* don't like her, *we* should, and it would be a good means of getting her out of this land of death, for all black people love Zanzibar." The rest need not be told; as a matter of course I had to appear very much gratified, and as the bowl went round, all became uproarious. I must wait a day or two, however, that a proper selection might be made; and when the marriage came off I was to chain the fair one two or three days, until she became used to me, else, from mere fright, she might run away. . . .

[30 March] To fulfill my engagement with the Queen, I walked off to her palace with stomach medicine, thinking we were now such warm friends, all pride and distant ceremonies would be dispensed with; but, on the contrary, I was kept waiting for hours till I sent in word to say, if she did not want medicine I wished to go home, for I was tired of Uganda and everything belonging to it. This message brought her to her gate, where she stood laughing till the Wahuma girls she had promised me, one of twelve and the other a little older, were brought in and made to squat in front of us. The elder, who was in the prime of youth and beauty, very large of limb, dark in color, cried considerably; whilst the younger one, though very fair, had a snubby nose and everted lips, and laughed as if she thought the change in her destiny very good fun. I had now to make my selection, and took the smaller one, promising her to Bombay as soon as we arrived on the coast, where, he said, she would be considered a Hubshi or Abyssinian. But when the queen saw what I had done, she gave me the other as well, saying the little one was too young to go alone, and, if separated, she would take fright and run away. Then with a gracious bow I walked off with my two fine specimens of natural history, though I would rather have had princes, that I might have taken them home to be instructed in England; but the Queen, as soon as we had cleared the palace, sent word to say that she must have another parting look at her son with his wives. Still laughing, she said, "That will do; you look beautiful; now go away home," and off we trotted, the elder sobbing bitterly, the younger laughing.

[26 April] We started early in the usual manner; the King paddling and steering himself with a pair of new white paddles, finally directed the boats to an island occupied by the Mgussa, or Neptune of the N'yanza, not in person—for Mgussa is a spirit—but by his familiar or deputy, the great medium who communicates the secrets of the deep to the king of Uganda. In another sense, he might be said to be the presiding priest of the source of the mighty Nile, and as such was, of course, an interesting person for me to meet. The first operation on shore was picnicking, when many large bugus of pombe were brought for the King; next, the whole party took a walk, winding through the trees, and picking fruit, enjoying themselves amazingly, till, by some unlucky chance, one of the royal wives a most charming creature, and truly one of the best of the lot, plucked a fruit and offered it to the King, thinking, doubtless, to please him greatly; but he, like a madman, flew into a towering passion, and said it was the first time a woman ever had the impudence to offer him anything, and ordered the pages to seize, bind, and lead her off to execution.

These words were no sooner uttered by the King than the whole bevy of pages slipped their cord turbans from their heads, and rushed like a pack of cupid beagles upon the fairy queen, who, indignant at the little urchins daring to touch her majesty, remonstrated with the King, and tried to beat them off like flies, but was soon captured, overcome, and dragged away, crying, in the names of the Kamraviona and Mzungu (myself) for help and protection; whilst Lubuga, the pet sister, and all the other women, clasped the King by his legs, and, kneeling, implored forgiveness for their sister. The more they craved for mercy, the more brutal he became, till at last he took a heavy stick and began to belabor the poor victim on the head.

Hitherto I had been extremely careful not to interfere with any of the King's acts of arbitrary cruelty knowing that such interference, at an early stage, would produce more harm than good. This last act of barbarism, however, was too much for my English blood to stand; and as I heard my name, "Mzungu," imploringly pronounced, I rushed at the King, and, staying his uplifted arm, demanded from him the woman's life. Of course I ran imminent risk of losing my own in thus thwarting the capricious tyrant; but his caprice proved the friend of both. The novelty of interference even made him smile, and the woman was instantly released. . . .

[3 May] I now received a letter from Grant to say he was coming by boat from Kitangule, and at once went to the palace to give the welcome news to the King. The road to the palace I found thronged with people; and in the square outside the entrance there squatted a multitude of attendants, headed by the King, sitting on a cloth, dressed in his national costume, with two spears and a shield by his side. On his right hand the pages sat waiting for orders, while on his left there was a small squatting cluster of women, headed by Wichwezis, or attendant sorceresses, offering pombe. In front of the King, in form of a hollow square, many ranks deep, sat the victorious officers lately returned from the war, variously dressed; the nobles distinguished by their leopard-cat skins and dirks, the commoners by colored mbugu and cow or antelope skin cloaks; but all their faces and arms were painted, red, black, or smoke color. Within the square of men immediately fronting the King, the war arms of Uganda were arranged in three ranks; the great war drum, covered with a leopard skin, and standing on a large carpeting of them, was placed in advance; behind this, propped or hung on a rack of iron, were a variety of the implements of war in common use, offensive and defensive, as spears—of which two were of copper, the rest iron—and shields of wood and leather; whilst in the last row or lot were arranged systematically, with great taste and powerful effect, the supernatural arms, the god of Uganda, consisting of charms of various descriptions and in great numbers. Outside the square again, in a line with the King, were the household arms, a very handsome copper kettledrum, of French manufacture, surmounted on the outer edge with pretty little brass bells depending from swan-neck-shaped copper wire, two new spears, a painted leather shield, and magic wands of various devices, deposited on a carpet of leopard skins—the whole scene giving the effect of true barbarous royalty in its uttermost magnificence.

Approaching, as usual, to take my seat beside the King, some slight sensation was perceptible, and I was directed to sit beyond the women. The whole ceremonies of this grand assemblage were now obvious. Each regimental commandant in turn narrated the whole services of his party distinguishing those subs who executed his orders well and successfully from those who either deserted before the enemy or feared to follow up their success. The King listened attentively, making, let us suppose, very shrewd remarks concerning them; when to the worthy he awarded pombe, helped with gourd cups from large earthen jars, which was n'yanzigged for vehemently; and to the unworthy, execution. When the fatal sentence was pronounced, a terrible bustle ensued, the convict wrestling and defying, whilst the other men seized, pulled and tore the struggling wretch from the crowd, bound him hands and head together, and led or rather tumbled him away. . . .

[3 July] The moment of triumph had come at last, and suddenly the road was granted! The King presently let us see the motive by which he had been influenced. He said he did not like having to send to Rumanika for everything: he wanted his visitors to come to him direct: moreover, Rumanika had sent him a message to the effect that we were not to be shown anything out of Uganda, and when we had done with it, were to be returned to him. Rumanika, indeed! who cared about Rumanika? Was not Mtesa the King of the country, to do as he liked? and we all laughed. Then the King, swelling with pride, asked me whom I liked best

—Rumanika or himself—an awkward question, which I disposed of by saying I liked Rumanika very much because he spoke well, and was very communicative; but I also liked Mtesa, because his habits were much like my own—fond of shooting and roaming about; whilst he had learnt so many things from my teaching, I must ever feel a yearning toward him.

On the way home, one of the King's favorite women overtook us, walking, with her hands clasped at the back of her head, to execution, crying *"N'yawo!"* in the most pitiful manner. A man was preceding her, but did not touch her; for she loved to obey the orders of her King voluntarily, and, in consequence of previous attachment, was permitted as a mark of distinction, to walk free. Wondrous world! it was not ten minutes since we parted from the King, yet he had found time to transact this bloody piece of business.

[7 July] Early in the morning the King bade us come to him to say farewell. Wishing to leave behind a favorable impression I instantly complied. On the breast of my coat, I suspended the necklace the Queen had given me, as well as his knife, and my medals. I talked with him in as friendly and flattering a manner as I could, dwelling on his shooting, the pleasant cruising on the lake, and our sundry picnics, as well as the grand prospect there was now of opening the country to trade, by which his guns, the best in the world, would be fed with powder—and other small matters of a like nature—to which he replied with great feeling and good taste. We then all rose with an English bow, placing the hand on the heart whilst saying adieu; and there was a complete uniformity in the ceremonial, for whatever I did, Mtesa, in an instant, mimicked with the instinct of a monkey.

We had, however, scarcely quitted the palace gate before the King issued himself, with his attendants and his brothers leading, and women bringing up the rear; here K'yengo and all the Wazina joined in the procession with ourselves, they kneeling and clapping their hands after the fashion of their own country. Mtesa, much pleased, complimented them on their goodly appearance, remarking that with such a force I would have no difficulty in reaching Gani, and exhorted them to follow me through fire and water; then, exchanging adieus again, he walked ahead in gigantic strides up the hill, the pretty favorite of his harem, Lubuga—beckoning and waving with her little hands and crying *"Bana! Bana!"*—trotting after him conspicuous amongst the rest, though all showed a little feeling at the severance. We saw them no more.

GORILLA HUNTING

by Paul du Chaillu

One of the most famous African explorers of the mid-nineteenth century was Paul du Chaillu. The son of a French African trader, he made his first expeditions while still in his teens. Later he traveled extensively in the "inextricable labyrinth" which is now French Equatorial Africa. He brought back information about many of the tribes that lived there and even more exciting, about the first specimens of the "King of the African Forest," the gorilla.

Du Chaillu wrote about his adventures with great charm and vividness, but his descriptions of cannibals, dwarfs and gorillas were at first denounced as impostures. Later, however, scientists like Sir Roderick Murchison and explorers like Stanley confirmed his observations. Here is his description of his first sight of the gorilla, taken from Adventures in the Great Forest of Equatorial Africa and of the Country of the Dwarfs.

TODAY (August 20, 1856), I sent back Dayoko's men, and am now in Mbene's power and at his mercy. He is a very good fellow, and I feel myself quite safe among his rough but kindly people. I have found it the best way to *trust* the people I travel among. They seem to take it as a compliment, and they are proud to have a white man among them. Even if a chief were inclined to murder, it would not be profitable in such a case, for the exhibition of his white visitor among the neighboring tribes does more to give him respect and prestige than his murder would.

They speak of me now as "Mbene's white man." Before, I was "Dayoko's white man." The title has comfort and safety in it, for it would be a great insult to Mbene for any stranger to molest *his* white man, and it is to his own honor to feed him as well as he can.

Of course, one must have tact enough to satisfy the chief with occasional little presents, given him generally in private, so that his people may not beg from him, and given, also, not as though you wished to conciliate—

From *Explorations and Adventures in Equatorial Africa*.

for it will not do to show any symptoms of fear, however much cause there may be—but apparently as friendly gifts.

This is the only safe way to get ahead in this country, and I never found a chief whose "white man" I was for the time but would help and further my plans and journeys.

Dayoko's men are to return to Mbene's camp in three months to look for me, and I have to be back, if possible, by that time.

The women have brought in a supply of the bitter palm seeds and of other fruits, mostly more palatable than that bitter abomination, but unfortunately not so plentiful.

Mbene had moved his village twice, his present removal making the third. I asked what reasons moved him to these changes. The first time, he said, a man had died there, and the place was "not good" after that. The second time he was forced to move because they had cut down all the palm-trees, and could get no more *mimbo* (palm wine), a beverage of which they are excessively fond, though they take no pains to preserve the trees out of the soft tops of which it is made.

The Mbondemo houses are mostly of uniform size, generally from twelve to fifteen feet long, and eight or ten feet wide. They are built on both sides of a long and tolerably wide street, and invariably join each other. The chief's house and the palaver house are larger than the others. The ends of the street are barricaded with stout sticks or palisades, and at night the *doors* or gates of the village are firmly closed, and persons approaching, if they cannot explain their intentions, are remorselessly shot down or speared. The houses have no windows, and doors only on the side toward the street; and when the door of the street is locked, the village is, in fact, a fortress.

Within, the Mbondemo house is divided by a bark partition into two rooms; one the kitchen, where also everybody sits or lies down on the ground about the fire; the other the sleeping apartment. This last is perfectly dark; and here are stowed their provisions and all their riches. To ascertain how large a family any Mbondemo householder has, you have only to count the little doors which open into the various sleeping apartments: "So many doors, so many wives," it was explained to me. The houses are made of bark and a kind of jointless bamboo, which is got from the trunk of a particular palm. The strips are tied to posts set firmly into the ground, with rope made from the vines of the forest. The roofing is made of matting.

Today (21st) my men have been getting ready their guns for enemies or game. The tribes of Africa have so many petty causes of quarrel that they are always in danger of a fight. They are so bound together by ridiculous superstitions of witchcraft, and by the entangling alliances of polygamy, and greatly also by their want of good faith in trade, that no man can say where or why an enemy is waiting for his life.

I have already spoken of the system of intermarriages by which a chief gains in power and friends. But there are other means of securing allies. For instance, two tribes are anxious for a fight, but one needs more force. This weakling sends one of its men secretly to kill a man or woman of some village, living near but having no share in the quarrel. The consequence is, *not*, as would seem most reasonable, that this last village takes its revenge on the murderer, but, strangely enough, that the murderer's people give them to understand that this is done because *another* tribe has insulted them, whereupon, according to African custom, the two villages join, and together march upon the enemy. In effect, to gain a village to a certain side in a quarrel, that side murders one of its men or women, with a purpose of retaliation on somebody else.

A man pays goods or slaves for his wife, and regards her therefore as a piece of merchandise. Young girls—even children in arms—are married to old men for political effect. The idea of love, as we understand it, seems unknown to these people. The inhabitant of the seacoast has no hesitation in bartering the virtue of his nearest female relatives, nor are the women averse from the traffic, if only they be well paid.

Adultery with a black man is punishable by fine among all the tribes, and this law, which is strictly executed, is the cause of a most singular state of things. Husband and wife combine to rob some fellow with whom the woman pretends to carry on an intrigue, making sure of being discovered by the husband, who thereupon obtains a recompense sufficient to heal his wounded honor, and upon which he and his wife and accomplice are able to live for some time.

Unlawful intercourse with the women of a neighboring tribe or village is the cause of nearly all the "palavers," and wars, and fights in Africa. If a tribe wants to fight, they *make* this the cause by getting one of their women to intrigue with a man of the other tribe or village; and even if they do not want to fight, they are often forced into it.

Then the system of intermarrying involves half a dozen tribes in the quarrel of two. Each chief calls on his fathers-in-law to assist, and thus the country is thrown into uproar; property is unsafe, and becomes almost valueless to them; agricultural operations are impeded, and whole villages gradually disappear from the scene of contention, either by migrating, starving out, or being killed out.

The women not only provide all the food, they are also the beasts of burden in this part of Africa. My party from Mbene's town consisted of Mbene's two sons, Miengai and Maginda, a young man named Pouliandai, and half a dozen stout women to bear my heavy chests and other luggage, and food for the journey.

We started at length on the morning of August 24. The natives had done what they could to gather food beforehand for the trip, but the result was poor enough. My own supplies were by this time completely exhausted. The half-dozen biscuits I had in reserve were for sickness or a great emergency. Besides this, they had succeeded in getting several large branches of plantains and a good many of the bitter palm nuts, and that was all the commissariat.

The packing of the women is a subject of great importance. They carry their loads in heavy, rude baskets, suspended down the back; and it is necessary that those should be carefully arranged, with three or four inches of soft tree fiber next to the back to prevent chafing.

When all was arranged—when everybody had taken leave of all his friends, and come back half a dozen times to take leave over again, or say something before forgotten—when all the shouting and ordering, and quarreling were done, and I had completely lost patience, we at last got away.

In about five miles' travel we came to the banks of the Noonday River, which is here a narrow, but clear and beautiful stream, so clear that I was tempted to shoot a fish of curious shape I saw swimming along as we stood on the bank.

I fired a charge of small shot into him; but no sooner had I pulled the trigger than I heard a tremendous crash on the opposite bank, above six or seven yards across, saw some small trees torn violently down, and then came the shrill trumpetings of a party of frightened elephants. They had been standing in dead silence on the opposite bank in the jungle, whether watching us or not we could not tell. I was sorry I fired, for we crossed the stream close by, and might have killed one but for the fright they got, which sent them out of our reach.

After crossing the Noonday, and traveling ten miles in a northeast direction, we reached a range of granite hills, which are a part of the Sierra del Crystal Mountains. The hills were very steep. I ate a few boiled plantains, then we ascended the crooked and poorly marked path uphill, which wound its devious course about immense boulders of granite and quartz, which, scattered along the declivity, gave the country a very strange look.

This range was about six hundred feet high, and the summit formed a tableland three miles long, which also was strewed with the immense quartz and granite boulders.

Passing this tableland, we came to another tier of hills, steeper and higher than the first, which also had to be surmounted. In this kind of traveling I find that the natives had a great advantage over me. They use their bare feet almost as monkeys do theirs. Long practice enables them to catch hold of objects with their toes, and they could jump from rock to rock without fear of falling, while I, with thick shoes on, was continually slipping.

We were yet on the first plateau when Miengai suddenly made me a sign to keep very still. He and I were in advance. I thought he had discovered a herd of elephants, or perhaps a leopard. He cocked his gun, and I mine, and there we stood for five minutes in perfect silence. Suddenly Miengai sent a "hurrah" rolling through the forest, which was immediately answered by shouts from many voices at no great distance, but whose owners were hid from us by the rocks and trees. Miengai replied with the fierce shout of the Mbondemo warriors, and was again answered. Going a little farther on, we came in sight of the encampment of a large party, who proved to be some of Mbene's people just returning from a trading expedition to the interior.

It was a curious picture. They lay encamped about their fires to the number of about a hundred—young and old, men and women; some gray and wrinkled, and others babes in arms. They had evidently traveled far, and were tired out. They had collected India rubber, and had in charge some ivory, and were now about to take these goods to Mbene or some other river chief, to be sent down from hand to hand to the "white man market."

Here even I noticed the cruel way in which the women are obliged to work. The Mbondemo men lay about the fires, handling their spears and guns, and talking or sleeping, while the women were doing the cooking and making the camp comfortable, and such of the children as could walk were driven out to collect firewood for the night.

Being tired ourselves, we built our campfires near the party, and I had the opportunity next day to see them get under way. The men carried only their arms, and most of them were armed to the teeth. The women and larger children carried, in the usual baskets, suspended along the back, the food—of which they seemed to have a good supply—the ivory and India rubber, and besides—still in the basket—such of the babies as could by no means get along alone. The old people were not exempt from light burdens, though they had to totter along with the help of long sticks.

The whole party were very thinly clothed, even for Africa. They had with them an old chief, to whom they seemed to pay much reverence, and *he* was constantly waited upon by his wives, of whom he seemed to have several with him. I gave them a little salt, for which they seemed very grateful.

Next morning we broke up before daylight, after eating a very scanty breakfast of a few cooked plantains. It rained all day, and consequently we tramped all day in the mud, wet through, and chilly. About noon we met another large party of traveling Mbondemo returning from the interior. They had never seen a white man before, and stared at me with all the eyes they had. I fear my appearance gave them but a poor idea of white people. I was clothed in only a blue drill shirt and trousers, both wet, and the latter muddy. They begged for some tobacco "to warm themselves," and a few leaves which I gave them made them perfectly happy.

Among this party were two fellows, named Ngolai and Yeava, who were from Mbene's village, and well known to Mbene's sons. These offered to go with us if we would give them food, as theirs was nearly gone, and Miengai and Maginda promising this much, they at once joined our party.

After a walk of about eighteen miles in the rain, through thick woods, and over a rough hilly country (and in a general direction of E.S.E.), we came to our camp, and to my delight found very large and commodious huts ready for us. This is a highway, it seems, of this country, though no signs of a road are visible, and different parties of traders had built and kept up these very neat and comfortable sheds.

We built great fires and made ourselves comfortable. I had three fires lit about my bed of brush, hung up my wet clothes to dry, and, after comforting myself with a little brandy, went to sleep in much more than usual snugness, not knowing the "palaver" which was in store for me on the morrow.

When we got up, much refreshed, my men came and said they were tired, and would not go a step farther if I did not pay them more cloth.

They seemed in earnest, and I was, as may be imagined, in considerable trouble of mind. To return now, when I had proceeded so far, was not to be thought of. To be left alone would have been almost certain death, and to give what they demanded was to set a bad precedent to my guides. Finally, I determined to put on a bold front. I went into the crowd, told them— pistols in hand—that I should not give them any more cloth; that neither could I permit them to leave me, because their father, Mbene, had given them to me to accompany me to the Fan tribe. So far, I told them, they must go with me, or else—here I motioned with my pistols—there would be war between us. But, I added, if they were faithful, I would give each something additional when the trip was done.

After a consultation among themselves, they finally said that they were pleased with what I said, and were my friends. Hereupon, with great lightness of heart at my escape from an ugly dilemma, I shook hands with them, and we set out on the journey.

It was ten o'clock before we made a start on this day. We were now approaching the second mountain range of the Sierra del Crystal, and passing through a wild country, densely wooded, rough, and strewn along the higher ground with immense boulders, which gave an additional wildness to the scene. Up, and up, and up we struggled, through a forest more silent than I recollect to have noticed in Africa before. Not even the scream of a bird or the shrill cry of a monkey to break the dark solitude— and either would have been welcome.

Nothing was heard but the panting breathings of our party, who were becoming exhausted by the ascent, till, at last, I thought I heard a subdued roar as of a fall of water. It grew plainer as we toiled on, and finally filled the whole air with its grand rush; soon turning a sharp corner of a declivity and marching on a little way, the torrent literally burst upon our sight. It was an immense mountain torrent dashing downhill at an angle of twenty-five or thirty degrees, for not less than a mile right before us, like a vast, seething, billowy sea. The river course was full of the huge granite boulders which lie about here as though the Titans had been playing at skittles in this country; and against these the angry waters dashed as though they would carry all before them, and, breaking, threw the milky spray up to the very tops of the trees which grew along the edge.

Where we stood at the foot of the rapids the stream took a winding turn down the mountain; but we had the whole mile of foaming rapid before us, seemingly pouring its mass of waters down upon our heads.

These were the headwaters of the Ntambounay.

Drinking a few handfuls of its pure, clear, cool water, we traveled onward, still uphill and partly along the edge of the rapids. In another hour we reached a clear space where a Mbondemo village had once stood; this was the summit.

From this elevation—about five thousand feet above the ocean level—I enjoyed an unobstructed view as far as the eye could reach. The hills we had surmounted the day before lay quietly at our feet, seeming mere molehills. On all sides stretched the immense virgin forests. And far away in the east loomed the blue tops of the farthest range of the Sierra del Crystal, and, as I strained my eyes toward those distant mountains which I hoped to reach, I began to think how this wilderness would look if only the light of civilization could once be fairly introduced among the black children of Africa. I dreamed of forests giving way to plantations of coffee, cotton, and spices; of peaceful Negroes going to their contented daily tasks; of farming and manufactures; of churches and schools; and, luckily raising my eyes heavenward at this stage of my thoughts, saw pendent from the branch of a tree beneath which I was sitting an immense serpent, evidently preparing to gobble up this dreaming intruder on his domains.

My dreams of future civilization vanished in a moment. Fortunately my gun lay at hand. I rushed out so as to "stand from under," and, taking good aim, shot my black friend through the head. He let go his hold, and, after dancing about a little on the ground, lay dead before me. He measured a little over thirteen feet in length, and his fangs proved that he was venomous.

And now that civilization of which I had mused so pleasantly a few minutes before received another shock. My men cut off the head of the snake, and, dividing the body into proper pieces, roasted it and ate it on the spot; and I—poor, starved, but *civilized* mortal!—stood by, longing for a meal, but after a while I had to learn also how to eat snake or starve.

When the snake was eaten, and I, the only empty-stomached individual of the company, had sufficiently reflected on the disadvantages of being bred in a civilized country, we began to look about the ruins of the village near which we sat. A degenerate kind of sugar cane was growing on the very spot where the houses had formerly stood, and I made haste to pluck some of this and chew it for the little sweetness it had. But, as we were plucking, my men perceived what instantly threw us all into the greatest excitement. Here and there the cane was beaten down, torn up by the roots, and lying about in fragments which had evidently been chewed.

I knew that these were fresh tracks of the gorilla, and joy filled my heart. My men looked at each other in silence, and muttered "*Nguyla*," which is as much as to say in Mpongwe "*Ngina*," or, as we say, "gorilla."

We followed these traces, and presently came to the footprints of the so-long-desired animal. It was the first time I had ever seen these footprints, and my sensations were indescribable. Here was I now, it seemed, on the point of meeting face to face that monster of whose ferocity, strength and cunning the natives had told me so much; an animal scarce known to the civilized world, and which no white man before had hunted. My heart beat till I feared its loud pulsations, and my feelings were really excited to a painful degree.

By the tracks it was easy to know that there must have been several gorillas in company. We prepared at once to follow them.

The women were terrified, and we left them a good escort of two or three men to take care of them and reassure them. Then the rest of us looked once more carefully at our guns—for the gorilla gives you no time to reload, and woe to him whom he attacks! We were armed to the teeth. My men were remarkably silent, as they were going on an expedition of more than usual risk; for the male gorilla is literally the king of the African forest.

As we departed from the camp, the men and women left behind crowded together, with fear written on their face. Miengai, Makinda, and Ngolai set out in one party, and myself and Yeava formed another, for the hunt. We determined to keep near each other, that in emergency we might be at hand to help each other. And for the rest, silence, coolness, and a sure aim were the only cautions to be given.

As we followed the tracks we could easily see that there were four or five of them; though none appeared very large. We saw where they had run along on all fours, the usual mode of progression of these animals; and where, from time to time, they had seated themselves to chew the canes they had borne off. The chase began to be very exciting.

We had agreed to return to the women and their guards, and consult upon final operations when we should have discovered their probable cause; and this was now done. To make sure of not alarming our prey, we moved the whole party forward a little way to where some leafy huts, built by passing traders, served for shelter and concealment. And having here stowed the women—who have a lively fear of the terrible gorilla, in consequence of various stories current among the tribes of women having been carried off into the woods by the fierce animal—we prepared once more to set out in chase, this time hopeful to get a shot.

Looking once more to our guns, we started off. I confess that I had never been more excited in my life. I had heard of the terrible roar of the gorilla, of its vast strength, its fierce courage, if, unhappily, only wounded by a shot. I knew that we were about to pit ourselves against an animal which even the leopard of these mountains fears.

We descended a hill, crossed a stream on a fallen log, and presently approached some huge boulders of granite. Alongside of this granite block lay an immense dead tree, and about this we saw many evidences of the very recent presence of the gorillas.

Our approach was very cautious. We were again divided into two parties. Makinda led one and I the other. We were to surround the granite block behind which Makinda expected the gorillas to be found. Guns cocked and in hand, we advanced through the dense wood, which cast a gloom even in midday over the whole scene. I looked at my men, and saw plainly that they were in even greater excitement than myself.

Slowly we pressed on through the dense brush, fearing almost to breathe lest we should alarm the beasts. Makinda was to go to the right of the rock, while I took the left. Unfortunately, he circled it at too great a distance. The watchful animals saw him. Suddenly I was startled by a strange, discordant, half-human, devilish cry, and beheld four young gorillas running toward the deep forests. We fired, but hit nothing. Then we rushed on in pursuit; but they knew the woods better than we. Once I caught a glimpse of one of the animals again, but an intervening tree spoiled my aim, and I did not fire. We ran till we were exhausted, but in vain. The alert beasts made good their escape. When we could pursue no more we returned slowly to our camp, where the women were anxiously expecting us.

As I saw the gorillas running—on their hind legs—they looked fearfully like hairy men: their heads down, their bodies inclined forward, their whole appearance was like men running for their lives. Take with this their awful cry, which, fierce and animal as it is, has yet something human in its discordance, and you will cease to wonder that the natives have the wildest superstitions about these "wild men of the woods."

In our absence the women had built large fires and prepared the camp, which was not so comfortable as last night's, but yet protected us from rain. I changed my clothes, which had become wet through by the frequent torrents and puddles we ran through in our eager pursuit, and then we sat down to our supper, which had been cooked meantime.

As we lay about the fire in the evening before going to sleep the adventure of the day was talked over, and of course there followed some curious stories of the gorillas. I listened in silence to the conversation, which was not addressed to me, and was rewarded by hearing the stories as they are believed, and not as a stranger would be apt to draw them out by questions.

One of the men told a story of two Mbondemo women who were walking together through the woods, when suddenly an immense gorilla stepped into the path, and, clutching one of the women, bore her off in spite of the screams and struggles of both. The other woman returned to the village, sadly frightened, and related the story. Of course, her companion was given up for lost. Great was the surprise, therefore, when, a few days afterward, she returned to her home. She related that the gorilla had misused her, but that she had eventually escaped from him. This and many similar stories I subsequently found to be devoid of all credit.

"Yes," said one of the men, "that was a gorilla inhabited by a spirit."

Which explanation was received with a general grunt of approval.

They believe, in all this country, that there is a kind of gorilla—known to the initiated by certain mysterious signs, but chiefly by being of extraordinary size—which is the residence of certain spirits of departed Negroes. Such gorillas, the natives believe, can never be caught or killed: and, also, they have much more shrewdness and sense than the common animal. In fact, in these "possessed" beasts, it would seem that the intelligence of man is united with the strength and ferocity of the beast. No wonder the poor African dreads so terrible a being as his imagination thus conjures up.

One of the men told how, some years ago, a party of gorillas were found in a cane field tying up the sugar cane in regular bundles, preparatory to carrying it away. The natives attacked them, but were routed, and several killed, while others were carried off prisoners by the gorillas; but in a few days they returned home uninjured, with this horrid exception: the nails of their fingers and toes had been torn off by their captors.

Some years ago a man suddenly disappeared from his village. It is probable that he was carried off, but as no news came of him, the native superstition invented a cause for his absence. It was related and believed that, as he walked through the wood one day, he was suddenly changed into a hideous large gorilla, which was often pursued afterward, but never killed, though it continually haunted the neighborhood of the village.

Here several spoke up and mentioned names of men now dead whose spirits were known to be dwelling in gorillas.

Finally, the story which is current among all the tribes who at all know the gorilla was rehearsed, viz.: that this animal lies in wait in the lower branches of trees, watching for people who go to and fro; and, when one passes sufficiently near, grasps the luckless fellow with his powerful feet, and draws him up into the tree, where he quietly chokes him.

Many of the natives agree, I say, in ascribing to the animal this trait of lying in wait for his enemies and drawing them up to him by his "lower hands," as they may properly be called. But I have little doubt that this story is incorrect. Of course, the secluded habits of this animal, which lives only in the darkest forests, and carefully shuns all approach to man, help to fill the natives with curious superstitions regarding it.

This day we traveled fifteen miles, ten of which were easterly, and five to the southeast.

The next day we went out on another gorilla hunt, but found no traces at all.

We rose early next morning, and trudged off breakfastless. There was not a particle of food among us. We crossed several streams, and traveled all day through a forest of an almost chilling gloom and solitude, ascending, in the midst, the steepest and highest hill we have so far met with. I suppose it to be part of the third range of the Sierra.

I felt vexed at the thoughtlessness of my men, who ought to have provided food enough to last us. But I ought to praise the poor fellows, for, though long hungry themselves, they gave me the greater part of the few nuts they found.

This is one of the hardest day's travel I had accomplished. We made twenty miles in a general direction of east, though some deductions must be made for deviations from a straight line.

The forest seemed deserted. Not a bird even to kill. We heard the chatter of a few monkeys, but sought in vain to get near them for a shot.

The next morning I woke up feeble, but found that the fellows had killed a monkey, which, roughly roasted on the coals, tasted delicious. To add to our satisfaction, Makinda presently discovered a beehive in the hollow of a tree. We smoked the bees out and divided the honey, which was full of worms, but was nevertheless all eaten up. We were so nearly famished that we could scarce wait for the hive to be emptied. No sooner was the honey spread out on leaves and laid on the grass, than every one of the men was ready to clutch the biggest piece he could lay his hand on and eat away. There might have been a fight, to prevent which I interposed, and divided the whole sweet booty into equal shares, reserving for myself only a share with the rest. This done, everyone—myself included—at once sat down and devoured honey, wax, dead bees, worms, dirt, and all, and our only sorrow was that we had not more.

We had a hard time getting through old elephant tracks, which were a better road then the path through the jungle. Saw no animals, but met with several gorilla tracks.

Toward two o'clock the men began to be very jolly, which I took to be a sign of our approach to a village. Presently they shouted, and, looking up toward the face of a hill before us, I saw the broad leaves of the plantain, the forerunner of an African town. Since we left Mbene's town these were the first human habitations we had met with, and I was not a little refreshed by the sight.

But alas! as we approached we found no one coming out to meet us, as is the hospitable way in Africa, and when we got to the place we found it entirely deserted. It was an old town of Mbene's people. Presently, however, some Mbicho people living near, relatives of Mbene's, came to see us, and gave us some plantains. But I could not get what I needed most—a fowl. The Mbichos were in great amazement. None had ever seen a white man before. They thought me very singular.

We spent the evening in our houses drying and warming ourselves. It was much better than the forest, even though it was only a deserted town.

I judged myself here about 150 miles from the coast. With the exception of a Mbicho town near by, we were now surrounded on three sides by Fan villages, and shall make the acquaintance of these cannibals in a very short time.

Next day Mbene came, which gave me great relief, for he is a steadier and more influential man than his sons. He was exhausted from his travels, and when I told him we needed food, he immediately set off to a Fan village a few miles off for a supply. Unable to wait for his return, I started off with my men to meet him, hoping perhaps to shoot something by the way. My hunger accelerated my movements, and pretty soon I found myself half a mile ahead of my companions and in sight of a chattering monkey, who dodged me whenever I took aim at him, and whom I vainly tried to get down off his perch on the high tree where he lived.

After watching this animal for some time, I happened to look down before me, and beheld a sight which drove the monkey out of my mind in an instant. Judge of my astonishment when before me I saw a Fan warrior, with his two wives behind him. I was at first alarmed, but immediately saw that all three were quaking with deadly terror. The man's shield shook and rattled, to such a degree was he frightened; his mouth stood open—the lips were fairly white; one of his three spears had fallen to the ground, and the other two he held in a manner betokening great fear.

The women had been carrying baskets on their heads, but these had been thrown to the ground, and they stood in perfect silence and terror looking at me.

They all thought, it appeared afterward, that I was a spirit who had just came down out of the sky. As for me, my first thought, when I took in the situation, was—Suppose these people grow desperate with fear, then I may have a poisoned arrow launched at me. And if they got over their terror ere my companions arrived, then I was likely to have a spear sent through me, unless I were quicker than my antagonist and shot him, which I by no means desired to do; for, aside from the hatred of unnecessary bloodshed, I should by such a course have endangered my life among his countrymen.

I smiled and tried to look pleasant, in order to reassure them a little; but this only made matters worse. They looked as though upon the point of sinking to the ground.

Then I heard the voices of my men behind coming up, and presently I was safe, and the Fan people were relieved of their terror. Miengai smiled to see it, and told the man he need not regard me as a spirit, for I was his father's white man, come from the seashore on purpose to visit the Fan. Then I gave the women some strings of white beads, which did more than anything else to ease their fears.

On our return we found that Makinda had brought some plantains, but no fowl. I had now been a week without tasting flesh, except only the monkey we shot on the way, and felt very much in need of something better.

For the rest of the day we held levee in my house. Great crowds of Fan from the neighboring villages came to see me. The men did not appear very much frightened, but the women and children were excessively so. But all kept at a very respectable distance. One glance from me toward a woman or child sufficed to make these run off.

If I was not frightened, I was at least as much surprised by all I saw as the Fan could be. These fellows, who now for the first time saw a white man, were to me an equal surprise, for they are real, unmistakable cannibals. And they were, by long odds, the most remarkable people I had thus far seen in Africa. They were much lighter in shade than any of the coast tribes, strong, tall, well made, and evidently active; and they seemed to me to have a more intelligent look than is usual to the African unacquainted with white men.

The men were almost naked. They had no cloth about the middle, but used instead the soft inside bark of a tree, over which in front was suspended the skin of some wildcat or other animal. They had their teeth filed, which gives the face a ghastly and ferocious look, and some had the teeth blackened besides. Their hair or "wool" was drawn out into long thin plaits; on the end of each stiff plait were strung some white beads, or copper or iron rings. Some wore feather caps, but others wore long queues made of their own wool and a kind of tow, dyed black and mixed with it, and giving the wearer a most grotesque appearance.

Over their shoulders was suspended the huge country knife, and in their hands were spears and the great shield of elephant hide, and about the necks and bodies of all was hung a variety of fetishes and grigris, which rattled as they walked.

The Fan shield is made of the hide of an *old* elephant, and only of that part which lies across the back. This, when dried and smoked, is hard and impenetrable as iron. The shield is about three feet long by two and a half wide.

Their fetishes consisted of fingers and tails of monkeys; of human hair, skin, teeth, bones; of clay, old nails, copper chains, shells; feathers, claws, and skulls of birds; pieces of iron, copper, or wood; seeds of plants; ashes of various substances; and I cannot tell what more. From the great variety and plenty of these objects on their persons, I suppose these Fan to be a very superstitious people.

The women, who were even less dressed than the men, were much smaller than they. These, too, had their teeth filed, and most had their bodies painted red, by means of a dye obtained from the bar wood. They carried their babies on their backs in a sling or rest made of some kind of treebark and fastened to the neck of the mother.

Such were the strange people who now crowded about me, examining every part of my person and dress that I would allow to be touched, but especially wondering at my hair and my feet. The former they could not sufficiently admire. On my feet I had boots; and as my trousers lay over these, they thought, naturally enough, that these boots were my veritable feet, and wondered greatly that my face should be of one color and the feet of another. I showed myself to as good advantage as I could, and surprised them very much—as I wished to do—by shooting a couple of swallows on the wing in their presence. This was thought a wonderful feat. They all went off at four o'clock, promising to return tomorrow and bring me some fowls.

I spent the day chiefly in looking about the town and neighborhood— really doing nothing. As I walked along, a Fan woman gravely asked me why I did not take off my clothes? She felt sure they must be a great hindrance to me, and if I would leave off these things I should be able to walk more easily.

The next day we went out all together for a gorilla hunt. The country hereabout is very rough, hilly, and densely crowded; consequently, hunting is scarcely to be counted sport. But a couple of days of rest had refreshed me, and I was anxious to be in at the death of a gorilla.

We saw several gorilla tracks, and about noon divided our party, in the hope of surrounding the resting place of one whose tracks were very plain. I had scarce got away from my party three hundred yards when I heard the report of a gun, then of three more, going off one after the other. Of course I ran back as fast as I could, and hoped to see a dead animal before me, but was once more disappointed. My Mbondemo fellows had fired at a female, had wounded her, as I saw by the clots of blood which marked her track, but she had made good her escape. We set out at once in pursuit; but these woods are so thick, so almost impenetrable, that pursuit of a wounded animal is not often successful. A man can only creep where the beast would run.

Night came upon us while we were still beating the bush, and it was determined to camp out and try our luck again on the morrow.

We started early, and pushed for the most dense and impenetrable part of the forest, in hopes to find the very home of the beast I so much wished to shoot. Hour after hour we traveled, and yet no sign of gorilla. Only the everlasting little chattering monkeys—and not many of these—and occasionally birds. In fact, the forests of this part of Africa—as the reader has seen by this time—are not so full of life as in some other parts to the south.

Suddenly Miengai uttered a little cluck with his tongue, which is the native's way of showing that something is stirring, and that a sharp lookout is necessary. And presently I noticed, ahead of us seemingly, a noise as of some one breaking down branches or twigs of trees.

This was the gorilla, I knew at once, by the eager and satisfied looks of the men. They looked once more carefully at their guns, to see if by any chance the powder had fallen out of the pans; I also examined mine, to make sure that all was right; and then we marched on cautiously.

The singular noise of the breaking of tree branches continued. We walked with the greatest care, making no noise at all. The countenances of the men showed that they thought themselves engaged in a very serious undertaking; but we pushed on, until finally we thought we saw through the thick woods the moving of the branches and small trees which the great beast was tearing down, probably to get from them the berries and fruits he lives on.

Suddenly, as we were creeping along, in a silence which made a heavy breath seem loud and distinct, the woods were filled with the tremendous barking roar of the gorilla.

Then the underbrush swayed rapidly just ahead, and presently before us stood an immense male gorilla. He had gone through the jungle on all fours; but when he saw our party, he raised himself erect and looked us boldly in the face. He stood about a dozen yards from us, and was a sight I think I shall never forget. Nearly six feet high (he proved four inches shorter), with immense body, huge chest, and great muscular arms, with fiercely glaring large deep gray eyes, and a hellish expression of face, which seemed to me like some nightmare vision; thus stood before us this king of the African forest.

He was not afraid of us. He stood there, and beat his breast with his huge fists till it resounded like an immense bass drum, which is their mode of offering defiance; meantime giving vent to roar after roar.

The roar of the gorilla is the most singular and awful noise heard in these African woods. It begins with a sharp *bark*, like an angry dog, then glides into a deep bass *roll* which literally and closely resembles the roll of distant thunder along the sky, for which I have sometimes been tempted to take it where I did not see the animal. So deep is it that it seems to proceed less from the mouth and throat than from the deep chest and vast paunch.

His eyes began to flash fiercer fire as we stood motionless on the defensive, and the crest of short hair which stands on his forehead began to twitch rapidly up and down, while his powerful fangs were shown as he again sent forth a thunderous roar. And now truly he reminded me of nothing but some hellish dream creature—a being of that hideous order, half-man, half-beast, which we find pictured by old artists in some representations of the infernal regions. He advanced a few steps—then stopped to utter that hideous roar again—advanced again, and finally stopped when at a distance of about six yards from us. And here, just as he began another of his roars, beating his breast in rage, we fired and killed him.

With a groan which had something terribly human in it, and yet was full of brutishness, he fell forward on his face. The body shook convulsively for a few minutes, the limbs moved about in a struggling way, and then all was quiet—death had done its work, and I had leisure to examine the huge body. It proved to be five feet eight inches high, and the muscular development of the arms and breast showed what immense strength it had possessed.

My men, though rejoicing at our luck, immediately began to quarrel about the apportionment of the meat—for they really eat this creature. I saw that they would come to blows presently if I did not interfere, and therefore said I would myself give each man his share, which satisfied all. As we were too tired to return to our camp of last night, we determined to camp here on the spot, and accordingly soon had some shelters erected and dinner going on. Luckily one of the fellows shot a deer just as we began to camp, and on its meat I feasted while my men ate gorilla.

I noticed that they very carefully saved the brain, and was told that charms were made of this—charms of two kinds. Prepared in one way, the charm gave the wearer a strong hand for the hunt, and in another it gave him success with women.

Part Four

TO
THE
POLES

TO THE NORTH POLE

by Robert E. Peary

It was the search for a passage to the Spice Islands of the East which led indirectly to the explorations culminating in Robert E. Peary's discovery of the North Pole on April 6, 1909.

Vasco da Gama had found a passage to the Indies south and east around the Cape of Good Hope. Magellan had reached the same destination by traveling south and west. As has been pointed out, the geographers reasoned that similar passages must exist to the northeast and northwest, or perhaps straight across the top of the earth. In 1818, the Englishman David Buchan sailed with instructions to proceed to the Sandwich Islands by way of the North Pole and to return, if possible, by the same route. He reached 80° 37′ North latitude before he came to the conclusion that the task he had been set was hopeless.

But if there was no northern passage across the Pole, the attainment of 90° North latitude became a goal in itself which was nearly a hundred years in acomplishment. The first of these great attempts was made by Sir Edward Parry in 1827. Parry had had experience in four Arctic voyages. He had been a leading figure in the attempts to find a northern passage to the Pacific. He traveled north in His Majesty's ship Hecla, sailing as far as possible via Spitsbergen. Then he took to small boats, their bottoms shod with iron. In open water the expedition sailed. Over the ice pack, the boats were dragged by seamen. Parry was defeated by southward currents, the drifts counteracting much of what he was able to gain. His farthest north of 82° 45′ was a record up to that time.

Another great name in Arctic exploration was that of Fridtjof Nansen, whose capacity for scientific observation and analysis resulted in a revolutionary plan of attack. It was his intention to build a ship capable of withstanding the pressure of the polar ice, to sail her across the top of Siberia, to freeze her in the pack and let the normal drift carry her toward the Pole.

At a high latitude, Nansen intended to leave the ship, journey across the ice to the Pole and continue to Spitsbergen without attempting to rejoin her. The plan was denounced as suicidal, but while Nansen failed to reach the Pole, his theories were sound in large degree. His ship the Fram was so designed that it easily resisted the pressure of the ice. The drift, however, proved erratic and Nansen took to dog sleds. He reached 86° 14′ North latitude, the highest attained up to that point, before being forced to turn back. After he left the Fram she drifted as he had predicted and reached 85° 57′ North. She was freed from the pack and in 1896, after a three-years trip, returned in safety to Norway. In 1911, incidentally, she was used by Amundsen during the trip on which he discovered the South Pole.

The last great name in the saga is that of Robert E. Peary of the American Navy, who reached the goal which had become the supreme aim of Arctic adventurers. His final dash was the culmination of years of experience and study. Peary came to the conclusion that the methods of existence and travel used by the Eskimos were best adapted to the environment. His diet consisted largely of pemmican—dried meat mixed with fat. He built snow huts for shelter and used dog sledges for transportation. These methods, combined with careful organization, resulted in a feat of discovery noteworthy for the absence of untoward or unexpected incidents. It is described below by Peary himself.

WITH every passing day even the Eskimos were becoming more eager and interested, notwithstanding the fatigue of the long marches. As we stopped to make camp, they would climb to some pinnacle of ice and strain their eyes to the north, wondering if the Pole was in sight, for they were now certain that we should get there this time.

We slept only a few hours the next night, hitting the trail again a little before midnight between the third and fourth of April. The weather and the going were even better than the day before. The surface of the ice, except as interrupted by infrequent pressure ridges, was as level as the glacial fringe from Hecla to Cape Columbia, and harder. I rejoiced at the thought that if the weather held good I should be able to get in my five marches before noon of the sixth.

Again we traveled for ten hours straight ahead, the dogs often on the trot and occasionally on the run, and in those ten hours we reeled off at least twenty-five miles. I had a slight accident that day, a sledge runner having passed over the side of my right foot as I stumbled while running beside a team; but the hurt was not severe enough to keep me from traveling.

Near the end of the day we crossed a lead about one hundred yards wide, on young ice so thin that, as I ran ahead to guide the dogs, I was obliged to slide my feet and travel wide, bear style, in order to distribute my weight, while the men let the sledges and dogs come over by themselves, gliding across where they could. The last two men came over on all fours.

I watched them from the other side with my heart in my mouth— watched the ice bending under the weight of the sledges and the men. As one of the sledges neared the north side, a runner cut clear through the ice, and I expected every moment that the whole thing, dogs and all, would go through the ice and down to the bottom. But it did not.

This dash reminded me of that day, nearly three years before, when in order to save our lives we had taken desperate chances in recrossing the "Big Lead" on ice similar to this—ice that buckled under us and through which my toe cut several times as I slid my long snowshoes over it. A man who should wait for the ice to be really safe would stand small chance of getting far in these latitudes. Traveling on the polar ice, one takes all kinds of chances. Often a man has the choice between the possibility of drowning by going on or starving to death by standing still, and challenges fate with the briefer and less painful chance.

That night we were all pretty tired, but satisfied with our progress so far. We were almost inside of the 89th parallel, and I wrote in my diary: "Give me three more days of this weather!" The temperature at the beginning of the march had been minus forty degrees. That night I put all the poorest dogs in one team and began to eliminate and feed them to the others, as it became necessary.

We stopped for only a short sleep, and early in the evening of the same day, the fourth, we struck on again. The temperature was then minus thirty-five degrees, the going was the same, but the sledges always haul more easily when the temperature rises, and the dogs were on the trot much of the time. Toward the end of the march we came upon a lead running north and south, and as the young ice was thick enough to support the teams, we traveled on it for two hours, the dogs galloping along and reeling off the miles in a way that delighted my heart. The light air which had blown from the south during the first few hours of the march veered to the east and grew keener as the hours wore on.

I had not dared to hope for such progress as we were making. Still the biting cold would have been impossible to face by anyone not fortified by an inflexible purpose. The bitter wind burned our faces so that they cracked, and long after we got into camp each day they pained us so that we could hardly go to sleep. The Eskimos complained much, and at every camp fixed their fur clothing about their faces, waists, knees, and wrists. They also complained of their noses, which I had never known them to do before. The air was as keen and bitter as frozen steel.

At the next camp I had another of the dogs killed. It was now exactly six weeks since we left the *Roosevelt*, and I felt as if the goal were in sight. I intended the next day, weather and ice permitting, to make a long march, "boil the kettle" midway, and then go on again without sleep, trying to make up the five miles which we had lost on the third of April.

During the daily march my mind and body were too busy with the problem of covering as many miles of distance as possible to permit me to enjoy the beauty of the frozen wilderness through which we tramped. But at the end of the day's march, while the igloos were being built, I usually had a few minutes in which to look about me and to realize the picturesqueness of our situation—we, the only living things in a trackless, colorless, inhospitable desert of ice. Nothing but the hostile ice, and far more hostile icy water, lay between our remote place on the world's map and the utmost tips of the lands of Mother Earth.

I knew of course that there was always a *possibility* that we might still end our lives up there, and that our conquest of the unknown spaces and silences of the polar void might remain forever unknown to the world which we had left behind. But it was hard to realize this. That hope which is said to spring eternal in the human breast always buoyed me up with the belief that, as a matter of course, we should be able to return along the white road by which we had come.

Sometimes I would climb to the top of a pinnacle of ice to the north of our camp and strain my eyes into the whiteness which lay beyond, trying to imagine myself already at the Pole. We had come so far, and the capricious ice had placed so few obstructions in our path, that now I dared to loose my fancy, to entertain the image which my will had heretofore forbidden to my imagination—the image of ourselves at the goal.

We had been very fortunate with the leads so far, but I was in constant and increasing dread lest we should encounter an impassable one toward the very end. With every successive march, my fear of such impassable leads had increased. At every pressure ridge I found myself hurrying breathlessly forward, fearing there might be a lead just beyond it, and when I arrived at the summit I would catch my breath with relief—only to find myself hurrying on in the same way at the next ridge.

At our camp on the fifth of April I gave the party a little more sleep than at the previous ones, as we were all pretty well played out and in need of rest. I took a latitude sight, and this indicated our position to be 89° 25', or thirty-five miles from the Pole; but I determined to make the next camp in time for a noon observation, if the sun should be visible.

Before midnight on the fifth we were again on the trail. The weather was overcast, and there was the same gray and shadowless light as on the march after Marvin had turned back. The sky was a colorless pall gradually deepening to almost black at the horizon, and the ice was a ghastly and chalky white, like that of the Greenland ice cap—just the colors which an imaginative artist would paint as a polar icescape. How different it seemed from the glittering fields, canopied with blue and lit by the sun and full moon, over which we had been traveling for the last four days.

The going was even better than before. There was hardly any snow on the hard granular surface of the old floes, and the sapphire blue lakes were larger than ever. The temperature had risen to minus fifteen degrees, which, reducing the friction of the sledges, gave the dogs the appearance of having caught the high spirits of the party. Some of them even tossed their heads and barked and yelped as they traveled.

Notwithstanding the grayness of the day, and the melancholy aspect of the surrounding world, by some strange shift of feeling the fear of the leads had fallen from me completely. I now felt that success was certain, and, notwithstanding the physical exhaustion of the forced marches of the last five days, I went tirelessly on and on, the Eskimos following almost automatically, though I knew that they must feel the weariness which my excited brain made me incapable of feeling.

When we had covered, as I estimated, a good fifteen miles, we halted, made tea, ate lunch, and rested the dogs. Then we went on for another estimated fifteen miles. In twelve hours' actual traveling time we made thirty miles. Many laymen have wondered why we were able to travel faster after the sending back of each of the supporting parties, especially after the last one. To any man experienced in the handling of troops this will need no explanation. The larger the party and the greater the number of sledges, the greater is the chance of breakages or delay for one reason or another. A large party cannot be forced as rapidly as a small party.

Take a regiment, for instance. The regiment could not make as good an average daily march for a number of forced marches as could a picked company of that regiment. The picked company could not make as good an average march for a number of forced marches as could a picked file of men from that particular company; and this file could not make the same average for a certain number of forced marches that the fastest traveler in the whole regiment could make.

So that, with my party reduced to five picked men, every man, dog, and sledge under my individual eye, myself in the lead, and all recognizing that the moment had now come to let ourselves out for all there was in us, we naturally bettered our previous speed.

When Bartlett left us the sledges had been practically rebuilt, all the best dogs were in our pack, and we all understood that we must attain our object and get back as quickly as we possibly could. The weather was in our favor. The average march for the whole journey from the land to the Pole was over fifteen miles. We had repeatedly made marches of twenty miles. Our average for five marches from the point where the last supporting party turned back was about twenty-six miles.

The last march northward ended at ten o'clock on the forenoon of April 6. I had now made the five marches planned from the point at which Bartlett turned back, and my reckoning showed that we were in the immediate neighborhood of the goal of all our striving. After the usual arrangements for going into camp, at approximate local noon, of the Columbia meridian, I made the first observation at our polar camp. It indicated our position as 89° 57′.

We were now at the end of the last long march of the upward journey. Yet with the Pole actually in sight I was too weary to take the last few steps. The accumulated weariness of all those days and nights of forced marches and insufficient sleep, constant peril and anxiety, seemed to roll across me all at once. I was actually too exhausted to realize at the moment that my life's purpose had been achieved. As soon as our igloos had been completed and we had eaten our dinner and double-rationed the dogs, I turned in for a few hours of absolutely necessary sleep, Henson and the Eskimos having unloaded the sledges and got them in readiness for such repairs as were necessary. But, weary though I was, I could not sleep long. It was, therefore, only a few hours later when I woke. The first thing I did after awakening was to write these words in my diary: "The Pole at last. The prize of three centuries. My dream and goal for twenty years. Mine at last! I cannot bring myself to realize it. It seems all so simple and commonplace."

Everything was in readiness for an observation at 6 P.M., Columbia meridian time, in case the sky should be clear, but at that hour it was, unfortunately, still overcast. But as there were indications that it would clear before long, two of the Eskimos and myself made ready a light sledge carrying only the instruments, a tin of pemmican, and one or two skins; and drawn by a double team of dogs, we pushed on an estimated distance of ten miles. While we traveled, the sky cleared, and at the end of the journey, I was able to get a satisfactory series of observations at Columbia meridian midnight. These observations indicated that our position was then beyond the Pole.

Nearly everything in the circumstances which then surrounded us seemed too strange to be thoroughly realized; but one of the strangest of those circumstances seemed to me to be the fact that, in a march of only a few hours, I had passed from the Western to the Eastern Hemisphere and had verified my position at the summit of the world. It was hard to realize that, in the first miles of this brief march, we had been traveling due north, while, on the last few miles of the same march, we had been traveling south, although we had all the time been traveling precisely in the same direction. It would be difficult to imagine a better illustration of the fact that most things are relative. Again, please consider the uncommon circumstance that, in order to return to our camp, it now became necessary to turn and go north again for a few miles and then to go directly south, all the time traveling in the same direction.

As we passed back along that trail which none had ever seen before or would ever see again, certain reflections intruded themselves which, I think, may fairly be called unique. East, west, and north had disappeared for us. Only one direction remained and that was south. Every breeze which could possibly blow upon us, no matter from what point of the horizon, must be a south wind. Where we were, one day and one night constituted a year, a hundred such days and nights constituted a century. Had we stood in that spot during the six months of the Arctic winter night, we should have seen every star of the Northern Hemisphere circling the sky at the same distance from the horizon, with Polaris (the North Star) practically in the zenith.

All during our march back to camp the sun was swinging around in its ever-moving circle. At six o'clock on the morning of April 7, having again arrived at Camp Jesup, I took another series of observations. These indicated our position as being four or five miles from the Pole, toward Bering Strait. Therefore, with a double team of dogs and a light sledge, I traveled directly toward the sun an estimated distance of eight miles. Again I returned to the camp in time for a final and completely satisfactory series of observations on April 7 at noon, Columbia meridian time. These observations gave results essentially the same as those made at the same spot twenty-four hours before.

I had now taken in all thirteen single, or six and one-half double, altitudes of the sun, at two different stations, in three different directions, at four different times. All were under satisfactory conditions, except for the first single altitude on the sixth. The temperature during these observations had been from minus eleven degrees Fahrenheit to minus thirty degrees Fahrenheit, with clear sky and calm weather (except as already noted for the single observation on the sixth).

In traversing the ice in these various directions as I had done, I had allowed approximately ten miles for possible errors in my observations, and at some moment during these marches and countermarches, I had passed over or very near the point where north and south and east and west blend into one.

Of course there were some more or less informal ceremonies connected with our arrival at our difficult destination, but they were not of a very elaborate character. We planted five flags at the top of the world. The first one was a silk American flag which Mrs. Peary gave me fifteen years ago. That flag has done more traveling in high latitudes than any other ever made. I carried it wrapped about my body on every one of my expeditions northward after it came into my possession, and I left a fragment of it at each of my successive "farthest norths": Cape Morris K. Jesup, the northernmost point of land in the known world; Cape Thomas Hubbard, the northernmost known point of Jesup Land, west of Grant Land; Cape Columbia, the northernmost point of North American lands; and my farthest north in 1906, latitude 87° 6' in the ice of the polar sea. By the time it actually reached the Pole, therefore, it was somewhat worn and discolored.

A broad diagonal section of this ensign would now mark the farthest goal of earth—the place where I and my dusky companions stood.

It was also considered appropriate to raise the colors of the Delta Kappa Epsilon fraternity, in which I was initiated a member while an undergraduate student at Bowdoin College, the "World's Ensign of Liberty and Peace," with its red, white, and blue in a field of white, the Navy League flag, and the Red Cross flag.

After I had planted the American flag in the ice, I told Henson to time the Eskimos for three rousing cheers, which they gave with the greatest enthusiasm. Thereupon, I shook hands with each member of the party—surely a sufficiently unceremonious affair to meet with the approval of the most democratic. The Eskimos were childishly delighted with our success. While, of course, they did not realize its importance fully, or its worldwide significance, they did understand that it meant the final achievement of a task upon which they had seen me engaged for many years.

Then, in a space between the ice blocks of a pressure ridge, I deposited a glass bottle containing a diagonal strip of my flag and records of which the following is a copy:

> 90 N. LAT., NORTH POLE
> April 6, 1909

Arrived here to-day, 27 marches from C. Columbia.

I have with me 5 men, Matthew Henson, colored, Ootah, Egingwah, Seegloo, and Ookeah, Eskimos; 5 sledges and 38 dogs. My ship, the S. S. *Roosevelt*, is in winter quarters at C. Sheridan, 90 miles east of Columbia.

The expedition under my command which has succeeded in reaching the Pole is under the auspices of the Peary Arctic Club of New York City, and has been fitted out and sent north by the members and friends of the club for the purpose of securing this geographical prize, if possible, for the honor and prestige of the United States of America.

The officers of the club are Thomas H. Hubbard, of New York, President; Zenas Crane, of Mass., Vice-president; Herbert L. Bridgman, of New York, Secretary and Treasurer.

I start back for Cape Columbia to-morrow.

> ROBERT E. PEARY,
> *United States Navy*

> 90 N. LAT., NORTH POLE
> April 6, 1909

I have to-day hoisted the national ensign of the United States of America at this place, which my observations indicate to be the North Polar axis of the earth, and have formally taken possession of the entire region, and adjacent, for and in the name of the President of the United States of America.

I leave this record and United States flag in possession.

> ROBERT E. PEARY,
> *United States Navy*

If it were possible for a man to arrive at 90° North latitude without being utterly exhausted, body and brain, he would doubtless enjoy a series of unique sensations and reflections. But the attainment of the Pole was the culmination of days and weeks of forced marches, physical discomfort, insufficient sleep, and racking anxiety. It is a wise provision of nature that the human consciousness can grasp only such degree of intense feeling as the brain can endure, and the grim guardians of earth's remotest spot will accept no man as guest until he has been tried and tested by the severest ordeal.

Perhaps it ought not to have been so, but when I knew for a certainty that we had reached the goal, there was not a thing in the world I wanted but sleep. But after I had a few hours of it, there succeeded a condition of mental exaltation which made further rest impossible. For more than a score of years that point on the earth's surface had been the object of my every effort. To its attainment my whole being, physical, mental, and moral, had been dedicated. Many times my own life and the lives of those with me had been risked. My own material and forces and those of my friends had been devoted to this object. This journey was my eighth into the Arctic wilderness. In that wilderness I had spent nearly twelve years out of the twenty-three between my thirtieth and my fifty-third year, and the intervening time spent in civilized communities during that period had been mainly occupied with preparations for returning to the wilderness. The determination to reach the Pole had become so much a part of my being that, strange as it may seem, I long ago ceased to think of myself save as an instrument for the attainment of that end. To the layman this may seem strange, but an inventor can understand it, or an artist, or anyone who has devoted himself for years upon years to the service of an idea.

But though my mind was busy at intervals during those thirty hours spent at the Pole with the exhilarating thought that my dream had come true, there was one recollection of other times that, now and then, intruded itself with startling distinctness. It was the recollection of a day three years before, April 21, 1906, when after making a fight with ice, open water, and storms, the expedition which I commanded had been forced to turn back from 87° 6′ North latitude because our supply of food would carry us no further. And the contrast between the terrible depression of that day and the exaltation of the present moment was not the least pleasant feature of our brief stay at the Pole. During the dark moments of that return journey in 1906, I had told myself that I was only one in a long list of Arctic explorers, dating back through the centuries, all the way from Henry Hudson to the Duke of the Abruzzi, and including Franklin, Kane, and Melville—a long list of valiant men who had striven and failed. I told myself that I had only succeeded, at the price of the best years of my life, in adding a few links to the chain that led from the parallels of civilization toward the polar center, but that, after all, at the end the only word I had to write was "failure."

But now, while quartering the ice in various directions from our camp, I tried to realize that, after twenty-three years of struggles and discouragement, I had at last succeeded in placing the flag of my country at the goal of the world's desire. It is not easy to write about such a thing, but I knew that we were going back to civilization with the last of the great adventure stories—a story the world had been waiting to hear for nearly four hundred years, a story which was to be told at last under the folds of the Stars and Stripes, the flag that during a lonely and isolated life had come to be for me the symbol of home and everything I loved—and might never see again.

The thirty hours at the Pole, what with my marchings and counter-marchings, together with the observations and records, were pretty well crowded. I found time, however, to write to Mrs. Peary on a United States postal card which I had found on the ship during the winter. It has been my custom at various important stages of the journey northward to write such a note in order that, if anything serious happened to me, these brief communications might ultimately reach her at the hands of survivors. This was the card, which later reached Mrs. Peary at Sydney:

90 NORTH LATITUDE, April 7th

MY DEAR JO,

I have won out at last. Have been here a day. I start for home and you in an hour. Love to the "kidsies."

BERT

In the afternoon of the seventh, after flying our flags and taking our photographs, we went into our igloos and tried to sleep a little, before starting south again.

I could not sleep and my two Eskimos, Seegloo and Egingwah, who occupied the igloo with me, seemed equally restless. They turned from side to side, and when they were quiet I could tell from their uneven breathing that they were not asleep. Though they had not been specially excited the day before when I told them that we had reached the goal, yet they also seemed to be under the same exhilarating influence which made sleep impossible for me.

Finally I rose, and telling my men and the three men in the other igloo, who were equally wakeful, that we would try to make our last camp, some thirty miles to the south, before we slept, I gave orders to hitch up the dogs and be off. It seemed unwise to waste such perfect traveling weather in tossing about on the sleeping platforms of our igloos.

Neither Henson nor the Eskimos required any urging to take to the trail again. They were naturally anxious to get back to the land as soon as possible—now that our work was done. And about four o'clock on the afternoon of the seventh of April we turned our backs upon the camp at the North Pole.

Though intensely conscious of what I was leaving, I did not wait for any lingering farewell of my life's goal. The event of human beings standing at the hitherto inaccessible summit of the earth was accomplished, and my work now lay to the south, where four hundred and thirteen nautical miles of ice-floes and possibly open leads still lay between us and the north coast of Grant Land. One backward glance I gave—then turned my face toward the south and toward the future.

PEOPLE OF THE STONE AGE

by Vilhjalmur Stefansson

Although Arctic exploration naturally lost much of its intensity after Peary had attained the great goal, one subsequent explorer made substantial contributions to our knowledge of the North. From 1913 to 1918, Vilhjalmur Stefansson led an expedition into the western American Arctic. He himself was a trained anthropologist and his expedition was planned along scientific lines. It resulted in the gathering of a fund of geological, oceanographic, and anthropological information. Stefansson, who continues to be an authority on the Arctic, was at the time a young man of powerful physique as well as a mighty hunter. He developed Peary's theory of living like the natives to a point where he could exist in comfort where others found only barren desolation. He here writes of an expedition he made to the Coronation Gulf, where he was the first white man the inhabitants had ever seen.

O N THE twenty-first of April, 1910, we finally made the long-planned start from Langton Bay on our trip toward Coronation Gulf.

We were now fairly started for the unknown, but no one but myself was very enthusiastic over the enterprise. The reluctance of my people was

From *My Life with the Eskimo* by Vilhjalmur Stefansson. Copyright 1912, 1913, by Harper & Brothers and used with the permission of The Macmillan Company.

due in part only (and in less part) to their fear of finding the unknown country gameless—they feared to find it inhabited by a barbarous and bloodthirsty race, of which the Baillie Islands Eskimos had been telling us grotesque tales. These dreaded people were the Nagyuktogmiut, the "People-of-the-Caribou-Antler," who lived far to the east, and who used to come in semihostile contact with the Baillie Islanders long ago.

"These people bear the name of the caribou antler," they had told us, "because of a peculiar custom. When a woman becomes of marriageable age her coming-out is announced several days in advance. At the appointed time she is made to take her place in an open space out of doors, and all the men who want wives form a circle round her, each armed with the antler of a large bull caribou. The word is given, and they all rush at her, each trying to hook her toward him with the antler. Often the woman is killed in the scrimmage, but if someone succeeds in getting her alive from the others he takes her for wife. As strength and the skill which experience gives are the main requirements for success, some of the Nagyuktogmiut have a great many wives, while most of them have none. Because so many women are killed in this way there are twice as many men as women among them. We know many stories, of which this is one, to show what queer people these Easterners are. They also kill all strangers." That was the way all stories about the Easterners ended. Like Cato's *"Delenda est Carthago,"* "They kill all strangers" were the unvarying words that finished every discussion of the Nagyuktogmiut by the Baillie Islanders.

No matter how fabulous a story sounds there is usually a basis of fact; when we at last got to these Easterners we found that the kernel of truth consisted in the fewness of women as compared with men, but this had nothing to do with caribou antlers.

When we finally made our start for the east we were in many respects poorly equipped for spending a year away from any possible sources of supplies other than those which the Arctic lands themselves can furnish. When I had planned this undertaking in New York, I had counted on having good dogs, but the good dogs were now dead. I had counted on having a silk tent and other light equipment for summer use, and the lightest and most powerful rifles and high-power ammunition, but during one of our winter periods of shortage of food I had been compelled to abandon many of these things at a distance from which they could not now be fetched.

When our little party of three Eskimos and myself had finally started for the east, they felt, and expressed it, and I felt, but tried to refrain from expressing it, that we had embarked on a serious venture. At Cape Lyon,

April 27, we left behind the farthest point of the mainland upon which any of the American whalers were known to have landed, though some had cruised as far east as the western end of Dolphin and Union Straits in summer, standing well offshore, of course, and never seeing any people.

We had with us on starting from Langton Bay only about two weeks' supplies. From the outset, therefore, we tried to provide each day food for that day from the animals of the land. In carrying out such a program for a party of four, each had to do his share. My main reliance was the Alaskan man Natkusiak, and the woman Pannigabluk; the Mackenzie River boy Tannaumirk was cheerful and companionable, but without initiative and (like many of his countrymen nowadays) not in the best of health.

Our general plan was that the three Eskimos took care of the sledge, one, usually the woman, walking ahead to pick out a trail through the rough sea ice, and the other two steadying the load and pulling in harness at the same time to help the dogs. If they saw a seal or a bear one of them would go after him while the other two waited at the sledge, cooked a lunch if it was near midday, or made camp if night was approaching. If by camp time no game had yet been seen, Pannigabluk would stay by the camp to cook supper, while the two men went off in different directions to hunt.

That the two should go in different directions was wise, for it doubled the chances of seeing game, but it at times caused unnecessary waste of ammunition and the killing of more meat than was needed. The very first time that both men went out to hunt in this manner, for instance, Natkusiak killed two seven- or eight-hundred-pound bearded seals in one shot, and Tannaumirk a big, fat grizzly bear in four shots. This was meat enough for several weeks if we had (Eskimo-fashion) stayed there to eat it up; traveling as we were, heavily loaded through rough ice, we could not take with us more than a hundred pounds of the meat.

Although the Eskimos frequently killed an animal or two if they happened on them along the line of march, the chief responsibility of food providing was mine. Their main business was getting the sledge ahead as rapidly as convenient, which was seldom over fifteen miles in a working day averaging perhaps eight hours. We were in no hurry, for we had no particular distance to go and no reason to hasten back, but expected to spend the summer wherever it overtook us, and the winter similarly in its turn.

Crossing Darnley Bay on the ice we had, of course, seen no caribou; at Cape Lyon the Eskimos saw one yearling, but were unable to get it; and at Point Pierce, five days out from Langton Bay, we were stopped by an easterly blizzard without having yet secured any. The Eskimos, who had "known" all along that we were going into a gameless country, felt sure that the fawn they had seen at Lyon was the most easterly member of the species inhabiting the coast; it would therefore be wise to turn about now, they argued, before the journey back got too long and we got too weak from hunger—all this over huge troughs of boiled meat and raw blubber of the seals killed two days before, on which we were gorging ourselves, for much eating was always our chief pastime when delayed by a blizzard that the dogs would not face. As a matter of fact, what my Eskimos dreaded was not so much hunger, as the possibility of our success in the quest of what to me were the scientifically interesting "people who had never seen a white man," but to them were the dreaded Nagyuktogmiut.

Generally it is only in times of extreme need that one hunts caribou in a blizzard. Not that nine-tenths of the blizzards in the Arctic need keep a healthy man indoors. In the present instance my reason for looking for caribou was that I wanted to kill a few for the moral effect it would have on my party; for in the midst of abundance they would be forced to fall back on their fear of the Nagyuktogmiut as the only argument for retreat, and this they were a bit ashamed of doing, even among themselves. It was therefore great luck that after a short hunt through the storm I ran into a band of seven cows and young bulls, about five miles inland, southwest from Point Pierce. I came upon them quite without cover, but saw them through the drifting snow at three hundred yards before they saw me—the human eye is a great deal keener than that of the caribou, wolf, or any other four-footed animal with which I have had experience, except the mountain sheep.

By stepping back a few paces till the drifting snow had hidden the caribou again, and then guardedly circling them to leeward, I found a slight ridge which allowed safe approach to within about two hundred yards of where they had been. The main thing in stalking caribou that are not moving is the ability to keep in mind their situation accurately, while you are circling and winding about so as to approach them from a new direction, behind cover of irregular hills and ridges that are of course unfamiliar to you. In this case my plans came suddenly to naught through the caribou appearing on the skyline two hundred yards off. I shot three of them, though we could not possibly use more than the meat of one. The moral effect on my Eskimos of having food to throw away would, I knew, be invaluable to me.

On the journey eastward along the deserted coast beyond Point Pierce, the

Eskimos handled the sledge, made camp and cooked, while I kept the job of food provider. On breaking camp in the morning, I used to get a start ahead of them by leaving while they were packing up and striking about five miles inland, then walking rapidly on my snowshoes parallel to the coast, keeping it and the sledge in sight as best I could.

There were not many adventures fortunately. An adventure is interesting enough in retrospect, especially to the person who didn't have it; at the time it happens it usually constitutes an exceedingly disagreeable experience. On May 2, near Point Deas Thompson, through incompetence of my own, I came near to having a serious one; that it did not end badly for me was due to the incompetence of a polar bear. After completely outmaneuvering me at the start, he allowed a fondness for grandstand play to lose him the game at the critical moment.

It happened in the afternoon. As usual, I was hunting caribou eastward along the sea front of the Melville Mountains that lie parallel to the coast a few miles inland. The sledge and the Eskimos were traveling more slowly along the coast and were several miles behind—for one thing, the load was heavy and the ice rough; for another, they used to stop an hour or so each day to cook a lunch. I had seen no caribou all day nor the day before, and our meat was low; therefore I stopped whenever I came to the top of a commanding hill to sweep the country carefully with my binoculars. For several days we had had small luck and food was running low. Ptarmigan there were, but they are uneconomical for a party of four that is to go a year on nine hundred and sixty rounds of ammunition; even the foxes were too small for our notice, though their meat is excellent; but a wolf that came within two hundred yards seldom got by, for a fat one weighs a hundred pounds, and all of us preferred them at this season to caribou—except Pannigabluk, who would not taste the meat because it is taboo to her tribe.

This day the wolves did not come near, and the first hopeful sign was a yellow spot on the sea ice about three miles off. It was difficult to determine whether or not it were merely yellow ice. Had my party been abreast of me, or ahead, I should have given up and moved on, but as they were several miles behind I put in a half-hour watching this thing that was a bit yellower than ice should be. Now and then I looked elsewhere, for a caribou or grizzly may at any time come out from behind a hill, a polar bear from behind a cake of ice, or a seal out of his hole. On perhaps the sixth or seventh sweep of the entire horizon with the field glasses, I missed the yellow spot. It had moved away and must therefore have been a polar bear that had been lying down; after sleeping too long in one position he had stood up and lain down again behind an ice cake.

In a moment I was running as hard as I could in the direction of the bear, for there was no telling when he would start traveling or how fast he would go. As soon as I began to suspect what the yellow spot might be, I had taken careful note of the topography of the land with relation to the rough sea ice, for it is as difficult to keep a straight line toward an invisible object among pressure ridges as it is in a forest. I kept glancing back at the mountains as I ran and tried to guide myself toward the bear by their configuration. Every three or four hundred yards I would climb a high pressure ridge and have a look round with the glasses, but nothing was to be seen. I did not, in fact, expect to see anything, unless the bear had commenced traveling, in which case he would perhaps expose himself by crossing a high ridge.

When at last I got to the neighborhood of where I thought the animal would be, I climbed an especially high ridge and spent a longer time than usual sweeping the surroundings with the glasses and studying individual ice cakes and ridges, with the hope of recognizing some of those I had seen from the mountains. But everything looked different on near approach, and I failed to locate myself definitely. I decided to go a quarter of a mile or so farther before beginning to circle in quest of the bear's tracks. My rifle was buckled in its case slung across my back, and I was slowly and cautiously clambering down the far side of a pressure ridge, when I heard behind me a noise like the spitting of a cat or the hiss of an angry goose. I looked back and saw, about twenty feet away and almost above me, a polar bear.

Had he come the remaining twenty feet as quietly and quickly as a bear can, the literary value of the incident would have been lost forever. For, as the Greek fable points out, a lion does not write a book. From his eye and attitude, as well as the story his trail told afterward, there was no doubting his intentions; the hiss was merely his way of saying, "Watch me do it!" Or at least that is how I interpreted it; possibly the motive was chivalry, and the hiss was his way of saying *"Garde!"* Whichever it was, it was the fatal mistake in a game played well to that point. No animal on earth can afford to give warning to a man with a rifle. And why should he? Has a hunter ever played fair with one of them?

Afterward the snow told plainly the short—and for one of the participants, tragic—story. I had overestimated the bear's distance from shore, and had passed the spot where he lay, going a hundred yards or two to windward.

On scenting me he had come up the wind to my trail, and had then followed it, walking about ten paces to leeward apparently smelling my tracks from a distance. The reason I had not seen his approach was that it had not occurred to me to look back over my own trail. I was so used to hunting bears that the possibility of one of them assuming my own role and hunting me had been left out of consideration. A good hunter, like a good detective, should leave nothing out of consideration.

On May 9, nineteen days out from Langton Bay, we came upon signs that made our hearts beat faster. It was at Point Wise, where the open sea begins to be narrowed into Dolphin and Union Straits by the near approach of the mountainous shores of Victoria Island. The beach was strewn with pieces of driftwood, on one of which we found the marks of recent choppings with a dull adz.

The night after this discovery we did not sleep much. The Eskimos were more excited than I was, and far into the morning they talked and speculated on the meaning of the signs. Had we come upon traces of the Nagyuktogmiut who "kill all strangers"?

Fortunately, my long-entertained fear that traces of people would cause a panic in my party was not realized. In spite of all their talk, and in spite of being seriously afraid, the curiosity as to what these strange people would prove to be like—in fine, the spirit of adventure, which seldom crops out in an Eskimo—was far stronger than their fears. We were therefore up early the next morning and were soon on the road.

All that day we found along the beach comparatively fresh traces of people, chiefly wood shavings and chips. None seen that day were of the present winter, though some seemed to be of the previous summer. But the next morning, just east of Point Young, we found at last human footprints in the crusted snow and sledge tracks that were not over three months old. That day at Cape Bexley we came upon a deserted village of over fifty snow houses; their inhabitants had apparently left them about midwinter, and it was now the twelfth of May.

The size of the deserted village took our breath away. Tannaumirk, the young man from the Mackenzie River, had never seen an inhabited village among his people of more than twelve or fifteen houses. All his old fears of the Nagyuktogmiut who "kill all strangers" now came to the surface afresh; all the stories that he knew of their peculiar ways and atrocious deeds were retold by him that evening for our common benefit.

A broad, but three months' untraveled, trail led north from this village site across the ice toward Victoria Island. My intentions were to continue east along the mainland into Coronation Gulf, but I decided nevertheless to stop here long enough to make an attempt to find the people at whose abandoned homes we were encamped. We would leave most of our gear on shore, with Pannigabluk to take care of it, while the two men and myself took the trail across the ice. This was according to Eskimo etiquette —on approach to the country of strange or distrusted people, noncombatants are left behind, and only the able men of the party advance to a cautious parley.

Tannaumirk was so thoroughly frightened by his own recital of the atrocities committed by the Nagyuktogmiut upon his ancestors long ago, that he let his pride go by the board and asked that he, too, might stay on shore at the camp. I told him he might, and Natkusiak and I prepared to start alone with a light sledge, but at the last moment he decided that he preferred to go with us, as the Nagyuktogmiut were likely in our absence to discover the camp, to surprise it by night, and to kill him while he slept. It would be safer, he thought, to go with us.

Pannigabluk was much the coolest of the three Eskimos; if she was afraid to be left alone on shore she did not show it; she merely said that she might get lonesome if we were gone more than three or four days. We left her cheerfully engaged in mending our worn footgear, and at 2:30 P.M., May 13, 1910, we took the old but nevertheless plain trail northward into the rough sea ice.

We made about six miles per hour, which brought us in less than two hours to another deserted village, about a month more recent than the one at Cape Bexley.

As we understood dimly then and know definitely now, each village on the winter migration trail of a sealing people should be about ten miles from the one preceding, and about a month more recent.

The village of a people who hunt seal on level bay ice must not be on shore, for it is not convenient for a hunter to go more than five miles at the most from camp in search of seal holes, and naturally there are no seal holes on land. The inhabitants of a sea village can hunt through an entire circle whose radius is about five miles; the inhabitants of a shore village can hunt through only half a circle of the same radius.

When the frost overtakes the seals in the autumn, each of them, wherever he happens to be, gnaws several holes in the thin ice, one not far from the other, and rises to them whenever he needs to breathe. As the ice thickens he keeps the holes open by continuous gnawing, and for the whole of the winter that follows he is kept a prisoner in their neighborhood; for if he ever went to a considerable distance he would be unable to find a place to reach the air, and would die of suffocation. By the aid of their dogs the Eskimos find these breathing holes of the seals underneath the snow that hides them in winter, and harpoon the animals as they rise for air. In a month or so the hunters of a single village will have killed all the seals within a radius of about five miles; they must then move camp about ten miles, so that a five-mile circle round their next camp shall be tangent to the five-mile circle about their last one; for if the circles overlapped there would be that much waste territory within the new circle of activities. If, then, you are following such a winter migration trail and come to a village about four months old, you will expect to find the people who made it not more than forty miles off.

In the present case our task was simplified, for the group we were following had been moving in a curve and had made their fourth camp west of the second. Standing on the roofs of the houses of the second camp, we could see three seal hunters a few miles to the west, each sitting on his block of snow by a seal hole waiting for a rise.

The seal hunters and their camp were up the wind, and our dogs scented them. As we bore swiftly down upon the nearest of the sealers the team showed enthusiasm and anticipation as keen as mine, keener by a great deal than did my Eskimos.

As the hunter was separated from each of his fellow huntsmen by a full half-mile, I thought he would probably be frightened if all of us were to rush up to him at the top speed of our dogs. We therefore stopped our sledge several hundred yards away. Tannaumirk had become braver on near approach, for the lone stranger did not look formidable, sitting stooped forward on his block of snow beside the seal hole. He accordingly volunteered to act as our ambassador, saying that the Mackenzie dialect (his own) was probably nearer the stranger's tongue than Natkusiak's. This seemed likely, so we told him to go ahead. The sealer sat motionless as Tannaumirk approached him; I watched him through my glasses and saw that he held his face steadily as if watching the seal hole, but that he raised his eyes every second or two to the strange figure of the man approaching. He was evidently tensely ready for action.

Tannaumirk had by now got over his fears completely, and would have walked right up to the sealer, but when five paces or so intervened between them the sealer suddenly jumped up, grasped a long copper-bladed knife that had lain on the snow beside him, and poised himself as if to receive an attack or to be ready to leap forward. This scared our man, who stopped abruptly and began excitedly and volubly to assure the sealer that he and all of us were men of excellent character and intentions.

I was, of course, too far away to hear, but Tannaumirk told me afterward that on the instant of jumping up the sealer began a monotonous noise, which is not a chant, nor is it words—it is merely an effort to ward off dumbness. For if a man who is in the presence of a spirit does not make at least one sound each time he draws his breath, he will be stricken permanently dumb. This is a belief common to the Alaskan and Coronation Gulf Eskimos. For several minutes Tannaumirk talked excitedly, and the sealer kept up the moaning noise, quite unable to realize, apparently, that he was being spoken to in human speech. It did not occur to him for a long time, he told us afterward, that we might be something other than spirits, for our dogs and dog harness, our sledges and clothes, were such as he had never seen in all his wanderings. Besides, we had not, on approaching, used the peace sign of his people, which is holding the hands out to show that one does not carry a knife.

After what may have been anything from five to fifteen minutes of talking and expostulation by Tannaumirk, the man finally began to listen and then to answer. The dialects proved to differ rather less than Norwegian does from Swedish, or Spanish from Portuguese. After Tannaumirk had made him understand that we were of good intent and character, and had indicated by lifting his own coat that he had no knife hidden, the sealer approached cautiously and felt of him, partly (as he told us later) to assure himself that he was not a spirit and partly to see if there were not a knife hidden somewhere under his clothes. After a careful examination and some further parley he told Tannaumirk to tell us that they two would precede us to the village, with Natkusiak and me following as far behind as we were now. When they got to the village we were to remain outside it till the people could be informed that we were visitors with friendly intentions.

As we proceeded toward the village other seal hunters gradually converged toward us from all over the neighboring four or five square miles of ice and joined Tannaumirk and his companion, who walked about two hundred yards ahead. As each of these was armed with a long knife and a seal harpoon, it may be imagined that the never very brave Tannaumirk was pretty thoroughly frightened—to which he owned up freely that night and the few days following, though he had forgotten the circumstance completely by next year, when we returned to his own people in the Mackenzie district, where he is now a drawing-room lion on the strength of his adventures in the remote east.

When we approached the village every man, woman, and child was outdoors waiting for us excitedly, for they could tell from afar that we were no ordinary visitors. The man whom we had first approached—who that day acquired a local prominence which still distinguishes him above his fellows—explained to an eagerly silent crowd that we were friends from a distance, who had come without evil intent, and immediately the whole crowd (about forty) came running toward us. As each came up he would say: "I am So-and-so. I am well disposed. I have no knife. Who are you?" After being told our names in return, and being assured that we were friendly, and that our knives were packed away in the sledge and not hidden under our clothing, each would express his satisfaction and stand aside for the next to present himself. Sometimes a man would present his wife, or a woman her husband, according to which came up first. The women were in more hurry to be presented than were the men, for they must, they said, go right back to their houses to cook us something to eat.

After the women were gone the men asked whether we preferred to have our camp right in the village or a little outside it. On talking it over we agreed that it would be better to camp about two hundred yards from the other houses, so as to keep our dogs from fighting with theirs. When this was decided, half a dozen small boys were sent home to as many houses to get their fathers' snow knives and house-building mittens.

We were not allowed to lend a hand to anything in camp-making, but stood idly by, surrounded continually by a crowd who used every means to show how friendly they felt and how welcome we were, while a few of the best house-builders set about erecting for us the house in which we were to live as long as we cared to stay with them. When it had been finished and furnished with the skins, lamp, and the other things that go to make a snowhouse the cosiest and most comfortable of camps, they told us they hoped we would occupy it at least till the last piece of meat in their storehouses had been eaten, and that as long as we stayed in the village no man would hunt seals or do any work until his children began to complain of hunger. It was to be a holiday, they said, for this was the first time their people had been visited by strangers from so great a distance that even their country was unknown.

These simple, well-bred, and hospitable people were the savages whom we had come so far to seek. That evening they saw for the first time the lighting of a sulphur match, and the next day I showed them the marvels of my rifle.

Our first day among the Dolphin and Union Straits Eskimos was the day of all my life to which I had looked forward with the most vivid anticipations. I now look back to it with equally vivid memories, for it introduced me, a student of mankind and of primitive men especially, to a people of a bygone age. Mark Twain's Connecticut Yankee went to sleep in the nineteenth century and woke up in King Arthur's time, among knights who rode in clinking mail to the rescue of fair ladies; we, without going to sleep at all, had walked out of the twentieth century into the country of the intellectual and cultural contemporaries of a far earlier age than King Arthur's. These were not such men as Cæsar found in Gaul or in Britain; they were more nearly like the still earlier hunting tribes of Britain and of Gaul living contemporaneous to, but oblivious of, the building of the first pyramid in Egypt. Their existence on the same continent with our populous cities was an anachronism of ten thousand years in material development. They gathered their food with the weapons of the Stone Age, they thought their simple, primitive thoughts, and lived their insecure and tense lives—lives that were to me the mirrors of the lives of our far ancestors, whose bones and crude handiwork we now and then discover in river gravels or in prehistoric caves. Such archæological remains, found in various parts of the world, tell a fascinating story to him whose scientific imagination can piece it together and fill in the wide gaps; but far better than such dreaming was my present opportunity. I had nothing to imagine; I had merely to look and listen; for here were not remains of the Stone Age, but the Stone Age itself, with its men and women, very human, entirely friendly, who welcomed us to their homes and talked with us.

Like our distant ancestors, no doubt, these people fear most of all things the evil spirits that are likely to appear to them at any time in any guise, and next to that they fear strangers. Our first meeting had been a bit doubtful and dramatic through our being mistaken for spirits, but now they had touched us and talked with us, and knew we were men. Strangers we were, it is true, but we were only three among forty of them, and were therefore not to be feared. Besides, they told us, they knew we could harbor no guile from the freedom and frankness with which we came among them; for, they said, a man who plots treachery never turns his back to those whom he intends to stab from behind.

Before the house they were building for us was quite ready, children came running from the village to announce that their mothers had dinner cooked. The houses were so small that it was not convenient to invite all three of us into the same one to eat; besides, it was not etiquette to do so, as we now know. Each of us was therefore taken to a different place. My host was the seal hunter whom we had first approached on the ice.

His wife was not a talkative nor inquisitive person, but motherly, kindly, and hospitable, like all her countrywomen. Her first questions were not of the land from which I came, but of my footgear. Weren't my feet just a little damp, and might she not pull my boots off for me and dry them over the lamp? Would I not put on a pair of her husband's dry socks, and was there no little hole in my mittens or coat that she could mend for me? She had boiled some seal meat for me, but she had not boiled any fat, for she thought I might prefer my blubber raw. They always cut it in small pieces and ate it raw themselves; but the pot still hung over the lamp, and anything she put into it would be cooked in a moment.

When I told her that my tastes quite coincided with theirs—as, in fact, they did—she was delighted. People were much alike, then, after all, though they came from a great distance. She would, accordingly, treat me exactly as if I were one of their own people come to visit them from afar —and, in fact, I *was* one of their own people, for she had heard that the wicked Indians to the south spoke a language no man could understand, and I spoke with but a slight flavor of strangeness.

When we entered the house the boiled pieces of seal meat had already been taken out of the pot and lay steaming on a side table. On being assured that my tastes in food were not likely to differ from theirs, my hostess picked out for me the lower joint of a seal's foreleg, squeezed it firmly between her hands to make sure nothing should later drip from it, and handed it to me, along with her own copper-bladed knife; the next most desirable piece was similarly squeezed and handed to her husband, and others in turn to the rest of the family.

As we ate we sat on the front edge of the bed-platform, each holding his piece of meat in the left hand and the knife in the right. This was my first experience with a knife of native copper. I found it more than sharp enough and very serviceable. As the house was only the ordinary oval snow dome, about seven by nine feet in inside dimensions, there was only room for the three of us on the front edge of the two-foot-high snow platform, over which reindeer, bear, and ovibos skins had been spread to make the bed. The children, therefore, ate standing up on the small, open floor space to the right of the door as one enters; the lamp and cooking gear and frames for drying clothing over the lamp took up all the space to the left of the door. In the horseshoe-shaped three-foot-high doorway stood the three dogs of my host, side by side, waiting for some one to finish the picking of a bone. As each of us in turn finished a bone we would toss it to one of the dogs, who retired with it to the alleyway, and returned to his position in line again as soon as he had finished it. When the meal was over they all went away unbidden, to curl up and sleep in the alleyway or outside.

Our meal was of two courses: the first, meat; the second, soup. The soup is made by pouring cold seal blood into the boiling broth immediately after the cooked meat has been taken out of the pot, and stirring briskly until the whole comes nearly (but never quite) to a boil.

After I had eaten my fill of fresh seal meat and drunk two pint cupfuls of blood soup, my host and I moved farther back on the bed-platform, where we could sit comfortably propped up against bundles of soft caribou skins while we talked of various things. He and his wife asked but few questions, and only such as could not be considered intrusive, either according to their standards as I learned them later or according to ours. It must be a very long way to the land from which we came; were we not satiated with traveling and did we not think of spending the summer with them? Of course, the tribes who lived farther east would also be glad to see us, and would treat us well, unless we went too far to the east and fell in with the Netsilik Eskimos (King William Island), who are wicked, treacherous people who—strange to say—have no chins. Beyond them, they had heard, lived the white men (Kablunat), of whom, no doubt, we had never heard, seeing we came from the west.

The white men, they told me, are farthest of all people to the east. They were said to have various physical deformities; they had heard that some of them had but one eye and that in the middle of the forehead, but of this they were not sure, because stories that come from afar are always doubtful. The white men were said to be of a strangely eccentric disposition; sometimes when they gave valuable things to an Eskimo they would take no pay for them; and at other times they wanted exorbitant prices for useless articles or mere curiosities. They would not eat good, ordinary food, but subsisted on various things which a normal person could not think of forcing himself to swallow except in case of starvation. And this in spite of the fact that the white men could have better things to eat if they wanted to, for seals, whales, fish, and even caribou abound in their country.

It was to be expected that men coming from so great a distance would have customs different from theirs. As for them, they were glad to answer my questions, and I should have to stay many days before they got tired of doing whatever they could to show they were glad I had come. After the meal was finished we sat and talked perhaps an hour, until a messenger came (it was always the children who carried messages) to say that my companions had gone to the house that had been built for us, and that the people hoped I would come there too, for it was a big house, and many could sit in there at once and talk with us. On arriving home I found that, although over half the village was already there, still we had plenty of room within doors for the four or five who had come along with me to see me home. The floor of the inner half of the house had been raised into the usual two-foot-high snow sleeping platform, covered with skins, partly ours and partly contributed by various households for our comfort. A seal-oil lamp for heating and lighting had been installed. It was a cozy place, heated by the lamp to fifty degrees Fahrenheit in spite of being well ventilated by a door that was never closed day or night, and a hole in the roof that was also always open. On the bed-platform there was room for twelve or fifteen persons to sit Turkish fashion, and on the floor in front another fifteen or twenty could stand.

Although the house was full of guests at my homecoming, they stayed only a few minutes, for someone suggested that we were no doubt tired and sleepy and would like to be left alone. In the morning, they said, we should have plenty of time for talking.

When they were all gone, however, we did not go to sleep, but sat up fully half the night discussing the strange things we had seen. My Eskimos were considerably more excited over it all than I. It was, they said, as if we were living through a story such as the old men tell in the assembly house when the sun is away in winter. What kindly, inoffensive-looking people these were, but no doubt they were powerful and dangerous magicians such as the stories tell about, and such as my companions' fathers had known in their youth. Tannaumirk had, in fact, heard something to prove this. He had eaten supper in the house of a man who last winter had dropped his knife into a seal hole through the ice where the sea was very deep, but so powerful was the spell he pronounced that when he reached down the water came only to his elbow and he picked the knife off the ocean bottom. And this, Tannaumirk commented, where the ice alone was at least a fathom thick, and the water so deep that a stone dropped into it would take a long time to sink to the bottom.

Did they believe all this, I asked my men, though I knew what the answer would be. Of course they did. Why should I ask? Had they not often told me that their own people were able to do such things until a few years ago, when they abjured their familiar spirits on learning from the missionary that no one can attain salvation who employs spirits to do his bidding? It was too bad that salvation and the practice of magic were incompatible; not that such trivial things as the recovery of lost articles were of moment, but in the cure of sickness and control of weather prayers seemed so much less efficient than the old charms. . . .

One of the things that interested me was to see some shooting with their strong-looking bows and long copper-tipped arrows. I therefore said that I should like to have them illustrate to me the manner in which they killed caribou, and I would in turn show them the weapons and method used by us. Half a dozen of the men at once sent home for their bows, and a block of snow to serve as a target was set up in front of our house. The range at which a target a foot square could be hit with fair regularity turned out to be about thirty or thirty-five yards, and the extreme range of the bow was a bit over one hundred yards, while the range at which caribou are ordinarily shot was shown to be from thirty-five to seventy-five yards.

When their exhibition was over I set up a stick at about two hundred yards and fired at it. The people who stood round had no idea what I was about to do. When they heard the loud report of my gun all the women and children made a scramble for the houses, while the men ran back about fifteen or twenty yards and stood talking together excitedly behind a snow wall. I at once went to them and asked them to come with me to the stick and see what had happened to it. After some persuasion three of them complied. But unfortunately for me it turned out that I had failed to score. At this they seemed much relieved, but when I told them I would try again they protested earnestly, saying that so loud a noise would scare all the seals away from their hunting grounds, and the people would therefore starve.

It seemed to me imperative, however, to show them I could keep my word and perforate the stick at two hundred yards. In spite of their protests I got ready to shoot again, telling them that we used these weapons in the west for seal hunting, and that the noise was found not to scare seals away. The second shot happened to hit, but the mark of the bullet on the stick impressed them far less than the noise. In fact, they did not seem to marvel at it at all. When I explained that I could kill a polar bear or a caribou at even twice the distance the stick had been they exhibited no surprise, but asked me if I could with my rifle kill a caribou on the other side of a mountain. When I said that I could not, they told me that a great shaman in a neighboring tribe had a magic arrow by which he could kill caribou on the other side of no matter how big a mountain. In other words, they considered the performance of my rifle nothing wonderful.

Perhaps I might here digress to point out that the Eskimos' refusal to be astonished by the killing at a great distance of a caribou or a bear by a rifle bullet whose flight was unerring and invisible, was not an isolated case. When I showed them later my binoculars that made faraway things seem near and clear, they were, of course, interested; when I looked to the south or east and saw bands of caribou that were to them invisible, they applauded. Then followed the suggestion: "Now that you have looked for the caribou that are here today and found them, will you not also look for the caribou that are coming tomorrow, so that we can tell where to lie in ambush for them?" When they heard that my glasses could not see into the future, they were disappointed and the reverse of well impressed. For their own medicine men, they told us, had charms and magic paraphernalia that enabled them to see things the morrow was to bring forth.

At another time, in describing to them the skill of our surgeons, I told that they could put a man to sleep, and while he slept take out a section of his intestines or one of his kidneys, and the man when he woke up would not even know what had been done to him, except as he was told and as he could see the sewed-up opening through which the part had been removed. Our doctors could even transplant the organs of one man into the body of another. These things I had never actually seen done, but that they were done was common knowledge in my country.

It was similar in their country, one of my listeners told me. He himself had a friend who suffered continually from backache until a great medicine man undertook to treat him. The next night, while the patient slept, the medicine man removed the entire spinal column, which had become diseased, and replaced it with a complete new set of vertebræ, and— what was most wonderful—there was not a scratch on the patient's skin or anything to show that the exchange had been made. This the narrator had not seen done, but the truth of it was common knowledge among his people. Another man had had his diseased heart replaced with a new and sound one.

The Eskimos believed in the truth of what he told us as thoroughly as I believed what I had told him. Neither of us had seen the things actually done, but that they were done was a matter of common belief among our respective countrymen.

LAST MARCH

by Robert Falcon Scott

The history of Antarctic exploration is in large part a story of discovery in reverse—discovery of the fact that the land mass which was once supposed to cover the entire southern portion of the earth and which had been given the name "Terra Australis," did not exist except as the relatively small section now known as Antarctica.

The original concept of the ancient geographers had been summed up by Ptolemy, the Alexandrian scholar, who lived about 150 A.D. His influence was enormous and as a result medieval geographers believed that the South was one vast continent, which linked Asia and Africa and made the Indian Ocean an inland sea. The theory died hard. When Vasco da Gama sailed around the Cape of Good Hope to reach the Indies, many believed that he had simply discovered a strait dividing the two continents. Magellan sailed through his name straits and it was considered that Tierra del Fuego was part of the Southern Continent. Tasman believed that New Zealand was part of this same continent, but when Schouten went round the Horn and discovered only water to the south, it was realized that Antarctica was much smaller than had been supposed. Captain Cook sailed nearly around the world below the latitude of Cape Horn and again Antarctica shrank on the maps.

In the early nineteenth century, Yankee whalers and sealers, as well as Russian sailors, extended our knowledge. The British navigator who gave his name to the Weddell Sea, the three Antarctic expeditions of Sir James Clark Ross (for whom the Ross Sea was named) and an American naval expedition under Lieutenant Charles Wilkes, all contributed to a more realistic appraisal of the true facts.

The stage for the race to the Pole was now set and its discovery was accompanied by happenings infinitely more dramatic than Peary's rather prosaic journey. This Southern epic, for epic it may truly be termed, involved international rivalries, a secret shift of plans, a test between two techniques of polar travel, incredible heroism in the face of danger and tragic death.

Captain Robert Falcon Scott, from whose diaries the next selection is taken, first became acquainted with the Antarctic on an expedition which he commanded in 1901. This trip, in the ship Discovery, lasted three years, explored the Antarctic plateau and reached farthest south up to that time, 82° 17'. One of the members of the expedition was Ernest Shackleton, who was later knighted. In 1908, he led his own expedition, attempting a dash to the Pole. He made the mistake of using Manchurian ponies instead of dogs. The ponies had to be abandoned, the men became draft animals and the party barely managed to return safely to base.

Scott meanwhile had continued his career in the British Navy. However, he remained engrossed in all things Antarctic, and in 1911, having financed and outfitted an expedition, he made his final try. All England and the Empire cheered him on. Elaborate equipment was available, but some of it was unwisely chosen. Scott had gone to Norway to ask the advice of Dr. Nansen, who had urged him to use dogs for transport. Instead, Scott chose motor sledges, Manchurian ponies and manpower—and all were to fail him in the end.

Meanwhile another strand in the story, which was to lead to the South Pole itself, was being woven. Roald Amundsen, author of a selection in the first section of this book, had spent his life in polar exploration. As commander of the Gjoa, he had been the first person in history actually to navigate the Northwest Passage to the Pacific, a feat which had baffled explorers for centuries. Later he was to negotiate the Northeast Passage also. He was planning an attempt on the North Pole in Nansen's ship the Fram when word reached him that Peary had been successful. He knew that Scott was preparing an assault on the South Pole and continued to announce that he was going north on a purely scientific expedition. Only when he was well at sea did his brother cable to Scott, then in Australia, "AM GOING SOUTH—AMUNDSEN." By choosing a more favorable base and by the use of excellent dogs, Amundsen was able to beat his rival to the South Pole by thirty-eight days. It is against this background that the excerpt from Scott's last diary should be read.

SUNDAY, February 18.—R. 32. Temp. −5.5°. At Shambles Camp. We gave ourselves 5 hours' sleep at the lower glacier depot after the horrible night, and came on at about 3 today to this camp, coming fairly easily over the divide. Here with plenty of horsemeat we have had a fine supper, to be followed by others such, and so continue a more plentiful era if we can keep good marches up. New life seems to come with greater food almost immediately, but I am anxious about the Barrier surfaces.

Monday, February 19.—Lunch T. −16°. It was late (past noon) before we got away today, as I gave nearly 8 hours sleep, and much camp work was done shifting sledges[1] and fitting up new one with mast, &c., packing horsemeat and personal effects. The surface was every bit as bad as I expected, the sun shining brightly on it and its covering of soft loose sandy snow. We have come out about 2′ on the old tracks. Perhaps lucky to have a fine day for this and our camp work, but we shall want wind or change of sliding conditions to do anything on such a surface as we have got. I fear there will not be much change for the next 3 or 4 days.

R. 33. Temp. −17°. We have struggled out 4.6 miles in a short day over a really terrible surface—it has been like pulling over desert sand, not the least glide in the world. If this goes on we shall have a bad time, but I sincerely trust it is only the result of this windless area close to the coast and that, as we are making steadily outward, we shall shortly escape it. It is perhaps premature to be anxious about covering distance. In all other respects things are improving. We have our sleeping-bags spread on the sledge and they are drying, but, above all, we have our full measure of food again. Tonight we had a sort of stew fry of pemmican and horseflesh, and voted it the best hoosh we had ever had on a sledge journey. The absence of poor Evans is a help to the commissariat, but if he had been here in a fit state we might have got along faster. I wonder what is in store for us, with some little alarm at the lateness of the season.

Monday, February 20.—R. 34. Lunch Temp. −13°; Supper Temp. −15°. Same terrible surface; four hours' hard plodding in morning brought us to our Desolation Camp, where we had the four-day blizzard. We looked for more pony meat, but found none. After lunch we took to ski with some improvement of comfort. Total mileage for day 7—the ski tracks pretty plain and easily followed this afternoon. We have left another cairn behind. Terribly slow progress, but we hope for better things as we clear the land. There is a tendency to cloud over in the S.E. tonight, which may turn to our advantage. At present our sledge and ski leave deeply plowed tracks which can be seen winding for miles behind. It is distressing, but as usual trials are forgotten when we camp, and good food is our lot. Pray God we get better traveling as we are not so fit as we were, and the season is advancing apace.

Tuesday, February 21.—R. 35. Lunch Temp. +9½°; Supper Temp.

[1] Sledges were left at the chief depots to replace damaged ones.

—11°. Gloomy and overcast when we started; a good deal warmer. The marching almost as bad as yesterday. Heavy toiling all day, inspiring gloomiest thoughts at times. Rays of comfort when we picked up tracks and cairns. At lunch we seemed to have missed the way, but an hour or two after we passed the last pony walls, and since, we struck a tent ring, ending the march actually on our old pony-tracks. There is a critical spot here with a long stretch between cairns. If we can tide that over we get on the regular cairn route, and with luck should stick to it; but everything depends on the weather. We never won a march of 8½ miles with greater difficulty, but we can't go on like this. We are drawing away from the land and perhaps may get better things in a day or two. I devoutly hope so.

Wednesday, February 22.—R. 36. Supper Temp. —2°. There is little doubt we are in for a rotten critical time going home, and the lateness of the season may make it really serious. Shortly after starting today the wind grew very fresh from the S.E. with strong surface drift. We lost the faint track immediately, though covering ground fairly rapidly. Lunch came without sight of the cairn we had hoped to pass. In the afternoon, Bowers being sure we were too far to the west, steered out. Result, we have passed another pony camp without seeing it. Looking at the map tonight there is no doubt we are too far to the east. With clear weather we ought to be able to correct the mistake, but will the weather get clear? It's a gloomy position more especially as one sees the same difficulty recurring even when we have corrected this error. The wind is dying down tonight and the sky clearing in the south, which is hopeful. Meanwhile it is satisfactory to note that such untoward events fail to damp the spirit of the party. Tonight we had a pony hoosh so excellent and filling that one feels really strong and vigorous again.

Thursday, February 23.—R. 37. Lunch Temp. —9.8°; Supper Temp. —12°. Started in sunshine, wind almost dropped. Luckily Bowers took a round of angles and with help of the chart we fogged out that we must be inside rather than outside tracks. The data were so meager that it seemed a great responsibility to march out and we were none of us happy about it. But just as we decided to lunch, Bowers' wonderful sharp eyes detected an old double lunch cairn, the theodolite telescope confirmed it, and our spirits rose accordingly. This afternoon we marched on and picked up another cairn; then on and camped only 2½ miles from the depot. We cannot see it, but, given fine weather, we cannot miss it. We are, therefore, extraordinarily relieved. Covered 8.2 miles in 7 hours, showing we can do 10 or 12 on this surface. Things are again looking up, as we are on the regular line of cairns, with no gaps right home, I hope.

Friday, February 24.—Lunch. Beautiful day—too beautiful—an hour after starting loose ice crystals spoiling surface. Saw depot and reached it middle forenoon. Found store in order except shortage oil—shall have to be *very* saving with fuel—otherwise have ten full days' provision from tonight and shall have less than 70 miles to go. Note from Meares who passed through December 15, saying surface bad; from Atkinson, after fine marching (2¼ days from pony depot), reporting Keohane better after sickness. Short note from Evans, not very cheerful, saying surface bad, temperature high. Think he must have been a little anxious.[2] It is an immense relief to have picked up this depot and, for the time, anxieties are thrust aside. There is no doubt we have been rising steadily since leaving the Shambles Camp. The coastal Barrier descends except where glaciers press out. Undulation still, but flattening out. Surface soft on top, curiously hard below. Great difference now between night and day temperatures. Quite warm as I write in tent. We are on tracks with half-march cairn ahead; have covered 4½ miles. Poor Wilson has a fearful attack snow-blindness consequent on yesterday's efforts. Wish we had more fuel.

Night camp R. 38. Temp. −17°. A little despondent again. We had a really terrible surface this afternoon and only covered 4 miles. We are on the track just beyond a lunch cairn. It really will be a bad business if we are to have this pulling all through. I don't know what to think, but the rapid closing of the season is ominous. It is great luck having the horsemeat to add to our ration. Tonight we have had a real fine "hoosh." It is a race between the season and hard conditions and our fitness and good food.

Saturday, February 25.—Lunch Temp. −12°. Managed just 6 miles this morning. Started somewhat despondent; not relieved when pulling seemed to show no improvement. Bit by bit surface grew better, less sastrugi, more glide, slight following wind for a time. Then we began to travel a little faster. But the pulling is still *very* hard; undulations disappearing but inequalities remain.

Twenty-six Camp walls about 2 miles ahead, all tracks in sight—Evans' track very conspicuous. This is something in favor, but the pulling is tiring us, though we are getting into better ski drawing again. Bowers hasn't quite the trick and is a little hurt at my criticisms, but I never doubted his heart. Very much easier—write diary at lunch—excellent meal —now one pannikin very strong tea—four biscuits and butter.

Hope for better things this afternoon, but no improvement apparent.

[2] He was already stricken with scurvy.

Oh! for a little wind—E. Evans evidently had plenty.

R. 39. Temp. −20°. Better march in afternoon. Day yields 11.4 miles —the first double figure of steady dragging for a long time, but it meant and will mean hard work if we can't get a wind to help us. Evans evidently had a strong wind here, S.E. I should think. The temperature goes very low at night now when the sky is clear as at present. As a matter of fact this is wonderfully fine weather—the only drawback the spoiling of the surface and absence of wind. We see all tracks very plain, but the pony-walls have evidently been badly drifted up. Some kind people had substituted a cairn at last camp 27. The old cairns do not seem to have suffered much.

Sunday, February 26.—Lunch Temp. −17°. Sky overcast at start, but able see tracks and cairn distinct at long distance. Did a little better, 6½ miles to date. Bowers and Wilson now in front. Find great relief pulling behind with no necessity to keep attention on track. Very cold nights now and cold feet starting march, as day footgear doesn't dry at all. We are doing well on our food, but we ought to have yet more. I hope the next depot, now only 50 miles, will find us with enough surplus to open out. The fuel shortage still an anxiety.

R. 40. Temp. −21°. Nine hours' solid marching has given us 11½ miles. Only 43 miles from the next depot. Wonderfully fine weather but cold, very cold. Nothing dries and we get our feet cold too often. We want more food yet and especially more fat. Fuel is woefully short. We can scarcely hope to get a better surface at this season, but I wish we could have some help from the wind, though it might shake us up badly if the temp. didn't rise.

Monday, February 27.—Desperately cold last night: −33° when we got up, with −37° minimum. Some suffering from cold feet, but all got good rest. We *must* open out on food soon. But we have done 7 miles this morning and hope for some 5 this afternoon. Overcast sky and good surface till now, when sun shows again. It is good to be marching the cairns up, but there is still much to be anxious about. We talk of little but food, except after meals. Land disappearing in satisfactory manner. Pray God we have no further setbacks. We are naturally always discussing possibility of meeting dogs, where and when, &c. It is a critical position. We may find ourselves in safety at next depot, but there is a horrid element of doubt.

Camp R. 41. Temp. −32°. Still fine clear weather but very cold— absolutely calm tonight. We have got off an excellent march for these days (12.2) and are much earlier than usual in our bags. 31 miles to depot, 3 days' fuel at a pinch, and 6 days' food. Things begin to look a little better; we can open out a little on food from tomorrow night, I think.

Very curious surface—soft recent sastrugi which sink underfoot, and between, a sort of flaky crust with large crystals beneath.

Tuesday, February 28.—Lunch. Thermometer went below −40° last night; it was desperately cold for us, but we had a fair night. I decided to slightly increase food; the effect is undoubtedly good. Started marching in −32° with a slight northwesterly breeze—blighting. Many cold feet this morning; long time over foot gear, but we are earlier. Shall camp earlier and get the chance of a good night, if not the reality. Things must be critical till we reach the depot, and the more I think of matters, the more I anticipate their remaining so after that event. Only 24½ miles from the depot. The sun shines brightly, but there is little warmth in it. There is no doubt the middle of the Barrier is a pretty awful locality.

Camp 42. Splendid pony hoosh sent us to bed and sleep happily after a horrid day, wind continuing; did 11½ miles. Temp. not quite so low, but expect we are in for cold night (Temp. −27°).

Wednesday, February 29.—Lunch. Cold night. Minimum Temp. −37.5°; −30° with northwest wind, force 4, when we got up. Frightfully cold starting; luckily Bowers and Oates in their last new finnesko; keeping my old ones for present. Expected awful march and for first hour got it. Then things improved and we camped after 5½ hours marching close to lunch camp—22½. Next camp is our depot and it is exactly 13 miles. It ought not to take more than 1½ days; we pray for another fine one. The oil will just about spin out in that event, and we arrive 3 clear days' food in hand. The increase of ration has had an enormously beneficial result. Mountains now looking small. Wind still very light from west—cannot understand this wind.

Thursday, March 1.—Lunch. Very cold last night—minimum −41.5°. Cold start to march, too, as usual now. Got away at 8 and have marched within sight of depot; flag something under 3 miles away. We did 11½ yesterday and marched 6 this morning. Heavy dragging yesterday and *very* heavy this morning. Apart from sledging considerations the weather is wonderful. Cloudless days and nights and the wind trifling. Worse luck, the light airs come from the north and keep us horribly cold. For this lunch hour the exception has come. There is a bright and comparatively warm sun. All our gear is out drying.

Friday, March 2.—Lunch. Misfortunes rarely come singly. We marched to the [Middle Barrier] depot fairly easily yesterday afternoon, and since that have suffered three distinct blows which have placed us in a bad position. First we found a shortage of oil; with most rigid economy it can scarce carry us to the next depot on this surface [71 miles away]. Second, Titus Oates disclosed his feet, the toes showing very bad indeed, evidently bitten by the late temperatures. The third blow came in the night, when the wind, which we had hailed with some joy, brought dark overcast weather. It fell below −40° in the night, and this morning it took 1½ hours to get our foot gear on, but we got away before eight. We lost cairn and tracks together and made as steady as we could N. by W., but have seen nothing. Worse was to come—the surface is simply awful. In spite of strong wind and full sail we have only done 5½ miles. We are in a *very* queer street since there is no doubt we cannot do the extra marches and feel the cold horribly.

Saturday, March 3.—Lunch. We picked up the track again yesterday, finding ourselves to the eastward. Did close on 10 miles and things looked a trifle better; but this morning the outlook is blacker than ever. Started well and with good breeze; for an hour made good headway; then the surface grew awful beyond words. The wind drew forward; every circumstance was against us. After 4¼ hours things so bad that we camped, having covered 4½ miles. [R. 46.] One cannot consider this a fault of our own—certainly we were pulling hard this morning—it was more than three parts surface which held us back—the wind at strongest, powerless to move the sledge. When the light is good it is easy to see the reason. The surface, lately a very good hard one, is coated with a thin layer of woolly crystals, formed by radiation no doubt. These are too firmly fixed to be removed by the wind and cause impossible friction on the runners. God help us, we can't keep up this pulling, that is certain. Amongst ourselves we are unendingly cheerful, but what each man feels in his heart I can only guess. Putting on foot gear in the morning is getting slower and slower, therefore every day more dangerous.

Sunday, March 4.—Lunch. Things looking *very* black indeed. As usual we forgot our trouble last night, got into our bags, slept splendidly on good hoosh, woke and had another, and started marching. Sun shining brightly, tracks clear, but surface covered with sandy frost-rime. All the morning we had to pull with all our strength, and in 4½ hours we covered 3½ miles. Last night it was overcast and thick, surface bad; this morning sun shining and surface as bad as ever. One has little to hope for except perhaps strong dry wind—an unlikely contingency at this time of year. Under the immediate surface crystals is a hard sastrugi surface, which must have been excellent for pulling a week or two ago. We are about 42 miles from the next depot and have a week's food, but only about 3 to 4 days' fuel—we are as economical of the latter as one can possibly be, and we cannot afford to save food and pull as we are pulling. We are in a very tight place indeed, but none of us despondent *yet*, or at least we preserve every semblance of good cheer, but one's heart sinks as the sledge stops dead at some sastrugi behind which the surface sand lies thickly heaped. For the moment the temperature is on the −20°—an improvement which makes us much more comfortable, but a colder snap is bound to come again soon. I fear that Oates at least will weather such an event very poorly. Providence to our aid! We can expect little from man now except the possibility of extra food at the next depot. It will be real bad if we get there and find the same shortage of oil. Shall we get there? Such a short distance it would have appeared to us on the summit! I don't know what I should do if Wilson and Bowers weren't so determinedly cheerful over things.

Monday, March 5.—Lunch. Regret to say going from bad to worse. We got a slant of wind yesterday afternoon, and going on 5 hours we converted our wretched morning run of 3½ miles into something over 9. We went to bed on a cup of cocoa and pemmican solid with the chill off. (R. 47.) The result is telling on all, but mainly on Oates, whose feet are in a wretched condition. One swelled up tremendously last night and he is very lame this morning. We started march on tea and pemmican as last night—we pretend to prefer the pemmican this way. Marched for 5 hours this morning over a slightly better surface covered with high moundy sastrugi. Sledge capsized twice; we pulled on foot, covering about 5½ miles. We are two pony marches and 4 miles about from our depot. Our fuel dreadfully low and the poor Soldier nearly done. It is pathetic enough because we can do nothing for him; more hot food might do a little, but only a little, I fear. We none of us expected these terribly low temperatures, and of the rest of us Wilson is feeling them most; mainly, I fear, from his self-sacrificing devotion in doctoring Oates' feet. We cannot help each other, each has enough to do to take care of himself. We get cold on the march when the trudging is heavy, and the wind pierces our warm garments. The others, all of them, are unendingly cheerful when in the tent. We mean to see the game through with a proper spirit, but it's tough work to be pulling harder than we ever pulled in our lives for long hours, and to feel that the progress is so slow. One can only say "God help us!" and plod on our weary way, cold and very miserable, though outwardly cheerful. We talk of all sorts of subjects in the tent, not much of food now, since we decided to take the risk of running a full ration. We simply couldn't go hungry at this time.

Tuesday, March 6.—Lunch. We did a little better with help of wind yesterday afternoon, finishing 9½ miles for the day, and 27 miles from depot. [R. 48.] But this morning things have been awful. It was warm in the night and for the first time during the journey I overslept myself by more than an hour; then we were slow with foot gear; then, pulling with all our might (for our lives) we could scarcely advance at rate of a mile an hour; then it grew thick and three times we had to get out of harness to search for tracks. The result is something less than 3½ miles for the forenoon. The sun is shining now and the wind gone. Poor Oates is unable to pull, sits on the sledge when we are track-searching—he is wonderfully plucky, as his feet must be giving him great pain. He makes no complaint, but his spirits only come up in spurts now, and he grows more silent in the tent. We are making a spirit lamp to try and replace the primus when our oil is exhausted. It will be a very poor substitute and we've not got much spirit. If we could have kept up our 9-mile days we might have got within reasonable distance of the depot before running out, but nothing but a strong wind and good surface can help us now, and though we had quite a good breeze this morning, the sledge came as heavy as lead. If we were all fit I should have hopes of getting through, but the poor Soldier has become a terrible hindrance, though he does his utmost and suffers much I fear.

Wednesday, March 7.—A little worse I fear. One of Oates' feet *very* bad this morning; he is wonderfully brave. We still talk of what we will do together at home.

We only made 6½ miles yesterday. [R. 49.] This morning in 4½ hours we did just over 4 miles. We are 16 from our depot. If we only find the correct proportion of food there and this surface continues, we may get to the next depot [Mt. Hooper, 72 miles farther] but not to One Ton Camp. We hope against hope that the dogs have been to Mt. Hooper; then we might pull through. If there is a shortage of oil again we can have little hope. One feels that for poor Oates the crisis is near, but none of us are improving, though we are wonderfully fit considering the really excessive work we are doing. We are only kept going by good food. No wind this morning till a chill northerly air came ahead. Sun bright and cairns showing up well. I should like to keep the track to the end.

Thursday, March 8.—Lunch. Worse and worse in morning; poor Oates' left foot can never last out, and time over foot gear something awful. Have to wait in night foot gear for nearly an hour before I start changing, and then am generally first to be ready. Wilson's feet giving trouble now, but this mainly because he gives so much help to others. We did 4½ miles this morning and are now 8½ miles from the depot—a ridiculously small distance to feel in difficulties, yet on this surface we know we cannot equal half our old marches, and that for that effort we expend nearly double the energy. The great question is, What shall we find at the depot? If the dogs have visited it we may get along a good distance, but if there is another short allowance of fuel, God help us indeed. We are in a very bad way, I fear, in any case.

Saturday, March 10.—Things steadily downhill. Oates' foot worse. He has rare pluck and must know that he can never get through. He asked Wilson if he had a chance this morning, and of course Bill had to say he didn't know. In point of fact he has none. Apart from him, if he went under now, I doubt whether we could get through. With great care we might have a dog's chance, but no more. The weather conditions are awful, and our gear gets steadily more icy and difficult to manage. At the same time of course poor Titus is the greatest handicap. He keeps us waiting in the morning until we have partly lost the warming effect of our good breakfast, when the only wise policy is to be up and away at once; again at lunch. Poor chap! it is too pathetic to watch him: one cannot but try to cheer him up.

Yesterday we marched up the depot, Mt. Hooper. Cold comfort. Shortage on our allowance all round. I don't know that anyone is to blame. . . .

This morning it was calm when we breakfasted, but the wind came from the W.N.W. as we broke camp. It rapidly grew in strength. After traveling for half an hour I saw that none of us could go on facing such conditions. We were forced to camp and are spending the rest of the day in a comfortless blizzard camp, wind quite foul. [R. 52.]

Sunday, March 11.—Titus Oates is very near the end, one feels. What we or he will do, God only knows. We discussed the matter after breakfast; he is a brave fine fellow and understands the situation, but he practically asked for advice. Nothing could be said but to urge him to march as long as he could. One satisfactory result to the discussion; I practically ordered Wilson to hand over the means of ending our troubles to us, so that any one of us may know how to do so. Wilson had no choice between doing so and our ransacking the medicine case. We have 30 opium tabloids apiece and he is left with a tube of morphine. So far the tragical side of our story. [R. 53.]

The sky completely overcast when we started this morning. We could see nothing, lost the tracks, and doubtless have been swaying a good deal since—3.1 miles for the forenoon—terribly heavy dragging—expected it. Know that 6 miles is about the limit of our endurance now, if we get no help from wind or surfaces. We have 7 days' food and should be about 55 miles from One Ton Camp tonight, 6 × 7 = 42, leaving us 13 miles short of our distance, even if things get no worse. Meanwhile the season rapidly advances.

Monday, March 12.—We did 6.9 miles yesterday, under our necessary average. Things are left much the same, Oates not pulling much, and now with hands as well as feet pretty well useless. We did 4 miles this morning in 4 hours 20 min.—we may hope for 3 this afternoon, 7 × 6 = 42. We shall be 47 miles from the depot. I doubt if we can possibly do it. The surface remains awful, the cold intense, and our physical condition running down. God help us! Not a breath of favorable wind for more than a week, and apparently liable to head winds at any moment.

Wednesday, March 14.—No doubt about the going downhill, but everything going wrong for us. Yesterday we woke to a strong northerly wind with temp. −37°. Couldn't face it, so remained in camp [R. 54] till 2, then did 5¼ miles. Wanted to march later, but party feeling the cold badly as the breeze (N.) never took off entirely, and as the sun sank the temp. fell. Long time getting supper in dark. [R. 55.]

This morning started with southerly breeze, set sail and passed another cairn at good speed; half-way, however, the wind shifted to W. by S. or W.S.W., blew through our wind clothes and into our mits. Poor Wilson horribly cold, could [not] get off ski for some time. Bowers and I practically made camp, and when we got into the tent at last we were all deadly cold. Then temp. now midday down −43° and the wind strong. We *must* go on, but now the making of every camp must be more difficult and dangerous. It must be near the end, but a pretty merciful end. Poor Oates got it again in the foot. I shudder to think what it will be like tomorrow. It is only with greatest pains rest of us keep off frostbites. No idea there could be temperatures like this at this time of year with such winds. Truly awful outside the tent. Must fight it out to the last biscuit, but can't reduce rations.

Friday, March 16 *or Saturday* 17.—Lost track of dates, but think the last correct. Tragedy all along the line. At lunch, the day before yesterday, poor Titus Oates said he couldn't go on; he proposed we should leave him in his sleeping-bag. That we could not do, and we induced him to come on, on the afternoon march. In spite of its awful nature for him he struggled on and we made a few miles. At night he was worse and we knew the end had come.

Should this be found I want these facts recorded. Oates' last thoughts were of his Mother, but immediately before he took pride in thinking that his regiment would be pleased with the bold way in which he met his death. We can testify to his bravery. He has borne intense suffering for weeks without complaint, and to the very last was able and willing to discuss outside subjects. He did not—would not—give up hope till the very end. He was a brave soul. This was the end. He slept through the night before last, hoping not to wake; but he woke in the morning—yesterday. It was blowing a blizzard. He said, "I am just going outside and may be some time." He went out into the blizzard and we have not seen him since.

I take this opportunity of saying that we have stuck to our sick companions to the last. In case of Edgar Evans, when absolutely out of food and he lay insensible, the safety of the remainder seemed to demand his abandonment, but Providence mercifully removed him at this critical moment. He died a natural death, and we did not leave him till two hours after his death. We knew that poor Oates was walking to his death, but though we tried to dissuade him, we knew it was the act of a brave man and an English gentleman. We all hope to meet the end with a similar spirit, and assuredly the end is not far.

I can only write at lunch and then only occasionally. The cold is intense, −40° at midday. My companions are unendingly cheerful, but we are all on the verge of serious frostbites, and though we constantly talk of fetching through I don't think any one of us believes it in his heart.

We are cold on the march now, and at all times except meals. Yesterday we had to lay up for a blizzard and today we move dreadfully slowly. We are at No 14 pony camp, only two pony marches from One Ton Depot. We leave here our theodolite, a camera, and Oates' sleeping-bags. Diaries, &c., and geological specimens carried at Wilson's special request, will be found with us or on our sledge.

Sunday, March 18.—Today, lunch, we are 21 miles from the depot. Ill fortune presses, but better may come. We have had more wind and drift from ahead yesterday; had to stop marching; wind N.W., force 4, temp. −35°. No human being could face it, and we are worn out *nearly*.

My right foot has gone, nearly all the toes—two days ago I was proud possessor of best feet. These are the steps of my downfall. Like an ass I mixed a small spoonful of curry powder with my melted pemmican—it gave me violent indigestion. I lay awake and in pain all night; woke and felt done on the march; foot went and I didn't know it. A very small measure of neglect and have a foot which is not pleasant to contemplate. Bowers takes first place in condition, but there is not much to choose after all. The others are still confident of getting through—or pretend to be—I don't know! We have the last *half* fill of oil in our primus and a very small quantity of spirit—this alone between us and thirst. The wind is fair for the moment, and that is perhaps a fact to help. The mileage would have seemed ridiculously small on our outward journey.

Monday, March 19.—Lunch. We camped with difficulty last night, and were dreadfully cold till after our supper of cold pemmican and biscuit and a half a pannikin of cocoa cooked over the spirit. Then, contrary to expectation, we got warm and all slept well. Today we started in the usual dragging manner. Sledge dreadfully heavy. We are 15½ miles from the depot and ought to get there in three days. What progress! We have two days' food but barely a day's fuel. All our feet are getting bad—Wilson's best, my right foot worst, left all right. There is no chance to nurse one's feet till we can get hot food into us. Amputation is the least I can hope for now, but will the trouble spread? That is the serious question. The weather doesn't give us a chance—the wind from N. to N.W. and −40° temp. today.

Wednesday, March 21.—Got within 11 miles of depot Monday night;[3] had to lay up all yesterday in severe blizzard. Today forlorn hope, Wilson and Bowers going to depot for fuel.

Thursday, March 22 *and* 23.—Blizzard bad as ever—Wilson and Bowers unable to start—tomorrow last chance—no fuel and only one or two of food left—must be near the end. Have decided it shall be natural—we shall march for the depot with or without our effects and die in our tracks.

Thursday, March 29.—Since the 21st we have had a continuous gale from W.S.W. and S.W. We had fuel to make two cups of tea apiece and bare food for two days on the 20th. Every day we have been ready to start for our depot 11 *miles* away, but outside the door of the tent it remains a scene of whirling drift. I do not think we can hope for any better things now. We shall stick it out to the end, but we are getting weaker, of course, and the end cannot be far.

It seems a pity, but I do not think I can write more.

R. SCOTT

Last entry.

For God's sake look after our people.

---

[3] The 60th camp from the Pole.

we shall stick it out
to the end but we
are getting weaker of
course and the end
cannot be far.
It seems a pity but
I do not think I can
write more —

R Scott

Last Entry

For Gods Sake look
after our people

SOUTH

by Sir Ernest Shackleton

The geographical and geological problems of the Antarctic plateau were far from solved by the exploits of Amundsen and Scott. Shackleton, who had failed to reach the Pole in 1908, decided in 1913 on a new method. He planned a two-pronged expedition. One prong was to follow the traditional route to McMurdo Sound; the other, which Shackleton meant to lead personally, was to set up a base on the Weddell Sea, then sledge inland across the Pole and continue to the bases on the other side. As with Scott, the British public reacted enthusiastically and nearly five thousand men—of whom only fifty could be accepted—volunteered for service.

As the expedition prepared to sail in 1914, war was declared and Shackleton offered his party for duty. The First Lord of the Admiralty, Winston Churchill, answered with one word, "Proceed," and Shackleton's ship the Endurance made for the Weddell Sea. She forced her way in, but tossed by storm and ice she was finally shaken to pieces and sank. With three small boats and some provisions, Shackleton set up a camp on the drifting ice pack and finally managed to make shore on Elephant Island, a rocky spot of land north of the South Shetlands. Now in order to obtain help, Shackleton embarked on one of the most celebrated of open-boat voyages. His own account of this voyage follows.

THE increasing sea made it necessary for us to drag the boats farther up the beach. This was a task for all hands, and after much labor we got the boats into safe positions among the rocks and made fast the painters to big boulders. Then I discussed with Wild and Worsley the chances of reaching South Georgia before the winter locked the seas against us. Some effort had to be made to secure relief. Privation and exposure had left their mark on the party, and the health and mental condition of several men were causing me serious anxiety. Blackborrow's feet, which had been frost-

From South: the Story of Shackleton's Last Expedition by Sir Ernest Shackleton.
Reprinted by permission of William Heinemann Ltd.

bitten during the boat journey, were in a bad way, and the two doctors feared that an operation would be necessary. They told me that the toes would have to be amputated unless animation could be restored within a short period. Then the food supply was a vital consideration. We had left ten cases of provisions in the crevice of the rocks at our first camping place on the island. An examination of our stores showed that we had full rations for the whole party for a period of five weeks. The rations could be spread over three months on a reduced allowance and probably would be supplemented by seals and sea elephants to some extent. I did not dare to count with full confidence on supplies of meat and blubber, for the animals seemed to have deserted the beach and the winter was near. Our stocks included three seals and two and a half skins (with blubber attached). We were mainly dependent on the blubber for fuel, and, after making a preliminary survey of the situation, I decided that the party must be limited to one hot meal a day.

A boat journey in search of relief was necessary and must not be delayed. That conclusion was forced upon me. The nearest port where assistance could certainly be secured was Port Stanley, in the Falkland Islands, 540 miles away, but we could scarcely hope to beat up against the prevailing northwesterly wind in a frail and weakened boat with a small sail area. South Georgia was over eight hundred miles away, but lay in the area of the west winds, and I could count upon finding whalers at any of the whaling stations on the east coast. A boat party might make the voyage and be back with relief within a month, provided that the sea was clear of ice and the boat survived the great seas. It was not difficult to decide that South Georgia must be the objective, and I proceeded to plan ways and means. The hazards of a boat journey across eight hundred miles of stormy subantarctic ocean were obvious, but I calculated that at worst the venture would add nothing to the risks of the men left on the island. There would be fewer mouths to feed during the winter and the boat would not require to take more than one month's provisions for six men, for if we did not make South Georgia in that time we were sure to go under. A consideration that had weight with me was that there was no chance at all of any search being made for us on Elephant Island.

The case required to be argued in some detail, since all hands knew that the perils of the proposed journey were extreme. The risk was justified solely by our urgent need of assistance. The ocean south of Cape Horn in the middle of May is known to be the most tempestuous storm-swept area of water in the world. The weather then is unsettled, the skies are dull and overcast, and the gales are almost unceasing. We had to face these conditions in a small and weather-beaten boat, already strained by the work of the months that had passed. Worsley and Wild realized that the attempt must be made, and they both asked to be allowed to accompany me on the voyage. I told Wild at once that he would have to stay behind. I relied upon him to hold the party together while I was away and to make the best of his way up to Deception Island with the men in the spring in the event of our failure to bring help. Worsley I would take with me, for I had a very high opinion of his accuracy and quickness as a navigator, and especially in the mapping and working out of positions in difficult circumstances—an opinion that was only enhanced during the actual journey. Four other men would be required, and I decided to call for volunteers, although, as a matter of fact, I pretty well knew which of the people I would select. Crean I proposed to leave on the island as a right-hand man for Wild, but he begged so hard to be allowed to come in the boat that, after consultation with Wild, I promised to take him. I called the men together, explained my plan, and asked for volunteers. Many came forward at once. Some were not fit enough for the work that would have to be done, and others would not have been much use in the boat since they were not seasoned sailors, though the experiences of recent months entitled them to some consideration as seafaring men. McIlroy and Macklin were both anxious to go but realized that their duty lay on the island with the sick men. They suggested that I should take Blackborrow in order that he might have shelter and warmth as quickly as possible, but I had to veto this idea. It would be hard enough for fit men to live in the boat. Indeed, I did not see how a sick man, lying helpless in the bottom of the boat, could possibly survive in the heavy weather we were sure to encounter. I finally selected McNeish, McCarthy, and Vincent in addition to Worsley and Crean. The crew seemed a strong one, and as I looked at the men I felt confidence increasing.

The decision made, I walked through the blizzard with Worsley and Wild to examine the *James Caird*. The twenty-foot boat had never looked big; she appeared to have shrunk in some mysterious way when I viewed her in the light of our new undertaking. She was an ordinary ship's whaler, fairly strong, but showing signs of the strains she had endured since the crushing of the *Endurance*. Where she was holed in leaving the pack was, fortunately, about the water line and easily patched. Standing beside her, we glanced at the fringe of the storm-swept, tumultuous sea that formed our path. Clearly, our voyage would be a big adventure. I called the carpenter and asked him if he could do anything to make the boat more seaworthy. He first inquired if he was to go with me, and seemed quite pleased when I said "Yes." He was over fifty years of age and not altogether fit, but he had a good knowledge of sailing boats and was very quick. McCarthy said that he could contrive some sort of covering for the *James Caird* if he might use the lids of the cases and the four sledge runners that we had lashed inside the boat for use in the event of a landing on Graham Land at Wilhelmina Bay. This bay, at one time the goal of our desire, had been left behind in the course of our drift, but we had retained the runners. The carpenter proposed to complete the covering with some of our canvas, and he set about making his plans at once.

Noon had passed and the gale was more severe than ever. We could not proceed with our preparations that day. The tents were suffering in the wind and the sea was rising. We made our way to the snow slope at the shore-ward end of the spit, with the intention of digging a hole in the snow large enough to provide shelter for the party. I had an idea that Wild and his men might camp there during my absence, since it seemed impossible that the tents could hold together for many more days against the attacks of the wind; but an examination of the spot indicated that any hole we could dig probably would be filled quickly by the drift. At dark, about 5 P.M., we all turned in, after a supper consisting of a pannikin of hot milk, one of our precious biscuits, and a cold penguin leg each.

The gale was stronger than ever on the following morning (April 20). No work could be done. Blizzard and snow, snow and blizzard, sudden lulls and fierce returns. During the lulls we could see on the far horizon to the northeast bergs of all shapes and sizes driving along before the gale, and the sinister appearance of the swift-moving masses made us thankful indeed that, instead of battling with the storm amid the ice, we were required only to face the drift from the glaciers and the inland heights. The gusts might throw us off our feet, but at least we fell on solid ground and not on the rocking floes. Two seals came up on the beach that day, one of them within ten yards of my tent. So urgent was our need of food and blubber that I called all hands and organized a line of beaters instead of simply walking up to the seal and hitting it on the nose. We were prepared to fall upon this seal *en masse* if it attempted to escape. The kill was made with a pick handle, and in a few minutes five days' food and six days' fuel were stowed in a place of safety among the boulders above high-water mark. During this day the cook, who had worked well on the floe and throughout the boat journey, suddenly collapsed. I happened to be at the galley at the moment and saw him fall. I pulled him down the slope to his tent and pushed him into its shelter with orders to his tent mates to keep him in his sleeping bag until I allowed him to come out or the doctors said he was fit enough. Then I took out to replace the cook, one of the men who had expressed a desire to lie down and die. The task of keeping the galley fire alight was both difficult and strenuous, and it took his thoughts away from the chances of immediate dissolution. In fact, I found him a little later gravely concerned over the drying of a naturally not overclean pair of socks which were hung up in close proximity to our evening milk. Occupation had brought his thoughts back to the ordinary cares of life.

There was a lull in the bad weather on April 21, and the carpenter started to collect material for the decking of the *James Caird*. He fitted the mast of the *Stancomb Wills* fore and aft inside the *James Caird* as a hogback and thus strengthened the keel with the object of preventing our boat "hogging" —that is, buckling in heavy seas. He had not sufficient wood to provide a deck, but by using the sledge runners and box lids he made a framework extending from the forecastle aft to a well. It was a patched-up affair, but it provided a base for a canvas covering. We had a bolt of canvas frozen stiff, and this material had to be cut and then thawed out over the blubber stove, foot by foot, in order that it might be sewn into the form of a cover. When it had been nailed and screwed into position it certainly gave an appearance of safety to the boat, though I had an uneasy feeling that it bore a strong likeness to stage scenery, which may look like a granite wall and is in fact nothing better than canvas and lath. As events proved, the covering served its purpose well. We certainly could not have lived through the voyage without it.

Another fierce gale was blowing on April 22, interfering with our preparations for the voyage. The cooker from No. 5 tent came adrift in a gust, and, although it was chased to the water's edge, it disappeared for good. Blackborrow's feet were giving him much pain, and McIlroy and Macklin thought it would be necessary for them to operate soon. They were under the impression then that they had no chloroform, but they found some subsequently in the medicine chest after we had left. Some cases of stores left on a rock off the spit on the day of our arrival were retrieved during this day. We were setting aside stores for the boat journey and choosing the essential equipment from the scanty stock at our disposal. Two ten-gallon casks had to be filled with water melted down from ice collected at the foot of the glacier. This was a rather slow business. The blubber stove was kept going all night, and the watchmen emptied the water into the casks from the pot in which the ice was melted. A working party started to dig a hole in the snow slope about forty feet above sea level with the object of providing a site for a camp. They made fairly good progress at first, but the snow drifted down unceasingly from the inland ice, and in the end the party had to give up the project.

The weather was fine on April 23, and we hurried forward our preparations. It was on this day I decided finally that the crew for the *James Caird* should consist of Worsley, Crean, McNeish, McCarthy, Vincent, and myself. A storm came on about noon, with driving snow and heavy squalls. Occasionally the air would clear for a few minutes, and we could see a line of pack ice, five miles out, driving across from west to east. This sight increased my anxiety to get away quickly. Winter was advancing, and soon the pack might close completely round the island and stay our departure for days or even for weeks. I did not think that ice would remain around Elephant Island continuously during the winter, since the strong winds and fast currents would keep it in motion. We had noticed ice and bergs going past at the rate of four or five knots. A certain amount of ice was held up about the end of our spit, but the sea was clear where the boat would have to be launched.

Worsley, Wild, and I climbed to the summit of the seaward rocks and examined the ice from a better vantage point than the beach for our purposes, and I decided that, unless the conditions forbade it, we would make a start in the *James Caird* on the following morning. Obviously the pack might close at any time. This decision made, I spent the rest of the day looking over the boat, gear, and stores, and discussing plans with Worsley and Wild.

Our last night on the solid ground of Elephant Island was cold and uncomfortable. We turned out at dawn and had breakfast. Then we launched the *Stancomb Wills* and loaded her with stores, gear, and ballast, which would be transferred to the *James Caird* when the heavier boat had been launched. The ballast consisted of bags made from blankets and filled with sand, making a total weight of about one thousand pounds. In addition we had gathered a number of round boulders and about 250 pounds of ice, which would supplement our two casks of water.

The stores taken in the *James Caird*, which would last six men for one month, were as follows:

> 30 boxes of matches
> 6½ gallons paraffin
> 1 tin methylated spirit
> 10 boxes of flamers
> 1 box of blue lights

2 Primus stoves with spare parts and prickers
1 Nansen aluminum cooker
6 sleeping bags
A few spare socks
A few candles and some blubber oil in an oil bag

Food:
3 cases sledging rations = 300 rations
2 cases nut food = 200 rations
2 cases biscuits = 600 biscuits
1 case lump sugar
30 pacqets of Trumilk
1 tin of Bovril cubes
1 tin of Cerebos salt
36 gallons of water
112 lbs. of ice

Instruments:

Sextant	Sea anchor
Binoculars	Charts
Prismatic compass	Aneroid

The swell was slight when the *Stancomb Wills* was launched and the boat got under way without any difficulty; but half an hour later, when we were pulling down the *James Caird*, the swell increased suddenly. Apparently the movement of the ice outside had made an opening and allowed the sea to run in without being blanketed by the line of pack. The swell made things difficult. Many of us got wet to the waist while dragging the boat out—a serious matter in that climate. When the *James Caird* was afloat in the surf she nearly capsized among the rocks before we could get her clear, and Vincent and the carpenter, who were on the deck, were thrown into the water. This was really bad luck, for the two men would have small chance of drying their clothes after we had got under way. Hurley, who had the eye of the professional photographer for "incidents," secured a picture of the upset, and I firmly believe that he would have liked the two unfortunate men to remain in the water until he could get a "snap" at close quarters; but we hauled them out immediately, regardless of his feelings.

The *James Caird* was soon clear of the breakers. We used all the available ropes as a long painter to prevent her drifting away to the northeast, and then the *Stancomb Wills* came alongside, transferred her load, and went back to the shore for more. As she was being beached this time the sea took her stern and half filled her with water. She had to be turned over and emptied before the return journey could be made. Every member of the crew of the *Stancomb Wills* was wet to the skin. The water casks were towed behind the *Stancomb Wills* on this second journey, and the swell, which was increasing rapidly, drove the boat onto the rocks, where one of the casks was slightly stove in. This accident proved later to be a serious one, since some sea water had entered the cask and the contents were now brackish.

By midday the *James Caird* was ready for the voyage. Vincent and the carpenter had secured some dry clothes by exchange with members of the shore party (I heard afterward that it was a full fortnight before the soaked garments were finally dried), and the boat's crew was standing by waiting for the order to cast off. A moderate westerly breeze was blowing. I went ashore in the *Stancomb Wills* and had a last word with Wild, who was remaining in full command, and with directions as to his course of action in the event of our failure to bring relief, but I practically left the whole situation and scope of action and decision to his own judgment, secure in the knowledge that he would act wisely. I told him that I trusted the party to him and said good-by to the men. Then we pushed off for the last time, and within a few minutes I was aboard the *James Caird*. The crew of the *Stancomb Wills* shook hands with us as the boats bumped together and offered us the last good wishes. Then, setting our jib, we cut the painter and moved away to the northeast. The men who were staying behind made a pathetic little group on the beach, with the grim heights of the island behind them and the sea seething at their feet, but they waved to us and gave three hearty cheers. There was hope in their hearts and they trusted us to bring the help that they needed.

I had all sails set, and the *James Caird* quickly dipped the beach and its line of dark figures. The westerly wind took us rapidly to the line of pack, and as we entered it I stood up with my arm around the mast, directing the steering, so as to avoid the great lumps of ice that were flung about in the heave of the sea. The pack thickened and we were forced to turn almost due east, running before the wind toward a gap I had seen in the morning from the high ground. I could not see the gap now, but we had come out on its bearing and I was prepared to find that it had been influenced by the easterly drift. At four o'clock in the afternoon we found the channel, much narrower than it had seemed in the morning but still navigable. Dropping sail, we rowed through without touching the ice anywhere, and by 5:30 P.M. we were clear of the pack with open water before us. We passed one more piece of ice in the darkness an hour later, but the pack lay behind, and with a fair wind swelling the sails we steered our little craft through the night, our hopes centered on our distant goal. The swell was very heavy now, and when the time came for our first evening meal we found great difficulty in keeping the Primus lamp alight and preventing the hoosh splashing out of the pot. Three men were needed to attend to the cooking, one man holding the lamp and two men guarding the aluminum cooking pot, which had to be lifted clear of the Primus whenever the movement of the boat threatened to cause a disaster. Then the lamp had to be protected from water, for sprays were coming over the bows and our flimsy decking was by no means watertight. All these operations were conducted in the confined space under the decking, where the men lay or knelt and adjusted themselves as best they could to the angles of our cases and ballast. It was uncomfortable, but we found consolation in the reflection that without the decking we could not have used the cooker at all.

The tale of the next sixteen days is one of supreme strife amid heaving waters. The Subantarctic Ocean lived up to its evil winter reputation. I decided to run north for at least two days while the wind held and so get into warmer weather before turning to the east and laying a course for South Georgia. We took two-hourly spells at the tiller. The men who were not on watch crawled into the sodden sleeping bags and tried to forget their troubles for a period; but there was no comfort in the boat. The bags and cases seemed to be alive in the unfailing knack of presenting their most uncomfortable angles to our rest-seeking bodies. A man might imagine for a moment that he had found a position of ease, but always discovered quickly that some unyielding point was impinging on muscle or bone. The first night aboard the boat was one of acute discomfort for us all, and we were heartily glad when the dawn came and we could set about the preparation of a hot breakfast.

This record of the voyage to South Georgia is based upon scanty notes made day by day. The notes dealt usually with the bare facts of distances, positions, and weather, but our memories retained the incidents of the passing days in a period never to be forgotten. By running north for the first two days I hoped to get warmer weather and also to avoid lines of pack that might be extending beyond the main body. We needed all the advantage that we could obtain from the higher latitude for sailing on the great circle, but we had to be cautious regarding possible ice streams. Cramped in our narrow quarters and continually wet by the spray, we suffered severely from cold throughout the journey. We fought the seas and the winds and at the same time had a daily struggle to keep ourselves alive. At times we were in dire peril. Generally we were upheld by the knowledge that we were making progress toward the land where we would be, but there were days and nights when we lay hove to, drifting across the storm-whitened seas and watching, with eyes interested rather than apprehensive, the uprearing masses of water, flung to and fro by Nature in the pride of her strength. Deep seemed the valleys when we lay between the reeling seas. High were the hills when we perched momentarily on the tops of giant combers. Nearly always there were gales. So small was our boat and so great were the seas that often our sail flapped idly in the calm between the crests of two waves. Then we would climb the next slope and catch the full fury of the gale where the wool-like whiteness of the breaking water surged around us. We had our moments of laughter—rare, it is true, but hearty enough. Even when cracked lips and swollen mouths checked the outward and visible signs of amusement we could see a joke of the primitive kind. Man's sense of humor is always most easily stirred by the petty misfortunes of his neighbors, and I shall never forget Worsley's efforts on one occasion to place the hot aluminum stand on top of the Primus stove after it had fallen off in an extra heavy roll. With his frostbitten fingers he picked it up, dropped it, picked it up again, and toyed with it gingerly as though it were some fragile article of lady's wear. We laughed, or rather gurgled with laughter.

The wind came up strong and worked into a gale from the northwest on the third day out. We stood away to the east. The increasing seas discovered the weaknesses of our decking. The continuous blows shifted to box lids and sledge runners so that the canvas sagged down and accumulated water. Then icy trickles, distinct from the driving sprays, poured fore and aft into the boat. The nails that the carpenter had extracted from cases at Elephant Island and used to fasten down the battens were too short to make firm the decking. We did what we could to secure it, but our means were very limited, and the water continued to enter the boat at a dozen points. Much bailing was necessary, and nothing that we could do prevented our gear from becoming sodden. The searching runnels from the canvas were really more unpleasant than the sudden definite douches of the sprays. Lying under the thwarts during watches below, we tried vainly to avoid them. There were no dry places in the boat, and at last we simply covered our heads with our Burberrys and endured the all-pervading water. The bailing was work for the watch. Real rest we had none. The perpetual motion of the boat made repose impossible; we were cold, sore, and anxious. We moved on hands and knees in the semidarkness of the day under the decking. The darkness was complete by 6 P.M., and not until 7 A.M. of the following day could we see one another under the thwarts. We had a few scraps of candle, and they were preserved carefully in order that we might have light at mealtimes. There was one fairly dry spot in the boat, under the solid original decking at the bows, and we managed to protect some of our biscuit from the salt water; but I do not think any of us got the taste of salt out of our mouths during the voyage.

The difficulty of movement in the boat would have had its humorous side if it had not involved us in so many aches and pains. We had to crawl under the thwarts in order to move along the boat, and our knees suffered considerably. When a watch turned out it was necessary for me to direct each man by name when and where to move, since if all hands had crawled about at the same time the result would have been dire confusion and many bruises. Then there was the trim of the boat to be considered. The order of the watch was four hours on and four hours off, three men to the watch. One man had the tiller ropes, the second man attended to the sail, and the third bailed for all he was worth. Sometimes when the water in the boat had been reduced to reasonable proportions, our pump could be used. This pump, which Hurley had made from the Flinders bar case of our ship's standard compass, was quite effective, though its capacity was not large. The man who was attending the sail could pump into the big outer cooker, which was lifted and emptied overboard when filled. We had a device by which the water could go direct from the pump into the sea through a hole in the gunwale, but this hole had to be blocked at an early stage of the voyage, since we found that it admitted water when the boat rolled.

While a new watch was shivering in the wind and spray, the men who had been relieved groped hurriedly among the soaked sleeping bags and tried to steal a little of the warmth created by the last occupants; but it was not always possible for us to find even this comfort when we went off watch. The boulders that we had taken aboard for ballast had to be shifted continually in order to trim the boat and give access of the pump, which became choked with hairs from the moulting sleeping bags and finnesko. The four reindeer-skin sleeping bags shed their hair freely owing to the continuous wetting, and soon became quite bald in appearance. The moving of the boulders was weary and painful work. We came to know every one of the stones by sight and touch, and I have vivid memories of their angular peculiarities even today. They might have been of considerable interest as geological specimens to a scientific man under happier conditions. As ballast they were useful. As weights to be moved about in cramped quarters they were simply appalling. They spared no portion of our poor bodies. Another of our troubles, worth mention here, was the chafing of our legs by our wet clothes, which had not been changed now for seven months. The insides of our thighs were rubbed raw, and the one tube of Hazeline cream in our medicine chest did not go far in alleviating our pain, which was increased by the bite of the salt water. We thought at the time that we never slept. The fact was that we would doze off uncomfortably, to be aroused quickly by some new ache or another call to effort. My own share of the general unpleasantness was accentuated by a finely developed bout of sciatica. I had become possessor of this originally on the floe several months earlier.

Our meals were regular in spite of the gales. Attention to this point was essential, since the conditions of the voyage made increasing calls upon our vitality. Breakfast, at 8 A.M., consisted of a pannikin of hot hoosh made from Bovril sledging ration, two biscuits, and some lumps of sugar. Lunch came at 1 P.M., and comprised Bovril sledging ration, eaten raw, and a pannikin of hot milk for each man. Tea, at 5 P.M., had the same menu. Then during the night we had a hot drink, generally of milk. The meals were the bright beacons in those cold and stormy days. The glow of warmth and comfort produced by the food and drink made optimists of us all. We had two tins of Virol, which we were keeping for an emergency; but, finding ourselves in need of an oil lamp to eke out our supply of candles, we emptied one of the tins in the manner that most appealed to us, and fitted it with a wick made by shredding a bit of canvas. When this lamp was filled with oil it gave a certain amount of light, though it was easily blown out, and was of great assistance to us at night. We were fairly well off as regarded fuel, since we had 6½ gallons of petroleum.

A severe southwesterly gale on the fourth day out forced us to heave to. I would have liked to have run before the wind, but the sea was very high and the *James Caird* was in danger of broaching to and swamping. The delay was vexatious, since up to that time we had been making sixty or seventy miles a day; good going with our limited sail area. We hove to under double-reefed mainsail and our little jigger, and waited for the gale to blow itself out. During that afternoon we saw bits of wreckage, the remains probably of some unfortunate vessel that had failed to weather the strong gales south of Cape Horn. The weather conditions did not improve, and on the fifth day out the gale was so fierce that we were compelled to take in the double-reefed mainsail and hoist our small jib instead. We put out a sea anchor to keep the *James Caird's* head up to the sea. This anchor consisted of a triangular canvas bag fastened to the end of the painter and allowed to stream out from the bows. The boat was high enough to catch the wind, and, as she drifted to leeward, the drag of the anchor kept her head to windward. Thus our boat took most of the seas more or less end on. Even then the crests of the waves often would curl right over us and we shipped a great deal of water, which necessitated unceasing bailing and pumping. Looking out abeam, we would see a hollow like a tunnel formed as the crest of a big wave toppled over onto the swelling body of water. A thousand times it appeared as though the *James Caird* must be engulfed; but the boat lived. The southwesterly gale had its birthplace above the Antarctic Continent, and its freezing breath lowered the temperature far toward zero. The sprays froze upon the boat and gave bows, sides, and decking a heavy coat of mail. This accumulation of ice reduced the buoyancy of the boat, and to that extent was an added peril; but it possessed a notable advantage from one point of view. The water ceased to drop and trickle from the canvas, and the spray came in solely at the well in the after part of the boat. We could not allow the load of ice to grow beyond a certain point, and in turns we crawled about the decking forward, chipping and picking at it with the available tools.

When daylight came on the morning of the sixth day out we saw and felt that the *James Caird* had lost her resiliency. She was not rising to the oncoming seas. The weight of the ice that had formed in her and upon her during the night was having its effect, and she was becoming more like a log than a boat. The situation called for immediate action. We first broke away the spare oars, which were encased in ice and frozen to the sides of the boat, and threw them overboard. We retained two oars for use when we got inshore. Two of the fur sleeping bags went over the side; they were thoroughly wet, weighing probably forty pounds each, and they had frozen stiff during the night. Three men constituted the watch below, and when a man went down it was better to turn into the wet bag just vacated by another man than to thaw out a frozen bag with the heat of his unfortunate body. We now had four bags, three in use and one for emergency use in case a member of the party should break down permanently. The reduction of weight relieved the boat to some extent, and vigorous chipping and scraping did more. We had to be very careful not to put ax or knife through the frozen canvas of the decking as we crawled over it, but gradually we got rid of a lot of ice. The *James Caird* lifted to the endless waves as though she lived again.

About 11 A.M. the boat suddenly fell off into the trough of the sea. The painter had parted and the sea anchor had gone. This was serious. The

James Caird went away to leeward, and we had no chance at all of recovering the anchor and our valuable rope, which had been our only means of keeping the boat's head up to the seas without the risk of hoisting sail in a gale. Now we had to set the sail and trust to its holding. When the *James Caird* rolled heavily in the trough, we beat the frozen canvas until the bulk of the ice had cracked off it and then hoisted it. The frozen gear worked protestingly, but after a struggle our little craft came up to the wind again, and we breathed more freely. Skin frostbites were troubling us, and we had developed large blisters on our fingers and hands. I shall always carry the scar of one of these frostbites on my left hand, which became badly inflamed after the skin had burst and the cold had bitten deeply.

We held the boat up to the gale during that day, enduring as best we could discomforts that amounted to pain. The boat tossed interminably on the big waves under gray, threatening skies. Our thoughts did not embrace much more than the necessities of the hour. Every surge of the sea was an enemy to be watched and circumvented. We ate our scanty meals, treated our frostbites, and hoped for the improved conditions that the morrow might bring. Night fell early, and in the lagging hours of darkness we were cheered by a change for the better in the weather. The wind dropped, the snow squalls became less frequent, and the sea moderated. When the morning of the seventh day dawned there was not much wind. We shook the reef out of the sail and laid our course once more for South Georgia. The sun came out bright and clear, and presently Worsley got a snap for longitude. We hoped that the sky would remain clear until noon, so that we could get the latiude. We had been six days out without an observation, and our dead reckoning naturally was uncertain. The boat must have presented a strange appearance that morning. All hands basked in the sun. We hung our sleeping bags to the mast and spread our socks and other gear all over the deck. Some of the ice had melted off the *James Caird* in the early morning after the gale began to slacken, and dry patches were appearing in the decking. Porpoises came blowing round the boat, and Cape pigeons wheeled and swooped within a few feet of us. These little black-and-white birds have an air of friendliness that is not possessed by the great circling albatross. They had looked gray against the swaying sea during the storm as they darted about over our heads and uttered their plaintive cries. The albatrosses, of the black or sooty variety, had watched with hard, bright eyes, and seemed to have a quite impersonal interest in our struggle to keep afloat amid the battering seas. In addition to the Cape pigeons an occasional stormy petrel flashed overhead. Then there was a small bird, unknown to me, that appeared always to be in a fussy, bustling state, quite out of keeping with the surroundings. It irritated me. It had practically no tail, and it flitted about vaguely as though in search of the lost member. I used to find myself wishing it would find its tail and have done with the silly fluttering.

We reveled in the warmth of the sun that day. Life was not so bad, after all. We felt we were well on our way. Our gear was drying, and we could have a hot meal in comparative comfort. The swell was still heavy, but it was not breaking and the boat rode easily. At noon Worsley balanced himself on the gunwale and clung with one hand to the stay of the mainmast while he got a snap of the sun. The result was more than encouraging. We had done over 380 miles and were getting on for halfway to South Georgia. It looked as though we were going to get through.

The wind freshened to a good stiff breeze during the afternoon, and the *James Caird* made satisfactory progress. I had not realized until the sunlight came how small our boat really was. There was some influence in the light and warmth, some hint of happier days, that made us revive memories of other voyages, when we had stout decks beneath our feet, unlimited food at our command, and pleasant cabins for our ease. Now we clung to a battered little boat, "alone, alone, all, all alone, alone on a wide, wide sea." So low in the water were we that each succeeding swell cut off our view of the skyline. We were a tiny speck in the vast vista of the sea—the ocean that is open to all and merciful to none, that threatens even when it seems to yield, and that is pitiless always to weakness. For a moment the consciousness of the forces arrayed against us would be almost overwhelming. Then hope and confidence would rise again as our boat rose to a wave and tossed aside the crest in a sparkling shower like the play of prismatic colors at the foot of a waterfall. My double-barreled gun and some cartridges had been stowed aboard the boat as an emergency precaution against a shortage of food, but we were not disposed to destroy our little neighbors, the Cape pigeons, even for the sake of fresh meat. We might have shot an albatross, but the wandering king of the ocean aroused in us something of the feeling that inspired, too late, the Ancient Mariner. So the gun remained among the stores and sleeping bags in the narrow quarters beneath our leaking deck, and the birds followed us unmolested.

The eighth, ninth, and tenth days of the voyage had few features worthy of special note. The wind blew hard during those days, and the strain of navigating the boat was unceasing, but always we made some advance toward our goal. No bergs showed on our horizon, and we knew that we were clear of the ice fields. Each day brought its little round of troubles, but also compensation in the form of food and growing hope. We felt that we were going to succeed. The odds against us had been great, but we were winning through. We still suffered severely from the cold, for, though the temperature was rising, our vitality was declining owing to shortage of food, exposure, and the necessity of maintaining our cramped positions day and night. I found that it was now absolutely necessary to prepare hot milk for all hands during the night, in order to sustain life till dawn. This meant lighting the Primus lamp in the darkness and involved an increased drain on our small store of matches. It was the rule that one match must serve when the Primus was being lit. We had no lamp for the compass and during the early days of the voyage we would strike a match when the steersman wanted to see the course at night; but later the necessity for strict economy impressed itself upon us, and the practice of striking matches at night was stopped. We had one watertight tin of matches. I had stowed away in a pocket, in readiness for a sunny day, a lens from one of the telescopes, but this was of no use during the voyage. The sun seldom shone upon us. The glass of the compass got broken one night, and we contrived to mend it with adhesive tape from the medicine chest. One of the memories that comes to me from those days is of Crean singing at the tiller. He always sang while he was steering, and nobody ever discovered what the song was. It was devoid of tune and as monotonous as the chanting of a Buddhist monk at his prayers; yet somehow it was cheerful. In moments of inspiration Crean would attempt "The Wearing of the Green."

On the tenth night Worsley could not straighten his body after his spell at the tiller. He was thoroughly cramped, and we had to drag him beneath the decking and massage him before he could unbend himself and get into a sleeping bag. A hard northwesterly gale came up on the eleventh day (May 5) and shifted to the southwest in the late afternoon. The sky was overcast and occasional snow squalls added to the discomfort produced by a tremendous cross sea—the worst, I thought, that we had experienced. At midnight I was at the tiller and suddenly noticed a line of clear sky between the south and southwest. I called to the other men that the sky was clearing, and then a moment later I realized that what I had seen was not a rift in the clouds but the white crest of an enormous wave. During twenty-six years' experience of the ocean in all its moods I had not encountered a wave so gigantic. It was a mighty upheaval of the ocean, a thing quite apart from the big white-capped seas that had been our tireless enemies for many days. I shouted, "For God's sake, hold on! It's got us!"

Then came a moment of suspense that seemed drawn out into hours. White surged the foam of the breaking sea around us. We felt our boat lifted and flung forward like a cork in breaking surf. We were in a seething chaos of tortured water; but somehow the boat lived through it, half full of water, sagging to the dead weight and shuddering under the blow. We bailed with the energy of men fighting for life, flinging the water over the sides with every receptacle that came to our hands, and after ten minutes of uncertainty we felt the boat renew her life beneath us. She floated again and ceased to lurch drunkenly as though dazed by the attack of the sea. Earnestly we hoped that never again would we encounter such a wave.

The conditions in the boat, uncomfortable before, had been made worse by the deluge of water. All our gear was thoroughly wet again. Our cooking stove had been floating about in the bottom of the boat, and portions of our last hoosh seemed to have permeated everything. Not until 3 A.M., when we were all chilled almost to the limit of endurance, did we manage to get the stove alight and make ourselves hot drinks. The carpenter was suffering particularly, but he showed grit and spirit. Vincent had for the past week ceased to be an active member of the crew, and I could not easily account for his collapse. Physically he was one of the strongest men in the boat. He was a young man, he had served on North Sea trawlers, and he should have been able to bear hardships better than McCarthy, who, not so strong, was always happy.

The weather was better on the following day (May 6), and we got a glimpse of the sun. Worsley's observation showed that we were not more than a hundred miles from the northwest corner of South Georgia. Two more days with a favorable wind and we would sight the promised land. I hoped that there would be no delay, for our supply of water was running very low. The hot drink at night was essential, but I decided that the daily allowance of water must be cut down to half a pint per man. The lumps of ice we had taken aboard had gone long ago. We were dependent upon the water we had brought from Elephant Island, and our thirst was increased by the fact that we were now using the brackish water in the beaker that had been slightly stove in in the surf when the boat was being loaded. Some sea water had entered at that time.

Thirst took possession of us. I dared not permit the allowance of water to be increased since an unfavorable wind might drive us away from the island and lengthen our voyage by many days. Lack of water is always the most severe privation that men can be condemned to endure, and we found, as during our earlier boat voyage, that the salt water in our clothing and the salt spray that lashed our faces made our thirst grow quickly to a burning pain. I had to be very firm in refusing to allow anyone to anticipate the morrow's allowance, which I was sometimes begged to do. We did the necessary work dully and hoped for the land. I had altered the course to the east so as to make sure of our striking the island, which would have been impossible to regain if we had run past the northern end. The course was laid on our scrap of chart for a point some thirty miles down the coast. That day and the following day passed for us in a sort of nightmare. Our mouths were dry and our tongues were swollen. The wind was still strong and heavy sea forced us to navigate carefully, but any thought of our peril from the waves was buried beneath the consciousness of our raging thirst. The bright moments were those when we each received our one mug of hot milk during the long, bitter watches of the night. Things were bad for us in those days, but the end was coming. The morning of May 8 broke thick and stormy, with squalls from the northwest. We searched the waters ahead for a sign of land, and though we could see nothing more than had met our eyes for many days, we were cheered by a sense that the goal was near at hand. About ten o'clock that morning we passed a little bit of kelp, a glad signal of the proximity of land. An hour later we saw two shags sitting on a big mass of kelp, and knew then that we must be within ten or fifteen miles of the shore. These birds are as sure an indication of the proximity of land as a lighthouse is, for they never venture far to sea. We gazed ahead with increasing eagerness, and at 12:30 P.M., through a rift in the clouds, McCarthy caught a glimpse of the black cliffs of South Georgia, just fourteen days after our departure from Elephant Island. It was a glad moment. Thirst-ridden, chilled, and weak as we were, happiness irradiated us. The job was nearly done.

We stood in toward the shore to look for a landing place, and presently we could see the green tussock grass on the ledges above the surf-beaten rocks. Ahead of us and to the south, blind rollers showed the presence of uncharted reefs along the coast. Here and there the hungry rocks were close to the surface, and over them the great waves broke, swirling viciously and spouting thirty and forty feet into the air. The rocky coast appeared to descend sheer to the sea. Our need of water and rest was well-nigh desperate, but to have attempted a landing at that time would have been suicidal. Night was drawing near, and the weather indications were not favorable. There was nothing for it but to haul off till the following morning, so we stood away on the starboard tack until we had made what appeared to be a safe offing. Then we hove to in the high westerly swell.

The hours passed slowly as we awaited the dawn, which would herald, we fondly hoped, the last stage of our journey. Our thirst was a torment and we could scarcely touch our food; the cold seemed to strike right through our weakened bodies. At 5 A.M. the wind shifted to the northwest and quickly increased to one of the worst hurricanes any of us had ever experienced. A great cross sea was running, and the wind simply shrieked as it tore the tops off the waves and converted the whole seascape into a haze of driving spray. Down into valleys, up to tossing heights, straining until her seams opened, swung our little boat, brave still but laboring heavily. We knew that the wind and set of the sea was driving us ashore, but we could do nothing. The dawn showed us a storm-torn ocean, and the morning passed without bringing us a sight of the land; but at 1 P.M., through a rift in the flying mists, we got a glimpse of the huge crags of the island and realized that our position had become desperate. We were on a dead lee shore, and we could gauge our approach to the unseen cliffs by the roar of the breakers against the sheer walls of rock. I ordered the double-reefed mainsail to be set in the hope that we might claw off, and this attempt increased the strain upon the boat. The *James Caird* was bumping heavily, and the water was pouring in everywhere. Our thirst was forgotten in the realization of our imminent danger, as we hailed unceasingly, and adjusted our weights from time to time; occasional glimpses showed that the shore was nearer. I knew that Annewkow Island lay to the south of us, but our small and badly marked chart showed uncertain reefs in the passage between the island and the mainland, and I dared not trust it, though as a last resort we could try to lie under the lee of the island. The afternoon wore away as we edged down the coast, with the thunder of the breakers in our ears. The approach of evening found us still some distance from Annewkow Island, and dimly in the twilight, we could see a snow-capped mountain looming above us. The chance of surviving the night, with the driving gale and the implacable sea forcing us onto the lee shore, seemed small. I think most of us had a feeling that the end was very near. Just after 6 P.M., in the dark, as the boat was in the yeasty backwash from the seas flung from this iron-bound coast, then, just when things looked their worst, they changed for the best. I have marveled often at the thin line that divides success from failure and the sudden turn that leads from apparently certain disaster to comparative safety. The wind suddenly shifted, and we were free once more to make an offing. Almost as soon as the gale eased, the pin that locked the mast to the thwart fell out. It must have been on the point of doing this throughout the hurricane, and if it had gone nothing could have saved us; the mast would have snapped like a carrot. Our backstays had carried away once before when iced up and were not too strongly fastened now. We were thankful indeed for the mercy that had held that pin in its place throughout the hurricane.

We stood off shore again, tired almost to the point of apathy. Our water had long been finished. The last was about a pint of hairy liquid, which we strained through a bit of gauze from the medicine chest. The pangs of thirst attacked us with redoubled intensity, and I felt that we must make a landing on the following day at almost any hazard. The night wore on. We were very tired. We longed for day. When at last the dawn came on the morning of May 10 there was practically no wind, but a high cross sea was running. We made slow progress toward the shore. About 8 A.M. the wind backed to the northwest and threatened another blow. We had sighted in the meantime a big indentation which I thought must be King Haakon Bay, and I decided that we must land there. We set the bows of the boat toward the bay and ran before the freshening gale. Soon we had angry reefs on either side. Great glaciers came down to the sea and offered no landing place. The sea spouted on the reefs and thundered against the shore. About noon we sighted a line of jagged reef, like blackened teeth, that seemed to bar the entrance to the bay. Inside, comparatively smooth water stretched eight or nine miles to the head of the bay. A gap in the reef appeared, and we made for it. But the fates had another rebuff for us. The wind shifted and blew from the east right out of the bay. We could see the way through the reef, but we could not approach it directly. That afternoon we bore up, tacking five times in the strong wind. The last tack enabled us to get through, and at last we were in the wide mouth of the bay. Dusk was approaching. A small cove, with a boulder-strewn beach guarded by a reef, made a break in the cliffs on the south side of the bay, and we turned in that direction. I stood in the bows directing the steering as we ran through the kelp and made the passage of the reef. The entrance was so narrow that we had to take in the oars, and the swell was piling itself right over the reef into the cove; but in a minute or two we were inside, and in the gathering darkness the *James Caird* ran in on a swell and touched the beach. I sprang ashore with the short painter and held on when the boat went out with the backward surge. When the *James Caird* came in again three of the men got ashore, and they held the painter while I climbed some rocks with another line. A slip on the wet rocks twenty feet up nearly closed my part of the story just at the moment when we were achieving safety. A jagged piece of rock held me and at the same time bruised me sorely. However, I made fast the line, and in a few minutes we were all safe on the beach, with the boat floating in the surging water just off the shore. We heard a gurgling sound that was sweet music in our ears, and, peering around, found a stream of fresh water almost at our feet. A moment later we were down on our knees drinking the pure, ice-cold water in long drafts that put new life into us. It was a splendid moment.

CLOUD FULL OF ROCKS

by William H. Kearns, Jr., and Beverley Britton

By contrast with Shackleton's expedition, modern exploration at both Poles is carried on in large part by airplane and photographic equipment. One of the leading exponents of this type of exploration with the latest and best scientific equipment, was Admiral Richard E. Byrd. On several expeditions, he made permanent contributions to our geographic, geological and meteorological knowledge of Antarctica. His record of one solitary sojourn in an isolated station which lasted for months and which is entitled Alone is a classic in polar literature.

As long as things go well, the work under modern conditions is usually done in comfort and with relatively enormous speed. But things do not always go well. Modern machines and the men who operate them are not perfect and, as we see in "Cloud Full of Rocks," man and nature are again cast in their ancient role of enemies.

WHEN man took to the skies in quest of Antarctica's secrets, he put on seven-league boots which would have filled earlier explorers with envy. Now he could step across vast distances in a single stride. One flight in an airplane could show him more of the continent than all his predecessors combined had seen in their long journeys by ship and by sledge.

The plane added a new dimension to exploration. It gave man a broad look at the continent, revealing its shape and extent. It laid bare rugged

From *The Silent Continent* by William Kearns and Beverley Britton. Copyright 1955 by William H. Kearns, Jr. and Beverley L. Britton. Reprinted by permission of Harper & Brothers.

areas which sledging parties might never reach. Although a flier could not bring back detailed geological or magnetic data, he could view the land as a whole and place its significant features in perspective. Where early voyagers had made their discoveries piece by piece, the man in the air could relate them in a coherent pattern.

In thus widening man's range, the flying explorer also took on new perils. He must fly through the world's worst weather, without the assistance of range or weather stations, and risk take-offs and landings on the ice fields. He must use skill and judgment to overcome the handicaps of polar navigation, which is tricky at best. His compasses became unreliable near the Pole, and sometimes refused to work at all; the earth's rotational force upset the regularity of his gyrocompasses. And the danger of icing rode with him always.

Worst of all, he must face the possibility of a crash or a forced landing. This eventuality dims the wonder of seven-league boots, for rescue becomes correspondingly more doubtful. If he survives, he is lost in an uninhabited world, unmarked by civilization. Medical aid is not likely to be close at hand. There is little he can do to help himself. He must wait while search parties, if there are any, comb thousands of uncharted square miles to reach him. His chances are slim indeed.

No aviator ever expects his plane to crash. But knowing the risks involved, he must prepare for the worst. In Antarctica, his first mistake may be his last—so he must learn all he can about staying alive under the most hostile conditions of nature.

In 1936, the world held its breath as the radio flashed word that a plane was down somewhere in the barren eastern sector of Antarctica. The aircraft was carrying Lincoln Ellsworth, an American explorer making his third attempt to fly across the Palmer Peninsula, and his pilot, Herbert Hollick-Kenyon. For weeks, as word failed to come from the Silent Continent, Ellsworth's fate preyed heavily on people's minds.

The Australian, British and New Zealand governments joined in sending a ship from Australia to aid the search. Other countries stood ready to lend assistance. Then Ellsworth startled the world by walking safe and unharmed into the camp at Little America which Admiral Byrd had used the year before. His plane had run out of gasoline just sixteen miles short of the Bay of Whales, and had landed safely on an ice plateau. For nine days they had wandered on the ice plain, their direction confused and uncertain. The rest of the time, they had waited for help to arrive.

Ten years later, world attention was focused again on Antarctica, and the

fate of another American plane. This time, nine Americans were involved
—officers and men of the U.S. Navy, engaged in "Operation Highjump"
under the direction of Admiral Byrd. They had disappeared on a mapping
flight over the so-called Phantom Coast, which borders the Bellingshausen
Sea. If they were still alive, they had been swallowed up within the icy
maw of the Silent Continent.

The missing plane was a Martin Mariner, one of three big patrol bombers
operating from the seaplane tender *Pine Island*, near Peter I Island. It was
part of the Eastern Task Group of the expedition, assigned to map and
explore the eastern half of the continent. Crews of other planes were
covering similar fan-shaped stretches, each hundreds of miles long.

It was not unusual for bombers to be exploring in an area thousands
of miles from the waters for which they were designed. Weapons of war
have frequently been used as weapons of exploration—and these planes
were engaged in a warlike assault on Antarctica. From three sides, man-made
machines were attacking the forces of nature.

The lost Mariner, known as *George One*, was a monster compared to
the frail Northrup in which Lincoln Ellsworth had flown against the
Antarctic fortress. She was 90 feet long and 18 high, and her wing span
was 118 feet. Loaded, she weighed close to thirty-five tons. Her engines'
four thousand horsepower could keep her in the air nearly eighteen hours
at a stretch, and she could float indefinitely in open water.

George One was a virtual flying laboratory, carrying radar and other
equipment far more elaborate than old-time explorers had dreamed of.
Nine cameras were set up within her huge frame. Her emergency supplies
included food packets, sleeping bags, field tents, medical equipment and
a survival sled. Within the sled were stored additional rations, warm clothing
and small arms.

The plane and its crew had left the *Pine Island* in the best of shape.
Most of the men had had previous polar flying experience, in the far
northern reaches of Greenland and the Canadian Arctic. All were well
drilled in the techniques of survival in polar climates. Except for the newly
assigned flight engineer, they had flown as a team and developed a high
degree of co-ordination. They had kept *George One* as mechanically perfect
as she could be.

Lieutenant "Frenchy" LeBlanc, a lanky Cajun from Louisiana, was pilot
of *George One*. The copilot was Lieutenant Bill Kearns of Boston, and
the navigator Ensign Max Lopez of Newport. The five enlisted crewmen

included a chief photographer's mate, Owen McCarty; two radiomen, Jim Robbins and Wendell Hendersin; a crew chief, Bill Warr; and a flight engineer, Fred Williams.

George One also carried a high-ranking passenger. Captain Howard Caldwell, the *Pine Island's* skipper, had decided at the last minute to go along as an observer. A flier himself, he had grown restive while the ship idled, with her planes tied down by foul weather. With the first favorable forecast, *George One* got flying orders—and Captain Caldwell "volunteered."

The plane was airborne just before three o'clock on the morning of December 30, 1946. There was as much light as there would be at this time of year, but in spite of the forecast the weather looked anything but promising. They flew three hours, through conditions that were bad even for the Antarctic, before they picked up the coastline. For a while it looked as if it might clear. Kearns took over the controls to give LeBlanc a rest, and they continued southward.

Then without warning, *George One* ran into what explorers call ice blink—a condition caused by trapped sunlight streaming through clouds. There was a shallow overcast above, and a fine driving snow obscured the land below. Light filtered eerily through the clouds and bounced off the snow in a million directions, as if each ice fragment were a tiny mirror. The brilliant white glare obliterated any visual horizon. It was like flying in a bowl of milk.

Just then the instruments began acting up. The altimeters, which measure height from the ground, started to give different readings. The men had no way of telling visually how high they were. The heavy weight of ice covering the wings and skin made the plane react sluggishly, as if many hands were conspiring to pull it down.

"I don't like the look of this," said Kearns to Frenchy LeBlanc. "Let's get the hell out of here."

Frenchy agreed, and Kearns banked the big Mariner for the turn.

Just then, a crunching shock ran through the plane and reverberated all along the hull. It wasn't a violent blow, but they had grazed something very solid. Kearns immediately slammed home the throttles and LeBlanc gave full low pitch to the propellers, to aid pulling power. With both men straining back on the yoke, careful not to stall her in a steep ascent, *George One* climbed like a homesick angel.

Bill Kearns looked over at LeBlanc and breathed a sigh of relief. But it was premature. At almost the identical moment, a tremendous explosion literally blew the plane apart.

"Something grabbed me squarely by the seat of the pants," Bill Kearns said later, "and threw me upward against the cockpit glass. In that split second, I knew I was headed straight for the starboard propeller. How I missed that meat cleaver, I'll never know. But when I came to, I was all in one piece—just full of pain, and nearly frozen."

None of the others knew, either, how they had been spared. Not one of them was wearing a parachute, but the soft drifting snow cushioned their fall. Kearns, whose safety belt was unfastened for the first time in years of flying, landed like a ski jumper, tumbling down a long incline covered with powdery snow over a hard crust. When he recovered consciousness, he was desperately afraid he was the only survivor. But up the slope he saw flames, and stumbled toward them in search of his shipmates.

Bill Warr and Jim Robbins, who had been riding just aft of the control room, had landed close to the wreckage of *George One*. They were almost unscathed. Captain Caldwell, whose seat was in the very nose of the plane, had picked himself up near by with only a slight knee injury. McCarty found himself sitting in the snow, holding his head, which was bloody from a scalp gash. Kearns had a head cut too, and his right shoulder throbbed so painfully he was sure it was broken. They looked at each other numbly in the blinding snowstorm, lighted eerily by angry fires in the wreckage. They were so dazed and shocked they didn't realize the plight of Frenchy LeBlanc.

Then an agonizing scream cut through the wail of the wind. It was Frenchy's voice. Robbins and Kearns ran toward the plane's midsection, tilted crazily with its top torn open to sky and storm. Frenchy's body dangled helplessly in the cockpit, held firmly by his safety belt while gasoline flames leapt up at him.

Kearns pushed through the fire and tried to loosen the belt. But his injured right arm wouldn't work, and finally, with a boost from Robbins, he reached across LeBlanc and unfastened the belt with his left hand. Warr came in to help, and the three dragged LeBlanc free. His clothing was on fire, but by beating at it with their gloved hands, they managed to smother the flame.

Frenchy's face, arms and legs were burned black and were already starting to swell. He was only half-conscious, writhing in pain and muttering unintelligibly. Kearns knelt to help him, and covered him with a parachute while the others went off to search for the missing.

Probing in the blinding blizzard, they found the inert bodies of Ensign Lopez, Hendersin and Williams. Apparently all had died instantly. Nothing could be done for them now, and the survivors turned their attention to their own welfare. Instinct told them they must rig some shelter or freeze to death.

The only possible shelter was what remained of *George One*. The big plane had broken into three sections, scattered over the slope like some giant's toys. The wings and center panel were intact. Driving snow had nearly smothered the fire in the flight deck section, which lay about twenty feet forward of the wings. Forty feet behind this, tossed on its port side, the waist was still attached to the tail section. By careful squeezing, they decided, all could get inside.

Some sort of luck was with them, for in the drifting snow they found sleeping bags, still neatly rolled in their khaki containers. Robbins and Warr rigged one for Frenchy and carried him into the severed waist. Then the rest crowded in. They were jammed tightly together, but that meant added warmth. McCarty spread parachutes to cover the exposed openings, and the six exhausted men dropped off into unconsciousness.

Some eighteen hours later, the men began to stir. Robbins and Warr, the young "eager beavers" of the group, scoured the wreckage for food but came up only with some dried fruit. This furnished a cheerless New Year's Eve dinner for the men of *George One*, and after the brief repast they bedded down again.

The situation of the survivors was anything but hopeful. They had crashed in an unknown sector of the continent, and already a screaming blizzard was covering the blackened wreckage of their only island of safety. Three of their men were dead, and a fourth seemed almost certain to die unless he got prompt medical care. They were certain in their minds that search procedures would already have started back at the *Pine Island*, but even so there were only two planes within 2,500 miles that could join in the hunt. They might almost have been stranded on the far side of the moon.

But sleep brought a rise in their spirits, and the next morning they wryly wished each other a Happy New Year—1947. Robbins and Warr, the energetic scroungers, found more bits of food but reported that snow had almost completely covered the wreck. However, there was some hope that the storm might end soon, for the wind had dropped.

Captain Caldwell was afraid the storm had driven them off course, and the searchers might direct their efforts to another area.

"We sent a position report about fifteen minutes before we hit," Kearns reassured him. "I'm sure we stayed on course, Captain."

"Just where would you say we are now?"

"I think this is what the chart calls Cape Dart," said Kearns. "It's just east of Thurston Peninsula and due south of the *Pine Island*."

"Hope you're right," said Captain Caldwell, shaking his head. "But the chart didn't even show these mountains. We're in for a rough time."

Kearns shrugged his shoulders. He couldn't deny Caldwell's point.

"I guess you're right, Captain. That last cloud was sure full of rocks!"

Robbins outdid himself in his scavenging that afternoon. He had already found a stove, but no fuel. Now he came back with four loaves of bread, a gallon can of peanut butter, some soup and canned heat. That evening, the men had their first real meal since the crash—spinach soup, and a slice of bread with peanut butter.

Next day the snow stopped, and all but LeBlanc and Kearns went outside. Their first job was to cover their dead shipmates with snow, just where they had fallen. Then they searched the wreck systematically. They found much of the survival gear—including two trail tents and the emergency sled—but nothing of the cameras, surveying equipment and charts. They also found more food; now they had pemmican, canned ham, pickles and more soup. Best of all, they discovered that the port bomb-bay tank hadn't exploded. That meant nearly five hundred gallons of aviation gas for the stove.

With the storm over and living conditions improved by their findings, Captain Caldwell suggested a system of rationing food and responsibilities. His idea was to keep everyone occupied with some job, preferably one he liked.

"You take over the galley, Robbins," he said, recognizing the radioman's penchant for cooking. "And you, Bill—you're bunged up, so you be Frenchy's nurse and get some extra sack time yourself."

"Aye, aye, sir," Kearns grinned.

"I'll keep the log, Captain," McCarty volunteered. "I've got a notebook, and keeping a diary is an old habit of mine."

"Fine, Mac," said the captain. "Everyone can have more room, too, if we use the trail tents. You and I can take one, and Robbins and Warr the other. Bill and Frenchy had better stay inside."

Routine helped to lend reality to the situation. By now they were also getting used to the biting cold, though most of the time they continued to stay buttoned up in their sleeping bags, dozing and talking. Time moved slowly. The waiting and the uncertainty were their chief enemies.

LeBlanc's pain had abated by this time, and he slept for long hours at a stretch. He clung to life with amazing tenacity, but everyone knew his condition was bad. His burned eyelids were closed tight so that he couldn't see, and his companions feared the flames had got to the eyes themselves. His face was covered with a hard black crust and swollen to inhuman shape. His hands were bloated like fat sausages. Kearns examined him closely, and found his thighs and back a mass of angry burns left by the searing gasoline. Kearns found some cooking oil and rubbed it on Frenchy's feet each day, hoping to keep them from freezing.

Everyone had an incessant thirst, but LeBlanc's was much the worst. The burns had dehydrated his body, and it took large quantities of snow, melted on the stove, to get him even a mouthful of water. They tried at first to keep a cup of water handy for Frenchy at night, but it would freeze solid in a few minutes. All of them knew better than to eat the snow itself, for it could cause frostbite inside the mouth.

But Frenchy LeBlanc was far from being counted out. In his more lucid moments he cheered the others with his dogged optimism.

"Don't you guys worry," he would say. "They'll find us soon, and we'll all be eating steaks."

But Frenchy often went into delirium, and then he'd lift himself to his blistered feet and mumble that he was "going below to see the doc." His companions would have to force him back into his sleeping bag—not an easy task, with a badly burned man of his size.

Near the end of the first week, skua gulls began to hover around the camp site. The skua is a big ugly bird, almost as large as an albatross, and is a known scavenger. They circled slowly overhead like evil omens, dipping occasionally toward the area where the dead men were buried. It was a sickening sight to watch. McCarty finally drove them off with a blast from a broken shotgun found in the wreckage. Firing it was dangerous but it succeeded in keeping the birds away.

After that, Captain Caldwell suggested a more proper burial for their dead comrades. Even assuming that rescue would come, it would be impossible to carry them out. Just getting Frenchy and themselves to safety would be a major task.

The next day was clear and sunny, and the men went about their sad duty as if they were rendering a final salute. They moved the three close together near the starboard wingtip, with their heads facing to the south. Then they covered the dead men with a deep blanket of pure white snow. Captain Caldwell placed a flag at the head of the grave, with a note telling how the three had died, and the rest stood for a moment in silent prayer.

The ceremony set the others to pondering their own fate. They dared not look at one another, for fear they would give away the growing dread that haunted them. For a week now, they had kept an unceasing watch for the rescue plane. But there was no sign. It seemed that all they could do was hope.

One of their regular daily tasks was to keep the snow brushed off the plane's dark metal surfaces, so that it could be seen. This was a brief chore, but a vitally important one. Their chances of rescue depended on remaining at the wreckage; they had no means of transporting themselves elsewhere—and if they did, they would be totally without shelter in the vast spaces of the frozen plain. The plane was big enough to provide a radar target for reflection—and if the snow were kept clear, the dark blue color should stand out like a beacon in the whiteness.

They continued to search the wreckage for useful finds, and were amazed to discover what a catalogue of knowledge they retained in their minds. If they thought of some piece of needed equipment, they could almost invariably locate it on the first try. Sometimes the equipment was barely identifiable, but when they found the plane's compass it was completely undamaged.

One of their most hopeful finds was an emergency transmitter, known as a "Gibson Girl" because of its hourglass shape. This is a hand-wound gadget that sends signals on five hundred kilocycles, the international distress frequency. When they turned the hand generator, they were elated to see that the output light flashed, indicating it was working properly. They sent regular messages giving their estimated position. But as days went by the signals brought no response.

The survivors had about given up on the Gibson Girl when Robbins found parts of the plane's radio transmitter. By combining some coils and a dynamotor, he got it in shape to operate provided they could get sufficient power. Robbins hooked up the generator to the radio, and the men cheered as the dynamotors began to hum. Then he connected to the generator a voltmeter he had salvaged. This would show whether or not they had the power necessary to transmit.

Captain Caldwell ground the hand crank energetically, working up a heavy perspiration. The others watched as the needle climbed. It rose steadily, then hovered and finally stopped a scant four volts short of the necessary twenty-four. No matter how hard the captain cranked, the needle wouldn't budge. Robbins sank back on his heels and swore.

For the next two days, Robbins kept digging in the snow in a desperate effort to find more batteries. But none turned up. Unless someone had picked up the Gibson Girl transmissions, the little group was still out of touch with the world.

Meanwhile, the rest of the men dragged out all the dark objects they could find to provide a better target for sighting by a search plane. They broke out radar reflectors—six large aluminum-foil frames specifically designed to bounce back radar waves in a prominent target—and scattered them in a wide circle. This should attract any plane within range of them. The men racked their brains for other methods of making themselves known.

While they were at it, they painted on *George One's* wrecked wings a message for the rescuers: "Lopez, Hendersin, Williams dead. LeBlanc hurt." It would tell any plane at once the seriousness of the situation.

By this time they had recovered about four-fifths of their emergency food, and if necessary they could make this last for nearly thirty days. But they took the extra precaution of keeping to tight rations—a cup of soup a day, and half a slice of bread while it lasted.

Robbins had become an excellent cook, and his companions cheered him for making pemmican edible. This standard survival ration is highly nourishing, but to the men of *George One* it tasted like a mixture of stale liverwurst and Limburger. One night Robbie concocted a thick stew by boiling snow with dried pemmican, and the men devoured every bit of it. If they had only had a little coffee, they might have felt luxuriously fed.

They made "dinner" a real occasion each day. The stove was set up in the tunnel-like section where LeBlanc and Kearns were quartered, and when Robbins crawled through the flap to start it as evening came on, a feeling of well-being settled over the stranded men. They had to move around in a hunched-over position, carefully stepping over one another, but the atmosphere was warm and friendly. While they waited for the pot to boil, they talked as if they hadn't seen one another for a year.

The smell of the stew and the buzz of conversation usually woke Frenchy, and often he would join in. On the evening of the ninth day, as Captain Caldwell came through the parachute curtain, Frenchy said, "Wipe your feet before you come in the house, Captain." Everyone just laughed at first, then suddenly they realized who had said it.

Frenchy was lying there in his sleeping bag with his eyes open. He could see! This was the first bit of good news in several days, and everyone made the most of it. LeBlanc not only had his sight back, but remained lucid and chatted all through the meal.

"How's it go with you, Frenchy?" Kearns asked.

"Not bad a-tall," said the lanky Southerner, with something like a smile on his blackened face. "We're gonna get out of here soon."

In spite of Frenchy's improved sight, he was growing worse; the nights when he woke in delirium and called for a doctor became more frequent. They knew rescue must come soon, for his sake. The only first-aid supplies which had survived the crash, a package of sulfa tablets, had been exhausted.

"This is a helluva ship," LeBlanc would mutter to Bill Kearns in his delirium. "A *helluva* ship! Where's the doc?"

"He's making his rounds, Frenchy," Kearns would tell him rather lamely. "He'll get to you soon, boy."

One night, in a clear interval, LeBlanc asked Kearns to look at his feet. They had been bothering him lately, and he was finding it hard to wiggle his toes. Kearns crawled over to him and pulled off his friend's boots. What he saw made his stomach turn over.

Under his socks, Frenchy's feet had turned a sickly gray-white color. They were ice-cold to the touch. They had a withered look that told Kearns they were frozen, and a pungent odor that indicated gangrene had set in. This time, Kearns was thankful when Frenchy lapsed back into delirium. He didn't have to tell him.

During the second week of their stranding, there were three successive days of heavy fog. The following day it snowed again. There was no chance of rescue while the weather was bad, for a rescue plane could never spot them. In the evenings the temperature often dropped to thirty below zero, and cheer was a scarce commodity as the little band of men huddled around their stove.

The weather began to break on the twelfth day. Patches of blue appeared in the sky, and by noon the sun was beating down. For the first time, they got a good look at their surroundings.

Under other conditions, this would have been a beautiful spot. They were high on a mountain ridge, and at their backs rose other higher mountains, merging in the far distance into an unending whiteness almost without horizon. Beneath them, the ever-moving sea ice was broken occasionally by open leads that showed dark water, and interspersed with great "growler" bergs that crashed and groaned as they shifted with the currents. Except for the reverberating noises of the bergs, and the whisper of shifting snow, silence pressed around them like a blanket.

It was always cold—so cold that it hurt to breathe deeply. The men could often see ice crystals forming as they exhaled. But on this day, the sun was near its height—about forty-five degrees above the horizon—and the temperature rose to nearly thirty-five above. The men's spirits improved correspondingly. Captain Caldwell and Lieutenant Kearns pored over a chart that had turned up in the wreckage, and Kearns again reassured the captain.

"If you're right, Bill," said Caldwell, "the *Pine Island* should be due north of us."

"That's what I figure, Captain. About 350 to 400 miles due north."

Captain Caldwell hiked to the top of the ridge that afternoon for a better look, and McCarty went with him. They came back dog-tired, but sure that Kearns' estimate was right. That put everyone in a good humor. McCarty brought out a hoarded cigar and gave it to the captain; Robbins found a camera and posed all of them for a picture; the snow on the wreckage melted, and the men's flight suits suddenly were uncomfortably warm.

Bill Warr came up with a mirror from the plane, and in spite of their gruesome appearance, the men had some laughs as they looked at themselves. Even though they had seen each other, each was amazed to see his own unwashed face, matted hair, icy beard and eyebrows. Kearns decided that his nose, which was twisted to one side, was definitely broken. His arm was less painful now, but it was undoubtedly fractured.

High spirits prevailed at the end of the day. It had been like a holiday, and all of the survivors felt confident of rescue.

Next morning, as Bill Kearns sat in his sleeping bag changing socks, he suddenly became aware of a new sound. He couldn't be sure, but in the intense silence he listened hard. It was like the beat of props that comes before you catch the full engine sound. For a moment it died out, and he thought his imagination was playing tricks. Then it was there again. He was positive this time.

Grabbing his boots, Kearns clawed his way outside and yelled at the top of his lungs: "Airplane! Airplane! It's a plane!"

McCarty was there too, and stood in the snow pointing upward.

"There it is! There it *is!*"

About two miles away, and no higher than three thousand feet, they saw a PBM just like *George One*, headed right over their position. Everyone shouted, and Bill Warr waved the brightest colored cloth he could find, an orange life-raft cover. Robbins fired the Verys' pistol; McCarty set off the smoke grenades. But the PBM continued on its course.

It was too much to take. After two weeks of waiting, had they muffed their only chance of rescue? As the plane disappeared over the horizon,

Bill Warr threw himself onto the snow, yelling crazily, "They didn't see us!" McCarty shook his fist toward the sky and called for the plane to return. Captain Caldwell stood dumfounded on the wing of *George One*.

Even in their disappointment, the men quickly recognized their possibly fatal error. They had failed to check the most important detail of all. In the desert of whiteness, Captain Caldwell had been sure the dark wreckage would stand out like a beacon. Even if it were not so conspicuous, he had counted on the reflectors, the flares and smoke grenades. With an entire plane crew scanning the ground, he thought they couldn't miss the plane and the little group of men beside it.

But they had overlooked the obvious thing. Their smoke grenades had come from life rafts and were designed for use at sea. They made a grayish-white smoke that couldn't possibly be seen against a snowy background.

They had bungled their main chance, but they might have another. As they talked it over, they felt sure the plane was not on a routine mapping mission; its low altitude indicated that it was conducting a search. Probably it was a standard "ladder search"—which, when laid out on a chart, looks just like a ladder. The pilot's next position should be about ten miles away, but he would be able to see them if they made a smoke signal that would show—black instead of white.

Captain Caldwell galvanized the group into action. They dragged out a rubber life raft and filled it with anything that would burn—manila line, cardboard, wood, paper. Then they poured gasoline over it, and set up a watch around the horizon. Nothing must go wrong this time.

At ten-twenty by Bill Kearns' watch, just two hours after the first sighting, Captain Caldwell cried, "There she is, lads!" This time the PBM was about six miles away, flying on an angular course at much higher altitude. Robbins dropped a match into the life-raft pyre and McCarty stood by, ready to set off the bomb-bay gas tank if necessary.

A column of heavy black smoke shot into the air. It rose straight up to more than three hundred feet, then fanned out in a long tail.

But still the plane continued on its course.

The watching men held their breaths and prayed hard. They stood in deathly silence, their eyes glued on the big blue Mariner. It was perhaps the longest moment of their lives. Then suddenly the pilot rocked his wings in recognition and began a long shallow dive over them.

"We're saved!" McCarty shouted, and tears ran unchecked down his face. Kearns rolled in the snow, laughing almost hysterically. Robbins and Warr joined hands in a wild dance, and even Captain Caldwell did a caper.

Then they remembered Frenchy. They had left him alone for nearly an hour, and Kearns ran back to tell him the news. But Frenchy had heard the laughter and the roar of the plane, and had pulled himself to the opening in the wreckage.

"What'd I tell you guys?" His voice almost swaggered. "I knew we'd get out of this mess."

Supplies came parachuting down—food, clothes, cigarettes, bedding, whisky, a rifle and ammunition. Copilot Bob Goff even pulled off his own flight suit and sent it hurtling down. The plane circled, then headed north to find a landing place. Minutes later it was back, and dropped a note wrapped around a tin of sardines. Robbins dashed over to recover it, and handed it to the captain, who read it aloud:

Open water ten air miles to north. If you can make it on foot, join hands in circle. If not, form straight line. Don't lose courage, we'll pick you up.

It was signed by the pilot, Lieutenant James Ball.

The big problem, of course, was Frenchy LeBlanc; he would have to be pulled on the survival sled. But the captain was also anxious about Kearns, whose injuries were fairly serious, and who would have to travel on his own steam.

"How do you feel, Bill? Think you can make it?" His rugged features were all concern. "If you're strong enough, we'll try. If not, we'll wait for them to get here."

Kearns looked at the eager faces around him: Robbins and Warr, full of pep and ready to go; McCarty, less energetic but eager to try; Captain Caldwell, a man like a rock but considerate of others. Even if he were not in shape, he couldn't say no.

"Let's go," said Kearns, and they formed their circle in the snow.

Before starting, the men had a good meal from their fresh supplies. Then they loaded the sled with sleeping bags, alpenstocks, a water breaker, and the candy and cigarettes that had been dropped. They took the compass salvaged from the wreck. Last of all they lashed LeBlanc securely to the sled, as comfortably and warmly as they could. Frenchy sat in an upright position, with sleeping bags under and behind him to lend support and protection for his raw skin.

"All set?" Captain Caldwell asked Frenchy as they prepared to start.

"All set," he repeated. "Let's put this show on the road."

They struck out to the north at a leisurely pace, for they knew it would be a tough journey. With LeBlanc, the sled weighed more than two hundred pounds, and there were only four men pulling it; Kearns had all he could do to lead, setting the pace. The plan was to march fifteen minutes and rest five.

For a while, the going was easy. They stuck to the top of a ridge, where six inches of powdery snow covered a hard crust and gave them some footing. After slogging for two hours, including several rests, they had made about a mile. Then they came to the downward slope of the ridge, and turned for a last look at *George One*. It was a tiny speck in a vast white sea, and they wondered how the rescue plane had seen them at all.

As they started down the slope, the PBM was overhead again to drop another message. It was running low on fuel and would return to the ship. Another plane, piloted by Lieutenant Commander John D. Howell, was already on its way out. In almost no time, Howell was there making more drops. The wind carried some away, and they let them go rather than waste their strength. When one fell on their course, they'd stop to eat, for even the short pulls were leaving them winded and exhausted.

"Don't stuff yourselves, boys," Captain Caldwell warned. "When you've been low on rations, you have to eat lightly at first."

It was a temptation to eat everything in sight. Evidently the captain couldn't resist either, for he downed a whole tin of meat without stopping.

"Is that the way you mean, Captain?" McCarty needled him.

"That's the way *not* to do," laughed the captain. But they all followed suit before starting again.

Fortunately, the weather continued good—and so did their spirits. The temperature was below freezing, for their water breaker rattled with ice. But the sun was so warm and the exertion so strenuous that they discarded some of their heavy clothing. Some were down to just woolen shirts.

The jostling sled gave Frenchy a rough ride, and now and then he threw his head back and winced with pain. But his spunk never deserted him. His shipmates offered him water at every halt, but after taking a sip or two, he would pass it back.

"I'm O. K.," said Frenchy. "You guys need it more than I do."

After six hours the slogging men reached the end of the ridge and dropped to the snow to relax their aching muscles. The exertion had sapped their vitality, and now they were coming to an area crossed with treacherous crevasses. They knew it would be dangerous, with their reflexes slowed, but they had no choice; they had to get to the plane.

They roped themselves together, each man with a knot tied both in front and back, so that if one fell, the rope would not bind but slip up to the chest, under the arms. Then Kearns led the way down the slope, testing every foot of the way with an alpenstock. Captain Caldwell and McCarty, being the heaviest, held back the sled by digging their heels into the snow.

Up to now they had been making good time, but here they had to advance by yards. Near the bottom, they were brought up short by a sheer sixty-foot drop. Without the sled, they might have roped their way down; for Frenchy's sake, they had to find another way.

Warr took over watching Frenchy and the sled, and the others scouted to the northeast. They plowed into deeper and deeper snow, until it was nearly waist-high and they could progress only by lunging their way forward, pulling those behind. Every bone and muscle cried for rest, but rest was dangerous now; it was growing colder as the day waned, and the land was becoming more rugged.

McCarty, who was short and heavy-set, had a particularly difficult time. He couldn't seem to lift his legs high enough in the deep snow, and fell several times. Once he broke through the crust, and dangled at the end of his line for a long minute while Caldwell, Robbins and Kearns all struggled to pull him to safety. It was a nerve-shattering experience, and they decided to try another direction.

As they turned, they got their first sight of the rescue plane—and this gave them a new burst of energy. It lay far off to the north, riding easily in open water. But danger loomed beyond it: a tremendous fog bank, miles long and at least a thousand feet deep. Within an hour or two, it would cover the take-off area. They searched desperately for a way down.

Finally, about four hundred yards away, they found what they were seeking. A large shoulder of ice had slipped from the cliff, and formed a perfect roadway down the grade. Kearns rested at the bottom while the others went back for Frenchy.

On the way down, the four men had to work the sled across a small crevasse. Robbins slipped momentarily, and the lurch tumbled the compass into the chasm, before anyone could grab it. If the fog caught them now, they had no way to tell direction. Somehow they found the strength to step up their speed another notch.

After McCarty's fall, they had stayed roped together. But this had disadvantages too. When anyone fell, the rope would drag back the man in front of him, and throw all of them into a jumbled heap. The men would struggle to their feet, sobbing and cursing, then start out again.

They hadn't stopped to rest for nearly an hour now, and were making good progress. Kearns had been guiding the party by watching a big iceberg about a thousand yards beyond the plane. When fog obliterated the berg, he shifted his reference point to a nunatak between them and the PBM, and plodded on. When they reached the nunatak, they sank to the snow in exhaustion. They felt they couldn't walk another step.

This last burst had taken nearly everything the weary men had, and they rolled on their backs in the snow. The fog was closing in now and would cover them in a matter of minutes, but they felt powerless to make another move. Then suddenly in the vast silence they heard something unbelievable: the sharp crack of a pistol shot.

Robbins jumped up and looked in the direction of the sound.

"Someone's coming!" he shouted. "I can see them!"

They forgot weariness and leapt to their feet. Half a mile away, they saw two men dragging a sled. The tired men waved and called, and the pair dropped the sled ropes and ran toward their shipmates. They were "Dixie" Howell and Chief Photographer's Mate Dick Conger.

The men of *George One* were overcome with happiness, but they stood silent, almost afraid to believe what had happened. There didn't seem to be any words appropriate to such an occasion—or the words wouldn't come out. Unashamed tears came to their eyes as they shook hands with their rescuers.

Dick Conger had brought his cameras with him, and stepped back to take a picture. Maybe the sight was too gruesome, or perhaps he was a bit emotional too. Anyway, he put the camera away. Instead, he threw his arms around Kearns' and McCarty's shoulders.

"I'm damned glad to see you," was all he said.

Howell and Conger took over the pulling of Frenchy's sled, and the rest followed their tracks in the snow, through the dense fog which had now covered the area. Two hours later they reached the edge of the ice. They had made the ten-mile trek in just a little over twelve hours.

Fog had now completely hidden the plane, and they would have to wait for it to lift. They heated some mushroom soup and ate it greedily. After their long march, the survivors found they couldn't stay still; their muscles demanded that they keep moving. For eight interminable hours they waited for the weather to clear.

LeBlanc was barely conscious as his shipmates rowed him out to the plane in a life raft. When all were safely aboard, the big Mariner headed back to the *Pine Island*. As they landed alongside and were hoisted to the ship's deck, they had the warm feeling of coming home again; the entire ship's company was on hand to greet them. Frenchy was quickly taken to sick bay, and the other four turned in too, for a rest from their harrowing adventure.

The next day was New Year's Day aboard the Pine Island. It didn't matter that the calendar said January 13. It was an all-hands holiday and everyone ate turkey—the dinner they had postponed after *George One* hit that "cloud full of rocks." In spite of the three lives lost, the world's most remote plane crash had had a far happier conclusion than anyone expected.

Note: Lieutenant Ralph P. (Frenchy) LeBlanc recovered from his burns, but lost both feet, which were amputated above the ankle for frostbite. Later he and the other survivors—with the exception of Captain Caldwell, who remained to command his ship—were flown back to the United States. LeBlanc is now retired from the Navy and lives in Louisiana. Kearns, Robbins and Warr were decorated for saving his life when they pulled him from the wreckage of *George One*.

Part Five

ABOVE
THE
SNOW
LINE

FIRST CLIMB OF THE MATTERHORN

by Edward Whymper

In the history of mountaineering there is no more fascinating story than that
of Edward Whymper's conquest of the Matterhorn in 1865. All the elements
of melodrama are here—the lonely and majestic peak which is regarded with
awe and fear by the near-by inhabitants; the belief, amounting to superstition,
that it is unassailable; the wandering British artist who becomes engrossed
with the problem; the six separate attacks and defeats over a period of four
years; the final victory which culminates in disaster and death. Whymper's
story is a classic which stands beside those of Herzog, of Mallory and Irvine
and of Tenzing and Hilary.

He saw the Matterhorn first in 1860, but contented himself with observing its face and studying the problems of the climb. At the time of his
first actual encounter with it, in 1861, he met the redoubtable Alpine guide,
Jean-Antoine Carrel and attempted without success to hire him. He described
Carrel as the finest rock climber he had ever seen, the only man, himself
excluded, who believed the mountain was "not inaccessible." Choosing another guide, Whymper made an attempt, but the guide, turning panicky at
what Whymper considered an ordinary difficulty, refused to go on. "I told
him he was a coward," says Whymper, "and he mentioned his opinion of
me." That climb left Whymper "longing to make the ascent and determined to return . . . to lay siege to the mountain until one or the other
was vanquished."

In the summer of 1862, Whymper tried four separate times to make the
climb. For the first of these, he made elaborate plans and took four companions, but an accident to one of the guides and a sudden hurricane defeated him. The very next day he set out again, this time with Carrel and
one other guide. Again there was cowardice—the second guide complained

From *Scrambles Among the Alps in the Years 1860-69.*

of illness at the same spot where the first guide had lost his nerve. Carrel stated that for a party to go with only one guide was impossible and the expedition collapsed. Now came the solitary reconnoitering expedition and the fourth climb, which Whymper describes below.

IT is unnecessary to enter into a minute description of the Matterhorn, after all that has been written about that famous mountain. Those by whom this book is likely to be read will know that that peak is nearly fifteen thousand feet high, and that it rises abruptly, by a series of cliffs which may properly be termed precipices, a clear five thousand feet above the glaciers which surround its base. They will know too that it was the last great Alpine peak which remained unscaled—less on account of the difficulty of doing so, than from the terror inspired by its invincible appearance. There seemed to be a cordon drawn around it, up to which one might go, but no farther. Within that invisible line jinns and afreets were supposed to exist—the Wandering Jew and the spirits of the damned. The superstitious natives in the surrounding valleys (many of whom still firmly believe it to be not only the highest mountain in the Alps, but in the world) spoke of a ruined city on its summit wherein the spirits dwelt; and if you laughed, they gravely shook their heads; told you to look yourself to see the castles and the walls, and warned one against a rash approach, lest the infuriate demons from their impregnable heights might hurl down vengeance for one's derision. Such were the traditions of the natives. Stronger minds felt the influence of the wonderful form, and men who ordinarily spoke or wrote like rational beings, when they came under its power seemed to quit their senses, and ranted, and rhapsodized, losing for a time all common forms of speech.

1862. Three times I had essayed the ascent of this mountain, and on each occasion had failed ignominiously. I had not advanced a yard beyond my predecessors. Up to the height of nearly thirteen thousand feet there were no extraordinary difficulties; the way so far might even become "a matter of amusement." Only eighteen hundred feet remained; but they were as yet untrodden, and might present the most formidable obstacles. No man could expect to climb them by himself. A morsel of rock only seven feet high might at any time defeat him, if it were perpendicular. Such a place might be possible to two, or a bagatelle to three men. It was evident that a party should consist of three men at least. But where could the other two men be obtained? Carrel was the only man who exhibited any enthusiasm in the matter.

The weather became bad again, so I went to Zermatt on the chance of picking up a man, and remained there during a week of storms. Not one of the good men, however, could be induced to come.

My tent had been left rolled up at the second platform, and whilst waiting for the men it occurred to me that it might have been blown away during the late stormy weather; so I started off on the eighteenth to see if this were so or not. The way was by this time familiar, and I mounted rapidly, astonishing the friendly herdsmen—who nodded recognition as I flitted past them and the cows—for I was alone, because no man was available.

The tent was safe, although snowed up; and I turned to contemplate the view, which, when seen alone and undisturbed, had all the strength and charm of complete novelty.

Time sped away unregarded, and the little birds which had built their nests on the neighboring cliffs had begun to chirp their evening hymn before I thought of returning. Half mechanically I turned to the tent, unrolled it, and set it up; it contained food enough for several days, and I resolved to stay over the night. I had started from Breil without provisions, or telling Favre—the innkeeper, who was accustomed to my erratic ways—where I was going. Shivering, at last I entered the tent and made my coffee. The night was passed comfortably, and the next morning, tempted by the brilliancy of the weather, I proceeded yet higher in search of another place for a platform. . . .

The first step was a difficult one. The ridge became diminished to the least possible width—it was hard to keep one's balance—and just where it was narrowest, a more than perpendicular mass barred the way. Nothing fairly within arm's reach could be laid hold of; it was necessary to spring up, and then to haul oneself over the sharp edge by sheer strength. Progression directly upward was then impossible. Enormous and appalling precipices plunged down to the Tiefenmatten Glacier on the left, but round the right-hand side it was just possible to go. . . .

An innocent gully was an untrodden vestibule which led to a scene so wild that even the most sober description of it must seem an exaggeration. There was a change in the quality of the rock, and there was a change in the appearance of the ridge. The rocks (talcose gneiss) below this spot were singularly firm; it was rarely necessary to test one's hold; the way led over the living rock, and not up rent-off fragments. But here, all was decay and ruin. The crest of the ridge was shattered and cleft, and the feet sank in the chips which had drifted down; while above, huge blocks, hacked and carved by the hand of time, nodded to the sky, looking like the gravestones of giants. Out of curiosity I wandered to a notch in the ridge, between two tottering piles of immense masses, which seemed to need but a few pounds on one or the other side to make them fall; so nicely poised that they would literally have rocked in the wind, for they were put in motion by a touch; and based on support so frail that I wondered they did not collapse before my eyes. In the whole range of my Alpine experience I have seen nothing more striking than this desolate, ruined, and shattered ridge at the back of the Great Tower. . . .

The Tower was now almost out of sight. So far, I had no doubts about my capacity to descend that which had been ascended; but, in a short time, on looking ahead, I saw that the cliffs steepened, and I turned back (without pushing on to them, and getting into inextricable difficulties), exulting in the thought that they would be passed when we returned together, and that I had, without assistance, got considerably higher than any one had been before. My exultation was a little premature.

About 5 P.M. I left the tent again, and thought myself as good as at Breil. I lowered myself through the Chimney by making a fixture of the rope, which I then cut off, and left behind, as there was enough and to spare. My ax had proved a great nuisance in coming down, and I left it in the tent. It was not attached to the baton, but was a separate affair,—an old navy boarding-ax. While cutting up the different snow beds on the ascent, the baton trailed behind fastened to the rope; and, when climbing, the ax was carried behind, run through the rope tied round my waist, and was sufficiently out of the way. But in descending, when coming down face outward (as is always best where it is possible), the head or the handle of the weapon caught frequently against the rocks, and several times nearly upset me. So, out of laziness if you will, it was left in the tent. I paid dearly for the imprudence.

The Col du Lion was passed, and fifty yards more would have placed me on the "Great Staircase," down which one can run. But on arriving at an angle of the cliffs of the Tête du Lion, while skirting the upper edge of the snow which abuts against them, I found that the heat of the two past days had nearly obliterated the steps which had been cut when coming up. The rocks happened to be impracticable just at this corner, so nothing could be done except make the steps afresh. The snow was too hard to beat or tread down, and at the angle it was all but ice. Half a dozen steps only were required, and then the ledges could be followed again. So I held to the rock with my right hand, and prodded at the snow with the point of my stick until a good step was made, and then, leaning round the angle, did the same for the other side. So far well, but in attempting to pass the corner (to the present moment I cannot tell how it happened) I slipped and fell.

The slope was steep on which this took place, and was at the top of a gully that led down through two subordinate buttresses toward the Glacier du Lion—which was just seen, a thousand feet below. The gully narrowed and narrowed, until there was a mere thread of snow lying between two walls of rock, which came to an abrupt termination at the top of a precipice that intervened between it and the glacier. Imagine a funnel cut in half through its length, placed an angle of forty-five degrees, with its point below and its concave side uppermost, and you will have a fair idea of the place.

The knapsack brought my head down first, and I pitched into some rocks about a dozen feet below; they caught something and tumbled me off the edge, head over heels, into the gully; the baton was dashed from my hands, and I whirled downward in a series of bounds, each longer than the last; now over ice, now into rocks; striking my head four or five times, each time with increased force. The last bound sent me spinning through the air, in a leap of fifty or sixty feet, from one side of the gully to the other, and I struck the rocks, luckily, with the whole of my left side. They caught my clothes for a moment, and I fell back onto the snow with motion arrested. My head fortunately came the right side up, and a few frantic catches brought me to a halt, in the neck of the gully, and on the verge of the precipice. Baton, hat, and veil skimmed by and disappeared, and the crash of the rocks—which I had started—as they fell onto the glacier, told how narrow had been the escape from utter destruction. As it was, I fell nearly two hundred feet in seven or eight bounds. Ten feet more would have taken me in one gigantic leap of eight hundred feet onto the glacier below.

The situation was sufficiently serious. The rocks could not be left go for a moment, and the blood was spirting out of more than twenty cuts. The most serious ones were in the head, and I vainly tried to close them with one hand, whilst holding on with the other. It was useless; the blood jerked out in blinding jets at each pulsation. At last, in a moment of inspiration, I kicked out a big lump of snow, and stuck it as a plaster on my head. The idea was a happy one, and the flow of blood diminished. Then, scrambling up, I got, not a moment too soon, to a place of safety, and fainted away. The sun was setting when consciousness returned, and it was pitch-dark before the Great Staircase was descended; but, by a combination of luck and care, the whole 4,800 feet of descent to Breil was accomplished without a slip, or once missing the way. I slunk past the cabin of the cowherds, who were talking and laughing inside, utterly ashamed of the state to which I had been brought by my imbecility, and entered the inn stealthily, wishing to escape to my room unnoticed. But Favre met in the passage, demanded "Who is it?" screamed with fright when he got a light, and aroused the household.

The news of the accident brought Jean-Antoine Carrel up to Breil, and, along with the haughty chasseur came one of his relatives, a strong and able young fellow named Cæsar. With these two men and Meynet I made another start on the twenty-third of July. We got to the tent without any trouble, and on the following day had ascended beyond the Tower, and were picking our way cautiously over the loose rocks behind (where my traces of the week before were well apparent) in lovely weather, when one of those abominable and almost instantaneous changes occurred, to which the Matterhorn is so liable on its southern side. Mists were created out of invisible vapors, and in a few minutes snow fell heavily. We stopped, as this part was of excessive difficulty, and, unwilling to retreat, remained on the spot several hours, in hopes that another change would occur; but, as it did not, we at length went down to the base of the Tower, and commenced to make a third platform, at the height of 12,992 feet above the sea. It still continued to snow, and we took refuge in the tent. Carrel argued that the weather had broken up, and that the mountain would become so glazed with ice as to render any attempt futile; and I, that the change was only temporary, and that the rocks were too hot to allow ice to form upon them. I wished to stay until the weather improved, but my leader would not endure contradiction, grew more positive, and insisted that we must go down. We went down, and when we got below the Col his opinion was found to be wrong; the cloud was confined to the upper three thousand feet, and outside it there was brilliant weather.

Carrel was not an easy man to manage. He was perfectly aware that he was the cock of the Val Tournanche, and he commanded the other men as by right. He was equally conscious that he was indispensable to me, and took no pains to conceal his knowledge of the fact. If he had been commanded, or if he had been entreated to stop, it would have been all the same. But, let me repeat, he was the only first-rate climber I could find who believed that the mountain was not inaccessible. With him I had hopes, but without him none; so he was allowed to do as he would.

[*One more attempt was made by Whymper in 1862. With a companion, the indomitable hunchback Meynet, he climbed higher than anyone had ever gone before. But just below the shoulder of the upper mountain, they found themselves "spread-eagled on the all but perpendicular face and were forced to descend."*

In 1863, Whymper made his sixth attack, accompanied by Carrel, Meynet and three others.]

1863. Carrel had *carte blanche* in the matter of guides, and his choice fell upon his relative Cæsar, Luc Meynet, and two others whose names I do not know. These men were now brought together, and our preparations were completed, as the weather was clearing up.

We rested on Sunday, August 9, eagerly watching the lessening of the mists around the great peak, and started just before dawn upon the tenth, on a still and cloudless morning, which seemed to promise a happy termination to our enterprise.

By going always, though gently, we arrived upon the Col du Lion before nine o'clock. Changes were apparent. Familiar ledges had vanished; the platform, whereupon my tent had stood, looked very forlorn, its stones had been scattered by wind and frost, and had half disappeared: and the summit of the Col itself, which in 1862 had always been respectably broad, and covered by snow, was now sharper than the ridge of any church roof, and was hard ice. Already we had found that the bad weather of the past week had done its work. The rocks for several hundred feet below the Col were varnished with ice. Loose, incoherent snow covered the older and harder beds below, and we nearly lost our leader through its treacherousness. He stepped on some snow which seemed firm and raised his ax to deliver a swinging blow, but, just as it was highest, the crust of the slope upon which he stood broke away, and poured down in serpentine streams, leaving long, bare strips, which glittered in the sun, for they were glassy ice. Carrel, with admirable readiness, flung himself back onto the rock off which he had stepped, and was at once secured. He simply remarked, "It is time we were tied up," and, after we had been tied up, he went to work again as if nothing had happened. . . .

We went on gaily, passed the second tent platform, the Chimney, and the other well-remembered points, and reckoned, confidently, on sleeping that night upon the top of "the shoulder"; but, before we had well arrived at the foot of the Great Tower, a sudden rush of cold air warned us to look out.

It was difficult to say where this air came from; it did not blow as a wind, but descended rather as the water in a shower bath! All was tranquil again; the atmosphere showed no signs of disturbance; there was a dead calm, and not a speck of cloud to be seen anywhere. But we did not remain very long in this state. The cold air came again, and this time it was difficult to say where it did *not* come from. We jammed down our hats as it beat against the ridge, and screamed amongst the crags. Before we had got to the foot of the Tower, mists had been formed above and below. They appeared at first in small, isolated patches (in several places at the same time), which danced and jerked and were torn into shreds by the wind, but grew larger under the process. They were united together, and rent again —showing us the blue sky for a moment, and blotting it out the next; and augmented incessantly, until the whole heavens were filled with whirling, boiling clouds. Before we could take off our packs, and get under any kind of shelter, a hurricane of snow burst upon us from the east. It fell very heavily, and in a few minutes the ridge was covered by it. "What shall we do?" I shouted to Carrel. "Monsieur," said he, "the wind is bad; the weather has changed; we are heavily laden. Here is a fine *gîte*; let us stop! If we go on we shall be half-frozen. That is *my* opinion." No one differed from him; so we fell to work to make a place for the tent. The clouds had blackened during that time, and we had hardly finished our task before a thunderstorm broke upon us with appalling fury. Forked lightning shot out at the turrets above, and at the crags below. It was so close that we quailed at its darts. It seemed to scorch us—we were in the very focus of the storm. The thunder was simultaneous with the flashes; short and sharp, and more like the noise of a door that is violently slammed, multiplied a thousandfold, than any noise to which I can compare it.

The wind during all this time seemed to blow tolerably consistently from the east. It smote the tent so vehemently (notwithstanding it was partly protected by rocks) that we had grave fears our refuge might be blown away bodily, with ourselves inside; so during some of the lulls, we issued out and built a wall to windward. At half-past three the wind changed to the northwest, and the clouds vanished. We immediately took the opportunity to send down one of the porters (under protection of some of the others, a little beyond the Col du Lion), as the tent would accommodate only five persons. From this time to sunset the weather was variable. It was sometimes blowing and snowing hard, and sometimes a dead calm.

We passed the night comfortably—even luxuriously—in our blanket bags, but there was little chance of sleeping, between the noise of the wind, of the thunder, and of the falling rocks. I forgave the thunder for the sake of the lightning. A more splendid spectacle than its illumination of the Matterhorn crags I do not expect to see.

We turned out at 3:30 A.M. on the eleventh and were dismayed to find that it still continued to snow. At 9 A.M. it ceased to fall, and the sun showed itself feebly, so we packed up our baggage, and set out to try to get upon "the shoulder." We struggled upward until eleven o'clock, and then it commenced to snow again. We held a council; the opinions expressed at it were unanimous against advancing, and I decided to retreat. . . .

[*Then in 1865, came the final attempt, one of the greatest feats in the history of mountaineering. On this climb Whymper was accompanied by a party including Charles Hudson, Vicar of Skillington in Lincolnshire, of whom Whymper says that he was considered the best amateur of his time. The joy of victory was lost in the tragedy which followed. It became a cause célèbre in England and on the Continent, and resulted in a sort of semidisgrace from which Whymper never entirely recovered.*]

1865. My thoughts were fixed on the Matterhorn, and my guides knew that I wished them to accompany me. They had an aversion to the mountain, and repeatedly expressed their belief that it was useless to try to ascend it. "*Anything* but Matterhorn, dear sir!" said Almer; "*anything* but Matterhorn." He did not speak of difficulty or of danger, nor was he shirking *work.* He offered to go *anywhere;* but he entreated that the Matterhorn should be abandoned. Both men spoke fairly enough. They did not think that an ascent could be made; and for their own credit, as well as for my sake, they did not wish to undertake a business which, in their opinion, would only lead to loss of time and money.

I sent them by the short cut to Breil, and walked down to Val Tournanche to look for Jean-Antoine Carrel. He was not there. The villagers said that he, and three others, had started on the sixth to try the Matterhorn by the old way, on their own account. They will have no luck, I thought, for the clouds were low down on the mountains; and I walked up to Breil, fully expecting to meet them. Nor was I disappointed. About halfway up I saw a group of men clustered around a chalet upon the other side of the torrent, and, crossing over, found that the party had returned. Jean-Antoine and Cæsar were there, C. E. Gorret, and J. J. Maquignaz. They had had no success. The weather, they said, had been horrible, and they had scarcely reached the Glacier du Lion.

I explained the situation to Carrel, and proposed that we, with Cæsar and another man, should cross the Théodule by moonlight on the ninth, and that upon the tenth we should pitch the tent as high as possible upon the east face. He was unwilling to abandon the old route, and urged me to try it again. I promised to do so provided the new route failed. This satisfied him, and he agreed to my proposal. I then went up to Breil, and discharged Almer and Biener—with much regret, for no two men ever served me more faithfully or more willingly. On the next day they crossed to Zermatt.

The eighth was occupied with preparations. The weather was stormy; and black, rainy vapors obscured the mountains. Toward evening a young man came from Val Tournanche, and reported that an Englishman was lying there, extremely ill. On the morning of Sunday the ninth I went down the valley to look after the sick man. On my way I passed a foreign gentleman, with a mule and several porters laden with baggage. Amongst these men were Jean-Antoine and Cæsar, carrying some barometers. "Hello!" I said, "what are you doing?" They explained that the foreigner had arrived just as they were setting out, and that they were assisting his porters. "Very well; go on to Breil, and await me there; we start at midnight as agreed." Jean-Antoine then said that he should not be able to serve me after Tuesday the eleventh, as he was engaged to travel "with a family of distinction" in the valley of Aosta. "And Cæsar?" "And Cæsar also." "Why did you not say this before?" "Because," said he, "it was not settled. The engagement is of long standing, but *the day* was not fixed. When I got back to Val Tournanche on Friday night, after leaving you, I found a letter naming the day." I could not object to the answer; still the prospect of being left guideless was provoking. They went up, and I down, the valley.

The weather continued bad upon the tenth, and I returned to Breil. The inn was lonely. I went to bed early, and was wakened the next morning by the invalid inquiring if I had "heard the news." "No; what news?" "Why," said he, "a large party of guides went off this morning to try the Matterhorn, taking with them a mule laden with provisions."

I went to the door, and with a telescope saw the party upon the lower slopes of the mountain. Favre, the landlord, stood by. "What is all this about?" I inquired, "who is the leader of this party?" "Carrel." "What! Jean-Antoine?" "Yes; Jean-Antoine." "Is Cæsar there too?" "Yes, he is there." Then I saw in a moment that I had been bamboozled and humbugged; and learned, bit by bit, that the affair had been arranged long beforehand. The start on the sixth had been for a preliminary reconnaissance; the mule, that I passed, was conveying stores for the attack; the "family of distinction" was Signor F. Giordano, who had just despatched the party to facilitate the way to the summit, and who, when the facilitation was completed, was to be taken to the top along with Signor Sella!

I was greatly mortified. My plans were upset; the Italians had clearly stolen a march upon me, and I saw that the astute Favre chuckled over my discomfiture, because the route by the eastern face, if successful, would not benefit his inn. What was to be done? I retired to my room, and soothed by tobacco, restudied my plans, to see if it was not possible to outmaneuver the Italians. "They had taken a mule's load of provisions." That is *one* point in my favor, for they will take two or three days to get through the food, and, until that is done, no work will be accomplished." "How is the weather?" I went to the window. The mountain was smothered up in mist. "Another point in my favor." "They are to facilitate the way. Well, if they do that to any purpose, it will be a long job." Altogether, I reckoned that they could not possibly ascend the mountain and come back to Breil in less than seven days. I got cooler, for it was evident that the wily ones might be outwitted after all. There was time enough to go to Zermatt, to try the eastern face, and, should it prove impracticable, to come back to Breil before the men returned; and then, it seemed to me, as the mountain was not padlocked, one might start at the same time as the Messieurs, and yet get to the top before them.

About midday on Tuesday the eleventh a large party hove in sight from Zermatt, preceded by a nimble young Englishman, and one of old Peter Taugwalder's sons. I went at once to this gentleman to learn if he could dispense with Taugwalder. He said that he could not, as they were going to recross to Zermatt on the morrow, but that the young man should assist in transporting my baggage, as he had nothing to carry. We naturally got into conversation. I told my story, and learned that the young Englishman was Lord Francis Douglas, whose recent exploit—the ascent of the Gabelhorn—had excited my wonder and admiration. He brought good news. Old Peter had lately been beyond the Hörnli, and had reported that he thought an ascent of the Matterhorn was possible upon that side. Almer had left Zermatt, and could not be recovered, so I determined to seek for old Peter. Lord Francis Douglas expressed a warm desire to ascend the mountain, and before long it was determined that he should take part in the expedition.

We descended to Zermatt, sought and engaged old Peter, and gave him permission to choose another guide. When we returned to the Monte Rosa Hotel, whom should we see sitting upon the wall in front but my old *guide chef*, Michel Croz. I supposed that he had come with Mr. B——, but I learned that that gentleman had arrived in ill health, at Chamounix, and had returned to England. Croz, thus left free, had been immediately engaged by the Rev. Charles Hudson, and they had come to Zermatt with the same object as ourselves—namely, to attempt the ascent of the Matterhorn!

Lord Francis Douglas and I dined at the Monte Rosa, and had just finished when Mr. Hudson and a friend entered the *salle à manger*. They had returned from inspecting the mountain, and some idlers in the room demanded their intentions. We learned that Mr. Hudson intended to set out on the morrow at the same hour as ourselves. We left the room to consult, and agreed it was undesirable that two independent parties should be on the mountain at the same time with the same object. Mr. Hudson was therefore invited to join us, and he accepted our proposal. Before admitting his friend—Mr. Hadow—I took the precaution to inquire what he had done in the Alps, and, as well as I remember, Mr. Hudson's reply was, "Mr. Hadow has done Mont Blanc in less time than most men." He then mentioned several other excursions that were unknown to me, and added, in answer to a further question, "I consider he is a sufficiently good man to go with us." Mr. Hadow was admitted without any further question, and we then went into the matter of guides. Hudson thought that Croz and old Peter would be sufficient. The question was referred to the men themselves, and they made no objection.

We started from Zermatt on the thirteenth of July, at half-past five, on a brilliant and perfectly cloudless morning. We were eight in number—Croz, old Peter and his two sons, Lord F. Douglas, Hadow, Hudson, and I. To ensure steady motion, one tourist and one native walked together. The youngest Taugwalder fell to my share, and the lad marched well, proud to be on the expedition, and happy to show his powers. The wine bags also fell to my lot to carry, and throughout the day, after each drink, I replenished them secretly with water, so that at the next halt they were found fuller than before! This was considered a good omen, and little short of miraculous.

Before twelve o'clock we had found a good position for the tent, at a height of eleven thousand feet. Croz and young Peter went on to see what was above, in order to save time on the following morning. They cut across the heads of the snow slopes which descended towards the Furggengletscher, and disappeared round a corner; but shortly afterward we saw them high up on the face, moving quickly. We others made a solid platform for the tent in a well-protected spot, and then watched eagerly for the return of the men. The stones which they upset told that they were very high, and we supposed that the way must be easy. At length, just before 3 P.M., we saw them coming down, evidently much excited. "What are they saying, Peter?" "Gentlemen, they say it is no good." But when they came near we heard a different story. "Nothing but what was good; not a difficulty, not a single difficulty! We could have gone to the summit and returned today easily!"

We passed the remaining hours of daylight—some basking in the sunshine, some sketching or collecting; and when the sun went down, giving, as it departed, a glorious promise for the morrow, we returned to the tent to arrange for the night. Hudson made tea, I coffee, and we then retired each one to his blanket bag; the Taugwalders, Lord Francis Douglas, and myself, occupying the tent, the others remaining, by preference, outside. Long after dusk the cliffs above echoed with our laughter and with the songs of the guides, for we were happy that night in camp, and feared no evil.

We assembled together outside the tent before dawn on the morning of the fourteenth, and started directly it was light enough to move. Young Peter came on with us as a guide, and his brother returned to Zermatt. We followed the route which had been taken on the previous day, and in a few minutes turned the rib which had intercepted the view of the eastern face from our tent platform. The whole of this great slope was now revealed, rising for three thousand feet like a huge natural staircase. Some parts were more, and others were less, easy; but we were not once brought to a halt by any serious impediment, for when an obstruction was met in front it could always be turned to the right or to the left. For the greater part of the way there was, indeed, no occasion for the rope, and sometimes Hudson led, sometimes myself. At 6:20 we had attained a height of 12,800 feet, and halted for half an hour; we then continued the ascent without a break until 9:55, when we stopped for fifty minutes, at a height of fourteen thousand feet. Twice we struck the N.E. ridge, and followed it for some little distance—to no advantage, for it was usually more rotten and steep, and always more difficult than the face. Still, we kept near to it, lest stones perchance might fall.

We had now arrived at the foot of that part which, from the Riffelberg or from Zermatt, seems perpendicular or overhanging, and could no longer continue upon the eastern side. For a little distance we ascended by snow upon the arête—that is, the ridge—descending toward Zermatt, and then, by common consent, turned over to the right, or to the northern side. Before doing so, we made a change in the order of ascent. Croz went first, I followed, Hudson came third; Hadow and old Peter were last. "Now," said Croz, as he led off, "now for something altogether different." The work became difficult, and required caution. In some places there was little to hold, and it was desirable that those should be in front who were least likely to slip. The general slope of the mountain at this part was *less* than forty degrees and snow had accumulated in, and had filled up, the interstices of the rock face, leaving only occasional fragments projecting here and there. These were at times covered with a thin film of ice, produced from the melting and refreezing of the snow. It was a place over which any fair mountaineer might pass in safety, and Mr. Hudson ascended this part, and, as far as I know, the entire mountain, without having the slightest assistance rendered to him upon any occasion. Sometimes, after I had taken a hand from Croz, or received a pull, I turned to offer the same to Hudson; but he invariably declined, saying it was not necessary. Mr. Hadow, however, was not accustomed to this kind of work, and required continual assistance. It is only fair to say that the difficulty which he found at this part arose simply and entirely from want of experience.

This solitary difficult part was of no great extent. We bore away over it at first, nearly horizontally, for a distance of about four hundred feet; then ascended directly toward the summit for about sixty feet; and then doubled back to the ridge which descends toward Zermatt. A long stride round a rather awkward corner brought us to snow once more. The last doubt vanished! The Matterhorn was ours! Nothing but two hundred feet of easy snow remained to be surmounted!

You must now carry your thoughts back to the seven Italians who started from Breil on the eleventh of July. Four days had passed since their departure, and we were tormented with anxiety lest they should arrive on the top before us. All the way up we had talked of them, and many false alarms of "men on the summit" had been raised. The higher we rose, the more intense became the excitement. What if we should be beaten at the last moment? The slope eased off, at length we could be detached, and Croz and I, dashing away, ran a neck-and-neck race, which ended in a dead heat. At 1:40 P.M. the world was at our feet, and the Matterhorn was conquered. Hurrah! Not a footstep could be seen.

It was not yet certain that we had not been beaten. The summit of the Matterhorn was formed of a rudely level ridge, about 350 feet long, and the

Italians might have been at its farther extremity. I hastened to the southern end, scanning the snow right and left eagerly. Hurrah! again; it was untrodden. "Where were the men?" I peered over the cliff, half doubting, half expectant. I saw them immediately—mere dots on the ridge, at an immense distance below. Up went my arms and my hat. "Croz! Croz!! come here!" "Where are they, Monsieur?" "There, don't you see them, down there?" "Ah! the *coquins*, they are low down." "Croz, we must make those fellows hear us." We yelled until we were hoarse. The Italians seemed to regard us —we could not be certain. "Croz, we *must* make them hear us; they *shall* hear us!" I seized a block of rock and hurled it down, and called upon my companion, in the name of friendship, to do the same. We drove our sticks in, and prized away the crags, and soon a torrent of stones poured down the cliffs. There was no mistake about it this time. The Italians turned and fled.

Sill, I would that the leader of that party could have stood with us at that moment, for our victorious shouts conveyed to him the disappointment of the ambition of a lifetime. He was *the* man, of all those who attempted the ascent of the Matterhorn, who most deserved to be the first upon its summit. He was the first to doubt its inaccessibility, and he was the only man who persisted in believing that its ascent would be accomplished. It was the aim of his life to make the ascent from the side of Italy, for the honor of his native valley. For a time he had the game in his hands: he played it as he thought best; but he made a false move, and he lost it. Times have changed with Carrel. His supremacy is questioned in the Val Tournanche; new men have arisen; and he is no longer recognized as *the* chasseur above all others: but so long as he remains the man that he is today, it will not be easy to find his superior.

We remained on the summit for one hour—

One crowded hour of glorious life.

It passed away too quickly, and we began to prepare for the descent.

Hudson and I again consulted as to the best and safest arrangement of the party. We agreed that it would be best for Croz to go first, and Hadow second; Hudson, who was almost equal to a guide in sureness of foot, wished to be third; Lord F. Douglas was placed next, and old Peter, the strongest of the remainder, after him. I suggested to Hudson that we should attach a rope to the rocks on our arrival at the difficult bit, and hold it as we descended, as an additional protection. He approved the idea, but it was not definitely settled that it should be done. The party was being arranged in the above order whilst I was sketching the summit, and they had finished, and were waiting for me to be tied in line, when someone remembered that our names had not been left in a bottle. They requested me to write them down, and moved off while it was being done.

A few minutes afterward I tied myself to young Peter, ran down after the others, and caught them just as they were commencing the descent of the difficult part. Great care was being taken. Only one man was moving at a time; when he was firmly planted the next advanced, and so on. They had not, however, attached the additional rope to rocks, and nothing was said about it. The suggestion was not made for my own sake, and I am not sure that it even occurred to me again. For some little distance we two followed the others, detached from them, and should have continued so had not Lord F. Douglas asked me, about 3 P.M., to tie on to old Peter, as he feared, he said, that Taugwalder would not be able to hold his ground if a slip occurred.

A few minutes later, a sharp-eyed lad ran into the Monte Rosa hotel, to Seiler, saying that he had seen an avalanche fall from the summit of the Matterhorn onto the Matterhorngletscher. The boy was reproved for telling idle stories; he was right, nevertheless, and this was what he saw.

Michel Croz had laid aside his ax, and in order to give Mr. Hadow greater security, was absolutely taking hold of his legs, and putting his feet, one by one, into their proper positions. As far as I know, no one was actually descending. I cannot speak with certainty, because the two leading men were partially hidden from my sight by an intervening mass of rock, but it is my belief, from the movements of their shoulders, that Croz, having done as I have said, was in the act of turning round to go down a step or two himself; at this moment Mr. Hadow slipped, fell against him, and knocked him over. I heard one startled exclamation from Croz, then saw him and Mr. Hadow flying downward; in another moment Hudson was dragged from his steps, and Lord F. Douglas immediately after him. All this was the work of a moment. Immediately we heard Croz's exclamation, old Peter and I planted ourselves as firmly as the rocks would permit: the rope was taut between us, and the jerk came on us both as on one man. We held; but the rope broke midway between Taugwalder and Lord Francis Douglas. For a few second we saw our unfortunate companions sliding downward on their backs, and spreading out their hands, endeavoring to save themselves. They passed from our sight uninjured, disappeared one by one, and fell from precipice to precipice on to the Matterhorngletscher below, a distance of nearly four thousand feet in height. From the moment the rope broke it was impossible to help them.

So perished our comrades! For the space of half an hour we remained on the spot without moving a single step. The two men, paralyzed by terror, cried like infants, and trembled in such a manner as to threaten us with the fate of the others. Old Peter rent the air with exclamations of "Chamounix! Oh, what will Chamounix say?" He meant, Who would believe that Croz could fall? The young man did nothing but scream or sob, "We are lost! we are lost!" Fixed between the two, I could neither move up nor down. I begged young Peter to descend, but he dared not. Unless he did, we could not advance. Old Peter became alive to the danger, and swelled the cry, "We are lost! we are lost!" The father's fear was natural—he trembled for his son; the young man's fear was cowardly—he thought of self alone. At last old Peter summoned up courage, and changed his position to a rock to which he could fix the rope; the young man then descended, and we all stood together. Immediately we did so, I asked for the rope which had given way, and found, to my surprise—indeed, to my horror—that it was the weakest of the three ropes. It was not brought, and should not have been employed, for the purpose for which it was used. It was old rope, and, compared with the others, was feeble. It was intended as a reserve, in case we had to leave much rope behind, attached to rocks. I saw at once that a serious question was involved, and made him give me the end. It had broken in mid-air, and it did not appear to have sustained previous injury.

For more than two hours afterward I thought almost every moment that the next would be my last; for the Taugwalders, utterly unnerved, were not only incapable of giving assistance, but were in such a state that a slip might have been expected from them at any moment. After a time, we were able to do that which should have been done at first, and fixed rope to firm rocks, in addition to being tied together. These ropes were cut from time to time, and were left behind. Even with their assurance the men were afraid to proceed, and several times old Peter turned with ashy face and faltering limbs, and said, with terrible emphasis, "*I cannot!*"

About 6 P.M. we arrived at the snow upon the ridge descending toward Zermatt, and all peril was over. We frequently looked, but in vain, for traces of our unfortunate companions; we bent over the ridge and cried to them, but no sound returned. Convinced at last that they were neither within sight nor hearing, we ceased from our useless efforts; and, too cast down for speech, silently gathered up our things, and the little effects of those who were lost, preparatory to continuing the descent. When, lo! a mighty arch appeared, rising above the Lyskamm, high into the sky. Pale, colorless, and noiseless, but perfectly sharp and defined, except where it was lost in the clouds, this unearthly apparition seemed like a vision from another world; and, almost appalled, we watched with amazement the gradual development of two vast crosses, one on either side. If the Taugwalders had not been the first to perceive it, I should have doubted my senses. They thought it had some connection with the accident, and I, after a while, that it might bear some relation to ourselves. But our movements had no effect upon it. The spectral forms remained motionless. It was a fearful and wonderful sight; unique in my experience, and impressive beyond description, coming at such a moment.

I was ready to leave, and waiting for the others. They had recovered their appetites and the use of their tongues. They spoke in patois, which I did not understand. At length the son said in French, "Monsieur." "Yes." "We are poor men; we have lost our Herr; we shall not get paid; we can ill afford this." "Stop!" I said, interrupting him, "that is nonsense; I shall pay you, of course, just as if your Herr were here." They talked together in their patois for a short time, and then the son spoke again. "We don't wish you to pay us. We wish you to write in the hotel book at Zermatt, and to your journals, that we have not been paid." "What nonsense are you talking? I don't understand you. What do you mean?" He proceeded—"Why, next year there will be many travelers at Zermatt, and we shall get more *voyageurs*."

Who would answer such a proposition? I made them no reply in words, but they knew very well the indignation that I felt. They filled the cup of bitterness to overflowing, and I tore down the cliff, madly and recklessly, in a way that caused them, more than once, to inquire if I wished to kill them. Night fell; and for an hour the descent was continued in the darkness. At half-past nine a resting place was found, and upon a wretched slab, barely large enough to hold the three, we passed six miserable hours. At daybreak the descent was resumed, and from the Hörnli ridge we ran down to the chalets of Buhl, and on to Zermatt. Seiler met me at his door, and followed in silence to my room. "What is the matter?" "The Taugwalders and I have returned." He did not need more, and burst into tears; but lost no time in useless lamentations, and set to work to arouse the village. Ere long a score of men had started to ascend the Hohlicht heights, above Kalbermatt and Z'Mutt, which commanded the plateau of the Matterhorngletscher. They returned after six hours, and reported that they had seen the bodies lying motionless on the snow. This was on Saturday; and they proposed that we should leave on Sunday evening, so as to arrive upon the plateau at daybreak on Monday. Unwilling to lose the slightest chance, the Rev. J. M'Cormick and I resolved to start on Sunday morning.

We started at 2 A.M. on Sunday the sixteenth. By 8:30 we had got to within sight of the corner in which we knew my companions must be. As we saw one weather-beaten man after another raise the telescope, turn deadly pale, and pass it on without a word to the next, we knew that all hope was gone. We approached. They had fallen below as they had fallen above—Croz a little in advance, Hadow near him, and Hudson some distance behind; but of Lord F. Douglas we could see nothing. We left them where they fell; buried in snow at the base of the grandest cliff of the most majestic mountain of the Alps.

THE SUICIDE CLIMBERS

by James Ramsey Ullman

A horrifying episode, drawn from a short-lived phase of the history of mountaineering, is described in the next selection by James Ramsey Ullman.

CLIMBING is fundamentally neither a standardized nor a competitive sport, but in recent years, along with its other developments, it has had a tendency to become so. One of the concomitants—part cause, part effect—has been an elaborate system of grading ascents, which originated in the Alps in the 1920's and has since spread over most of the world. By this method, climbs of all descriptions are ranked according to their degree of difficulty, beginning with a First Degree for an easy walk-up and culminating in a Sixth, which has been aptly defined as "an ascent recognized as impossible until someone does it without being killed." Inherently, perhaps, there is nothing wrong with such a system; at least it helps a climber in the selection of his route and lets him know roughly what he may expect. But it was soon perverted to the purposes of competition, and by the thirties the Alps were full of glory-seeking young climbers who looked down with contempt on anything less than a certified Super-Sixth. The Eigerwand, the north wall of the Grandes Jorasses, the north and west faces of the Matterhorn and various of the rock pinnacles in the Dolomites achieved a notorious celebrity as "impossible" ascents, and it was on them in particular that the new order of Alpine cragsmen concentrated and struggled —and often died.

Aiding and abetting this suicidal insanity was a rising tide of nationalism. To be sure, mountaineering, since its earliest days, has suffered from ugly and senseless rivalries (witness the stories of Mont Blanc and the Matterhorn), but the jingoistic fervor that developed in the decade before the Second World War touched new heights of absurdity. Inevitably, it was the Germans and Italians who carried it to its furthest extreme. Aflame with the hero-philosophy of Nazi-Fascism and egged on by flag-wavers and tub-thumpers at home, brown- and black-shirted young climbers began vying with one another in what they conceived to be feats of courage and skill. All or nothing was their watchword—victory or death. No risk was too great, no foolhardiness to be condemned, so long as their exploits brought kudos to *Vaterland* or *patria*.

As a result of all this, Alpine mountaineering—at least in its more "expert" phases—became an activity with scarcely any relationship to the usual concept of sport. Competion was everything: competition literally to the death. Each year saw scores of new attempts at "record climbs," hundreds of reckless youngsters clinging to precipices and cliff faces which a centipede could scarcely have surmounted, much less a man. And each year, inevitably, the fatalities mounted, until two, three or four hundred lives a season came to be accepted as the usual toll. The Alps had once been looked upon as a playground; then as a laboratory. Now they had become a battlefield. Seldom has there been an unhappier example of how hysterical and perverted nationalism can infect even the most unpolitical of human activities.

One glimpse of this "all-or-nothing" type of climbing is more than enough. The time is mid-July of 1936; the scene the mile-high precipice of the Eigerwand—the Wall of the Ogre—that rises close by the Jungfrau in the heart of the Bernese Oberland. . . .

For years the Eigerwand had been famous throughout Europe as one of the few great unclaimed "prizes" of the Alps. Many parties of daredevil climbers—most of them Germans—had tried to force a way up its appalling pitches of rock and ice; but none had succeeded, and almost every venture had ended in the death of one or more participants. Still the suicidal at-

tempts went on—"victory or annihilation"; "for *Führer* and *Vaterland*."[1]
And on the morning of July 20 crowds of sight-seers again thronged the
terrace of the Kleine Scheidegg Hotel, in the valley below, staring upward
through the telescopes. For yet another assault was under way.

High on the mountain wall the figures of the climbers could be seen,
clinging to the rock like minute black insects. There were four of them—
two Bavarians and two Austrians—all of them young, all with records of
many sensational climbs behind them, all resolved to win fame and glory by
accomplishing "the most difficult ascent in the Alps." By the time the
telescopes picked them up on the morning of the twentieth they had already
been on the precipice for two full days. Hour after hour they had inched
their way upward, digging fingers and toes into tiny crevices, driving pitons
where no crevices existed at all, dangling in space at rope's end as they
struggled with vertical cliffs and bulging overhangs. The first night they
spent standing upright, lashed to a rockwall with pitons and rope. On the
second a storm swooped down, and the whole mountainside around them
was sheathed in a whirling fury of ice and snow. The watchers below gave
them up as lost, but at daybreak they were still there alive—still able to
move. And the third day began.

Throughout the morning they crept on and by noon were almost within a
thousand feet of their goal. There, however, their good luck ended. Storm
and cold and the savage, perpendicular wall must at last have taken their
toll of the climbers' strength, for they were seen to remain motionless for
a long time and then begin to descend. But their downward progress did
not last long either, and presently they were motionless again—four in-
finitesimal specks transfixed against the wall. Apparently they were unable
to move either up or down.

A council of war was held in the valley below, and four guides set out
as a rescue party. Following the tracks of the Jungfrau Railway, which bores
through the rock of the Eiger, they came out on the precipice through
an opening in the tunnel wall and began working their way across it
toward the point where the climbers were trapped. Soon they were near
enough to see the four of them clearly. They were clinging to the merest
wrinkles in the ice-coated rockface, one above the other, tied together and
supported by a mass of ropes and pitons. Their clothing was in tatters and
their faces scarcely recognizable from the effects of exposure and exhaustion.
Above them was a sheer, almost holdless wall, down which they had some-

---

[1] Hitler himself announced that gold medals would be awarded to the first scalers
of the Eigerwand, in conjunction with the Berlin Olympic Games of 1936.

how managed to lower themselves. Below was an overhanging precipice and an abyss of blue space.

Slowly, with deliberation and care, the rescue party drew nearer, but while they were still some distance away the inevitable happened. The uppermost of the four Germans lost his hold and toppled backward into thin air, arms and legs twisting grotesquely. The coils of the rope, spinning down after him, caught the next man around the neck, almost wrenching his head from his shoulders, while a third, still lower, was struck by the falling body of his companion. Then the rope went taut and snapped. The first man plummeted on for four thousand feet to the valley below; the second and third stayed motionless where they had fallen, half lying, half hanging from the ropes and pitons. In five seconds it was all over. And one man was left alive.

Still the horrified guides kept on. Hacking their way diagonally across a sixty-degree ice slope, they at last reached a point only a few yards away from the sole survivor—a Bavarian soldier named Kurz. But before they could begin the delicate work of rescue another storm bore down on the mountain, and they were forced to beat a retreat. Kurz was left to spend his third night on the precipice, his body suspended over space and tied to the corpses of two of his companions.

The next morning, miraculously, he was still alive, but so weak that he was scarcely able to speak or move. Again the guides began the grim work of reaching him and this time succeeded in establishing themselves on a narrow ledge some one hundred feet below his position. Farther, however, they could not go. The stretch that still separated them from Kurz was an ice-glazed overhang, and to have ventured so much as a step onto it would have been obvious suicide. They called up the Kurz to cut himself loose from the bodies of his companions. This he did, using the point of his ice-ax; then, summoning his last reserves of strength, he knotted several ropes together and lowered them to the guides. He was so feeble by this time that these two operations took him three hours.

On the ropes dangling from above the guides sent up a specially devised sling. As there was no possible way of their reaching him, it was up to Kurz to lower himself on it—if he had the strength left. Slowly and patiently he wrapped the coils about his body, leaned out into space, started down. The men below could hear his hoarse breathing and see his boot nails scraping weakly against the rock. In a few moments he was so close that one of the guides, balancing on the others' shoulders, could almost touch his feet.

Then suddenly the rope sling jammed and Kurz's downward progress ceased. For a desperate, straining moment he clung with fingers and toes to the ice-smooth bulge of the overhang; but the last of his strength was gone. His ice ax dropped from his hand and went spinning downward. An instant later he himself swung out from the mountain wall into space. And hanging there at rope's end, he died.

This miserable disaster was only one among many of similar nature that occurred in the Alps in prewar years. The Eigerwand was finally climbed in the summer of 1938, and those other famous "impossibles," the north wall of the Grandes Jorasses and the northern and western faces of the Matterhorn, also yielded at last to climbers with more luck than sense. For each success, however, there were many failures and many lives lost; and, far from being deterred by the endless list of catastrophes, there appeared to be an ever-growing supply of young men eager to devise still more spectacular and gruesome ways of killing themselves. The coming of war had at least one good effect, in that it put pretty much of an end to this sort of lunatic extreme in mountaineering. True, there are still plenty of accidents in the Alps. "Impossible" ascents are still attempted, and occasionally made. But at least a measure of sanity has been restored; the hordes of storm-trooper heroes have disappeared, and the mountains are being given back again to those who understand and love them.

MOUNT McKINLEY, THE GREAT ONE

by James Ramsey Ullman

We journey to the Western Hemisphere, to the highest peak in North America. The story of how it was climbed contains elements both comic and tragic. It is written by James Ramsey Ullman, a mountaineer of note

From *The Age of Mountaineering* by James Ramsey Ullman. Copyright, 1941, 1954, by James Ramsey Ullman. Published by J. B. Lippincott Company.

who has written fascinatingly about mountains in both novels and works of nonfiction.

IN THE faraway frozen heart of Alaska stands the highest mountain in North America. We know it as Mount McKinley. Men of other races, however, have had other, and better, names for it. To many of the aboriginal Indian tribes of the region it was known as Denali—"The Home of the Sun." Others referred to it as Tralaika, still others as Doleyka, and the Russians, when they came, called it Bulshaia Gora. Significantly these three names, in three different tongues, meant the same thing—"The Great One."

For this remote snow peak in our own Northwest is not merely the culminating point of the North American Continent; it is also one of the greatest single mountains on earth. The giants of the Himalayas and Andes are higher—twenty-two thousand to twenty-nine thousand feet, as against McKinley's 20,300—but these figures indicate total heights above sea level, and the mountains usually rise from lofty plateaus that are themselves ten to fifteen thousand feet high. McKinley, however, has no such headstart. The valley of the Yukon River, from which its northern slopes spring, is a scant fifteen hundred feet above the sea, and the wilderness of forests and glaciers to the south is only slightly more elevated. The mountain soars up in one gigantic, unbroken sweep of rock and ice to its full height—three and a half miles straight up from base to peak.

But the greatness of McKinley is more than a matter of arithmetic. Every traveler who has laid eyes on it, from near or far, has declared it to be one of the most impressive sights in the world. From Cook Inlet on the Pacific, two hundred miles to the south, its snowy crest dominates the northern horizon; from Fairbanks, a hundred and fifrty miles north, it appears like a great white giant crouched against the sky. Except for its immediate neighbor, seventeen-thousand-foot Mount Foraker, it has not a single rival. Its cloud-hung battlements tower, lone and immense, over three hundred thousand square miles of central Alaska.

This colossus among mountains has now been climbed ten times. The records of these ascents, together with those of the several near-misses, make a story that, for achievement and disappointment, tragedy and comedy, heroism and even villainy, are unsurpassed in the annals of mountaineering.

So far as we know, the first white man to look upon McKinley was the English navigator, George Vancouver. While exploring the southern coast of Alaska in 1794 he saw "distant, stupendous snow mountains" to the north. He did not, however, approach any nearer, nor did any other white men, so far as we know, for almost a hundred years. The Russians, who owned and occupied the territory for the first two-thirds of the last century, obviously knew of the peak, since they gave it a name, but there is no record of any exploration in its vicinity. In 1867 the United States purchased Alaska for what then seemed the enormous sum of $7,200,000—the famous "Seward's Folly." During the next twenty years traders and prospectors trickled in, and towns and trading posts were established. But they hugged the coasts. It was not until the 1890's that the interior wilderness began to be opened up, and Americans discovered that they had acquired not only a vast Arctic storehouse of gold, fish and fur, but the highest mountain on the continent as well.

Most of the pioneers of central Alaska were men in search of gold. One of these, Frank Densmore, penetrated the McKinley region in 1889 and returned with such fabulous descriptions of the mountain that it was known for years among the Yukon prospectors as Densmore's Peak. Another, W. A. Dickey, followed in 1896, reaching the outer edge of the mountain's great skirt of glaciers. Presumably Dickey was ignorant of the already-existing names for the peak—or perhaps he was merely a good Republican. In either case, he named it in honor of William McKinley, who was then candidate for President of the United States. And the name stuck.

In the next ten years several individuals and expeditions approached the mountain, among them George Eldridge and Robert Muldrow, of the U.S. Geological Survey, who measured it by triangulation and fixed its height at 20,300 feet. The first actual attempt at ascent took place in 1903. Under the leadership of Judge Wickersham, one of the foremost citizens of the new boom town of Fairbanks, a party of four men packed in to the base of the mountain and began to climb it. They were unfortunate in their choice of route, however, for they were halted almost immediately by unscalable walls of ice, and soon turned back. Thereafter Judge Wickersham was often heard to declare that the summit would never be reached except by an airplane or a balloon. Thereafter, that is, until it was climbed.

The next man to enter the expanding saga of McKinley was one of the strangest figures in the history of exploration and mountaineering. This was Dr. Frederick Cook, who was later to win world-wide notoriety as the bogus "Discoverer of the North Pole." At this time, however, Dr. Cook was concentrating on becoming the equally bogus "Conqueror of Mount

McKinley." His first expedition to the mountain was in the same year as Judge Wickersham's, but it was little more than a reconnaissance of the surrounding passes and glaciers. Then in 1906 he returned and plunged energetically into the business of making his own particular brand of history.

Ironically, Cook's companions at the outset of this second venture were two men of complete honor and integrity. They were Herschel Parker and Belmore Browne, whose later battles with McKinley form one of the brightest, most heroic chapters of mountain history. On this occasion, however, they and Cook bogged down in the great wilderness south of the peak and were forced to withdraw without finding even a way of approach to the heights.

Then began Cook's audacious hoax. With only one companion, a packer named Edward Barrill, he returned to the base of the mountain, was unheard from for a few weeks, and reappeared with the claim that he had reached the summit. Neither Parker, Browne nor anyone else who knew McKinley believed him. He had not, for one thing, had enough time for the ascent, and, furthermore, his description of his experiences did not tally with their own observations. But Cook was a fraud who knew his business. Undeterred by suspicions and accusations, he returned to civilization and began systematically to reap the rewards of his "feat." He wrote a book called *To the Top of the Continent*, in which he described his struggles on the ascent and the magnificence of the view from the top. He showed photographs which he said he had taken on the summit. He lectured before public gatherings and learned societies. As far as the world was concerned, he was what he claimed to be—the "Conqueror of McKinley."

Seven years passed before the fraud was finally exposed. Parker and Browne could not conclusively prove their suspicions, and it remained for Hudson Stuck and his companions, who in 1913 made the true first ascent, to settle the matter once and for all. Stuck was Archdeacon of the Yukon, a man above suspicion in every way, and his description of McKinley refuted Cook's in countless details. From this point on the evidence piled up rapidly. Barrill, Cook's packer, after years of silence, signed a sworn statement that his employer's claims were untrue. An insignificant foothill peak was found, which coincided so completely with Cook's supposed photographs of McKinley's summit that it became obvious they had been made there. Within a short time the "conqueror's" claims were thoroughly discredited. Then, a few years later, came the still more sensational exposure of his faked discovery of the North Pole, and Cook's fantastic career reached its end. He dropped into obscurity—a dishonored, broken man.

Meanwhile the fight against The Great One went on. The bogus conquest had, if nothing else, aroused widespread interest in the greatest American mountain, and the attack was on in full force.

First in the field was a group of men who put even the incredible Dr. Cook to shame. They are known in climbing history as the Sourdough Expedition, and no stranger or more haphazard exploit than theirs has ever occurred on any major mountain in the world. By every accepted standard they should not only have made a fiasco of their attempt, but all should have been killed five times over. Instead, they missed immortality by a hairbreadth—or, to be accurate, three hundred feet—and, in addition, performed what is undoubtedly one of the greatest exploits in the annals of mountaineering.

The sourdoughs of McKinley were a half-dozen prospectors and miners of the vicinity of Fairbanks. None of them had ever been on a mountain in his life, but they were typical Alaskan frontiersmen, with frontiersmen's strength and pride, and when they heard of Cook's claims they snorted in disbelief and decided it was high time they took a hand in the affair themselves. "If McKinley is going to be climbed," they decided in effect, "we're the boys who are going to do it."

And in the spring of 1910, off they went.

The venture was organized in a way that would make a good Alpine Club member's hair stand on end. Or, rather, it wasn't organized at all. The five hundred dollars which was the bulk of their capital was put up by one Billy McPhee, a public-spirited saloonkeeper of Fairbanks. There was no leader, no prearranged plan of attack, and by the time they reached the base of the mountain half the party had come to blows with the other half and left for home. There was no scientific knowledge among them, no proper clothing or equipment, in fact nothing whatever of the things which a mountaineer is supposed to possess—save two. They had pluck and they had luck.

Their first great good fortune was in selecting the Muldrow Glacier as their way of approach. This vast tongue of ice extends from the northern foothills up into the very heart of the McKinley range, and, for forty years to come, it was the only practical route that was found giving access to the upper reaches of the mountain. The sourdoughs' experience was small, but their instinct was right. Day after day, they toiled up the gigantic ice slope of the Muldrow, hacking steps, bridging crevasses, moving slowly on and up into a silent, frozen world where no living thing had ever moved before.

At last they reached the glacier's head. They were now eleven thousand feet above the sea, but barely at the base of the mountain proper, and above them the white ridges and precipices of McKinley towered almost another two miles into the sky. By this time only three members of the expedition were left—Pete Anderson, Billy Taylor and Charley McGonogol —but these three, as they were soon to prove, were men of herculean strength and determination. For several days they camped at the head of the glacier, studying the vertical wilderness above them and awaiting favorable weather. Then, at two in the morning of April 10, they started off.

It should perhaps be mentioned, at this point, that an assault on a mountain as huge as McKinley is a vastly different proposition from climbing in a range like the Alps, where the distances are small and huts and shelters abound. Here, climbing itself is only one of the problems involved; more than half the battle is the establishment of high camps and the bringing up of reserve supplies, so that the climbers will not starve or freeze to death in the event of a mishap or a storm. On the great Himalayan peaks one of the greatest difficulties has always been that of porterage. On McKinley, every normal expedition has spent weeks preparing the way for the final assault. Such finicky, tenderfoot precautions, however, were not in the line of the Messrs. Anderson, Taylor and McGonogol. With the food and equipment that an average person might take along for a picnic lunch, they climbed from their glacier camp to within three hundred feet of the highest point of North America and back—*all in one day*.[1]

The sourdoughs, unlike most mountaineers, have left no written record of their venture, and the details of their astonishing ascent are very vague. It is known, however, that their route was roughly that followed by most subsequent expeditions: from the head of the Muldrow, up the great ice spine that was later to be called Karstens Ridge, and into the upper ice basin near the mountain's summit. It was when they reached this basin— now known as Harper Glacier—that they made a choice that was to cheat them of world-wide fame. McKinley is a mountain of two peaks—the south, or true summit, 20,300 feet high, and the north, a scant three hundred feet lower. Standing between them on that day, already at seventeen thousand feet and with victory in their grasp, the sourdoughs chose the wrong one.

What prompted their choice has never been satisfactorily explained. It may have been that they thought the north peak was the higher. It may have been the knowledge that half the population of central Alaska was

---

[1] In the Arctic, in spring and summer, the climbing day is limited only by the endurance of the climbers. Instead of darkness, nighttime brings merely a gray twilight, and it is possible to climb safely at any hour.

watching through telescopes in Fairbanks, from which the north peak alone is visible. At all events, the north peak it was. McGonogol, near collapse, had to turn back within five hundred feet of the goal, but Anderson and Taylor struggled on up the ice slope, in subzero cold, until they reached the top. There they unfurled the Stars and Stripes on a fourteen-foot flagstaff they had miraculously carried with them and planted it firmly on the topmost pinnacle. This done, they started down, picked up the exhausted McGonogol, and descended the nine thousand feet to the Muldrow Glacier without a single stop. And in another week or so they were safe and sound in Billy McPhee's Fairbanks saloon, telling all about it to anyone who would buy them a drink.

Confronted with a performance like this, the usual rules and standards of mountaineering collapse into the wastebasket, Indeed, the whole story of their ascent seemed so fantastic that for several years it was generally disbelieved—those same years, ironically, during which Dr. Cook was still a national hero. It remained again for Archdeacon Stuck to clear things up. In his ascent of the true summit in 1913 he had ample opportunity to view the top of the north peak, and what he saw completely vindicated the claims of the sourdoughs. The American flag was gone, to be sure, long since torn to shreds in the wild Arctic winds; but the flagstaff was still there—"plain, prominent and unmistakable."

The sourdoughs never went back to McKinley. They were prospectors, not mountaineers, and one fling at The Great One was enough for them. That they could have reached the true summit had they tried no one who has known them or the mountain has ever doubted. But the fact remains that they didn't. The highest point in the continent still stood, lofty and untrodden, awaiting its next attackers.

And they were not long in coming.

Indeed, in the same year as the Sourdough Climb Herschel Parker and Belmore Browne were again in the vicinity of the mountain. As in 1906, they approached it from Cook's Inlet, on the south, fighting their way through almost impassable country, and this time they reached McKinley's base—only to find above them a sheer fifteen thousand feet of precipice and avalanche slope. Convinced that the peak could never be climbed from that side, they turned dejectedly away. And since then The Great One has never been challenged from the south.

But Parker and Browne were not through yet. McKinley had cast its spell upon them, and in 1912, six years after their first attempt, they were back again for their third and last. This time, profiting from experience, they approached McKinley from the north, by the same general route that the sourdoughs had used. But there any resemblance between their expedition and that of the doughty pioneers ended. Both of them were thoughtful, highly educated men—Parker, a physicist and university professor and Browne, a distinguished painter—and their attack was as reasoned and carefully planned as the sourdoughs' had been haphazard. For months in advance they pored over maps, planned their marches and camps, assembled their supplies and equipment. Then, with Merle La Voy and Arthur Aten, two Alaskans who had been with them in 1910, they set out for their goal.

From late February until late May they mushed in by dogsled from Seward, on the coast, to the inner fastnesses of the mountain. After much reconnoitering they found a pass through the northern ridge, came out on the Muldrow Glacier and began its steep, laborious ascent. The Muldrow was long and broad, but it could never be mistaken for a paved avenue. It lunged down from the heights like a colossal ski jump, and its surface was an ice-choked wilderness of humps and hollows. In some places huge seracs, a thousand feet high, had to be surmounted; in others were yawning, seemingly bottomless crevasses that they circumvented. Often the sled dogs would tumble headlong into them and hang howling by their harnesses until they were pulled out.

Back and forth, back and forth, went the men and dogs and sleds, establishing camps and bringing up supplies. But slowly they advanced, and at last, in the first week of June, they reached the head of the glacier. Here, at eleven thousand feet, the great northeast ridge of McKinley began its skyward climb. Leaving the dogs behind, with Aten to take care of them, Parker, Browne and La Voy set foot at last upon the mountain proper.

Almost immediately they encountered the frightful weather that was to plague them during their whole ordeal on the peak. A blizzard howled down, the ice cliffs cracked and groaned, and avalanches roared about them like artillery. For four days the men huddled in their tent, rubbing one another's bodies to keep from freezing to death, clinging to the guy ropes so that they would not be blown into eternity. When the storm had passed they resumed the ascent and for a week crept upward. Uncounted thousands of steps had to be hacked in the glazed snow of the ridge. Backbreaking loads had to be carried in relays to higher camps. At one point their food supply ran so low that they had to descend all the way to the glacier to replenish it. But they pushed on doggedly and at last gained the upper basin, at a height of about sixteen thousand feet.

Here another storm imprisoned them for days, but they bided their time hopefully, for they were confident that the worst of McKinley was beneath them. And, indeed, when the weather finally cleared, the last four thousand feet of the south peak appeared as merely a gentle slope into the sky, easy of access and presenting no major difficulties. At six in the morning of June 29 they began the summit dash with high hearts.

Dash, to be sure, is scarcely the word. It was still necessary for them to hack out footholds in the cone of ice and to halt every few steps, gasping, in the thin, freezing air. But they made steady progress and within four hours had gained half the distance. The summit point of North America stood out near and clear above them. "It rose," Browne declared later, "as innocently as a tilted snow-covered tennis court, and as we looked at it we grinned with relief—we *knew* the peak was ours."

Then the last blow fell. With paralyzing suddenness the wind sprang up into a howling gale, the sky darkened and the blizzard resumed. By the time they had struggled up another thousand feet they could no longer see one another at five yards through the blinding snow, and the sixty-mile wind threatened to hurl them at any moment from the mountainside. Bent double, frost-crippled, scarcely able to breathe, they still crept on until they reached the limit of human endurance. To have gone another step upward would have been suicide. At a height of twenty thousand feet —a mere three hundred from their goal—they turned back.

Somehow they succeeded in descending to their highest camp, and two days later they made a second attempt. But again the elements defeated them. A thick, freezing fog closed in about them, in which they could neither see nor breathe, and they were stopped at 19,300 feet. The next day, both their supplies and strength exhausted, they began the descent of the mountain. "I remember," said Browne, "only a feeling of dull despair."

Thus ended one of the most gallant unsuccessful ventures in the story of mountaineering. That it did not end in final and complete tragedy was merely a stroke of the greatest luck. For in that summer of 1912 the volcano Katmai, four hundred miles away, was in eruption, and the shock of its explosions was felt throughout the plains and ranges of central Alaska. Only a few days after they had descended to the lowlands, the weary, discouraged men were startled by a vast thunder of sound, so great that it seemed the earth itself were splitting open. And, indeed, it was. Behind them, as they watched, the whole north face and ridges of McKinley, on which they had so recently stood, gave a monstrous shudder, detached themselves from the main mass of the mountain and plunged wildly into the valleys below.

That was their last view of McKinley—roaring defiance at its challengers.

Mountains are not greatly concerned with human concepts of justice. Parker and Browne devoted years of their lives to the exploring and ascent of McKinley, only to meet ultimate defeat. Its next assailants spent a total of two months on its forbidding terrain—and conquered it.

Not that there was anything fortuitous in the triumph of Archdeacon Hudson Stuck. He and his companions were mountaineers of the first order; he had made many ascents in the American and Canadian Rockies, and for years past, during his journeys among the Indians of Alaska, he had seen McKinley from afar and yearned to climb it. Then, at last, in the spring of 1913 Stuck received leave of absence from his duties and set out from the mission station of Nenana to achieve his ambition. His companions were Harry Karstens, a sturdy sourdough who had come to Alaska in the Klondike gold rush and was later to become superintendent of McKinley National Park; Robert Tatum, a twenty-one-year-old missionary from Tennessee; Walter Harper, a strong, cheerful, young half-breed, who had been Stuck's dog driver and interpreter for several years; and two Indian youngsters from the Nenana mission school named Johnny and Esaias.

With dogs and sleds they mushed across the white plains of central Alaska, crossed the outer spurs and ridges that guard McKinley and came out at last on the Muldrow Glacier, as the other expeditions had done before them. Here Esaias, having done his bit, was sent back to Nenana, Johnny remaining to take care of the dogs. Slowly and carefully the little party threaded its way up the steep maze of the glacier, probing and zigzagging to avoid the great crevasses, suffering greatly from cold and snowstorms and the fierce wind that swooped down on them from the heights.

Presently, however, they reached the head of the glacier and stood staring upward at the huge white wilderness of the upper mountain. But, as they stared, they realized something was wrong. The great ridge which was to be their route was not at all as the previous expeditions had described it—a thin, clean knife-edge cutting into the sky. What they saw instead was an indescribable chaos of pinnacles and chasms and great tumbled ice-masses piled crazily upon each other as far as the eye could see. And then they realized what had happened. The great earth tremors of the previous year, from which Parker and Browne had barely escaped with their lives, had indeed blown to bits what had formerly been the northeast ramparts of the mountain. The ridge that the other parties had ascended had completely ceased to be. Instead of following a route which others had pioneered before them, they were faced with the necessity of becoming pioneers themselves.

What Stuck and his companions did then was quite simply this: they cut a three-mile staircase in the ice. With patience and endurance they hacked and chopped and clawed their way from the eleven thousand foot altitude of the Muldrow's head to the sixteen thousand foot heights of the upper basin. They surmounted ice blocks as large as three-story houses, they edged around cornices that hung in space a mile above the glaciers; they struggled up with their supplies on their backs, descended again, struggled up with more. None of them ventured to count the thousands or tens of thousands of steps they cut, but Stuck later estimated that each member of the party, in going back and forth, had climbed at least sixty thousand feet—or three times the total height of McKinley.

After days of toil the savage earthquake-shattered ridge was at last behind them. On June third they camped at 16,500 feet in the middle of the upper basin, between the twin peaks of the mountain, and three days later at eighteen thousand feet on the slopes just beneath the summit. And now the blessing that had been so cruelly withheld from Parker and Browne was granted to them: the day of the final assault was clear and fine. They started at three in the morning and for hour after hour crept upward through the frozen gray silence of the arctic heights. Sometimes it was still necessary to hack steps with their axes; at other times their crampons sufficed, biting deeply into the hard-crusted slope. At eleven o'clock they passed the point at which Parker and Browne had been turned back by the blizzard. At one they stepped up upon the horseshoe ridge that forms the summit of the peak. And a few moments later—

—there still stretched ahead of us, [wrote Stuck] and perhaps one hundred feet above us, another small ridge with a north and south pair of little haycock summits. This is the real top. With keen excitement we pushed on. Walter Harper, who had been in the lead all day, was the first to scramble up; a native Alaskan, he is the first human being to set foot on the top of Alaska's great mountain, and he had well earned the lifelong distinction. Karstens and Tatum were hard upon his heels, but the last man on the rope had almost to be hauled up the last few feet, and fell unconscious for a moment upon the floor of the little snow basin that occupies the top of the mountain.

Four men stood at last on the summit of North America.

Their first act was to thank God for permitting them to achieve their goal. "This prime duty done," to quote the reverend archdeacon, they set up the instruments that they had carried with them and took thermometer and barometer readings. Then they let their eyes sweep out over the stupendous panorama that no man had ever seen before—more than fifty thousand square miles of Alaska, peaks and ranges, glaciers and valleys, rivers and plains, from the ice-locked arctic interior to the sea.

But it is not alone for the sake of a "view" that men struggle up to the high places of the earth. Let us allow the conqueror of McKinley to describe the mountaineer's reward, for few men have described it better:

> Only those who have for long years cherished a great and almost inordinate desire, and have had that desire gratified . . . can enter into the deep thankfulness and content that filled the heart. . . . There was no pride of conquest . . . no gloating over good fortune that had hoisted us a few hundred feet higher than others who had struggled and been discomfited. Rather was the feeling that a privileged communion with the high places of the earth had been granted; that not only had we been permitted to lift up eager eyes to these summits, secret and solitary since the world began, but to enter boldly upon them, to take place, as it were, domestically in their hitherto sealed chambers, to inhabit them, and to cast our eyes down from them, seeing all things as they spread out from the windows of heaven itself.

They constructed a rough cross of birch staves which they had carried with them, thrust it deep into the snow, and, gathering around it, spoke the solemn, joyful words of the Te Deum. Then they started down, the tiredest and happiest of men.

For nineteen years after its conquest no one approached McKinley. Then, in the spring of 1932, two separate expeditions converged upon it at the same time. One was successful in every respect. The other culminated tragically in the only deaths that have occurred on the mountain.

The successful party was composed of Erling Strom, a well-known Norwegian-American skier, Alfred Lindley, a Minneapolis attorney, Harry Liek, superintendent of McKinley National Park, and Grant Pearson, a park ranger. They reached the upper basin by substantially the same route as the earlier parties and successfully scaled both north and south peaks, thus becoming the first party to reach both summits of McKinley.

High on Karstens Ridge the Strom-Lindley party discovered a thermometer left by Stuck. It had been the archdeacon's belief that McKinley, in winter, was the coldest place in the world, and on his descent of the mountain he had cached a minimum thermometer at a point where he hoped the next party would find it. The climbers of 1932 proved that he had been right. The indicator of the instrument had dropped past the end of the scale, which was ninety-five degrees below zero, and was stuck in the bulb, where it could go no farther. It appeared obvious, therefore, that at one time or another during the winters of the intervening years, the temperature had sunk to at least one hundred degrees below zero— the greatest natural cold ever recorded anywhere on earth.

The second 1932 expedition to McKinley did not arrive on the scene until the first was already high on the mountain. This was the so-called "Cosmic Ray" expedition, which planned to undertake extensive scientific observations at great altitudes and was led by Allan Carpé, one of the most accomplished young American mountaineers. These climbers brought a startling modern innovation to the technique of mountaineering. And on the same day they found Stuck's thermometer on Karstens Ridge, Strom and his companions stared down the face of a precipice to see a plane landing supplies at the head of the Muldrow Glacier, four thousand feet below. This was the first time in climbing history such a feat had been attempted, much less accomplished.

During the next week, while the first party successfully scaled both the north and south peaks, they saw nothing more of Carpé and his expedition. When at last they descended to the head of the Muldrow, the plane was gone, but two tents were standing near the former site of one of their own camps. And the tents were deserted.

"Immediately," Strom had said, "we felt that something had gone wrong. Inside one tent we found two open sleeping bags and a pot half full of frozen mulligan stew. From the other tent, containing cosmic ray apparatus, we could hear a little mechanism slowly ticking."

From a diary found in one of the sleeping bags they learned that the only occupants of the tents had been Carpé and one companion, Theodore Koven. There being no sign of either man, they pushed on down the glacier, and it was not long before their fears were confirmed. A mile and a half below the camp they spied a tiny dark object against the white immensity of snow. It was Koven's body. One leg had been injured and also the side of his head. He had obviously fallen into a crevasse, but had managed to climb out again, only to collapse and die from exposure.

Carpé's body has never been found.

ANNAPURNA

by Maurice Herzog

To the casual reader, the story of mountaineering in the Himalayas centers on one peak only, Mount Everest. Like the Matterhorn, Everest has become the stuff of legend, with religious fear, international rivalries and unsuccessful attempts all playing their parts. Perhaps the most tragic episode in its history was the death of Mallory and Irvine in 1924, when, only hundreds of feet from the summit, they suddenly disappeared from the view of those below and were never seen again.

But this story has become so well known through all the media of mass communication that another selection has been chosen, the record, by one who made the climb, of the assault on Annapurna. While many climbers have been articulate, none has succeeded in describing more vividly the consuming urge for conquest, and the price that is sometimes exacted, than has Maurice Herzog in the article which follows.

ON THE third of June, 1950, the first light of dawn found us still clinging to the tent poles at Camp V. Gradually the wind abated, and with daylight, died away altogether. I made desperate attempts to push back the soft, icy stuff which stifled me, but every movement became an act of heroism. My mental powers were numbed: thinking was an effort, and we did not exchange a single word.

What a repellent place it was! To everyone who reached it, Camp V became one of the worst memories of their lives. We had only one thought —to get away. We should have waited for the first rays of the sun, but at half-past five we felt we couldn't stick it any longer.

"Let's go, Biscante," I muttered. "Can't stay here a minute longer."

"Yes, let's go," repeated Lachenal.

Which of us would have the energy to make tea? Although our minds worked slowly we were quite able to envisage all the movements that would

be necessary—and neither of us could face up to it. It couldn't be helped
—we would just have to go without. It was quite hard enough work to get
ourselves and our boots out of our sleeping bags—and the boots were
frozen stiff so that we got them on only with the greatest difficulty. Every
movement made us terribly breathless. We felt as if we were being stifled.
Our gaiters were stiff as a board, and I succeeded in lacing mine up;
Lachenal couldn't manage his.

"No need for the rope, eh, Biscante?"

"No need," replied Lachenal laconically.

That was two pounds saved. I pushed a tube of condensed milk, some
nougat and a pair of socks into my sack; one never knew, the socks might
come in useful—they might even do as balaclavas. For the time being I
stuffed them with first-aid equipment. The camera was loaded with a black
and white film; I had a color film in reserve. I pulled the movie camera
out from the bottom of my sleeping bag, wound it up and tried letting
it run without film. There was a little click, then it stopped and jammed.

"Bad luck after bringing it so far," said Lachenal.

In spite of our photographer, Ichac's, precautions taken to lubricate it
with special grease, the intense cold, even inside the sleeping bag, had
frozen it. I left it at the camp rather sadly: I had looked forward to taking
it to the top. I had used it up to 24,600 feet.

We went outside and put on our crampons, which we kept on all day.
We wore as many clothes as possible; our sacks were very light. At six
o'clock we started off. It was brilliantly fine, but also very cold. Our super-
lightweight crampons bit deep into the steep slopes of ice and hard snow
up which lay the first stage of our climb.

Later the slope became slightly less steep and more uniform. Sometimes
the hard crust bore our weight, but at others we broke through and sank
into soft powder snow which made progress exhausting. We took turns in
making the track and often stopped without any word having passed between
us. Each of us lived in a closed and private world of his own. I was suspicious
of my mental processes; my mind was working very slowly and I was
perfectly aware of the low state of my intelligence. It was easiest just to
stick to one thought at a time—safest, too. The cold was penetrating; for
all our special eiderdown clothing we felt as if we'd nothing on. Whenever
we halted, we stamped our feet hard. Lachenal went as far as to take off
one boot which was a bit tight; he was in terror of frostbite.

"I don't want to be like Lambert," he said. Raymond Lambert, a
Geneva guide, had to have all his toes amputated after an eventful climb

during which he got his feet frostbitten.[1] While Lachenal rubbed himself hard, I looked at the summits all around us; already we overtopped them all except the distant Dhaulagiri. The complicated structure of these mountains, with which our many laborious explorations had made us familiar, was now spread out plainly at our feet.

The going was incredibly exhausting, and every step was a struggle of mind over matter. We came out into the sunlight, and by way of marking the occasion made yet another halt. Lachenal continued to complain of his feet. "I can't feel anything. I think I'm beginning to get frostbite." And once again he undid his boot.

I began to be seriously worried. I realized very well the risk we were running; I knew from experience how insidiously and quickly frostbite can set in if one is not extremely careful. Nor was Lachenal under any illusions. "We're in danger of having frozen feet. Do you think it's worth it?"

This was most disturbing. It was my responsibility as leader to think of the others. There was no doubt about frostbite being a very real danger. Did Annapurna justify such risks? That was the question I asked myself; it continued to worry me.

Lachenal had laced his boots up again, and once more we continued to force our way through the exhausting snow. The whole of the Sickle Glacier was now in view, bathed in light. We still had a long way to go to cross it, and then there was that rock band—would we find a gap in it?

My feet, like Lachenal's, were very cold and I continued to wriggle my toes, even when we were moving. I could not feel them, but that was nothing new in the mountains, and if I kept on moving them it would keep the circulation going.

Lachenal appeared to me as a sort of specter—he was alone in his world, I in mine. But—and this was odd enough—any effort was slightly *less* exhausting than lower down. Perhaps it was hope lending us wings. Even through dark glasses the snow was blinding—the sun beating straight down on the ice. We looked down upon precipitous ridges which dropped away into space, and upon tiny glaciers far, far below. Familiar peaks soared arrow-like into the sky. Suddenly Lachenal grabbed me:

"If I go back, what will you do?"

A whole sequence of pictures flashed through my head: the days of marching in sweltering heat, the hard pitches we had overcome, the tremendous efforts we had all made to lay siege to the mountain, the daily

---

[1] In May, 1952 Lambert, with the Sherpa Ang-Tsering, reached 28,215 feet on Mount Everest, possibly the highest point yet attained. (Translators' note.)

heroism of all my friends in establishing the camps. Now we were nearing our goal. In an hour or two, perhaps, victory would be ours. Must we give up? Impossible! My whole being revolted against the idea. I had made up my mind, irrevocably. Today we were consecrating an ideal, and no sacrifice was too great. I heard my voice clearly: "I should go on by myself."

I would go alone. If he wished to go down it was not for me to stop him. He must make his own choice freely.

"Then I'll follow you."

The die was cast. I was no longer anxious. Nothing could stop us now from getting to the top. The psychological atmosphere changed with these few words, and we went forward now as brothers.

I felt as though I were plunging into something new and quite abnormal. I had the strangest and most vivid impressions, such as I had never before known in the mountains. There was something unnatural in the way I saw Lachenal and everything around us. I smiled to myself at the paltriness of our efforts, for I could stand apart and watch myself making these efforts. But all sense of exertion was gone, as though there were no longer any gravity. This diaphanous landscape, this quintessence of purity—these were not the mountains I knew: they were the mountains of my dreams.

The snow, sprinkled over every rock and gleaming in the sun, was of a radiant beauty that touched me to the heart. I had never seen such complete transparency, and I was living in a world of crystal. Sounds were indistinct, the atmosphere like cotton wool.

An astonishing happiness welled up in me, but I could not define it. Everything was so new, so utterly unprecedented. It was not in the least like anything I had known in the Alps, where one feels buoyed up by the presence of others—by people of whom one is vaguely aware, or even by the dwellings one can see in the far distance.

This was quite different. An enormous gulf was between me and the world. This was a different universe—withered, desert, lifeless; a fantastic universe where the presence of man was not foreseen, perhaps not desired. We were braving an interdict, overstepping a boundary, and yet we had no fear as we continued upward. I thought of the famous ladder of St. Theresa of Avila. Something clutched at my heart.

Did Lachenal share these feelings? The summit ridge drew nearer, and we reached the foot of the ultimate rock band. The slope was very steep and the snow interspersed with rocks.

"Couloir!"

A finger pointed. The whispered word from one to another indicated the key to the rocks—the last line of defense.

"What luck!"

The couloir up the rocks though steep was feasible.

The sky was a deep sapphire blue. With a great effort we edged over to the right, avoiding the rocks; we preferred to keep to the snow on account of our crampons and it was not long before we set foot in the couloir. It was fairly steep and we had a minute's hesitation. Should we have enough strength left to overcome this final obstacle?

Fortunately the snow was hard, and by kicking steps we were able to manage, thanks to our crampons. A false move would have been fatal. There was no need to make handholds—our axes, driven in as far as possible, served us for an anchor.

Lachenal went splendidly. What a wonderful contrast to the early days! It was a hard struggle here, but he kept going. Lifting our eyes occasionally from the slope, we saw the couloir opening out on to . . . well, we didn't quite know, probably a ridge. But where was the top—left or right? Stopping at every step, leaning on our axes we tried to recover our breath and to calm down our racing hearts, which were thumping as though they would burst. We knew we were there now—that nothing could stop us. No need to exchange looks—each of us would have read the same determination in the other's eyes. A slight detour to the left, a few more steps— the summit ridge came gradually nearer—a few rocks to avoid. We dragged ourselves up. Could we possibly be there?

Yes!

A fierce and savage wind tore at us.

We were on top of Annapurna! 8,075 meters, 26,493 feet.

Our hearts overflowed with an unspeakable happiness.

"If only the others could know . . ."

If only everyone could know!

The summit was a corniced crest of ice, and the precipices on the far side which plunged vertically down beneath us, were terrifying, unfathomable. There could be few other mountains in the world like this. Clouds floated halfway down, concealing the gentle, fertile valley of Pokhara, 23,000 feet below. Above us there was nothing!

Our mission was accomplished. But at the same time we had accomplished something infinitely greater. How wonderful life would now become! What an inconceivable experience it is to attain one's ideal and, at the very same moment, to fulfill oneself. I was stirred to the depths of my being. Never had I felt happiness like this—so intense and yet so pure. That brown rock, the highest of them all, that ridge of ice—were these the goals of a lifetime? Or were they, rather, the limits of man's pride?

"Well, what about going down?"

Lachenal shook me. What were his own feelings? Did he simply think he had finished another climb, as in the Alps? Did he think one could just go down again like that, with nothing more to it?

"One minute, I must take some photographs."

"Hurry up!"

I fumbled feverishly in my sack, pulled out the camera, took out the little French flag which was right at the bottom, and the pennants. Useless gestures, no doubt, but something more than symbols—eloquent tokens of affection and good will. I tied the strips of material—stained by sweat and by the food in the sacks—to the shaft of my ice ax, the only flagstaff at hand. Then I focused my camera on Lachenal.

"Now, will you take me?"

"Hand it over—hurry up!" said Lachenal.

He took several pictures and then handed me back the camera. I loaded a color film and we repeated the process to be certain of bringing back records to be cherished in the future.

"Are you mad?" asked Lachenal. "We haven't a minute to lose: we must go down at once."

And in fact a glance round showed me that the weather was no longer gloriously fine as it had been in the morning. Lachenal was becoming impatient.

"We must go down!"

He was right. His was the reaction of the mountaineer who knows his own domain. But I just could not accustom myself to the idea that we had won our victory. It seemed inconceivable that we should have trodden those summit snows.

It was impossible to build a cairn; there were no stones; everything was frozen. Lachenal stamped his feet; he felt them freezing. I felt mine freezing too, but paid little attention. The highest mountain to be climbed by man lay under our feet! The names of our predecessors on these heights raced through my mind: Mummery, Mallory and Irvine, Bauer, Welzenbach, Tilman, Shipton. How many of them were dead—how many had found on these mountains what, to them, was the finest end of all?

"Come on, straight down," called Lachenal.

He had already done up his sack and started going down. I took out my pocket aneroid: 8,500 meters. I smiled. I swallowed a little condensed milk and left the tube behind—the only trace of our passage. I did up my sack, put on my gloves and my glasses, seized my ice ax; one look around and I, too, hurried down the slope. Before disappearing into the couloir I gave one last look at the summit which would henceforth be all our joy and all our consolation.

Lachenal was already far below; he had reached the foot of the couloir. I hurried down in his tracks. I went as fast as I could, but it was dangerous going. At every step one had to take care that the snow did not break away beneath one's weight. Lachenal, going faster than I thought he was capable of, was now on the long traverse. It was my turn to cross the area of mixed rock and snow. At last I reached the foot of the rock band. I had hurried and I was out of breath. I undid my sack. What had I been going to do? I couldn't say.

"My gloves!"

Before I had time to bend over, I saw them slide and roll. They went further and further straight down the slope. I remained where I was, quite stunned. I watched them rolling down slowly, with no appearance of stopping. The movement of those gloves was engraved in my sight as something irredeemable, against which I was powerless. The consequences might be most serious. What was I to do?

"Quickly, down to Camp V."

Rébuffat and Terray would be there. My concern dissolved like magic. I now had a fixed objective again: to reach the camp. Never for a minute did it occur to me to use as gloves the socks which I always carry in reserve for just such a mishap as this.

On I went, trying to catch up with Lachenal. It had been two o'clock when we reached the summit; we had started out at six in the morning, but I had to admit that I had lost all sense of time. I felt as if I were running, whereas in actual fact I was walking normally, perhaps rather slowly, and I had to keep stopping to get my breath. The sky was now covered with clouds, everything had become gray and dirty-looking. An icy wind sprang up, boding no good. We must push on! But where was Lachenal? I spotted him a couple of hundred yards away, looking as if he was never going to stop. And I had thought he was in indifferent form!

The clouds grew thicker and came right down over us; the wind blew stronger, but I did not suffer from the cold. Perhaps the descent had restored my circulation. Should I be able to find the tents in the mist? I watched the rib ending in the beaklike point which overlooked the camp. It was gradually swallowed up by the clouds, but I was able to make out the spearhead rib lower down. If the mist should thicken I would make straight for that rib and follow it down, and in this way I should be bound to come upon the tent.

Lachenal disappeared from time to time, and then the mist was so thick that I lost sight of him altogether. I kept going at the same speed, as fast as my breathing would allow.

The slope was now steeper; a few patches of bare ice followed the smooth stretches of snow. A good sign—I was nearing the camp. How difficult to find one's way in thick mist! I kept the course which I had set by the steepest angle of the slope. The ground was broken; with my crampons I went straight down walls of bare ice. There were some patches ahead—a few more steps. It was the camp all right, but there were *two tents!*

So Rébuffat and Terray had come up. What a mercy! I should be able to tell them that we had been successful, that we were returning from the top. How thrilled they would be!

I got there, dropping down from above. The platform had been extended, and the two tents were facing each other. I tripped over one of the guy ropes of the first tent; there was movement inside, they had heard me. Rébuffat and Terray put their heads out.

"We've made it. We're back from Annapurna!"

Rébuffat and Terray received the news with great excitement.

"But what about Biscante?" asked Terray anxiously.

"He won't be long. He was just in front of me! What a day—started out at six this morning—didn't stop . . . got up at last."

Words failed me. I had so much to say. The sight of familiar faces dispelled the strange feeling that I had experienced since morning, and I became, once more, just a mountaineer.

Terray, who was speechless with delight, wrung my hands. Then the smile vanished from his face: "Maurice, your hands!" There was an uneasy silence. I had forgotten that I had lost my gloves: my fingers were violet and white and hard as wood. The other two stared at them in dismay—they realized the full seriousness of the injury. But, still blissfully floating on a sea of joy remote from reality, I leaned over toward Terray and said confidentially, "You're in such splendid form, and you've done so marvelously, it's absolutely tragic you didn't come up there with us!"

"What I did was for the Expedition, my dear Maurice, and anyway you've got up, and that's a victory for the whole lot of us."

I nearly burst with happiness. How could I tell him all that his answer meant to me? The rapture I had felt on the summit, which might have seemed a purely personal, egotistical emotion, had been transformed by his words into a complete and perfect joy with no shadow upon it. His answer proved that this victory was not just one man's achievement, a matter for personal pride; no—and Terray was the first to understand this—it was a victory for us all, a victory for mankind itself.

"Hi! Help! Help!"

"Biscante!" exclaimed the others.

Still half intoxicated and remote from reality I had heard nothing. Terray felt a chill at his heart, and his thoughts flew to his partner on so many unforgettable climbs; together they had so often skirted death, and won so many splendid victories. Putting his head out, and seeing Lachenal clinging to the slope a hundred yards lower down, he dressed in frantic haste.

Out he went. But the slope was bare now; Lachenal had disappeared. Terray was horribly frightened, and he could only utter unintelligible cries. It was a ghastly moment for him. A violent wind sent the mist tearing by. Under the stress of emotion Terray had not realized how it falsified distances.

"Biscante! Biscante!"

He had spotted him, through a rift in the mist, lying on the slope much lower down than he had thought. Terray set his teeth, and glissaded down like a madman. How would he be able to brake without crampons, on the wind-hardened snow? But Terray was a first-class skier, and with a jump turn he stopped beside Lachenal, who was suffering from concussion after his tremendous fall. In a state of collapse, with no ice ax, balaclava, or gloves, and only one crampon, he gazed vacantly around him.

"My feet are frostbitten. Take me down . . . take me down, so that Oudot can see to me."

"It can't be done," said Terray sorrowfully. "Can't you see we're in the middle of a storm. . . . It'll be dark soon."

But Lachenal was obsessed by the fear of amputation. With a gesture of despair he tore the ax out of Terray's hands and tried to force his way down; but soon saw the futility of his action and resolved to climb up to the camp. While Terray cut steps without stopping, Lachenal, ravaged and exhausted as he was, dragged himself along on all fours.

Meanwhile I had gone into Rébuffat's tent. He was appalled at the sight of my hands, and, as rather incoherently I told him what we had done, he took a piece of rope and began flicking my fingers. Then he took off my boots with great difficulty for my feet were swollen, and beat my feet and rubbed me. We soon heard Terray giving Lachenal the same treatment in the other tent.

For our comrades it was a tragic moment: Annapurna was conquered, and the first eight-thousander had been climbed. Every one of us had been ready to sacrifice everything for this. Yet, as they looked at our feet and hands, what can Terray and Rébuffat have felt?

Outside the storm howled and the snow was still falling. The mist grew thick and darkness came. As on the previous night we had to cling to the poles to prevent the tents being carried away by the wind. The only two air mattresses were given to Lachenal and myself while Terray and Rébuffat both sat on ropes, rucksacks, and provisions to keep themselves off the snow. They rubbed, slapped and beat us with a rope. Sometimes the blows fell on the living flesh, and howls arose from both tents. Rébuffat persevered; it was essential to continue painful as it was. Gradually life returned to my feet as well as to my hands, and circulation started again. Lachenal, too, found that feeling was returning.

Now Terray summoned up the energy to prepare some hot drinks. He called to Rébuffat that he would pass him a mug, so two hands stretched out toward each other between the two tents and were instantly covered with snow. The liquid was boiling though scarcely more than 60° centigrade (140° Fahrenheit). I swallowed it greedily and felt infinitely better.

The night was absolute hell. Frightful onslaughts of wind battered us incessantly, while the never-ceasing snow piled up on the tents.

Now and again I heard voices from next door—it was Terray massaging Lachenal with admirable perseverance, only stopping to ply him with hot drinks. In our tent Rébuffat was quite worn out, but satisfied that warmth was returning to my limbs.

Lying half unconscious I was scarcely aware of the passage of time. There were moments when I was able to see our situation in its true dramatic light, but the rest of the time I was plunged in an inexplicable stupor with no thought for the consequences of our victory.

As the night wore on the snow lay heavier on the tent, and once again I had the frightful feeling of being slowly and silently asphyxiated. I tried, with all the strength of which I was capable, to push off with both forearms the mass that was crushing me. These fearful exertions left me gasping for breath and I fell back into the same exhausted state. It was much worse than the previous night.

"Rébuffat! Gaston! Gaston!"

I recognized Terray's voice.

"Time to be off!"

I heard the sounds without grasping their meaning. Was it light already? I was not in the least surprised that the other two had given up all thought of going to the top, and I did not at all grasp the measure of their sacrifice.

Outside the storm redoubled in violence. The tent shook and the fabric flapped alarmingly. It had usually been fine in the mornings: did this mean the monsoon was upon us? We knew it was not far off—could this be its first onslaught?

"Gaston! Are you ready?" Terray called again.

"One minute," answered Rébuffat. He did not have an easy job: he had to put my boots on and do everything to get me ready. I let myself be handled like a baby. In the other tent Terray finished dressing Lachenal whose feet were still swollen and would not fit into his boots. So Terray gave him his own, which were bigger. To get Lachenal's on to his own feet he had to make slits in them. As a precaution he put a sleeping bag and some food into his sack and shouted to us to do the same. Were his words lost in the storm? Or were we too intent on leaving this hellish place to listen to his instructions?

Lachenal and Terray were already outside.

"We're going down!" they shouted.

Then Rébuffat tied me on the rope and we went out. There were only two ice axes for the four of us, so Rébuffat and Terray took them as a matter of course. For a moment as we left the two tents of Camp V, I felt childishly ashamed at leaving all this good equipment behind.

Already the first rope seemed a long way down below us. We were blinded by the squalls of snow and we could not hear each other a yard away. We had both put on our *cagoules,* for it was very cold. The snow was apt to slide and the rope often came in useful.

Ahead of us the other two were losing no time. Lachenal went first and, safeguarded by Terray, he forced the pace in his anxiety to get down. There were no tracks to show us the way, but it was engraved on all our minds— straight down the slope for four hundred yards then traverse to the left for one hundred fifty to two hundred yards to get to Camp IV. The snow was thinning and the wind less violent. Was it going to clear? We hardly dared to hope so. A wall of seracs brought us up short.

"It's to the left," I said, "I remember perfectly."

Somebody else thought it was to the right. We started going down again. The wind had dropped completely, but the snow fell in big flakes.

The mist was thick, and, not to lose each other, we walked in line: I was third and I could barely see Lachenal who was first. It was impossible to recognize any of the pitches. We were all experienced enough mountaineers to know that even on familiar ground it is easy to make mistakes in such weather. Distances are deceptive, one cannot tell whether one is going up or down. We kept colliding with hummocks which we had taken for hollows. The mist, the falling snowflakes, the carpet of snow, all merged into the same whitish tone and confused our vision. The towering outlines of the seracs took on fantastic shapes and seemed to move slowly around us.

Our situation was not desperate, we were certainly not lost. We would have to go lower down; the traverse must begin further on—I remembered the serac which served as a milestone. The snow stuck to our *cagoules*, and turned us into white phantoms noiselessly flitting against a background equally white. We began to sink in dreadfully, and there is nothing worse for bodies already on the edge of exhaustion.

Were we too high or too low? No one could tell. Perhaps we had better try slanting over to the left! The snow was in a dangerous condition, but we did not seem to realize it. We were forced to admit that we were not on the right route, so we retraced our steps and climbed up above the serac which overhung us. No doubt, we decided, we should be on the right level now. With Rébuffat leading, we went back over the way which had cost us such an effort. I followed him jerkily, saying nothing, and determined to go on to the end. If Rébuffat had fallen I could never have held him.

We went doggedly on from one serac to another. Each time we thought we had recognized the right route, and each time there was a fresh disappointment. If only the mist would lift, if only the snow would stop for a second! On the slope it seemed to be growing deeper every minute. Only Terray and Rébuffat were capable of breaking the trail and they relieved each other at regular intervals, without a word and without a second's hesitation.

I admired this determination of Rébuffat's for which he is so justly famed. He did not intend to die! With the strength of desperation and at the price of superhuman effort he forged ahead. The slowness of his progress would have dismayed even the most obstinate climber, but he would not give up, and in the end the mountain yielded in face of his perseverance.

Terray, when his turn came, charged madly ahead. He was like a force of nature: at all costs he would break down these prison walls that penned us in. His physical strength was exceptional, his will power no less remarkable. Lachenal gave him considerable trouble. Perhaps he was not quite in his right mind. He said it was no use going on; we must dig a hole in the snow and wait for fine weather. He swore at Terray and called him a madman. Nobody but Terray would have been capable of dealing with him—he just tugged sharply on the rope and Lachenal was forced to follow.

We were well and truly lost.

The weather did not seem likely to improve. A minute ago we had still had ideas about which way to go—now we had none. This way or that . . . We went on at random to allow for the chance of a miracle which appeared increasingly unlikely. The instinct of self-preservation in the two fit members of the party alternated with a hopelessness which made them completely irresponsible. Each in turn did the maddest things: Terray traversed the steep and avalanchy slopes with one crampon badly adjusted. He and Rébuffat performed incredible feats of balance without the least slip.

Camp IV was certainly on the left, on the edge of the Sickle. On that point we were all agreed. But it was very hard to find. The wall of ice that gave it such magnificent protection was now ironical, for it hid the tents from us. In mist like this we should have to be right on top of them before we spotted them.

Perhaps if we called, someone would hear us? Lachenal gave the signal, but snow absorbs sound and his shout seemed to carry only a few yards. All four of us called out together: "One . . . two . . . three . . . Help!"

We got the impression that our united shout carried a long way, so we began again: "One . . . two . . . three . . . Help!" Not a sound in reply!

Now and again Terray took off his boots and rubbed his feet; the sight of our frostbitten limbs had made him aware of the danger and he had the strength of mind to do something about it. Like Lachenal, he was haunted by the idea of amputation. For me, it was too late: my feet and hands, already affected from yesterday, were beginning to freeze up again.

We had eaten nothing since the day before, and we had been on the go the whole time, but men's resources of energy in face of death are inexhaustible. When the end seems imminent, there still remain reserves, though it needs tremendous will power to call them up.

Time passed, but we had no idea how long. Night was approaching, and we were terrified, though none of us made any complaint. Rébuffat and I found a way that we thought we remembered, but were brought to a halt by the extreme steepness of the slope—the mist turned it into a vertical wall. We were to find next day that at that moment we had been only thirty yards from the camp, and that the wall was the very one that sheltered the tent which would have been our salvation.

"We must find a crevasse."

"We can't stay here all night!"

"A hole—it's the only thing."

"We'll all die in it."

Night had suddenly fallen and it was essential to come to a decision without wasting another minute; if we remained on the slope, we should be dead before morning. We would have to bivouac. What the conditions would be like, we could guess, for we all knew what it meant to bivouac above 23,000 feet.

With his ax Terray began to dig a hole. Lachenal went over to a snow-filled crevasse a few yards further on, then suddenly let out a yell and disappeared before our eyes. We stood helpless: should we, or rather would Terray and Rébuffat, have enough strength for all the maneuvers with the rope that would be needed to get him out? The crevasse was completely blocked up save for the one little hole which Lachenal had fallen through.

"Lachenal!" called Terray.

A voice, muffled by many thicknesses of ice and snow, came up to us. It was impossible to make out what it was saying.

"Lachenal!"

Terray jerked the rope violently; this time we could hear.

"I'm here!"

"Anything broken?"

"No! It'll do for the night! Come along."

This shelter was heaven-sent. None of us would have had the strength to dig a hole big enough to protect the lot of us from the wind. Without hesitation Terray let himself drop into the crevasse, and a loud "Come on!" told us he had arrived safely. In my turn I let myself go: it was a regular toboggan slide. I shot down a sort of twisting tunnel, very steep, and about thirty feet long. I came out at great speed into the opening beyond and was literally hurled to the bottom of the crevasse. We let Rébuffat know he could come by giving a tug on the rope.

The intense cold of this minute grotto shriveled us up, the enclosing walls of ice were damp and the floor a carpet of fresh snow; by huddling together there was just room for the four of us. Icicles hung from the ceiling and we broke some of them off to make more head room and kept little bits to suck—it was a long time since we had had anything to drink.

That was our shelter for the night. At least we should be protected from the wind, and the temperature would remain fairly even, though the damp was extremely unpleasant. We settled ourselves in the dark as best we could. As always in a bivouac we took off our boots; without this precaution the constriction would cause immediate frostbite. Terray unrolled the sleeping bag which he had had the foresight to bring, and settled himself in relative comfort. We put on everything warm that we had, and to avoid contact with the snow I sat on the movie camera. We huddled close up to each other, in our search for a hypothetical position in which the warmth of our bodies could be combined without loss, but we couldn't keep still for a second.

We did not open our mouths—signs were less of an effort than words. Every man withdrew into himself and took refuge in his own inner world. Terray massaged Lachenal's feet; Rébuffat felt his feet freezing too, but he had sufficient strength to rub them himself. I remained motionless, unseeing. My feet and hands went on freezing, but what could be done? I attempted to forget suffering by withdrawing into myself, trying to forget the passing of time, trying not to feel the devouring and numbing cold which insidously gained upon us.

Terray shared his sleeping bag with Lachenal, putting his feet and hands inside the precious eiderdown. At the same time he went on rubbing. Anyhow the frostbite won't spread further, he was thinking.

None of us could make any movement without upsetting the others, and the positions we had taken up with such care were continually being altered so that we had to start all over again. This kept us busy. Rébuffat persevered with his rubbing and complained of his feet; like Terray he was thinking: We mustn't look beyond tomorrow—afterward we'll see. But he was not blind to the fact that "afterward" was one big question mark.

Terray generously tried to give me part of his sleeping bag. He had understood the seriousness of my condition, and knew why it was that I said nothing and remained quite passive; he realized that I had abandoned all hope for myself. He massaged me for nearly two hours; his feet, too, might have frozen, but he didn't appear to give the matter a thought. I found new courage simply in contemplating his unselfishness; he was doing so much to help me that it would have been ungrateful of me not to go on struggling to live. Though my heart was like a lump of ice itself, I was astonished to feel no pain. Everything material about me seemed to have dropped away. I seemed to be quite clear in my thoughts and yet I floated in a kind of peaceful happiness. There was still a breath of life in me, but it dwindled steadily as the hours went by. Terray's massage no longer had any effect upon me. All was over, I thought. Wasn't this cavern the most beautiful grave I could hope for? Death caused me no grief, no regret—I smiled at the thought.

After hours of torpor a voice mumbled, "Daylight!"

This made some impression on the others. I only felt surprised—I had not thought that daylight would penetrate so far down.

"Too early to start," said Rébuffat.

A ghastly light spread through our grotto and we could just vaguely make out the shapes of each other's heads. A queer noise from a long way off came down to us—a sort of prolonged hiss. The noise increased. Suddenly I was buried, blinded, smothered beneath an avalanche of new snow. The icy snow spread over the cavern, finding its way through every gap in our clothing. I ducked my head between my knees and covered myself with both arms. The snow flowed on and on. There was a terrible silence. We were not completely buried, but there was snow everywhere. We got up, taking care not to bang our heads against the ceiling of ice, and tried to shake ourselves. We were all in our stockinged feet in the snow. The first thing to do was to find our boots.

Rébuffat and Terray began to search, and realized at once that they were blind. Yesterday they had taken off their glasses to lead us down and now they were paying for it. Lachenal was the first to lay hands upon a pair of boots. He tried to put them on, but they were Rébuffat's. Rébuffat attempted to climb up the chute down which we had come yesterday, and which the avalanche had followed in its turn.

"Hi, Gaston! What's the weather like?" called up Terray.

"Can't see a thing. It's blowing hard."

We were still groping for our things. Terray found his boots and put them on awkwardly, unable to see what he was doing. Lachenal helped him, but he was all on edge and fearfully impatient, in striking contrast to my immobility. Terray then went up the icy channel, puffing and blowing, and at last reached the outer world. He was met by terrible gusts of wind that cut right through him and lashed his face.

Bad weather, he said to himself, this time it's the end. We're lost . . . we'll never come through.

At the bottom of the crevasse there were still two of us looking for our boots. Lachenal poked fiercely with an ice ax. I was calmer and tried to proceed more rationally. We extracted crampons and an ax in turn from the snow, but still no boots.

Well—so this cavern was to be our last resting place! There was very little room—we were bent double and got in each other's way. Lachenal decided to go out without his boots. He called frantically, hauled himself up on the rope, trying to get a hold or to wiggle his way up, digging his toes into the snow walls. Terray from outside pulled as hard as he could. I watched him go; he gathered speed and disappeared.

When he emerged from the opening he saw the sky was clear and blue, and he began to run like a madman, shrieking, "It's fine, it's fine!"

I set to work again to search the cave. The boots *had* to be found, or Lachenal and I were done for. On all fours, with nothing on my hands or feet I raked the snow, stirring it around this way and that, hoping every second to come upon something hard. I was no longer capable of thinking —I reacted like an animal fighting for its life.

I found one boot! The other was tied to it—a pair! Having ransacked the whole cave I at last found the other pair. But in spite of all my efforts I could not find the movie camera, and gave up in despair. There was no question of putting my boots on—my hands were like lumps of wood and I could hold nothing in my fingers; my feet were very swollen—I should never be able to get boots on them. I twisted the rope around the boots as well as I could and called up the chute: "Lionel . . . Boots!"

There was no answer, but he must have heard for with a jerk the precious boots shot up. Soon after the rope came down again. My turn. I wound the rope around me. I could not pull it tight so I made a whole series of little knots. Their combined strength, I hoped, would be enough to hold me. I had no strength to shout again; I gave a great tug on the rope, and Terray understood.

At the first step I had to kick a notch in the hard snow for my toes. Further on I expected to be able to get up more easily by wedging myself across the runnel. I wriggled up a few yards like this and then I tried to dig my hands and my feet into the wall. My hands were stiff and hard right up to the wrists and my feet had no feeling up to the ankles, the joints were inflexible and this hampered me greatly. Somehow or other I succeeded in working my way up, while Terray pulled so hard he nearly choked me. I began to see more distinctly and so knew that I must be nearing the opening. Often I fell back, but I clung on and wedged myself in again as best I could. My heart was bursting and I was forced to rest. A fresh wave of energy enabled me to crawl to the top. I pulled myself out by clutching Terray's legs; he was just about all in and I was in the last stages of exhaustion. Terray was close to me and I whispered: "Lionel . . . I'm dying!"

He supported me and helped me away from the crevasse. Lachenal and Rébuffat were sitting in the snow a few yards away. The instant Lionel let go of me I sank down and dragged myself along on all fours.

The weather was perfect. Quantities of snow had fallen the day before and the mountains were resplendent. Never had I seen them look so beautiful —our last day would be magnificent.

Rébuffat and Terray were completely blind; as he came along with me Terray knocked into things and I had to direct him. Rébuffat, too, could not move a step without guidance. It was terrifying to be blind when there was danger all around. Lachenal's frozen feet affected his nervous system. His behavior was disquieting—he was possessed by the most fantastic ideas:

"I tell you we must go down . . . down there . . ."

"You've nothing on your feet!"

"Don't worry about that."

"You're off your head. The way's not there . . . it's to the left!"

He was already standing up; he wanted to go straight down to the bottom of the glacier. Terray held him back, made him sit down, and though he couldn't see, helped Lachenal put his boots on.

Behind them I was living in my own private dream. I knew the end was near, but it was the end that all mountaineers wish for—an end in keeping with their ruling passion. I was consciously grateful to the mountains for being so beautiful for me that day, and as awed by their silence as if I had been in church. I was in no pain, and had no worry. My utter calmness was alarming. Terray came staggering toward me, and I told him: "It's all over for me. Go on . . . you have a chance . . . you must take it . . . over to the left . . . that's the way."

I felt better after telling him that. But Terray would have none of it: "We'll help you. If we get away, so will you."

At this moment Lachenal shouted: "Help! Help!"

Obviously he didn't know what he was doing . . . Or did he? He was the only one of the four of us who could see Camp II down below. Perhaps his calls would be heard. They were shrieks of despair, reminding me tragically of some climbers lost in the Mont Blanc massif whom I had endeavored to save. Now it was our turn. The impression was vivid: we were lost.

I joined in with the others: "One . . . two . . . three . . . *Help!* One . . . two . . . three . . . *Help!*" We tried to shout together, but without much success; our voices could not have carried more than ten feet. The noise I made was more of a whisper than a shout. Terray insisted that I should put my boots on, but my hands were dead. Neither Rébuffat nor Terray, who were unable to see, could help much, so I said to Lachenal: "Come and help me to put my boots on."

"Don't be silly, we must go down!"

And off he went once again in the wrong direction, straight down. I was not in the least angry with him; he had been sorely tried by the altitude and by everything he had gone through.

Terray resolutely got out his knife, and with fumbling hands slit the uppers of my boots back and front. Split in two like this I could get them on, but it was not easy and I had to make several attempts. Soon I lost heart—what was the use of it all anyway since I was going to stay where I was? But Terray pulled violently and finally he succeeded. He laced up my now gigantic boots, missing half the hooks. I was ready now. But how was I going to walk with my stiff joints?

"To the left, Lionel!"

"You're crazy, Maurice," said Lachenal, "it's to the right straight down."

Terray did not know what to think of these conflicting views. He had not given up like me, he was going to fight; but what, at the moment, could he do? The three of them discussed which way to go.

I remained sitting in the snow. Gradually my mind lost grip—why should I struggle? I would just let myself drift. I saw pictures of shady slopes, peaceful paths, there was a scent of resin. It was pleasant—I was going to die in my own mountains. My body had no feeling—everything was frozen.

"Aah . . . aah!"

Was it a groan or a call? I gathered my strength for one cry: "They're coming!" The others heard me and shouted for joy. What a miraculous apparition! "Schatz . . . it's Schatz!"

Barely two hundred yards away Marcel Schatz, waist-deep in snow, was coming slowly toward us like a boat on the surface of the slope. I found this vision of a strong and invincible deliverer inexpressibly moving. I expected everything of him. The shock was violent, and quite shattered me. Death clutched at me and I gave myself up.

When I came to again the wish to live returned and I experienced a violent revulsion of feeling. All was not lost! As Schatz came nearer my eyes never left him for a second—twenty yards—ten yards—he came straight toward me. Why? Without a word he leaned over me, held me close, hugged me, and his warm breath revived me.

I could not make the slightest movement—I was like marble. My heart was overwhelmed by such tremendous feelings and yet my eyes remained dry.

"It is wonderful—what you have done!"

I was clear-headed and delirious by turns, and had the queer feeling that my eyes were glazed. Schatz looked after me like a mother, and while the others were shouting with joy, he put his rope around me. The sky was blue—the deep blue of extreme altitude, so dark that one can almost see the stars—and we were bathed in the warm rays of the sun. Schatz spoke gently: "We'll be moving now, Maurice, old man."

I could not help obeying him, and with his assistance succeeded in getting up and standing in balance. He moved on gradually, pulling me after him. I seemed to make contact with the snow by means of two strange stiltlike objects—my legs. I could no longer see the others; I did not dare to turn around for fear of losing my balance, and I was dazzled by the reflection of the sun's rays.

Having walked about a couple of hundred yards, and skirted around an ice wall, suddenly, and without any sort of warning we came upon a tent. We had bivouacked two hundred yards from the camp. Couzy got up as I appeared, and without speaking held me close and embraced me, Terray threw himself down in the tent and took off his boots. His feet, too, were frostbitten; he massaged them and beat them unmercifully.

The will to live stirred again in me. I tried to take in the situation: there was not much that we could do—but we would do whatever was possible. Our only hope lay in Dr. Oudot; only he could save our feet and hands by the proper treatment. I heartily agreed to Schatz's suggestion that we should go down immediately to the lower Camp IV which the Sherpas had re-established. Terray wanted to remain in the tent, and as he flailed his feet with the energy of despair he cried out: "Come and fetch me tomorrow if necessary. I want to be whole, or dead!"

Rébuffat's feet were affected too, but he preferred to go down to Oudot immediately. He started the descent with Lachenal and Couzy, while Schatz continued to look after me—for which I was deeply grateful. He took the rope and propelled me gently along the track. The slope suddenly became very steep, and the thin layer of snow adhering to the surface of the ice gave no foothold; I slipped several times, but Schatz, holding me on a tight rope, was able to check me.

Below there was a broad track: no doubt the others had let themselves slide straight down toward the lower Camp IV, but they had started an avalanche which had swept the slope clear of snow, and this hardly made things easier for me. As soon as we drew in sight of the camp the Sherpas came up to meet us. In their eyes I read such kindliness and such pity that I began to realize my dreadful plight. They were busy clearing the tents which the avalanche had covered with snow. Lachenal was in a corner massaging his feet; from time to time Pansy comforted him, saying that the Doctor Sahib would cure him.

I hurried everyone—we must get down—that was our first objective. As for the equipment, well it could not be helped; we simply must get off the mountain before the next onslaught of the monsoon. For those of us with frostbitten limbs it was a matter of hours. I chose Aila and Sarki to escort Rébuffat, Lachenal and myself. I tried to make the two Sherpas understand that they must watch me very closely and hold me on a short rope. For some unknown reason, neither Lachenal nor Rébuffat wished to rope.

While we started down, Schatz, with Ang-Tharkey and Pansy, went up to fetch Terray who had remained on the glacier above. Schatz was master of the situation—none of the others were capable of taking the slightest initiative. After a hard struggle he found Terray:

"You can get ready in a minute," he said.

"I'm beginning to feel my feet again," replied Terray, now more amenable to reason.

"I'm going to have a look in the crevasse. Maurice couldn't find the camera and it's got all the shots he took high up."

Terray made no reply; he had not really understood, and it was only several days later that we fully realized Schatz's heroism. He spent a long time searching the snow at the bottom of the cavern, while Terray began to get anxious. At last he returned triumphantly carrying the camera which contained the views taken from the summit. He also found my ice ax and various other things, but no movie camera. So our last film shots would stop at 23,000 feet.

The descent began—Ang-Tharkey was magnificent, going first and cutting comfortable steps for Terray. Schatz, coming down last, carefully safeguarded the whole party.

Our first group was advancing slowly. The snow was soft and we sank in up to our knees. Lachenal grew worse; he frequently stopped and moaned about his feet. Rébuffat was a few yards behind me.

I was concerned at the abnormal heat, and feared that bad weather would put an end here and now to the epic of Annapurna. It is said that mountaineers have a sixth sense that warns them of danger—suddenly I became aware of danger through every pore of my body. There was a feeling in the atmosphere that could not be ignored. Yesterday it had snowed heavily, and the heat was now working on these great masses of snow which were on the point of sliding off. Nothing in Europe can give any idea of the force of these avalanches. They roll down over a distance of miles and are preceded by a blast that destroys everything in its path.

The glare was so terrific that without glasses it would have been impossible to keep one's eyes open. By good luck we were fairly well spaced out, so that the risk was diminished. The Sherpas no longer remembered the different pitches and oftentimes, with great difficulty, I had to take the lead and be let down on the end of the rope to find the right way. I had no crampons and I could not grasp an ax. We lost height far too slowly for my liking, and it worried me to see my Sherpas going so slowly and carefully and at the same time so insecurely. In actual fact they went very well, but I was so impatient I could no longer judge their performance fairly.

Lachenal was a long way behind us and every time I turned around he was sitting down in the track. He, too, was affected by snow-blindness, though not so badly as Terray and Rébuffat, and he found difficulty in seeing his way. Rébuffat went ahead by guesswork, with agony in his face, but he kept on. We crossed the couloir without incident, and I congratulated myself that we had passed the danger zone.

The sun was at its height, the weather brilliant and the colors magnificent. Never had the mountains appeared to me so majestic as in this moment of extreme danger.

All at once a crack appeared in the snow under the feet of the Sherpas, and grew longer and wider. A mad idea flashed into my head—to climb up the slope at speed and reach solid ground. Then I was lifted up by a superhuman force, and, as the Sherpas disappeared before my eyes, I went head over heels. I could not see what was happening. My head hit the ice. In spite of my efforts I could no longer breathe, and a violent blow on my left thigh caused me acute pain. I turned round and round like a puppet. In a flash I saw the blinding light of the sun through the snow which was pouring past my eyes. The rope joining me to Sarki and Aila curled round my neck —the Sherpas shooting down the slope beneath would shortly strangle me, and the pain was unbearable. Again and again I crashed into solid ice as I went hurtling from one serac to another, and the snow crushed me down. The rope tightened around my neck and brought me to a stop. Before I had recovered my wits I began to pass water, violently and uncontrollably.

I opened my eyes to find myself hanging head downwards with the rope around my neck and my left leg, in a sort of hatchway of blue ice. I put out my elbows toward the walls in an attempt to stop the unbearable pendulum motion which sent me from one side to the other, and I caught a glimpse of the last slopes of the couloir beneath me. My breathing steadied, and I blessed the rope which had stood the strain of the shock.

I simply *had* to try to get myself out. My feet and hands were numb, but I was able to make use of some little nicks in the wall. There was room for at least the edges of my boots. By frenzied jerky movements I succeeded in freeing my left leg from the rope, and then managed to right myself and to climb up a yard or two. After every move I stopped, convinced that I had come to the end of my physical strength, and that in a second I should have to let go.

One more desperate effort, and I gained a few inches. I pulled on the rope and felt something give at the other end—no doubt the bodies of the Sherpas. I called, but hardly a whisper issued from my lips. There was a deathlike silence. Where was Rébuffat?

Conscious of a shadow, as from a passing cloud, I looked up instinctively, and low and behold! two scared black faces were framed against the circle of blue sky. Aila and Sarki! They were safe and sound, and at once set to work to rescue me. I was incapable of giving them the slighest advice. Aila disappeared, leaving Sarki alone at the edge of the hole; they began to pull on the rope, slowly, so as not to hurt me, and I was hauled up with a power and steadiness that gave me fresh courage. At last I was out. I collapsed on the snow.

The rope had caught over a ridge of ice and we had been suspended on either side. By good luck the weight of the two Sherpas and my own had balanced. If we had not been checked like this we should have hurtled down for another fifteen hundred feet. There was chaos all around us. Where was Rébuffat? I was mortally anxious, for he was unroped. Looking up I caught sight of him less than a hundred yards away:

"Anything broken?" he called out to me.

I was greatly relieved, but I had no strength to reply. Lying flat, and semi-conscious, I gazed at the wreckage about me with unseeing eyes. We had been carried down for about five hundred feet. It was not a healthy place to linger in—suppose another avalanche should fall! I instructed the Sherpas: "Now—Doctor Sahib. Quick, very quick!"

By gestures, I tried to make them understand that they must hold me very firm. In doing this I found that my left arm was practically useless. I could not move it at all, the elbow had seized up—was it broken? We should see later. Now, we must push on to Oudot.

Rébuffat started down to join us, moving slowly; he had to place his feet by feel alone. Seeing him walk like this made my heart ache; he too had fallen and he must have hit something with his jaw, for blood was oozing from the corners of his mouth. Like me, he had lost his glasses and we were forced to shut our eyes. Aila had an old spare pair which did very well for me, and without a second's hesitation Sarki gave his own to Rébuffat.

We had to get down at once. The Sherpas helping me up, I advanced as best I could, reeling about in the most alarming fashion, but they realized now that they must hold me from behind. I skirted round the avalanche to our old track which started again a little further on.

We now came to the first wall. How on earth should we get down? Again, I asked the Sherpas to hold me firmly: *"Hold me well because . . ."* And I showed them my hands.

"Yes, sir," they replied together like good pupils. I came to the piton; the fixed rope attached to it hung down the wall and I had to hold on to it—there was no other way. It was terrible: my wooden feet kept slipping on the ice wall, and I could not grasp the thin line in my hands. Without letting go I endeavored to wind it around my hands, but they were swollen and the skin broke in several places. Great strips of it came away and stuck to the rope and the flesh was laid bare. Yet I had to go on down, I could not give up halfway.

"Aila! Pay attention! . . . Pay attention!"

To save my hands I now let the rope slide over my good forearm and lowered myself like this in jerks. On reaching the bottom I fell about three feet and the rope wrenched my forearm and my wrists. The jolt was severe and affected my feet. I heard a queer crack and supposed I must have broken something—no doubt it was the frostbite that prevented me from feeling any pain.

Rébuffat and the Sherpas came down and we went on but it all seemed to take an unconscionably long time, and the plateau of Camp II seemed a long way off. I was just about at the limit of my strength. Every minute I felt like giving up; and why, anyway, should I go on when for me everything was over? My conscience was quite easy: everyone was safe, and the others would all get down. Far away below I could see the tents. Just one more hour—I gave myself one more hour and then, wherever I was, I would lie down in the snow. I would let myself go, peacefully. I would be through with it all, and could sleep content.

Setting this limit somehow cheered me on. I kept slipping, and on the steep slope the Sherpas could hardly hold me—it was miraculous that they did. The track stopped above a drop—the second and bigger of the walls we had equipped with a fixed rope. I tried to make up my mind, but I could not begin to see how I was going to get down. I pulled off the glove I had on one hand, and the red silk scarf that hid the other, which was covered with blood. This time everything was at stake—and my fingers could just look after themselves. I placed Sarki and Aila on the stance from which I had been accustomed to belay them, and where the two of them would be able to take the strain of my rope by standing firmly braced against each other. I tried to take hold of the fixed rope; both my hands were bleeding, but I had no pity to spare for myself and I took the rope between my thumb and forefinger, and started off. At the first move I was faced at once with a painful decision: if I let go, we should all fall to the bottom: if I held on what would remain of my hands? I decided to hold on.

Every inch was a torture I was resolved to ignore. The sight of my hands made me feel sick; the flesh was laid bare and red, and the rope was covered with blood. I tried not to tear the strips right off: other accidents had taught me that one must preserve these bits to hasten the healing process later on. I tried to save my hands by braking with my stomach, my shoulders, and every other possible point of contact. When would this agony come to an end?

I came down to the nose of ice which I myself had cut away with my ax on the ascent. I felt about with my legs—it was all hard. There was no snow beneath. I was not yet down. In panic I called up to the Sherpas: "Quick . . . Aila . . . Sarki . . . !"

They let my rope out more quickly and the friction on the fixed rope increased.

My hands were in a ghastly state. It felt as though all the flesh was being torn off. At last I was aware of something beneath my feet—the ledge. I had made it! I had to go along it now, always held by the rope; only three yards, but they were the trickiest of all. It was over. I collapsed, up to the waist in snow—no longer conscious of time.

When I half-opened my eyes Rébuffat and the Sherpas were beside me, and I could distinctly see black dots moving about near the tents of Camp II. Sarki spoke to me, and pointed out two Sherpas coming up to meet us. They were still a long way off, but all the same it cheered me up.

I had to rouse myself; things were getting worse and worse. The frostbite seemed to be gaining ground—up to my calves and my elbows. Sarki put my glasses on for me again, although the weather had turned gray. He put one glove on as best he could; but my left hand was in such a frightful state that it made him sick to look at it, and he tried to hide it in my red scarf.

The fantastic descent continued and I was sure that every step would be my last. Through the swirling mist I sometimes caught glimpses of the two Sherpas coming up. They had already reached the base of the avalanche cone, and when, from the little platform I had just reached, I saw them stop there, it sapped all my courage.

Snow began to fall, and we now had to make a long traverse over very unsafe ground where it was difficult to guard anyone; then, fifty yards further, we came to the avalanche cone. I recognized Foutharkey and Angawa mounting rapidly toward us. Evidently they expected bad news, and Angawa must have been thinking of his two brothers, Aila and Pansy. The former was with us all right—he could see him in the flesh—but what about Pansy? Even at this distance they started to ask questions, and by the time we reached them they knew everything. I heaved a deep sigh of relief. I felt now as if I had laid down a burden so heavy that I had nearly given way beneath it. Foutharkey was beside me, smiling affectionately. How can anyone call such people "primitive," or say that the rigors of their existence take away all sense of pity? The Sherpas rushed toward me, put down their sacks, uncorked their flasks. Ah, just to drink a few mouthfuls! Nothing more. It had all been such a long time . . .

Foutharkey lowered his eyes to my hands and lifted them again, almost with embarrassment. With infinite sorrow, he whispered: "Poor Bara Sahib—Ah . . ."

These reinforcements gave me a fresh access of courage, and Camp II was near. Foutharkey supported me, and Angawa safeguarded us both. Foutharkey was small and I hung on around his neck and leaned on his shoulders, gripping him close. This contact comforted me and his warmth gave me strength. I staggered down with little jerky steps, leaning more and more on Foutharkey. Would I ever have the strength to make it even with his help? Rousing what seemed my very last ounce of energy, I begged Foutharkey to give me yet more help. He took my glasses off and I could see better then. Just a few more steps—the very last . . .

Part Six

ABOVE
AND
BELOW
THE
EARTH'S
CRUST

FIFTY FATHOMS DOWN

by Jacques Yves Cousteau

Exploration is usually thought of in purely geographical terms as dealing with oceans, land masses, lakes and rivers on the earth's surface. The articles in the previous sections have been chosen with such a conception in mind. There is, however, still another field of exploration—of the territory under the surface of the earth and above it. For generations miners have burrowed into the depths, even tunneling under the ocean to follow the coal seams of Cornwall. But the life and geography beneath the surface of the oceans has until recently been all but unknown. The sponge fishermen of the Mediterranean ventured down a few fathoms and men in old-fashioned diving suits went a few fathoms more but they made few observations. Now, with new techniques of echo sounding, the hills and valleys, precipices and tremendous deeps of the ocean are being charted in some detail. Currents and "river systems" are being mapped. Geological and biological samplings are being studied. Best of all, man has invented methods of seeing with his own eyes.

The first of these methods was devised by William Beebe. In a reinforced iron ball large enough to hold two men, he traveled "Half Mile Down" at the end of a steel cable, but the limitations on movement and observation were great. The bathyscaphe, a submersible craft lowered and raised by control of weights magnetically attached to the hull, was developed by Auguste Piccard and Max Cosyns in collaboration with the French Navy. To a great extent it overcame the limitations of Beebe's device. But the technique of free-swimming observation to depths of several hundred feet invented by Jacques Yves Cousteau has proved most successful of all. With this method, the hitherto hidden vista below the surface is spread before the fascinated eyes of the observer. No one who has ever mask-dived is likely ever to forget his sensations on exploring a new world which he has never known

before. Something about this technique and a good deal about its excitement
are conveyed in the following articles by Cousteau himself.

W E CONTINUED to be puzzled with the rapture of the depths and
felt that we were challenged to go deeper. Didi's deep dive in 1943
had made us aware of the problem, and the Group had assembled detailed
reports on its deep dives. But we had only a literary knowledge of the full
effects of *l'ivresse des grandes profondeurs* as it must strike lower down. In
the summer of 1947 we set out to make a series of deeper penetrations.

Here I must say that we were not trying for record descents, although the
dives did set new world marks. We have always placed a reasonable premium
on returning alive. Even Didi, the boldest among us, is not a stunt man.
We went lower because that was the only way to learn more about the
drunken effect, and to sample individual reactions on what aqualung work
could be done in severe depths. The attempts were surrounded with careful
preparations and controls, in order to obtain clear data. The objective range
we set was three hundred feet or fifty fathoms. No independent diver had yet
been deeper than Dumas's two hundred and ten feet.

The dives were measured by a heavy shotline hanging from the *Élie
Monnier*. On the line at sixteen-and-one-half-foot intervals (five meters)
there were white boards. The divers carried indelible pencils to sign their
names on the deepest board they could reach, and to write a sentence
describing their sensations.

To save energy and air, the test divers descended the shotline without
undue motion, carried down by ten-pound hunks of scrap iron. They retarded their descent by holding the line. When a man reached the target
depth, or the maximum distance he could stand, he signed in, jettisoned his
weight, and took the line back to the surface. During the return the divers
halted at depths of twenty and ten feet for short periods of stage decompression to avoid the bends.

I was in good physical condition for the trial, trained fine by an active
spring in the sea, and with responsive ears. I entered the water holding the
scrap iron in my left hand. I went down with great rapidity, with my right
arm crooked around the shotline. I was oppressively conscious of the
Diesel generator rumble of the idle *Élie Monnier* as I wedged my head into
mounting pressure. It was high noon in July, but the light soon faded. I
dropped through the twilight, alone with the white rope, which stretched
before me in a monotonous perspective of blank white signposts.

At two hundred feet I tasted the metallic flavor of compressed nitrogen and was instantaneously and severely struck with rapture. I closed my hand on the rope and stopped. My mind was jammed with conceited thoughts and antic joy. I struggled to fix my brain on reality, to attempt to name the color of the sea about me. A contest took place between navy blue, aquamarine and Prussian blue. The debate would not resolve. The sole fact I could grasp was that there was no roof and no floor in the blue room. The distant purr of the Diesel invaded my mind—it swelled to a giant beat, the rhythm of the world's heart.

I took the pencil and wrote on a board, "Nitrogen has a dirty taste." I had little impression of holding the pencil, childhood nightmares overruled my mind. I was ill in bed, terrorized with the realization that everything in the world was thick. My fingers were sausages. My tongue was a tennis ball. My lips swelled grotesquely on the mouth grip. The air was syrup. The water jelled around me as though I were smothered in aspic.

I hung witless on the rope. Standing aside was a smiling jaunty man, my second self, perfectly self-contained, grinning sardonically at the wretched diver. As the seconds passed the jaunty man installed himself in my command and ordered that I unloose the rope and go on down.

I sank slowly through a period of intense visions.

Around the two-hundred-and-sixty-four-foot board the water was suffused with an unearthly glow. I was passing from night to an intimation of dawn. What I saw as sunrise was light reflected from the floor, which had passed unimpeded through the dark transparent strata above. I saw below me the weight at the end of the shotline, hanging twenty feet from the floor. I stopped at the penultimate board and looked down at the last board, five meters away, and marshaled all my resources to evaluate the situation without deluding myself. Then I went to the last board, two hundred and ninety-seven feet down.

The floor was gloomy and barren, save for morbid shells and sea urchins. I was sufficiently in control to remember that in this pressure, ten times that of the surface, any untoward physical effort was extremely dangerous. I filled my lungs slowly and signed the board. I could not write what it felt like fifty fathoms down.

I was the deepest independent diver. In my bisected brain the satisfaction was balanced by satirical self-contempt.

I dropped the scrap iron and bounded like a coiled spring, clearing two boards in the first flight. There, at two hundred and sixty-four feet, the rapture vanished suddenly, inexplicably and entirely, I was light and sharp, one man again, enjoying the lighter air expanding in my lungs. I rose through the twilight zone at high speed, and saw the surface pattern in a blaze of platinum bubbles and dancing prisms. It was impossible not to think of flying to heaven.

However, before heaven there was purgatory. I waited twenty feet down for five minutes of stage decompression, then hurried to ten feet where I spent ten shivering minutes. When they hauled in the shotline I found that some impostor had written my name on the last board.

For a half-hour afterward I had a slight pain in the knees and shoulders. Philippe Tailliez went down to the last board, scribbled a silly message, and came up with a two-day headache. Dumas had to overcome dramas of heavy rapture in the fifty-fathom zone. Our two tough sailors, Fargues and Morandière, said they could have done short easy labor around the bottom. Quartermaster Georges visited the bottom board and was dizzy for an hour or so afterward. Jean Pinard felt out of condition at two hundred and twenty feet, signed in, and sensibly returned. None of us wrote a legible word on the deep board.

In the autumn we undertook another series of deep dives, with marker boards extending below fifty fathoms. We planned to venture beyond with lines tied to the waist, and a safety man stationed on deck, completely equipped to jump in and give aid in case of difficulty.

Diving master Maurice Fargues dived first. On deck we regularly received the reassuring conventional signal Fargues gave by tugging on the line, "*Tout va bien*" (All is well). Suddenly there was no signal. Anxiety struck us all at once. Jean Pinard, his safety man, went down immediately, and we hauled Fargues up toward one hundred and fifty feet, where they would meet. Pinard plunged toward an inert body, and beheld with horror that Fargues' mouthpiece was hanging on his chest.

We worked for twelve hours trying to revive Fargues, but he was dead. Rapture of the depths had stolen his air tube from his mouth and drowned him. When we brought up the shotline we found Maurice Fargues's name written on the three-hundred-and-ninety-six-foot board. Fargues gave his life a hundred feet below our greatest penetrations, deeper than any helmet diver breathing unmixed air has ever gone in the sea.

He had shared our unfolding wonderment of the ocean since the early days of the Research Group; we retained the memory of his prodigal comradeship. Dumas and I owed our lives to Maurice Fargues, who had resurrected us from the death cave at Vaucluse. We will not be consoled that we were unable to save him.

The death of Fargues and the lessons of the summer showed that three hundred feet is the extreme boundary of compressed-air diving. Amateurs can be trained in a few days to reach one hundred and thirty feet, and there professionals, observing decompression tables, may do almost any sort of hard work. In the next zone down to two hundred and ten feet experienced divers may perform light labor and make short explorations if rigid safety rules are followed. In the zone of rapture below only the highly skilled aqualunger may venture for a brief reconnaissance. Free divers could range considerably beyond the fifty-fathom layer by breathing oxygen mixed with lighter gases such as helium and hydrogen. While it has been proved that helium removes the causes of depth drunkenness, such dives would still require long tedious hours of decompression.

Dumas slightly improved the standing free-diving record in 1948 on a mission that had no such intent. He was called out to survey an obstacle believed to be an uncharted wreck, that had fouled the drag cables of a minesweeper. When he came aboard he learned that the depth had been sounded at three hundred and six feet. Dumas kicked up his fins and swam down in ninety seconds. The cable was snagged on a low rock. He studied the situation for a minute and returned as quickly as he had descended. He had not been subjected to enough nitrogen saturation to cause the bends.

Dumas planned the diving courses for the fleet aqualung divers, two of whom are to be carried on each French naval vessel. He immerses the novices first in shallow water to bring them through the fetal stage that took us years—that of seeing through the clear window of the mask, experiencing the ease of automatic breathing, and learning that useless motion is the enemy of undersea swimming. On his second dive the trainee descends fifty feet on a rope and returns, getting a sense of pressure change and testing his ears. The instructor startles the class with the third lesson. The students go down with heavy weights and sit on the floor fifty feet down. The teacher removes his mask and passes it around the circle. He molds the mask again, full of water. One strong nasal exhalation blows all the water through the flanges of the mask. Then he bids the novices emulate him. They learn that it is easy to stop off their nasal passages while the mask is off and breathe as usual through the mouthgrip.

A subsequent lesson finds the class convened at the bottom and again their attendance is assured by weights. The professor removes his mask. Then he removes his mouthpiece, throws the breathing tube loop back over his head and unbuckles the aqualung harness. He lays all his diving equipment on the sand and stands naked except for his breechclout. With sure, unhurried gestures he resumes the equipment, blowing his mask and swallowing the cupful of water in the breathing tubes. The demonstration is not difficult for a person who can hold a lungful of air for a half-minute.

By this time the scholars realize they are learning by example. They remove their diving equipment entirely, put it back on, and await the praise of the teacher. The next problem is that of removing all equipment and exchanging it among each other. People who do this gain confidence in their ability to live under the sea.

At the end of the course the honor students swim down to a hundred feet, remove all equipment and return to the surface naked. The baccalaureate is an enjoyable rite. As they soar with their original lungful, the air expands progressively in the journey through lessening pressures, issuing a continuous stream of bubbles from puckered lips.

The first foreign naval officer to visit us officially at Toulon was Lieutenant Hodges of the Royal Navy, who became an enthusiastic free diver and cinematographer. In 1950 there befell to him a tragic task—locating the sunken submarine H.M.S. *Truculent*. In a January fog in the Thames estuary the small Swedish tanker *Divina* rammed and sank the submarine with eighty men aboard. Fifteen of the crew escaped with Davis lungs; from their reports it did not seem difficult to locate the wreck. But the river was cold and filthy with a strong current running. Helmet divers made repeated descents and were swung away in the current, without making contact with the hull. Hodges volunteered to dive with the aqualung. He went in upstream at a point calculated in relation to the speed of the current and the supposed location of the *Truculent*, and went sailing giddily down in the turbulent darkness. He hit the submarine on his first pass. Unfortunately the trapped men were dead when the submarine was raised.

During the summer of Liberation I came home from Paris with two miniature aqualungs for my sons, Jean-Michel, then seven, and Philippe, five. The older boy was learning to swim but the younger had only been wading. I was confident that they would take to diving, since one does not need to be a swimmer to go down with the apparatus. The eyes and nose are dry inside the mask, breathing comes automatically and the clumsiest kick will do for locomotion.

We went to the seashore and I delivered a short technical lecture, which the boys did not hear. Without hesitation they accompanied me to a shallow rocky bottom, amidst sea wrack, spiny urchins and bright fish. The peaceful water resounded with screams of delight as they pointed out all the wonders to me. They would not stop talking. Philippe's mouthpiece came loose. I crammed it back in place and jumped to Jean-Michel to restore his breathing tube. They tugged at me and yelled questions as I shuttled between them, shoving the grips back between their teeth. In a short time they absorbed a certain quantity of water, and it was apparent that nothing short of drowning would still their tongues. I seized the waterlogged infants and hauled them out of the water.

I gave another lecture on the theme that the sea was a silent world and that little boys were advised to shut up when visiting it. It took several dives before they learned to hold their volleys of chatter until they had surfaced. Then I took them deeper. They did not hesitate to catch octopi with their hands. On seaside picnics Jean-Michel would go down thirty feet with a kitchen fork and fetch succulent sea urchins. Their mother dives too, but without the same enthusiasm. For reasons of their own, women are suspicious of diving and frown on their menfolk going down. Dumas, who has starred in seven underwater films, has never received a fan letter from a woman.

CAVE DIVING

by Jacques Yves Cousteau

OUR worst experience in five thousand dives did not come in the sea but in an inland water cave, the famous Fountain of Vaucluse near Avignon. The renowned spring is a quiet pool in a crater under a six-hundred-foot limestone cliff above the River Sorgue. A trickle flows from it the year round, until March comes; then the Fountain of Vaucluse erupts in a rage of water which swells the Sorgue to flood. It pumps furiously for five weeks, then subsides. The phenomenon has occurred every year of recorded history.

The fountain has evoked the fancy of poets since the Middle Ages. Petrarch wrote sonnets to Laura by the Fountain of Vaucluse in the fourteenth century. Frédéric Mistral, our Provençal poet, was another admirer of the spring. Generations of hydrologists have leaned over the fountain, evolving dozens of theories. They have measured the rainfall on the plateau above, mapped the potholes in it, analyzed the water, and determined that it is an invariable fifty-five degrees Fahrenheit the year round. But no one knew what happened to discharge the amazing flood.

One principle of intermittent natural fountains is that of an underground siphon, which taps a pool of water lying higher inside the hill than the water level of the surface pool. Simple overflows of the inner pool by heavy rain seeping through the porous limestone, did not explain Vaucluse, because it did not entirely respond to rainfall. There was either a huge inner reservoir or a series of inner caverns and a system of siphons. Scientific theories had no more validity than Mistral's explanation: "One day the fairy of the Fountain changed herself into a beautiful maiden and took an old strolling minstrel by the hand and led him down through Vaucluse's waters to an underground prairie, where seven huge diamonds plugged seven holes. 'See these diamonds?' said the fairy. 'When I lift the seventh, the fountain rises to the roots of the fig tree that drinks only once a year.'" Mistral's theory, as a matter of fact, possessed one more piece of tangible evidence than the scientific guesses. There is a rachitic hundred-year-old fig tree hooked on the vertical wall at the waterline of the annual flood. Its roots are watered but once a year.

A retired army officer, Commandant Brunet, who had settled in the near-by village of Apt, became an addict of the Fountain as had Petrarch six hundred years before. The Commandant suggested that the Undersea Research Group dive into the Fountain and learn the secret of the mechanism. In 1946 the Navy gave us permission to try. We journeyed to Vaucluse on the twenty-fourth of August, when the spring was quiescent. There seemed to be no point in entering a violent flood, if its source might be discovered when the fountain was quiet.

The arrival of uniformed naval officers and sailors in trucks loaded with diving equipment, set off a commotion in Vaucluse. We were overwhelmed by boys, vying for the privilege of carrying our air cylinders, portable decompression chamber, aqualungs and diving dresses up the wooded trail to the Fountain. Half the town, led by Mayor Garcin, dropped work and accompanied us. They told us about the formidable dive into the Fountain made by Señor Negri in 1936. What a bold type was this Señor Negri! He had descended in a diving suit with a microphone inside the helmet through which he broadcast a running account of his incredible rigors as he plunged one hundred and twenty feet to the inferior elbow of a siphon. Our friends of Vaucluse recalled with a thrill the dramatic moment when the voice from the depths announced that Señor Negri had found Ottonelli's zinc boat!

We knew about Negri and Ottonelli, the two men who had preceded us into the Fountain, Ottonelli in 1878. We greatly admired Ottonelli's dive in the primitive equipment of his era. We were somewhat mystified by Señor Negri, a salvage contractor of Marseilles, who had avoided seeing us on several occasions when we sought firsthand information on the topography of the Fountain. We had read his diving report, but we felt deprived of the details he might have given us personally.

The helmet divers described certain features to be found in the Fountain. Ottonelli's report stated that he had alighted on the bottom of a basin forty-five feet down and reached a depth of ninety feet in a sloping tunnel under a huge triangular stone. During the dive his zinc boat had capsized in the pool and slid down through the shaft. Negri said he had gone to one hundred and twenty feet, to the elbow of a siphon leading uphill, and found the zinc boat. The corrosion-proof metal had, of course, survived sixty years of immersion. Negri reported he could proceed no further because his air pipe was dragging against a great boulder, precariously balanced on a pivot. The slightest move might have toppled the rock and pinned him down to a gruesome death.

We had predicated our tactical planning on the physical features described by the pioneer divers. Dumas and I were to form the first *cordée*—we used the mountain climber's term because we were tied together by a thirty-foot cord attached to our belts. Negri's measurements determined the length of our guide rope—four hundred feet—and the weights we carried on our belts, which were unusually heavy to allow us to penetrate the tunnel he had described and to plant ourselves against currents inside the siphon.

What we could not know until we had gone inside the Fountain was that Negri was overimaginative. The topography of the cavern was completely unlike his description. Señor Negri's dramatic broadcast was probably delivered just out of sight of the watchers, about fifty feet down. Dumas and I all but gave our lives to learn that Ottonelli's zinc boat never existed. That misinformation was not all of the burden we carried into the Fountain: the new air compressor with which we filled the breathing cylinders had prepared a fantastic fate for us.

We adjusted our eyes to the gloom of the crater. Mayor Garcin had lent us a Canadian canoe, which was floated over the throat of the Fountain, to anchor the guide rope. There was a heavy pig-iron weight on the end of the rope, which we wanted lowered beforehand as far as it would go down. The underwater entry was partially blocked by a huge stone buttress, but we managed to lower the pig iron fifty-five feet. Chief Petty Officer Jean Pinard volunteered to dive without a protective suit to attempt to roll the pig iron down as far as it was possible. Pinard returned lobster-red with cold and reported he had shoved the weight down to ninety feet. He did not suspect that he had been down further than Negri.

I donned my constant-volume diving dress over long woolens, under the eyes of an appreciative audience perched around the rocky lip of the crater. My wife was among them, not liking this venture at all. Dumas wore an Italian Navy frogman outfit. We were loaded like donkeys. Each wore a three-cylinder lung, rubber foot fins, heavy dagger and two large waterproof flashlights, one in hand and one on the belt. Over my left arm was coiled three hundred feet of line in three pieces. Dumas carried an emergency micro-aqualung on his belt, a depth gauge and a *piolet*, the Alpinist's ice ax. There were rocks slopes to be negotiated: with our heavy ballast we might need the *piolet*.

The surface commander was the late Lieutenant Maurice Fargues, our resourceful equipment officer. He was to keep his hand on the guide line as we transported the pig iron down with us. The guide rope was our only communication with the surface. We had memorized a signal code. One tug from below requested Fargues to tighten the rope to clear snags. Three tugs meant pay out more line. Six tugs was the emergency signal for Fargues to haul us up as quickly as possible.

When the *cordée* reached Negri's siphon, we planned to station the pig iron, and attach to it one of the lengths of rope I carried over my arm. As we climbed on into the siphon, I would unreel this line behind me. We believed that our goal would be found past Negri's teetering rock, up a long sloping arm of the siphon, in an air cave, where in some manner unknown the annual outburst of Vaucluse was launched.

Embarrassed by our pendent gadgetry and requiring the support of our comrades, we waded into the pool. We looked around for the last time. I saw the reassuring silhouette of Fargues and the crowd jutting around the amphitheater. In their forefront was a young *abbé*, who had come no doubt to be of service in a certain eventuality.

As we submerged, the water liberated us from weight. We stayed motionless in the pool for a minute to test our ballast and communications system. Under my flexible helmet I had a special mouthpiece which allowed me to articulate under water. Dumas had no speaking facility, but could answer me with nods and gestures.

I turned face down and plunged through the dark door. I rapidly passed the buttress into the shaft, unworried about Dumas's keeping pace on the thirty-foot cord at my waist. He can outswim me any time. Our dive was a trial run: we were the first *cordée* of a series. We intended to waste no time on details of topography but proceed directly to the pig iron and take it on to the elbow of Negri's siphon, from which we would quickly take up a new thread into the secret of the Fountain. In retrospect I can also find that my subconscious mechanism was anxious to conclude the first dive as soon as possible.

I glanced back and saw Didi gliding easily through the door against a faint green haze. The sky was no longer our business. We belonged now to a world where no light had ever struck. I could not see my flashlight beam beneath me in the frightening dark—the water had no suspended motes to reflect light. A disc of light blinked on and off in the darkness, when my flashlight beam hit rock. I went head down with tigerish speed, sinking by my overballast, unmindful of Dumas. Suddenly I was held by the belt and stones rattled past me. Heavier borne than I, Dumas was trying to brake his fall with his feet. His suit was filling with water. Big limestone blocks came loose and rumbled down around me. A stone bounced off my shoulder. I remotely realized I should try to think. I could not think.

Ninety feet down I found the pig iron standing on a ledge. It did not appear in the torch beam as an object from the world above, but as something germane to this place. Dimly I recalled that I must do something about the pig iron. I shoved it down the slope. It roared down with Dumas's stones. During this blurred effort I did not notice that I lost the lines coiled on my arm. I did not know that I had failed to give Fargues three tugs on the line to pay out the weight. I had forgotten Fargues, and everything behind. The tunnel broke into a sharper decline. I circled my right hand continuously, playing the torch in spirals on the clean and polished walls. I was traveling at two knots. I was in the Paris subway. I met nobody. There was nobody in the Metro, not a single rock bass. No fish at all.

At that time of year our ears are well trained to pressure after a summer's diving. *Why did my ears ache so?* Something was happening. The light no longer ran around the tunnel walls. The beam spread on a flat bottom, covered with pebbles. It was earth, not rock, the detritus of the chasm. I could find no walls. I was on the floor of a vast drowned cave. I found the pig iron, but no zinc boat, no siphon and no teetering rock. My head ached. I was drained of initiative.

I returned to our purpose, to learn the geography of the immensity that had no visible roof or walls, but rolled away down at a forty-five-degree incline. I could not surface without searching the ceiling for the hole that led up to the inner cavern of our theory.

I was attached to something, I remembered. The flashlight picked out a rope which curled off to a strange form floating supine above the pebbles. Dumas hung there in his cumbersome equipment, holding his torch like a ridiculous glowworm. Only his arms were moving. He was sleepily trying to tie his *piolet* to the pig-iron line. His black frogman suit was filling with water. He struggled weakly to inflate it with compressed air. I swam to him and looked at his depth gauge. It read one hundred and fifty feet. The dial was flooded. We were deeper than that. We were at least two hundred feet down, four hundred feet away from the surface at the bottom of a crooked slanting tunnel.

We had rapture of the depths, but not the familiar drunkenness. We felt heavy and anxious, instead of exuberant. Dumas was stricken worse than I. This is what I thought: *I shouldn't feel this way in this depth. . . . I can't go back until I learn where we are. Why don't I feel a current? The pig-iron line is our only way home. What if we lose it? Where is the rope I had on my arm?* I was able in that instant to recall that I had lost the line somewhere above. I took Dumas's hand and closed it around the guide line. "Stay here," I shouted. "I'll find the shaft." Dumas understood me to mean I had no air and needed the safety aqualung. I sent the beam of the flashlight around in search of the roof of the cave. I found no ceiling.

Dumas was passing under heavy narcosis. He thought I was the one in danger. He fumbled to release the emergency lung. As he tugged hopelessly at his belt, he scudded across the drowned shingle and abandoned the guide line to the surface. The rope dissolved in the dark. I was swimming above, mulishly seeking for a wall or a ceiling, when I felt his weight tugging me back like a drifting anchor, restraining my search.

Above us somewhere were seventy fathoms of tunnel and crumbling rock. My weakened brain found the power to conjure up our fate. When our air ran out we would grope along the ceiling and suffocate in dulled agony. I shook off this thought and swam down to the ebbing glow of Dumas's flashlight.

He had lost the better part of his consciousness. When I touched him, he grabbed my wrist with awful strength and hauled me toward him for a final experience of life, an embrace that would take me with him. I twisted out of his hold and backed off. I examined Dumas with the torch. I saw his protruded eyes rolling inside the mask.

The cave was quiet between my gasping breaths. I marshaled all my remaining brain power to consider the situation. Fortunately there was no current to carry Dumas away from the pig iron. If there had been the least current we would have been lost. *The pig iron must be near.* I looked for that rusted metal block, more precious than gold. And suddenly there was the stolid and reassuring pig iron. Its line flew away into the dark, toward the hope of life.

In his stupor, Didi lost control of his jaws and his mouthpiece slipped from his teeth. He swallowed water and took some in his lungs before he somehow got the grip back into his mouth. Now, with the guide line beckoning, I realized that I could not swim to the surface, carrying the inert Dumas, who weighed at least twenty-five pounds in his waterlogged suit. I was in a state of exhaustion from the mysterious effect of the cave. We had not exercised strenuously, yet Dumas was helpless and I was becoming idiotic.

I would climb the rope, dragging Dumas with me. I grasped the pig-iron rope and started up, hand over hand, with Dumas drifting below, along the smooth vertical rock.

My first three hand holds on the line were interpreted correctly by Fargues as the signal to pay out more rope. He did so, with a will. I regarded with utter dismay the phenomenon of the rope slackening and made superhuman efforts to climb it. Fargues smartly fed me rope when he felt my traction. It took an eternal minute for me to form the tactic that I should continue to haul down rope, until the end of it came into Fargues's hand. He would never let that go. I hauled rope in dull glee.

Four hundred feet of rope passed through my hands and curled into the cavern. And a knot came into my hands. Fargues was giving us more rope to penetrate the ultimate gallery of Vaucluse. He had efficiently tied on another length to encourage us to pass deeper.

I dropped the rope like an enemy. I would have to climb the tunnel slope like an Alpinist. Foot by foot I climbed the fingerholds of rock, stopping when I lost my respiratory rhythm by exertion and was near to fainting. I drove myself on, and felt that I was making progress. I reached for a good hand hold, standing on the tips of my fins. The crag eluded my fingers and I was dragged down by the weight of Dumas.

The shock turned my mind to the rope again and I received a last-minute remembrance of our signals: six tugs meant pull everything up. I grabbed the line and jerked it, confident that I could count to six. The line was slacked and snagged on obstacles in the four hundred feet to Maurice Fargues. *Fargues, do you not understand my situation?* I was at the end of my strength. Dumas was hanging on me. *Why doesn't Dumas understand how bad he is for me? Dumas, you will die, anyway. Maybe you are already gone. Didi, I hate to do it, but you are dead and you will not let me live. Go away, Didi.* I reached for my belt dagger and prepared to cut the cord to Dumas.

Even in my incompetence there was something that held the knife in its holster. *Before I cut you off, Didi, I will try again to reach Fargues.* I took the line and and repeated the distress signal, again and again. *Didi, I am doing all a man can do. I am dying too.*

On shore, Fargues stood in perplexed concentration. The first *cordée* had not been down for the full period of the plan, but the strange pattern of our signals disturbed him. His hard but sensitive hand on the rope had felt no clear signals since the episode a few minutes back when suddenly we wanted lots of rope. He had given it to us, eagerly adding another length. *They must have found something tremendous down there,* thought Fargues. He was eager to penetrate the mystery himself on a later dive. Yet he was uneasy about the lifelessness of the rope in the last few minutes. He frowned and fingered the rope like a pulse, and waited.

Up from the lag of rope, four hundred feet across the friction of rocks, and through the surface, a faint vibration tickled Fargues's finger. He reacted by standing and grumbling, half to himself, half to the cave watchers, *"Qu'est-ce que je risque? De me faire engueuler?"* ("What do I risk? A bawling out?") With a set face he hauled the pig iron in.

I felt the rope tighten. I jerked my hand off the dagger and hung on. Dumas's air cylinders rang on the rocks as we were borne swiftly up. A hundred feet above I saw a faint triangle of green light, where hope lay. In less than a minute Fargues pulled us out into the pool and leaped in the water after the senseless Dumas. Tailliez and Pinard waded in after me. I gathered what strength I had left to control my emotions, not to break down. I managed to walk out of the pool. Dumas lay on his stomach and vomited. Our friends stripped off our rubber suits. I warmed myself around a flaming caldron of gasoline. Fargues and the doctor worked over Dumas. In five minutes he was on his feet, standing by the fire. I handed him a bottle of brandy. He took a drink and said, "I'm going down again." I wondered where Simone was.

The Mayor said, "When your air bubbles stopped coming to the surface, your wife ran down the hill. She said she could not stand it." Poor Simone had raced to a café in Vaucluse and ordered the most powerful spirit in the house. A rumor monger raced through the village, yelling that one of the divers was drowned. Simone cried, "Which one? What color was his mask?"

"Red," said the harbinger.

Simone gasped with relief—my mask was blue. Then she thought of Didi of the red mask and her joy collapsed. She returned distractedly up the trail to the Fountain. There stood Didi, a miracle to her.

Dumas's recuperative powers put the color back on him and his mind cleared. He wanted to know why we had been drugged in the cavern. In the afternoon another *cordée*, Tailliez and Guy Morandière, prepared to dive, without the junk we had carried. They wore only long underwear and light ballast, which rendered them slightly buoyant. They planned to go to the cavern and reconnoiter for the passage which led to the secret of Vaucluse. Having found it they would immediately return and sketch the layout for the third *cordée*, which would make the final plunge.

From the diving logs of Captain Tailliez and Morandière, I am able to recount their experience, which was almost as appalling as ours. Certainly it took greater courage than ours to enter the Fountain from which we had been luckily saved. In their familiarization period just under the surface of the pool, Morandière felt intense cold. They entered the tunnel abreast, roped together. Second *cordée* tactics were to swim down side by side along the ceiling.

When they encountered humps sticking down from the roof, they were to duck under and return to follow closely the ceiling contour. Each hump they met promised to level off beyond, but never did. They went down and down. Our only depth gauge had been ruined, but the veteran Tailliez had a sharp physiological sense of depth. At an estimated one hundred and twenty feet he halted the march so they might study their subjective sensations. Tailliez felt the first inviting throbs of rapture of the depths. He knew that to be impossible at a mere twenty fathoms. However, the symptoms were pronounced.

He hooted to Morandière that they should turn back. Morandière maneuvered himself and the rope to facilitate Tailliez's turnabout. As he did so, he heard that Tailliez's respiratory rhythm was disorderly, and faced his partner so that Tailliez could see him give six pulls on the pig-iron rope. Unable to exchange words under water, the team had to depend on errant flashlight beams and understanding, to accomplish the turn. Morandière stationed himself below Tailliez to conduct the Captain to the surface. Tailliez construed these activities to mean that Morandière was in trouble. Both men were slipping into the blank rapture that had almost finished the first *cordée*.

Tailliez carefully climbed the guide line. The rope behind drifted aimlessly in the water and a loop hung around his shoulders. Tailliez felt he had to sever the rope before it entangled him. He whipped out his dagger and cut it away. Morandière, swimming freely below him, was afraid his mate was passing out. The confused second *cordée* ascended to the green hall light of the Fountain. Morandière closed in, took Tailliez's feet and gave him a strong boost through the narrow door. The effort upset Morandière's breathing cycle.

We saw Tailliez emerge in his white underwear, Morandière following through the underwater door. Tailliez broke the surface, found a footing and walked out of the water, erect and wild-eyed. In his right hand he held his dagger, upside down. His fingers were bitten to the bone by the blade and blood flowed down his sodden woolens. He did not feel it.

We resolved to call it a day with a shallow plunge to map the entrance of the Fountain. We made sure that Didi, in his anger against the cave, could not slip down to the drowned cavern that had nearly been our tomb. Fargues lashed a one-hundred-and-fifty-foot line to Dumas's waist and took Didi's dagger so he couldn't cut himself loose and go down further. The final reconnaissance of the entrance shaft passed without incident.

It was an emotional day. That evening in Vaucluse the first and second *cordées* made a subjective comparison of cognac narcosis and rapture of the Fountain. None of us could relax, thinking of the enigmatic stupor that had overtaken us. We knew the berserk intoxication of *l'ivresse des grandes profondeurs* at two hundred and twenty feet in the sea, but why did this clear, lifeless limestone water cheat a man's mind in a different way?

Simone, Didi and I drove back to Toulon that night, thinking hard, despite fatigue and headache. Long silences were spaced by occasional suggestions. Didi said, "Narcotic effects aren't the only cause of diving accidents. There are social and subjective fears, the air you breathe. . . ." I jumped at the idea. "The air you breathe!" I said. "Let's run a lab test on the air left in the lungs."

The next morning we sampled the cylinders. The analysis showed 1/2000 of carbon monoxide. At a depth of one hundred and sixty feet the effect of carbon monoxide is sixfold. The amount we were breathing may kill a man in twenty minutes. We started our new Diesel-powered free-piston air compressor. We saw the compressor sucking in its own exhaust fumes. We had all been breathing lethal doses of carbon monoxide.

Further expeditions were made to the caves of Chartreux and Estramar which taught us much about the problems of cave diving. But we still had not gone through a siphon or the mechanism that shot water earthward. In 1948, while most of us were away on the *Bathyscaphe* expedition, three members of the Group finally achieved the goal, Lieutenant Jean Alinat, Dr. F. Devilla and CPO Jean Pinard, this time assisted by the Army Corps of Engineers. The spring of Vitarelles near Gramat was the object of their large cave expedition.

Vitarelles is a subterranean spring. The surface of the water is three hundred and ninety feet down. The engineers carried out a full-scale dry-cave operation before the divers reached the water. First the soldiers descended an air shaft two hundred and seventy feet deep, lowering pontoons, duck-boards, aqualungs, constant-volume suits, lines, electric-lighting equipment, and food. From this landing they conveyed the equipment down another hole, narrow and almost vertical, one hundred and twenty feet to an underground chamber. From this base they were required to lay duck-boards and pack the gear sixteen hundred feet through partially flooded galleries, including a dangerous cramped passage thirty feet long. Only then did they reach the surface of the spring, into which the divers were to continue for hundreds of feet more. The engineers established a pontoon pier in the pool, with diving ladders, and the sailors prepared to dive.

Alinat's plan was to send divers down one at a time, on safety ropes of progressively greater lengths. Using measuring lines, flashlights, compasses, depth gauges and sketch blocks, the divers mapped the water tunnel, each one advancing further than the man before. The scheme worked smoothly, and the chart moved league-by-league into the void. The culminating tenth dive was made by Alinat on the twenty-ninth of October, 1948.

The diver before him had reached the entrance to a siphon. Alinat went down, fastened to a four-hundred-foot safety line, and rapidly swam to the limit of the chart. The gallery rose at a twenty-degree angle. Alinat swam into the narrow tunnel. He passed uphill through forty feet of rather turbid water in a darkness pierced only by his narrow flashlight beam. He felt his head part a gentle tissue and water resistance ceased. Through his mask, now blurred like a windshield in rain, he saw that his head was in air. He was in a sealed clay vault one hundred and fifty feet long. He removed his mouth piece and mask and breathed natural air. Where water flows, even in a sealed pocket beneath the earth, there is air.

He climbed out on a slippery strand that ranged down one side of the long room. He was the first living thing in the vault of water, earth and air, where no sun had ever brought the gift of life. He walked along the shore, measuring and sketching, elated with the victory of our campaigns against the fountains.

At the far end, Alinat received a bitter revelation. Plain under the clear water was the aperture of another siphon. The mechanism of Vitarelles held further secrets. Alinat sat down and thought of the cost of penetrating the new labyrinth. The divers would have to transport equipment nearly four hundred feet under water to set up an advanced camp in the clay room, before they could plunge into the second siphon.

Alinat finished his sketch and walked back to the entrance, imprinting rubber frog tracks on the hidden beach. He spit in the mask and sloshed it in the water. He molded the mask over his face and inserted the mouth grip. He slipped into the water, turned up his flukes and sailed head down through the current of the first siphon. In a few minutes his exhalations sputtered out on the surface. Nothingness was restored in the cave. The tracks of man vanished into darkness.

LISTEN! THE WIND

by Anne Morrow Lindbergh

A controllable flying machine to conquer the realm of the air was first developed by the Wright brothers in their historic flight at Kitty Hawk, and the invention has completely revolutionized the technique of exploration. Jungles inacessible to man have been mapped and photographed in detail. Polar wastes have been comfortably observed by men soaring over them, although as we have seen in "Cloud Full of Rocks" the method is by no means without its dangers. Innumerable individuals, on seeing their own homes and cities from the air, have observed that never before have they truly known the localities in which they have lived, sometimes all their lives.

Of the many records of aerial exploration, we have chosen a selection from Anne Morrow Lindbergh's memorable Listen! the Wind. In a Foreword, Charles A. Lindbergh tells us something of the purpose and significance of the expedition, and Mrs. Lindbergh's own account conveys in a unique manner the sensations and emotions of flight. Three times they had attempted the transatlantic crossing. In the Cape Verde Islands, the winds had been too strong for their single-motored airplane to take off with a sufficient load of fuel. They turned back to Bathurst on the coast of Africa but here there was insufficient wind to lift them. Lindbergh, however, had "a few tricks" including the dumping of excess fuel and every ounce of unnecessary supplies. Then came the morning of the last try they would be able to make, and finally they were airborne.

FOREWORD

by Charles A. Lindbergh

Listen! the Wind is the story of a survey flight around the North Atlantic Ocean in 1933. It is a true and accurate account of various incidents which occurred in flying from Africa to South America. The purpose of the flight was to study the air routes between America and Europe. At that time, the air routes of the world were entering their final stage of development. The countries had already been crossed and the continents connected. It remained only for the oceans to be spanned. Their great over-water distances constituted the last major barrier to the commerce of the air.

The North Atlantic is the most important, and also the most difficult to fly, of all the oceans crossed by the trade routes of men. Distance and climate have combined to place obstacles in the path of those who wish to travel over it. Where the distance is short, the climate is severe, as in the north; while in the south, great distances counteract the advantages of a milder season. There are three natural air routes across the North Atlantic. They may be designated as the "Greenland Route" in the north, the "Azores Route" in the south, and the "Great Circle Route" in the center. We were to survey them all.

Our flight began at New York in July, and after following the "Great

Circle Route" to Newfoundland, turned north along the coast of Labrador. We crossed to Europe over the "Northern Route," making our first continental landing at Copenhagen. The following weeks were spent in the countries of Europe, and in flights along the coasts of Norway, Scotland, Ireland, Spain, and Portugal.

We reached the Azores too late in the year to fly to Newfoundland or Bermuda with the facilities which then existed. The risk would have been unnecessarily great. So, after a few days in these islands, we set our course south to Africa and the less difficult route which passes over the Equator to South America. *Listen! the Wind* is written about our homeward trip, or rather that portion of it which lay between Africa and South America. It describes the people we met and the problems we encountered in making a long over-water flight without advance organization and with a plane originally constructed for continental flying. . . .

Our flight lasted for nearly six months. This book covers only ten days of that time. It is about a period in aviation which is now gone, but which was probably more interesting than any the future will bring. As time passes, the perfection of machinery tends to insulate man from contact with the elements in which he lives. The "stratosphere" planes of the future will cross the ocean without any sense of the water below. Like a train tunneling through a mountain, they will be aloof from both the problems and the beauty of the earth's surface. Only the vibration from the engines will impress the senses of the traveler with his movement through the air. Wind and heat and moonlight take-offs will be of no concern to the transatlantic passenger. His only contact with these elements will lie in accounts such as this book contains.

M Y HUSBAND swung up into the cockpit. He started the engine. I felt under my feet for obstructions; saw that the control wires were free; sat on my extra shirt, stuffed the lunch in the aluminum case; put the radio bag in the seat beside me. There now, fasten the belt. Ready.

We pushed out into the bay. It was not such a strange world tonight. We had been here before. I greeted old landmarks. There were the lights of the town. There was the path of the moon.

We taxied over our take-off stretch. We tried out the engine; we throttled down; we swung into the wind. That pause for breath. The last look out: the palms outlined dimly above the town; the moon, a bright path ahead; and the wind—the wind was rising—

"All set?"

"All right."

Here we go. Hold on. The roar, the spray over the wings. Look at your watch. Won't be more than two minutes. Then you'll know. You can stand two minutes. Look at your watch. That's your job. Listen—listen—the spray has stopped. We are spanking along. We are up on the step—faster, faster—oh, much faster than before. Sparks from the exhaust. We're going to get off! But how long it takes. Spank, spank—we're off? Not yet—spank—almost. Splutter, choke—the engine? My God—it's coming then—death. He's going on just the same. We're off—no more spanks. Splutter—splutter. What is wrong? Will he turn? Will we land? The wobble pump? Gas? Mixture? Never mind, your job, the watch. Just two, Greenwich. Yes—we're off—we're rising. But why start off with an engine like that?

But it smooths out now, like a long sigh, like a person breathing easily, freely. Like someone singing ecstatically, climbing, soaring—sustained note of power and joy. We turn from the lights of the city; we pivot on a dark wing; we roar over the earth. The plane seems exultant now, even arrogant. We did it, we did it! We're up, above you. We were dependent on you just now, River, prisoners fawning on you for favors, for wind and light. But now, we are free. We are up; we are off. We can toss you aside, you there, way below us, a few lights in the great dark silent world that is ours —for we are above it.

The lights flashed on in the front cockpit, outlining my husband's head and shoulders. Then off again quickly. He was looking at the chart. We turned low over the shadowy land. I reached up and wrenched back the sliding cockpit cover, shutting out the noise and wind. The papers in my lap stopped fluttering wildly. I took out my large pad. Still taut from excitement, I wrote down by moonlight, "Took off Bathurst 2:00 GMT." Looking at the sentence scrawled unevenly across the top of the big sheet of blank paper, I said sternly to myself, "Well, you needn't get so excited—After all, we've got the whole flight ahead of us. Heaven knows if we'll get there." But I could not help feeling that the worst was over, now we were off, that after this all would be easy.

It was just as well, however, to be pulled down to practical affairs. There was no time now for fear or exaltation, for speculation or doubt. The windless bay, the docks, the lights, the palm trees, had dropped off behind us. I was concerned with them no longer. Neither was the great dark world outside my cockpit cover any business of mine. The moon, the stars, the wind, the formless stretch of land we were crossing, the vast ocean we were headed toward—all these I must shut out. For me they did not exist. All that existed now was this small cockpit, pulled over me like the shell of a snail. From now on until we reached the other side of the ocean, there I should stay curled down, oblivious to the outside world, touching it only through those faint squeaks in the earphones, through the light taps of my fingers.

It is strange how one's place of work, anywhere, becomes an all-important world—how it becomes, even more than that, a shelter and a home, enclosing and buttressing you on all sides, giving you a sense of security, no matter how precarious it may actually be—even hurtling blindly through the air.

This little cockpit of mine became extraordinarily pleasing to me, as much so as a furnished study at home. Every corner, every crack, had significance. Every object meant something. Not only the tools I was working with, the transmitter and receiver, the key and the antenna reel; but even the small irrelevant objects on the side of the fuselage, the little black hooded light, its face now turned away from me, the shining arm and knob of the second throttle, the bright switches and handles, the colored wires and copper pipes: all gave me, in a strange sense, as much pleasure as my familiar books and pictures might at home. The pleasure was perhaps not aesthetic but came from a sense of familiarity, security, and possession. I invested them with an emotional significance of their own, since they had been through so much with me. They made up this comfortable, familiar, tidy, compact world that was mine.

There were, in the first place, the oval sides of the fuselage, curving up around me in a way that was curiously comforting and secure. They seemed to surround me in a warmer, more friendly fashion than the straight inanimate walls of a room, so that I felt as snug as a bird in a nest.

There was my curved metal seat, securely rooted in the floor, wide and comfortable with its creased leather cushion. When I was not flying the plane, or bent over the receiver, I could squat, kneel, or curl up in it. There was plenty of room besides, in the corners, for my radio bag, an extra sweater or two, a package of sandwiches, pencils, pads, mittens, coils that I was changing—everything, in fact, that I needed. It was the only safe place to put things, where I could keep my hands on them, and be sure nothing would get lost or fall down on the floor. I was always afraid that a lunchbox or a coil would get wedged in the controls and cause an accident. The seat would bounce up or bump down as I pulled a cable underneath. I preferred it down so that I could work at the receiver. And when down, I was completely buried in the cockpit, only the top of my head, my eyes and nose emerging. It was, of course, the center of my world and seemed much more than a seat to me. It attained the importance of that special armchair, or bed, or corner, which is to a child his ship or his house.

Directly in front of me, between my legs, was the aluminum stick, with its corrugated rubber cap on top to grip. I could twist this out of its socket and fasten it into a clamp at the side when I was operating radio, as it interfered with the pad on my lap. In front of the stick was the box holding the sextant, which slid into grooves fastened to the floor. On either side of the sextant box were the rudders. At my right hand was the board which held the shiny black sending key, and the drift meter with its eyepiece to peer down at the waves below.

On the right side of the cockpit, about the height of my knees, was the receiver, a long narrow black box, mounted on springs and sponge rubber. In smooth air, its top served as a temporary shelf for notes and sandwiches passed between my husband and myself, although it was rather unsafe, and things were apt to jiggle off onto the floor. When operating the radio, as the box was rather low, I had to bend way over in order to watch and adjust the dials. At the same time, I had to keep a pad balanced on my lap for taking down messages. Receiving was still quite difficult. Except for familiar words and expressions, I could not yet translate the messages in my head and was forced to write them letter by letter as the sounds came to my ear. My pencil and not my mind apparently did the translating, hopping busily across the page. When the pencil stopped I would look down and see what had been written.

At the right side of the seat, out of sight but well within reach, was the box for the transmitter coils. The transmitter itself, a square black box, mounted like the receiver, was in front of me on my left. Its door let down and formed a convenient ledge for the coils as I was changing them. Then there was the antenna reel on the floor below this, its copper wire running down through a hole in the footboards. When we took off, this was wound up tightly, the ball weight on the end pulled snugly against the outside of the fair lead. But once we were up, it trailed in the air behind us.

A constant worry of mine was lest we lose the ball weight on the end of the antenna. It could easily be snapped off by a sudden impact with the water if we landed unexpectedly, or flew too near the surface of the waves before I had time to reel in. This had happened to me once before in an emergency landing at night in Alaska. I remembered quite well frantically winding the handle with an aching arm, racing against the descent of the plane; then the ominous jerk as the ball weight spun off into the sea; and, as I continued to wind, the unaccustomed lightness with which the frayed end of wire snapped back airily into the cockpit. For such a contingency there was an extra weight in the repair box in my husband's cockpit.

Looking forward, midway between my husband's cockpit and mine, and slightly raised from the floor, was the aperiodic compass, the one instrument I could clearly see and fly by, watching its swinging parallel white lines and figures as I pushed the rudders. Then, ahead, was my husband's cockpit. I could see him, his back at least, in segments; his helmet above the cockpit, through our sliding covers. Then, through the cockpit itself, his shoulder and arm, the shiny black back of his seat, the Duralumin tubes on which it slid up and down, and the V-shaped rubber cords that helped support it. Although he was only a few inches from me, communication was not easy. He could turn around and shout back to me but I could never, even with the wildest shriek, make myself heard above the engine's roar. I would write little notes, poke my husband in the back with a pencil (the degree of poke depending on my state of excitement) and pass him the paper, firmly held so it would not blow out of the cockpit.

But it was not only by sight that my little room was known to me. It was even more intimately known by touch. Everything was within arm's reach. Everything obeyed my hand: the stick which twisted down into the socket in the floor, the edges of whose rubber handle I had dog-eared fondly; the rudders, answering to one's feet like stirrups; but also, more personally mine, the little round flat disk, that was my radio key. Smooth and polished as a counter, it fitted lightly between my fingers, as comfortable, as familiar, as a pencil; obedient as any tool, and, as a tool, giving one a sense of pleasure to use it, play with it, master it, ride it.

Without sight, my fingers also knew the precise shape and spin of the small screws to open the radio boxes. My hand knew the plump smooth wooden handle of the antenna reel, and the cold square metal brake to fasten it. I could even change the coils by touch alone, running my finger over the polished spool and the ribbed surface of tightly wound wires, judging by the number of turns the wave length of the coil.

Tonight, I must do all by touch. The moonlight, which bloomed luminous on my white pad and dimly outlined the objects in the cockpit, did not brush into the darkest corners, did not throw any more light on the coil-box or the antenna reel. And though I could switch on the little hooded light, and might need to later on, to read by, I did not want to use it while we were still over land. The artificial glow might reflect into the front cockpit and take away some fraction of my husband's meager vision. Flying on the night mail, he once told me, I remembered, that the dimmest light in the cockpit might blind you temporarily.

I ran my fingers over the coils, found the right ones, jiggled them out of their places and pressed them (smelling faintly of shellac) into their sockets in the transmitter box. I clamped down the earphones over my ears. I switched on the receiver. The luminous dials glowed warmly out of the dark. I reached for the plump handle of the antenna reel. I put my fingers on the smooth key. "Darr dit darr dit, dit darr dit—" My work had begun. Outside the night rushed by. How nice to be in your own little room, to pull your belongings around you, to draw in like a snail in his shell, to work!

"CRKK CRKK [Porto Praia] DE KHCAL [The call letters of our plane]." It was 2:15. I had just time to call Porto Praia before my regular hourly and half-hourly schedule with the Pan American stations on the coast of South America. The heavy dragging buzz of my own sending rang closely in my ears. Then silence. Listening, fingering the bright dials in the darkness of the cockpit. No answer. Only the crashes of static in my earphones. I tried again. No answer. Perhaps he never got the telegram, I thought, on that timeless island. What time was it, anyway? Two-fifteen, Greenwich; one-fifteen, here. It was the middle of the night, of course. Why *should* he be watching for us?

I reeled in the antenna. I changed the coils. I reeled out for another resonance point on another wave. I would start calling the Pan American stations on the coast; not that I expected to get an answer as early as this, but simply because we had agreed to send on the hour and half-hour. It was now two-thirty.

"PVC PVC [Ceara] DE KHCAL." No answer, except the crashes of static, from that outer world. For to put on your earphones and tap into the radio waves is to open a window to another world, to have a peephole to the outside, an earhole. Tonight it was a very different world from the one in which I was sitting. Here all was still, snug and ordered. My husband sat calmly at the controls; I was curled up in my seat. Moonlight bathed the cabin; the night was clear; the plane bored its way steadily through a cloudless sky. But out there, in that outer cosmos, so it seemed to me listening, worlds were crashing; planets were breaking up. I could hear the tossing and hurling, the cracking and breaking, the terror and night.

Frightful static, I thought to myself, I wonder what that means—Storms? And I made a note on my fluttering featherweight radio pad: "Nil hrd [Nothing heard] QRN [*Atmospherics*]." No, I couldn't hear anything through that, but I might as well send out "blind" our time of take-off. Someone might pick it up, even though there didn't seem much chance. It was like putting a message into a corked bottle and throwing it overboard in a storm.

"PVC PVC DE KHCAL TOOK OFF BATHURST 02:00 GMT."
No answer in the earphones, only those stars clashing in the distance, those moons cart-wheeling through space. For you seem to hear distance and space on the radio. Sounds punctuate the silence, like stars the dark, giving you a sense of perspective.

But I was beginning to hear something else besides the cosmic crashes, faint squeaks against the welter of noise, precise scratchings upon the blurred surface of sound. So dim and faint, they were no more than a twig's tapping on a windowpane during a storm; no more than a crab's track on sand, partly erased by a wave; or a dead leaf's tracing on new-fallen snow. They were living, however; they were human, I was sure. They were dot-dash, Morse-code letters, words, messages of a human being.

I put my pencil on the page and let it jot down stray letters where I thought I could hear them between crashes: "O - - - - T - - - - C - - - FN - - - R - - - - K - - - L." Then suddenly, through the welter of sounds, I heard no longer letters but my name, or so it sounded to me, "KHCAL," the call letters of the plane. Across an ocean and through the night, my name! More thrilling than to hear your nickname in a room full of strangers, or your own language in a street of foreigners. Someone was calling us, an ocean away. Someone had heard us—in our little cabin, flying in the dark in a plane thousands of miles away. Who was it?

"SORRY CAN'T COPY   QRS [Please send more slowly]," I answered and pressed the phones to my ears.

"Dit darr dit—dit darr dit [R—received OK]," I heard dimly through the crashes. Then, "PVB BAHIA."

PVB, Pan American station at Bahia, South America. Right on the watch —good man! I switched on the light and poked my husband in the back with a pencil (rather excitedly I am afraid, for he jumped) and handed him a note.

"Can *just* hear PVB, Bahia, but think he hears me ok. Have you any msg [message]?"

He sent back "Very good" with his first message which I tapped out firmly, double-sending, across the ocean to Bahia.

"TOOK OFF 2:00 GMT [Greenwich Mean Time]
  POSN [Position at] 3:00 GMT
  12° 17′ N
  17° 50′ W
  COURSE 224° TRUE"
"Dit darr dit—dit darr dit [R—received OK]," came back the faint clicks.

He got it! Over two thousand miles away. We really were in contact with South America. We had jumped the distance, touched hands between hemispheres.

I felt as though the voyage were now not unguided. A path had opened up through the night. There was our goal. Hitherto it had been unseen, unheard, theoretical. It was a point on a compass, a dot on a map, convincing enough to my husband, but to me, not nearly as tangible as this— this faint, fluctuating, but friendly eye of a distant lighthouse.

From now on through three hours of night, I sat hunched over the lighted dials. Only once did I look out, a brief backward glance which told me we were well out over the water, for there, in the vast darkness underneath, were the twinkling lights of a ship far below us. How long would it be until I saw another boat, I thought in passing, and turned quickly back to my work. My hand on the knobs, the earphones pressed close against my ears, I sat straining to hear through the crashes of static. It was maddening. You could almost hear, almost, and then a crash would blot out everything. It was like trying to find something in the dark by lighting little matches whose flare petered out just as you were about to put your hand down. Or like trying to pick up a shell in the glossy smooth stretch of sand in the tail of a receiving wave. Before you could quite get there another wave crashed over.

I reeled in and out the antenna; I changed coils; I tapped out positions, repeating twice, three times, over and over again for the man at the other end who was also straining to hear.

"POSN 4:00 GMT
11° 05′ N
19° 05′ W
COURSE 224° TRUE
1/10 OVERCAST AT 2000 FEET   VISIBILITY UNLIMITED   WIND 10
KNOTS 30°   ALTITUDE 1200 FEET   MAKING 100 KNOTS."

I did not dare look up. In that half-second some whisper in the air might escape me. But I could tell it was still good weather by the moonlight over my shoulder. By this light I would write and send my own messages. I had to switch on the cabin light for receiving, which was literally a kind of deciphering of hieroglyphics my pencil had automatically jotted down on the page. What could I glean from those scattered letters? At first, nothing, a few stray words only of the weather reports they were trying to send me: "MOON - - - WIND - - NORTHEAST." Then gradually more. After much repetition I got some weather from Rio. (PVB, Bahia, had "passed me on" to Rio.) Things were going better. I breathed more easily, stretched myself and looked at my watch. Almost five—three hours since we took off—we were over three hundred miles out over the Atlantic—could it be possible! I felt as if I had hardly caught my breath, hardly stopped to realize we were off, on our way to South America. Relaxing a little, I realized also that I was very tired. I was sending with my eyes closed.

"POSN 5:00 GMT
09° 50′ N
20° 15′ W
COURSE 224° TRUE
9/10 OVERCAST   VISIBILITY 10 MILES
WIND 10 KNOTS 30°   ALTITUDE 1200."

It was a rest to send. Sleepy already, and I had the whole day to go through! But that would be *day*. Night was the hardest. It would be all right once it was day, I kept saying. (Just as I had said in Bathurst, it will be all right once we get off.)

We began to hit clouds. I could tell without looking up, for the plane bumped slightly from time to time, first one wing down and then the other. And the moon blackened out for short periods. Then for longer periods. I could not see to write my messages. I stiffened, dimly sensing fear—the old fear of bad weather—and looked out. We were flying under clouds. I could still find a kind of horizon, a difference in shading where the water met the clouds. That was all. But it seemed to be getting darker. Storms? Were those clouds or was it the sky? We had lost the water. We were flying blind. I turned off the light quickly (to give my husband a little more vision), and sat waiting, tense, peering through the night. Now we were out again. There were holes through which one could see the dark water, and holes through which one could see the dark sky. It was all right, I felt, as long as there were holes.

More blind flying. This is it, I thought, this is what people forget. This is what it means to fly across an ocean, blind and at night. But day is coming. It ought to be day before long. I tried to figure out—one hour off Greenwich. When did the sun rise? In an hour? Could we go through this for an hour?

We were climbing up through the clouds. The static hissed in my ears. I could not see the pad to write and I did not seem able to control my fingers to send steadily. But I must keep contact. "QRX—QRX [Please stand by]" I sent out, postponing my usual contact, "GOING THRU CLOUDS—MIN PSE [Please wait a minute]." We came out into the stars. My hand steadied. "QRX—ALL OK," I sent blindly. Again clouds ahead; again blind flying;

again we were climbing. I was shivering. It was cold, that was it; we were higher. Never let yourself get cold when you're frightened, I reminded myself, it just makes it worse.

I put on my extra shirt and tried to work again. But I could not read my messages in pitch blackness, and I did not dare turn on the light. It might make it harder to fly. "QRX—QRX—ALL OK."

A slip of paper was scratching my knee. My husband had pushed back a note, a message to send. I switched on the light.

"8/10 overcast," I read. "Scattered squalls—Visibility 3 miles— Daybreak."

Daybreak! what a miracle. I didn't see any sign of day and yet it must be lighter. The clouds were distinguishing themselves more and more from water and sea.

Daybreak—thank God—as if we had been living in eternal night—as if this were the first sun that ever rose out of the sea.

"POSN 7:00 GMT [Five hours gone now.]
  07° 25′ N
  22° 30′ W
  COURSE 224° TRUE
  9/10 OVERCAST AT 1000   FREQUENT SQUALLS   VISIBILITY UNLIMITED
  AWAY FROM SQUALLS   SEA CALM   WIND ZERO."

At the word *unlimited*, I looked up. Lovely word, which opens like a window from the straight walls of a radio report. How often, standing in some station on a wet field, with the sky a gray and lowering curtain, listening to the weather reports coming in from the west, I had waited for that word. "Newark—Newark—overcast—local storms," the monotonous voice on the radio would drone out. "Sunbury—Sunbury—visibility two miles—" (Down on the mountains.) "Bellefonte—lower broken clouds—ceiling estimated 3,000 feet." (That's better.) "Cleveland—Cleveland—ceiling and visibility unlimited—"(Good—we could go!)

Unlimited, my breath quickens at the sound of it. For it suggests more than the technically perfect, "ceiling and visibility unlimited." It calls up pictures of a soft wide cloudless sky, the morning of an endless summer day, a smooth and rippleless sea, spread silken to the horizon.

Not that this was the picture I saw now, looking out of the cockpit, but still, the weather was definitely better. Or perhaps it was the light. I could see the clouds that we had been going through, black pillowy thunderclouds that we grazed under, bumping heavily. They stretched out on all sides, a dark curtain pressing down on our heads. But underneath you could see clearly; and beyond, it looked brighter. Yes—"visibility unlimited"—now everything would be easy.

The radio was better, too. I was hearing well enough to receive, through triple-sending and a good deal of repetition, a message from Rio about the landing arrangements at Natal. It seemed incredible to think about landing when we were more than half an ocean away. Yet there was the message on my pad. It read like a professional telegram:

"RIO JANEIRO DECEMBER 6TH LINDBERGHS KHCAL PAA BARGE AT NATAL [Would we ever really get there?] LOCATED ON RIVER AT SOUTHWEST EDGE OF CITY STOP BETWEEN CITY AND LARGE AERO POSTALE HANGAR AND RAMP STOP [As though finding it would be any difficulty once we were there.] CAUTION TALL RADIO MASTS AT AERO POSTALE HANGAR STOP [Caution! radio masts in full daylight—caution—after that moonlight take-off!] FEW SPARE PARTS AVAILABLE ON BARGE."

"Few spart parts available." They evidently *did* expect us at the other end. The very attention to details seemed to bring the goal nearer. Natal began to materialize before my eyes. I felt lighthearted. I ate one of my sandwiches. I began writing cheerful notes to my husband. There had not been time before this.

"I still can't believe we got off." I wrote excitedly, "What was all that spluttering?"

"Insufficient gas feed," he scribbled back.

"I thought motor failure on take-off! Will we get out of the storms by and by?" ran my next question.

"By and by," was his noncommittal answer.

"I think you are wonderful," I added in a burst of enthusiasm.

The only comment on this last item was a heavy pencil mark. It looked like a firm laconic check.

Well—it was all wonderful, the take-off, the day, and the weather. I did not even mind the storms. I rather enjoyed bumping under the clouds. It was like a mild roller coaster, and added to my general good spirits. The sky grew brighter; I tapped out messages regularly.

"POSN 8:00 GMT [Six hours behind us, now.]
    06° 15′ N
    23° 40′ W
    COURSE 224° TRUE
    9/10 OVERCAST AT 1500   FREQUENT SQUALLS   VISIBILITY UNLIMITED
    OUTSIDE SQUALLS   SEA CALM   WIND ZERO   ALTITUDE 1000."

Suddenly, in the middle of my usual contact with Rio, I heard a loud note barging in over the radio, like heavy clumping footsteps filling the air. Who was it, knocking on my door?

"KHCAL DE WCC."

WCC—I couldn't believe it! WCC was thousands of miles away. It was that big station in Massachusetts. I looked it up to make sure. Yes, Chatham, Massachusetts, was calling us.

"ANSWER [on] 36 [meters] or 54 [meters]," went on the heavy voice.

Could it be Chatham, Massachusetts, as loud as that? It was completely unreal. But the whole night was unreal, so I answered quite casually on 57 meters (the wave length I was using), not bothering to change to the shorter wave.

He answered immediately, the notes pounding through, clear and strong, every word intact. I did not need his triple-sending but hardly dared interrupt. Chatham, Massachusetts, nearly four thousand miles away—think how thrilling!

Slowly the message dribbled onto the page: "WOULD YOU ANSWER ANSWER ANSWER FEW FEW FEW QUESTIONS QUESTIONS QUESTIONS FIRST RADIO INTERVIEW FROM FROM FROM AIRPLANE."

Newspapers here too, out in the middle of the ocean—what a disappointment. My thrilling contact with Chatham was just an interview. It was like a dream in which the door knob slowly turns into a grinning face. The night was more unreal than ever now.

"SORRY," I tapped back, "TOO BUSY HERE MUST GET WEATHER FROM PVJ."

Had I lost PVJ in the excitement? I began calling him insistently, reeling in and out the antenna and changing coils. Finally, I heard him faintly on 36 (meters) and sent out hurriedly our last position.

"POSN 09:00 GMT
05° 00′ N
24° 45′ W
COURSE 224° TRUE
2/10 OVERCAST AT 1500   9/10 OVERCAST AT 8000   VISIBILITY UNLIMITED   SEA CALM   WIND ZERO   ALTITUDE 1200."

Yes, he got it; now for the weather from Natal.

"WEA [weather] NATAL——," he started to give me in return. But the rest of his message faded out, smothered in silence. I pressed my earphones against my head; I bent over the dials; I could not hear it. The game of blindman's buff had started again.

Ten o'clock—eight hours behind us, eight ahead; we were halfway. By now the sun was well up at our back. The day was good. There were no more storms, only a few clouds left wandering at our own level. And far above, the sky was a broken overcast. Bits of blue showed through its gray folds. The sea below, rippled with little waves, looked peaceful and calm as far as one could see. It was still "unlimited."

But I was very tired, the thought of the whole day ahead seemed an unbearable burden. I was sending all the time now with my eyes closed. To open them again to write was like lifting day and night. Time, in hours, minutes, and seconds, like an ever-increasing weight of sand, piled on my lids. Sleep settled on me like a fall of feathers. One more feather and I should go under, be drowned in that delicious sea.

Now, you *mustn't* go to sleep, I would shake myself. Suppose the pilot went to sleep at the controls? You must keep contact.

But there was nothing on the radio to keep me awake. All sounds had faded out. Sleep seemed to have fallen, also, on that outer world. Even the crashes of static had disappeared. I would have been glad even to hear them. Anything but this still deathlike cotton-wool void, in which no creature was alive but me.

I changed the coils, I reeled in and out the antenna. I tapped out my positions "blind," hoping that the Pan American stations at the other end could hear me even if I could not hear them (which, in fact, was the case). But I could wake no reply.

"NIL HRD [nothing heard] on 36

POSN 10:00 GMT

04° 00′ N

26° 00′ W

9/10 OVERCAST   VISIBILITY UNLIMITED   SEA CALM   WIND 10 KNOTS

135°   ALTITUDE 800."

Perhaps I *was* asleep, I thought at times, and that was why I couldn't hear anything. I certainly was not very quick at turning the dials and changing the coils. My back ached from that perpetually bent-over position and my ears hurt from the clamp of the phones. (I had fastened my helmet over the phones and pulled it down tightly, hoping to shut out all outside noise and pin myself more closely to the radio world.) My thumb and finger, too, had sore dents in them from pressing the key too hard in my intensity. None of these things was difficult in itself. They were trifling annoyances, easily overlooked or overcome by a little will power. But when you are very tired your will is tired too. It seems to go more quickly than the mind. My thoughts were clear; I knew what I should do but it did not seem worth the effort.

Come now, you must do something about this, I would say to myself.

Yes, but what? Nothing I do will help. It takes all the strength I have just to stay where I am.

Well, try something, anyway, even if you don't think it will do any good. First get the canteen, a drink of water. A little on the handkerchief to wipe off your face. Then a sandwich.

It *did* help, surprisingly, and I felt more awake. But the radio was as dead as ever.

"NIL HRD ON 36   PSE [please] GO 53."

In the middle of my efforts I got a note from my husband. He would like to take some "sun sights" with the sextant, to check our position. Would I fly for a while?

I certainly would. I put my pad away and jiggled the stick into its socket on the floor between my legs. If I couldn't contact anyone on the radio, I might as well make myself useful some other way. I straightened up to the stick, I stretched my legs out to meet the rudders, pushing them gently this way and that. What a relief to change my position, to push, to do something active.

It was pleasant to look out, too. We were skimming along near the water. The sea was mottled, now, with sunshine and deep purple shadows. The gray overcast curtain above had broken into big loose white clouds, piled up in a bright blue sky. My eye wandered from the brightness of the clouds to the dark shadows of the cockpit, where the compass stood on the floor ahead of me. That swinging arrow must be kept parallel to the white lines if we were to continue straight on our course. And the ship must be steady while my husband held the sextant to his eye. My hands stiffened on the stick, my feet on the rudders. Now please, I would think, trying to wheedle the plane like a pony, don't buck or kick for a few minutes.

I left my earphones on and the antenna trailing, so that in between the "sights" I could try to contact stations. The sun was over our heads, hot on our backs. The middle of the day. A deep noonday sleep still swathed the radio. I sent out our position "blind" again.

"POSN 11:00 GMT [Nine hours behind us; seven to go.]

02° 50′ N

27° 10′ W

COURSE 224° TRUE

6/10 OVERCAST AT 10000   VISIBILITY UNLIMITED   SEA LIGHT   WIND

10 KNOTS 135°   ALTITUDE 800."

There was no answer. "Nil hrd on 36—nil hrd on 54—Nil hrd 600 to 900 —nil—nil," were the notes on my pad.

How about the sights? I peered forward at my husband and tried to read his face. He did not look satisfied. Was he working out calculations on his pad? No, he was taking the sextant to pieces on his lap! Something had gone wrong then; the sights were no good. We were over halfway across and it was vital to have radio. I reeled out again.

"PVJ   PVJ   DE KHCAL."

I swept the dial. *There*—yes, there *was* a squeak. There were some signals, an answer.

"KHCAL [But it wasn't PVJ, a different note, a different place on the dial.] DE CRKK."

CRKK—Porto Praia, behind us! Now farther away than the South American stations. Was it the "Chef," I wondered, sitting up in the radio shack? It might, of course, be that pale little operator. But I thought not. Somehow, I was convinced it was the "Chef" in his loose gray coat. He *had* received the telegram and was "on watch" for us. "WE LISTEN YOU ALL TIME," he had once said. "POSN PSE [Please give position]," he asked now.

"POSN 12:00 GMT [Ten hours passed; six ahead.]

01° 30′ N

28° 20′ W

4/10 OVERCAST   VISIBILITY UNLIMITED   SEA LIGHT   CAN YOU TELL PFX [Fernando de Noronha] TO LISTEN FOR ME."

"Dit darr dit, dit darr dit [Received OK]. QSK [What time will you call me again?]"

"QSK [I will call you again at] 12:45   MNI TKS [Many *thanks*]," I sent out gratefully.

"OK   QSK   12:45 [Till 12:45]," came back the friendly clicks from the radio towers on top of the hill in Santiago.

That was really our good-by to the island. For try as I might at twelve-forty-five, I never heard him again.

I would have to put out a CQ (general call), I thought in desperation, after another unsuccessful attempt at twelve-forty-five to contact Porto Praia. Perhaps some boat would answer me. I would sign it *Lindbergh Plane*, this time, instead of KHCAL. That might bring results. It sometimes worked. Stations apparently stone-deaf to KHCAL would speak up quickly to *Lindbergh Plane*. I only used this unprofessional signature as a last resort. I thought it a little unfair, somehow, not exactly sporting, like using live bait on your fishing rod instead of a regulation fly.

But, now, I didn't care. The Pan American stations might, of course, be hearing me all the time, even though I couldn't hear them, but I wanted some kind of an answer, something tangible.

"CQ   CQ [general call to all stations] LISTENING 28 to 48 [meters] LINDBERGH PLANE."

"LINDBERGH   LINDBERGH   LINDBERGH," I hardly had the bait in the water before I got a bite!

"DDEA SS CAPARCONA BOUND RIO   QRK [I receive you well. Your signals are good.]."

A ship, answering us—loud clear notes. Good, I had someone at last. They gave us their weather and position and then asked for ours.

"POSN 13:00 GMT [Eleven hours behind us: five more to go. Five hours was not as long as a flight from New York to St. Louis, I thought as I tapped.]

00° 15′ N

29° 25′ W

1/10 OVERCAST   VISIBILITY UNLIMITED   SEA LIGHT   WIND 10 KNOTS 135°   ALTITUDE 800   COULD YOU RELAY LAST POSN TO PVJ [Rio] OR PVB [Bahia]."

"OK," they answered, "WHERE BOUND?"

Where bound? Why, Natal, of course—BOUND NATAL. So indelibly stamped on my mind was our destination, it seemed surprising even to be asked the question. It had been our goal for weeks now. That half-forgotten ride down the coast of Africa, on the back of the wind; the long dusty wait at Santiago; the sultry trials at Bathurst; that fierce moonlit drive across the windless bay; the long night of work just behind us—it had all been to get to Natal.

The words, though, as I sent them over the radio, gave me an acute flash of excitement. They sounded clipped, sharp and swift, like the ping of an arrow, leaving its string. For today we were really bound for Natal like that, pointed at it, speeding toward it, like an arrow sprung from its bow: "BOUND NATAL."

The plane rocked gently. It was my husband moving the stick to attract my attention. I sat up quickly. What was it? His right hand pointed, out of the cockpit, to the north. There on the blue horizon was a ship! The first we had seen since those solitary lights below us in the dark off Bathurst, eleven hours before. A tiny speck only on the horizon, it was comforting as the first sight of land and bright as a beacon fire.

It is strange how the smallest touch of human life in the wilderness will light a landscape. Flying over the wastes of Arizona or New Mexico, I have noticed, even a deserted shack, a pile of stones hand-placed, or a patch of land once cultivated by man, shines out of the wilderness like a distant field in a ray of sunshine. It is lit with a strange brightness which is not explained by differences of color and light, but seems more to be a kind of warmth left there by the touch of humanity, a glowing ember of Promethean fire.

But this, the first ship on the South American side of the Atlantic, was more than an ember. It was a spark of life itself. It seemed the central point of an orbit, with the sky and sea rayed out from it in all directions. It lit the ocean like a lamp.

"POSN 14:00 GMT [Twelve hours behind us; only four to go.]

01° 00' S [We had crossed the Equator!]

30° 10' W

COURSE 226° TRUE

MAKING 100 KNOTS   8/10 OVERCAST   VISIBILITY UNLIMITED."

"Unlimited"—we could see as far as a ship on the edge of the round ocean.

I looked up from the radio again. What were we doing now? We were going down. My husband was pointing at something straight ahead. I could not see from the back cockpit. Yes—there was another ship, this time right on our course, a freighter, steaming along slowly, pulling a white wake behind. We were fast catching up to her, now diving down, down, down. (What did they think of us coming out of the sky with no warning? Did we give them as much thrill as they gave us? A second ship! We must be well across the ocean, in the converging lanes to South America.) Now on top of her, the masts and smokestack came up to meet us. Roaring over her, for one second we were in her world. She there, we here; separated from each other by days of slow sea travel but for this second together, sharing the time, the place. The blue star on her funnel, the decks, the cargo, someone waving, we could see. And on the side of the hull—yes—I could read as we passed, her name, *Aldebaran*—(Aldebaran, lovely star—a good omen!)

Up, up, up, we were climbing back into our own world, our own time. The *Aldebaran* was left behind, dropped back in the water, painfully plodding along. Bound for South America, too, how long would she take to get there? While *we*, I thought, as we roared away—we would be at Natal tonight, this afternoon even. Only four hours to go.

"Arcturus, Aldebaran, Alpheratz," I repeated reminiscently as we leveled out and straightened our course again. Perhaps that first white speck on the horizon was *Arcturus,* and the next ship we passed would be *Alpheratz.*

The next ship, however, was not *Alpheratz.* It was the *Westfalen,* the German catapult ship stationed in the Atlantic for the transoceanic flying service. She had passed Fernando de Noronha, that tiny island off the coast of Brazil, in the morning, and lay almost on our course. We were in contact with them (DDWE) for about two hours, sending weather and position reports, and transmitting on long wave for radio bearings. They gave us our bearing from their ship, and we turned slightly off course and headed in their direction.

"QRT [Stop sending]," the ship's operator broke off abruptly, "SEE YOU ON OUR PORT SIDE."

I looked out over the edge of the cockpit. There it was—a broad ship, steaming ahead of us, its plane, the catapult track, and the crooked arm of its derrick perched incongruously on top, looking like miniature toys from this height. We were diving down to meet them.

Suddenly I was aware of the men on deck, many bare arms waving, and steam puffing from a stack, visible sign of the blasts of salute we could not hear through the roar of our engine.

I held up my arm and waved frantically, conscious of that supreme thrill of communication. It is the most exciting thing in life anyway, whether you find it in a book or in conversation or in the understanding of two minds. But this, the momentary synthesis of two kinds of communication, was almost unbearable in its intensity. All night and all day I had been struggling to speak over a radio. I had been able to contact people only through my fingers, and my ears, like someone who is blind. But now, suddenly, I could see. A veil had dropped away. I could see, face to face. One of those men waving on deck was the radio operator I had been talking to. I raised my arm again—wonderful!

Now we were past. We were climbing up again, back to blind communication.

"MANY THANKS ALL HELP," I signaled back.

The operator on the *Westfalen* answered, giving us a bearing to Fernando de Noronha and to Natal. Then, "XMAS WISHES AND HAPPY NEW YEAR," he signed off, "FROM ALL ON DDWE." (Those bare arms waving from the deck.) "Xmas wishes"—on that tropical sea! I had never felt so far away from Christmas. But, of course, it was December, I recalled, December sixth. It was even possible that we might get home for Christmas. I let myself think about it; it was so near. "The men are sailing home from Troy," I thought, "And all the lamps are lit." The line jingled in my head as it always did when I was going home. It had danced to the rhythm of the train, coming back from school. It had throbbed in the engines of a steamer, coming into port. And now, again:

> The men are sailing home from Troy,
> And all the lamps are lit.[1]

I was very happy. We were only forty miles from Fernando de Noronha. The day was clear and cool. I did not feel sleepy at all. I could have gone on indefinitely, and the flight was almost over. We were coasting downhill, I felt, into Natal. Now over Fernando de Noronha, that bare little island with one steep peak sticking up like a long French roll on end. Now bumping around its steep sides. Now off straight for Natal. Now in contact with the Pan American station at Ceara again.

"POSN 16:45 GMT [Almost fifteen hours behind us—an hour to go.]
    04° 40′ S
    33° 40′ W
    CLEAR AND UNLIMITED   SEA LIGHT   WIND 15 KNOTS 60°."

Only an hour to go! An hour was nothing. An hour could be measured easily.

My husband was wobbling the stick again. I looked up. The first dim line of land was pushing up over the horizon—South America. It did not really give me as much thrill as the boats. It was then I realized, for the first time, that we were on the other side. As for South America—well, I expected it to appear—and there it was.

Nevertheless I kept my eye on that dim line, watching it harden from a stationary cloud rim to the fixed, irregular outline of a shore.

> ; The men are sailing home from Troy,
> And all the lamps are lit.

We would be there in no time. I turned back to the radio; Ceara was calling again. They had a message for us. I took it down. It was the one we had received almost ten hours before from Rio while we were still in the dark, on the other side of the ocean. I passed it forward to my husband. How strange to read it again, now we were almost there:

"PAA BARGE AT NATAL [The coast of Brazil spread low and green in the slight haze ahead.] LOCATED ON RIVER [We came on it very quickly, following

[1] From "My Heart" by Elizabeth Madox Roberts.

the coast for only a few minutes.] AT SOUTH WEST EDGE OF CITY STOP [There was Natal at last—that group of white houses running up a green hill, those palms on the skyline.] BETWEEN CITY AND LARGE AERO POSTALE HANGAR AND RAMP STOP [My husband looked back and signaled with his hand, 'Five minutes more.'] CAUTION TALL RADIO MASTS—[There they were, there was the hangar; we were circling!] FEW SPARE PARTS AVAILABLE ON BARGE [I could see it now, a square white barge on the river, flying an American flag.]"

We were spiraling down fast. I had hardly time to signal Ceara that we were landing. Quick, reel in the antenna before it hits the water. Fasten the brake, turn off the switches. Unplug the earphones. (At last! How sore my ears were from the pressure.) Now, fix up a little. Water on a handkerchief. Wipe my face. Comb my hair. Put on the helmet again and fasten the belt for landing.

Just in time. We were skimming over the surface of the water. The engine throttled, the propeller whirring idly, we were settling down gently like a gull coming to rest. There, we had clipped the water, riding along it with little slaps like a skipping stone. Now, sinking back in it. The rush of water over the pontoons as we slowed down. The surge forward as we came to a floating position. The blast of air as the plane started again, turning heavily, charging slowly through the water toward the barge. Creature of water again, now, no longer a bird of the air.

I took out my pad and, in the jolting motion of the waves, wrote unsteadily, "Landed Natal 17:55 GMT."

GOING INTO SPACE

by Arthur C. Clarke

A decade ago all but a tiny band of enthusiasts would have derided the idea that experiments in interplanetary flight might change the destiny of the human race. Now, far from laughter, an increasing number believe that initial flights will take place during their own lifetimes and that colonization of other planets will follow inevitably. Prognostication is not easy as the problems to be solved are enormously complicated. Nevertheless, the patterns for exploration of the surface of the earth have been set; and it is therefore fitting that this book should close with an article on the last great area of exploration, in which man may duplicate in actual fact the imaginary voyagings described by a Verne, a Wells or a contemporary writer of science fiction.

MAN is the great explorer. Perhaps a million years ago, our remote ancestors began to spread over the face of the world until at last they had made their homes in every continent except the frozen Antarctic. The final chapter in the long story of Earth's exploration was not written until our own age. Now, thanks to the conquest of the air, no spot on the globe is more than a few hours' distance from any other, and soon it will be possible to circle the world inside a single day.

It is hard for us to remember that, only fifty years ago, there were great areas of the Earth where no man had ever been. Our grandfathers could dream, when they read such adventure stories as *King Solomon's Mines*, of strange countries and peoples still waiting to be discovered. Now that the airplane is rapidly filling in the last blanks on the map, the mystery and romance which always surround the unknown have been swept away. The world is a more humdrum and a less exciting place.

Or so it seems at first sight. The truth of the matter is that, although we may have explored the continents, we have scarcely scratched the surface even of our own planet. The ocean deeps—three-quarters of the Earth—are still as unknown as was Darkest Africa a century ago. And in the other direction, above the atmosphere, lies the enormous emptiness of space. Shining out there in the darkness we can see other worlds than ours—the Moon, the planets, and the still more distant stars. Not long ago, it seemed that only dreams could reach them. "Crying for the Moon" meant asking for something that was utterly impossible. In the past generation, all that has changed. We know now, in theory at least, how we may escape from our native world and go voyaging out into space. When men have imagined something, sooner or later they have always done it, as the discovery of flight has proved. For the same reason, since we now have the means to travel into space, it is only a matter of time before the first Columbus of the future sets course for the Moon.

The development of the rocket during the Second World War has made it possible to talk seriously about voyages to the planets. But first of all, let us look for a moment into the past to find out how the idea of interplanetary flight first arose.

In ancient times, before the invention of the telescope, no one knew that there *were* any other worlds besides our own. There were many theories to explain the Sun, Moon, and stars, but there was no way of proving which of them was correct. If you go out at night under a clear sky and look up at the heavens, you would never be able to guess—if someone had not already told you!—that those twinkling points of light were blazing suns, most of them millions of times larger than the world on which we live. Such an idea seems against all common sense, so it is not surprising that it was a long time before anyone could prove it was true, and longer still before everybody else believed them.

Even the Moon, our nearest neighbor, is too far away for the unaided eye to tell us much about it, though some of the Greek scientists more than two thousand years ago had been able to make a good estimate of its size. They knew that it must be a world of its own, and not just a small globe only a few miles away; but what kind of a world it was, they could not tell.

The invention of the telescope changed all this. A century before, Columbus had discovered a new world in the West, and the First Elizabethan Age had seen the great explorations of such adventurers as Drake and Raleigh. Then, in 1609, the Italian scientist Galileo looked through his crude, home-made telescopes and discovered new lands in the sky. Although the best instrument Galileo used was not as good as a pair of modern field glasses, he could see the mountains and plains on the Moon and was even able to map its surface. After that date, men knew definitely that the Earth was not the only world that existed, and they also began to wonder if we were the only people in the universe. To *that* question, we still do not know the answer—but one day we will.

It is not surprising that the discoveries of Galileo and later astronomers excited enormous interest. Men began to ask themselves what it was like in the new lands they could dimly see through their feeble telescopes. They tried to imagine the kinds of creatures that might live there. And, before long, they started wondering if explorers would ever be able to cross space as they had already crossed the sea.

This, remember, was three hundred years ago. We think of space-flight as a modern idea, and so it is rather startling to discover that several stories of voyages to the Moon (and the Sun!) were written by the French author Cyrano de Bergerac as long ago as 1656.

During the next two hundred years, many other writers produced tales of journeys to the Moon, but few of them were intended at all seriously. At the same time, astronomical knowledge steadily increased. A good deal had been discovered about the Earth's atmosphere—that invisible blanket which enables us to breathe and which protects us from space—and the forces which make the planets move were better understood.

The first man to use all this new knowledge was the famous French writer Jules Verne, who foresaw so many of our modern inventions, such as the submarine and the helicopter. His novel *From the Earth to the Moon,* which was published in 1865, contained a remarkable amount of accurate scientific information, and is still well worth reading today (much of it is also highly amusing). Verne knew that nothing depending upon the air could possibly fly to the Moon, so that ruled out balloons and machines using wings or propellers. But if one could build an enormous gun, and fire a shell from it in the right direction *and* with enough speed, it would be possible to hit the Moon. It is not hard to calculate what starting speed the shell would need or how long the journey would take, and Verne was very careful to get all his figures right. Where he let his imagination go, however, was in pretending that men could travel in such a shell without being killed by the concussion when the gun was fired, no matter how well padded and protected they might be.

And there was another objection to Verne's mammoth gun, not so well known in his time as it is today. As experiments in supersonic flight have shown, anything moving through our atmosphere at very high speeds meets tremendous resistance, and so becomes very hot. For this reason, the fastest jet planes now have to be fitted with refrigeration. But Jules Verne's shell would have traveled *thirty* times as fast as any jet flying today. It would not simply have become hot—it would have melted almost immediately, even before it left the barrel of the gun!

However, though we of today may pick holes in his story, Verne's ideas were brilliantly worked out and they must have made many people think seriously about travel through space. The shell inside which his voyagers circled the Moon was fitted with apparatus to supply oxygen, observation windows through which the travelers could watch the stars, and—the most modern touch of all—rockets for steering. Almost a hundred years ago, Verne realized that rockets could be used to give a "push" in the vacuum of space, something that many people do not understand even today.

We do not require any wonderful new inventions to enable us to reach the planets. The tool for the job has been known for over seven hundred years, since the Chinese made the first gunpowder rockets around the year 1200. But until recent times, the rocket was little more than a firework, its main practical use being for shooting lines to shipwrecked mariners. During the nineteenth century it was employed as a weapon for a short period, but when more accurate guns were built war rockets soon became obsolete. They played no important part at all in the 1914-1918 War.

There are many reasons why interest in the rocket revived from 1920 onward. In the first place, Man had now conquered the air and so achieved one of his oldest dreams. Flying had always been considered impossible by most people: when the Wright brothers started to make their first short hops in 1903, newspaper editors refused to print the story because they *knew* it couldn't be true! Yet now, after 1920, airplanes were flying all over the world. After the air, the next step could only be—Space.

But space was airless, so some new form of engine would have to be used, an engine that would carry *all* its fuel and wouldn't have to "push" against something outside it in order to move forward. An airplane can reach only a certain height, usually less than ten miles, because it depends on the atmosphere around it.

Balloons, floating in the air like a cork on water, can do considerably better than this. If they are carrying only small loads, they can reach heights of twenty-five miles before the air can no longer support them. At this altitude, the air is so thin that, even if it were compressed a hundredfold, it would not be as dense as it is down here at sea level. Beyond this region, only rockets can ever fly.

Although, as we have already seen, Jules Verne knew this back in 1865, few scientists gave the rocket any serious thought until the end of the First World War. Even then, it was first looked upon merely as a way of sending automatic instruments far above the Earth, as had already been done with balloons. The idea that it could carry men as well was, for a long time, rather too fantastic to accept, but by 1930 nearly everyone knew that if we ever *did* succeed in building spaceships, they would be rocket-propelled....

Space-flight will not be the adventure into the unknown that is often imagined. It will be a step-by-step process; one must learn to walk before one can run. The Wright brothers didn't attempt to build a transatlantic airliner when they started their experiments on flying—and astronautics won't begin right away with someone trying to make a ship that can fly to the Moon.

After the high-speed, high-altitude rockets, the next important step is the rocket that can go around the world. For that opens up new and tremendous possibilities, and brings us into the realm of space-stations— permanent artificial bases circling the Earth beyond the atmosphere. But before that we shall use world-circling rockets in an operation that is really the key to the whole problem of space-flight—*refueling in space*.

Most of the things we see in our daily life we take for granted and never give them any thought. Consider the Moon, for example, as it hangs there in the sky on a brilliant, clear night. How many people bother to ask themselves what keeps it up?

There are planets that have no moon at all. If someone from such a world came to Earth, he might be very surprised to see the great silver disc of our satellite floating overhead, and if he knew no astronomy he might well wonder what prevented it from falling down.

The answer to this question, which is of fundamental importance in space-flight, was discovered some three hundred years ago by the great scientist Sir Isaac Newton. The Moon is kept securely in its place by the same force that holds us to the Earth: gravity.

There is a common impression that at a certain height gravity disappears. That's quite untrue; Earth's gravity reaches to the remotest stars. But it gets steadily weaker with distance, and when one is a few million miles away it is so feeble that, for almost all practical purposes, it can be ignored.

Newton's law of gravitation, like most great discoveries, can be put into very simple words. It states that, as one goes away from the Earth, gravity decreases according to the square of one's distance from Earth's center. In other words, doubling your distance reduces the force of gravity to a *quarter*; increasing it tenfold reduces gravity to a *hundredth*.

When we talk of gravity, we ordinarily think of the force that holds us to this Earth. But every planet—every body in the universe, in fact—has a gravity of its own. Its value on any world depends on the size and mass of that world. The giant planet Jupiter has almost three times as powerful a gravity as Earth's; the Moon's gravity, on the other hand, is only a sixth of ours.

Now let us return to the problem: "What keeps the Moon up?"

The mutual gravity of Earth and Moon draws the two bodies together with a force of millions of tons. If it had no movement around the Earth, the Moon would soon crash into us.

But the Moon *has* such a movement, and that is why it doesn't fall down. It's swinging round the Earth in a great circle, moving at a speed of over two thousand m.p.h. As long as it maintains that speed (and, since there's no air resistance in space, it can't lose it) it can never fall down.

Everyone knows that if you tie a stone at the end of a piece of string, you can set it whirling in a circle with very little effort. This is a crude working model of what happens with the Moon. Here, the pull of gravity plays the same role as the tension of the string.

To sum up, then, the Moon's velocity saves it from falling down, and Earth's gravity prevents it from flying off into space.

It may sound rather a delicate juggling feat, but it isn't anything of the sort. If for any reason the Moon altered its distance slightly, the speed would automatically adjust itself, so there's no danger of anything suddenly going wrong. Indeed, such variations are continually taking place, because the Moon's orbit is not exactly circular.

Now, there is no reason at all why the Moon should be at the particular distance it is. It could be much closer, or much further away—as long as its speed was correctly adjusted to balance gravity at that point. To return to our stone-and-string analogy, we know that the shorter the string, the faster the stone has to be moved. The same rule applies to moons revolving round planets, and to planets revolving round the Sun. Mercury, the nearest planet to the Sun, rushes along at thirty miles a second, whereas remote Pluto, at the borders of the solar system, needs only a tenth of this speed to maintain itself in its orbit. Some planets have at least a dozen moons scattered at all sorts of distances and revolving quite happily in their various orbits. There is no law of nature stopping us from having a moon only a couple of hundred miles up, instead of a quarter of a million miles away.

Such a moon would have to move almost ten times as quickly as the real Moon does, since gravity is much stronger so close to the Earth. But if it were given the correct speed—about eighteen thousand miles an hour—it would continue to circle our world forever, taking only an hour and a half to complete one revolution.

All this may seem to have very little to do with space-flight, but actually it is of the utmost importance. For it follows that if we could give any object this speed of eighteen thousand miles an hour just above the atmosphere, it would remain up there in space forever and could never fall down again. It wouldn't need any fuel to maintain it there—after all, the Moon has no rocket motors! In fact, a considerable amount of work would have to be done to *bring it down again*, since it could return to Earth only if its speed were neutralized in some way.

Now let's see how this idea can be used to take us along the road to the planets.

Eighteen thousand miles an hour is a tremendous speed, more than three times as fast as any rocket has traveled up to the present. But with improved motors and the use of multistep construction, it should be possible to achieve it. . . . The first rockets to reach "orbital speed," as it is called, will be very small and will carry nothing more than a few pounds of radio equipment. They will broadcast instrument readings back to Earth, just as present rockets do, but these satellite missiles won't fall back after a few minutes but will remain aloft forever.

The next stage will be for man-carrying rockets to get into an orbit. The vehicles that do this will be the upper steps of giant rockets very much bigger than themselves. These rockets will be launched over the sea so that the empty stages, as they fall back to Earth, will not drop on inhabited territory. They will probably descend by parachute and be towed back to land so that they can be used again.

So now we have our little spaceship, its fuel tanks almost exhausted, spinning around the Earth like a tiny Moon. It would be a fascinating experience, watching the whole world turn beneath you in only ninety minutes. But we're not interested in traveling all this way merely to look at the scenery!

Let's suppose that a second rocket—a "tanker" carrying fuel—were to take off from Earth and fly up into the same orbit. When it turned off its motors, it too would be circling the Earth in just the same way as the first vehicle. They would both be moving in the same direction and at the same speed—eighteen thousand miles an hour. *They would therefore, be at rest with respect to each other.* If they could be connected together by pipe line, it would be possible to transfer fuel from one rocket to the other. In this way, the tanks of the first ship could be replenished. It might be necessary for the tanker rocket to make a number of trips up from the ground before the job could be completed; alternatively, several tankers could be employed. In any case, there would be no great hurry, since the spaceships will go on circling Earth happily as long as we want them to, in exactly the same orbit.

The whole operation is just like refueling in the air, which has been successfully carried out for many years. In some ways, it would be simpler. Out in space, there would be no air resistance to buffet the vehicles and their connecting pipes. Indeed, as they swept silently around Earth, there would be no sense of motion at all. And, still more important, the spaceships and everything in them would be weightless, which would greatly simplify the transfer of fuel and stores.

If a rocket is to escape from the Earth and never come back, it must reach a speed of twenty-five thousand miles an hour. The circling spaceship, two hundred miles up, is already moving at eighteen thousand miles an hour—nearly three-quarters of this speed. *An extra seven thousand miles an hour is therefore all that is required.* The fact that the ship is only two hundred miles away doesn't matter. Once it's reached escape velocity Earth can never hold it back and it will coast on out into space.

Spaceships returning to Earth may also go into these orbits, instead of attempting to land directly. They will be met in space by small "ferry" rockets, to which their crews will be transferred for the trip down to Earth. The big spaceships will be left circling above the atmosphere until they are refueled and ready for their next mission.

The great advantage of this is that the short climb through the atmosphere and the long trip across space really require two entirely different sorts of spaceship, and it's very inefficient trying to make one vehicle do the entire trip. It would be like trying to combine the characteristics of bulldozer and racing car. So we will see two kinds of spaceship being developed. The first will be the carefully streamlined, winged vehicle which will leave Earth and climb into the orbit above the atmosphere with its load of fuel and stores for the *real* spaceships already waiting out there. These will not be streamlined at all, and may look very odd objects indeed—perhaps collections of spheres and cylinders held together with struts.

So far we've considered how our spaceships will get into the orbit around the Earth, but we haven't stopped to see how they will get safely back again. Unless they lose their speed, they can't fall down, so one way of making them return would be to employ rocket *braking*—in other words, firing the rockets against the direction of the spaceship's motion.

That would work all right, but it would be extremely expensive in terms of fuel if we had to get rid of all the spaceship's velocity by this means. We would have to carry up a considerable amount of fuel just to make the return journey, and to lift *that* would require a far huger quantity of fuel at the take-off. Fortunately, there is another way.

By using quite a small amount of rocket braking—cutting its speed from eighteen thousand to, say, sixteen thousand miles an hour—the spaceship would swing closer to the Earth and would pass through the upper layers of the atmosphere. This would make it lose still more speed owing to air resistance, until before long it would be impossible for it to remain out in space. It would race through the upper air, fifty miles above the Earth, and circle the world several times as a supersonic glider before it came down into the lower atmosphere and landed at no greater speed than an ordinary aircraft. All its original velocity would have been whittled away by air resistance, and it would have become very hot in the process. However, if special heat-resisting materials were used for the parts of the wings and fuselage most affected, the maneuver could be carried out safely without the ship melting down like a meteor.

The first of the other worlds which men will reach and explore will undoubtedly be the Moon, for it is so much closer to us than any other body in space. Even Venus, nearest of the planets, is more than a hundred times further away. Because of its closeness, we also know a great deal more about the Moon than any other world, so our first explorers will not be going completely into the unknown. Let's follow them now on one of those voyages—those great adventures of the future which many of you who are reading these words will live to see . . .

It's four minutes to take-off, and you're trying to tell yourself that you aren't *really* afraid. The pilot has finished checking his instruments, and from time to time a voice from the control tower comes through a loudspeaker. Otherwise it is quiet—almost too quiet. To occupy your mind, you examine the masses of instruments and try to decide what they all do. Some of them, the fuel, pressure, and temperature gauges, for example, are obvious, but there are others of which you can't make head or tail. You wonder how anyone can ever learn what they're all for. Just suppose the pilot made a mistake and pressed the wrong button. . . .

Suddenly, an electric motor starts to whir close at hand. Then things begin to happen all over the place: switches click, powerful pumps begin to whine, and valves start to snap open down in the heart of the great rocket in whose streamlined nose you are sitting. With each new noise you think, "This is it!"—but still you don't move. When the voyage finally begins, you aren't prepared for it.

A long way off, it seems, there's a noise like a thousand waterfalls, or a thunderstorm in which the crashes follow each other so quickly that there's no moment of silence between them. The rocket motors have started, but are not yet delivering enough power to lift the ship. Quickly the roar mounts, the cabin begins to vibrate, and the spaceship rises from the face of the desert. Outside, the Arizona sands are being sprayed with flame for a hundred yards around.

Something seems to be pushing you down, quite gently, into the thick padding of your couch. It isn't at all uncomfortable, but the pressure mounts until your limbs seem to be made of lead and it takes a deliberate effort to keep breathing. You try to lift your hand, and the effort needed to move it even a few inches is so tiring that you let it drop back beside you. You lie limp and relaxed, waiting to see what will happen next. You're no longer frightened: it's too exciting for that, this feeling of infinite power sweeping you up into the sky.

There's a sudden fall in the thunder of the rockets, the sensation of immense weight ebbs away, and you can breathe more easily. Power is being reduced; in a few moments, Earth will no longer be able to recapture you. A minute later silence comes flooding back as the motors cut out completely, and all feeling of weight vanishes. For a few minutes the pilot checks his instruments; then he turns round and smiles.

"Nicely on course; we'll make our rendezvous in forty minutes. You can get up if you want to."

Gingerly, you ease yourself out of the couch, holding on to it with one hand. You feel rather like a captive balloon as you float there in space; then you pluck up courage and gently push yourself across the cabin. You float slowly over to the observation port, anxious to have a look at Earth.

You'd expected to see a great globe hanging in space, with the seas and continents clearly visible—just like one of those globes you find in map-sellers' windows, except that there wouldn't be any lines of longitude and latitude. What you *do* see, however, is so unexpected and so wonderful that it takes your breath away. Almost filling the sky is a tremendous, blinding crescent, the shape of a new moon but hundreds of times bigger. The rocket is passing over the night side of Earth, and most of the planet is in darkness. You can see it dimly as a vast, shadowy circle eclipsing the stars. Here and there are patches of phosphorescence—the lights of great cities.

As you wait, the narrow crescent slowly grows until presently you are looking down on the sunlit side of the planet. It's taken you just over forty minutes to travel halfway round the world! Then the pilot tells you to go back to your couch while he "homes" on the spaceship that is already circling up here, waiting for you to go aboard.

It's an ugly-looking machine, nothing like the sleek, streamlined torpedo that carried you up from Earth. In fact, it's a stubby cylinder, rounded at one end and with a shock-absorbing undercarriage at the other. The rounded end is fitted with several windows and a lot of radio equipment, while between the undercarriage legs you can see the jets of rocket nozzles.

This is the Lunar Shuttle, built up here in space in exactly the same way as the space-stations were constructed. Its job is to circle the Earth and take aboard passengers and supplies for the colony on the Moon. Moving in its orbit above the atmosphere at eighteen thousand miles an hour, it can then build up the extra seven thousand miles an hour that will let it escape from the Earth. Its rocket motors are far too weak to enable it to land on Earth or take off again, but they are powerful enough to fight the Moon's much weaker gravity, so that the Shuttle can make the trip down to the Moon and back again to its orbit around Earth.

It's several hours later, and you're now aboard the Shuttle waiting for the *real* journey to begin. The rocket that carried you up from Earth has returned to its base, having fallen back into the atmosphere and landed as a glider. The first lap of your journey is over; climbing that hundred miles has taken more fuel than the quarter of a million miles that remains.

The Shuttle is quite large, and several passengers are already aboard. They came up, you gather, on earlier ferry flights. Since the journey is going to last several days, there are little bunks in which you can sleep, and there's a tiny lounge in which you can sit and read or look at the stars.

At last everything is ready. The pilot waits for the carefully calculated instant and starts the motors. This time, the force urging you down into your couch is very gentle—hardly enough, in fact, to give you your normal weight. The Shuttle is taking its time to build up speed, to add the extra seven thousand miles an hour that will tear it away from Earth. The vibration of the rockets lasts for many minutes; then silence falls and your weight vanishes once more. It will not return until you reach the Moon.

Yet everything still seems exactly the same. The Earth hasn't moved, and you still appear to be going around it just as you were before. You'll have to wait for a while if you want to see any change.

An hour later there's no doubt about it. Earth is a good deal smaller; it's slowly falling astern. You're traveling outward on the long curve which, without any more effort on the part of the rockets, will take you to the Moon. . . .

Space-travel may sound exciting, but I'm afraid you'll be rather bored before the five days of the journey are up. All that will happen is that Earth will slowly shrink astern, while the Moon slowly grows ahead. Since, of course, there is no sensation of motion whatsoever, only logic tells you that you are really approaching the Moon. The nose of the ship isn't pointing anywhere in particular; in fact, as it travels along, the Shuttle very slowly turns end over end. Not until it is time to land will the pilot bother to check the ship's spin.

That time has come at last. For some hours, the gravity field of the Moon has been increasing—and so has the ship's speed. But you can't feel this, since you are still weightless as the ship is in free fall.

The Moon is now only a few hundred miles away, and so enormous that it seems to fill the sky. Indeed, it's no longer a globe hanging in space but a jagged landscape spread out far below. You can see countless mountains and craters, many of whose names you've learned from the maps in the past few days. They're beginning to look much too close for comfort . . .

The ship is falling at over five thousand miles an hour toward that inhospitable world. Since there is scarcely a trace of atmosphere, you can't use wings or parachutes to land, and will therefore have to rely entirely on the rockets. That means turning the ship around in space so that the jets —and the elaborate shock-absorbing equipment of the undercarriage—point downward.

You have strapped yourself in your couch when the pilot begins the landing maneuvers. The stars sweep around you as the ship turns in space. Nothing has happened to its speed yet, but the low-powered steering jets have swung the Shuttle around into the right position for landing. The pilot is watching his instruments intently—but he is not touching the controls, for the final landing is quite automatic. It is controlled by a radar set in the ship, which measures the distance to the ground and passes this information on to the automatic pilot controlling the jets. The human pilot merely stands by in case something goes wrong—in which case he would use his judgment to try to make an emergency landing or to climb out into space again.

With a roar that seems doubly impressive after the long hours of silence, the motors thunder into life. There's a sudden feeling of returning weight, and through the observation window you can just glimpse the white-hot pillar of flame that's checking your headlong fall against the Moon, still many miles below. The spaceship is dropping toward the heart of a great ring of mountains. Presently, when the roar of the rocket ceases, some of the taller peaks already seem to be towering above the ship. For a few seconds you are falling free once more, and for a horrible moment you wonder if power has failed and you are about to crash on those cruel hills. Then the

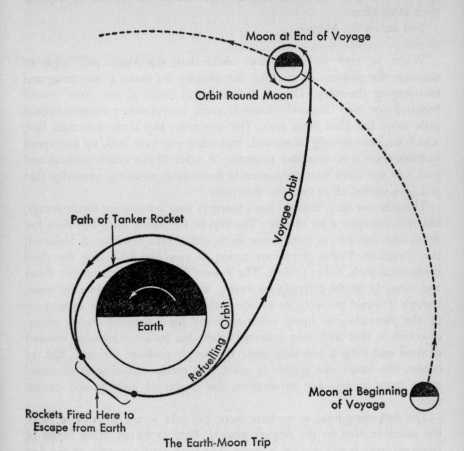

Moon at End of Voyage

Orbit Round Moon

Path of Tanker Rocket

Voyage Orbit

Earth

Refuelling Orbit

Moon at Beginning
of Voyage

Rockets Fired Here to
Escape from Earth

The Earth-Moon Trip

rockets flare out again, and the scene below vanishes in fire and clouds of dust blasted up by the jet. A moment later there's the gentlest of impacts, then utter silence.

You are on the Moon.

When we start looking further afield than the Moon and begin to consider the problem of reaching the planets, we make a surprising and encouraging discovery. Though the distances involved are often several hundred—or even thousand—times as great, interplanetary voyages require little more fuel than lunar ones. The reason for this is the fortunate fact, which we have already mentioned, that once you have built up any speed in space there is no resistance to destroy it again. If you simply sit back and wait, you will reach your destination in due course, assuming, naturally, that you have started off in the right direction!

There is one snag, though. Such journeys may not require much energy, but they consume a lot of time. The trip to the Moon takes less than five days—and only two or three if one starts with a little extra speed. However, the voyage to Venus, if you are trying to save fuel by taking the most economical path, lasts 145 days. The journey to Mars is even longer, about 250 days. It would certainly be boring to spend all that time in space, though it would probably be no worse than spending a winter snowed up in the Antarctic, as many polar explorers have done. A more serious objection is that such long journeys would use up a considerable amount of food and oxygen and thus make the supply problem difficult. And, of course, the longer one spends in space, the greater the chances of something going wrong—not to mention the danger of meteors and cosmic rays. . . .

The first spaceships, as we have seen, will take several months to make the journeys even to the nearest planets. But, as for all other forms of transport, speeds will steadily increase. The long, lonely months of the first pioneers will be carved down to weeks, and eventually to days. There is no limit to speed in space, at least, according to Einstein's theory of relativity, not until one begins to approach the velocity of light. And as *that* is 670,000,000 miles an hour, it's not a speed limit that will worry us for a long time to come! At a thousandth of this velocity, one would get to Mars in a few days.

As greater speeds become available, they would not merely shorten the voyages to the nearer planets; they would also make it possible to travel to more distant worlds such as Jupiter and Saturn. Eventually though this may well take several hundred years, spaceships from Earth will have reached all the planets of the Sun, from scorched Mercury to eternally frozen Pluto and the unknown worlds that may lie beyond it.

Fantastic? Certainly not, when one thinks of all that has happened in the last hundred years, and remembers that thousands—indeed, millions —of years lie ahead of us.

One day, all the planets of the Sun will have been explored, just as all the Earth is today. Mars, Venus, Ganymede, Titan, Phobos will be names as familiar as New Zealand, Canada, Peru, South Africa—countries which were once unknown, which once took longer to reach than will the planets a hundred years from now. The frontier will move outward from Earth, past the frozen worlds at the fringes of the solar system, until at last men are looking out across the great abyss, with all the planets behind and nothing between them and the incredibly distant stars. Across that gulf, light itself, the fastest thing in the universe, takes years to travel. Yet out there must lie other solar systems, some of them with planets much more like Earth than are any of the other worlds of our own Sun. And somewhere among the thousands of millions of stars scattered throughout space there must, surely, be other intelligent races, many of them far in advance of our own. One day we shall meet them: it may not be for thousands of years, but that is the ultimate goal of astronautics.

We may never actually meet them face to face; contact may be made by automatic spaceships that will return to Earth many generations after they have set out, bringing back the knowledge their cameras and recorders have obtained. Or perhaps medical science may discover ways of permitting the spaceship crews to "hibernate," so that they may be able to travel on journeys lasting for centuries. Or perhaps, though all the evidence is against it, the speed of light may prove to be no greater obstacle than the speed of sound, so that we may achieve such velocities that men will be able to travel to the stars and return in a single lifetime.

We do not know—but we can be sure that, even if we never reach the stars, the planets of our own solar system will keep all our scientists and explorers busy for as far ahead as imagination can go.

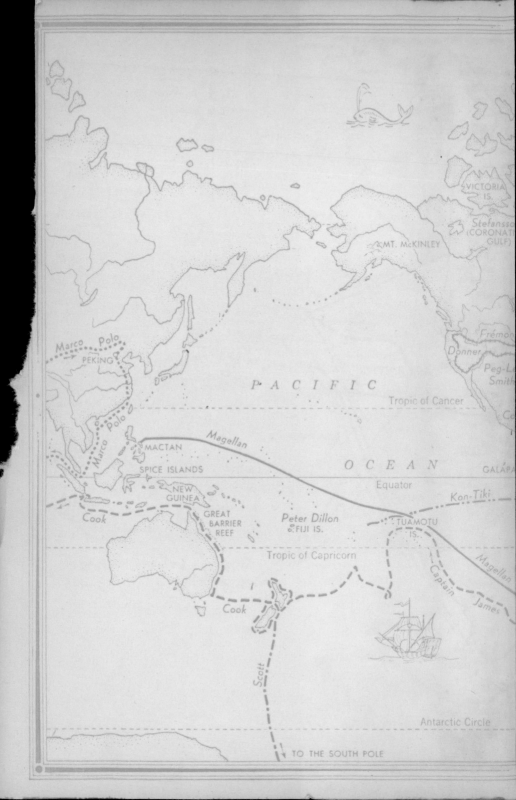